JAZZ
PROFILES

The

Spirit

of the

Nineties

BILLBOARD
BOOKS

Reginald CARVER
Lenny BERNSTEIN

Dedications

*I dedicate this book to my wife and best friend, Ann, and
to my daughter, Caroline. I love you both with all my heart.*

*I also dedicate this to Mom, Pops, and Sheila for helping me
understand what it means to attain soul.*

*Finally I dedicate this to all the artists who participated in this project.
You all have touched me in ways in which you will never know.*

RC

*To my wife, Evelyn, and my daughter, Lisa, for their encouragement
and support, and for being there whenever I needed them.*

LB

REGINALD CARVER is a jazz fan and attorney practicing in Atlanta, GA.

LENNY BERNSTEIN is a photographer whose photographs have been published in such publications as *The New York Times*, *New York* magazine, *Vanity Fair*, *Interview*, and *Harper's*. He lives in Capitola, CA.

Copyright © 1998 by Reginald Carver and Lenny Bernstein
First published in 1998 in New York by Billboard Books, an imprint of Watson-Guptill Publications, a division of BPI Communications,
1515 Broadway, New York, NY 10036

Library of Congress Cataloging in Publication Data

Carver, Reginald.
Jazz profiles: the spirit of the nineties / by Reginald Carver
and Lenny Bernstein.

Each of 40 musician profiles includes photograph, biographical sketch, interview, and discography.
Includes index.

Contents: The trumpeters — The saxophonists — The trombonists —
The clarinetist — The guitarists — The pianists and organist —
The bassists — The drummers — The vocalists.

ISBN 0-8230-8338-1 (hc)

1. Jazz musicians.   2. Jazz—1991-2000—History and criticism.
I. Bernstein, Lenny.   II. Title.
ML394.C37   1998
781.65'092'2—dc21 98-30133 [B] CIP MN

Manufactured in the United States

1 2 3 4 5 6 7 8 9/06 05 04 03 02 01 00 99 98

Senior Editor: Bob Nirkind
Editor: Liz Harvey
Production Manager: Ellen Greene
Design: Farenga Design Group

Contents

Acknowledgements

There are many, many people who have contributed to the completion of this book. I wish to thank first of all my co-author Lenny Bernstein, who eagerly agreed to undertake this project with me and who always has given his all. I also wish to thank my agent, Lee Beitchman, whose guidance and patience have been major contributions. Thank you to my editors, Bob Nirkind and Liz Harvey of Billboard Books, for understanding this project and giving it a chance.

Thanks to the many people who have contributed much time and effort in helping me with whatever I asked, including Tom Bradshaw of the National Endowment for the Arts, my friend Vinnie D'Agostino, Lisa Bernstein, Alex Bach, and Joel Turry and the folks at WORDZXPRESSED. A very special thanks to Marie Curry and Judy Cato for going way beyond the call of duty. Another kind of thanks to my law partners John Bach and Bob Hulsey for allowing me to take time away from my practice to pursue this project.

A very special thanks to Russell Malone, Branford Marsalis, and Joshua Redman, who agreed to interviews when this was still a speculative project. You all helped get this ball rolling, and I appreciate it. And thanks to all the musicians, and their managers and agents, for giving me time out of your busy schedules.

Finally I wish to give thanks to my wife, Ann, for her enthusiastic support and patience throughout this project.

RC

First and foremost, to my wife, Evelyn, and my daughter, Lisa, for many unrewarded hours. Without them, I couldn't have done this book.

To my co-author Reggie Carver, whom I never seemed to have any disagreements with, and who always made my tasks easier.

To my agent Lee Beitchman, who always had an open line for me and believed in the project.

To my editors at Billboard Books, Bob Nirkind and Liz Harvey, who had so many good suggestions that they can't but help the book be better.

To Tim Jackson and the crew at Kuumbwa Jazz Center and the Monterey Jazz Festival; Julie, the light and sound engineer at Kuumbwa and Monterey; Chris, Kurt, and the volunteers at Kuumbwa, who have been so kind and gracious over the years; and Paul Fingerote at Monterey.

To Bay Photo Lab, particularly Chris Humm, Bryan Hitchcock, Brandon Bowen, and Charlie Daniels, for their professional help.

To the folks at Yoshi's: Yoshi and Kaz, for always being pleasant and accommodating despite the hectic work of running a jazz club; Dan Pettit, production manager, who always made sure that the lighting was "right" for me; and Jason Olaine, Bob Cole, and Marshall Lamm, who saw to it that I had a good seat from which to work.

Last, to the musicians, those still with us and those who are gone, who pioneered this great American music, nurtured it, and kept it alive—to those who passed on the heritage and to the younger artists in this book who are carrying it on. Thank you for graciously allowing me to photograph you, to capture and share the spirit of the moment.

LB

Foreword

Reginald Carver and Lenny Bernstein have brought a visionary spirit to their book, *Jazz Profiles: The Spirit of the Nineties*. As we approach the new millennium, it is a special treat to see Mr. Bernstein's photographs, read Mr. Carver's interviews, and experience the coming of age of the contemporary jazz artists identified within these pages.

I first heard about Lenny Bernstein and his work through a colleague named John Purcell. At the time John, who performs extensively with the World Saxophone Quartet, and I were engaged in the formation of a jazz academy. John remembered Bernstein's work because he had taken a series of photographs involving other members of the World Saxophone Quartet, and John had been particularly impressed with photographs taken of fellow jazz saxophonist Oliver Lake. Later, after developing the curriculum for the West Coast Jazz Academy, we decided to decorate the walls of our facility. It is in this circumstance that Bernstein's name resurfaced, and I gave him a call.

My first meeting with Lenny Bernstein was an extraordinary affair. He came to my office bursting with enthusiasm and energy for developing the Jazz Academy, and seemingly as an afterthought brought out a few examples of his photographic work. I still can remember how exciting it was for me to see his photographs of jazz musicians, which expressed to me some very special lyrical and dynamic qualities. Our first meeting led to further conversations in which he described how and why he came to develop his individualistic style. He told me how he traveled from Santa Cruz to his favorite sites in Oakland and the Monterey Jazz Festival. And as you will soon read, he planned each photograph by sight lines and sat for hours listening and waiting for the particular instrument and musician in order to get the right shot.

As you can tell from the color photographs on the front and back covers of this book, Bernstein has developed a special way of shooting his images. His photographs bring you directly into the experience of being in a jazz club or listening to a jazz performance at a festival. His use of color in capturing this ephemeral moment accurately enhances this experience and documents a special moment. When looking at one of his images, you are immediately transported to center stage. The photographs create the sense of a continuous performance. The musicians are captured in a transcendent moment, and seem to be still playing.

Add to Bernstein's images the interviews Reginald Carver conducted and wrote, and you have an almost complete picture of the contemporary jazz musician. Through his writings, Carver produces a snapshot in literary form of each of these musicians, and he reveals how they approach their craft. The caption that accompanies each image helps bring to life the educational path and sacrifice required on the road to becoming a jazz musician. You can almost sense, with young musicians like Joshua Redman, Roy Hargrove, and Wynton Marsalis, what it feels like to be on the road ten months out of the year. You can also read how vocalists like Dee Dee Bridgewater, Kurt Elling, and Kevin Mahogany got started in the music business. Each interview is followed by a select discography that will help you discover more about these contemporary jazz musicians by listening to their music.

In this book, you will view and read about some of the famous, as well as the not-so-famous and soon-to-be-famous, musicians of our time. Bernstein and Carver have caught them in the "act." These two together have created an outstanding montage on the life of jazz musicians doing what they do best: performing on stage. Laypeople and professionals, and teachers and students, will gain tremendous insight from these glimpses into the lives of these contemporary jazz musicians. Many people familiar with some of the recordings of these musicians will experience a freshness and clarity in viewing their favorite musicians and reading the interviews in this book. Those unfamiliar with the lives of these musicians will discover a treasure of superb material and will embark on a journey to new areas of auditory and visual landscapes in jazz.

As a music educator, I predict this book will become a substantial resource for all people interested in the creativity and endurance of jazz music.

Richard Bains

Richard Bains is the director of the Music and Performing Arts Institute, and a founding member of California State University at Monterey Bay.

Introduction

The idea for this book hit me all at once. I was sitting at my desk in my law office one afternoon in October, 1996. As I often do, I was listening to one of many jazz CDs I play while I work. I don't remember the particular tune or even the CD, but I do remember that I was listening to a group made up of jazz artists my age. I love this generation of artists. I feel a bond with these musicians because I know we've grown up with many of the same experiences and share many of the same influences.

A few weeks before, I'd spoken to Lenny Bernstein for the first time. I'd been looking for some photographs of jazz artists to place beside my favorite one of John Coltrane, which hangs in my office. At that time Lenny had placed an ad in *DownBeat* magazine about his performance photography. I called him and ordered several proofs and had since been mulling over which ones to buy.

As I sat in my office that October, the idea for this book emerged. I'd always felt (and I still do) that with the exception of a few notables, the jazz artists of my generation get very little recognition. For years I had been buying their CDs, enjoying their music, and studying their careers. I knew I was a fanatic, but I was saddened that few people knew much about the music and the artists who mean so much to me.

It was time to do something about my feelings. That afternoon I pieced together in my mind what I would like to present in a book. I wanted to profile today's top younger generation jazz artists, and for each one I wanted to include brief biographical data, an interview, a discography, and a photograph. I wanted to introduce others to the artists I'd grown to love.

I called Lenny late the same day and reintroduced myself. He remembered me, and we started talking about our love for jazz music and the younger generation artists. I soon realized that he was an even bigger fan of the music than I was. Now in his seventies, Lenny told me he'd been photographing jazz musicians in performance for the last forty years. He knew many jazz musicians young and old, the legends and the young lions.

I sprang my book idea on him and asked if he would consider being my co-author and provide the photography. He agreed without hesitation. At that moment we'd talked only briefly once before. We didn't know each other at all really, but I think each of us sensed a sincerity in the other's voice. We both knew immediately how we felt about jazz music, the artists, and the idea of a book. We also knew we would get much satisfaction out of creating it.

From the outset we agreed on the goals for the book. The first goal is an impossible one to attain. We're trying to capture in words and pictures the spirit and soul of jazz music and its artists.

As anyone knows, this can be completely accomplished only through the music. Knowing that we would fail, we still wanted to try.

One way we've attempted to accomplish this first goal is through the chapter format. Brief biographical data introduces the artist. This is followed by excerpts from interviews I conducted with each artist over the last year and a half. We chose to do interviews because, like jazz music, the conversations here are mostly improvised. We've endeavored to introduce readers to each musician's influences, background, and views on various issues in jazz. We've also included a performance photograph of each artist. Again, rather than a staged shot, this will, we hope, help capture the look and feel of jazz performance. Finally we've included a select discography for each artist.

The second goal of this book is to introduce readers to the forty artists chosen for this project. These artists represent a wide range of jazz musicians with various styles, backgrounds, and tastes. We've chosen musicians on each primary instrument in jazz, plus vocalists. Most of the artists presented here are leaders of their own groups and have released recordings as a leader. All have been hailed by critics and knowledgeable fans as top artists in the genre. Each artist in this book is one of the best jazz musicians working today.

For my part, I thoroughly enjoyed this project. The musicians I've met and interviewed all have been warm, enthusiastic, and insightful. Each is an artist in every sense of the word—totally committed to his or her craft.

RC

About the Photographs

The question I'm most frequently asked when I'm shooting in a club is, "What speed film are you using?" People are aware that I can't use a flash because it would disturb the performance (the musicians and the audience) and that the low-light conditions dictate my using fast film. I suppose they want to know how they, too, can take the type of photographs they see in publications and on display. Some other less-frequent inquiries pertain to the camera, lens, etc. Without appearing to be impolite, I usually try to respond by saying that these things have little to do with taking a good photograph. There is an axiom that 90 percent of getting the photograph you want has hardly anything to do with photographic equipment or technique.

I read once that if we were more aware and stayed open to all our senses, we would see things better and clearer. Although smell, touch, and taste sometimes influence my picture selections, my hearing helps me most when I shoot a jazz photograph. That seems obvious. After all, music is mostly sound—although the performance isn't all sound. I recently saw Max Roach's *So What* brass quintet perform. At one point in the program, Mark Taylor, the French horn player, was soloing on "My Funny Valentine." The song seemed to have been written just for the instrument that evening. It sounded so beautiful. Taylor had such a look of beatitude on his face while he was playing that I had to try to capture that look. I was really satisfied with how that photograph turned out.

But there was also another scene going on. Roach was so entranced listening to Taylor that I had to try to record this look, too. Although I've taken many photographs of Roach before, I think this one is the best. The look on his face made the photograph for me. There was a whole lot of luck and good audience reaction that made all of that possible. It's times like these that I try to make pictures, not just take pictures.

I view jazz photography as a trilogy—that is, a combination of the contribution from three sources: 1) the musician or musicians being photographed, 2) the music being played, and 3) the performance interpreted by the photographer and then captured at a very precise moment in time in order to preserve it. My purpose is to get as close to the feeling I had when I was listening to the music. My goal is that when I look at the photograph after processing, the photograph brings back the memories and emotion of the performance.

With this purpose and goal in mind, I took the photographs in this book in live performance in intimate club settings. Under these conditions, I believe, I have a better chance of *listening* to the music and the musician(s), rather than just *hearing* the sounds. I'm using the term "listening" to mean an interaction between me and the performers, which includes reacting either actively or passively, as opposed to hearing but not responding. I believe that the audience usually plays an important role in affecting the performance. This interaction, in turn, will affect the quality of the photograph that captures the performance.

There are some photographs whose main purpose is to memorialize the jazz event. I wouldn't call these jazz photographs. They probably are better described as documentary, archival, event, or journalistic photographs. None of this type is included in this book. Then there is some portraiture that is called jazz photography primarily because the subject is a jazz musician with or without a musical instrument included in the picture. This type of photograph is most often seen in advertising and other forms of publicity, as well as on album covers, etc. I would no more refer to one of these images as a jazz photograph than I would call a shot of a surgeon, with or without a scalpel, a medical photograph, or a scuba diver pictured with gear a marine photograph. This style of "musical photography" rarely, if ever, speaks to me of anything about the musician, music, or photographer.

The black-and-white photographs in the book were originally taken in color in order to preserve the mood and feeling of the performance. My intention regarding the conversion from color to black and white was threefold. First, I wanted to preserve the integrity and quality of the original color photograph. Second, my requirement was that the emotion and feeling of the musician wasn't compromised by the conversion. And lastly, the intimacy of the performance ambiance had to be maintained. I was satisfied that although there was some intangible loss as measured by the aforementioned criteria, the overall effect was minimal. Imagine, if you can, seeing some of your favorite works of art that were originally printed in color being viewed in black and white.

The photographs were taken primarily in three locations: Yoshi's Nite Spot in Oakland, California; Kuumbwa Jazz Center in Santa Cruz, California; and the Monterey Jazz Festival, also in California. Yoshi's is a highly acclaimed Japanese restaurant and nightclub in the San Francisco Bay area that has for a long time showcased the best in jazz from all over the United States and the world. Yoshi's has an intimate setting for approximately 250 people, and the acoustics and lighting are second to none. Yoshi's recently moved to its present location in Jack London Square from its previous address in Oakland. Although food and drink waitpersons are on the floor throughout the performances, they are relatively unobtrusive and respectful of the music. All in all, it is an excellent venue in which to capture the feeling of the music, both in its sound and in being photograph-friendly.

Kuumbwa is second only to the Village Vanguard in New York City in being the longest continuously operating jazz club in the United States. Kuumbwa recently celebrated its twentieth anniversary. It is run as a nonprofit organization and serves no hard liquor, but does serve beer, wine, and food. No waitpersons means fewer visual or audio distractions for the musicians and audience, compared with many other venues.

The capacity of Kuumbwa is approximately 250, not too large to disrupt the intimacy. Many of the musicians who have performed there have said it is one of their favorite clubs. Neither Kuumbwa nor Yoshi's allows smoking, which the musicians really appreciate.

The Monterey Jazz Festival is held in late September each year in a beautiful location on the magnificent California coast. It's a great place to hear music and take photographs. Within the grounds, the performers play on several stages. The main stage is in an outdoor arena that holds several thousand people, and performances are under normal daylight and artificial light. Small venues on the grounds include an outdoor Garden Stage, where several hundred in the audience can watch and listen while seated on the grass, in addition to three nightclub and coffee gallery locations on the grounds, with a capacity of fewer than 300 persons. The atmosphere, location, lighting, and general facilities are instrumental in producing the highest-quality music and photographs.

One final note. Where I could, I tried to scope out the stage before the performance. I'd look for where the piano and drums were located, and also, where any other large instruments (such as bass or vibes) might be. They wouldn't likely be moved come performance time. On the basis of this information and who and what I wanted to photograph, I would choose a location to sit and *stay there* throughout the entire performance.

I remember one time that a photographer kept moving around the front of the stage through most of the performance, much to the annoyance of the audience. He chose not to heed their pleas. Afterward one of the musicians told me that it felt like a butterfly was flitting around in front of him. I try not to disturb the audience or distract the musicians, and not to become part of the performance, but merely to be an observer. There were times when I felt that I wanted shots from another vantage point. On these occasions, I would wait until the next set to change my location.

All of the artists' photographs were taken in an attempt to capture the performers' feelings while playing the music at that special moment. Every musician has his or her own particular sound. I hope you hear my "sound" as you look at these photographs. My intent is also that after viewing the photographs, you can hear the performance and see the music.

If you have any questions or comments, you may contact me on the Internet at: www.jazzjonesphotos.com

LB

CHAPTER 1

JAZZ PROFILES

Terence Blanchard

Roy Hargrove

Wynton Marsalis

Nicholas Payton

Wallace Roney

THE TRUMPETERS

Biography

TEREN

A native and, after having lived in New York for almost sixteen years, current resident of New Orleans, Terence Blanchard (DOB 3/13/62) is not only one of today's most acclaimed jazz trumpeters, but also one of his generation's most prolific composers. He began in music on the piano at age five and switched to trumpet in the third grade after seeing trumpeter Alvin Alcorn during a school assembly jazz performance. Blanchard's musical heroes include Miles Davis, Clifford Brown, John Coltrane, Thelonious Monk, and Duke Ellington.

BLANCHARD

Early in his professional career, Blanchard was a member of legend Art Blakey's Jazz Messengers. Upon leaving Blakey's band, he and saxophonist Donald Harrison, also a Jazz Messengers' veteran, formed a band and released five recordings as co-leaders during the mid-1980s. Since the early 1990s, Blanchard has recorded and performed almost exclusively with his own bands. In addition to film scores, Blanchard has released six recordings as sole leader, his latest of which, *The Heart Speaks* (Columbia Records/SONY), was nominated for a Grammy in 1996.

The 1990s brought about an additional career path for Blanchard. Beginning in 1990 with *Mo' Better Blues* (Columbia Records/SONY), also nominated for a Grammy, Blanchard has composed the scores for numerous Spike Lee films, including *Jungle Fever* (Universal Pictures), *Malcolm X* (Warner Bros.), *Crooklyn* (Universal Pictures), *Get on the Bus* (Universal Pictures) and the Oscar-nominated *Four Little Girls* (HBO Films), for which Blanchard has received an Emmy nomination. Blanchard has also scored for the directors of *Sugar Hill* (Twentieth Century Fox), the Emmy-nominated score of *The Promised Land* (HBO Pictures), *Gia* (BBC/Discovery), *Free of Eden* (Showtime), and *Eve's Bayou* (MCA/Universal). A serious artist with the talent to match, Terence Blanchard is definitely one of the premier artists working today.

TERENCE
BLANCHARD

INTERVIEW, APRIL 9, 1997

You've experienced intense study with Art Blakey. How did you become involved with him, and what is it about Blakey's influence that's so strong with young musicians?

The way I got in the band is that they had open auditions. Donald Harrison and I went down to audition, and we won the auditions. In terms of how he taught people, he had a unique way of giving you the experience by letting you fall on your face a bit. He would let us do things. He'd let us compose the music for the band. . . . And he would talk to us. He'd constantly talk to us about his experiences with Billy Eckstine, his experiences with Louis Armstrong, and all the other musicians he had ever played with. So, in a sense, it was very much like the African tradition of the storytellers.

We gained a lot of experience and knowledge just by being around him and watching him. I watched him nightly. I would see how, even though he could be really sick, running a fever with the flu, he would get up and play his heart out on the drums. That was never an excuse for him.

Have you thought about the things he may have taught musicians other than musical development, just life lessons, for example?

Oh, yes. One of the things you always learned from him is just to be who you are, be truthful. Don't talk down to people or talk above them; just be the best person you can be. He always said if you have something to offer, the world will beat a path to your door. And he had a lot to offer off the bandstand, because he was such a personable guy. And he was a great teacher. One of the things I always noticed about Art Blakey was the fact that he was a very humble person. Extremely. I remember walking by a homeless person [with him], and Art Blakey whispered to himself, "But by the grace of God, there go I."

Since the 1980s we've seen a strong resurgence in the popularity of jazz music, and you've definitely been a part of that. Have you thought about what it is that made jazz more popular over this time period?

I've been trying to think about it. I don't think I have a real grasp of it. I think probably it's just the fact that some of the guys in our generation, including myself, have been socially acceptable, for lack of a better phrase. We're college-educated, which means a lot to a certain segment of society. We're "articulate." That was the story that was told over and over again. The frustrating part about it for us is that all of our heroes were just as articulate or more so. They just weren't college-educated. So it put us in a rare predicament of constantly having to refer the public back to the fact that there were some great musicians who came before us because people were calling us the young lions, the new breed. For me personally, I just felt like I hadn't measured up to the level of the people who came before me. So, it's a constant struggle.

Did your generation of musicians will jazz to be more popular again, or is it just something that happened for whatever reason?

It's something that we actually went out and willed. We actually went out and campaigned for it because at a time when the industry was trying to make us pop musicians or fusion musicians, we resisted. And we said, look, we grew up listening to [pop and fusion], and there's nothing wrong with it, but we like playing this. And I think that's one of the first times that had happened in jazz. Before then, everybody was going along with the flow.

Things would change and everybody thought that was a new direction to go in. And I think our generation was the first to come along and say, okay, those electric instruments are fine; as a matter of fact, we played in some bands like that. But, you know what, we'd rather do this.

I read in another interview of you that you felt like you had two careers, one being a jazz musician and another a composer of film scores. How did your career scoring films come about?

It came up totally by accident. I was a session player on Spike Lee's *Do the Right Thing*, and we were working on *Mo' Better Blues*, and he heard one of my songs I was playing at the piano entitled "Sing Soweto," and he asked me if he could use it. So we recorded it, and then he asked me if I could write an orchestral arrangement for it, and I did that. He then called me to do *Jungle Fever*, which led to *Malcolm X*. And *Malcolm X* led to a lot of work. I then got an agent, and things just kind of snowballed from there.

Let me ask you about a jazz musician developing his own sound. That's pretty much the goal of a jazz musician. How is it that a jazz musician develops that?

That's one of the things that has fascinated me about this music. If you take John Coltrane and put him on any tenor saxophone, he's going to sound like John Coltrane. If he could take the same twelve notes as Sonny Rollins plays, it would sound totally different. I think a lot of it has to do with just putting in a lot of time and effort into finding out what it is that you like about music. And that's the hardest thing to do because a lot of times people don't want to be honest with themselves as to what they like about music. . . .
[For example], how do I want to approach this? What type of rhythm is it that I really love? What type of harmony is it that I like to use? When you start to put all of those things together over a course of time, that's when you start to really develop your sound.

When did you realize you'd developed your own sound?

I still don't know that I have. That's always the eternal quest. I don't know if I've really gotten there yet. A lot of people say that I have, and a lot of people say they can recognize my compositions or recognize my sound.

I feel you have. It takes a person awhile to be able to recognize a particular musician's sound, but, for example on one of your latest recordings, Romantic Defiance, I knew the first time I heard it that that was Terence Blanchard. There's just no question.

That's a great compliment.

Who are some of the musicians you've most enjoyed working with?

Wow, man, the list is endless. All the great trumpeters, Clark Terry, Dizzy Gillespie, Woody Shaw, Freddie Hubbard, Doc Cheatham. Those are all fun. In terms of other players, I played a gig once with Elvin [Jones], and I had a great time playing with him. I played with Sonny Rollins at Carnegie Hall and was scared to death! Never got a chance to play with McCoy [Tyner], Chick [Corea], or Herbie [Hancock]. But I've played with Hank Jones, Ron Carter, and Cedar Walton, and I've had a great time playing with them all.

Who are some trumpet players you may know that the rest of us don't, and who are artists we should be on the lookout for?

There's a young guy in New Orleans now who's very talented. His name is Irvin Mayfield. He's a very energetic and serious musician. He's only seventeen or eighteen years old. I think he's going to do very well.

What advice would you have for someone wanting to make a career of being a jazz musician?

I would tell them, in order to get started, you have to think of being a jazz musician as like learning a foreign language. You have to know how to pronounce the words, which is the same thing as being able to play scales and arpeggios on the instrument, then you have to learn the grammar, which is the same with jazz in terms of learning theory; and then you have to learn how to put phrases together, which is by listening to somebody. So you listen to musicians, and you start to learn the language.

And the thing about it that really matters the most is that you could sit down to learn it from a book, but if you learn French from a book, you won't speak French until you actually start to speak to a Frenchman and hear the inflections in the voice and hear how the phrases are spoken. So you have to spend a lot of time with the music, listening to it. It's not magic, and it takes a lot of time and effort. But anybody can do it if they really put the time into it.

TERENCE BLANCHARD
SELECT DISCOGRAPHY

As a Leader
- *The Heart Speaks*— Columbia Records/SONY
- *Romantic Defiance*— Columbia Records/SONY
- *The Billie Holiday Songbook*—Columbia Records/SONY
- *The Malcolm X Jazz Suite*—Columbia Records/SONY
- *Simply Stated*—Columbia Records/SONY
- *Terence Blanchard*— Columbia Records/SONY
- *Jubilant*—with Jubilant Sykes—SONY Classical
- *Black Pearl*— with Donald Harrison— Columbia/CBS Records
- *Crystal Stair*— with Donald Harrison— Columbia/CBS Records

Soundtracks/Film Scores
- *Eve's Bayou*— Sonic Images
- *Clockers*—Columbia Records/SONY
- *The Original Motion Picture Soundtrack of Malcolm X*— Columbia/SONY
- *Mo' Better Blues*— Columbia Records/SONY

Biography

ROY

A Texas native who now lives in New York City, Roy Hargrove is one of today's leading jazz trumpeters. He began playing cornet in his elementary school band, switched to trumpet, and began listening to such masters as Louis Armstrong, Maynard Ferguson, Clifford Brown, Freddie Hubbard, Miles Davis, and Dizzy Gillespie. After high school, Hargrove studied at the prestigious Berklee School of Music while at the same time traveled back and forth to New York for steady work in jazz clubs.

Hargrove established his unique voice early on. With a sound equally forceful and lyrical, he has released numerous recordings as a leader and sideman, and all have enjoyed critical acclaim. His latest release, *Habana* (Verve), won a Grammy in 1998 for Latin Jazz Album.

HARGROVE

INTERVIEW, AUGUST 5, 1997

You said in an interview which appeared a couple years ago in DownBeat that one reason you didn't stay in the Berklee School of Music was because, in some respects, music schools are just creating clones. Do you still feel that way?

Well, that's the feeling I have at times, but I do believe that education is important. It depends on how you apply it.

Whom would you name as your greatest influences, and why?

I would have to say people like Clifford Jordan, and Jackie McLean, Slide Hampton, Jon Faddis, and Freddie Hubbard. These are all musicians I got a chance to play with and just be around and observe the things they would do. A lot of times it wouldn't be about how many notes they were playing. Sometimes it would just be about the amount of space they might leave—to set up the next phrase, to make that phrase much more meaningful.

I would just stand by and listen to these cats, and later on when I would go and play with my quintet or sextet or whatever group I'd be playing with, I could transfer the information I got from the elder statesmen to my peers.

In terms of being a jazz musician, what do you like best: composing, performing, recording?

I like to perform, and I also like to compose. They are two different worlds. With composition, I get a chance to develop that when I'm working with a big band. Because you can always have different kinds of dynamics when you have that many musicians together. You can work with the dynamics and change the sound of the whole composition.

As far as performance goes, I've been working with this group, the inspiration for which came from my traveling to the Havana Jazz Festival in Cuba last year.

ROY
HARGROVE

Yes—your band called the Crisol.

Yes. We'll be working on the road, and we're playing basically the same repertoire every night, but it's different, too, because depending on the vibe of the audience or how everybody's feeling that day, it's always different. It's a challenge just to learn how to be consistent.

You mentioned the vibe of the audience. What kind of effect does an audience have on a performance?

It depends on where you are. For example, in a New York club, people are very contained with their response in how they react to the music. But, for example, in Dallas, you'll have people in [the club] shouting and testifying.

Which do you like better?

I like them both. With [the contained audience], it's more of a challenge. But sometimes you can get them yelling, too. It depends on what's happening that night.

Tell me about your process of composing.

Sometimes I sit at the piano and play chords, and I work out a composition first using the chord changes. Then I figure out the melody on my trumpet, or maybe, vice versa. I think the piano is very important to be able to compose. Also, it wouldn't hurt to learn how to play some other instruments as well because then you can really understand the different ranges you are dealing with when writing.

If you're writing a part for bass, for example, how much of it do you actually write note-for-note, and how much of it is just an idea you want the player to explore?

The basic structure will be the harmony, and I'll write in little specific parts of the music. You may have a certain rhythm you want that bass player to play, and you write that. But for the most part it's all based on improvisation, and if you have good musicians and especially ones who have worked together a few times, [it will] come together and sound like an arrangement.

In the last ten to fifteen years, we've seen a strong resurgence in the popularity of jazz music. Have you thought about the reasons for that?

I think a lot of people are looking back at the history. For me, when I look at a photograph of John Coltrane, Charlie Parker, that gives me a lot of motivation because I say, wow, this is a great person who did something, who really dedicated his life to something. That inspires me to want to do the same. I think that's what's happening now. People are paying attention. The music never left. The listeners left. There have always been cats coming on the scene. People just weren't paying attention at certain points in time.

Do you think there is any particular reason people are now looking back to jazz?

I don't know. When I go out and play jazz festivals, there is less and less jazz being played at these festivals. It's very minimal. Because people are in a panic. They really want to sell these tickets. And with the onslaught of technology, the internet, no one wants to go out and spend money to sit down and hear live music when they can sit at home and get the video, buy the CD, whatever. It's an interesting thing to see cats who are used to working all the time trying to get a gig.

What advice might you have for a someone interested in a professional music career?

I would say to practice as much as you can. Do all the rudimental things you hate doing. Just continue to develop that because when you get out there on the road, there's no time to practice really. You have time to do a routine or something in the morning, but it's not like you have time to sit down and work out something. Because you've got to get up and go to the gig, and get on the plane, and make the train, and get on the bus.

I also would say, just listen, listen. Be still and listen. Absorb.

Throughout the history of jazz, we've had many different periods: bebop, free jazz, etc. Do you see any kind of new movement on the horizon?

I think a lot of people are getting into the old world music vibe and adding elements of the foundation of cultures in music, like from the West Indies, from Brazil, from Cuba, and from Africa. I'm seeing a lot of cats getting into that. Dizzy [Gillespie] was talking about this. I read it in an interview magazine from the 1980s.

[Gillespie] said it would really be hip if a band could come out that was dealing with all the different cultures of rhythm, including the African-American vibe. The folk vibe.

It is said of you that you have an eclectic music taste. Is that true and do you think it's important for your development as a jazz musician to listen to other kinds of music as well?

Yes, I think it's important if you are going to be a musician, period, to listen to other forms of music. It's such a vast world, why ignore certain parts of it? It's into infinity, the amount of things that can be done with music. I think music has a very healing power. It brings people together.

What other kinds of music do you enjoy listening to?

Well, I like listening to a little country and western every now and then.

Your Texas roots come out in you there.
You know, I say—[singing] Austin, Texas.

I wish we could capture this on text.
[Laughs and continues singing.]

ROY HARGROVE
SELECT DISCOGRAPHY

As a Leader
- *Habana*—with Roy Hargrove's Crisol—Verve
- *Extended Family*—Verve
- *Family*—Verve
- *With the Tenors of Our Time*—Verve
- *Approaching Standards*—Novus
- *Of Kindred Souls*—Novus
- *The Vibe*—Novus
- *Public Eye*—Novus
- *Diamond in the Rough*—Novus

Collaborations With Other Artists
- *Young Lions & Old Tigers*—with Dave Brubeck—Telarc
- *Oscar Peterson Meets Roy Hargrove and Ralph Moore*—with Niels-Henning Orsted Pedersen and Lewis Nash—Telarc

Biography

WYNT

The contributions to jazz music by Wynton Marsalis (DOB 10/18/61) are immeasurable. Born in New Orleans, he now resides in New York City where he serves as the artistic director of the acclaimed "Jazz at Lincoln Center" program. Still in his mid-thirties, Marsalis is one of the most recognized figures in all the arts today.

Marsalis began studying the trumpet seriously around age twelve. At seventeen he moved to New York City to attend the prestigious Juilliard School. Soon after arriving, however, he accepted an offer to join Art Blakey's Jazz Messengers and began touring the world. A couple of years later, he began forming his own groups, and he has maintained a relentless recording and touring schedule ever since. In 1987 Marsalis co-founded "Jazz at Lincoln Center," and it recently was named a full constituent organization, the first to earn the distinction since 1969.

MARSALIS

Marsalis has garnered awards of all kinds from numerous sources. He has received the Grand Prix du Disque of France, the Edison Award of the Netherlands, and eight Grammys for jazz and classical music (including Grammys in both jazz and classical the same year). In 1996 he won a Peabody Award for his twenty-six-part National Public Radio series, "Making the Music," and his four-part PBS-TV series, "Marsalis on Music." The same year *TIME* magazine named him one of America's 25 Most Influential People. He was awarded the Pulitzer Prize in 1997 for his epic work, *Blood on the Fields* (Columbia), which he recorded with the Lincoln Center Jazz Orchestra. In 1998 Marsalis was given the Young Star Award at the Turner Broadcasting Systems' Trumpet Awards, which recognizes outstanding African-American achievement.

Despite his young age, Marsalis already is one of the greatest figures in jazz. Continually pursuing his goals of recording and performing music at the highest levels, as well as educating today's youth, he is indeed worthy of all the recognition he has received so far and will undoubtedly continue to receive.

INTERVIEW WITH WYNTON MARSALIS,
FEBRUARY 22, 1997

***When did you decide you wanted to make a career
in music, and what led you to that decision?***

I'd say about the time I was thirteen, just because
of my father. That's the main thing, my father playing music.

***Who are some of the people who have had
the most influence in your life, and why?***

Both my parents. First, just my father—just to have
an opportunity to be around a musician of that caliber, that
type of man with a lot of integrity and not really pretentious
at all. Someone who really loves music and believes in it and
whose belief in music is not predicated on his position in it
because he was always struggling just to make ends meet
to feed that big family he had.

But he didn't get jaded because he still had belief
in the music. So he would say, "Well, I might not be making
money, but this music is great." And my mother— just the type
of investment in time she put into us going to music lessons
and taking us to concerts and stuff that she didn't really
necessarily want to do.

Then all the many teachers I had. . . . I had so many
trumpet teachers. And then all the musicians that I knew
when I was growing up. They were kind of like my uncles
even though they maybe didn't know the type of impact
they had on me. Just to always be around them.

And then musicians like Art Blakey. [He] had a
tremendous impact on me. The opportunity to work and
understand what it means to go to work every night and
play and not joke around, like be serious about swinging
and playing with a vibe at all times, playing with a certain
intensity and feeling.

And musicians like Clark Terry, I would meet them when
I was in high school. And he sent me a postcard once. Just
musicians who keep you inspired, you know. So many people.
I could just go on and on. . . . There are so many musicians.
I know so many people I've met who were very inspirational.

Recently I've had the opportunity to talk with several jazz musicians. I've talked to guys like Eric Reed, Steve Turre, Nicholas Payton, and Christian McBride. Every one of these guys acknowledges that jazz music has enjoyed a resurgence in popularity. And each one of these guys is adamant about the fact that you should get a lot of credit for that. And what I want to know is did you start out at some point some years ago with a plan, "I'm going to make jazz music more popular," or was it just something that happened along the way of your career?

I never really thought, "I'm going to make jazz music more popular." I just wanted to play. Whenever I had the opportunity to get publicity, I would speak very strongly on behalf of playing. And of course, you know, I had to be criticized for ten years. You just get criticized. Your words get twisted around. You get character-assassinated and misrepresented, but I wanted to play. I wanted to represent all the people who never had a chance like my father and all those musicians that I knew. They never had a chance to speak.

And the generation that I was from, too, from a racial standpoint, there are certain things I just didn't have to take and wasn't going to take it, especially when I was younger. I had so much fire then, man. You know I've mellowed as I got old and as I got tired. I mean, I'm not tired really, but it's not like when I was twenty, or twenty-one, or nineteen.

So that made me get more publicity. And in addition to the publicity, I was always playing. A lot of years I'd be the only band at a jazz festival playing jazz. We'd go out and play, and we'd be playing jazz. Everything would be pop, funk, or R & B, fusion, but I didn't care. I mean, I was going to play. It didn't make a difference to me.

I would always try to go to a school and try to teach the musicians, you know, talk about the music just because that's what I believed in. It wasn't so much that I'm going to save jazz, but it was what I had seen my father do. Some say I'm on a messianic trip and all that. It's not like that. You just go into a city, play a gig, and go to a school, give a class. If somebody asks you a question, you answer it. And you do that in city after city after city, and it starts to have an impact. And then it gets pushed through the media, and they put their spin on it, whatever it is, and they turn it into something else, and it just happened like that.

WYNTON
MARSALIS

You co-founded "Jazz at Lincoln Center," and you now serve as its artistic director. And recently it was named as a new constituent organization, the first time since 1969. In your opinion, what does that mean for the popularity of jazz music, maybe the future popularity of jazz music?

Nothing, really. It doesn't mean anything for it. It means more for the future of Lincoln Center than it means for jazz music. The question of "Jazz at Lincoln Center" is what Rob Gibson [co-founder] and I do. We still have to do our job. The question is what are we going to do. Maybe if we have the opportunity, if we do our jobs well, and then we bring the music to more people and we're successful in our endeavor to present the music properly, with education events, then maybe we can have an impact on the popularity of jazz.

But jazz music has been out for years; millions of great records have been selling for a hundred years. It would be very arrogant for us to think the fact that we were named a constituent makes jazz music popular. In one way, it's a belated aesthetic recognition. But that recognition was given years ago. See, Duke Ellington, going to the Midwest in the 1930s, they had a big sign up saying, "Lovers Of Art Welcome Duke Ellington." So they were recognizing him in 1930. People were doing that. So, you know, it is just another forum for us to present the music in. I mean, it's a powerful forum, but still. . . .

You've reached a level of musicianship that most people, and probably even most professional musicians, only dream about. I'm under the impression that you've attained this through, obviously, talent, and then just a ton of hard work. . . . Was it a struggle to get to this point?

Yeah, it was hard. It's not just the practice, man. Practice is first. That first six or seven years of practicing, like when you have to get up at 6 o'clock and you're going to bed at 2 o'clock or 3 o'clock in the morning after a gig and trying to do all your homework and trying to cope with whatever your personal situation is.

Then moving to New York. I had never been away from home. I was seventeen, struggling, you know, just trying to find an apartment and work, trying to support myself, man, and live. Then all of the dealing with the musicians. And, you know, at one point, everybody loves you. You first come up thinking you're from New Orleans and can play, and then realizing you can't play. I always thought I could play until I really heard myself. Then I realized I couldn't play. Then I had to figure out why was I sad because I was serious about learning how to play. But it was just basic things about the music I hadn't figured out.

Then going from being liked to being vilified because of my opinions and views. You know, not so much that I felt like I was a victim because I was on the attack, too, but just, you know, to have to really face it. It's one thing to attack. It's another thing for that attack to be returned, to have to deal with the return, to always be playing and defending something, and to be sabotaged by the media constantly for years, unrelenting. And just pressure on me, cats in the band and not being able to keep a band together, just all that jealousy and animosity.

You have to deal with people in your field. Going through personal changes at the same time with various women and children. Still trying to maintain your belief in what you're doing even though people around you don't believe in it, whether it's the record company or—yeah, it's hard man. I mean, but even all of that I'm saying is not as hard as being in Kenner, Louisiana, working at Clay's Gas Station. You know, I mean it's hard, but it ain't as hard as picking cotton. That's what my great uncle used to always say, "It ain't as hard as picking cotton."

And there's other stuff, too, you know, just mental-tripping that you're going through. Especially at first when you're young, you get a lot of publicity. You say, "Man, I don't deserve to have this publicity. I can't play." You feel guilty. You go in a short time from just being a cat out here to somebody who people know. . . .

They accused me of anti-Semitism, accused me of racism. The black people accuse you of Tomming. I mean, you have to be really prepared to deal with the fact that the opinion of you will be shaped by something that has nothing to do with you so much.

Then the real negative articles you'll get. You'll meet people for years—man, I would meet people, and they would be like, "Wow, we didn't know you were like this." That used to irritate me to no end, man. . . .

I'm thirty-five, and I've been on the road since I was twenty with my own band, including Art Blakey since I was eighteen. My whole life is just being a musician. So that's the stuff that has nothing to do with just what it takes to—staying up all night writing music, or getting up practicing, or going to the gig, riding in the van and the bus, getting on the plane, dealing with cats that are wanting to be home with their family and not wanting to be on the road, trying to keep the music together. . . . Yeah, it's hard, man. I'd be lying if I said it wasn't.

Do you have any specific plans for what you want to do in the future at Lincoln Center?

Yes, we have a lot we want to do, and all of them entail just presenting a broad range of the music and presenting a canon—saying these are the attributes, these are the pieces that we feel best identify jazz music. So that the students and those who want to know what jazz is, we'll at least put them in the ballpark. We have all the components of our program. We're getting up our education department. We want to do more things that involve a broader segment of the population, and we're doing free concerts in the park. You know, all these are things that Rob [Gibson] and I talk about all the time. That's what we're dedicated to.

And we want to use the forum to just do what we can to bring our music to more people, and the feeling of the music, too. Because when you talk about it, it's one thing, but when you're doing it, it's another thing. You want to have fun doing it, too.

WYNTON
MARSALIS
SELECT DISCOGRAPHY

As a Leader

- *Blood on the Fields*— Columbia
- *In This House, On This Morning*—Columbia
- *Citi Movement*—Columbia
- *Blue Interlude*—Columbia
- *The Majesty of the Blues*— Columbia
- *Soul Gestures in Southern Blue*—Columbia

  Volume 1—Thick in the South

  Volume 2—Uptown Ruler

  Volume 3—Levee Low Moan
- *Marsalis Standard Time*— Columbia
- *Standard Time Volume 2— Intimacy Calling*— Columbia
- *Standard Time Volume 3— The Resolution of Romance*—Columbia
- *Standard Time Volume 5— The Midnight Blues*— Columbia
- *Joe Cool's Blues*—with Ellis Marsalis—Columbia

Collaborations With Other Artists

- *Lincoln Center Jazz Orchestra—Portraits by Ellington*—Columbia
- *Deep in the Shed*—with Marcus Roberts—Novus

Biography # NICHOLAS

Photo Notes

Nicholas Payton (DOB 9/26/73) was born into a musical family in a musical city. From the birthplace of jazz, New Orleans, Louisiana, Payton's earliest influences were his father, bassist Walter Payton, and his mother, Maria, who was a classical pianist. He began playing trumpet at the tender age of four and has developed a sound and maturity far beyond his twenty-something years.

At age eight, Payton played his first professional gig, a Mardi Gras parade with the Young Tuxedo Brass Band. By age twelve, he was performing regularly around New Orleans. In addition to his education on the bandstand, Payton studied with trumpeter Clyde Kerr, Jr., at the acclaimed New Orleans Center for the Creative Arts and with Ellis Marsalis at the University of New Orleans.

I was very excited about seeing Nicholas Payton when I first heard he was coming to Kuumbwa to play with the Ellis Marsalis Quartet. This was to be an opportunity for me to hear one of the wunderkinds from Louisiana who studied with Ellis Marsalis himself. That night in Santa Cruz, Payton was very reserved, probably in deference to his teacher.

The following year, 1996, he came to Yoshi's, where this photograph was taken. By that time, he was leading his own group, and it felt to me that he was "coming out." He appeared very shy. So many of the talented musicians I've met seem to be most comfortable speaking through their music and instruments.

Payton's group at this gig consisted of Jesse Davis, alto sax; Reuben Rogers, bass; Anthony Wonsey, piano; and Adonis Rose, drums, all very young musicians. The group was playing very quietly and without Payton. It seemed that they were trying to feel each other out at the start of a new gig.

Payton was standing at the side of the stage. He walked to center stage, picked up his horn, and out of this relative stillness his sound shattered the room. For a moment I felt transported to the Louis Armstrong of my youth, a "blast from the past."

PAYTON

In his young career, Payton has performed
and recorded with such jazz legends as Clark Terry,
Elvin Jones, Joe Henderson, and Doc Cheatham
(with whom he was awarded a Grammy in 1998), as
well as younger generation artists like Wynton Marsalis,
Marcus Roberts, and Christian McBride. These days
Payton performs and records with his own band and
performs regularly in "Jazz at Lincoln Center" programs.
With a sound that evokes the spirit of New Orleans,
Payton embodies the essence of the modern jazz
trumpeter.

INTERVIEW, JANUARY 18, 1997

I understand that you were given a trumpet at age four as a Christmas present you'd requested. How is it that you decided on the trumpet as your instrument?

The trumpet just appealed to me the most out of all the instruments that I grew up seeing. Both my parents are musicians. My father plays the bass; my mother is an operatic singer and also plays classical piano. So I grew up at my father's rehearsals listening to some of the greatest jazz musicians in New Orleans. New Orleans has always been noted as the town for trumpeters, and I witnessed some of the best trumpeters in my father's living room. The instrument has sort of a regal quality to it. In a lot of bands, the trumpet takes the lead. So I guess it just stuck out to me the most.

You're known as someone who has always practiced incessantly. I've heard that you'll even practice ten hours a day. Do you enjoy the actual practicing, or do you see it as a necessary means to an end?

There was a certain period when I was practicing ten hours a day. I was in my early teens, and I really fell in love with jazz as I said before. . . . I wish I could or had the time or the discipline to practice ten hours a day now. I'm sure I could use it. But it's hard now. It's hard for me to practice being on the road.

Did you decide early on as a kid that you wanted to be a professional musician?

I knew I loved music, and I liked playing my trumpet. But my father started me off taking formal lessons when I was about eight. Up until then he had been coaching me because my father is a retired school teacher so he knew a bit about the instrument. But at that time he thought it would be best for me to get further teaching from a professional musician.

But it was at that point where, now that I had to do it, I didn't want to do it. At first it was at my leisure. I would just pick up the horn whenever and ask my dad to show me something. Now that I had weekly lessons, I had a regimen that I had to be on to do it. I just totally rebelled against it.

I didn't want to do it. He used to force me to practice.
He backed off a bit and said, well, hey, whatever.

There was a time when I was eleven years old—I was
looking through my father's collection, and I was looking
through trumpet players, and Miles Davis was someone who
stood out in my mind. So I picked out an album of his called
Four & More, and I dropped that needle, and I heard his sound
and the way that band sounded. I knew right then and there
I wanted to play jazz.

*There are sort of two paths to being a jazz musician.
I think one is the academic path, and the other one is
playing on the road with other musicians. Do you feel like
one is more beneficial than the other?*

Definitely. The best way to learn how to play jazz music
is by doing it and being in an environment where you are
surrounded by people who love doing it and who are playing it.
The academic thing is cool. The thing that is great about the
academic part of education is this: it gives you a controlled
environment to deal with.

For instance, when I was going to the University
of New Orleans, the best thing about that was that I had a
situation where I knew I would be in combo Tuesdays and
Thursdays. I knew how many musicians I'd be dealing with.
Everyone was coming, and I could prepare for that. We
could develop something on a consistent basis for those
people who may not be in regular bands. I really developed
a lot of compositional skills as well because I was able to
bring in tunes every week. I mean every session I would bring
in something new. And that really helped me to develop in
that way.

NICHOLAS
PAYTON

A lot of the older generation musicians, they only had the on-the-road-type education. Do you feel now though that it would be almost impossible to be a jazz musician professionally without the academic component as well?

I think the academic component is a road for a lot of people who otherwise don't have an opportunity to get their thing together. For instance, many years ago, there would be a lot of other things that musicians could do without necessarily having to go to school. The scene was different. The process that musicians, young musicians, have to learn now are totally different than say thirty, forty, fifty years ago. There aren't many bands, working bands, for younger musicians to really have an opportunity to play. I was fortunate enough to be in situations where I was able to. There are a lot of talented young musicians in New York and Chicago and New Orleans, all over the country, and there are no gigs for them, you know what I mean?

And also the scene was different because a lot of musicians used to get together, you know, at someone's house. Like the scene in New York in the '40s—you know, Dizzy [Gillespie] and Miles [Davis] and all these guys, they would go to someone's house all day and talk about music and listen to music and practice and play together. There's not that kind of camaraderie between musicians nowadays. It's really cliquish and individualistic.

I really think things could be so much better for the jazz scene and the musicians in general if everyone could just pool their energies together to try to work together. And everyone doesn't have to like everyone's playing or play the same. But I think the mutual respect, there should be more mutual respect and adoration for what other people are doing in the business. It's lacking in that, I think.

Many folks credit Wynton Marsalis as inspiring a lot of the younger generation artists of today. Was he an influence on your development, and if so, how?

Definitely. I mean, of course, my primary influences would be my parents, particularly my father who is a jazz musician. I met Wynton around when I was twelve or thirteen years old. That was really when I started listening to him. . . . He was an inspiration to me because I just think he represented to me that jazz can be a music of younger people as well. It always seemed that whenever you saw jazz on television, it was older musicians. Or even the community I lived in. Primarily those who were doing what I wanted to do were older musicians. And it was just nice to have someone whom I could relate to and who was closer to my age level. It made me feel like I had more of a chance to have a part in this music.

Other than your parents and Wynton, who would you credit as a great influence or inspiration for you to become a musician?

Clark Terry. He was very helpful to me—even still to this day. I met him around the same time, when I was about twelve or thirteen years old. Ironically, I met him when I was subbing on a gig playing trombone for somebody because the leader played trumpet, and he didn't want two trumpeters. So it was later on he came to New Orleans, and I was at a session he was at. I played trumpet and ever since then, he has taken me under his wing. . . . Even still today, people call me and say we were looking for a trumpet player, and Clark recommended you. But he's been helpful to a lot of other people. A lot of great trumpeters and other musicians as well.

Would you have any advice to pass along to somebody who's thinking about being a professional musician? What would you tell them that maybe you wish somebody had told you?

The best thing I can say for someone trying to play this music is you have to stay focused and keep your goals in line regardless. This is a tough music to try to succeed in. This is a tough business to break into. One thing I can say is that if you're in it for financial reasons, this is one of the worst things to get involved in, this particular music. Because while the financial rewards can be great at times, maybe they might not be. Nothing is guaranteed to anyone. A record contract is not necessarily guaranteed to you. A gig is not guaranteed to you. For some people, it takes longer than others to hook things up a certain way. But you just have to know that you have to stay focused and committed to it. There may be a lot of hard times, but hopefully, eventually, if it's for you, it will pay off.

NICHOLAS PAYTON
SELECT DISCOGRAPHY

As a Leader
- *Payton's Place*—Verve
- *From This Moment*—Verve
- *Doc Cheatham/Nicholas Payton*—Verve
- *Fingerpainting*—with Christian McBride and Mark Whitfield—Verve

Collaborations With Other Artists
- *Big Band*—with Joe Henderson—Verve
- *Kansas City—The Original Motion Picture Soundtrack*—Verve
- *They Came to Swing*—"Jazz at Lincoln Center"—Columbia
- *Underground*—Courtney Pine—Antilles

Biography

WALLACE

A native of Philadelphia, Wallace Roney (DOB 5/25/60) now lives in New York City. Steeped in jazz music from early childhood, he began playing trumpet around age five. While in Philadelphia, he studied at the Philadelphia Settlement Music School, and in his teens he studied at the Duke Ellington School for the Arts after his family moved to Washington, DC. He went on to study at Howard University and the acclaimed Berklee School of Music.

During his career, Roney has performed and recorded with some of jazz's all-time greats. He has worked with Art Blakey and the Jazz Messengers, Miles Davis, Tony Williams, Herbie Hancock, Wayne Shorter, and Ron Carter. These days Roney plays with his own group and also collaborates with his wife, jazz pianist Geri Allen.

Sometimes I get lucky taking a photograph. Thi shot of Wallace Roney fal into that category. When clicked the shutter, I wasr sure what I would see wh the film was processed. For a few seconds, while composing, I could see Roney in a contemplative, dream-like stance while h was listening to the other musicians. I quickly adjusted the aperture opening and shutter spee and took the photograph.

I was pleasantly surpris when I saw the finished product. To this day, I'm n sure whether the result wa due to the camera setting light or both, but it woulc extremely difficult for me duplicate the shot. The bottom line is that Roney looked the way I hoped h would but doubted I woul so lucky to get.

Sometime later, I submi this photograph, along wit dozen others, for exhibitio a show in a prestigious gallery. This was the only o that was accepted. Later th curator told me they weren looking for the type of photographs that I had submitted, but that this one had a very "mysterious appearance and so they decided to include it.

Roney was appearing on trumpet at Kuumbwa in January, 1993, with the Tony Williams Quintet. The other musicians were Billy Pierce on tenor sax, Mulgrew Miller on piano, and Ira Coleman on bass.

RONEY

INTERVIEW, OCTOBER 21, 1997

Tell me about some of the earliest musical experiences you can remember.

Earliest musical experiences would be jazz and my father. I lived in north Philadelphia. Every weekend, from Friday to Sunday, at the end of the work week, guys would come over to certain people's houses, and all the friends would bring in jazz records, and they would sit and listen to the latest jazz records.

My father had to have the latest trumpet players' records; his friend, Charlie, had to have the latest drummers' records. His friend, Rob, had the latest tenor saxophonists' records. Clarence had the latest piano players' records or whatever the thing was. And every week they did this. And they compared notes and listened.

And the wives would come over, and my mother would be friends with all the wives. And then her sisters would come over. So they'd have this thing going along simultaneously with my father's doings, and then they would all eat. It was just a big party.

And my house wasn't the only one like this. Next door neighbors and their friends did that, the neighbors on the other side, and it was the whole community. If you stepped outside, you'd hear jazz all day, and that's the way it was. I grew up in that, and I loved it, and I participated in it from the day I could make sounds. I was grooving with it.

Your music education, you've had both a formal type training—music schools, and you've had the on-the-road-type training with some of the most wonderful legends of the music. There were Miles Davis, Art Blakey, Herbie Hancock, McCoy Tyner, Tony Williams. Do you have an opinion as to which of those educational types would benefit a jazz musician the most?

Let me say it like this. I got a problem with the word "formal." Let me tell you why. I'm only estimating that when European music was at its best and at its most vibrant, in order to learn how to play that music or learn how to master that music or its instruments, you had to be with the master musicians. And they didn't call that formal at the time. You were an apprentice.

Somehow when it got to European music and that way of learning, it became "formal." With jazz at its most vibrant now and its doing the same thing or has never stopped doing the same thing that European music did before they called it something else. It's called an apprenticeship, and you're learning from the masters.

I did have lessons from music school. My first teacher was the principal trumpeter of the Philadelphia Orchestra in the 1920s and 1930s. He was a great teacher. But I learned as much or more about correct trumpet playing from Clark Terry. And it wasn't a "by the rope thing." He taught me things, you know. And Dizzy Gillespie taught me more about theoretic harmony than Howard [University] and Berklee [School of Music]. And Miles Davis taught me more about how to be an artistic master because he showed me more things.

So it's your opinion that the apprenticeship route is more beneficial than the school route?

I think both are necessary. I think the school route is the beginning, but if you're serious, you have to do the apprenticeship. You've got to do it. There's no other way to learn how those people feel and to get to the heart of mastering it. There's no other way. I can't see it being any other way.

Tell me who would be some of the people who have influenced your life the most.

First the family influence. And overall your parents are the ones who brought you here, so they're the ones who guided you and allowed you to be moved by people. So you're talking about my father, and my mother, and my grandmother. Those three were probably the ones who really made it possible for me to exist, who shaped the qualities of my life. And then Art Blakey along with them because he was like family.

Then the musical influence. Miles Davis is my biggest musical influence. And Bird, Coltrane, Clifford Brown, Dizzy Gillespie, Ornette Coleman, and Don Cherry.

And third, boxing. My father was a boxer. I like Sugar Ray Robinson and Muhammad Ali. I like boxing a lot.

Tell me the story about your hooking up with Miles Davis.

Let me tell the whole story. One day around October, 1983, I went to see a concert at the Bottom Line. It was Steve Smith's group, Vital Information, and Billy Carlton. And George Butler happened to be there. I had known George Butler for a couple years, and he says to me, "Hey, Wallace, how you doing?" I said, "I'm doing fine." He says, "Listen, there's going to be a retrospective of Miles Davis's life." I'm thinking, wow, my idol. He says, "Would you like to participate?" I said, "Wow, sure." He said he had an idea of having seven trumpet players each come up and play a couple choruses of the blues, and then you all get together and play this fanfare and that would be the announcement for Miles.

Now mind you, I wasn't working that much at the time. I was on the scene. And I was playing, but I didn't have a steady gig. [Butler] is asking me to play a fanfare. I said, "Look, I'll play a fanfare. I'll shine his trumpet if you want me to."

So I get to rehearsal, and the band that's going to do it is Herbie [Hancock], Ron [Carter], and Tony [Williams]. I said, "I don't believe this. This is just too much." So after we rehearsed, we got in the concert, and each one of [the trumpeters] played, and the way I played I got more response out of Tony and Herbie and Ron than the other guys because I was probably one of the only ones who really played that way. The people seemed to really like my playing.

And that's how it happened. Afterwards, Art Farmer took me backstage to meet Miles. And that's how I met Miles, and that began our relationship or mentorship that was very fruitful.

A lot of people are saying we're in the midst of a resurgence in the popularity of jazz music. Do you agree with that?

I don't agree with it because if there were [a resurgence], it would translate in sales of records and attendance. My attendance has been pretty strong. I don't know if my records do great or not. Maybe they are doing great, but if they are, it shouldn't just be my records. It should be every musician's records. I would think if there's a great popularity among jazz fans, [the jazz fans] would want to check out everybody who's doing something, you know, spend their money and see what's going on. And if they don't like a certain artist, they just don't buy it the next time. It seems like only two or three people are breaking a certain mark—so that doesn't tell me there's a resurgence. Maybe we can do more to make that happen or to make it translate because if it were, the jazz record industry wouldn't be doing what they're doing, trying to tell artists what to do because of sales.

What advice would you have for someone wanting to be a jazz musician?

Be committed to it, and play music because you love playing music, not for any kind of reward. Rewards are fine, and it's nice to look for it later on, but don't start out playing music for that.

Play music for the sheer inspiration and love and expression, musical expression, the commitment of it. Music is supposed to be an extension of your feelings. If you have a need to express yourself and you're a musician, then that's why you do it, and have the commitment that it takes to learn your instrument so you can be true to your own feelings.

And the most important part is the more you become dedicated to that, the better your music is. Then you have to dedicate that to the one that made you because then the music belongs to God because anything of beauty must reflect that.

WALLACE
RONEY
SELECT DISCOGRAPHY

Solo Albums
- *Village*—Warner Bros.
- *Wallace Roney*—Warner Bros.
- *Misterios*—Warner Bros.
- *The Standard Bearer*—Muse
- *Intuition*—Muse
- *Verses*—Muse
- *Munchin'*—Muse
- *Crunchin'*—Muse
- *Seth Air*—with the Miles Davis Tribute Band—Muse
- *Obsession*—Muse

Collaborations With Other Artists
- *A Tribute to Miles*—Miles Davis Tribute Band—Qwest/Reprise
- *Miles & Quincy Live at Montreux*—with Miles Davis—Warner Bros.
- *Tokyo Live*—with Tony Williams—Blue Note
- *Neptune*—with Tony Williams—Blue Note
- *Eyes . . . in the Back of Your Head*—with Geri Allen—Blue Note
- *Maroons*—with Geri Allen—Blue Note
- *Remembering Bud Powell*—with Chick Corea—Stretch Records
- *Warner Jams Vol. 1*—with Brad Mehldan, Joshua Redman, Kenny Garrett, and Wallace Roney—Warner Bros.

JAZZ PROFILES

THE SAXOPHONISTS/CLARINETIST

Biography

JAMES

J ames Carter (DOB 1/4/69) is the youngest of five children born into a musical family from Detroit. The owner of more than sixty woodwind instruments, he is best known for his saxophone work. In addition to the soprano, alto, tenor, and baritone saxes, he plays the clarinet, bass clarinet, oboe, and bass flute. His musical taste also runs the gamut— from straight-ahead, to swing, to free jazz.

In 1990 Carter moved to New York City. He made a name for himself quickly, and in 1995 was named one of *Rolling Stone* magazine's hottest artists. He has collaborated extensively with legends Lester Bowie and Julius Hemphill. Carter also has performed and recorded with some of today's top jazz artists, including Wynton Marsalis and the Lincoln Center Jazz Orchestra, the Mingus Big Band, Harry "Sweets" Edison, Buddy Tate, and Hamiet Bluiett. Carter has made five recordings as a leader and performs regularly with his own quintet.

Photo Notes

The first time I saw James Carter, he was playing at Yoshi's at the Eddie Moore Festival in August, 1995, with the New York Organ Ensemble. That group included Lester Bowie on trumpet, Amina Claudine Myers on organ, Frank Lacy on trombone, Kelvyn Bell on guitar, Don Moye on drums, and Carter on all the saxophones. Carter was the youngest of the group, and the other musicians seemed protective of him. He didn't seem to need the protection, however. He carried himself on and off the stage like a musician experienced well beyond his years. This photograph is from that performance.

About a week later the group played again at Kuumbwa, and I showed Carter the photographs I had taken of him. The other musicians looked at them and said, "That's James, Mister Blur." His playing matched the photographs—very high-energy. The photograph of him on the front cover of this book was taken about a year later, in September, 1996, at Yoshi's. This time he appeared with his own group. He played all the saxophones again. Craig Taborn was on piano, Jaribu Shadid on bass, and Tani Tabal on drums. The night was electric. Many in attendance were the Bay area musicians eager to check Carter out.

CARTER

INTERVIEW, SEPTEMBER 18, 1997

You speak highly of a former teacher, Donald Washington. You've said that one of the great things he passed on to you was a spiritual direction.

Teachers nowadays really stick to the academics of what helps you to produce music—you know, the reed goes here, and this is the C scale, blah, blah, blah—these are chords, these are progressions, things like that, just to make sure you are able to make the changes and play in all the right keys, etc.

But there is a story behind certain things, and [Washington] always talked about music as life, and he mentioned good cases in point about Charlie Parker, for example, and he encouraged reading biographies so that you knew that the influence of individuals went beyond just what they recorded as an end result. Like "Body and Soul," what was Coleman Hawkins doing before October 11, 1939, that led up to that point? Those are important things everybody should know about. And it doesn't necessarily have to be musicians, but it could be everybody. You never know what might be a turning point for an individual.

You are somewhat of a rarity in that you play soprano, alto, tenor and baritone saxophone, flute, oboe, clarinet, and bass clarinet. You also play in a wide variety of styles. Is this just a function of your personality in that you like so many different things, or is it more of just the challenge of doing all those things?

I would say it is all the above. But at the helm of it, once again, is Mr. Washington, also a multi-instrumentalist. Just by hearing the different voices he had coming out of each instrument, as well as the individuals he was steering me towards as far as listening and eventually coming to know personally and playing with. . . . It came as a result of just the natural cultivation of having it around and just feeling inclined to play more than one instrument.

What are some of the most memorable gigs or recordings you can recall?

One gig that really sticks out to me is seeing the World Saxophone Quartet in 1982. This was during the time

they came to the Detroit Institute of Arts as part of a series. Just to see the viability of the saxophone standing on its own—no rhythm section to propel it, nothing like that, just four saxophones, four individuals up there, and that's it, it took me for the biggest loop of my life.

In the last ten to fifteen years we've seen a strong resurgence in the popularity of jazz music. Have you given any thought as to why that is?

I think it is people starving for truth. And I feel that there is truth in all music. But for me it seems the biggest truth comes out in jazz. For example, when you look at certain songs like Billie Holiday's "Strange Fruit" or "Fables of Faubus." These are music interpretations of events. And this is how they manifested themselves by song.

I know you're asked about this often, but tell me about your collection of saxophones.

Let's see, early on I became fascinated with the saxophone. It was a physical attraction to them as well as what I was hearing. The person directly responsible for [the fascination] is Charles Green. He used to play with my oldest brother's group called Nature's Divine, which was like an R & B group back in the late '70s.

Green was a boarder at your home for a while, right?

Right. And out of all the instruments he had, one stood out. It was a Selmer Mark VI alto he had—it was gold-plated, and it had all this engraving on it. I was like, "Ooh," you know. I had little love affairs with his horns, as far as picking them up, not necessarily playing them. And I got caught.

[Green] wound up picking out my first alto, which was a King from the late 1920s. Silver with a gold bell. And it was subject to tarnishing and oxidation, right? So one day I decided to—I had seen those Tarn-X commercials, they were rampant around this time for some reason. It was like Tarn-X commercials couldn't be squelched for some reason—but, anyhow I was able to find a bottle of Tarn-X around the house. And I got a screwdriver and started taking the instrument apart. And then another love affair happened—the ability to clean and start repairing instruments happened. It was

curiosity that pretty much killed the cat, but I was just cleaning the horn at this time. And it took like seven hours to do this. And I got it down to—just to take it apart and put it back together—I got it down to a half hour.

So I started looking around for other instruments. My second saxophone was a [Selmer] Mark VI tenor. And I think before that I had that alto, a flute, a clarinet, and the others were borrowed from the school . . . . A good portion of what I've acquired has been through pawn shops, the classifieds, [people] getting rid of something for whatever reason.

How many instruments are you up to now?
I'm in the process of figuring that out.

You're over sixty though, aren't you?
Somewhere in that neck of the woods.

When you think about certain instruments, like one I just [obtained] is a 1938 Selmer Balanced Action, and the special thing about this horn is that this is the horn that Buddy Tate was playing in Count Basie's orchestra. So you think about tunes, such as "Tickle Toe" with Buster Young, "Rocket" by Basie, "Super Chief," all these tunes were recorded on this horn, with [Tate] playing featured solos.

I acquired it the day after Buddy turned eighty-five, went up there, and rapped with him, and just spent time with him because he hasn't been in good health. And so I have a piece of history put into my hands, and it's like a relay race that is being run; the baton is being passed on. It has that significance to it. And not only to be able to play it, but to recondition it, and take care of it, and put it back out there as opposed to it becoming a museum piece. That's where I feel the horn should be. It should be active and playing.

What advice would you have for a youngster who might want to become a jazz musician?
The first thing I would say is to keep your ears open and be true to yourself. Study the music, and listen to yourself. Keep your ears open because I'm not just influenced by the saxophone. I'm influenced by voices and everything that is audible, down to the "big bang" itself. And you incorporate

these things. You ingest them and make them your own, make them personal. That's what sets you apart.

And also, put up with other people who don't hear things the same way that you do, you know, within the media as well as personally. Because they are not living for you. There is only so much that they can do, even if it is negative. [For example], I have a whole lot of [critics] talking about circular breathing here, and multiphonics this, and gimmicks that. But these same individuals won't put their butts out on the line either. They won't put themselves on stage; they would rather stay behind a desk pencil-pushing, saying so and so was there and he had this, that, and the other to offer, but that's it. But march that critic up on the stage, and put a horn in his hand, and see how he feels.

So bear in mind that it becomes a lot easier to be honest with yourself because you have that whole other foreign or outer influence in check as far as within your mind, so that you can go on with what you have to do and what voices you hear with what the Creator has given you to use as tools of creativity.

Study the music in terms of knowing where you are going, knowing where you come from, how the music has evolved in your particular instrument as well as other instruments. And, more importantly, [knowing] that this music wasn't born out of a secular situation, such as the first time it was amplified was the sporting houses and the brothels as opposed to like a Carnegie-Hall-type situation, which didn't happen until later. And folks had been trying to say, oh, it's a music from the Devil's workshop as opposed to classical. That was all the design. And that whole concept needs to be omitted.

And anytime I get a chance to, I always tell folks that this music was about solidifying people and celebrating, celebrating life and the circle of life.

JAMES CARTER
SELECT DISCOGRAPHY

As a Leader
- *In Carterian Fashion—* Atlantic Records
- *Conversin' with the Elders—*Atlantic Jazz
- *The Real Quietstorm—* Atlantic Jazz
- *Jurassic Classics—* Columbia/DIW
- *JC on the Set—* Columbia/DIW

Collaborations With Other Artists
- *Saxemble—*with Saxemble—Qwest/ Warner Bros.
- *Rush & Hustle—*with Wendell Harrison— Wenlta
- *Five Chord Stud—*with Julius Hemphill—Black Saint
- *The Fat Man and the Hand Blues—*with Julius Hemphill—Black Saint
- *Funky T, Cool T—*with Lester Bowie—DIW
- *Organizer—*with Lester Bowie—DIW

Biography

CRAIG

A resident of Union City, New Jersey, Craig Handy is a product of two acclaimed arts institutions, the Berkeley High School jazz program and North Texas State University. He began on piano at age eight and started to play saxophone at twelve. He counts his father's jazz and classical record collection as an early major influence.

Handy began to seriously consider jazz music as a career while in college on a Charlie Parker Scholarship. At the famed Fort Worth jazz club, Caravan of Dreams, he met jazz legends, such as Art Blakey, McCoy Tyner, and Betty Carter, as well as artists of his generation, including Ralph Moore, Donald Harrison, and Terence Blanchard. At Moore's urging, Handy moved to New York City in the summer of 1986. His big break came just after Christmas when legend Roy Haynes was looking for a tenor sax player. Handy got the gig and promptly began touring with Haynes. As Handy put it, "That was the end of my struggling days."

Since breaking into the national scene, Handy has played with the likes of Abdullah Ibrahim, the Mingus Dynasty Band, Art Blakey, Betty Carter, and Herbie Hancock, as well as lead his own groups.

Craig Handy is a homegrown talent out of the Berkeley, Californ high school system, alon with some other young lions, Peter Apfelbaum, Joshua Redman, and Ber Green. Every time I've see Handy play it has been ir the San Francisco Bay are with many family and friends in the audience. This has made for a "pla) at your best" situation. I knew that under these conditions it would be very good for me to photograph him.

The first time I saw Handy was in 1994 at the Eddie Moore Festival at Yoshi's. He was playing tenor sax with Ralph Peterson on drums, and Charles Fambrough on bass. The presence of mar other talented musicians the festival pushed him t play up to his potential. Two years later, in the fal of 1996, he came to the Monterey Jazz Festival wit Herbie Hancock on piano, Dave Holland on bass, anc Gene Jackson on drums. Shortly thereafter Handy was back at Yoshi's to pla) with some Berkeley High School stars and some old friends he'd played with when he was younger. Thi= photograph is from the Monterey performance.

Playing with Hancock, Holland, and Jackson here before a large festival audience seemed to prope him to an enthusiasm tha I saw only a few times before.

HANDY

INTERVIEW, MAY 16, 1997

Tell me about the earliest musical experiences you can remember.

I started the saxophone when I was twelve. I fell in love with the saxophone. I heard a recording of Dexter Gordon playing on the radio, and I don't remember what the tune was, but I remember that he had this amazing sound—this incredible sound just hit me right in the chest. It was just the coolest thing I have ever heard. I knew I had to check that out, so I begged my parents to buy me a saxophone. They said, well, why don't you try it at school. I said, no, please, I've got to play this instrument. They again said, go to school, and learn it in school, and see how it works with the instrument. I didn't think I was going to get a saxophone. They surprised me—I forget whether it was Christmas or my birthday, but they bought me a saxophone. And that was it, man. I was practicing every day for like, four or five hours after I came home from school. . . .

I listened to the radio and listened to everything that was current, too. James Brown, Motown, and funk music, whatever. Then, as well, my father is a big jazz fan, a huge jazz fan, so he has a very large collection of jazz records. I can remember hearing jazz before I could speak. He liked to listen to classical music as well. Every Sunday was classical day. So it was largely through the influence of music that I heard on the radio or on records that I got into jazz—into music in general.

How did you decide that you wanted to make your career as being a professional musician?

I never really decided it until it was sort of decided for me—I didn't really know what else to do. I didn't really like doing anything else. . . . It wasn't until I was in college that I said this is what I want to do and why waste time fighting it and trying to learn some other skill and get a degree and do something else. My parents always said if music doesn't work out, you can fall back on something else. But my attitude was, well, it's going to work out. It's just a matter of how it's going to work out. I didn't really see it as needing to fall back on anything else. It was just a matter of if this avenue doesn't

work, I'll do something else in music. I'm going to have to do something [in music], otherwise I'm going to jump off a bridge.

CRAIG HANDY

There's probably a lot of uncertainty in being a professional musician; it isn't one of the more stable careers. Do you find that exhilarating, or is it something that bothers you?

On the one hand, I think it's important to make plans and to have goals, so there are things that I want to achieve in the next five or ten years. At the same time, you learn in life in general, nobody can really say what they are going to be doing in five or ten years. Obviously the best-laid plans sometimes go off course, and you end up somewhere that's even better than you thought it was or it could happen that you end up somewhere that is a lot worse. It just depends on your attitude, I think, and what you make of the situation that you have in front of you. To make the most of each situation and try and gain the most out of it is, I think, the most important thing. And to learn from it.

What are some of the goals and aspirations you have for yourself?

Number one would be to have a band that tours at least six months out of the year. Number two is to have some kind of outlet for my writing, and what I mean by that is to have some kind of a commercial outlet for it as well as for the band that would be touring.

I would like to get more involved with film and TV. I've worked with [Bill] Cosby. . . . He asked me to play the '94-'95 theme for "The Cosby Show." Each year he would use a different artist to record the same theme. So I went in and recorded it, and that started kind of a long association I've had with him. . . . I recorded a couple records with him. . . . I actually ended up writing and producing the music for "The Cosby Mysteries. . . ." I'd like to do more of that kind of work.

As we speak, you are on tour with Herbie Hancock. He is obviously one of the masters. What specifically have you learned from him, and how has the tour been?

We've been working together since last March, 1996. He's great. He's one of my all-time greatest heroes. To have the

chance to work with him and actually go back each night and work with him again is like I'm dreaming every night. It took me six months to get used to the fact that that was Herbie Hancock who was four feet away from me playing this amazing piano solo. It would be my turn to play and I would be like—huh? What? I've got to follow that? What am I going to do?

Herbie is a really, really unique individual. He's not only my musical hero, but he's also one of my all-around heroes because he's figured out a way to do all those things he's wanted to do—or maybe not all of them, but at least enough where people have an idea about him. He's involved in so many things, and he does them all really well. He has an amazing ability to really focus on what it is that he wants to get done in a particular time and accomplish it. That's a lesson in itself—just watching him work and the way he does it.

Who would you count as your heroes on the tenor saxophone?

Oh, man, that's like listing the *Who's Who of Music Anthology*. Anybody who has ever picked up a saxophone. That's a hard one. I'd leave so many people out if I started naming names. Sonny Rollins, John Coltrane, Hank Crawford, Charlie Parker, Eddie "Lockjaw" Davis—if I started writing these down now, by December I could probably fill the list out. The list is so long, it just doesn't really make any sense to do it. And it's not just straight-ahead jazz players. It would also include guys who played popular music and played it well.

Have you thought about why we are seeing a resurgence of the popularity of traditional jazz?

I think that the number of people who aspire to play straight-ahead jazz is probably pretty constant. What you see is a reflection of the market responding to it. By that I mean, when you have somebody who has the right story, the right package, the right profile, like a Wynton Marsalis, who comes along who has a great story. His father is a fixture in the education community. All of his brothers are great musicians. He himself is one of the best classical interpreters, and he can play jazz at the same time. It is a sure thing. You can't go wrong with it; he's intelligent and well-spoken.

So when you get a guy like that, who's got it all together, and you put him out there, people are attracted to him. It's easier to market than a guy who's just playing his instrument very well. I think what happened was he created this whole kind of atmosphere where it was cool to like jazz again. Plus, he came along, and he was wearing a suit and tie, which gave it some loftier type of appeal. He appealed to people who were theatergoers, classical music lovers. He appealed to a—not a highbrow clientele, but to people who were more inclined to think along those lines, perhaps. And that again is a great appeal and I'm sure that the record executives sit back and go, well, this is our guy. This is what we're looking for. This is going to work for now.

But anywhere you go in the country, there is going to be a handful of people, young people, who are going to be wanting to learn how to play jazz. They are going to find out about Duke Ellington, Thelonious Monk, and Coltrane, and go, man—Miles Davis, and go, wow, this is really—what is that? Whom do I talk to? Where do I go? And so you have an outlet in people like Wynton and Herbie, too, who make it okay to do it. And make it okay to like it, that's the thing, make it okay for John Q. Public and Suzie Q. Public to go ahead and buy the records. They make it cool; they actually make it like a hip thing. . . .

As far as a resurgence, I don't think it's so much a resurgence as much as it's just the media picking up on wherever it's happening, and they're exploiting it now. It's going on all the time, okay, well, let's go find out where it is, so, now it's popular. Okay, great. So here it is. I think it's that type of thing. The spotlight is on it right now. Because when I was coming up, the guys I came up with, Benny Green, and tons of other kids, they are scattered around still playing jazz. So, it isn't dead and hasn't gone anywhere. It's just waiting for people to go, okay, we're going to like this now.

CRAIG HANDY

SELECT DISCOGRAPHY

As a Leader
- *Introducing Three for All*—Arabesque
- *Acoustic Masters II*—with Bobby Hutcherson, Lenny White, Jerry Gonzales—Atlantic Jazz

Collaborations With Other Artists
- *Hello Friends: To Ennis With Love*—with Bill Cosby—Verve
- *Kansas City—The Original Motion Picture Soundtrack*—Verve
- *Gunslinging Birds*—with the Mingus Big Band—Dreyfus Records
- *Tenor Conclave: A Tribute to Hank Mobley*—with Grand Central—Evidence
- *Chartbusters: Volume 1*—with Chartbusters—NYC

Biography

BRANFORD

Photo Notes

Branford Marsalis (DOB 8/26/60) is one of the most creative musicians of his generation. The firstborn son of New Orleans pianist Ellis Marsalis, he began piano lessons at age four, moved to the clarinet, and settled on the saxophone in his mid-teens. He has studied jazz at some of the most prestigious music schools in the United States, including the New Orleans Center for the Creative Arts and Boston's Berklee School of Music.

Marsalis's recording career began in 1981 when he recorded *Fathers and Sons* (Columbia) with his father, his brother Wynton, and Chico and Von Freeman. The same year Branford and Wynton toured and recorded with the great Art Blakey and his Jazz Messengers, as well as with legendary pianist Herbie Hancock. Since Marsalis's early professional days, he has made numerous recordings as both leader and sideman, and all have enjoyed raving commercial and critical success.

I photographed Branford Marsalis during his week-long engagement at the old Yoshi's Nite Spot on Claremont Avenue in Oakland, California, in December, 1996. His new trio consisted of Marsalis on tenor and soprano saxophones, Jeff "Tain" Watts on drums, and Reginald Veal on bass. At the beginning of the first set on opening night Marsalis spotted me in the front row and announced over the mike, "We're being photographed for a magazine cover." I replied "We should be so lucky!"

This photograph of Marsalis was taken during that night's gig. When he plays, he's all business, yet his humor really connects with the audience. In spite of the low light throughout the performance, I was able to adequately photograph him, probably because of the inspiration given by the music, and the rapport between musician and audience.

MARSALIS

Marsalis has garnered several Grammy nominations and was awarded a Grammy in 1993 for Jazz Instrumental Performance, Individual or Group, for his album *I Heard You Twice the First Time* (Columbia) and another in 1994 for Pop Instrumental Performance for "Barcelona Mona," a single he recorded with Bruce Hornsby for the 1992 Olympic Games in Barcelona, Spain.

In addition to composing, recording, and performing, Marsalis pursues numerous other music-related projects. In 1990, he hosted and narrated a National Public Radio (NPR) series on the history of jazz entitled "Bass Lines: The Reflections of Milt Hinton." Also during the early 1990s Marsalis was the music director and arranger of NBC's "The Tonight Show with Jay Leno." In 1996 and 1997, he was a guest lecturer at Michigan State University as the first recipient of the Catherine Herrick Cobb Distinguished Lectureship. Last year he was named a creative consultant to Columbia Jazz, where he is involved in forming the creative direction of the label. He currently hosts "Jazzset," a weekly NPR series featuring jazz performances by top artists.

Marsalis has made a lifetime's worth of contributions to the music world and is still only in his thirties. He has few peers in his generation, and the jazz community is blessed to have him.

**BRANFORD
MARSALIS**

INTERVIEW, DECEMBER 6, 1996

Tell me something about your earliest musical experiences.

I used to play piano. My father tried to make me practice, and I wouldn't. And he told me [one night] I was going to sit on the piano all night until I practiced. So I fell asleep at the piano because I wasn't going to practice. And that could possibly be where I get my aversion to practicing
up to this very day.

I was in a recital with a young lady named Barbara Krauss. I didn't practice, but I knew the music. I knew it, and I knew I knew it. But my mother, not being a musician, she's an academician, and they believe in that ridiculous ritual of hard work brings forth excellence, which I agree with. But when they say "hard work" they mean physical work, the appearance of labor. So if you're sitting there practicing all day, you're going to be good. But I think even at an early age, I kind of knew that that was bull.

It just sort of came to you naturally?

Well, no. I thought about the song in my head. That's what came naturally, the thought process. The song wasn't that hard. It wasn't like we were playing Chopin. I was seven years old, eight, nine. And it was one of those cute duet things. I played it a couple of times with Barbara and I knew it. I would sing it every night in my head. So when it came time to play, I just played it.

So when we did the concert, my mother was so nervous she got up and walked out and peered through the door. She's always been that way. I didn't miss a note. And then when we finished, I stuck my tongue out at her bowing on the stage. And people probably had no idea what that was about because they didn't see her get up and leave. Just a little

punk—what's this punk kid sticking his tongue out for? Who's he sticking his tongue out at, you know?

Music education, in jazz anyway, has two avenues. You can go a formal-education route or you can go a more informal, on-the-road route, playing with other musicians. You've done both. Do you think one is more beneficial than the other?

No. Because the thing that makes successful jazz musicians is intellectual application. I can think of a whole lot of people who played with great musicians, and we never heard of them again. Records are full of them. Everybody talks about Wynton and I playing with Art Blakey and Billy Pierce, but Art Blakey had bands from 1971, '72, '76, '77, '78, '79, '80, and no one even knows who those guys were. So playing with Art Blakey or playing with Dizzy Gillespie isn't the secret.

Sort of goes back to what you were just saying. You can sit down and practice all day.

You can sit down and practice all day. That's the difference between a great instrumentalist and a great musician. Great musicians develop over a certain period of time. But you have to think about your craft in a way. You have to really hone your skills and do a tremendous amount of research.

And listening is the key. Listening isn't emphasized anywhere. It's almost like you have to just figure it out on your own. But from talking to those musicians—that's the thing that was invaluable for me playing with Miles [Davis] and playing with Dizzy [Gillespie] and playing with Art Blakey. It's not really the gig. It's the conversations before and after the gig. That's what gave me an inkling.

Playing with Ron Carter and Herbie Hancock and talking about listening and who they used to listen to and how it influenced them. And the combination of Bud Powell, Wynton Kelly, and Debussy. Herbie would talk about how it changed his music. So that gives me an inkling. I'd say, okay, listening. That's the key. My father, he talked about listening.

Academic education in classical music and jazz should stress listening first and everything else second. And that is why you have so many dull and unimaginative players in jazz and in classical music. There's an absolute paucity of quality classical soloists because these guys don't know how to listen to music. They don't know how to interpret the music that is in front of them. They just know how to play it.

It's like you use all of the tools that are at your disposal. One of the things that we can do is we can get a lot more information than Bird and those cats could because we have their recordings. . . .

Did your father and brothers, other people in your family, have an influence on the way you played or your development as a musician?

Yes, but not from a musical standpoint—from an intellectual standpoint of view. If you want to really know why we play jazz the way we do, you should sit at our dinner table and hear the conversations that we have that don't pertain to jazz. That gives you a major inkling into the people.

There has been a lot of comparison lately of younger generation jazz artists to what I would say are the legends, Coltrane, Miles Davis, etc. And I think that a lot of the comparison has come from writers and critics. Do you think there's too much of that going on, and do you think that that might inhibit some of the younger generation's creativity?

Anybody who is a student of this music realizes that it is absolutely absurd to compare a twenty-two-year-old kid to the geniuses of the music. Any serious student of the music would know that, and if any serious musician allows his creativity or his ability to be changed by a handful of writers, handful of hack writers, or former musicians, they don't deserve to be musicians.

The way I used to look at it is that quid pro quo. You know, every guy who would compare me to Coltrane, I would compare his writing to Hemingway, compare his writing to Faulkner. And some of them, I'd even tell them that. Say, man, I was comparing your work to Faulkner. Man, you've really got a way to go.

There are ones that I get along with personally, guys I go golfing with, guys I'll call and talk about their families and all that stuff. But what they write about, they write about. You know, Leonard Feather was like my favorite. I'd go to his house, then he'd come and give me a shitty review. And I thought that was great. I thought it was the way it should be because it's great when you meet somebody whose journalistic ethic allows them to separate their personal relationship with you from what they feel as a critic.

I told a guy when I was twenty-four, he was talking about you know, do you think you have your own voice? I'm like, what a ridiculous notion for a twenty-four-year-old to have his own voice. Come and check on me when I'm thirty. And when I was thirty I started to have one. . . . And now, I mean, I got it.

Tell me a little bit about life on the road. You play a week somewhere, and you have to move somewhere else. Some musicians feel that while they get to go to a lot of cities, they don't get to really visit any of them.

If you do jazz clubs, I mean, how can you not see the city? You can see any city four or five hours a day for a six-night span. When you do one-nighters, it's a lot more difficult. I do one-nighters, but [with this tour] I chose to do a jazz-club tour. These are the best days because we go on the road for a month, and we only have to fly five times. The original thing [one-nighters], you go on the road for a month, you fly twenty times. That's bad. But the joy of playing music, the joy of expressing yourself can't be touched, you know.

BRANFORD MARSALIS
SELECT DISCOGRAPHY

As a Leader
- *The Dark Keys*—Columbia
- *Bloomington*—Columbia
- *I Heard You Twice the First Time*—Columbia
- *The Beautiful Ones Are Not Yet Born*—Columbia
- *Crazy People Music*—Columbia
- *Trio Jeepy*—Columbia
- *Random Abstract*—Columbia
- *Renaissance*—Columbia
- *Royal Garden Blues*—Columbia
- *Scenes in the City*—Columbia

Collaborations With Other Artists
- *Music Evolution*—with Buckshot LeFonque—Columbia
- *Buckshot LeFonque*—Columbia

Biography

JOSHUA

Photo Notes

With a recording career that began only in 1993, Joshua Redman (DOB 2/1/69), the son of tenor legend Dewey Redman, quickly has become one of the premier saxophonists of his generation. Redman got his first tenor saxophone at age ten and became one of the featured soloists of Berkeley High School's widely acclaimed jazz ensemble. In 1991 he graduated summa cum laude from Harvard College, where he also was elected to membership into Phi Beta Kappa. Setting his sights on becoming a lawyer, he achieved a perfect score on the Law School Admission Test and was accepted to Yale Law School.

I photographed Joshua Redman many times between 1993 and 1997. Although he always played with excellent musicians during that period, it seemed he was experimenting to find a compatible group.

The night that I took this photograph, the group was playing at Kuumbwa on February 26, 1996. The stage was lit with very, very low lights and a preponderance of reds. Redman was soloing on a standard that could have been included in one of those "Jazz for Lovers" albums. The lighting on his tenor sax and on one side of his face helped to create a romantic mood. These conditions, coupled with blue backlighting, reminded me of Surrealistic paintings.

This photograph of Redman was taken while he was playing with his current group as of this writing (Peter Martin on piano, Peter Bernstein on guitar, Brian Blade on drums, and Christopher Thomas on bass), the same one he played with at the Monterey Jazz Festival in September, 1996.

At Redman's closing performance, with his own group, he said, "I've been dreaming of playing on this stage, at the Monterey Jazz Festival, for five years and it's a wonderful moment for me, a dream come true."

REDMAN

Before entering law school, Redman moved to New York City with some musician friends and practiced and performed regularly. He also took first place in the 1991 Thelonious Monk Institute of Jazz Saxophone Competition. Because Redman enjoyed these experiences so much, he decided to postpone law school to become a professional musician. He hasn't looked back since.

Redman has released six recordings as a leader in just five years, and each has enjoyed overwhelming success. In his young career, he has performed and recorded with some of the biggest names in jazz, including Dave Brubeck, the Carnegie Hall Jazz Band, B. B. King, Clark Terry, and McCoy Tyner. Redman is a truly gifted individual, artistically and intellectually. His quick, meteoric rise is unusual yet well deserved.

INTERVIEW, NOVEMBER 21, 1996

Please describe some of your earliest music experiences.

My earliest musical experience was listening to music. And I think I've been listening to music and loving music since the day I was born. . . . [M]y mom remembers that I always had an inclination for music, was always attracted to music, always liked to move my body to music. . . .

And when I was five, my mom took me to this place called the Center for World Music in Berkeley, California, which offered introductory courses in a lot of different world musics. . . . After that, I guess the first Western instrument I played was the recorder. I probably picked that up when I was seven or something like that. . . . I was fooling around on the piano. At one point, I took classical piano lessons for a few months. . . . I played guitar before I ever played a wind instrument. I didn't get very far in it but learned some good power chords, you know, strummed along with Beatles tunes. And then I picked up the clarinet in the fourth grade and saxophone in the fifth grade.

And then it all was the saxophone pretty much after that?

Yes. I think even before I picked up a saxophone, I had an affinity for the instrument. I loved the sound of the instrument as it was played by great saxophonists like [John] Coltrane and [Sonny] Rollins, and Lester Young, and Stanley Turrentine, and my father [Dewey Redman], and all the people that I was listening to when I was young.

And I always wanted to try the tenor saxophone because the sound of the instrument was so rich and so powerful to me. And when I tried it, I fell in love with it and knew that, to the extent that I was going to be a musician—I didn't think I was going to be a professional musician at the time—but to the extent that I was going to be one, I knew the saxophone would be my main instrument.

Many career opportunities have come your way. You were Phi Beta Kappa at Harvard. You were accepted to Yale Law School. Is there any one thing that you can point to that made you shift gears and decide you were going to be a professional musician?

There's not one thing, but I would say more than anything was the opportunity to make music with and learn from and also be encouraged by idols of mine, great musicians whom I had always idolized. People like Charlie Haden, Jack DeJohnette, Elvin Jones, Paul Motian, Clark Terry, Milt Jackson, Pat Metheny, Billy Higgins. These were people whom I had a chance to play with all, basically, during the first year of my career—before I really even realized that I had a career. It was the opportunity to make music with these people and learn from them, and the inspiration I got from playing with them that convinced me to pursue music and choose that track.

Ever since your career's beginning, both colleagues and critics have said that you are a future legend. You are a future Coltrane or Rollins. You also, though, have a very eclectic musical taste, and that's evidenced by your recordings. . . . [D]oes your conscience struggle in balancing the traditional with exploring new things?

I've never felt there needs to be a struggle or a conflict between tradition and innovation. I've always believed that through music you can resolve that contradiction. In fact, I think that all great music, all honest music, contains both the tradition and innovation. Because if you're playing music and you're playing honestly, your own experiences can never deny the past. You can never deny your influences and the history and the language of your art form.

By the same token, if you're playing honestly from your soul and playing your own experiences, you will have something original to say because each one of us is an original. Each one of us is an individual. And in that sense, I believe each one of us is an innovator. Each one of us has something new to offer.

JOSHUA REDMAN

So I've always felt that the less you think about, well, how do I want to position myself relative to a tradition or against a tradition, the less you think about that, the more naturally you will be able to embrace a tradition, but also depart from that tradition and extend it and maybe do things that are innovative and maybe do things that, in a sense, are opposed to the tradition. Part of the tradition of jazz is going beyond the tradition. I think innovation is part of the tradition. With any creative music, I think they're completely commingled, and you can't and shouldn't even really try to separate them.

I think that's the beauty of music. If you look at the intellectual problem, you see innovation relative to the future and tradition relative to the past. But music isn't about that, music has its own logic. . . .

I also want to say that as far as the whole notion of inheriting a legacy or my generation inheriting a legacy of the Coltranes, and the Rollinses, and the Miles Davises, and the Charlie Parkers, I mean, obviously, I and anyone else in my generation, we're always honored to be compared to those legends. But for me, I would never think about trying to live up to their standards because I think that, one, if you try to live up to someone else's standards, if you try to be the next somebody else, then you're destined to fail because you're never—I'm never going to, in my own eyes or in anyone else's eyes, I'm never going to be another Sonny Rollins or another John Coltrane. They are singular individuals just like Sonny Rollins and John Coltrane were not another Charlie Parker, and Charlie Parker was not another Lester Young.

I think that I and everyone else in my generation, we have to be careful not to be overwhelmed by the grand tradition and the grand legacy of our music. . . . I think excessive comparison of this generation with the tradition that's come before it can be dangerous, can be detrimental to the creativity that's happening now.

And I sense a little bit of that in the climate of jazz today. Everyone seems to be trying to refer what's going on now to something that happened in the past. And I think that's a dangerous trend. I don't think that musicians

are directly responsible for it. I don't think the industry is directly responsible for it. I don't think that writers are directly responsible for it. But everyone together I think has kind of made this almost like a self-reflexive period. Jazz, in a lot of people's minds, is looking back on itself. And that's definitely something which I don't have any desire to do.

I love listening to old music, but I'm not necessarily looking far into the future either. I'm trying to deal with the present and look into the here and now. And what it is that I feel. And what it is that my generation feels. You know, how can we come together and make music which embodies our whole experience and at the same time is uniquely ours?

You've described life on the road as one big packing and unpacking experience; and you've said that you get to a lot of cities, but don't visit them really. And also, you feel like being on the road takes a lot of life out of you. Do you still have that perspective, or how do you feel nowadays about being on the road?

. . . I feel incredibly fortunate that I've had these opportunities to perform around the world, for people around the world, and lead a band and tour with the band around the world. By no means am I taking that for granted. And I'm always grateful for that.

But life on the road is difficult. And it's gotten to a point, for me, where I've realized that in order to continue to be a creative, inspired musician and in order to continue to be an inspired human being, I need to, at least over the next year or so, cut back a little bit on the amount of time I spend on the road. I spend pretty much the whole year on the road now; and I've realized that I need to take, not a giant step back, but a bit of a step back or a step in another direction and make sure that I have time for practice, for composition, and for life outside of music. That's very, very important.

What about the future? Future projects for you and your band? Do you have a specific path that you're going to go down, or do you just sort of take it as it comes?

Well, I think that I never try to plan concretely too far in advance because music is an adventure, and you've got to let whatever happens happen. This record that we've done now and the tour that we're doing ["Freedom in the Groove"], it didn't come out as I had expected it to come out. It came out better and different. And so I try not to plan too much.

Right now, with this band, in terms of the things that I'm writing, we're very interested in trying to preserve the spirit of acoustic jazz which is improvisation, interaction, spontaneity, that freedom of jazz, but extend it into stylistic territory and, in particular, into rhythmic territory that isn't considered part of the jazz tradition. So I feel that we are moving in a direction which is away from mainstream jazz without in any way abandoning the spirit of jazz. So I'd like to continue in that direction. That's one project I'd like to do.

There are so many different things I'd like to do. Basically, I just have to try to follow my own soul. And if I'm inspired to do something, I do it.

JOSHUA REDMAN
SELECT DISCOGRAPHY

As a Leader

- *Timeless Tales (For Changing Times)*— Warner Bros.
- *Freedom in the Groove*— Warner Bros.
- *Spirit of the Moment (Live at the Village Vanguard)*—Warner Bros.
- *Moodswing*— Warner Bros.
- *Wish*—Warner Bros.
- *Joshua Redman*— Warner Bros.

Collaborations With Other Artists

- *Young Lions and Old Tigers*—with Dave Brubeck—Telarc
- *Gettin' to It*—with Christian McBride—Verve
- *With the Tenors of Our Time*—with the Roy Hargrove Quintet—Verve
- *Tenor Legacy*—with Joe Lovano—Blue Note

Biography | # DAVID

Photo Notes

B orn and raised in Puerto Rico, David Sanchez (DOB 9/3/68) is one of the most exciting and enthusiastic saxophonists of his generation. Initially interested in percussion, he began studying the saxophone while attending La Escuela Libra de Musica in Puerto Rico. Trained classically as a youngster, Sanchez became interested in jazz after hearing recordings of Miles Davis, John Coltrane, Billie Holiday, and Cannonball Adderly.

Sanchez began serious jazz studies at Rutgers University, which led him to an opportunity to play with Eddie Palmieri. Soon thereafter Sanchez began working steadily with Dizzy Gillespie and his United Nations Orchestra and also in smaller group settings until Gillespie's retirement in 1992.

I first saw David Sanche after Dizzy Gillespie's deat in 1993. Sanchez is from Puerto Rico, and as a resul he is often thought of as a Latin-jazz musician. You would hardly know that, however, when he leads his own groups.

This photograph is from such a date, this time at Yoshi's in October, 1996. Although his group consisted of musicians all thought of as playing Latin-jazz—Sanchez on all the saxophones; Richie Flores, percussion; Adam Cruz, drums; Edsel Gomez, piano; and John Benitez, bass—the music this evening was more bop than Latin.

When Sanchez leads his own group, there seems to be little frivolity in his demeanor. It looks like it's all business. A little over a year later, I was with my daughter, Lisa, who is a vocalist and musician, when we saw Sanchez play with McCoy Tyner's Latin All Stars. She commented that Sanchez sounded better than she'd ever heard him. Later, Charlie Fishman, Sanchez's manager, told us that Sanchez always seems more relaxed when playing with someone else's group. I've learned from photographing him many times now that in looking at the photographs later, I can always tell if he was playing with his own group or someone else's.

SANCHEZ

During Sanchez's young career, he has performed with many of jazz's greatest legends, including Slide Hampton, Kenny Barron, Jimmy Heath, Hank Jones, McCoy Tyner, and Elvin Jones. Sanchez has released four recordings as a leader and spends most of his time these days performing with his own quintet.

DAVID
SANCHEZ

INTERVIEW, DECEMBER 2, 1997

Tell me how you became interested in jazz.

You know, I'm asked that question a lot, but I always find it hard to answer because I don't really know. One day I found one of my sister's records, *Basic Miles*, which was basically a compilation of different things. . . . And this record touched me in a way—when I checked the record, I said, man, I really want to play, I really want to focus on the saxophone, and I really would like to play jazz some day.

And that's when I really started buying books and talking to different people in Puerto Rico who were also interested in the same type of music. It's a little hard because there were no jazz schools, no formal training you could get in terms of jazz. But on the other hand it was good because I was really listening to a lot of records and getting things from records. That helped me a lot in the long run.

How did you first garner the attention of Dizzy Gillespie?

I first joined Dizzy because of a recommendation of Paquito D'Rivera and other members of the United Nations Orchestra.

I was playing with Eddie Palmieri at the time. It was my third year playing with Eddie, and it was great, a great band, great learning experience also. And one good thing about Eddie besides all the things I learned was the exposure was great. We used to play at jazz festivals, world-music festivals, things like that. And because of that I had the opportunity to meet many musicians. They were all responsible for my being able to join Dizzy Gillespie.

You've played with a lot of jazz legends. Tell me some of the things you've learned from them.

From Dizzy I learned how to be dedicated to what you are doing, to have some kind of discipline. In many ways I learned that from him. He was probably seventy-one-years-old when I joined the band. And he would get up every day and do his routine. He'd have breakfast, and then he'd warm up and sit down at the piano all the time. He stayed focused. These things you pick up as you go along.

And from Eddie Palmieri, I learned about rhythmic concepts. And I learned a lot of his whole philosophy of music. These are things you don't even realize you're learning until years go by and then it's sort of, wow, I picked this up from when I used to play in these situations.

You're still in your twenties, and you've released four recordings as a leader and all have been critically acclaimed. Are you surprised at all the attention you've received while you're still at such a young age?

Yes, I'm really surprised because, I've got to tell you, in New York City, in the whole United States and the world, there are so many great musicians, and not just saxophone players, but trumpet players, piano players. And the only reason I came to the United States was for the learning. The rest was secondary. And when I started working and people started calling me, I was very surprised. I just came here happy to be here and just happy to be surrounded by a bunch of great and talented musicians.

What are your goals in terms of establishing your own voice?

Well, I'm working on it. This is a lifetime procedure I would say. But I'm finding it little by little. And I'm focusing on melodies and rhythm lately. Little by little, I'll find my voice.

Which saxophone players have most influenced your style?

I would say Dexter Gordon, Sonny Rollins, and [John] Coltrane. They are the main three who have influenced my playing. But also Ben Webster and Joe Henderson. I'm just talking about tenor saxophonists here, but I've been influenced by all sorts of players.

You came to New York in 1988. Since that time have you noticed a surge in the popularity of jazz music?

Yes, definitely. There are more and more players, very young players.

Have you given any thought to why it's now more popular?

Yes. Realize that in the 1980s and 1990s, the whole movement, Wynton [Marsalis], Terence [Blanchard], and Branford [Marsalis] and all those people, brought a different vibe, and they influenced us. Then there were Kenny Garrett and a bunch of others. I would have to be here a long time to name all the people. But all these people influenced us. And now there's a different vibe. I don't know exactly why, but there's a lot of people coming on the scene.

Tell me what advice you would have for a young person who might be thinking of becoming a jazz musician.

The main thing to use is tradition. Just check out the past and where [these musicians] were coming from. Study that, and use it as a tool to really do something new with it because that's what jazz is about. It's about bringing in your perspective. It's freedom, but, of course, you've got to know your past. You've got to know where you've come from. That's the main thing. Use the past as a tool to build the future, to come up with new ideas and new perspectives.

DAVID SANCHEZ
SELECT DISCOGRAPHY

As a Leader
- *Obsesión*—Columbia
- *Street Scenes*—Columbia
- *Sketches of Dreams*—Columbia
- *The Departure*—Columbia

Collaborations With Other Artists
- *To Bird With Love*—with Dizzy Gillespie—Telarc
- *Bird Songs*—with Dizzy Gillespie—Telarc
- *Dedicated to Diz*—with Slide Hampton & The JazzMasters—Telarc
- *Habana*—with Roy Hargrove's Crisol—Verve
- *The Journey*—with Danilo Perez—RCA/Novus
- *The New Arrival*—with Charlie Sepulveda—Antilles
- *Algo Nuestro*—with Charlie Sepulveda—Antilles
- *Villa Hidalgo*—with Giovanni Hidalgo—Messidor
- *Kenny Drew, Jr.*—with Kenny Drew, Jr.—Antilles
- *Hilton Ruiz*—with Hilton Ruiz—Telarc
- *Rachel Z.*—with Rachel Z.—Columbia

Biography

BOBBY

From Lawrence, Kansas, Bobby Watson (DOB 8/23/53) was first exposed to, and influenced by, the music of his church and the spirituals his mother played on the piano. He began on the clarinet and later switched to alto sax, with which he has made his name. After studying at the University of Miami, Watson moved to New York in 1976 and soon joined Art Blakey and the Jazz Messengers. He also has worked with many other legends, including Max Roach, Joe Williams, and Lou Rawls.

A multifaceted artist, Watson has produced recordings by younger generation artists, including David Sanchez and Ryan Kisor. He composed the original music for the score for Robert DeNiro's directorial debut, *A Bronx Tale* (Sony Pictures). He also finds time to serve as an adjunct professor at the Manhattan School of Music. Watson has released numerous recordings as a leader and sideman.

Offstage, Bobby Watson is the happiest musician I ever knew. He is laughing and bubbling all the time Onstage, however, he hardly cracks a smile. He is always taking care of business while playing, and at those times he is Mr. Serious. When he is leading his own groups, Horizon and The High Court of Swing, he is especially concentrating on music.

I remember seeing him with Charli Persip's Superband, Panama Francis's Savoy Sultans, and also with the 29th Street Saxophone Quartet, where he didn't have total musical-planning responsibility. At those times the jovial Watson was again evident.

In October and December, 1997, he was playing with the T. S. Monk Big Band at Kuumbwa and Yoshi's, respectively, on a tribute tour to Thelonious Monk, Sr. There were thirteen to fifteen musicians in the band, including two vocalists, Nnenna Freelon and Dianne Reeves. Sometimes Watson would stand up to give the band directions. This photograph was taken at Kuumbwa. This is classic Bobby Watson, playing the music he loves.

WATSON

INTERVIEW, NOVEMBER 5, 1997

Do you recall how you became interested in jazz music?

I've always naturally wanted to improvise, and the way I got into it is not the way you're going to hear it from everybody else. I didn't come from a jazz family. [Mine] was a highly religious family. I would say orthodox for lack of a better word. And there were always spirituals, so I just always wanted to express myself on an instrument, bottom line, because music always gave me a feeling. And there was just something there—I was attracted to it. The first time I performed in public was at the church. I played "Battle Hymn of the Republic" on the clarinet. And I souped it up my way.

I'd listen to the radio for hours listening to this clarinet thing, "Stranger on the Shore," and I'd try to play it on my clarinet. And I'd always be playing things I heard. When I got into high school, I really got a formal introduction to jazz and heard Charlie Parker for the first time when I was in the eleventh grade. My high school American History teacher was a jazz drummer who moonlighted during the night, and he decided the second half of the year to make the American History into Jazz History. The whole second half of the year we had to read this book, *Jazz Masters of the Thirties and Forties.*

And he brought records, and he played them. And it sort of just went from the beginning up to the present. At that time it was 1970, and he brought us up to the present. And that was something. I was like, wow, you know, this is what I've been looking for.

How do you feel about the state of jazz education today?

I think it's better than it ever has been. There are a lot of people who have contributed to the history of the music by way of records and being out there and have walked with some of the originators. They are now in some of the jazz schools. . . . A lot of people who know what they're talking about are getting involved in education. I think that's healthy. These people are preparing those who want to for the real world because there's no substitute for experience.

Tell me what advice you find yourself giving most to youngsters who want to become jazz musicians.

I tell them to be patient and trust the voice inside them. Get rid of that man with the gun—that little man with the gun who's standing there getting ready to blow your head off or something. You know, learn to love yourself, and learn to love your sound, and don't let anyone put you down. Go straight ahead and believe what you hear.

But at the same time, after you check the minutes of the last meeting, which means listening to all those records. You've got to listen to those records. And once you listen to those records and once you get the gist of what's going on on those records, I say put them down. Listen to them for your enjoyment and for your own education in terms of your repertoire, but in terms of how you approach the repertoire, you should approach it your own way because I think life's too short to be imitating and trying to sound like somebody else.

Yes, I read an interview of yours where you said the younger generation needs to focus on learning from the masters but not duplicating what they played, and to try to create their own tradition. Do you think so far the younger generation has been successful at this?

They're all very serious. I don't hear too much originality, and the reason is because they're being recorded at a stage where they shouldn't have. You know, we all went through that stage—I went through a stage where everything I did was like Cannonball Adderly. I wanted to play Miles [Davis]; I wanted to play Cannonball. That's because at some point when you learn this, you want to see how it feels to swing. You want to capture that feeling you got on the record. To see what it feels to have [the music] surround you. And there's nothing wrong with that, but you shouldn't be on a major label while you're doing that. But I think it's imperative that young people go through that stage; that's the tradition of it.

Do you think a lot of that stems from pressure from the labels?

Yes. And then, not so much pressure, it's just that you can't bring out what's not in their heads. They haven't lived long enough. They're going to do what they know, which is those records. And the labels see someone young, someone they can ride. It's almost like athletes. You know, youth and athleticism, that concept is drifting over into music, and I don't like it.

[With musicians], the older you get, the better you get. As long as you're taking care of yourself, the older you get, the better you get. I wouldn't want to go back and be twenty-two again for nothing.

And I feel they're disrupting an ancient tradition called apprenticeship. Before all of this, people were going and standing under someone and learning with their hands. And that's really how I learned and all the guys my age, and that's how [the younger generation] will have to learn. The depth, that takes time.

Do you agree that there's been a strong resurgence in the popularity of jazz music in the last ten to fifteen years?

Yes. And I always thought from the minute I got into jazz back in the 1970s and really became passionate about it, I couldn't figure out why it wasn't more popular. And I just knew that one day it would become popular again. And I think that [jazz music is more popular] because it evokes feelings, not just anxious feelings like a lot of pop music. . . . But jazz, you can put it on to wake up, you can put it on to go to sleep, you can put it on to pay your bills, or to sweep the floor, or to just sit and look. And because the world is moving so fast, jazz does have a healing [component] to it. And in these times, it is drawing people to it.

Tell me what your favorite part of your job is: composing, recording, performing?

Oh, gosh, all of it. I think my favorite part of the job is composing. That's the dreaming part of it, coming up with something new and then hearing it come to light. That's wonderful. That's a feeling that you can't describe.

BOBBY
WATSON
SELECT DISCOGRAPHY

As a Leader
- *Urban Renewal*—Kokopelli
- *Midwest Shuffle*—Columbia
- *Tailor Made*—Columbia
- *Present Tense*—Columbia
- *Post-Motown Bop*—Blue Note
- *The Inventor*—Blue Note
- *No Question About It*—Blue Note
- *Love Remains*—Red Records
- *Advance*—Enja
- *Appointment in Milano*—Red Records
- *Gumbo*—Evidence
- *Jewel*—Evidence
- *Round Trip*—Red Records
- *Solo Saxophone Album*—Red Records
- *Beatitudes*—with Curtis Lundy—Evidence

Biography

DON

D on Byron is probably the most widely acclaimed jazz clarinetist working today. He regularly is voted the top clarinetist in *DownBeat* magazine's Critics Poll and in 1991 was named its Jazz Artist of the Year. A true innovator, Byron brings to his art an eclectic taste.

Byron grew up in the Bronx, New York, and counts his father, a bassist, and mother, a pianist, as early musical influences. He has studied both European classical and jazz music and attended the New England Conservatory of Music. He has been a part of groups of all kinds, including straight-ahead jazz, Latin ensembles, and the Klezmer Conservatory Band.

In addition to extensive collaboration with guitarist Bill Frisell, Byron has performed with numerous artists, such as Cassandra Wilson, Hamiet Bluiett, Geri Allen, Reggie Workman, Steve Coleman, and Ralph Peterson. Byron has been featured in many jazz festivals throughout the United States and Europe. These days Byron records and performs with his own groups.

Don Byron is one of several musicians I would go far out of my way to see. His playing is animated, unstrained, and true. It's a challenge to capture him on film showing all that emotion and enthusiasm. Byron first came to my attention in 1992 when he was playing the music of Mickey Katz with a klezmer band. He seems to have a penchant for playing different kind of music and an ability to carry it off.

This photograph was taken during the second set at Yoshi's on April 26, 1995. The lights were very low, very harsh—too many reds—and there were areas of disparate intensities of light. I expected Byron to be very tired during the second set because of his recent traveling and scheduling, so I almost called it a night as far as picture-taking went after the first set. Luckily I decided to stay and was rewarded accordingly when he came out for the second set; he seemed to be reinvigorated. Byron was out of his klezmer phase that night. (Byron says he is never in or out of any phase—that he just keeps changing.) When I took this photograph, he was soloing on his version of a Monk standard.

BYRON

INTERVIEW, JANUARY 18, 1997

Did you know as a youngster that you wanted to be a professional musician, or what time period in your life did you know you wanted to play professionally?

I always liked math. I'd say right until I got into high school, I was thinking a lot about some kind of math-derived career. At that time, computers weren't—there was no such thing. By the time I got out of high school, I probably felt more than anything like I wanted to play the clarinet. At that time, I wasn't thinking about playing jazz or anything like that. I was just trying to learn how to play the clarinet, and I guess I kind of had fantasies about playing a lot of new music. Kind of like twentieth-century classical. That was my interest.

Who were your earliest inspirations in terms of music?

My father had a lot of records around the house. And even though I didn't intend to be a jazz musician, no one had ever stopped me from liking any music. So I liked what I liked. I liked Miles [Davis], and I liked Cannonball [Adderly], and I liked some of the Oscar Peterson stuff that he had. And then I loved Motown music. Loved Aretha's [Franklin] music. I was a kid. Anything that I heard that I liked, I liked it.

My favorite group was a group called Mandrill. In a way, they were kind of like the prototype for the kind of musician that I tried to be. They had a lot of interests—like they would play some funk, they would play some stuff that sounded kind of more rockish, they would play Latin things, calypso things. And they seemed to reflect the kind of varied interests that I— it's not even like I tried to develop a varied interest; I just always had them.

I think some people grow up, and they think that there is a part of what they liked as a kid that they're supposed to outgrow. It's like I used to like Led Zeppelin but now I'm into Sonny Rollins. So that other stuff wasn't really valid. I was just too young to know any better. I think I kind of have always felt

like I had a certain amount of taste. I liked Mandrill; I didn't like the Monkees that much. I just didn't make bad choices, and I never outgrew them. I liked Eddie Palmieri, and I didn't like Larry Harlow. I just always have been making choices, but I made choices in each kind of sub-genre that I was interested in. I made educated choices in each one.

What do you like best about being a musician? Do you like the playing, the composing, recording, performing? What's your favorite part?

I don't know if I have a favorite part, but I think I make good records. In a lot of ways I could say that I've produced all of the records that I have done. They were all my ideas and my calls for who to bring in and my choices of music and my choices of sequence and the records and the way that they looked. I like that process. Not because I do a whole lot of technical trickery, but there is something about it I like. Usually when you do a recording, you have money. You can get who you want to be where you want when you want them. Other times that can be really hard to do.

From what I know of you, you have a very eclectic musical taste. A lot of times from both musicians' and listeners' standpoints, folks categorize themselves like "I'm a jazz listener" or "I'm a jazz musician," or "I'm a classical listener" or "I'm a classical musician." And I think you're unlike that. For whatever reason, this phenomenon seems only to be a part of music. When people go to movies, they don't say, "I only go to comedies." And when people read books, they don't say, "I only read crime novels." But for some reason, folks tend to want to like one kind of music to the exclusion of others.

Not only that, but people tend to think of music as an imitative art. Which is really—that doesn't exist. It's like nobody wants to see somebody's copy of Picasso.

Have you thought about why that is? Why people want just to listen to one type or play one type of music?

I think why people want to listen to one kind of music makes more sense to me. Because music is a pretty environmental thing. It gets into people, you know, their eyes can be crossed, they can be half asleep. But somehow music gets in, and people take it and tend to personalize it and identify with the kind of person that they think the musician is. Which I think is one of the real problems that I have had because, for example, if I'm playing Klezmer stuff, people can think that I'm all these different kinds of people that I'm not. They can think I'm down with killing Palestinians, but I'm not. They can think that, you know, because that's the person that they project me to be. And usually it has more to do with them than it has to do with me. And I see myself do it.

A couple of years ago Dionne Farris came out with her record, and I identified with the kind of person that she must be to put that message out. So even I, who pride myself on a certain amount of objectivity, I find myself identifying with some people more than other people. I can tell when that is, and I'd like to be able to listen to someone who I don't think that I like or identify with as a person and say, well, you know, he's an asshole, but he sure can play. He's an asshole, but he sure can write. He was a member of the Nazi party, but that section there is bad. I think the Jewish thing, especially, it was almost like I'd set up such an enigmatic thing just by being myself and doing that music—it almost became a Rorschach test for people. They were projecting whatever they figured I must be like. And most times, that has nothing to do with the person that I am.

Why is it do you think that critics want to categorize everything. . . . It's like critics and writers have said, "This is a jazz musician, and this is a jazz record." Or "This is a classical musician." They sort of almost inhibit the creative process I think of some, if musicians are swayed at all by the critics—

You know they are.

They may, if they think, "Well, this isn't really going to be accepted as a jazz record, so I've got to limit the way I do this composition."

Most critics get into writing about music to write about a certain music that they relate to—that they're empathic to over others. There are basically two ways that I think we could objectify the whole thing. One is if critics had to write about— a music critic had to write about classical shit. And he had to write about pop shit. That there was no division. Then we would be more in the ballpark of what I'm talking about for myself.

The other thing is if we structured music criticism in the kind of *New York Times Book Review* way, where people that were working in a similar idiom or in a similar way were the only people that were writing about my work. So I don't know who it would be. If Bill Frisell were criticizing my stuff, or Henry Threadgill, or Muhal Richard Abrams, or somebody like that were writing about it—then we would get information.

I think what's happening now is kind of a disproving of everything that's left of straight-ahead jazz. It's like we need to disprove it. Or if we like it—if you like David Murray, then you believe that he plays chords really great. You know what I mean? You can like him, and he may not be able to play chords really great. So it's like this all-or-nothing thing.

If we like somebody, if we like Ornette [Coleman]—oh, well, he used to play like Bird [Charlie Parker]. Well maybe he didn't play just like Bird. Maybe we just like him because whatever musical endeavor that he's finally come up with on his own is valid. It doesn't mean he can play the shit out of rhythm changes. It doesn't mean he understands everything. It doesn't mean he knows everything. But those are the terms. Right now, those are the terms.

The terms are if I give it up to "X" musician here as a real jazz musician, then he can do everything. And he knows everything. It's like when we were doing the filming of *Kansas City* and were playing "Moten Swing." It was like two of the people in the band who were considered the "outest" cats knew that one of the chords that we were playing was wrong. Me and James Carter, we were the only cats that knew that, like in that period, there was a certain chord in a certain place. Everybody else was just playing. Some of these cats are like—everybody would say, "Oh, they were in a tradition and blah blah blah." If I can do something that you like, it doesn't mean I know everything. . . .

What's put out there now is this kind of very narrowed definition of what a jazz musician is. To me, what's interesting about James Carter is that he kind of is skittering all over the fence. He gives it up to some of the outer cats which probably of half the people that are setting up that definition of what a jazz musician is, they'll tolerate it but they're not in love with it. They like it better that he plays all that Ben Webster stuff. God bless him for like keeping that whole spectrum of stuff kind of in his mind and under his fingers.

Anything you can think of that you would for sure want the young musician to know?

Well, in a general kind of way, the conservatories especially are very narrow, especially when you're dealing with a lot of classical musicians. Classical musicians in conservatories are saying stuff like, "If you read a piece of jazz, you lose your sound, you lose your ability to play classical music. Whenever anybody says anything like that, it just can't be true because as soon as you get out of school, you just have to deal with making money. Just making money. Just making some kind of money.

As soon as I left school, I had to play more saxophone than I had planned. As soon as I left school, I just fell in with cats who maybe weren't that close to my aesthetics. But I had to make it work. The school thing is always one thing. And what you'll have to do to actually make it as a musician and maybe what you'll end up being successful at doing are two different things.

DON
BYRON
SELECT DISCOGRAPHY

As a Leader
• *Nu Blaxploitation*—Don Byron & Existential Dred—Blue Note
• *Bug Music*—Nonesuch
• *No-Vibe Zone*—Knitting Factory
• *Music for Six Musicians*—Nonesuch
• *Don Byron Plays the Music of Mickey Katz*—Nonesuch
• *Tuskegee Experiments*—Nonesuch

Collaborations With Other Artists
• *Have a Little Faith*—with Bill Frisell—Nonesuch
• *This Land*—with Bill Frisell—Nonesuch
• *Ornettology*—with Ralph Peterson—Blue Note

JAZZ PROFILES

Craig Harris

Steve Turre

THE TROMBONISTS

Biography # CRAIG

B orn in Hempstead, Long Island, Craig Harris (DOB 9/10/53) currently resides in Manhattan. He began playing and studying the trombone around age ten. He attended the State University of New York—Old Westbury— and studied with Makanda Ken McIntyre and Warren Smith.

Harris's first major break into jazz came with the legendary Sun Ra, with whom he traveled the world. He also has worked with acclaimed pianist/vocalist Abdullah Ibrahim, David Murray, Henry Threadgill, Muhal Richard Abrams, and Lester Bowie. Harris has garnered many grants and awards for his work, including a Rockefeller Foundation MAP grant, a New York Foundation for the Arts Fellowship, and a John Simon Guggenheim Memorial Foundation Fellowship. These days Harris performs with his own groups, touring all over the United States and the world. A true innovator, he is one of the premier trombonists of his generation.

I loved photographing Craig Harris. He was so animated and ominous-looking, I figured that if luck was with me, I would end up with many good photographs.

This photograph is from an appearance with David Murray's Octet at Yoshi's in August, 1996. The octet consisted of David Murray on tenor sax and bass clarinet, James Spaulding on alto sax, Winston Bird on trumpet, Hugh Ragin on trumpet, Fred Hopkins on bass, D. D. Jackson on piano, Ranzel Merritt on drums, and Harris on trombone.

There was a very eclectic audience that night because the group was playing music from a recently recorded CD entitled *Dark Star—The Music of the Grateful Dead*. This performance in the San Francisco Bay area, the home of the Grateful Dead, attracted many rock aficionados, as well as jazz fans. It made for an interesting evening, to say the least.

HARRIS

INTERVIEW, FEBRUARY 14, 1998

What sparked your interest in jazz?

Playing a lot of R & B music, there were limitations on you as a horn player as to your function in the music. And so if you're really going to be a horn player and you want to play— I think if you want to hear horn players who have to challenge themselves and learn more about the instrument, you have to listen to other kinds of music. So that's how I came to it. When you start hearing people like Curtis Fuller, J. J. Johnson, Bennie Green, just people like that, you just know that it takes more than just learning a couple lines on the instrument. You have to really involve yourself.

I guess one of your biggest breaks was playing with Sun Ra. Could you tell me some of the things he taught you?

That connection was Pat Patrick, one of Sun Ra's original band members. Pat was teaching at the university I attended. He invited me on; in the summer of 1976, he said come sit in with the band. And I had seen Sun Ra before. It used to amaze me how all the people would get up there and just play their music for four or five hours straight.

And so when I went down, I remember I sat in with the band for the first time at The Bottom Line. And I just sat in. I didn't know the book. I didn't know anything. And I just got up, and he gave me a little space to play. That's how they auditioned you, test by fire. And we got off the bandstand, and he said, "We're going to Europe in three weeks. Do you have a passport?" I said no, and I went and got one. And I went to Europe in the summer of '76, my first time out of the country. . . .

I guess learning the process just came naturally by watching and listening. Sun Ra was a great speaker. He was a historian. And he would just talk and talk. The rehearsals would be playing 50 percent and 50 percent, we listened. And they would go on for hours and hours. And it was a real intense period because we were on the road, and we rehearsed every day.

CRAIG
HARRIS

Sun Ra would write music every day. Just watching Sun Ra, I learned discipline. . . . And just to hear John Gilmore play every night was like a lesson. It was an invaluable lesson.

To listen to Sun Ra talk about the history [of jazz music]. He always talked about tradition, and he'd go all the way back to Fletcher Henderson, which was his connection. He worked with Fletcher Henderson. And then you became part of that lineage. And he would tell those stories about Fletcher Henderson's band. We would play a lot of Fletcher Henderson and Duke Ellington's music from the 1920s. And we would play Sun Ra's more contemporary music at that time. So it was like we were a sponge. He would never tell you exactly what to play. You just had to learn by observation. And it was a real healthy music environment, that summer of '76.

A lot of people have said that during the 1980s and 1990s there has been a strong resurgence in the popularity of jazz music. Do you agree with that?

Well, that term has become so broad, and means so many different things to different people.

You mean "jazz?"

Yes. That's a hard one to define.

But I'm still seeing that there's not enough work for all the great musicians I know out here. We're still giving benefits for people because they can't make a living in this country. We still don't have major labels investing major money into the talent out here. We still work very little in this country. There's not enough commercial TV and radio exposure. I'm not being pessimistic, but I'm trying to be realistic when people say that [there's been a resurgence]. I'm just talking about being a musician and talking to musicians every day or going out to places and seeing all the great talent living in New York City, sitting home and not working.

So if it's improved that much, I just don't see it. In the music community, some are thriving. But overall the state of the industry is not going well. I don't think Americans are really

educated about this music to really understand this greatness and be able to support it to where people are financially surviving from it. We still do the majority of our work in Japan and Europe.

What do you think we can do to make Americans understand jazz a little better and to make it more popular?

First of all, the music has to be presented to children in schools by practitioners of the music; more radio and television exposure is a must. Also practitioners of the music have to stay fresh and encourage the evolution of the art form, technical and spiritual. Remembering the standards of our ancestors are high and only elevate influences from the universe.

You mentioned the problem with defining "jazz." How would you like to define it? What is it today?

I guess the most important thing is that improvisation is the basis of it. That's the root of it. Improvised music which in its basic sense was developed by people of African descent in America.

Tell me what your main goals as a musician and composer are.

First of all, you're trying to make a living in the United States of America. I'm just talking real basic. To pay your bills and survive and raise your family.

Then, instrumentally, you're trying every day to take all you've heard before, and use parts of this and parts of that, and make your own contribution to it in an improvised language. And I guess the same for composition and orchestration. You're just trying to take from what you've heard and what you've seen the masters do and just add to the great reservoir.

What advice would you have for someone wanting to make a career with this music?

Study. You have to start there. Listen to everything you can listen to. Be very openminded. You have to be very open, worldwide open. Study everything that's out there for you. Study computers, study your instrument, study writing, study languages. Just be real open.

Absorb everything you can. Go see the people who have excelled at what you want to do. If you can find some kind of apprenticeship, that's always good. That helps. Somebody to mentor you through a certain period.

And just never lose your dream. Just believe, that's it.

CRAIG HARRIS

SELECT DISCOGRAPHY

As a Leader

- *Craig Harris and the Nation of Imagination—*Double Moon
- *F-Stops—*Soul Note
- *Blackout in the Square Root of Soul—*Verve
- *Coldsweat Plays J. B.—*Polygram
- *Shelter—*Polygram
- *Black Bone—*Soul Note

Biography | # STEVE

Born in Omaha, Nebraska, Steve Turre (DOB 9/12/48) grew up in the San Francisco Bay area and now lives in Montclair, New Jersey. He studied music at Sacramento State University and has enjoyed associations with a varied list of jazz greats, including Ray Charles, Woody Shaw, Dizzy Gillespie, Cedar Walton, Art Blakey, Thad Jones, Mel Lewis, and Rahsaan Roland Kirk. He also has worked with McCoy Tyner, the Carnegie Hall Jazz Orchestra, Max Roach, Slide Hampton, and Billy Taylor.

Known mostly for his work on trombone, Turre also has garnered acclaim for his innovative work playing seashells. A prolific composer, he has released numerous recordings as both leader and sideman. He fronts several bands under his own name and also leads a seashell group known as Sanctified Shells. A true innovator, Turre is in a class by himself.

After seeing Steve Turre over many years playing with Chico Hamilton, Art Blakey, Woody Shaw, Rahsaan Roland Kirk, and Dizzy Gillespie, I finally got a chance to photograph him in the early 1990s. Although I have many excellent photographs of him, I chose the one from the most recent performance that I saw. He was playing at Yoshi's in January, 1998, with the McCoy Tyner Latin All Stars. He and David Sanchez were standing and playing next to each other throughout the performance, and often they were laughing and kidding each other. They seemed to be having a good time.

On many previous occasions I saw Turre when he was the leader of his own group or an apprentice in a "legends" band. I'm told that as a leader you usually have a great deal of responsibility that prevents you from relaxing completely during a performance. Playing with McCoy Tyner, not only was Turre not the leader, but he was surrounded by excellent musicians whom he knew well but seldom performed with. Believe me, he seemed relaxed throughout this performance. I'm sure it contributed to the quality of the photograph.

TURRE

INTERVIEW, FEBRUARY 10, 1997

How did you develop your interest in playing the shells, and how did you learn to play them?

I'm self-taught, just trial and error. You don't learn that in school, and there's nobody else doing it. So over the years, I just kind of discovered whatever it is that I do.

I actually was shy about playing the shells and didn't want to do it, except that other people encouraged me to, and mainly because I had worked with Roland Kirk, who played three saxophones at once. He was brilliant, a genius. I thought he was worth of all the accolades, but a lot of people didn't understand it or else they were jealous—whatever reason, he was accused at times of being a gimmick. And I worked with him, and I felt his pain. When that happened, I would see how it would hurt his feelings so much. And I became in tune with that, so to speak, and I was worried that people would say that the shells are a gimmick. So I was kind of reluctant to bring them out.

But I did play shell solos with Roland Kirk. I played shell solos with Art Blakey. I played shell solos with Chico Hamilton, Woody Shaw, Cedar Walton, Dizzy Gillespie, McCoy [Tyner], all kinds of people. But it wasn't until I went to Mexico with Woody Shaw, and I met my relatives there, and it just happened that that night Woody called a tune on the concert in Mexico City. It was a feature for the shells, and I played them, and the people loved it. As it's a part of their culture, I know and understand why they responded. And then afterwards they told me, "Did you know your ancestors used to play the shells?" I didn't know. And then I went to the pyramids and saw carvings of shells, and it kind of hit me over the head like a bell ringing. And I said, well, I guess I'm supposed to do this.

STEVE TURRE

This is something that's natural to me to hear this sound. And so I just said, well, I don't care what people think, I'm just going to do it because I have a need to. And lo and behold, everybody seems to like it, and I'm so grateful. Didn't have to turn out that way, but it did.

It's unbelievable the number of people you've played with and the experiences you've had. Tell me about some of the most memorable experiences.

I've been so fortunate that I would say the vast majority of gigs I've done have just been outstanding musical experiences—whether it's Dizzy Gillespie or Woody Shaw or Lester Bowie or Freddie Hubbard, Art Farmer, Dexter Gordon, Jackie McLean, or Roland Kirk or Pharoah Sanders or Archie Shepp. I've done all kinds of stuff. And they were all different, and they were all wonderful.

I think one of the deepest—not only because he's a father of the music and I learned so much from him on so many levels, but also just sheer having fun—working with Dizzy Gillespie has to be near the top. He would be there both musically and with having fun. That Dizzy was a cut-up, man. We had a ball. But, you know, he was also deep. You know, he could act like a fool, but when he put the horn up to his mouth, he was anything but.

Roland Kirk was super cool. Roland Kirk was, I think, the most profound. As a young man, that was a real changing point in my life, meeting and playing with Roland Kirk. I think that is the one experience that changed me the most because he got me on the track, you know. . . . He made me aware of the whole lineage [of jazz music] and explained it as such. Not just looking in the book and intellectualizing it as a scholar, but through understanding it as a playing musician so that you could play the different styles and still be yourself.

Another turning point experience was working with Woody Shaw. I did twelve albums with him in the course of my relationship with him, and my first solo on record is on one of his albums. And Woody encouraged me to find my own voice. And I traveled all over the world with him.

I worked a lot with Manny O'Quendo, and he is really a teacher in so many ways, not even by verbally explaining, but by playing with him—if you're listening, you pick it up. And he'll tell you if you ask him. And it really brought me to a new understanding of what clave is about and the whole experience.

Let me ask you some questions about the education of today's jazz musician. In the 1920s, '30s, and '40s, a musician's main source of education was playing with other musicians. Now you've got a lot of folks getting their beginnings in a more academic setting.

It's deeper than that, man.

Tell me about it.

Everybody started, for the most part, playing in school bands or marching bands. Drum and bugle corps and all that kind of stuff. And you've got to remember, too, acoustic instrumental music was the dance music of the day. Now they got all electronic stuff. It's very different.

[Before,] kids were playing in school bands, and if they got to a certain level and word got around, they'd come out and start sitting in, and then they might get some local gigs—even J. J. [Johnson] worked locally and ended up in a national band, then came to New York, and the rest is history. Same with Charlie Parker. . . .

But nowadays, they'll get a kid that's out of school, and they'll get him gigs and then totally overlook the other generation that had already paid their dues. It's simply about marketing. It's not the musician's fault. But it ain't right.

I think there has been a resurgence in the popularity of jazz music in the last ten to fifteen years.

Absolutely.

What's your opinion on why that is?

Well, I have several theories, and that's all it can really be; it's just my opinion. One way of looking at it is I feel that it was inevitable and that Roland Kirk was the prophet and that what he was saying about jazz being America's classical music—and Dizzy [Gillespie] was saying this, too—it has finally come to be a reality.

And I think the Wynton Marsalis phenomenon had a lot to do with it. . . . When he came to town [New York], everybody said, well, there's a phenomenal young musician; he's really talented, and he's going to Juilliard and that was a hook for the record companies because Miles [Davis] went to Juilliard and here they think, well, the next Miles Davis. . . .

But I really believe that if Wynton had just played jazz, he'd just be like the rest of the cats out here. He'd be another brother out here playing jazz, struggling, and doing the best— getting gigs and playing his ass off because he deserves it and he's great. But when he played classical music, too, all of a sudden this "made him legitimate." If he was just playing jazz, well, jazz is jazz—but since he played classical music, too— and then he became a spokesman for the music and because he had the ear of the powers, because they respected him because he played European classical music—when he started

laying the facts on the line that you can't argue with him, it's not something to debate. It's not a debate, these are just facts—jazz is America's classical music. The orchestra, the string quartet, all of that—that's European classical music, period. That evolved there; that's their music. It's beautiful, I love it, but it's European music.

Jazz is America's music. It evolved here, and everywhere else in the world you go, all the musicians, including the European musicians, know and feel that jazz is America's classical music. We get more money and respect outside of this country. Wynton Marsalis brought these points to light, and they gave it up. We got jazz in Lincoln Center. We got jazz at Carnegie Hall.

So I love [Wynton Marsalis]. He was able to bring all these points to light and made the people who run all the arts organizations and the record companies, he was able to get to them and make them understand the beauty and the power to save his music. He's a great speaker, and he's a smart man.

Tell me about your plans.

I just want to say that part of my philosophy is that music is a healing force, and musicians are supposed to be like a doctor. You're supposed to make people feel better. It's not really the same as a medical doctor, but the vibrations can really affect people. And I think it's a great privilege and an honor to play this music, and I feel very fortunate to be able to make my living doing it.

For me, it's more than entertainment. It's a very profound thing. If you look at all the great musics of the world, whether it's European classical music, or Indian classical music, or African classical music with the hand drums, or Japanese classical music, it's a reflection of a culture, and it's more than just entertainment. It's something that means something special to be part of this lineage and part of this continuum, and there's no one person who's greater than the music itself. We're all players in the continuum and its lineage, and I feel that it's also very important to pass it on and to keep it alive. I'm very much into young people and supporting them playing the music and helping them any way I can.

STEVE
TURRE
SELECT DISCOGRAPHY

As a Leader
- *Steve Turre*—Verve
- *Rhythm Within*—Verve
- *Sanctified Shells*—Antilles
- *Right There*—Antilles
- *Dedication*—Steve Turre and Robin Eubanks—JMT
- *Fire & Ice*—Stash 7
- *Viewpoints & Vibrations*—Stash 2

Collaborations With Other Artists
- *The Art Blakey Legacy*—with the Cedar Walton Sextet—Evidence
- *The Moontrane*—with Woody Shaw—32 Records
- *Journey*—with the McCoy Turner Big Band—Verve
- *Dizzy Gillespie*—with the United Nations Orchestra—Enja
- *Live at the Blue Note*—with Kenny Burrell & the Jazz Heritage All Stars—Concord
- *The Hard Bop Grandpop*—with Horace Silver—Impulse!

CHAPTER 4

JAZZ PROFILES

Bill Frisell

Russell Malone

John Scofield

Mark Whitfield

THE GUITARISTS

Biography

BILL

B orn in Baltimore, Maryland, Bill Frisell grew up in Denver, Colorado, and now makes his home in Seattle, Washington. He started playing music early in childhood, but it was the clarinet and not the guitar he played until college. He studied music at the University of Northern Colorado and also attended the acclaimed Berklee School of Music.

A prolific composer, Frisell has released more than twenty recordings as leader and has appeared on numerous others. He has collaborated with a varied group of artists, including Paul Motian, Don Byron, Paul Bley, Joe Lovano, and Julius Hemphill. Frisell's sound is definitely one of a kind. His music includes the sounds of traditional jazz, rock, folk, and country and western. A unique artist with a unique perspective of jazz, Bill Frisell is the epitome of a jazz man: he has carved out a trademark contribution to the world of music.

Seeing and hearing Bill Frisell nowadays, I would never think that he started his musical career by playing the clarinet. The guitar and the clarinet are very disparate instruments, and knowing his music now, I can't even imagine him playing anything other than the guitar. But it has to be his own kind of guitar, which looks different from everyone else's. Also, he holds it like no other guitar player. It's almost as if he's molded it to his body.

Frisell is a very inward kind of guy. When he plays he never looks at the audience. When I look at his face in this picture, I can't tell if that's pain, concentration, or shyness. But his music is way out. I tried to capture that in this photograph taken at Yoshi's in May, 1995, with his trio, including Kermit Driscoll on electric bass and Eyvind Kang on violin. Even the instrumental makeup of this trio was unusual.

FRISELL

INTERVIEW, SEPTEMBER 26, 1997

Tell me what you can remember about your introduction to music and some of your earliest musical experiences.

I think I've been interested in music from a very early age. I remember watching "The Mickey Mouse Club" on TV every afternoon and I remember waiting, there was this moment where, I think his name was Jimmy, and he was like the leader of all these kids, and he would come out with his guitar with Mickey Mouse painted on the front, and he would play a song with the kids. And I remember waiting for that moment just to look at his guitar. This was when I was four and five years old. I even made a guitar out of a piece of cardboard and put rubberbands on it when I was really little.

The first real serious time I spent, I was about ten, and I started playing clarinet with this school-music program, and I had a private teacher. I played in a marching band, and I seemed to take to that pretty easily. And I ended up playing clarinet all the way into a couple of years of college, actually. There was a moment where I was actually considering trying to be a clarinet player. By that time I had been playing guitar, and my heart was in that. So I played clarinet from when I was nine or ten until college, and a few years after that I got a guitar more as something on the side—it was more for fun. But years and years and years later after I was well into playing the guitar, I realized that the foundation that I got with the clarinet, that's really the bottom of everything that I do in music.

You have a very eclectic musical taste, and your music is very eclectic. How would you describe your music?

Boy. Yes, labels really make me uncomfortable because they exclude this or that, and that always bothers me. And these days what people call jazz, I'm not sure what it is anymore. But I feel pretty comfortable with thinking that that is where a lot of my—a lot but not all—of my kind of value system comes out of looking up to people like Miles [Davis] or Sonny Rollins or Charlie Parker. Trying to imagine, I've never

met these people, but I remember the time, I'm old enough now to remember waiting for the next Miles [Davis] record and wondering what he's going to do next. Trying to figure out what in the world he was thinking about. Just thinking about those people, [Thelonious] Monk, all the great jazz people, and learning those tunes, and thinking about them really has shaped the way I think about music.

And a lot of the eclecticism that you're talking about, that comes from them, too. I mean, Sonny Rollins, all of them would play any kind of music that was around. It wasn't like some kind of formal, this is jazz and this is not jazz. They were playing what reflected the circumstances around them. And that's really all I'm doing, just trying to be honest with where I've been my whole life and where I grew up. When I was growing up, there were The Beatles and The Rolling Stones or this blues thing or there is this or that. I played in marching bands. There is all that music that is part of my past.

What do you search for musically?

It's been this ongoing honesty, I guess. Trying to be honest with who I am. When I talk about all these influences, like, not to be afraid to let it come out. Years ago, when I first was getting into jazz, I would kind of shut off some of these little instincts that I would have, thinking, oh, that's not cool.

You mean other types of music?

Yes. I kind of had these blinders on. I just wanted to play within this one area. But then as I got older, it seemed like that wasn't really being honest or exposing the full experience I've had.

Do you recall a specific time when you decided you wanted to make a career in music?

I remember the moment. It was real clear. It was just kind of a simple thing, but I just said it. I remember saying to myself that this is what I'm going to do. I was maybe nineteen or twenty, something like that. It was a commitment I made to myself, thinking, I don't care what happens, I'm just going to go ahead and do this for the rest of my life.

Were your parents musicians?

No, but they were really supportive. I feel like I've been really lucky that they allowed me to do this. I had friends in high school, they would have to sneak out of their house to go play music. It's such a delicate—I remember there are so many little points along the way that if you don't get nudged in the right direction. . . . I remember one teacher I had at Berklee who was more of a discouraging way. I wrote a tune for the class, and he said it was terrible. He really put it down. And it sort of like—I didn't write another tune for like five years after that.

Your self-confidence takes a hit.

Yes. I was lucky to have a whole bunch of people who said, yes, that sounds good. You should keep doing this. If there had been a few other people who went the other way at some of those crucial times, it's very likely I might not even be playing. I'm doing all right, but there is an incredible amount of self-doubt that goes along with it.

What are some of your goals for the future?

It's about balance. It's still a struggle to spend as much time as I would like on developing my own music. Just playing with my own band is where I get the most fulfillment, from working on my own music and trying to figure out ways for us to play together. It's just to be able to get deeper and deeper into what I've been doing.

Describe the process you go through in composing music.

[Music] is just constantly coming out in little riffs all the time.

You mean you hear these things?

Yes, it's like a sea of music that is floating by all the time in my head. And, for me, writing is finding the time to sit down, and sitting down, and grabbing some of that music. It's more about just putting in the time and sitting there. Sometimes I will sit there, and I will get some little idea, and then that will shoot off into something else, and by the end it's something completely different from what I started with.

What advice would you have for someone wanting to make a career of playing music?

I have been asked that before, and I never know what to say. Just that thing about trying to be true to yourself. There is such huge pressure. The whole commercial world of music and radio and the way things are sold and fashioned and this and that. It's a pretty overwhelming, gigantic thing hanging over us all the time. If you get caught up in trying to figure out what that means, it can really take you away from the real music.

So you just try to listen to whatever that little thing is inside. If you are playing something or writing something or singing something, you try to keep hold of what keeps you going and gets you excited. And I think that's the only thing that can pull you through all this stuff. . . .

It just doesn't seem to work to run after trying to be "successful" or trying to make money. Maybe it will work for a second, but it's not going to be very lasting.

BILL
FRISELL
SELECT DISCOGRAPHY

As a Leader

- *Gone, Just Like a Train*— Nonesuch
- *Nashville*—Nonesuch
- *Quartet*—Nonesuch
- *Go West: Music for the Films of Buster Keaton*— Nonesuch
- *The High Sign/One Week: Music for the Films of Buster Keaton*—Nonesuch
- *This Land*—Nonesuch
- *Have a Little Faith*— Nonesuch
- *Where in the World?*— Bill Frisell Band— Elektra Entertainment
- *Is That You?*—Elektra Entertainment
- *Before We Were Born*— Elektra Musician
- *ECM Works*—ECM Records
- *Smash & Scatteration*— Rykodisc USA
- *Rambler*—ECM Records
- *In Line*—with Kermit Driscoll and Joey Baron—Gramavision Records
- *Lookout for Hope*—ECM Records
- *American Blood/Safety in Numbers*—with Victor Bruce Godsey and Brian Ales—Intuition Music

Biography

RUSSELL

A mostly self-taught musician, Russell Malone (DOB 11/08/63) was born and raised in the Deep South town of Albany, Georgia. He was first introduced to music in church, where his mother played the organ and guitar. He fell in love with the guitar the first moment he heard it, later discovering jazz guitar.

Malone's earliest professional gigs took him throughout the South with the Gospel Crusaders and later with Al Rylander. His career in jazz began in Atlanta, playing often with "Thumbs" Carlisle and Clarence Carter. In the late 1980s, Malone spent two years with legendary jazz organist Jimmy Smith, and the 1990s brought an extended relationship with Harry Connick, Jr. For the last couple of years, he has recorded and toured extensively with pianist/vocalist Diana Krall. Since Malone's debut in 1992, he has recorded four albums as a leader, and all have enjoyed critical acclaim and feature various idioms, including gospel, ballads, classics, and blues.

Of the many photographs that I've taken of jazz musicians, the ones I enjoy most are those in which the musician's emotion is evident. Sometimes I get an unconscious message from my body that says, "Take this shot." This usually happens when I find myself responding to the music and musician and begin to move with the rhythm. Looking at Russell Malone's face in this photograph, I think it is obvious that he was enjoying himself. Fans and musicians alike have told me that emotion in a photograph is what they like best.

This photograph of Russell Malone was taken at the Kuumbwa Jazz Center in Santa Cruz, California, in November, 1996, when he was accompanying pianist/vocalist Diana Krall. Backstage after the show, Malone asked me if I could hear him okay, and how did his guitar sound. He was very concerned because, he said, he was "breaking in a new guitar." I told him I thought he sounded great. Russell Malone is kind of a shy guy. He probably is happier playing than talking.

MALONE

INTERVIEW, OCTOBER 30, 1996

Tell me about your musical background.

My first introduction to music was in my church back in Albany. The guitar wasn't added to the church until . . . I must have been about four years old when I first heard the guitar played in the church. But prior to that, people were singing, and they were clapping their hands, and the drums were very prevalent. You'd even see a washboard being played with a coat hanger. Yeah, you know, the music wasn't that sophisticated; but there was a whole lot of emotion. . . .

Now when the guitar was added, that took [my interest] to a whole other level. Because first of all, I was totally taken by the sound of the instrument, not to mention the way it looked. There was just something about that instrument that attracted me to it.

I remember sitting at home one day in the living room playing, and my mother came in with a bag. And do you remember when you were a little kid whenever your mother would come in with a bag, the first thing you want to know is, well, Mom, what did you buy for me, you know? So I followed her into the kitchen. I still remember it. I followed her into the kitchen, and she pulled out this little guitar. It must have been about a foot and a half long. I remember it being green in color, and it had four little red strings on it. And that's how the love affair with the guitar started.

I would take my guitar to church every Sunday, and I'd sit over in the corner, and I'd watch the players. And I'd try to take what I could take from them. And then a couple of years later I was playing at the church. So that's where I first started to play music, in my church.

RUSSELL MALONE

Do you know why particularly you chose jazz as an art form?

Well, see, before I got into jazz, keep in mind that I was living in Albany, Georgia at the time. And in a town like that, jazz isn't a very prominent type—it's not very popular.

But there were other forms of music that caught my ear, such as—well, first of all, gospel. Some of the first music that I remember hearing was Sam Cooke with the Soul Stirrers. There were the Dixie Hummingbirds, Shirley Caesar, Dorothy Norwood, Albertina Walker.

And also country and western music, which was very popular. I got to see guys like Merle Travis performing on television, Roy Clark, Glen Campbell, because, you know, country music, I mean, that's guitar music, you know what I'm saying? Guitar music.

Then blues. The first time I saw B. B. King perform on TV . . . I was, like, oh, my goodness gracious. And I immediately identified with the way B. B. King sang and played because it was so similar to the way a minister would deliver a sermon. There was so much soul and conviction there. And the guitar, we don't even have to talk about his guitar playing. Now, the jazz thing, the first time I got hip to jazz was when I saw George Benson performing on television with Benny Goodman when I was twelve years old. And that did it for me. That's what did it.

So after I saw that, I remembered his name. I said, okay, George Benson. Say, I'm going to go out and see what else this man has on record. So the first record that I bought by him was *George Benson Cookbook*. And I just picked up every record I could find by him, and I remember reading the liner notes and coming across names like Miles Davis and Duke Ellington and Wes Montgomery, Charlie Christian, Django Reinhardt, [John] Coltrane.

And there was a guy in my church who was a Wes Montgomery fan, and he laid two albums on me. One was *Smoking at the Half Note* and *Boss Guitar*. Both of these records were by Wes Montgomery. So those are the records that I cut my teeth on.

What inspires you, typically, to write a tune? Is it how you're feeling, or is it a particular person or a combination of things? What do you think about when you write a song?

It's a combination of all those things. I'm not one of those kind of people who can sit down and just write a tune right off the top of my head. I know some guys are gifted that way. I'm not gifted that way.

There's a tune that's on my second record, a tune that I wrote, "After Her Bath." That's the only tune that I wrote on the spur of the moment like that because it was written for my daughter. My daughter had just been born, and I don't know—do you have any kids?

Yes, I have one girl, two years old.

Okay. So, you know, they have ways of just—they're just so beautiful. They have ways of making you grow up fast. They make you mature. And my daughter, she inspired me to write this tune. My wife was giving her a bath one night. She must have been maybe six months old. And after she gave her the bath, she just looked so peaceful sleeping in her crib. And then I started to hear this melody in my head. I heard it as I was watching her sleeping. She just looked so peaceful at that moment.

Let me ask you about one other song that interests me, "Flowers For Emmett Till." You have to know a little something about the civil rights movement to know who Emmett Till was. Do you know a lot about the civil rights movement, or did the Emmett Till story just strike you as particularly horrifying? What made you write that tune?

First of all, yes, I do know a lot about the civil rights movement. How could you be a black man—because I was born in 1963, which would make me old enough to know something about it.

The first time I heard about Emmett Till, I was thirteen years old, in the eighth grade, and I was taking a black history course at school. And my teacher at the time, a Mrs. Harris, I'll never forget her, she brought in this old copy of *Jet* magazine, and she told us the story about Emmett Till, about how he was murdered for supposedly whistling at a white woman.

This was back in 1955, you know. He was living up in Chicago, and he came down to visit his uncle in Mississippi. And he and one of his buddies went to the store, and word has it that he whistled at this white woman. And they came to his house, the woman's husband and another friend came to his house; and they got the boy and did all kinds of horrible things to him.

But the thing that really stuck out in my mind was the picture that they had of him in the magazine. It was an open-coffin funeral. It was a very—did you see the picture?

Yes, I've seen that. His mother, as a matter of fact, demanded that the casket be open. . . .

Yes, so the world could see the horrors they had done. . . . So when I saw that, it was something I could never get out of my mind. I'll never forget about that. I was thirteen years old when I saw that. It was tragic.

So that tune, I started hearing that tune in my head a long time ago. And over time it became more refined, and I got all the kinks worked out.

In your debut album [Russell Malone], there's a little piece written by Milt Hinton, and he says that for most of his life America "treated jazz musicians with a certain kind of disdain . . . , [b]ut a great deal has changed," he says, "because of the younger musicians like Russell . . . it's their behavior that's begun to change the image of jazz. . . ."

Well, things are a lot different [now] than they were years ago for us. Back then older musicians had to go through a lot of obstacles that we don't have to go through. Such as, well, the race factor for one thing. I mean, I don't know what it feels like to have to go in through the "colored" entrance or to have to play a gig and then after your gig is over having to sit in the kitchen. I don't know what that's like. So a lot of those guys had to go through a lot of nonsense, and, therefore, that turned them into very bitter people later on. You know what I'm saying?

[My generation of artists hasn't] had to go through any of that. So maybe that's why we behave the way we do. We're so happy—it's so good to be able to play this music. But I never forget that the reason why we are where we are today is because of the things that so many of the other guys had to go through. A lot of them, in order to deal with the things that they were going through, a lot of them turned to drugs and alcohol. We never had it that bad. So, therefore, all we have to do is just concentrate on our music. We don't get screwed around business-wise because we have managers; we have lawyers. A lot of us are very hip as far as taking care of our business.

Tell me, what do you think about life on the road?

Well, I tell you, I like being on the road. The hardest thing about being out here on the road is getting to the gig. Because a lot of times you may have to get up early in the morning and make—get up at 5 o'clock in the morning in order to make a 7 o'clock flight, the one-nighters here and there. Your luggage may get lost. The equipment may not be working properly. But if the music is fine, I can put up with the rest.

You have to be prepared for anything. Just take it as it comes, because it's inevitable that it's going to come, whatever. . . . But you have to keep a sense of humor in order to survive out here. Because if you're not able to do that, then you just won't survive.

RUSSELL MALONE
SELECT DISCOGRAPHY

As a Leader

- *Sweet Georgia Peach—* Impulse!
- *Wholly Cats—*Venus
- *Black Butterfly—* Columbia
- *Russell Malone—* Columbia

Collaborations With Other Artists

- *Love Scenes—*with Diana Krall—GRP/Impulse!
- *Habana—*with Roy Hargrove—Verve
- *Kaleidoscope—*with Benny Green—Blue Note
- *All for You—*with Diana Krall—GRP/Impulse!
- *Blue Light, Red Light—* with Harry Connick, Jr.— Columbia
- *We Are in Love—*with Harry Connick, Jr.— Columbia

Biography

JOHN

B orn in Dayton, Ohio, John Scofield (DOB 12/26/51) grew up in Connecticut and currently resides in northern Westchester County, New York. He began playing guitar at age eleven and attended the Berklee School of Music in Boston in the early 1970s.

In his distinguished career, Scofield has collaborated with many of the greatest artists in jazz, including Miles Davis, Herbie Hancock, Chick Corea, McCoy Tyner, Joe Henderson, and Pat Metheny. A prolific composer, Scofield has released twenty-five recordings as a leader and has appeared on numerous others. With an eclectic taste and enormous talent, Scofield is the embodiment of the consummate jazz artist: steeped in tradition, yet in constant pursuit of innovation and a unique voice.

John Scofield seems to be quite stretched out in different directions. He has a four-to-seven-piece woodwind and brass ensemble with which he plays an unamplified acoustic guitar. Sometimes he adds a three-piece rhythm section, which may or may not be electric. He frequently leads a quartet that includes a tenor saxophone. And he plays regularly with his trio. This photograph was taken when his quartet played Kuumbwa in April, 1993, consisting of Scofield on electric guitar, Joe Lovano on tenor saxophone, Dennis Irwin on acoustic bass, and Bill Stewart on drums. Several people have asked me to "explain" this photograph. One inquired about the musicians Scofield was playing with. Another asked about the "special lighting." Another photographer asked a lot of technical questions. Somebody even asked me why I "posed" Scofield this way. I found it very difficult to come up with satisfactory answers. What I do know is that the evening I photographed Scofield I found myself to be very much in touch with the music. I think that the horn-guitar interplay had some special meaning to me.

John Coltrane told me that when asked to "explain" his music, he was at a loss for words. That's how I feel about this shot.

SCOFIELD

INTERVIEW, JANUARY 30, 1998

A lot of the people I've interviewed for this project went to the Berklee School of Music in Boston. In your opinion, is that the school of jazz in the United States?

Yes. I think it is the school of music for jazz, and when I went to school, it was the only one. It was the only place you could go. Some universities were starting to have jazz departments then, just a handful. But [Berklee] is where you could go, and you didn't have to take other academics. You could just do jazz. And it was sort of like the next best thing to being a professional musician and, if you weren't ready for that, which none of us were quite there, that's where you went and you took courses that all related to what you wanted to do, which was play jazz music.

And I think that when you learn to play, you have to do it yourself, and no school can teach you. In a way, it's up to you. But Berklee, the information was true; it was correct. The people up there were good. Not only the teachers, but all the students. You would be up there with a few thousand kids trying to get it together and to be around that was very, very good.

Who would be your greatest influences on guitar?

I would have to start with B. B. King because that's the kind of playing, and his specifically, that I fell in love with when I was a teenager. Blues. In the mid-1960s, it was starting to work its way into white consciousness a little bit. Nothing like it is now, I mean, I still had to go to the black part of town to the record store to buy blues records.

B. B. King was my favorite. I used to go hear him and the soul and the way he played that stuff on the guitar, the way he transcended the instrument, you know. Still to this day, I think that the guitar was made for the blues.

And then when I got into jazz, there were a number of guys. Pat Martino, Wes Montgomery, Jim Hall, I would say were my three first real loves. And Jim Hall especially because I didn't feel like I had a natural, big technique, and Martino and Wes, they were so athletic.

It was so hard to do what they did. It's hard to do what Jim does, too, just like him. But he took a more lyrical approach and brought out the beauty of the guitar, and it was very thoughtful. And I thought, well, I can learn from this temperament, and it showed me that you didn't have to play fast like Pat Martino. And you could still swing. It reminded me of Miles Davis on the guitar. Those were the guys.

There has been a lot of discussion lately about there being a resurgence in the popularity of jazz over the last ten to fifteen years. Do you agree with that?

I don't know. To tell you the truth, I think that if there is more of an awareness, maybe it's because of education. But I think that jazz always stays the same. It's really special music, and what makes people like myself like it is that there is this stuff that takes a little bit more attention to get into, like classical music.

And you have to give it a little more to get it. It's not like a pop jingle or it's not like a pop tune with a hook. It's more subtle, and that's why it's not popular music. And one of the reasons we like it is because it is the crème de la crème. [Jazz music] is so hip that you've got to get with it to get with it.

But I also see right now, in 1998, because of the curve of styles and stuff, that young people are into liking things that are different. I think ten years ago young people were more into just following the norm. Now it's gone back to maybe a little bit like it was in the 1960s when the hippies thing started, and kids were listening to Indian music and free jazz, and all kinds of mind-expanding things. I think it's kind of like that right now, and I think that's really a healthy attitude, and I love to see that in young kids. I have a sixteen-year-old daughter, and I see that with her and her friends.

What's your favorite part of what you do: composing, recording, performing?

I like to play the guitar and improvise and have it work with other people. When the band connects, and we start to groove together in whatever way. I think that's an immediate fix, you know. It's just like, wow, this is great.

Composing is very hard work for me. And you have to put in a lot of time and when nothing is happening, it's painful, because you say, oh man, it was like a wasted day. And you don't get as much back, but when you do have a composition that you think is good, that is so rewarding because it's not as fleeting as taking a good solo. You can hold onto that for a longer time. So in that way, it's a different kind of reward and actually probably more rewarding. . . .

Since the turn of the century, jazz has gone through many eras. Many things, from bebop to free jazz. Do you feel there's any new era on the horizon?

I've been trying to figure this out along with all the writers and people that know about jazz and musicians. Probably musicians think about it less because they are mainly learning how to play their instruments, but I don't think there is one movement now in jazz like there was when the bebop movement started or free jazz.

And I think that the way I've thought about it is that jazz was this incredible invention really that happened at the last of the turn of the century. And it coincided with the invention of the phonograph—recording. So that's why it is where it is because improvised solos could be captured, and the idea of jazz spread and took over the world. It was like a mushroom; it changed music. . . .

But I think that the original idea of improvisation has permeated music so much, and the idea of swing has permeated music so much that a lot of the options have been taken from pure jazz as we say. So now I think the things that are going to happen are going to maybe be different from what we consider branches on the tree of jazz. And they might not fall specifically into the category of one exponent of jazz after another—one version after another of this nice little line that we can see of Dixieland, swing, bebop, free, whatever. . . . The days of one form after another in jazz are over.

I think maybe one reason it's not as popular as we would like is because it's hard to get a grasp of just what jazz music really is. How do you define it? It's the hardest damn thing I can think of to try to define.

Yes. And everybody's concept of jazz is different. It's almost like I don't want to even try to define it. I really don't. I just want to play.

A lot of folks don't like naming names, but I just wonder if you could tell me some of the most memorable gigs you've had.

Oh, there have been so many, my God. I think I've really been lucky that way. Do you want me to start from the beginning? I remember them all! [Laughs]

That's all right. I just thought maybe a few would stick out in your mind.

I think that playing with Miles Davis, my idol, was something that I will certainly never forget, but a lot of my career, I've been lucky enough to play with Gerry Mulligan, [Charles] Mingus, Chet Baker, Joe Henderson, Herbie Hancock recently. And playing with Joe Lovano and Bill Stewart in recent years, and guys my own age, Pat Metheny, Bill Frisell, these guys.

Steve Swallow, my teacher. It's not just been the gigs, but the musical friendships and relationships, getting to play and improvise with these guys, and hook up and make a sound. It's better than just you by yourself. It's a group thing and that's what I like.

JOHN SCOFIELD
SELECT DISCOGRAPHY

As a Leader
- *A Go Go*—Verve
- *Quiet*—Verve
- *The Best of John Scofield*—Blue Note
- *Groove Elation*—Blue Note
- *Hand Jive*—Blue Note
- *I Can See Your House From Here*—Blue Note
- *Live*—Enja
- *What We Do*—Blue Note
- *Grace Under Pressure*—Blue Note
- *Meant to Be*—Blue Note
- *Time on My Hands*—Blue Note
- *Who's Who*—One Way Records
- *Slo Sco: Best of the Ballads*—Gramavision
- *Loud Jazz*—Gramavision Records
- *Blue Matter*—Gramavision Records

Biography

MARK

Photo Notes

A native of Long Island, New York, who now resides in Baton Rouge, Louisiana, Mark Whitfield is a virtuoso guitarist who counts George Benson, Wes Montgomery, and Kenny Burrell among his greatest musical influences. As a youngster, Whitfield studied both the acoustic bass and guitar and was awarded scholarships to the Berklee School of Music for both instruments. In 1983 he turned down an accelerated medical-school program at Georgetown University and attended Berklee School of Music on a guitar scholarship.

Mark Whitfield is a one-of-a-kind guitarist. To me, he sounds like a cross between John Scofield and Bill Frisell, both of whom are also featured in this book. He can take you out there like Frisell or play with the dedication and consistency of Scofield, but all the time, he's distinctively his own person.

I saw Whitfield live in early January, 1996, at Yoshi's, where this photograph was taken. He seemed oblivious to anything or anyone around him at the time, except the musicians he was playing with. I liked that. His group consisted of Victor Atkins, piano; Roland Guerin, bass; and Donald Edwards, drums. Later in the month Whitfield performed at Kuumbwa with the same group. His playing appeared much more relaxed that night, but was equally excellent.

WHITFIELD

From Berklee, Whitfield moved to New York for professional opportunities. He has made the most of them, performing with such legends as George Benson, Ray Brown, Jimmy Smith, and Betty Carter, as well as some of the top jazz artists of his own generation, including Terence Blanchard, Donald Harrison, Nicholas Payton, Christian McBride, and Courtney Pine. Whitfield has released six recordings as a leader, including 1997's *Forever Love* (Verve), which features solo guitar to full orchestra arrangements. With his unique combination of talent and showmanship, Mark Whitfield is truly one of the most talented jazz guitarists working today.

MARK
WHITFIELD

INTERVIEW, SEPTEMBER 12, 1997

Tell me about the earliest musical experiences you can recall.

I was about seven years old, and finally I got my first guitar. My brother, who had just come back from Vietnam, had gotten it from my sister as a coming-home present because he's a big blues fan, but he quickly discovered that he didn't have any real natural ability for the guitar, so he gave it to me along with one his favorite blues records, which is a Lightnin' Hopkins record called *And Follows You After Blues*. And I took the guitar and tried to imitate what I heard on the recording. So there I was trying to play some of Lightnin' Hopkins blues riffs and things with his songs. My parents saw my interest and got me some lessons at a local music store.

Early on you were trained more in the classical genre. How is it that you decided you were going to go the jazz route?

I think jazz was always my favorite. You have to sort of wait until you have an opportunity to be part of an organized ensemble to really play jazz in schools.

Before attending Berklee School of Music on scholarship, you were at one point headed to Georgetown University on a pre-med scholarship. How did you make the decision to forgo Georgetown for Berklee?

Well, I actually did go to Georgetown, at a summer-entrance program for high-school juniors. The scholastic program I was involved in [at the time] had me a year ahead of my age group, so in tenth grade I went to this summer program at Georgetown, taking statistics, calculus, physics, and that kind of thing. I enjoyed being there very much, but I wasn't completely satisfied with the notion of actually going there right after high school and taking part in the six-year, undergrad pre-med program in which I had been accepted.

I think it had a lot to do with moving from New York to Seattle at that time, and there were a lot of other contributing factors. I had an acoustic guitar with me that summer while I was at [Georgetown], and I found myself spending almost the majority of my free time playing the guitar. And I was really starting to enjoy just playing the guitar for the sake of playing it. And I was starting to explore a lot of different possibilities and scraping the surface of what jazz was about as it relates to the guitar as an instrument. So I think when I got the opportunity to play in a jazz band, that really was what I needed to convince me that I wanted to take some time to see how well I would fare in that arena.

And with having the opportunity to go to Berklee on a scholarship and study—I had graduated high school at age sixteen—I felt I had time to go there, check it out for a while and, if I didn't like it, I could always still go back and enroll at Georgetown. I had been at Berklee about two weeks and realized there was no turning back for me. I was crazy about the idea.

Whom would you cite as your greatest musical heroes and inspirations?

I would have to credit Lightnin' Hopkins first just because he got me started actually. And then George Benson would be next because when I was about ten I saw him on PBS Broadcasting with his band and the Boston Pops orchestra, and they were playing the music from the *Breezin'* record in concert. And that show—sometimes you hear something, and in ten seconds you know you have found your direction, you know, if you're lucky. Minutes into that concert I knew that one day I wanted to do what George Benson was doing. And I set out to try to learn all I could about music and the guitar so that one day I would be able to play like him.

After that, when you're hit with the same curses, you just fall in love with all the great jazz musicians. There are way too many of them to list them all. But that's just from Jelly Roll Morton to Wes Montgomery. They were all instrumental in inspiring me to achieve some level of greatness as a musician and make some sort of contribution as an innovator to the legacy of jazz music.

You've traveled all over the world playing music. Can you tell me some of the differences you notice in the fans in different parts of this country or the world, and where are some of your favorite places to play?

You know, it's funny. I think the response and the interpretation of the music from an audience standpoint goes hand-in-hand with the personality of that area. So the places I actually like to visit the most just as a tourist are often the places that I enjoy playing the most. New York, for instance. The northwest, like Seattle, Vancouver, Toronto, places like that. Places in southern Europe, Brazil—the people in these places seem to be very open to trying to enjoy things that they don't necessarily understand.

A lot of people are turned off or frightened or whatever, just intimidated or ultimately turned off by things they don't necessarily understand. But when you go to some places, in Japan or wherever, the people, it's not that they have a greater understanding of what it is you do, but the fact that they don't understand doesn't mean they won't try to enjoy it and take something from it.

Beginning with the late 1980s and certainly through the 1990s, we've seen a strong resurgence in the popularity of jazz music. Have you given any thought as to why that is?

I think jazz benefits from the same things as in everyday society. Things come in cycles. Whether it's every twenty, twenty-five years or so, I think jazz has a few very-high-profile figures who came to prominence about the same time. In jazz music, Wynton and Branford Marsalis and Harry Connick, Jr., and people like that who in very unique and individual ways brought a lot of attention to jazz music in the general press.

Jazz has always been popular in a specialty group. In the people who read jazz magazines and collect records and the whole thing. But every once in a while you get a wave of mainstream press. Let's say *USA Today* or *People* magazine and that kind of thing, regular television shows and *TIME* magazine articles that spotlight the accomplishments of a few, a select group of jazz musicians and that brings a lot

of attention to the whole scene. And, before that time, jazz had really sort of fallen out of the mainstream. So it's funny, people were calling it "new"; they were finding a way to talk about jazz as though it were something new.

You recently appeared in the Robert Altman film Kansas City. Then the Kansas City Band went on tour, and that probably was a rare chance for you and a lot of your contemporaries to be on the same stage at once.

You're right, it is rare. Tours like that are organized once a generation—they put together all the so-called young lions, all the musicians who are kind of popular on the scene at one time, and take them on the road. [With the Kansas City Band], the majority of the folks featured in the film were part of that tour. And it was an incredible experience for us because most of us came up together in some way, shape, or form. You know, the jazz community is pretty small. And being within the same age group, we all pretty much came up playing music together. So it was a big reunion; it was like a big party basically. We had a ball being part of that collective ensemble.

Your stage presence is really wonderful, and you look as though you're having a good time when you play. You also have a certain amount of showmanship when you play. Is this something that comes completely natural to you, or are you conscious of developing a stage presence?

Well, I appreciate the compliment, first of all. But I think it is very important that as an artist, when you take the stage, in any forum, that you have some sort of presence people can identify with. I think it's a problem if it's something you have to go out and find. I think one thing I've always been able to do is walk out in front of a lot of people and play music and enjoy myself. I enjoy playing for myself, and I enjoy playing for people. I've never really had to give much thought to putting together some sort of show. To reinforce that, you know, the fact that I genuinely really love to play and that that comes across, the music is enough, and maybe that's even better for people because I think they perceive it as being genuine.

Tell me some advice you might have for someone who might want to become a jazz musician.

I had the benefit of a lot of really good advice, and it came from a lot of different sources. I think the most important thing a young person can do in thinking about preparing for a career in jazz music is that you have to go about it with the same seriousness and preparation that you would use for any highly specialized skill—as if you wanted to be a neurosurgeon, an astronaut, something that requires a lot of study and a lot of dedication far beyond what is the normal call of duty. In this day and age, you have so many different avenues for information. There are tons of books and instructional videos, and I guess you can even now study over the Internet.

And prepare yourself before you even think about going to college. And when you go, you want to pick a place where you can go, and be prepared, and get the best education possible for what it is that you want to do. If you want to be a great basketball player, you don't want to go to the Berklee School of Music. I think if you dedicate a lot of time and effort and energy into it and you love it and you have the ability, it will pay off for you.

MARK WHITFIELD
SELECT DISCOGRAPHY

As a Leader
- *Forever Love*—Verve
- *7th Avenue Stroll*—Verve
- *True Blue*—Verve
- *Mark Whitfield*—Warner Bros.
- *Patrice*—Warner Bros.
- *The Marksman*—Warner Bros.
- *Fingerpainting*—with Christian McBride and Nicholas Payton—Verve

Collaborations With Other Artists
- *Damn*—with Jimmy Smith—Verve
- *From This Moment*—with Nicholas Payton—Verve
- *Underground*—with Courtney Pine—Antilles

CHAPTER 5:

JAZZ PROFILES

Geri Allen

Cyrus Chestnut

Joey DeFrancesco

Benny Green

Diana Krall

Danilo Perez

Eric Reed

Marcus Roberts

Stephen Scott

Jacky Terrasson

THE PIANISTS/ORGANISTS

Biography

GERI

Born in Pontiac, Michigan, Geri Allen (DOB 6/12/57) resides in New York City. Playing the piano since age seven, she studied music at Howard University in Washington, DC, and earned a master's degree from the University of Pittsburgh. An educator herself, she has taught at the acclaimed New England Conservatory of Music in Boston.

A prolific composer and recording artist, Allen has released numerous recordings both as a leader and with other artists. In addition to leading her own groups, she has collaborated extensively with Charlie Haden and Paul Motian, as well as her husband, jazz trumpeter Wallace Roney.

Allen is a consummate jazz artist. She knows the history of the art form, as well as her instrument. With this knowledge and her enormous talent, she is forging her unique contribution and voice.

I'm always surprised at how well Geri Allen plays with musicians of extremely varying styles and interests. She seems to make herself over anew with each group. She actually looks different with different groups.

At a performance in 1994 I showed her some photographs I'd taken of her two years earlier. She was very surprised at how she looked then, and she commented that the picture appeared to be from another life.

This photograph was taken at her trio performance at Yoshi's in November, 1995. She was playing then with Eric Allen on drums and Ralph Armstrong on bass. The piano that Allen was playing was located at the left of the stage, and she appeared to be physically isolated from the two other musicians. The bass and drums, however, were very much in sync with her directions. I could feel the oneness of the group. Just before I took this shot, Allen's head was bent over the keyboard, and she was deep into a solo. All of a sudden, she looked up as if to say, "Where am I?" She was staring at the other musicians but almost not seeing them. At this point, I released the shutter.

ALLEN

INTERVIEW, DECEMBER 4, 1997

Tell me what sparked your interest in jazz.

My father has a great collection of jazz, and he always did, and he's a big fan of the music. Very early on I heard the music as a little kid, as a little toddler, and maybe pre-birth even. So it was in me, you know. And I just found the personalities of the musicians to be intriguing and elegant and a big source of pride—the way they looked and their courage and the impact that they were having on the world, the world scene.

You have been involved in music education. When I think about jazz education, I think of two routes. I think of an in-school type education and an on-the-road education. Could you comment on the differences in those two types, and whether you think they're both being provided out there today?

I have done both. And a lot of my peers have at least dabbled in the education area as well. Many of them came away with degrees, and many of them didn't, but I think that was the road many of us took as a means of preparation, not as a means to an end, but as a means for preparation, to get ready for the road.

Let me just speak on my experience. Being at school did a lot for me in terms of giving me a place to grow up and to get my head on straight as a person as well as a player. I think that it was a helpful experience for me personally to have that cushion of time to develop. . . .

And it was a very informative environment for me outside of music as well, politically and culturally. . . . I think having a chance to go to [Howard University], which was totally international, it was a great experience for me. I felt that I had a real clear sense all the time when I went there of what I wanted. And I think that may be a problem with many students I've encountered.

GERI ALLEN

They might be in music because they're not quite sure what other things interest them?

They may think they know what they want out of music, but they're not really there with the commitment that's necessary. [Mine was] a generation who were prepared to sit down and practice and spend the time and deal with the discipline that was necessary to get that thing. And I get a sense that a lot of the kids today don't have that patience. They seem to want to have things come quickly, and they don't understand the value of repetition, and even just doing a small amount every day and what that can mean in the long run.

That's a big part of the difference that I see in the attitude of the kids today—a lot of my students. Now there are special students, and I'm sure there were special students in my time, too, who understood what was really necessary and were happy and found it joyful to sit down and work through a process like that. And I've had a couple who have given me a lot of hope for the music scene. And there are some really talented people out there. But I just think there is a difference in patience—the patience to sit down and learn an instrument.

Tell me who would be some of your greatest jazz piano influences.

I would say Herbie Hancock was my major influence. And I would say there's a lineage of players whom Herbie Hancock would be the direct descendant of. But Herbie is the most modern. He's taken the piano the furthest in terms of that lineage. I also am greatly influenced by Cecil Taylor and McCoy Tyner, who are also a part of another line of great players.

Tell me about some of your most memorable gigs you can recall.

I had a chance to play duo with McCoy [Tyner] once. That was extremely memorable. And the experience of sitting next to one of your idols, to hear the weight, his weight. We were playing duo, so there was this response back and forth, and it's just weight and quality and experiencing that.

Also playing with Ornette Coleman was a really great experience for the same reasons. The mastership and the wisdom in that voice. It's like hearing someone who really

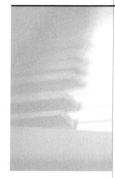

could tell a story, and they're telling it with some real clear knowledge and experience from years and years and years. And also having the chance to play with Tony Williams and Ron Carter, that was a moment that goes down for me as one of the greatest moments of my musical career.

Also working with my husband, Wallace [Roney]. We've been friends since Howard [University] days, and we developed a lot early on as kids. And then there was a period of time that we didn't work together. He was doing amazing things, and I was on my way in another direction. We both kind of came back together, and the musical exchange that I've had with him over the past four or five years also has just been greatly illuminating for me as a musician. It's been very exciting working in his band.

And working with Betty Carter was a great experience. With Jack DeJohnette and Dave Holland.

What is it about jazz that makes it such a unique art form? What does it offer that makes it stand out for you?

It's so many things. I think you get a real sense of the magnitude of the music when you start to travel around the world and see how greatly people are influenced by it. Based on what it represents here and what it has represented, it's been a source of great pride—it's like the best we have to offer in many respects.

People like to say the sciences and these intellectual pursuits are serious and music isn't serious. And you get this kind of thing, that it's really not necessary, so if you're going cut something, cut music and arts. But I think people are starting to realize that that is not an appropriate response, and it's not an intelligent response. It's not an aware response. Music and art, they make us know who we are. Other older cultures understand that, and they have understood that since their existence.

Jazz music has definitely been a beacon of light to the world. It is something that was created here and is totally unique, totally scientific, advanced, and intellectual, and spiritual. All the higher realms of what is good about being human is represented by this music. For me it certainly has been a path-setter. It's been a real clear map to me as to how to approach my life and how to approach trying to be a better musician. . . .

And one of the things the music has had to offer is this freedom of speech. I think that's a major thing to be held onto today that our music represents, too—the freedom to be who you are. And I really hope that as the new millennium approaches, the industry continues to support freedom of speech and freedom of artistic integrity. You know, they get behind the artist so that the artist leads the music and not the industry leading the direction of the music. I think that's been a problem in terms of where we've been the last ten years or so.

[The music industry] has concepts about what works. And I think that perhaps for the first time, the music has come out of the artists' hands. [Before] there was never a question of taking that power away from [the artists], but they always were able to make the direction, create the pace, and that's why the music has always been vibrant. And as long as the industry understands there has to be a balance. . . . I think it's possible. It has been done, so it's possible.

What advice would you have for someone interested in becoming a jazz musician?

There's a way that has worked and that has been done over and over again, and that's basically to search out the great musicians who are still here. Some of the originators are still with us. And to make it their point to be there whenever these people play. And if they're fortunate enough to be in these people's company, to ask a question. I think asking questions is the best way to learn.

There's plenty of literature, and the records are an amazing source of how people become acquainted. You have to really want to live inside the music, so you find out everything you can about it. There's really no shortcut to it. If you want it, you have to do what everybody else has done. And you find that the greater the artist is, the more detail they took in that process.

GERI
ALLEN
SELECT DISCOGRAPHY

As a Leader
- *The Gathering*—Verve
- *Eyes . . . in the Back of Your Head*—Blue Note
- *Some Aspects of Water*—Storyville
- *In the Middle*—Verve
- *Maroons*—Blue Note
- *The Nurturer*—Blue Note
- *Open on All Sides in the Middle*—Minor Music
- *Twylight*—Verve
- *Twenty One*—with the Geri Allen Trio—Blue Note
- *The Printmakers*—with the Geri Allen Trio—Minor Music
- *In the Year of the Dragon*—with Charlie Haden and Paul Motian—Verve
- *Live at the Village Vanguard*—with Charlie Haden and Paul Motian—DIW
- *Segments*—with Charlie Haden and Paul Motian—DIW

Biography

CYRUS

Photo Notes

The first time I saw Cyrus Chestnut, in 1992, he was accompanying Betty Carter. Four years later, in May, 1996, I saw him again at Yoshi's. This time he was playing with his own trio: himself on piano, Alvester Garnett on drums, and Steve Kirby on bass. Chestnut is completely in command—just look at the photograph to see the self assurance. It's his intensity and of course, his sincerity that got to me.

Here again, I was looking for something to connect to the music. Chestnut was playing church music at the time, and the audience responded in kind. I almost missed the shot because I, too, got caught up in being transported elsewhere.

E xtremely talented and one of the most versatile jazz pianists working today, Cyrus Chestnut (DOB 1/17/63) was born in Baltimore, Maryland, and currently lives in New York City. A prodigy, at age nine Chestnut studied at the Peabody Preparatory, a part of the acclaimed Peabody Conservatory in Baltimore. He earned a degree in jazz composition and arranging from the Berklee School of Music.

Chestnut has released seven recordings as a leader and has recorded with many other artists. His recordings have displayed a mastery of various styles from straight-ahead jazz, to funk, rhythm and blues, and gospel. He has collaborated with many of his contemporaries, including Dee Dee Bridgewater, Joshua Redman, and Courtney Pine. Chestnut is committed to bringing a wider audience to jazz. With his enormous talent, a small taste of his artistry will be all most will need to be jazz fans for life.

CHESTNUT

INTERVIEW, JANUARY 28, 1998

Describe for me some of your earliest musical experiences.

There was always music going on in the house. Mom tells me that my father would put me in the bassinet, and he would play the piano. He plays piano, and he was actually my first teacher. He would play for me, and I'm telling you, no matter what I was doing, I would get quiet and after awhile I would just go to sleep. And sometimes my father would play, and my mom would sing, and I would be in the bassinet.

Around age four, I was starting [to play piano], but I had a fascination with the bottom half of the piano. There was just something about it that I really liked. [Around this time] my father got me a piano book, and he started teaching me the piano. And by the time I was six I had my first official outing playing at church.

Early on were you trained in classical music?

No. I've always liked instrumental music. I have nothing against lyrics, but I just like instrumental music. In my house [growing up] there were Shirley Caesar, James Cleveland, Jackie Wilson, Sam Cooke, and King Curtis. I really liked listening to King Curtis because it was instrumental.

Age nine was an interesting year for me, too. I used to get like a two-dollar allowance, and I went to this five-and-dime store, and I went to the record bin, and I picked up this record because I liked the cover. The name of that record was *Thelonious Monk's Greatest Hits*. At that time I didn't know anything about Monk or what he was all about. I liked the cover. And so when I played the record, I was like, wow, this is nice. And again it was instrumental music. And I was listening to stuff like "Epistrophy," "Ruby My Dear," "Crepuscule with Nellie." I think on that record he played solo. So it was really nice. I think that was like the beginning between King Curtis and Monk, kind of one of those destiny-setters, you know?

CYRUS CHESTNUT

When did you know that you wanted to make a career out of playing piano?

I think that didn't happen until I was sixteen or seventeen. At first when I went to Berklee, just the general plan was to go study some music and maybe get a teaching degree. But once I got to school, it was like, wait a minute, there are a lot of things going on. And I just believed I could do it.

Besides King Curtis and Thelonious Monk, whom would you count as your greatest inspirations in jazz?

Those two were introductory. But when I'm asked about my influences, I say a lot of different people. I say Fats Waller, Red Garland, Tommy Flanagan, Hank Jones. I will also mention Art Tatum, Herbie Hancock, McCoy Tyner, Chick Corea. I will also mention Wynton Kelly, Ahmad Jamal, Marcus Roberts. A lot of different people: John Coltrane, Charlie Parker, Bud Powell—and the list goes on and on.

A lot of people have said we're in the midst of a resurgence in the popularity of jazz. Do you agree with this, and if you do, have you thought about why this may be?

Yes, I think the whole stigma behind jazz is starting to slow; those walls, those barriers are starting to get old and crumble down now. I think younger people are starting to realize that, hey, this music can be hip. This is not necessarily your mama's and daddy's, your grandma's and grandfather's music. It's starting to see that this could be music now. The face of jazz, as far as the musicians, also has received a makeover, too. I'm saddened because so many of the great legends and pioneers are starting to drift away, but in the way, here comes a new crowd of younger musicians who are still carrying the torch.

And so for those who say, oh, jazz is dead, I think they will be making a great big error because if that's true, then there wouldn't be Nicholas Paytons around. There wouldn't be Roy Hargroves around; there wouldn't be Joshua Redmans around. There wouldn't be Christian McBrides around.

Or Cyrus Chestnuts.

[Laughs] Yes.

What is your favorite part of your job? Would it be composing, recording, performing?

Putting smiles on peoples' faces. I like writing, but it is kind of gratifying to have someone come up to you and, in a very honest way, to really say I didn't know you before, I didn't know any of your music before, but what you have done this evening has really touched me, and thank you for making this evening so special. It is things like that that keep me going.

What about goals for yourself?

I wish to honestly and skillfully transcend these barriers of jazz. I believe that jazz is a musical idiom that is worth all the accolades. I think it is very much worth the support. It has taken time for the music industry to see that it's starting to come around, but I would like to be able to see the day when I could go into Radio City Music Hall for a week and pack it each night. To be able to play Madison Square Garden and have the whole place full of people to come see some jazz at Madison Square Garden. It may sound like a lot to chew, but a lot of people tell me that it can't be done, and I don't know if that's going to be done. I immediately have to say, you know what, let me show you. And I'll do everything I can to attempt it. If it doesn't work, then that means it wasn't meant to be, but at least I gave it my best shot.

What do you think the jazz community is going to have to do to reach that point?

Well I think that first off, the artists have to gain a lot of confidence in the music as being able to reach the masses. Not, well, it's just a jazz record, and I'm not going to have a large audience so I'm just going to do this music for myself. I think that's the wrong way to look at it. If the musician gains more confidence in the music and just simply presents him- or herself in an honest way, simply attempting to communicate with people, I think that is the first step of it.

Hopefully when that happens, the industry will say, okay, all right. There are some different things going on, and then they will be a little bit more willing to put in all the guns. Expose this music to a lot more people rather than just a dignified few.

Do you think the record companies are putting more money behind marketing of jazz records and allowing the artistic freedom that the musicians need?

I guess that if a record is selling well then the company probably would be a little more willing to put dollars behind it.

Someone has to make the first move.

Yes. It surely could be a lot better. I look at it at this time as I'm going to continue to hope for it. Things are really going well for me, but in order to achieve what I want to achieve, I'm at the point that I'm realizing that it has to be done one audience at a time. So the more of a following I can develop and the larger the audience base gets, then hopefully it will become a little easier.

CYRUS CHESTNUT
SELECT DISCOGRAPHY

As a Leader

- *Cyrus Chestnut—* Atlantic Jazz
- *Blessed Quietness: A Collection of Hymns, Spirituals & Carols—* Atlantic Jazz
- *Earth Stories—* Atlantic Jazz
- *The Dark Before the Dawn*—Atlantic Jazz
- *Revelation*—Atlantic Jazz
- *Another Direction*—Cyrus Chestnut Trio—Evidence
- *Nut*—Evidence

Collaborations With Other Artists

- *Underground*—with Courtney Pine—Antilles
- *Kansas City*—Original Motion Picture Soundtrack—Verve
- *Gettin' to It*—with Christian McBride—Verve
- *It's Not About the Melody*—with Betty Carter—Verve
- *Testimonial*—with Carl Allen—Atlantic Jazz
- *Black Pearl*—with Donald Harrison and Terence Blanchard— Columbia

Biography

JOEY

A native of Philadelphia, Joey DeFrancesco (DOB 4/10/71) has been playing the organ practically his whole life. His earliest influence was his father, who also plays jazz organ. DeFrancesco also counts Jimmy Smith, Miles Davis, and Frank Sinatra as major influences.

From a very early age, DeFrancesco has recorded and performed with some of jazz's greatest artists. Legendary trumpeter Miles Davis heard DeFrancesco play at age sixteen and asked the teenager to join his band. DeFrancesco toured the world with Davis, and it was also around this time that he signed with the Columbia label. These days DeFrancesco records and tours mostly with his own bands. He has released nine recordings as a leader and has appeared on numerous records. Still in his twenties, he is one of the premier jazz organists working today.

DEFRANCESCO

INTERVIEW, APRIL 9, 1997

You certainly started music very early; I think by age six you were playing a Hammond organ. How did it all get started for you?

It all got started because of my father. He's also a professional jazz musician—jazz organist in fact. The first instrument I ever played was the organ. I'm an organ player from the start. And my dad and his influences—I just loved the organ sound. For a long time when I was a kid, [organ music] was all that was playing through the house. I was naturally attracted to it and loved it and wanted to play.

You've said that a major turning point in your career was when you were called to lead the band for a local television show in Philadelphia called "Time Out." Miles Davis was a special guest on one of the shows. How old were you at the time?

At that time I was sixteen years old.

After seeing you on the show, Miles Davis called you. What was it like getting a call from Miles Davis?

He called, and I was out. [I was told that] Miles Davis called, and I didn't believe it. In fact it was my grandmother, who was not aware of who Miles Davis was, who said some man named Miles Davis called. And I said, yeah, right, it's one of my buddies. Christian McBride and I went to high school together, and I thought it was him or something like that.

I said, all right, let me call this number and see who this is. It was a New York number. And I called; sure enough, it was the man. And I said, wow, Miles, you know? He said, "Who are you playing with?" And I said, "I'm not playing with anybody; I'm seventeen years old. I'm still in high school." "Well, come on up to New York. When can you come? Today? Tomorrow?" I said, "I'll come tomorrow." "Come on up." I said, "All right."

So I went to New York the next day and sat down and he said, "Play something for me." Very warm, he hugged me, a very warm person, Miles. A lot of people probably don't know that, but he was. And he had a Fender Rhodes in there. And

I started to play something, and he picked up his horn and started playing with me. And I'll never forget that. "You want to play in the band?" I said, "Of course." So that's how it started.

JOEY DEFRANCESCO

Tell me about the experience of being with Miles Davis's band.

Well, it was incredible. To be around Miles—I was around him a lot, too, because we were just together a lot. . . . I used to ask him a billion questions about the old times, the music they used to play. And he always would talk about that. Much as he'd say he didn't want to go back, that's all he ever talked about. He was just a wonderful person to be around, and we had a great time. . . . It was just incredible. He was so really good to me.

Who have been your greatest musical influences?

My father, of course, first. If it weren't for him, I wouldn't have known any of this stuff. But then I'd have to say Jimmy Smith. Still to this day, you know, a very big influence. Not that I play a lot like that, but he is a big influence.

Miles Davis. I'm a Miles Davis fanatic. Very big fan. You know I love him a lot. I love him. His music is unbelievable. That's why I started playing trumpet, because of him.

John Coltrane. And I like singers a lot, too. I'm a very big fan of Frank Sinatra.

In the last ten to fifteen years, we've seen a strong resurgence in the popularity of jazz music. Have you given any thought as to why this may be?

I guess because maybe people are just tired of hearing the same old stuff all the time. Music that's here one day, gone the next day, and very limited talent abilities. And jazz is such a creative music, and you have to be a master of your instrument to play it. I think maybe it's just a new age. People want to hear something different. And to a lot of people [jazz] is very different. It's like me, people see me, "Wow, you play the organ? That's really cool, man." Organists have been playing in this tradition since the 1950s. . . .

And I think it's also because there are a lot of younger players, and a lot of the younger people identify. I think it's because they'll hear somebody like a Marsalis or maybe somebody else like a Josh Redman, and they may not have known about John Coltrane and other players . . . So I think it's good for all the eras. I think it's a wonderful thing. Like I feel very responsible for the resurgence of the organ because until my first record came out, it was really dying out. And it really sparked a big interest. And that made a lot of the other guys— they came up to me all the time telling me thanks. And I'm glad that happened. I'm glad it's happening, period, for jazz.

Do you think that the younger generation willed or intended it to happen, or do you think it's just something that happened along the way of your careers?

I don't know. I know when I started playing, I got signed at Columbia, and I was excited about it. I said I'm going to bring jazz—I mean, that was something in my mind. I want to bring this back. I hope people recognize this and realize this is the real deal. I think the young musicians, we're all serious about it. We love [jazz] so much that we play it. And I think we all wished there would be something like this happening. Of course.

Who are some of the younger generation musicians you've most enjoyed playing with?

I like playing with them all. I have fun whenever that opportunity comes up. I've played with Josh [Redman]; I've played with Christian McBride quite a bit. Roy Hargrove. I think we've all played together at one time or another, and I have a ball. There's not anyone that I like better than playing with any other. I think we just all have fun together.

Are there any young keyboard players out there you know that the public might not know yet and who we should look out for?

I played in Detroit a couple years ago. There was a little boy there; his name was Eddie Brown. And I had heard about him before. I think he was about eleven when I saw him. I had heard he could really play some organ, and he's a big fan of mine and all. So I asked him to play, and he played his little butt off. So don't be surprised if you hear about an Eddie Brown on organ pretty soon.

Would you have any specific advice for aspiring musicians, maybe something you wish somebody had told you?

I had my dad there, so I've been very fortunate. He's always telling me the right things, and I've been lucky with that. I think if I had to tell somebody something who wasn't aware of a lot of things, when you learn how to play this music, I think the main thing is just listening to records, and listening and listening and never stop listening. Because that's how you learn to play.

But, you know, too, I think to be able to swing is a natural thing. I don't think you can learn how to swing. I think you can learn how to play with real good time, and . . . the pulse will be there, but that swing that makes you move your neck and pat your foot, I think that's got to be within you. You're born with that.

JOEY DEFRANCESCO
SELECT DISCOGRAPHY

As a Leader
- *The Street of Dreams*— Big Mo Records
- *All About My Girl*—Muse
- *Live at the Five Spot*— Columbia
- *Reboppin'*—Columbia
- *Part III*—Columbia
- *All of Me*—Columbia
- *Where Were You?*— Columbia
- *All in the Family*— Joey DeFrancesco & "Papa" John DeFrancesco—HighNote
- *It's About Time*—with Jack McDuff—Concord Jazz

Collaborations With Other Artists
- *Marchel Ivery Meets Joey DeFrancesco*— with Marchel Ivery— Leaning House
- *Live Around the World*— with Miles Davis— Warner Bros. Records

Biography

BENNY

Photo Notes

This photograph was taken at Yoshi's in 1997 when Benny Green led an all-star group consisting of Gary Bartz on alto sax, Larry Coryell on guitar, Peter Apfelbaum on tenor sax, and others. Here Green was minutes from his hometown, and many old friends and family were in attendance. His playing was better than I'd ever heard.

Every time Green comes back to the (San Francisco) Bay Area, his stature grows larger. Being the shy guy that he is, he seems to be uncomfortable with all of the attention, and he becomes even humbler. I love to photograph him because when he sits down at the piano, he seems to forget everything but the music. For me, Green is one of the easiest subjects to photograph. He is intense most of the time, so I don't have to wait for the "right" time to photograph him. Unquestionably the other musicians playing with him that night, along with the hometown crowd, propelled him to new heights. It was a good photo night.

A California native who now lives in New York City, Benny Green (DOB 4/4/63) began an enriching jazz education with the heralded Berkeley, California, public system, where he developed a love for jazz while in elementary school. As a young adult, he started a series of extended apprenticeships under such jazz giants as Betty Carter, Art Blakey, Freddie Hubbard, Oscar Peterson, and Ray Brown.

For a player still in his thirties, Green has recorded an enormous amount of music, including eight releases as a leader. Green's playing consistently incorporates traditional jazz elements, yet he also brings a unique style to the piano, culminating in a signature sound. Since the early 1990s, Green has recorded and performed almost exclusively with his own bands. His raw talent combined with his education, experiences, and commitment make for the consummate jazz artist—grounded in tradition, yet always in pursuit of innovation.

GREEN

INTERVIEW, MAY 8, 1997

Tell me about the earliest experiences with music you can remember.

I grew up hearing music around the house through my father who plays tenor saxophone. I heard him playing his horn at home and also, very importantly, I was exposed to his jazz-record collection, which included artists like Thelonious Monk and Charlie Parker, Billie Holiday, Ray Charles and Bessie Smith, people like that. Before I knew that this music was an African-American art form, I associated these sounds with a lot of warmth around the house.

We got a piano in our home when I was about six years old, and I was very taken with the instrument—pretty much from the start—and I would sit at the piano and try to compose my own tunes. When my parents saw that I had this interest, they got a classical teacher for me. The lessons started when I was about seven and after a few years, my first classical teacher noticed that I tended toward improvisation, so she suggested to my parents that they try to find someone in the [San Francisco] Bay Area who could help me more in the arena of jazz improvisation. And when I went into the fourth grade and started attending Longfellow Elementary School in Berkeley, I came in contact with a man named Phil Hardeman, who was running a jazz department in all of the Berkeley public schools. And that's something that really made a strong connection for me. Up until that time I had associated this music with older people, like my father and the faces on his album covers. But seeing my peers trying to play a twelve-bar blues made me realize that maybe this was something that I could actualize, so that was an important connection.

You attended Berkeley High, and it has a widely acclaimed high-school jazz program. Did you know at the time that you were getting such a specialized jazz education?

I didn't have the awareness that I have now of just how unique the whole program was, but I did know that it was something special. . . . But I think the most important facet of the atmosphere Mr. Hardeman provided for us, starting at the elementary-school level and continuing up, was just seeing kids our own age trying to play the music and growing up together, coming up through this public-school system and being competitive with each other in a healthy kind of way, and all striving to get an opportunity to play with the high-school band if we could excel to that level by the time we attended high school.

You've been fortunate to have some of the great legends guiding you along the way. You've played with Art Blakey and Betty Carter, Ray Brown and Oscar Peterson. What does playing with these caliber musicians do for you?

In the case of both Betty Carter and Art Blakey, they really tried to emphasize the importance of developing my own individuality and not just being encumbered by trying to emulate pianists whom I had admired on recordings. To really try to begin to realize my own potential as an individual voice in the music, which is a very important part or significant part of the tradition of jazz. . . .

And both Betty and Art talked to me about the importance of writing my own music and steering clear from just being an imitator. Also, both of those band leaders talked to me about the importance of consistency in live performance, that if we were ever physically or emotionally fatigued in the course of a tour, how necessary it was to realize our higher purpose when we step on stage—as actually being instruments for the music and rising above anything that could possibly obstruct the flow of the music.

After playing with Art Blakey, I joined Freddie Hubbard's quintet and that was a unique experience for me because, with Freddie's dynamic personality, I never knew what direction we would take musically on any given night or for any particular set or tune for that matter. There was a kind of freedom I felt in the music that I never experienced before and, in certain ways, haven't experienced on that consistent of a level since. . . .

When I was with Ray Brown, which has been the longest tenure of all the bands I've worked with, while it might appear on the surface that what Ray would have exposed me to was more about the art of arranging for a piano trio, but in fact, what I think he laid on me of even more significance was a further facet of some of the things Betty and Art had touched on about developing a sound of my own. He pointed out to me that it's a calling of mine to nurture my relationship with my instrument and to begin to think about developing an individual sound as a pianist so that I could be recognizable in a few notes. Only a small handful of pianists in jazz have achieved this.

In the fall of 1992, Oscar Peterson received the Glenn Gould Foundation Award and then bestowed upon you the Protege prize. Tell me what is was like to receive that.

I don't really tend towards superlatives, but I really feel that with all the listening I've done to Oscar's music, in a sense, he's possibly the most dynamic pianist in jazz. When I say dynamic, I'm talking about the wide range of emotions he's able to touch on in his music. . . . Since getting to know Oscar as a friend, I've had the privilege of realizing that all of this beauty that we feel in Oscar's music is clearly a reflection of the human being, of the kind of soul this man has, and of his faith—and that's been an important lesson for me away from the piano, just realizing that all this emotion he's able to impart to us as listeners is only a reflection of what he has in his heart.

BENNY GREEN

Oscar's been a very deep inspiration to me in so many ways. For example, the fact that he mastered his instrument at a very early age but was never satisfied with that level he achieved early on. He continued to strive for deeper levels of expression throughout his development, and although he mastered the instrument so very long ago, he's remained very, very humble to the task of being a music-maker. He's a strong inspiration to me in that sense as well. . . .

And I realized as a young pianist that there are many players out there right now, my age, some a little older, some even younger now, who have something valid to say and to contribute to the heritage of this music. So what I don't want to do is utilize this inspiration or this affirmation that Oscar's given me as a way to try to consider myself to be of any kind of a mountain because I'm well aware that everyone has something of their own to contribute to this music. I'd rather just like to utilize this inspiration to work harder and consistently at realizing my own personal potential.

You've said before that you love being on the road. You're unlike a lot of musicians who say being on the road is the worst part about being a jazz musician.

There's actually a beauty I think in experiencing the road and experiencing feeling worn out, dealing with some elements that are unexpected and overcoming any kind of obstacle so that when we get on stage, we're able to impart a positive feeling to the listeners. And I think it's a beautiful kind of learning experience, and it helps to mature and shape your character as a player. And I'm grateful for the opportunity to travel, play music, because it's real—it's kind of a spiritual education. . . . It's clear to me that experience teaches, so it's invaluable to get to tour. And I think when we go into the studio to document our music and to make a statement for all times, I think the fact that we've been able to tour and come through these experiences really helps to shape and form the very substance of what we do.

What advice would you have for someone who is thinking about a career as a jazz musician?

I don't know how different what I have to say is from what I was told by my father because I think he really laid some important things on me. But I feel that whatever instrument a young person wants to play, it's very important to listen as much as possible to recordings. If you can't afford to buy a recording, listen to your local jazz radio station. Begin to get a feel for just how advanced this music is, and begin to cultivate a personal taste in the music, and become aware of how your instrument can function within an improvising jazz ensemble.

I think it's important to try to get the very best teachers you can—both classically in terms of learning your instrument and also if you can find a jazz instructor who's actually a player whom you respect, not just someone who teaches the music out of the book, but someone who can teach from actual experience whom you can relate to.

It's also important, I think, to try to play as much as possible with the best players you could possibly find. The best way to grow is by playing with people who are of a higher level of experience than yourself, but if that's not possible, even if you can just get together with your peers and play together, that's going to help you also.

I think being open and receptive to receiving constructive criticism from people who mean well and are aware of what you're doing and what you're working towards can also help you because sometimes we might have a very different sense in our own minds of where we are musically as contrasted with what other people are actually hearing. If you can listen to other people's objective viewpoints without feeling you are necessarily being put down, then that's going to be to your benefit as well.

I think it's very important, if you really want to be the best you can be in music, New York is an important place to investigate. . . . [I]f you can just experience New York, I think that will be beneficial wherever you ultimately make your home.

BENNY GREEN

SELECT DISCOGRAPHY

As a Leader

- *Kaleidoscope*—Blue Note
- *The Place to Be*—Blue Note
- *That's Right!*—Blue Note
- *Testifyin': Live at the Village Vanguard*—Blue Note
- *Greens*—Blue Note
- *Lineage*—Blue Note
- *In This Direction*—Criss Cross
- *Prelude*—Criss Cross
- *Oscar and Benny*—with Oscar Peterson—Telarc Jazz

Collaborations With Other Artists

- *Not Yet*—with Art Blakey and the Jazz Messengers—Soul Note
- *I Get a Kick Out of Bu*—with Art Blakey and the Jazz Messengers—Soul Note
- *Topsy*—with Freddie Hubbard—Alfa
- *Live at Fat Tuesday's*—with Freddie Hubbard—MusicMasters
- *Look What I Got*—with Betty Carter—Verve
- *Betty Carter and Her Trio*—with Betty Carter—Repertoire

Biography

DIANA

A native of Nanaimo, British Columbia, Diana Krall (DOB 11/16/64) is a rarity in jazz in that she is known equally well for her piano playing and for her singing. As a child, Krall was surrounded by music, including jazz from such artists as Nat "King" Cole, Fats Waller, and Frank Sinatra. Krall won a Vancouver Jazz Festival scholarship to study at the Berklee School of Music in Boston. She also has enjoyed apprenticeships with two legends, Ray Brown and Jimmy Rowles.

In 1990 Krall moved to New York City, and she has maintained a relentless recording and touring schedule ever since. She has released four recordings as a leader, including *All For You* (Impulse!), for which she received a Grammy nomination, and *Love Scenes* (Impulse!); both albums are enjoying overwhelming critical and commercial success.

When I saw Diana Krall for the first time at Kuumbwa in November, 1996, her reputation preceded her. She was getting a lot of publicity in the trade publications and had played to large audiences. I wondered how she would do in a small club like Kuumbwa. Russell Malone on guitar was playing along with her. It was a cold, damp evening, but to my pleasant surprise she played to the audience like a pro and really warmed them up. They responded to her and she to them. This photograph is from that appearance.

A year later, in September, 1997, she appeared, with Russell Malone again on guitar and John Clayton on bass, at the Monterey Jazz Festival. I didn't get the warmth of her playing on the big stage, but later that evening in a much smaller venue, the audience responded in a more intimate way.

KRALL

INTERVIEW, AUGUST 5, 1997

Tell me about the earliest experiences with music you remember and maybe some of the things that sparked your interest in music—jazz music in particular.

I don't remember my first piano lessons. I remember coloring piano keys in a coloring book from Mrs. Thomas, and she called them Popsicle sticks. And I was probably five or four and coloring—trying to color inside the lines of the piano keys. I remember sitting on the bench, but I do not remember playing the piano.

When did you know that you wanted to play jazz music as a career?

I don't know. I don't know if I ever knew. I think I was fifteen years old, and my mom took me down to audition for a gig that was changing over, and there was a bass player there who obviously wanted to keep his gig that he had previously, and therefore I was able to play with him. He was an older musician and a bass player who taught me a lot about songs, and about music, and how to play with a bass player.

And I just sort of started out playing, and there was never any doubt in my mind that I wanted to play music. I think jazz music was the music that had a swing feel to it. I don't even want to say "jazz" because it's kind of—I think Jimmy Rowles said to me that jazz is an adjective for a way of doing something. But I wanted to play the sort of music that had that feeling to it. That made me feel so good. I like the structure and the creativity within the structure.

Who have been some of your greatest inspirations and influences?

I've been lucky enough to have a series of mentors. There have been people who have been an influence on me indirectly who I haven't met, like Ahmad Jamal. Of course, I now have met him and had a chance to talk with him and Hank Jones. But people like Nat King Cole, Frank Sinatra, Billie Holiday, Carmen McRae, Sarah Vaughn, Ella Fitzgerald, and Bill Evans.

And the records of John Coltrane, Charlie Parker, Miles Davis, Herbie Hancock, Wayne Shorter, Wynton Kelly, Red Garland. The list goes on. I've checked out as much as I possibly can. Visual artists, poetry, the works of great composers.

I guess I could start with my family. From my father, the humor and joy that my father gets from the music and his own quiet enjoyment of the music. My mother, with her—right down to singing Lutheran hymns in church in almost perfect pitch with great strength. The love and the passion for just pure and simple—the passion for the music started at home.

And then expanded upon by my band director, Brian Stovell, who was also a bass player who taught me about Charlie Parker, John Coltrane, and Miles Davis. And then going to Berklee, Dave McKenna, who I was able to hear on a regular basis. Then Don Thompson, another great musician who taught me a lot of things—a lot of things that are just starting to sink in. And Jimmy Rowles. I think I was nineteen years old when

I went to see him, and he taught me about, most importantly, the beauty of the music.

Ray Brown is like a musical dad to me. In a way, like a godfather who is always present in my life, since I was nineteen. From talking about the same things, about the groove. As a guide he's been a real guide for me. . . . I'm influenced now strongly by my peers. Russell Malone is a great influence in my life right now, musically. As a partner, we're constantly searching. I've had the opportunity to meet with Tony Bennett and talk with him for a long time, Nancy Wilson and Abbey Lincoln, and it just keeps moving and moving and moving. It's a very exciting thing.

Not many artists play and sing. Does having to sing while you play making playing the piano more difficult?

No, I don't really think about that. I think it's just difficult to keep the two up. It's just that there are sometimes when I concentrate more on playing the piano than I do on singing. And there are times when I am really focusing on the lyric and singing. But it comes pretty natural to me to accompany myself.

I am just constantly striving to be a better pianist separate from just being my own best accompanist.

You've become somewhat of a jazz superstar. What kind of effect does your success have on an artist?

[Laughs] Only when I'm back in the United States and I'm doing interviews or when I'm doing interviews and people say you are somewhat of a—use that word "star," which just completely throws me because I don't have time to think about that sort of thing and, I guess, that's people's perception of where you are.

I think one of the things that Jeff Hamilton taught me very early on, and John Clayton, that I have not forgotten, is that you get to do this—you get to play, and the so-called success has enabled me to have the great, great opportunities to meet people and learn from people whom I admire. . . . We are not getting paid to play the music; we're getting paid to get on an airplane at six in the morning and have no sleep.

But I think that I am very lucky. You don't get into this art form for fame and fortune. You don't say, Mom and Dad, I want to grow up and I want to be a star jazz piano player and singer; you know, they'd laugh in your face.

It's an art form that is not considered stable in the eyes of a parent. You have passion and focus for what you are doing, and you keep focused and keep passionate about what you are doing. I believe that in life, if you are passionate about whatever you do, these things will come to you.

What kind of toll does touring nonstop take on you?

I take care of myself. I am not a person who will go back to the hotel room right after the gig and go right to bed. I am going to go out for dinner, hang out with my peers, or go to a jam session, and if I get three hours of sleep, fine, I'll sleep on the plane. Right now, I am still young enough that I am able to do that. Maybe I'll be young enough to do that when I'm seventy-five; hopefully, if it's in my mind. I am pretty curious, and I am always afraid I'm going to miss something.

Tell me about your plans.

One day at a time. I have things that I am thinking about, but I'm kind of private about it because I am working it out. But I am constantly searching.

What advice would you have for someone who is young and thinks he or she might want to be a jazz musician?

I think if at a certain time of your life—even if somebody told you at nineteen years old, it's about the beauty of the music, and you are struggling to play, you know, you're not really listening; you are still doing your own thing, and you're rebelling, and you're doing this—and it's going to sink in when you are thirty-two years old, great.

This sounds really simple, but I am really finding that simplicity is the most complex thing to achieve, and a lot of those things have to come in time. You have to go through one phase to get to the next. I think the only thing that I can say is that [whatever you're doing] be passionate about it, and be honest and sincere and love what you do. That's what my parents taught me. It's a very simple thing. It will take you there, where you want to go.

I think that it's whatever kind of music that is in your heart. Whether it's funk, or fusion, or whatever. Whether you are writing, whether you are arranging, if that's your passion, then follow that. Be constantly curious, and be constantly open to everything and listen. Get as much information as you possibly can to build your own self—find yourself through knowledge.

DIANA KRALL
SELECT DISCOGRAPHY

As a Leader
- *Love Scenes*—Impulse!
- *All For You*—Impulse!
- *Only Trust Your Heart*—GRP
- *Steppin' Out*—Justin Time

Collaborations With Other Artists
- *Forever Love*—with Mark Whitfield—Verve

Biography

DANILO

A native of Panama, Danilo Perez was born on December 29, 1966. His father's love of music made a great impression on him, and at age five he started studying the piano at the National Conservatory in Panama. He began studies at the Berklee School of Music in 1985. Perez counts Bill Evans as one of his earliest jazz influences.

Perez has enjoyed one of the most rewarding apprenticeships in jazz, studying with Donald Brown, Herb Pomeroy, and Charlie Bonacos, and performing with Jon Hendricks, Wynton Marsalis, Claudio Roditi, Paquito D'Rivera, and Dizzy Gillespie. He also has performed with such legends as Freddie Hubbard, James Moody, Jimmy Heath, and Slide Hampton. Perez currently records and performs with his own group, as well as teaches improvisation and jazz studies at the New England Conservatory of Music. To date Perez has released four recordings as a leader, and all are critically acclaimed. An exciting player and performer, he is a joy to listen to and watch.

I remember the evening in July, 1996, that Danilo Perez came to Kuumbwa with his trio, with Avashai Cohen on bass and Terri Lyne Carrington on drums. It was an extremely hot, muggy night, unusual for Santa Cruz, California. I was afraid that the uncomfortable humidity would put a damper on Perez's performance. In retrospect, worrying was silly; Danilo, raised in Panama, was probably a lot more used to this weather than I was. I'd never heard him live before. I wasn't disappointed. Kuumbwa, with its audience and ambiance, seems to bring out the best in jazz musicians.

In this photograph, that's not a smile you see on Perez's face, that's concentration. Although he'd recently recorded his CD Panamonk, the performance this night was more Monk than Panama. The concentration that you need to play Monk can easily make you forget your surroundings.

PEREZ

INTERVIEW, DECEMBER 8, 1997

Tell me about some of your earliest music experiences.

Most of my early musical experience was with my father and his playing guitar. I remember when my father used to take me when I was four or five years old to his rehearsals. I would go and play a little percussion.

There is one experience I'll never forget. It taught me how powerful music is. When I was a kid, my father and I were playing music, and this guy came by and was fixing the washing machine. He was about to leave but when you came to our house, you had to play some musical instrument, you know, a pot, fork, cowbell. So he played with us for about two hours, and when he was ready to go, my father asked how much he owed for the fixing of the washing machine. The man said, "If we're talking about money, I have to pay you because this feeling, I never had it playing music."

Any particular reason why you decided to go with the piano rather than percussion?

Wow, that's a good question. My father was a big fan of piano players. We could just do a duet, voice and piano, that's it, because in the piano, you have the orchestra.

What sparked your interest in jazz?

I think it just happened little by little. I was listening to all the great Latin piano players, and at one point I heard a piano player called Papo Lucca who was playing Latin music, but he was putting the bebop to it—that was the first thing that caught my ears. I think that was the beginning of me liking jazz. And just the way he was picking up stuff from Bud Powell and putting it into Latin. I didn't know what it was called; I just thought the music was really neat and cool. And there is another guy from Cuba called Peruchin. These type of piano players helped make my first connection.

I also had a neighbor in Panama who played all jazz records. He played them so loudly, it was like he wanted all of the neighborhood to listen. And that's when I really started hearing the music.

DANILO PEREZ

Do you think that the Thelonious Monk competition was one of your biggest breaks into jazz?

No. Before that I had spent two years with Jon Hendricks, and I would say that would be my entrance to jazz. The biggest one. The Thelonious Monk competition would be an extension of that. But being with Hendricks was like taking advanced courses in jazz.

You're a professor at the New England Conservatory teaching improvisation and jazz studies. Could you comment about the state of education for jazz today?

There are two parts to this. There is one part in which I feel the young musicians have a really big advantage. Academically today's students have an advantage. But you have to combine the academic education with the heart. The academic education is great, but if the kids don't have enough chances to experiment and assimilate what they have learned in the classroom through the heart, then there could be a problem with the future.

So how do you try to prevent that from happening to your students?

I focus a lot of my teaching on rhythms and body dance because I think the connection to music comes from the body. The body and the voice, the percussion first. So I make them dance if I have to, and I make them sing the stuff.

But, of course, a person needs a lot of basic stuff like ear training, and he needs to have a lot of things together. The instrument, too. But I always combine a little bit of the mysterious, like not giving them all the answers. I let them look for the answers.

A lot of people have said that since the early 1980s, there has been a strong resurgence in the popularity of jazz music. Do you agree?

I do. I think it has happened little by little. I think Americans are catching up to the European audiences. Jazz is the musical key of the century. . . . And I hope that

it will grow, but it has to grow for the best. I see a tendency to take the music and feed all of this market, too.

I do see schools starting up jazz programs. I see a lot of musicians doing a lot of clinics. I see a lot of people having more respect for the music.

People always want to compare the young musicians to musicians like Duke Ellington. I think that's a mistake because they were the leaders. All we are trying to do is keep the music alive.

One thing that is interesting about your playing is that when I hear your music, and I hear you playing the piano, especially if it's just the rhythm section playing, I can hear you scatting while you're playing. Is that something you do consciously?

Because of my father's influence, I always sang while I played the piano. But when I studied classical piano, I was told not to make noises. But once I started working in jazz, I was allowed once again to play the piano and sing what I was playing, and it made perfect sense. And what that does for me is just give me the right phrasing. And it has taught me a lot about space—something that Dizzy Gillespie also made a big remark about. Space is also music.

What do you want to accomplish in the future?

I hope to be able to keep doing what I'm doing, which is doing music that has a healing purpose, you know, music that makes people feel happy, makes people feel good. And keep developing the sense of bringing different cultures together. Nowadays you can go to New York, and you can meet every race that you ever imagined. And I would like to accomplish that in my music. I want to be a part of the world-music vibe that is going on without sacrificing the elements I believe in: rhythm, swing, groove. And definitely, more and more, I love the blues.

I also want to be able to leave a testament of Panamanian music in another arena. And that is something that I'm going to strive for. And to be able to do projects with a lot of great musicians. Just keep growing. The day I stop growing, I stop playing.

You know, jazz has moved into different stages or eras. For example, we've had bebop, acid jazz, fusion, etc. Do you see on the horizon a new era of jazz?

I have faith that we will. The music that represents the Americas—North America, South America, Central America—lately there has been more of a fusion of all those elements. It started in the United States with Jelly Roll Morton. That's why I say to people that what I'm doing is more related to Jelly Roll. Later the music became known as either jazz or Latin jazz. But if you go back to Jelly Roll Morton, there were some of those Latin elements already in.

So it kind of got into the Conga theme and the percussion, with the jazz solo on top. But lately, there has been a new movement. We Latin players have been playing with a lot of jazz musicians and learning a lot from the music. And then with the background of Latin, then you have the Latin tinge of jazz music—back to Jelly Roll basically.

Jelly Roll Morton called that the "Spanish tinge."

Exactly. And Dizzy Gillespie always said that the North Americans had to learn more about the Caribbean and Latin music. And nowadays I think definitely I am seeing some world-music groove, and a lot of people are grasping the elements. And when that happens, when the total absorption of those powerful rhythms and melodies or those genres of music happens, then I think you are playing a newborn music.

And it's going to be like the Afro-textures meeting. When you have all the African roots meeting again, that's when something new is going to happen, too. That change is going to be so intense because I've noticed that people are getting hip to Afro-African music again. And the audience will be ready for this.

DANILO
PEREZ
SELECT DISCOGRAPHY

As a Leader
- *Central Avenue*—Impulse!
- *Panamonk*—Impulse!
- *The Journey*—Novus
- *Danilo Perez*—Novus

Collaborations With Other Artists
- *Danzon*—with Arturo Sandoval—GRP
- *To Bird With Love*—with Dizzy Gillespie—Telarc Jazz
- *Live at the Royal Festival Hall*—with Dizzy Gillespie and the United Nations Orchestra—Enja
- *The New Arrival*—with Charlie Sepulveda & The Turnaround—Antilles
- *Street Scenes*—with David Sanchez—Columbia
- *Sketches of Dreams*—with David Sanchez—Columbia
- *Dedicated to Diz*—with Slide Hampton & The Jazz Masters—Telarc
- *Who's Smoking*—with Paquito D'Rivera—Candid
- *Havana Cafe*—with Paquito D'Rivera—Chesky
- *Reunion*—with Paquito D'Rivera—Messidor
- *Two of Sorts*—with Claudio Roditi—Candid

Biography | # ERIC

A native of Philadelphia who currently makes his home in Harlem, Eric Reed (DOB 6/21/70) is a virtuoso pianist with an unbridled enthusiasm for jazz music. His earliest musical influences were the sounds and songs of his childhood Holiness church and his father's gospel quartet. Classical music was also a major influence.

An integral part of the acclaimed Wynton Marsalis Septet, Reed continues to record and perform with Marsalis and the Lincoln Center Jazz Orchestra. Reed also has performed with jazz legends Charlie Haden, Benny Carter, Joe Henderson, and Freddie Hubbard.

In addition to his work with the Lincoln Center Jazz Orchestra, Reed currently spends most of his time composing, recording, and performing with his own groups. He has released five recordings as a leader, and all have enjoyed critical acclaim. Reed has made quite an impact in his young career. He most assuredly will make a greater one in the near future.

Photo Notes

In February, 1998, Eric Reed came to Berkel California, to play with the Lincoln Center Jazz Orchestra. This performance was quite different from the one I' seen him at almost three years earlier. This was a sixteen-piece orchestra of mostly contemporarie including Wynton Marsal Wycliffe Gordon, Wess Anderson, Walter Blandir Jr., Rodney Whitaker, Stefan Harris, and Herlin Riley. Reed's playing seemed much more forceful.

This photograph of Re is the only one in this boo that wasn't taken at an actual performance but rather during rehearsal. The orchestra was in the midst of a two-month world tour. The next morning, the musicians were leaving for Korea. Reed and his piano were at the left front of the enormous stage where he could see the entire orchestra.

At this rehearsal, Reed was "conducting" in Marsalis's absence. Reed had just finished giving the musicians instructions for a difficult passage and had now joined them at the piano. His ferocity of play staggered me. I almost stumbled over myself taking this shot because I had only a few seconds to capture the magic of the moment.

REED

INTERVIEW, FEBRUARY 11, 1997

Tell me a little bit about your earliest musical experiences and your musical training.

I was born in Philadelphia. And I always like to claim Philadelphia because that's where I'm from, and there's a long legacy of jazz musicians who come from there. And Philadelphia definitely has its own sound. You listen to somebody like McCoy Tyner, or Lee Morgan, or Philly Joe Jones, Benny Golson. Plus, Philadelphia was more or less a center for jazz—cats coming from the South, stopping through Philly, through Pittsburgh, and going on up to New York.

My main musical influences were gospel and classical. My father is a gospel singer. . . . He had his own group, and they would perform in and around Philadelphia, the tristate area.

I started playing the piano at about age two. It was a God-given gift. Thank God for it taking me a very, very long way. I started studying privately when I was five. And I basically would just pick up things that I heard on records. I would just listen to records and radio and sit at the piano and plunk them out the best way I could. I was always surrounded by music.

I don't want to embarrass you, but I want to quote something from the liner notes in your CD The Swing and I. This quote from Wynton Marsalis says that you possess "the highest levels of pure musical abilities which are matched with a devout belief in jazz music. This is what you hear when you listen to his playing."

First I can tell you that whole quote from Wynton is based on Wynton's ability to recognize musical ability. Wynton has an uncanny knack for being able to detect exactly the finest points of a person's playing. Certainly it's easy to listen to somebody and say he can't do this, and he can't do that. But

it's much more difficult to listen to somebody and say, well, he really does that well. Maybe if I hone in on that, he can develop even further. And that's what Wynton does. And that's one of his greatest, greatest talents.

ERIC REED

When I think of the younger generation of jazz artists, . . . there's a real special place in my heart for what I call the "Wynton Marsalis guys." When I think of people like you, Wessell [Anderson], [Reginald] Veal, Herlin [Riley], there's just something very special about that to me. For you, does playing with Wynton Marsalis's groups have special meaning?

Absolutely, because you know why? I think what happened is all of those records, and I'm talking about from the very first Wynton Marsalis record, the self-titled one, on to the latest one, *Blood on the Fields*, those records helped to create a movement. And it was very similar to what bebop did for young musicians in the '40s and '50s. When people heard Charlie Parker and Dizzy Gillespie, they were like, "Oh my God. What is this? Where is it coming from? And where has it been?" And some people were opposed to it, and some people just ate it right up, and other people were just more or less immune. They really didn't care either way.

Well, Wynton's music has had the same exact effect. I'm not talking about in terms of musical influence because certainly Charlie Parker is Charlie Parker. He's in a class by himself. . . . [But] the effect, more or less, in terms of the vibe, the look, the attitude about music, all of that whole movement was basically what made this thing very, very special for me.

And—I'll be perfectly honest. People would always put me in the Wynton Marsalis "camp" or the Wynton Marsalis "school" or whatever. And it used to bother me because I said, you know what, I can't get my own identity. People always

associate me with Wynton. Then I started to realize, you know what, that's a really good place to come from. There's nothing wrong with that, and I should be proud of that. And then thank God I started to be more aware of that and started to appreciate it more. . . .

So getting back to your question . . . Two records that I did were *Citi Movement* and *In This House, On This Morning.* Those particular records aren't going to have an effect until a very, very long time from now because Wynton is way ahead of his time, and he always has been. Something like *Black Codes (From the Underground)*, when it came out in '85, the effect began to take place a couple years after. All the musicians on the scene, the young ones, were trying to play like that group. Marvin "Smitty" Smith, Bob Hurst, Terence Blanchard, Donald Harrison, Cyrus Chestnut, they were all coming out of that. And the same thing with *Citi Movement* and *In This House, On This Morning*, that's something that's going to have more of an effect two or three years from now, maybe even ten because that music is really, really deep.

What's your favorite part about being a jazz musician: composing, playing, being on the road?

All of those things. I don't know if I have one—yes, I do. My favorite element about being a jazz musician is that when you sit down and play with other musicians, you never know what's going to happen. Some of my best playing, I think, has been with bassist Ben Wolfe and with Gregory Hutchinson, the drummer. When I sit down and play with them, I'm telling you, it's like the Rolls Royce of jazz musicians. I sit down, and I play with them, and it's so comfortable, and it swings so hard, and they just know how to play with me.

**ERIC
REED**

Tell me about your composing habits.

My thing is I work very well under pressure. So I know if I have something to write and somebody says, okay, a year from now, I want to hear this piece performed, well, like most of us, I won't start writing it until about a month before it's time to perform. And that's just the artistic flow. I think having the pressure put on me gets my creative juices flowing, gets the adrenaline pumping, etc. It makes it more imperative for me to try to come up with some decent music.

When you compose, for example, your release Musicale, and you set up the recording dates, and you have the musicians in that you want to perform on it, have they seen the music before they get into the studio

Generally, no.

So they basically learn all the tunes in the studio in a day or two?

Oh, sure. It depends on the musicians you have. See, the thing about writing music for me is I never just write tunes that sound good. I'm always writing songs for somebody else. If I write a song, then I've got somebody, some specific sound in mind. Somebody like Wess Anderson.

Yes, for like "Upper Wess Side"?

Exactly. I wrote that for him. I didn't write that for Jessie Davis. I love Jessie Davis. I love Jackie McLean. I love Antonio Hart. I love Vincent Herring. I didn't write it for any of them, though. I wrote it for Wess because I know what Wess sounds like, and that's exactly the sound I wanted to hear. That's not to say that the others couldn't play it and interpret it in their own wonderful way. But I wrote it for Wess. And that's what I always do. I like to write something specifically and personally for somebody. That way your music has a personal stamp on it.

What comes to mind as some of the most memorable experiences you've had as a professional musician?

I remember a week that I played with Joe Henderson at Catalina Bar and Grill out in Los Angeles. And the group was Joe Henderson, me, Charlie Haden on bass, and Joe Chambers on drums. And that was so incredible for me. That was such a wonderful experience for me because here are these three very influential musicians from the '60s who also were a part of their own movement that influenced a whole wave of young musicians. And I was definitely—I wasn't in this certain group of young musicians, but I definitely was a part of the aftermath of the trail they had paved for us.

Another moment would be a week also with Charlie Haden again, but this time Benny Carter was playing saxophone. It was just a trio. And it was billed as the Jazz Generations Trio because Benny Carter's about eighty, and Charlie's somewhere in his fifties, and then there was me, twenty-six. Any time you get to work with a Benny Carter or a Charlie Haden, that's always memorable.

And thank God, through Wynton, I was put in a position to be able to work with a lot of different musicians. I got to meet Charlie Rouse. I got to work with Elvin Jones. I got to work with Clark Terry. Thank God for "Jazz at Lincoln Center" because that puts you in a position to get the whole gambit of musicians. And thank God some of these guys are still alive, someone like Joe Henderson, Max Roach, or someone like that.

Have you thought a lot about what you want to do with the future?

I definitely want to become more involved in the educating of young people, not just of jazz, just in terms of being influential in their lives in terms of their life growth, their life pattern. And if music happens to come into play, then that's good, too.

ERIC
REED
SELECT DISCOGRAPHY

As a Leader
- *Pure Imagination—*
  GRP/Impulse!
- *Musicale—*
  GRP/Impulse!
- *The Swing and I—*MoJazz
- *It's All Right to Swing—*
  MoJazz
- *Soldier's Hymn—*Candid

Collaborations With Other Artists
- *Blood on the Fields—*
  with Wynton Marsalis
  and the Lincoln Center
  Jazz Orchestra—
  Columbia
- *In This House, On This Morning—*with Wynton
  Marsalis—Columbia
- *Citi Movement—*with
  Wynton Marsalis—
  Columbia
- *Warmdaddy in the Garden of Swing—*with
  Wessell Anderson—
  Atlantic Jazz
- *West Coast Jazz Summit—*with Bob
  Hurst, Jeff Hamilton,
  and Ralph Moore—
  Mons Records

Biography

MARCUS

M arcus Roberts (DOB 8/7/63) was born in Jacksonville, Florida, and continues to reside in Florida today. His first exposure to music was in the church where his mother sang in the gospel choir. He majored in music at Florida State University and studied under noted educator Leonidus Lipovetsky.

Early in his career, Roberts won two major jazz competitions. In 1982 he won the National Association of Jazz Educators annual jazz competition, and in 1987 he won the first Thelonious Monk International Jazz Piano Competition. Roberts first met Wynton Marsalis at that 1982 Jazz Educators' Conference and joined his band in 1985, recording and touring with him from 1985 to 1991.

A prolific composer, Roberts has released twelve recordings as a leader of his own groups, and all have enjoyed critical acclaim and much success. He was the first artist to have his first three recordings reach Number One on Billboard's traditional jazz chart.

On numerous occasions I've had a great deal of difficulty photographing Marcus Roberts. No, it wasn't because of one of the usual reasons, such as poor lighting, or the wrong film or equipment, or poor positioning, or similar logical explanations. These were performances when I had no problem taking photographs of other musicians in the group. I didn't know it at the time of the photo shoot, but I saw it in all the photographs after processing. I know this doesn't sound scientific or reasonable. It took me two or three shoots before I felt satisfied with the photographs of him. To this day I can't explain it.

This photograph is from a trio performance at Yoshi's in August, 1996. On this number Roberts was paying homage to his church roots. He and Jason Marsalis, his drummer, were engaged in an old-fashioned call-and-response. For a second or two, Roberts looked mesmerized. He leaned back on the piano stool, and I could see the reflection of the piano keys in his glasses. I was lucky to capture it.

ROBERTS

In 1996 Roberts released two recordings, the Grammy-nominated *Portraits in Blue* (SONY Classical), recorded with a full orchestra, and *Time and Circumstance* (Columbia), voted one of *TIME* magazine's ten best recordings of that year.

Today Roberts continues his busy touring schedule with his own groups. He records and performs in various formats: solo piano, trio, larger band ensembles, and piano with full orchestra. A very dedicated artist still in his mid-thirties, he has attained a level of achievement most artists aspire to reach in a lifetime.

**MARCUS
ROBERTS**

INTERVIEW, OCTOBER 31, 1997

*Describe for me some of your earliest experiences
with music.*

Most of those occurred in church. I used to try to play the
church piano a little bit after the service when I was even five
or six years old. I remember trying to do that. And just getting
five minutes here or there. And I used to go over to an aunt's
house every now and then and play a little bit on her piano.
I had an interest in the piano, and I kind of knew I wanted to
do it. My parents bought a piano when I was eight years old,
and I was self-taught from then until I began lessons at age
twelve or thirteen.

*Whom would you count as your greatest musical
inspirations and influences, and why?*

Well certainly I think gospel music has had a profound
impact on my piano style. That's just due to the fact that that's
where I started playing, in church. There are a lot of styles you
explore throughout your career. But for me, I would certainly
say that I have a very deep kinship to [Thelonious] Monk's
philosophy of piano playing. I have been very deeply affected,
both as a composer and as a pianist, by his work.

Duke Ellington. I've always loved Ellington. And
Jelly Roll Morton certainly because he consolidated all of the
New Orleans piano styles, so I've been very influenced by New
Orleans music, Jelly Roll Morton in particular. And James P.
Johnson is my inspiration for stride playing; he provides a real
basic concept of where that style is coming from. Ragtime
music and Scott Joplin—I've investigated that, too, and it
certainly has a role in my playing.

McCoy Tyner has strongly influenced my playing, especially when I'm playing trio or larger configurations. I also was influenced by the John Coltrane sound in general in my composition and playing. And Ahmad Jamal—my trio concept is very heavily based on his way of using the instrument, the way he breaks up the trio and the way he tends to expand forms and sections of forms. I've used that in a lot of my own arrangements. And probably Erroll Garner as well. He has been a big influence on me.

A lot of people have said that ever since the 1980s, we've seen a steady and strong resurgence in the popularity of jazz music. Do you agree with that, and have you given any thought as to why that might be?

I do agree with it, even though I feel that we have a lot of work to do—in terms of the presentation of the music and getting it to a wider audience. We still need to work on establishing what the standard level of achievement on the stage should be. Then it will be easier to measure and maintain the value of the music in our culture.

In terms of why the music is more popular, I think a lot of it has to do with some of the work that Wynton [Marsalis] started. It has been an active part of his mission, obviously. His career pretty much mirrors the period of resurgent interest that we're talking about. Since he's sort of taken the Miles Davis position in the music, it stands to reason that you would have to give most of the credit for building that to him.

I've studied the careers of a lot of your generation of jazz artists. With respect to your career and the career of a handful of others, a couple of things stand out: one, you seem to have a level of seriousness about the music that's greater than that of some of your contemporaries, and two, you seem to organize your career in such a way that you can get an incredible amount of work completed. You're playing classical and jazz, you're releasing a lot of recordings, you're composing, educating. How are you able to accomplish so much?

First of all, you make sure that all the things you're doing are based on the same belief system. By that I mean that I don't play any music that cannot be traced back to the roots of what the music is about. As an example, when I play "Rhapsody in Blue," I base it on concepts that I learned from listening to Monk and listening to New Orleans music. I'm addressing all of the traditional concepts that a jazz artist is dealing with. But with "Rhapsody in Blue," I obviously combine certain traces of European sensibility with that jazz heritage.

Whatever I'm playing, it's all organized under one belief system. I think that's the first thing that has to be clear in an artist's presentation: what you believe in. It should be easy to hear and consistent throughout the literature of your recordings. This underlying belief system permits you to expand much more rapidly in a number of directions because you have an anchor connecting everything.

I'm fortunate because the piano is a very versatile instrument that lends itself well to various types of presentations. And there's just a lot that's been done with the instrument you can use as inspirational material. I would argue that the pianist probably occupies the strongest position in Western music because most of the greatest composers, from Bach, to Mozart and Beethoven, either played piano or some keyboard instrument. Beethoven was a tremendous pianist who demonstrated the value of the piano in the thirty-two sonatas that he wrote for the instrument.

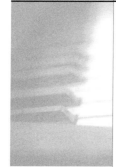

There's just a huge body of work for the piano. Chopin obviously could play. Liszt was a great pianist. In American music, we have the inspiration of the greatest ragtime composer, Scott Joplin—he played piano. We have the legacy of great pianists like James P. Johnson and Jelly Roll Morton. Duke Ellington's contribution to American music is unparalleled. And we can check out Fats Waller and Nat Cole.

In jazz you typically hear about the great band leader, and you hear about Louis Armstrong. He was clearly a foundation for the music and greatly responsible for 80 to 90 percent of the jazz vocabulary that we have, so I think that the trumpet has a very high position as well. But the piano has a high position both in Europe and in America. Its versatility and the great written and recorded legacy for the instrument give us a lot to draw from. That's what I try to build on every day.

What's your favorite part of your job: composing, recording, performing?

Definitely playing in front of an audience.

Do you have specific goals in mind you could share with us?

Goals only have meaning if you actually accomplish them, but I'd like to record all of Monk's music. I would like to continue to play widely in all of the different formats that I present—solo piano, trio, octet, piano, and the orchestra—and I would like to continue to explore all of those formats for the rest of my career.

Another goal that I have is to establish a written musical heritage for the piano in different formats that merges the philosophy of jazz with the European classical tradition—to put those two sensibilities together to generate a new sound in jazz. And, of course, a fundamental goal is to educate and expand the audience base for our music. And I'm always fighting for the piano and its role and position in American music every day.

What advice would you give someone who thinks he or she might want to pursue a career in jazz?

First you need to learn to use your ears to evaluate music. Listen to a lot of great jazz records. And then you need to work to learn how to play your instrument on a very, very high level.

MARCUS ROBERTS

SELECT DISCOGRAPHY

As a Leader

- *The Joy of Joplin—* SONY Classical
- *Blues for the New Millenium—*Columbia
- *Portraits in Blue—* SONY Classical
- *Time and Circumstance—* Columbia
- *Gershwin for Lovers—* Columbia
- *Marcus Roberts Plays Ellington—*Columbia
- *If I Could Be With You—* Novus
- *As Serenity Approaches—* Novus
- *Prayer for Peace—*Novus
- *Alone With Three Giants—* Novus
- *Deep in the Shed—*Novus
- *The Truth Is Spoken Here—* Novus

Collaborations With Other Artists

- *J Mood—*with Wynton Marsalis—Columbia
- *The Majesty of the Blues—* with Wynton Marsalis— Columbia
- *They Came to Swing—*with the Lincoln Center Jazz Orchestra—Columbia
- *The Fire of the Fundamentals—*with the Lincoln Center Jazz Orchestra—Columbia

Biography | # STEPH

B orn in Queens, New York, Stephen Scott (DOB 3/13/69) continues to live there today. He began playing the piano at age five, and by age twelve was taking private lessons at Juilliard. Scott was introduced to jazz music by a high-school classmate, jazz saxophonist Justin Robinson.

Scott's earliest major break was landing a long-term gig with legendary vocalist Betty Carter. He also has enjoyed extensive collaboration with saxophonist Sonny Rollins and bassist Ron Carter. Scott continues to play with Rollins and Carter today, and leads his own groups.

Scott has released six recordings as a leader. His music displays all his influences, including classical, jazz, salsa, and reggae. A true student of jazz music, Stephen Scott is one of the premier pianists of his generation.

SCOTT

INTERVIEW, FEBRUARY 13, 1998

Describe some of your earliest musical experiences.

One of the earliest memories I have is sitting on the staircase at the top of the stairs, and the piano was right at the bottom of the staircase. My sisters would sit there, and they'd be looking out the windows because they could hear their friends playing outside. The teacher would tell them to concentrate, and they would sit and play their Bach and Beethoven. That would go on for hours, however long they had their lesson. Then the teacher would leave, and I would go downstairs, and I would start to play by ear some of the lessons—a small part of the Bach and Beethoven that my sisters had started playing.

There was a lot of music in my house. My mother always wanted one of us to be a concert pianist because she loved the instrument. She loved European classical music.

How did you become introduced to jazz?

Once in high school I was looking for a practice room early in the beginning of the school year—all the rooms with grand pianos were taken at lunch period. The school had this one room that had sixteen to eighteen back-to-back upright pianos. So in this one room, there was this young saxophone player playing in the corner of the room. Nobody else was in there, and no one was playing the pianos. I said, hey, man, do you mind if I go over into this corner and play one of the pianos? He's like, cool, no problem. This young guy'sname is Justin Robinson. At that point, he had had a different upbringing. By the time he was twelve years old, he knew who Sonny Stitt was; he knew who Charlie Parker was. His father was an alto saxophone player. His mother loved jazz, too, so they brought him up through the music.

So by the time he got to high school, he already had memorized the Charlie Parker book and knew all the solos. So he was playing in the corner. He was bebopping. I was in the other corner playing. I'll never forget the tune, "Ribbon in the Sky" by Stevie Wonder. And the next thing I knew, we were jamming. And I decided, well, we'll loop this part and make that a solo section, and I started comping, and he started soloing over the changes, and I was like, yeah, man, what are you doing? How do I get that? He said, well, go out and buy some records. And I was like, okay. And that's how we started.

I started buying records every day. At some point I started experimenting with Miles Davis, Red Garland, Wynton Kelly, stuff like that. I was drawn to that. Later on that year, I got turned out by [Thelonious] Monk. That's the only way I can put it. I heard Monk's music for the first time, and I heard the strength of his music. I heard the character of his music and how it crossed lines. You couldn't put it here and say, well, it's bebop. Or you couldn't say it was like swing, or you couldn't say it was progressive bebop like Herbie [Hancock] and McCoy [Tyner], even though they're all my favorites as well. It just hit me, the sound that he got out of the piano, the colors that he chose to use.

One of your biggest breaks was accompanying Betty Carter. Tell me what you learned from her.

I learned from Betty how to be original, how to respect the history of the music, but how to find your own voice in it. She was very much into that. . . .

She would start playing a ballad, and come time for me to take a solo, I might start playing like Wynton Kelly or Herbie [Hancock]. She would turn around, microphone to her face, and say, no, kid, be honest, you know, right in front of the audience. I don't know if anybody else knew what that meant,

but what she was trying to tell me was I know you're young, but that doesn't matter. Surely there's something else for you to say other than what Wynton Kelly said in 1963. So that's something that always stuck in my mind to this day.

You've also played a lot with Ron Carter and Sonny Rollins. What have you learned from them?

The biggest thing I'm learning from Mr. Carter is about proper use of options. When you listen to Mr. Carter play on records, you realize that he doesn't repeat notes; he doesn't always play the same way. He doesn't always make the same harmonic choices. These are some of the things I've learned to develop by playing with him.

From Sonny Rollins I'm learning about the importance of melody, which is kind of a continuation of Ron Carter. Sonny Rollins is a master of melody. He's also a master of options, and he's a master of originality.

Do you think that in the past ten to fifteen years we've seen a resurgence in the popularity of jazz?

I don't know. The music has always been strong for me. But, then again, the people I work with have a strong following. Ron Carter's been around for thirty years. Every time I go to a gig with him, the house is packed. Sonny Rollins, forty years, so we always sell out, oversell. So it's hard for me to judge.

I think it's great that we still have an audience. I'm glad to see that the people love the music. I think we need to figure out how we can reach a younger audience without compromising the quality of the music. . . . We need a younger audience. It's a shame that I don't see a lot of young heads out there, not as many as I would like to see.

What are some of your goals?

Like [Ron] Carter would say, I'm still looking for some good notes to play. It's really true. That's really the objective. I want to perfect what it is I do. This is a good time for me right now, and I'm hungry to play some good notes. I'm really hungry to play some good music and to have some fun with what it is I do. I'm committed to what I do, and I love it.

STEPHEN SCOTT
SELECT DISCOGRAPHY

As a Leader

- *The Beautiful Thing*—Verve
- *Vikings of the Sunrise*—New Albion
- *Renaissance—Stephen Scott Trio*—Verve
- *Parker's Mood*—with Roy Hargrove and Christian McBride—Verve
- *Aminah's Dream*—Verve
- *Something to Consider*—Verve

Collaborations With Other Artists

- *The Bass and I*—with Ron Carter—Blue Note
- *Family*—with Roy Hargrove—Verve
- *Approaching Standards*—with Roy Hargrove—Novus
- *Remembrance: Live at the Village Vanguard*—with the Harper Brothers—Verve
- *Look What I Got!*—with Betty Carter—Verve
- *Lush Life*—with Joe Henderson—Verve

Biography

JACKY

J acky Terrasson (DOB 11/27/65) was born in Berlin, Germany, raised in Paris, France, and now lives in New York City. He began piano at age five and studied classical music exclusively until age twelve. Discovering his mother's record collection, which included Billie Holiday, Nat "King" Cole, and Duke Ellington, he became interested in jazz.

Terrasson's formal jazz studies began under pianist Jeff Gardner, an expatriate American living in Paris. Terrasson later attended Boston's widely acclaimed Berklee School of Music on scholarship. Extensive training came on the bandstand with such legends as drummer Arthur Taylor and vocalist Betty Carter.

Terrasson formed his own trio in 1993 with bassist Ugonna Okegwo and percussionist Leon Parker. That same year Terrasson won the Thelonious Monk International Jazz Piano Competition and was awarded a contract with the prestigious Blue Note label. In 1994 Terrasson was named by *The New York Times Magazine* as one of the thirty artists, thirty years old and under, most likely to change American culture for the next thirty years.

I first photographed Jacky Terrasson in 1996. I feel much more comfortable when I photograph musicians a second time, at a later set or performance, because I'm more familiar with their playing styles and habits then. This photograph was taken on October, 1997, right after the Monterey Jazz Festival. I knew Terrasson was coming to the new Yoshi's shortly with his new trio. He was with Ugonna Okegwo on bass and Leon Parker on drums. I was anxiously looking forward to hearing and seeing the trio (all of whom are featured in this book). I thought the music would be different from what I'd heard from Terrasson's group a year and a half ago, but I didn't know what to expect.

I wasn't disappointed: all three were ready to play. They seemed to be excited about a gig in such a new, well-equipped, intimate setting. Later, Terrasson told me that the setting and the audience were very important to the performance. He went on to say he really needed that audience just so he could go on composing and playing.

TERRASSON

INTERVIEW, JULY 29, 1997

You began piano at the age of five and studied classically exclusively until twelve. Tell me about your introduction to jazz.

The first introduction was really through records because I was living in Paris at that time. I was still young, so I wasn't really exposed to any kind of jazz scene. So my first introduction was through records that my mom had: Billie Holiday, Bessie Smith, a lot of singers, Miles Davis.

With your training as a classical musician, is that something you might go back to, or would you explore a career in classical music as well?

I don't think so. . . . I like to play classical for myself. I play classical music at home, but as far as pursuing a career, I don't think so. I think it's too late.

Do you think that if you play jazz, you sort of lose your classical chops, and if you play classical, you lose your jazz chops?

No. I don't think so. . . . Chops are chops. Chops are just techniques, technical stuff, and that's just something you need to maintain to have more freedom while improvising.

Who would you say are the persons who have influenced you the most musically?

Okay. I'm going to try to keep this one short. . . . I would say Bud Powell, Miles Davis, Herbie Hancock, Keith Jarrett, Billie Holiday, and John Coltrane.

What was it about them that made such an impression on you?

It seems like there were no compromises whatsoever. The number-one priority was music and experimenting, and those are two things that will make you progress. Also, they just played so well. And they have—Coltrane had that fire, that energy, and it's just beautiful to see that music could bring you to that, could make you enter another world. And I saw real footage of Bud Powell playing and it's just so intense.

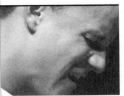

**JACKY
TERRASSON**

*Tell me why you chose jazz over any other genre of
music.*

That's a very good question. I think jazz is the most
honest, one of the most honest artistic forms of expression
because of the immediacy—that was very appealing. And also
it was for social reasons. As a teenager, I couldn't go to parties
because I didn't like the music. So I didn't really have a choice.
Jazz was what I liked, and I love the piano as an instrument.
In other forms of music, when I saw the piano, unless it was
classical or jazz, the piano was being burned or something. . . .
So I couldn't deal with that.

*In your release titled Reach, you recorded using the
"cello" sound system that Mark Levinson put together.
Tell me about that.*

Well, it's got a great advantage. It's that it allows the
musicians to really be comfortable. There are no separations.
There are no booths. There are no headphones. There's
nothing, so you just set up like you want. You don't have to
worry about not seeing someone or whatever. He used two
overhead microphones, and it was up to us to just take control
of the dynamics and all that. So what you hear is really—what
we do is what you get, and what you hear is exactly what went
down.

And no overdubbing or anything like that?

No, you can't even do it. It's not technically possible.

So you pretty much just count it off and go.

Yes. And it just felt natural. It was like we played in
someone's living room and a CD came out of it.

*I've loved music all my life, and I've met all kinds of
musicians. Jazz musicians stand out to me for a couple
reasons: they are very soulful people; they're very warm,
honest, and hip. Do you notice this as well?*

Yes, I kind of do. I think there's a community sense within
the jazz musicians. When everybody's out there on the road,
it's kind of fun to meet people in different parts of the world.
The music itself also demands studying, demands practicing—

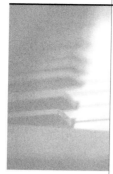

it requires that you really focus on it and do a little research. You're either in it or you're not, but I think if you like it, you just want to find more and more things about what went on and where it can go. And I do agree about the honesty. The fact is the music is very honest, so maybe that has to do with the people who play it. But, of course, many examples would contradict that.

What differences have you noticed between European jazz audiences and American jazz audiences?

In general, jazz music has always been fairly well received in Europe, and that is because it was recognized more as an art form earlier on. Forty years ago, being black and trying to make a living and playing music was nearly impossible. And a lot of musicians realized that when they went to Europe, they were treated well. People respected them, and they liked the music, and that's why actually a lot of American musicians went over there to live for quite some time.

Since the early 1980s, we've seen a strong resurgence in the United States in the popularity of jazz. Have you given any thought as to why that might be?

Yes. I think it's been mediatized more in the last ten, fifteen years. I think that's great. And I think record companies have been trying to put it out again—everybody says that it was kind of out of the markets and all that. . . . And I would probably credit Wynton [Marsalis] for that.

What do you see in terms of your future?

I just want to keep doing what I'm doing—I want to be better at it. I want to keep playing in the trio format, but I don't only want to do that. I've been focusing on that a lot of the last three years, and it's been great, but I think I'm ready to be more versatile in general as far as styles of music and as far as different groups and different situations. I also want to play some electric stuff.

I don't want to be the leader all the time. I just want to be versatile. I think it's good to be versatile. It keeps you on your toes.

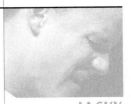

Is your father still playing classical piano?
No. They don't have a piano anymore.

Was he a professional musician?
No, just a weekend Mozart and Beethoven sonata player.

Was he somewhat disappointed when you went to jazz?
Yes. At the beginning, he was reluctant because he knows that it's not easy out there, in general. I mean it's hard, too, in the classical field. You know, people are trying to knife each other and all that, but now he's very happy for me.

How much of making it in the music business is raw talent versus hard work and dedication?
I think most people out there who are successful worked hard. Yes, I hope so. No, I'm pretty sure they did.

I mean some musicians are more gifted than others, and some have a natural thing for having something that's their own and not sounding like a copycat, but I think all the masters have worked, have practiced.

JACKY TERRASSON
SELECT DISCOGRAPHY

As a Leader
- *Alive*—Blue Note
- *Reach*—Blue Note
- *Jacky Terrasson*—Blue Note
- *Lover Man*—The Jacky Terrasson Jazz Trio—Venus
- *What's New*—Jacky Terrasson—J.A.R.
- *Rendezvous*—with Cassandra Wilson—Blue Note
- *Moon and Sand*—with Tom Harrell—J.A.R.

Collaborations With Other Artists
- *Heaven*—with Jimmy Scott—Warner Bros.
- *Blue Patches*—with Michael "Patches" Stewart—Hipbop
- *For One Who Knows*—with Javon Jackson—Blue Note
- *Quiet After the Storm*—with Dianne Reeves—Blue Note
- *Tenor Titans*—with Ravi Coltrane and Antoine Roney—Venus
- *Seth Air*—with Wallace Roney—Muse

CHAPTER 6

JAZZ PROFILES

Christian McBride

Ugonna Okegwo

Avery Sharpe

Reginald Veal

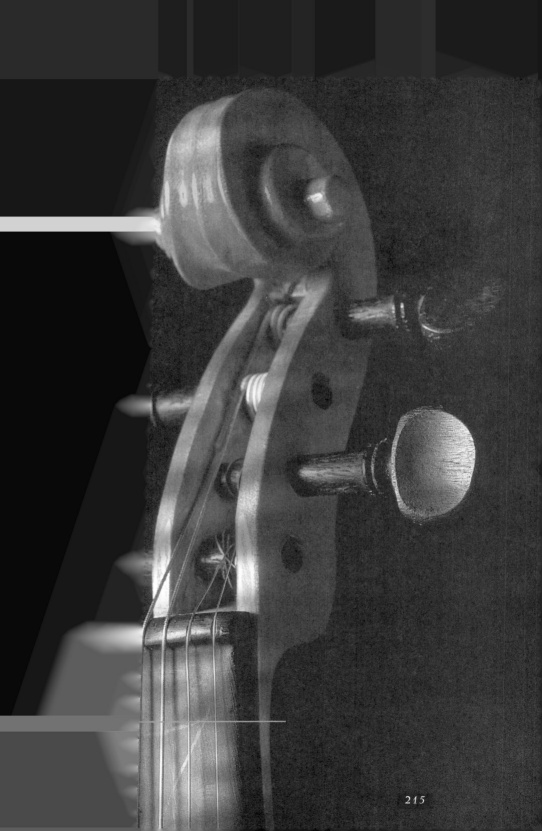

Biography

CHRISTIAN

S till in his twenties, Christian McBride (DOB 5/31/72) is one of the premier bassists working today. Born and raised in Philadelphia, he now lives in New York City. He has released five recordings as a leader and has made more than a hundred others.

McBride's inspiration came from his father, Lee Smith, who played with the likes of the Delfonics, Billy Paul, Blue Magic, and Major Harris, and his great uncle, Howard Cooper. McBride also counts James Brown as one of his greatest musical influences and heroes. He studied classical bass at Philadelphia's High School for the Performing Arts and with Neil Courtney of the Philadelphia Orchestra. He attended the Juilliard School of Music in Manhattan on scholarship.

Soon after he went to Juilliard, McBride began steady work in New York with such notable artists as Bobby Watson, Betty Carter, Wynton Marsalis, Freddie Hubbard, Benny Green, and Joshua Redman. McBride continues to play with all the top jazz artists working today.

Christian McBride is a true wunderkind. It was a pleasure to photograph him as a jazz musician from the time he was a teenage up to the present. He has always been photogenic, and his joyful spirit comes through in both music and photographs. But McBride also reveals a range of moods. In an early photograph I took of him in what an artist friend of mine calls my "Old Master style" (it is what I call black-and-white in color because it is only in red and black), McBride's serious side comes through.

This photograph was taken at Kuumbwa in June 1996, at the beginning of the second set. McBride was playing with his quartet: Tim Warfield on tenor sax, Joey Calderazzo on piano, and Greg Hutchinson on drums. The musicians were teasing him about being late, and he responded with a funky uptempo tune. Earlier that day, McBride had missed his flight out of New York and hadn't made it to the first set in Santa Cruz. Surprisingly, he was in great shape for the second set; he even had enough energy to sing and dance in addition to playing! I'd never before photographed McBride on the electric bass. It was a spirited evening, which inspired me in my photographs of every musician in his group that night.

MCBRIDE

INTERVIEW, JANUARY 17, 1997

With your father and your great-uncle both being bassists, it certainly seems natural that you would be attracted to that instrument. But did you ever seriously consider any other instrument?

From the minute—this is something I always tell people—from the minute that I first touched the bass, I didn't know where it would take me, but I knew that's what I wanted to do.

And how old were you when you first started playing?
I was eight years old.

Tell me a little bit about your early practice habits. Were you a guy who practiced just incessantly?

Yes. When I first started playing, I would just turn on the radio or get a record that I liked, and just listen to it, and wear the record out until I learned the bass line that was on the record. This was my electric bass now because I didn't even start playing acoustic bass until junior high school. So I would just take my electric bass, and just pick off the bass line, and just try to work it out because I couldn't read music. I was just trying to work it out by ear. This went on every day for about two years.

But the reason why I say I knew that I wanted to do this forever was because I remember the first song I ever learned how to play was "Papa Was a Rolling Stone." And it felt so natural to me. I'll never forget thinking, wow, you know. I didn't say to myself this is easy, but I said this isn't as hard as I thought it was going to be. From then on, I started learning almost every song I possibly could. I just remember the natural feeling I had. So that's when I knew I was going to play bass forever.

**CHRISTIAN
MCBRIDE**

In another interview that I read, you were asked to name some of your favorite recording sessions. . . . You said [pianist] Benny Green's recording sessions were all fun. What makes Benny Green's recording sessions sort of stick out in your mind as being fun?

Benny Green's group was the first group that I ever played in that was a band. Up until that point, I had played in Bobby Watson's band, which was already together by the time I moved to New York. I was just a replacement for the bass player that left. So I was never really "a part of the band." I was a part of it, but I was kind of a replacement.

And then after Bobby, I started working with Freddie Hubbard, and as much of an honor as it was to play in Freddie Hubbard's band, it was probably one of my greatest honors. I don't think that was a band because what you used to do in preparation for Freddie's gigs was you would just go home, and listen to his records, and kind of study the chord changes. And then you would get on the gig, and he would just kind of call the song. More just like five cats getting together and playing songs written by Freddie Hubbard. . . .

But Benny Green's group was the first group I played in where we rehearsed all the time. I used to feel special because I was a charter member. The other thing was because it was a trio, the bass stuck out a lot. I had a lot of room to stretch out and do my own thing, as well as play Benny's music.

What is it about James Brown that makes him your musical hero?

A number of things I assume. First of all, I've always thought James Brown was probably one of the greatest performing artists. You can take the music and put it somewhere by itself. But just to watch the man perform is something else entirely. That's one thing. But the first time I really got hooked on James Brown was—let's see if I can remember—yeah, my mother has a collection of 45s. She has like all these old singles. She had a huge closet; there must have been at least 500 to 600 in there. She had James Brown in there. There wasn't more of James Brown than there was anyone else. But for some reason, I was always listening to those James Brown 45s because there was just a certain intensity, a certain energy that came off of those records that— the same kind of energy didn't come from all the other ones. The first time I saw James Brown in person, it was really over.

In the past ten to fifteen years, we've seen a strong resurgence in the popularity of jazz music. And a lot of people give a lot of this credit to Wynton Marsalis. Do you think this one individual can have that kind of impact, or do you think maybe that even if we didn't have Wynton, would we still have had this resurgence?

I think I can be somewhat accurate when I say that Wynton—I honestly don't think there might have been such a resurgence because, speaking for me personally, as I said earlier, I always knew I wanted to play bass, and I always knew I wanted to be a musician.

Once I got to high school and started hooking up with guys like Joey DeFrancesco and a lot of the other band members that were in my school, then I started to love jazz. But I still wasn't really sure if that's what I wanted to play, that was the style I wanted to play. I didn't know if I wanted to play

R & B; I didn't know whether I wanted to play jazz or classical. But after meeting and admiring someone like Wynton for all his diversity, you know, playing classical and playing jazz. He was like a god to everyone, every young musician in high school at that time.

The first time I met Wynton and being around him and seeing his level of seriousness in everything that he does, especially when it comes to music, that did something to me. I remember listening to all of his albums when I was in high school. I just listened to everything he did, and I had all of his records, and I knew all of the songs off of his records. And then he invited me to sit in with his band. Wynton's group came to Philadelphia—I was in tenth grade.

That was a surprise to you, wasn't it, when he asked you up on stage?

Yeah, it was a big surprise. See, I would have to say Wynton gave a lot of the young musicians in my generation— he pointed us in the right direction. He had a big part to do with our development. I know I can speak for guys like Nicholas Payton and Roy Hargrove and James Carter. Wynton was there for us a long time ago.

Do you ever get to interact with other great bass players out there, Reginald Veal, Ben Wolfe, Rizzy Hurst, . . . or is your schedule such that you don't really get to interact with other bass players?

Well, it's a little like that now because all of us are working all the time. Ben is going on the road with Wynton here and there, and Robert's [Rizzy] out on the west coast doing "The Tonight Show." All those guys you just named are great friends, and I admire them, and I admire their work; I admire their talent. When we do get together, it's always a lot of fun. I think it's a learning experience for everyone, and it's a lot of fun.

As I was telling someone a few nights ago, I ran into Ben Wolfe last week in Chicago at the Jazz Educators' Convention, and I remember maybe four years ago Ben Wolfe, Christopher Thomas who plays bass with Joshua Redman, who was playing bass with Betty Carter at the time, that was one of our first times getting to see each other, especially all three of us together in one city. We decided we were going to a have a bassman's bonding night. So I remember we hung out, they came to my house, we listened to records, then we went to a club and stayed in there until about 5 o'clock in the morning. Then they came back to my house and listened to some more records, then had breakfast. I haven't had a night like that since.

With all your success, Christian, you must keep an extremely hectic schedule. Because of that, do you feel overworked and overwhelmed sometimes by it all, or are you able to make time for yourself personally and have some time to relax?

I used to feel like that, and I used to feel like that on a regular basis at one time. But then I decided I had to do something about that. What's wrong with this picture? So I sat down and figured out because see, I've always been a person that moved in the moment. I go with the flow. But I realize now that my schedule is such that I can't really do that anymore. I mean I can always live for and in the moment, but certain times I have to leave chunks of my time specifically for myself because I don't get it that often now.

I just moved into a new apartment about three months ago. This certainly has brought me lots more peace and head space. This is like my little retreat. . . . I'm feeling a lot more rested and under control now. I still have my grueling schedule, but I think I'm handling it better now.

Do you have any specific advice you can give to an aspiring musician?

I'll tell you, the only thing I can tell someone who's young, looking to play music, be serious about it; don't take it lightly. It's okay when you're young—it's just about having fun. You've got to have fun. If you're not having fun, you might as well not play music at all. That's what it's all about. But at the same time, don't have so much fun until you don't do your homework, you don't know what a major or minor scale is. Because that could be that fine line between no work and a lifetime's worth of work.

CHRISTIAN MCBRIDE
SELECT DISCOGRAPHY

As a Leader

- *A Family Affair*—Verve
- *Number Two Express*—Verve
- *Gettin' to It*—Verve
- *Parker's Mood*—with Roy Hargrove and Stephen Scott—Verve
- *Fingerpainting*—with Nicholas Payton and Mark Whitfield—Verve

Collaborations With Other Artists

- *Love Scenes*—with Diana Krall—GRP/Impulse!
- *Young Lions and Old Tigers*—with Dave Brubeck—Telarc
- *Big Band*—with Joe Henderson—Verve
- *Lush Life*—with Joe Henderson—Verve
- *Tenor Legacy*—with Joe Lovano—Blue Note
- *Quartets: Live at the Village Vanguard*—Blue Note
- *Moodswing*—with Joshua Redman—Warner Bros.
- *Joshua Redman*—with Joshua Redman—Warner Bros.

Biography

UGON

Born in London and raised in Germany, Ugonna Okegwo (DOB 3/15/62) lives in New York City. He grew up listening to an eclectic mix of African American musicians: James Brown, Jimi Hendrix, Miles Davis, Ornette Coleman, and Charles Mingus.

Okegwo played jazz throughout Europe until moving to New York in 1989. He received a B.F.A. degree from Long Island University in 1994. Soon after arriving in New York, he began working with legendary vocalist Jon Hendricks. In New York he also met and began collaborating with Jacky Terrasson and Leon Parker, an association that continues to this day.

Okegwo has performed with such jazz legends as Benny Carter, Dewey Redman, Oliver Lake, James Moody, and Clark Terry. Okegwo has also worked with many of his contemporaries, including Tom Harrell, Joshua Redman, and David Sanchez. He has appeared in jazz festivals all over the United States and the world, including JVC/New York, Montreal, Nice, North Sea, San Francisco, Vienna, and Mt. Fuji.

OKEGWO

INTERVIEW, AUGUST 7, 1997

You are a rarity in jazz in that you didn't start playing until you were in your teens, right?

No. I started playing electric bass when I was twenty. When I was twenty-one, I started playing acoustic bass.

And that was the first time you'd played an instrument?

I had fooled around on guitar before for a couple of years, but not seriously because I wasn't really into the instrument. It was an affordable instrument to buy for me. But guitar wasn't really what I wanted to play. Sometimes I tried to play some bass lines on it, but it was not serious. Once I got an electric bass, that's when it became serious for me. I started practicing and tried to develop my skills on the instrument.

Who has been most influential in your life?

I must say my mother because she was very supportive of whatever I wanted to do. After high school, I wasn't really sure whether or not I wanted to go to college right away. She wasn't pressing me to hurry up and find something, she gave me the feeling that she understood I needed to find something I really liked. . . . Once I found what I wanted to do, she was happy for me, and I felt she was always behind me.

And some of my teachers helped me out a lot. Jay Oliver and Walter Norris. Jay Oliver taught me that it's not just about playing the bass technically, but about being a musician and living the music. He taught me a lot about that. He taught me that music is an important part of your life and that when you play, you should bring everything you have to that experience. Walter Norris helped me understand the music, also more on a technical level. He showed me a lot about harmony, different approaches to playing tunes and constructing bass lines. He also taught me to experiment with different ways of practicing, different ways of approaching rhythm, melody, and harmony. All three of these artists are very involved musicians (unfortunately Jay Oliver has passed away), so being around those personalities was an education in itself.

UGONNA
OKEGWO

Later Cecil McBee further clarified the importance of letting yourself be absorbed in the intense experience of playing music.

Of your contemporaries today, who are some of the artists you most enjoy playing with?

I like playing with Jacky Terrasson a lot. He is a very creative pianist without fear of changing things. His concept of the trio is very open. It gives a possibility to all three members to explore the music and find a personal outlet—to try to express themselves very personally. The concept of the way we play is not really like a normal piano trio, not like an arrangement with a piano solo, then a bass solo and then drum solo. We have arrangements, but sometimes we all improvise on certain ideas without really having an arrangement, or we might change the arrangement. We also change forms and structures of compositions, which keeps the music very open. Jacky is also a very tasteful interpreter of ballads.

I also like playing with Leon Parker a lot because he's a strong and interactive drummer; the way he plays gives me a certain freedom. He has a very strong rhythmic feel, a strong cymbal beat, good ideas, a good ear, and he leaves a lot of space.

Also Tom Harrell. He's one of the greatest musicians, composers, and arrangers I've ever played with. Playing with him is a very deep experience for me. He's so humble and brings out this great music; it has made a big impression on me. To hear him play his music, to hear him improvise, and to come up with all these different ideas is a great musical experience. Ideas are just flowing out of him. He is amazing to me.

There are a lot of other musicians I like playing with. These three play a big part in my musical experiences at this time, and I am very thankful for that.

Tell me about your experiences with Jon Hendricks.

For him, it's very important to pay attention to the tradition of the music. The way he sings is very much rooted in bebop. He's a very strong improviser, and when he sings, his interpretation of a certain song is very personal and very strong. To listen to and play with a person who has lived through that period and played with some of the people who brought this music to life, who changed the music, was a very important part of my musical life.

What are some of your plans?

To try to play good music, as much as I can, try to be in musical situations that I like and that I can learn from. Keep on developing my own concept because I want to do some writing. Right now I don't feel strong enough yet to put something together.

What have you noticed about the differences about how jazz is received in Europe versus the United States?

When I first came [to the United States], I was shocked about how disrespectful the music is treated in this country. I couldn't believe the difference in the appreciation of the music. Now I've also found that the music is just experienced differently in the United States. It's not easy to generalize, but overall I've noticed that it is more a form of entertainment, and I want to say that without negative connotation. There might be dancing; there might be interaction with the musicians while they're playing, which sometimes gives the musician and the music a certain energy because it's like a direct feedback. In Europe the music is viewed more as an art form which can make the appreciation of it more respectful but also more reserved. But this is an oversimplification because I've seen all kinds of different reactions to music in different parts of the world.

What advice would you have to pass along to someone wanting to be a professional musician?

Try to be honest, and don't be afraid to find out how you are going to be able to express yourself personally. Learn from the tradition and check out everything you can; and try to see what people did before. But it's very important to find a personal approach to music, to find your own voice, which is hard to do, and it sometimes is not supported. A lot of times it's not supported by the record business because a lot of companies are more interested in fast payoff than building a listening audience over time. They might think that someone is more marketable if he or she sounds like "so and so" or a certain image can be sold. This way record deals are given to musicians who have not found their own voice yet. This is a big responsibility, and it is not easy to deal with the different pressures. A lot of times musicians aren't able to maintain control over artistic decisions. And that's dangerous because if you really want to explore within yourself what you have to offer, these outside pressures can hinder you from doing so. You cannot really find out about yourself if you don't try.

I think the most important thing is to have the time and space to try to find out what you can bring to the music. Music is really about personal development, expression, and life.

UGONNA OKEGWO
SELECT DISCOGRAPHY

Collaborations With Other Artists

- *Alive*—with Jacky Terrasson—Blue Note
- *Belief*—with Leon Parker—Columbia
- *Reach*—with Jacky Terrasson—Blue Note
- *The Jaunt*—with Steve Davis—Criss Cross Jazz
- *6 x 6*—with Royce Campbell and Larry Coryell—King Records
- *Above and Below*—with Leon Parker—Epicure
- *Jacky Terrasson*—with Jacky Terrasson—Blue Note
- *Boppin' at the Blue Note*—with Jon Hendricks and the All Stars—Telarc
- *Lover Man*—with The Jacky Terrasson Trio—Venus
- *Late Night*—with Tex Allen—Muse
- *Live in Berlin: At the Quasimodo, Volumes 1 & 2*—with Charles Tolliver—Strata East
- *The Art of Rhythm*—with Tom Harrell—RCA Victor
- *Awakening*—with Leon Parker—Columbia

Biography

AVERY

Photo Notes

A native of Georgia who now lives in Amherst, Massachusetts, Avery Sharpe (DOB 8/23/54) is not only an innovative bassist, but also an acclaimed composer, educator, and producer as well. He began on the piano at age eight, followed with the accordion, and then started bass at sixteen. His early musical influences and experiences were playing the gospel music of his church. In high school and college, he began performing many genres of music, including rhythm and blues, funk, jazz, big band, and gospel music for symphonic orchestra.

Avery Sharpe is one of my favorite bass players. I've photographed Sharpe at least a dozen times between 1991 and now, in many different musical configurations, but always with McCoy Tyner. These groups included the standard trio with Tyner on piano, Aaron Scott on drums, and Sharpe on bass; the same trio with Bobby Hutcherson on vibes or Michael Brecker on tenor sax; and various bop-oriented, all-star and Latin all-star groups. I've photographed Sharpe at Sweet Basil, at Kuumbwa and at Yoshi's.

This photograph, taken at Yoshi's on January 12, 1996, while Sharpe was playing with McCoy Tyner on piano, Michael Brecker on tenor sax, and Aaron Scott on drums. This shot shows one of Sharpe's typical performances. He is very photogenic, probably because of his intensity while playing. After the set was over, Sharpe told me that another voice in the trio, this time the tenor sax, inspires him in another direction. For this picture, I waited until he was soloing after a tenor solo. And after reviewing a series of photographs, Sharpe said, "You sure know how to capture my feelings." It is easy when you're photographing someone as expressive as Avery Sharpe.

SHARPE

A longtime veteran of legendary pianist McCoy Tyner's bands, Sharpe has performed and recorded with many of jazz's top artists, including Art Blakey, Dizzy Gillespie, Wynton Marsalis, Bobby McFerrin, Freddie Hubbard, Archie Shepp, and Yusef Lateef. He is also the leader of the Avery Sharpe Group, which has released four recordings.

In addition to Sharpe's performing and recording, music education and composition play a large role in his career. He has developed and regularly conducts seminars and workshops for all ages on a range of topics, such as the history of jazz and jazz improvisation. He also composes and arranges for numerous jazz ensembles and has scored films. Avery Sharpe is an artist who is committed to giving his talent and time back to his craft. Many have benefited from his generosity, and many more will in the future.

AVERY SHARPE

INTERVIEW, APRIL 3, 1997

We've seen a strong resurgence in the popularity of jazz music since the early 1980s, and you've been very much a part of that. What has caused this resurgence?

I think it's a number of reasons. It's funny when they say resurgence. I'm not quite sure if there was an actual resurgence, or if it's the media or the record companies just trying to make people more aware of it. I think, also, society as a whole, you can only feed people so much candy. That's the way I look at popular music, as kinds of candies and sweeteners. It's not really anything that has any substance per se. It can, but it just doesn't as a general rule. After a while you can only have so much candy, and then you have to have some nutrition there.

I think Wynton Marsalis, of course, is credited a lot with that because he fought hard with the record companies to push his plan ahead, which is to give jazz a more viable voice in America. And that was his plan all along. . . . And I think it's a good thing because there's an audience for it which should be cultivated. And I think sometimes the industry just forgets about that and doesn't realize that baby boomers are getting older and don't want to be force-fed candy all the time. I think it's great. I think that was one of the causes.

You said in one interview that part of the tradition of jazz is innovation, but before one can become innovative one must learn the history of jazz. Do you think the young people coming up today are learning their jazz history?

I think, yes, to a certain extent, but if they learn history, they may learn only about one or two people. For example, if you're a trumpet player, not only should you know about Lee Morgan or Louis Armstrong, but you should know that whole line of trumpet players, or whatever instrument it is that you play.

But not only just about that instrument, but just about the music in general. You should know as much as you can about

the history of music. Who was it, Churchill, who said that the further back you go in history, that's how much further ahead you can go in the future. It's the same with the music. The more you learn about it, the history and roots of this music and where it came from, the stronger and better player that it will make you. And also it will give you some sensitivity.

You have a very multifaceted career. Not only do you perform and record, but you also compose, including film scores. You also produce and present jazz educational workshops. Tell me about that.

The future of the music is our children. The future audience, the future people who carry this on, are our children. And I think one of the things that we need to do as musicians is to pass the word on, to get a truer sense of what is actually happening in terms of the history and in terms of the music. It's better to hear it straight from the horse's mouth rather than reading it from a third or fourth party.

Some of the programs I do involve children, not only teaching them some musical concepts about jazz and about improvisation, but also the historical component as well. And demonstrating how African elements are all interwoven in between the music, even the so-called hip-hop music. And even people who don't understand why the music makes them feel the way it does or why it moves them a certain way, I point out to them the historical aspect of the African movement that's still in the music.

Whom would you list as your greatest musical influences?

My mother's my first influence, and she was the first one to teach me piano when I started at eight years old. Being in the church, whether it was singing in the choir, and I didn't like singing so I thought of something that wasn't happening [in church], which was bass. In terms of my initial and biggest musical influence, that would be her.

In terms of jazz, it would probably have to be Reggie Workman because he was the first cat I saw, in terms of acoustic bass, of the caliber that I was trying to get to and that I work at now. And I was knocked out about that. And of course, you know, listening to [Charles] Mingus and Ron Carter, Jimmy Garrison.

And I would say in terms of the whole connection with [John] Coltrane, that was just a whole other thing, you know. And hearing McCoy [Tyner] and Garrison. It was really kind of a turnaround for me there as well.

In terms of today, one of my biggest heroes musically is Milt Hinton, who's the granddad of all in terms of the acoustic bass. Once you read through history, you realize that Milt Hinton basically influenced just about every bass player in the twentieth century.

Name some of the artists you've most enjoyed playing with.

In the last few years I've been fortunate enough to be working with and doing a lot of recording with Yusef Lateef—now probably about nine records with Yusef. He's probably one of the most knowledgeable and extraordinary musicians I know. I call him a walking encyclopedia. But not only that, he's an extremely great human being, an extremely sensitive human being, and it's always a pleasure to work with him because Yusef is a free spirit.

And people forget the amount of influence he's had. He's the first person in jazz to start playing oboe and that kind of thing in a jazz setting. And also different types of flutes and other different types of instruments in different settings.

But the thing I really love about Yusef is that each time I do a recording with him, there's this freedom of searching, searching for sounds, searching for composition, which is always inspiring. And every so often I just have to call him and let him know that it really is a pleasure and also very

enlightening and motivating to see someone his age just always searching for sound and always trying to come up with something new.

Being a jazz musician requires you to be on the road a lot and also makes for a complex schedule. Has this presented a lot of problems in terms of trying to balance family with your career?

I wouldn't say problems as much as a challenge, yes. It's definitely a challenge. Being married and having a family is a challenge for straight-life people, as they say, a "nine-to-five Joe." In some ways it's probably more difficult. People always think of it as more difficult to do it the way I do it, and maybe it is. But it all depends on how you approach it and how you approach life, number one.

Music is very important to me and is one of the most important things in my life. It's not the most important thing. Of course, I think it was Vince Lombardi who said "God, country, and the Green Bay Packers." Well, with me, it's God, family, and then music, and in that order. I think once people are aware of that and you make people aware of that, then I think it makes everything else a little easier to tolerate.

As artists, what we do is a very selfish thing because you have to spend a lot of time by yourself perfecting your craft, and then you spend a lot of time giving of yourself and of your craft to people who you don't even know and maybe never will meet again in life. So you do give a lot, but you also take a lot in order that you can give. And the folks around you really have to have an understanding of what it is that you do and that this is not just a game that you're playing.

So there are ways that you can balance. You know, my phone bill is outrageous, but my wife and kids have been in places that they might not have been if they hadn't been with me. And there's a certain part of life that [my children] learn from me as well because what I teach [them] is that Dad is going to do what he wants to do, in terms of my life, in terms of creativity. And I encourage them to do the same, just so it's something that you love or that you want to do, that you pursue it to the utmost. Because that's what I'm going to do. And whatever it is that you do, you should take it on with that same fervor and that interest.

What advice do you have for someone thinking about becoming a jazz musician?

Be a doctor. [Laughs] Actually it's funny you should ask because I'm having that situation with my son now who's in the eleventh grade and who's a really brilliant person. And my oldest daughter is actually a pre-med major, and I'm hoping she stays on that course. But my son is actually a very talented bass player. And now he's thinking about college, and he's thinking about possibly music schools, but he also loves sciences, too. And it's hard for me—I can't discourage him because, of course, this is what I do. And I also understand that once you get bit by the bug, it's a passion. You can't rest until you do it.

So a young person coming up, if you get bit by the bug, the music bug, to know that you've been bitten by the bug means that you would do this regardless. You know, if your friends tell you you're crazy or if you're worried about making a lot of money, but you want to pursue this as a form of expression more so than a form of career, I would just say pursue it to no end. In other words, see it being a reality and just make it a reality.

AVERY SHARPE

SELECT DISCOGRAPHY

As a Leader
- *Unspoken Words*—Sunnyside Records
- *Extended Family*—JKNM Records
- *Extended Family II (Thoughts of My Ancestors)*—JKNM Records
- *Epic Ebony Journey*—Avery Sharpe/John Blake Duet—JKNM Records

Collaborations With Other Artists
- *Infinity*—with McCoy Tyner—GRP/Impulse!
- *Journey*—with McCoy Tyner—Verve
- *Turning Point*—with McCoy Tyner—Verve
- *Remembering John*—McCoy Tyner-Enja Records
- *Yusef Lateef Plays Ballads*—with Yusef Lateef—YAL Records
- *Tenors Featuring Rene McLean*—with Yusef Lateef—YAL Records
- *Full Circle*—with Yusef Lateef—YAL Records

Biography | # REGINA

R eginald Veal (DOB 11/05/63) was born and raised in the heart of jazz, New Orleans, Louisiana. Known affectionately by his peers as "Swing Doom," he has made his name primarily on the acoustic and electric basses, but he also plays piano, trombone, and drums.

Veal began private piano lessons and also started playing electric bass around age eight. While a high-school senior, he studied at the New Orleans Center for the Creative Arts, concentrating on electric bass. He began playing professionally with Ellis Marsalis at this time.

VEAL

Veal attended Southern University in Baton Rouge, where he began to play acoustic bass. In July, 1986, he moved to New York City and quickly became a steady sideman for Terence Blanchard and Donald Harrison. A year later Veal landed a steady gig with Wynton Marsalis and has recorded and performed with him since.

Veal has played with jazz legends Elvin Jones, Lionel Hampton, Art Blakey, McCoy Tyner, Clark Terry, and Jimmy Heath, and contemporaries Marcus Roberts, Harry Connick, Jr., and Branford Marsalis. He also has recorded and toured extensively with the Lincoln Center Jazz Orchestra.

REGINALD VEAL

INTERVIEW, MARCH 11, 1997

Describe for me some of your earliest musical experiences you can recall.

My earliest experience with music would be being at home in New Orleans and having a piano there, at least something that I could participate in. We've always had a piano in my home, and that was the first instrument I really started playing. My experiences also included church music, records played in the house, my dad's guitar playing and his gospel quartet, and my brother and sister practicing their instruments. There was music at every holiday and function at my house and our friends and relatives' houses. There would be listening to music, singing, and gathering around the piano.

Growing up in New Orleans, I experienced street bands in street parades. Parade music in New Orleans and the public-school-system band is very important. That's like a big thing. So you go out to a parade, you hear marching bands, concert bands, and that kind of thing. I experienced all kinds of music, including pop, funk, and blues.

What is it about the bass that made it your instrument of choice?

I've always been attracted to the bass because I can tell you what started it is my dad played guitar. So at home he would always play guitar. I knew there was something missing. So he's playing the upper part, the treble guitar part, and I'm thinking about the bass lines in my head and sometimes singing it with him as he's playing.

And most music that I heard, instead of always humming the melody part, I'd always hum the bass part. I wouldn't walk around singing whatever tune. I would sing the bass part. So that's always been my instrument, the bottom end.

Who would be your greatest musical influences?

Well, I would say all of my family members, first of all my dad. But after all my family members, I would say Ellis Marsalis definitely because I stood on the bandstand professionally with him for quite some time playing the electric bass, seriously learning and developing and making the transition to acoustic bass. Also I went to the New Orleans Center for the Creative Arts, and I studied with him there. And either in the classroom or on the bandstand, that's like *the* education. So he was a great, great influence.

And then there are lots of musicians. But I guess if we're talking about bass players, I can go down the line from the very beginning: Pops Foster, Wellman Braud, Milt Hinton, Charles Mingus, Jimmy Garrison, Ray Brown, Ron Carter, Paul Chambers, Sam Jones, Slam Stewart, Major Holly.

Of the individuals you're naming, have you played or taken lessons with the majority of them, or was it just hearing their music?

Hearing their music. Some of the people I've named, they are no longer with us. . . . But some of them I named, like Milt Hinton, I did take a lesson from him. Milt Hinton is like this. When I was living in New York, I was trying to reach him to get with him and get a lesson or some information. So I kept trying. He was always out of town. So one day I called, and his wife answered the phone and said, "Milt will be home on Thursday. Call then." I called that Thursday, and Milt told me to come over. We got together, and we just played, and I asked him some questions and got a world of information on the bass, music, life, and on and on.

Milt taught me how to determine if you are getting the optimum sound performance from your bass. He struck a match, he put it up to the F hole of his bass, and said if the bass's sound post was set right or simply if you had a huge sound, you could blow out the match. Of course, Milt blew it out every time.

Just the fact that he took time out for me meant so much. I'll never forget Milt Hinton. Later, we sat down and ate some pork chops and greens that Milt himself cooked before my eyes. We talked some more. I have never had another official lesson since, but I see him from time to time, and, of course, seeing him and talking to him is a lesson in itself. The great Milt "Judge" Hinton.

I also went to Larry Ridley's house. Great man. Real cool, intelligent. He taught me about sound and really listening to your notes and playing with the most intensity with the least amount of effort.

Keeter Betts had me play in the dark—to get to know my instrument, even in the dark. It was deep. So I started practicing in the dark sometimes.

John Clayton gave me so much stuff to work on, it was incredible. He is a complete musician, very thorough, organized and willing to help others.

I went to Slam Stewart's house in upstate New York. He didn't play but discussed music and the bass. Great experience. I think Slam may have been sick then.

So most of the other people I'm talking about, I've seen them play in person but I wasn't able to get a lesson with them. And most of them I have tried. Like I've tried several times for Ray Brown. I've tried several times with Ron Carter, but it hasn't happened yet.

When did you decide you wanted to be a professional musician?

You know, it's ironic because I had decided that very early on, pretty much at the age of eight. I can remember—seven, eight, nine. I just didn't know what kind of professional musician that I wanted to be. . . . You have to understand, it's kind of difficult to go in a direction. I think a lot of times, the music chooses you. You know what I'm saying? Because although I had not been really playing jazz music, I had been playing and listening to all other types of music. And at one point, I had like a pop band, and I did all of that, and I thought maybe we'd become popular. But once I started playing jazz music seriously and listening to it, that was the end of it. I knew.

I'll never forget the first time when I auditioned for NOCCA, New Orleans Center for Creative Arts. And I brought my electric bass in, and Ellis [Marsalis] sat down to the piano. And what he wanted me to do was just to try to play a blues with him. And he started out for F blues. And he started playing these chords, these extended chords and all of that. And I heard that, I'm like, "Wow." And I kind of had heard that on record but never live like that, you know, right there in front of me. I was in love, man.

What do you like best about being a jazz musician?

For me, I really like just being on the bandstand playing the music. That's most important for me. If I had to say one thing, the greatest thing for me is to be on the bandstand playing the music and interacting with other musicians, creating and developing.

REGINALD VEAL

Tell me some of the musicians that you've most enjoyed working with.

Of course, Wynton Marsalis. Terence Blanchard, saxophonist Donald Harrison. Definitely Elvin Jones. You know, pretty much everyone that I've played with, I've enjoyed working with them. And that's a lot of people.

In the last ten to fifteen years, we've seen a tremendous resurgence in the popularity of jazz music, traditional jazz music. Have you given any thought to why that is?

Wynton Marsalis [is] a big part of that. And everyone else who has gained popularity by playing traditional jazz music has also contributed to that. But I think that, in general, jazz music is so profound, most people with a certain amount of intelligence, if they listen to [jazz music], you have to be pretty much hooked or intrigued, or even curious because it's different from any other type of music. I mean, it's a music that's pretty much addictive. Maybe addictive is a bad word, but I think it's real simple. For example, I've had friends who aren't musicians to start listening to jazz music and become jazz fanatics.

People want to hear good music. I think people discover it sometimes by accident. And it just grows on them. I think people really just want to hear good music because, if you'll notice, I think there's also a lot of younger non-musicians that are really checking out the music and listening to jazz music now more than ever before.

People need something different and something with some substance. There is music out here that has substance . . . and I'm not putting down any other type of music. But for me, especially jazz music, it's the highest level of music or free expression that I've experienced in my whole lifetime. If there is anything else out here, I wish somebody would let me know about it so I could get to it. Really.

Who are a couple—two or three—of your favorite jazz musicians of all time?

Of all time? Whew, that's really difficult. Okay. I'll just narrow it down. Let me see. Louis Armstrong. John Coltrane. This is very difficult. You're giving me three, right? . . . Duke Ellington. Charles Mingus. Miles Davis. Can I go on? Man, there are so many. I said Duke. I guess we can stop at that.

What would be some of your favorite recordings that you've made?

Well, my most recent recording was with Branford [Marsalis], *The Dark Keys*. It has become one of my favorite recordings for several reasons. It's because it is the first time that I've done a full record in a trio setting without a piano, which is very, very difficult and challenging for me as a bassist because with no piano, there's no harmony, and I have to outline the harmony, and I have to continue to swing, and make everything sound interesting. . . .

[Usually] the most current recordings are the ones that are my favorites because I look back on the old ones and I hear things that I could have done. Like a few years from now, I'm going to listen to these records that I made in '96 or '97 or whatever, and I'm going to be like, wow. I'm [always] going to like the recording I just made.

What specific goals do you have for the future?

First and foremost, I want to continue to develop as a bassist and to explore every aspect of bass playing. . . .

I know my role, and traditionally it plays a supportive role. It accompanies, and I love doing that, but I think there are some other things to be explored on the bass.

To become a great bass player, continue to practice, and to play with as many great people as possible, [because] we're losing a lot of the masters as you know. . . . But that's one thing I've always wanted to do is to get the opportunity to play with everyone that's not in my generation. . . . But I don't know if I'll ever have the opportunity to do that. . . .

I picked up my electric bass some time ago. So I want to be able to play electric in some situations, not necessarily an acoustic jazz situation, but whatever quality music I can find that would lend itself to electric bass. I would like to do that and to be known as a bassist who could do both, play electric bass and upright bass equally well. I would like for that to happen.

REGINALD VEAL
SELECT DISCOGRAPHY

Collaborations With Wynton Marsalis

- *In This House, On This Morning*—Columbia
- *Citi Movement*—Columbia
- *Blue Interlude*—Columbia
- *The Majesty of the Blues*—Columbia

Collaborations With Branford Marsalis

- *The Dark Keys*—Columbia
- *I Heard You Twice the First Time*—Columbia

Collaborations With the Lincoln Center Jazz Orchestra

- *Blood on the Fields*—with Wynton Marsalis—Columbia
- *The Fire of the Fundamentals*—Columbia
- *They Came to Swing*—Columbia
- *Portraits by Ellington*—Columbia

Collaborations With Other Artists

- *Underground*—with Courtney Pine—Antilles
- *Music Evolution*—with Buckshot LeFonque—Columbia
- *Buckshot LeFonque*—with Buckshot LeFonque—Columbia
- *Gershwin for Lovers*—with Marcus Roberts—Columbia

CHAPTER 7

JAZZ PROFILES

Cindy Blackman

Brian Blade

Gregory Hutchinson

Leon Parker

Jeff "Tain" Watts

THE DRUMMERS

Biography

CINDY

B orn in Young Springs, Ohio, Cindy Blackman (DOB 11/18/59) currently resides in New York City. She began studying percussion at a very early age and attended the Berklee School of Music in Boston. She counts Tony Williams as her greatest percussion influence.

Blackman maintains a very busy recording and performing schedule. She is called upon for recording and performing gigs by many of today's top jazz artists. Also a noted rock-n-roll drummer, for the last several years she has been the drummer for Lenny Kravitz's band. Squeezed in between these obligations are her composing, recording, and performing with her own groups. A versatile drummer, Blackman represents the best of the jazz artist—in constant pursuit of a unique form of her instrument's expression.

Photo Notes

In 1995 alto saxophoni Vincent Herring brought his quintet to northern California to play at Yoshi and Kuumbwa. The members of his group were Scott Wendholt, trumpet; Jessie Murphy, bass; Carlos McKinney, piano; and Cindy Blackma drums. I'd never seen any of these musicians, beside Blackman, perform live. I' heard of her recordings o the Muse label and saw h with Jackie McLean, Don Pullen, Joe Henderson, an Pharoah Sanders, but on the '95 gigs, she looked and sounded different. Many of you might know her from appearances on "The Late Show with Davi Letterman," "Saturday Night Live," or the "MTV Video Awards," but if you haven't seen her in a club live, try to catch her ther I hope this photograph w stimulate your interest.

The photographs of Blackman in this chapter and on the book's back cover were taken at Yoshi in April, 1995. Her spirit that evening was contagious. She was soloing in both of these pictures, and the audience was urging her on. I coul see that Blackman was photogenic, and I couldn resist continually clicking my camera shutter. What you see here is one of a series of very satisfying photographs.

BLACKMAN

INTERVIEW, FEBRUARY 7, 1998

Tell me what sparked your interest in jazz.

Jazz I fell in love with because it's so creative. And because you can interject your feelings and your personal opinion and your personality, and because of all the great people whom I admired—[jazz] is the music they loved. And [jazz] to me was the hippest music around.

Who would be some of your greatest influences in music?

I would say my greatest influence is Tony Williams, without a doubt. And I was influenced by him from a very early age because there was a friend of mine who was a guitar player, an older guy, and I was quite a bit younger, but this person, he said, hey you really want to be a drummer, then I've got a guy who you should check out. I know who the guy is. So he brought me to his house and took me to his basement where he had all of his records and stereo equipment, and he put a record on, and then he just went upstairs. And then he came back, and I said, "Oh, man, who was that? That was incredible." And he said, well, believe it or not, this guy was like seventeen on this record, sixteen or seventeen. And it was Tony Williams. And then he put on *Live in Europe*. And so from then on I was totally into Tony Williams.

And a couple years later I was fortunate enough to see him in a clinic, just Tony Williams and a bass player in a Connecticut drum store called Creative Music. I saw him there, and it was really, really incredible. I had never seen anything like that, and immediately I knew that that was the direction that, for me, drumming should go into and drumming should be.

The sound of his drums was just beautiful. His intelligence was very high, the highest. His techniquewas impeccable; his choice of notes around the kit and the variations with which he used all of his rudiments and all the expression around the kit was just amazing. I was really floored. And a lot of it I didn't understand because it was way over my head. But that was the feeling and, yes, that's Tony Williams. He's definitely my biggest influence and my favorite musician ever.

Since jazz music was created, it has gone through various periods that have been labeled bop, fusion, etc. Do you see jazz currently moving into any new definable phase?

Well, as Bird said, creativity is unlimited. And that's what I think jazz music is. It's creative music. So will it change? Of course it will change because life changes; the universe is in constant flux, you know; everything changes. And I think the universe is creative. And that's where I think jazz comes from, basically.

And it should change. It's a music that expresses where the people are at the time they are playing it, as well as where the music has been, as well as where the music is going. So jazz music will always change, and that is the beauty of it; that's one of the beauties of it to me.

And for people who want to make jazz a museum piece and a statement which says jazz existed in 1950 or 1947 or 1930 and didn't go anywhere else, to me that's a bore. If you want to check that out, you can check that out at home or turn on your Walkman or something. Study it. You should know it, but then you are not expressing life in your music. You are not giving the music life. To me the music is dead in that way, and it's a bore.

A lot of people say that jazz music has become a lot more popular in the last ten to fifteen years. Do you agree with that?

Has it become more popular? Well, probably. There are more young cats on the scene. In the 1970s there was quite a lull. And there weren't a lot of people on the scene. I know Al Foster told me at one point in the 1970s it was hard for him to find people to play with in terms of playing jazz. And he's a guy who was there in the 1960s, there in the 1970s. So he saw a difference in the scene.

Yes, it has changed because there are more people here to play it. Has it become more popular in terms of the populous and listening audience? I would say, to a degree, yes. Stereotypical jazz has become more popular. Creative jazz is not always more popular because that is something that requires people to do a lot of thinking, and it incites feeling and emotion within the listener. And sometimes people don't want to think or figure out what is going on. Sometimes people just want to have some background music and say, oh yes, I'm into jazz. Well, that's pretty superficial to me.

Creative music, it's a double-edged sword because it has gotten more popular. The most popular parts of it are pretty commercial in a sense. The most creative parts of it still are not as popular. But it's kind of an exclusive club almost because it takes a certain kind of person to really be into listening to that kind of level of creativity. But at the same time, I do think that if that was pushed the way more commercial music was pushed, then I think people would respond to it in an overwhelming fashion.

To hear something that is so creative is a beautiful thing. And to be involved in that, to even sit there and watch it happen, that's a great thing. To do it, to try earnestly with every ounce of sweat that you have, with every thought that you have in your brain, and every feeling that you have in your heart, and every emotion that you have picked up throughout your life, to try to create on a high level with all of those feelings and instincts and all of that knowledge, to really try to do that every moment, is pretty fantastic.

Do you think it is more difficult, even in this day and age, for women to make it in jazz than it is for men?

Well, things are changing, but they have not changed totally.

It seems to me maybe that female vocalists have had it easier than those playing instruments.

I tell you, it seems to me that if you play an instrument that people think it's okay [for a woman] to play, which sounds silly already, but if you do that—for example, if you're a vocalist or a pianist, play the violin, flute—then they deem that okay. And then your career is automatically in a different place because, since someone says that it's okay or if they think that it's all right for you to do that, then already you're able to do more with your career; you'll have more opportunities. And opportunities, they give you more of a chance to grow and to do things that you want to do, play music. If you play another instrument, then it becomes a little more difficult. But all in all, none of that is anything that I really even think about.

Hopefully, things are getting better.

Sure, it's getting better because times are changing. But it's still not there yet. And in terms of your instrument, it's harder for a bass player, and that goes beyond gender or color or whatever. It's harder for a bass player to get a contract. It's harder for a drummer to get a contract because people don't really consider drummers as the main focal point in terms of leaders.

Now there have been some great drummer leaders. Art Blakey, Philly Joe Jones, Tony Williams, Elvin Jones, even as far back as Chick Webb. I'm not trying to say there haven't been great drummer leaders; I just mean in my opinion, it's easier for a record company to look at a group and say, okay, the front man on trumpet or saxophone or guitar is going to lead this project because they can do trio or they can do whatever; the piano players can lead it. But in terms of a drummer leading it, there are more contracts I would say for people who play other instruments than there are for drums or bass. In terms of gender, I don't even care about that. That's really nothing that I—things happen, but they sometimes happen because of your color, sometimes because of your hairstyle, sometimes because of your gender, sometimes this or that. That exists across the board for different people at different times. But none of that is anything that I really focus on because to me that just holds you back. Because while you are thinking about that, you could have been practicing or studying something. You could have just been enjoying a moment which could have inspired you to play something else.

What advice would you have for a youngster who might want to be a jazz musician?

Go see as much music as possible. Study as many records as possible. Listen all the time, but seeing is also very important. There are a lot of things you will get from seeing people play that you won't get from hearing them on a record.

And for young players, it's also good for them to know that it's not only okay to play like someone great whom they admire, but they should—because if you don't know where your instrument came from, if you don't have a good grasp of that, then there is no way that you can truly push it forward and do something else with it because there is no way that you can develop your own style if you don't have anything to base it off of.

CINDY BLACKMAN
SELECT DISCOGRAPHY

As a Leader
- *The Oracle*—Muse
- *Telepathy*—Muse
- *Code Red*—Muse
- *Arcane*—Muse

**Collaborations
With Other Artists**
- *Sax Storm*—with Grand Central—Evidence
- *Tenor Conclave: A Tribute to Hank Mobley*—Evidence
- *Obsession*—with Wallace Roney—Muse
- *The Standard Bearer*—with Wallace Roney—Muse

Biography

BRIAN

F rom Shreveport, Louisiana, Brian Blade, son of a Baptist minister, was influenced early on by the music of his father's congregation and choir. Beginning in music on the violin, Blade began drumming around age thirteen. He counts Elvin Jones, Tony Williams, Max Roach, David Lee, Jr., and John Vidacovich as major percussion influences.

One of the most-sought-after drummers in jazz, Blade has enjoyed extensive collaborations with Joshua Redman and Kenny Garrett. Blade also has worked with legendary singer/songwriter Joni Mitchell. Still in his twenties, he already has established his own style and voice. Brian Blade is the epitome of the great jazz drummer, providing high energy and maximum swing. He truly enjoys his art and provides the same enjoyment for his listeners.

In January, 1998, Brian Blade was part of a trio (Blade on drums, Joshua Redman on saxophones, and Christian McBride on bass) accompanying McCoy Tyner at Yoshi's. This was departure for Blade because he'd played mos with his contemporaries the last six or seven year It must have been a new experience in many ways for him to play along wi Tyner, but he handled it very well.

Blade is quite photogenic, and his bod and facial expression ver much match the spirit o the moment. I've seen them change from the fi time I photographed hin in 1992, with the Delfea Marsalis Quintet, throug the groups led by Joshua Redman and Kenny Garr Here he's playing with th Kenny Garrett Trio, including Nat Reeves on bass, at Kuumbwa in September, 1996. Nowadays Blade mostly plays with Joshua Redma

BLADE

INTERVIEW, MARCH 24, 1997

Can you point to a specific big break in terms of your career?

There was one, and, of course, it didn't register. It was hindsight, like one or two years after that I realized it, but it was with George French and Emile Vinette. They're unsung heroes down home in New Orleans who trusted me enough to play with them. The trio, George French is a singer/bassist, and Emile plays piano. We were playing at a hotel for six nights a week during a summer while I was down at Loyola [University]. I realized that that summer of playing with them—music that I didn't think I wanted to play. We played everything from country sounds, to New Orleans R & B, to Thelonious Monk's music.

At the time I remember thinking, oh man, I'm sounding horrible, and I shouldn't be here. It wasn't until a year or two later that I realized that kind of took me to the next plateau of understanding and being able to interpret music in any situation that I was in. So that was a big breaking point for me.

And just playing with a lot of different people. I can't really cite another situation. Before George and Emile, [others] prepared me for tolerance and to be open wide.

How did you meet Joshua Redman?

We used to play in a band with Delfeayo Marsalis, who plays trombone. While Joshua was in school in Boston and I was down in New Orleans, [Joshua Redman] would come down to play in this band that Delfeayo had put together.

**BRIAN
BLADE**

Who are some of your favorites you've most enjoyed playing or recording with?

Definitely Kenny Garrett and Joshua [Redman]. Presently Joni Mitchell—that's beyond dreams. It feels as if she saved my life. When I was about sixteen, I discovered her music. And also Daniel Lanois, who's Canadian.

What is your favorite aspect about being a professional musician? Do you enjoy playing on the bandstand, recording, touring, composing? What is your favorite part of it all?

Definitely all of those things. But playing live, that's when the circle is completed because people come hoping to share, and they come hoping that you will share. And so it is completed then. That's [also] when it's most electric and the most fulfilling. Most times on the road, that's your only refuge, when you have that time together on the stage with everyone listening. So I think playing live, definitely.

How much time out of the year do you spend on the road?

The last four or five years, nine to ten months a year, broken throughout the year.

Do you like touring that much?

It's wearing thin. If there were some way to just reach a better balance—in terms of being a part of community, being wherever you live and then going out [on tour] every now and then, but then coming back, more so than being gone and forgetting where you were or what you were a part of. I don't know. It's a love/hate relationship. I'm sort of making my peace with it. But I definitely can't keep up a ten-months-a-year pace for much longer.

Tell me what a typical day on the road is like for you.

Wake up early; scrounge for food; hopefully, shuttle onto the bus, but [a bus] is rarely a luxury, so we get up even earlier to get to the airport and check all the baggage; sit there for an hour and a half—you wonder why you're doing what you're doing; get on the plane; probably fall asleep; wake up in another state, another city; get off [the plane]; into the hotel room hopefully for an hour just to get your sense about you; get ready for sound check; go and eat a horrible meal because you haven't had time to go out and get something of your own choosing. And then play that night and hopefully by some miracle have a conversation with one person. And then you go back to your room, go to sleep, and then do it again the next day.

Let me ask you about a resurgence in the popularity of jazz in the last ten to fifteen years. Do you have any thoughts as to why that is?

I don't know. That's a good question. It's just due to more people want to play [jazz music]. People like Wynton Marsalis coming about and Branford Marsalis. People like Mulgrew Miller and Kenny Garrett, who have been playing the music in the Duke Ellington Orchestra and with Art Blakey. They were concerned with hearing the music, making sure the music lives. So I think it's simply that there are more younger people who want to carry on a tradition or play the music that they think is important.

No matter what it is, I'm sure there is an equal—or actually probably three times or ten times—the number of musicians wanting to play rock and roll or wanting to play classical music. I think there's just more willingness and wanting [with music in general].

What specific goals do you have for yourself?

I want to continue writing music. Hopefully not lose faith in the possibilities of the music—healing people, and touching people, and getting better in what I do playing drums and crafting music. Hopefully, have a group of people that I can play with for as long as possible. Those are some long-term goals.

Do you see yourself as always being a jazz drummer, or would you like to have a different career at some point in your life?

I don't know. I like to think that everyone's been given some gifts by God, something they were put here to do. And figuring that out or learning what it is, I guess is part of the whole process. Living here, you are going to struggle through things. I feel as if [my being a musician] is definitely a gift, and I have to embrace it for as long as possible.

So I want to continue making music for as long as I'm able. I can't even think of choosing another career or—[but] I definitely want to study a million things, you know. I want to do a hundred things. But playing music gives me the most joy, and hopefully I can spread a little around by doing it.

What advice would you have for someone who's thinking about making a career of jazz music?

I think learning as much about music as you can early on is the wisest thing and rounding your awareness of other things. Get as much direction and information as you can get from musicians you know or people you can go and hear—hear music live, hear all music live, and lift your consciousness through as much literature as you can get, and as many people as you can come into contact with. If you go to school, make sure you're studying something else, aside from music, so that it's not all a one-way street.

BRIAN BLADE
SELECT DISCOGRAPHY

As a Leader

- *Brian Blade Fellowship*— Blue Note

- *New Orleans Collective*— with Nicholas Payton, Wessell Anderson, Christopher Thomas, and Peter Martin—Evidence

Collaborations With Other Artists

- *Freedom in the Groove*— with Joshua Redman— Warner Bros.

- *Spirit of the Moment: Live at the Village Vanguard*—with the Joshua Redman Quartet—Warner Bros.

- *Moodswing*—with Joshua Redman— Warner Bros.

- *Pursuance: The Music of John Coltrane*—with Kenny Garrett—Warner Bros.

- *Triology*—with Kenny Garrett—Warner Bros.

- *Black Hope*—with Kenny Garrett —Warner Bros.

Biography | GREGO

B orn in 1970 in Brooklyn, New York, Gregory Hutchinson grew up in a musical household. The son of a percussionist, Hutchinson was exposed to his father's playing, as well as his mother's large record collection that included jazz, soul, and Afro-Cuban music. Like that of many of his contemporaries, Hutchinson's first major break came with vocalist Betty Carter. Since then he has enjoyed extensive collaborations with Ray Brown and Roy Hargrove.

He also performs often with Christian McBride, Eric Reed, and Joshua Redman. One of the most in-demand percussionists today, Hutchinson loves music of all kinds and plays all styles of jazz.

HUTCHINSON

INTERVIEW, MAY 16, 1997

How do you view the role of a jazz drummer?

To lead the band. The drums and the bass—as they go, so goes the band. To play good time, not get in the way, to add colors to, and to enhance the soloist and inspire, add that fire. If you check out all the great drummers, they inspire, and they create a certain amount of energy up there. There is no way you cannot play off [their drumming.]

I like to fashion myself behind [Art] Blakey. Blakey led his bands. So that's the way I try to play; not in his style, but more so in the way that he directed.

Who are some of your musical heroes?

I definitely have to say Charlie Parker, Cannonball [Adderly], Miles [Davis]—I'm just talking about all the other instruments now, besides the drums. Wynton Kelly, definitely Freddie Hubbard. Blue Mitchell.

When you talk about drummers, Philly [Joe Jones], Max [Roach], and Art [Blakey]—I guess all the great drummers who lived before me.

In the last fifteen years, we've seen a resurgence in the popularity of jazz music. Jazz-record sales are up, and more people are going to jazz concerts. Have you given any thought as to why this might be?

I attribute a lot of the resurgence to when Wynton [Marsalis] came out. Here was a young guy who had a certain way about him, and younger people could relate to him. Then with the younger [musicians] coming up, [the people] start to see it more, and they said, hey, these guys are just like us. Let me go check this out. Young people need to have something they can relate to. With the younger generation playing now, you get not only the history of the music, but you also get what's happening now. . . .

GREGORY HUTCHINSON

Did Wynton Marsalis have the same effect on jazz musicians, or was it just the listeners?

I think it was on the listeners. I think that once you decide you want to play jazz, or once I decided I wanted to play jazz, it wouldn't have mattered what was happening. This was what I was going to do.

This is something I want to do, and it's a love that I have, so I can't really say in terms of [Marsalis] affecting a lot of musicians, but the public, definitely. I can remember walking up in a train station in front of this big billboard poster, and it said, "Wynton Is Coming." That's some different stuff for a jazz artist. You don't see that. . . .

Tell me why you chose jazz instead of another form of music.

I still enjoy all music. I enjoy everything. I just choose to make my living playing jazz. But I enjoy good R & B; you know, anything that is good music, I'll play. I don't limit myself. Some guys say, "All I do is play jazz." So you mean to tell me if you get called to go out on the road with, say, Eric Clapton or someone like that, you're not going to do it because all you do is play jazz? That doesn't make any sense. You are a musician; you play music.

The reason I've chosen jazz is because that's what I've been exposed to the most. Had I been exposed to R & B the most or another form of music, then I would have been in that field of music. But there are certain things I really, really enjoy about jazz. It has that freedom and the creativity. Also, jazz is a music that's really not for everyone. You have to be a special listener to really enjoy it. A lot of people try to enjoy it, and they just don't—this is not for them.

What do you think about being on the road as much as you are?

Oh, I love it. I was just talking about this the other night with a friend of mine. The fact that you have to get on a plane, get from one city to the next city, get off the plane, go to sound check, and then hit, and you have to pull that off as if you had a full day's rest—that's a challenge.

Also, you get to experience different cultures, and that affects the way you play. After you have traveled around the world and you come back, you ask yourself how you can draw from your travels. You see different people and the way they live. I've yet to get to Africa, but I can't wait because I know it's going to have a totally different effect on the way I play.

It seems that with jazz, there are very loose-knit bands. In other words, with rock music and pop music, for example, there are bands made up of folks who stick together their whole career. In jazz, you guys all record and play with others' bands. Why do you think there's that difference?

Just the need to be creative and to experience different people who are coming up. If you notice, with the rock and pop groups, they all have the same sound for as long as they are together, and there's nothing wrong with that. But to me, after a while I want to change. I would want to head in another direction. Like Miles [Davis], he was always changing. That's what made him so good—the fact that at any given moment you never knew what was going to happen. And the music always stayed fresh. That's my thing. As long as the music stays fresh. So if you can keep the same band and the music stays fresh, then that's fine, too.

You've played extensively with Ray Brown, Roy Hargrove, Eric Reed, and Christian McBride. Describe for me the personalities of those different bands.

Let's start with Ray Brown. Since he is older, someone I'm looking up to, it's already dictated how things are going to happen. He's open for suggestions, but he's been around so much, that [experience] just comes out in the way he leads the band. You just kind of follow what's happening.

I like playing with Roy Hargrove because then I can take on more of a Blakey-esque kind of role. I can lead the band. Even though [Hargrove's] the leader, I can still dictate what goes on the bandstand and how the cats are going to play. And that's cool, and he's open for that; he likes that. We play a lot of different styles of music, and it's really open. I get to just really explore how I want to play. [Playing with Roy Hargrove], those are some of the best times I've had playing.

Eric Reed's band, another trio, that's open, too. He has a certain way he writes his music, but he knows so much about music at such an early age that we play all kinds of styles. He has his own concept of the music, and that's really important.

And Christian McBride, he also already has his own concept. Christian and I are both funksters, we love R & B music, and that plays another important part in the way he plays. As you already know, he's an incredible bassist, and he's an incredible writer. It's fun playing with him, too, and that's what's great.

GREGORY HUTCHINSON
SELECT DISCOGRAPHY

Collaborations With Other Artists

- *Pure Imagination*—with Eric Reed—Impulse!
- *Musicale*—with Eric Reed—Impulse!
- *It's Alright to Swing*—with Eric Reed—MoJazz
- *The Swing and I*—with Eric Reed—MoJazz
- *The Sax Players*—with Ray Brown—Telarc
- *Seven Steps to Heaven*—with Ray Brown—Telarc
- *Joshua Redman*—with Joshua Redman—Warner Bros.
- *Family*—with Roy Hargrove—Verve
- *With the Tenors of Our Time*—with Roy Hargrove—Verve
- *Of Kindred Souls*—with Roy Hargrove—Verve
- *The Vibe*—with Roy Hargrove—Verve
- *Lush Life*—with Joe Henderson—Verve
- *I'm Yours/You're Mine*—with Betty Carter—Verve
- *Droppin Things*—with Betty Carter—Verve
- *Swingin*—with Arturo Sandoval—GRP

LEON

Photo Notes

I'd heard about Leon Parker for quite awhile before I had the opportunity to see him play or photograph him. I was looking forward to hearing this much-heralded minimalist drummer, who at various times has used very few drums, traps, or cymbals. In the fall of 1996 he'd brought a group into the Monterey Jazz Festival tha played in Dizzy's Den, one of the smaller venues on the site, a somewhat intimate setting to hear music and definitely photo-friendly. The group was in good spirits and played accordingly at thei first Monterey Jazz Festiva appearance. One month later, Parker came back to the San Francisco Bay area to play at Kuumbwa and the San Francisco Jazz Festival.

I took this photograph of Parker during the same set at Yoshi's, in October, 1997, at which I shot the photographs of Jacky Terrasson and Ugonna Okegwo (who are also featured in this book). the gig, when I gave Parker some of the photographs I'd taken of him the year before, he was surprised at how he looked when he played. Since I'd photographed him several times already, we were mutually comfortable while I took pictures of him during the gig. The result was the best series of photographs of him I've taken.

L eon Parker (DOB 8/21/65) is a percussionist who truly marches to his own beat. Known as a minimalist, Parker has performed with instrumentation ranging from one cymbal only to a full trap kit. Any way he plays, he provides a full accompaniment of rhythm and swing.

Growing up in White Plains, New York, Parker was first exposed to jazz as a child through his parents' record collection. He began drumming at age three, using Quaker Oatmeal boxes as drums. By his teen years, he was performing with jazz ensembles and also began studying classical percussion. After high school, he turned down a religion-and-philosophy scholarship to Fordham University, became a fixture of New York City jazz clubs, and began developing his own style and sound. He later spent most of the year in Spain and Portugal further exploring his craft.

At the beginning of the 1990s, Parker returned to New York City and soon began collaborations with saxophonist Dewey Redman, pianist Jacky Terrasson, and saxophonist Steve Wilson. Parker currently performs mostly as a solo and leader artists and emphasizes hand drumming, vocal body rhythms, and various percussion instruments.

PARKER

INTERVIEW, AUGUST 26, 1997

How is it that you evolved into choosing jazz as an art form?

My parents had a record collection, and it had just tons of classic jazz recordings. Growing up, I would periodically consult their records and try and understand what was going on. I don't know why I gravitated toward those records, but everything else was like stuff that was on the radio, but those records spoke to me. . . .

[My parents] had everything. They had Art Blakey, Max Roach. They had Count Basie, Duke Ellington, Miles Davis. It seemed like they had every classic jazz record. . . . So I would listen to this music and try to play along with it. So every couple of years I would reinvestigate it, and I would hear more. Every time I listened I would hear more and more.

By the time I was a teenager, I was starting to find other young musicians who played jazz. There is this thing called the Westchester Youth Jazz Ensemble . . . And I was the only African-American in the band. They were all suburban white kids. So I got into that and tried to jam a little bit. . . . But I didn't really play jazz with musicians until I was at least sixteen or seventeen when I began to meet some older musicians in the area who were playing in the clubs, which I didn't even know existed until I was about seventeen.

You're known as a minimalist; you've experimented with playing just a cymbal. Most of the time you're playing with a limited set. Tell me about how that came about and what do you think you've gained from that?

I started when I was young. Besides not using the tom-toms, just using fewer instruments because basically I was always carrying my drums with me somewhere, and it was just more practical—and also it was during a time in the early 1980s when the big drum-equipment boom happened, and everybody was just buying more and more drums. I just felt it was stupid. I couldn't understand it.

LEON
PARKER

It wasn't like people heard something and wanted to try it. It was just all of a sudden the drum companies could sell a lot, and people were buying it up. And I decided I wanted to go a more traditional, old-world traditional and Eastern route, which is the percussion concept versus the drum-set concept. And so I just started focusing on playing fewer instruments, and I really wanted to become close and have a personal relationship with my instrument. And that's when I got down to just playing the cymbal. So what that taught me was you grow to understand the basics in a deeper way.

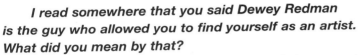

I read somewhere that you said Dewey Redman is the guy who allowed you to find yourself as an artist. What did you mean by that?

He basically lived and let live. He just leads by example. He plays the music and takes you with him. As does Tom Harrell. . . . He's not a controlling person who tells you what to play and how to play. He kind of lets the music show you the way.

Who would you count as your greatest jazz influences?

On my instrument I would say Ray White, Ben Riley, and Roy Haynes. Ray is my biggest influence musically because he always asks me to go deeper within myself. He knew my potential and he always asked me to follow it. He was a drummer himself, but he was on another level. He had not played professionally for years on the level that Ben Riley and Roy Haynes did, but he didn't have any remorse or regret. He was just happy to be a part of the scene as it was and to inspire younger musicians. And he had a beautiful spirit, and he always asked me to go deeper into my own resolve and find out what I really have to say and express. He never forgot about that—that's some old-school stuff. And that's what he asked of me, and I just accepted the challenge, always.

Ben [Riley] to me is like the perfect accompanist as far as doing what I aspire to do—to uplift the band—but he is never in the way. And he hasn't taken it for granted; he has so much humility, which is another quality we don't recognize today in music or in life. . . . And then Roy Haynes is just—he's it for me. He's just all rhythm and playing in the moment, in a very deep way.

And then influences overall?
Overall?

Yes. Not necessairily your instrument, but just if you had to pick a few people who were the most inspiration to you, and it doesn't have to be a musician, but I'm trying to get a feel for who has inspired you in your life.
In my life?

Yes.
Leon Parker.

That's a good answer.
[Laughs] . . . All the musicians [I've encountered]. They've all touched me.

Tell me, how do you view your role in a jazz group? What are you trying to accomplish on the bandstand?
Try to be supportive, and provide some kind of shape or form or structure into the music, or to outline it, that form or structure. And also to be involved and inspiring other musicians because rhythm has that quality to it.

I think we are in the midst of a strong resurgence in the popularity of jazz music. Do you agree?

Yes. I think the roots of jazz are about truth and culture and expression. It's a true art form. And it has a cultural basis as opposed to most of the other things in this country, which has to do with trend and materialism. It's like a tree that was planted, and all these weeds have been growing up around it, but it has kept growing. It's one of the true cultural art forms that this country has produced.

What are some of your plans?

Let me think. Good question. I don't really know because I didn't really see myself being in the position I'm in now. So I really don't know where it's going to lead me. . . . Basically I'm just trying to find balance in the midst of, as you said, this resurgence because it's a resurgence, but it's like everything else in this country: it's about how can everybody make money off of it. And in the process you siphon out the essence of what the art form is really about, so that's a real struggle to try to maintain it as an art form when it's being used as a commodity.

LEON PARKER
SELECT DISCOGRAPHY

As a Leader
- *Awakening*—Columbia
- *Belief*—Columbia
- *Above & Below*—Epicure

Collaborations With Other Artists
- *Alive*—with Jacky Terrasson—Blue Note
- *Reach*—with Jacky Terrasson—Blue Note
- *Jacky Terrasson*—with Jacky Terrasson—Blue Note
- *Sketches of Dreams*—with David Sanchez—Columbia
- *The Departure*—with David Sanchez—Columbia
- *The Real Quietstorm*—with James Carter—Atlantic Jazz
- *Young at Art*—with Jesse Davis—Concord Jazz
- *As We Speak*—with Jesse Davis—Concord Jazz
- *Choices*—with Dewey Redman—Enja
- *Sphere Music*—with Uri Caine—jMT
- *Morning Call*—with Bruce Barth—Enja
- *The Art of Rhythm*—with Tom Harrell—RCA
- *Other Spheres*—with Geoff Keezer—DIW
- *4/4 Time*—with Steve Wilson—CrissCross
- *In a Different Light*—with Harvey Swarz—Mesa/Blue Moon

JEFF "TAIN

Photo Notes

A native of Pittsburgh, Pennsylvania, Jeff "Tain" Watts is perhaps the most versatile drummer in jazz today, providing the color and swing for a wide array of today's top artists. He studied music at the University of Pittsburgh and later at the Berklee School of Music. He left Berklee to begin long-time associations with Wynton Marsalis and Branford Marsalis. Watts also records and performs with the patriarch of the Marsalis clan, legendary New Orleans pianist/educator Ellis Marsalis.

From straight-ahead to funk and fusion, Watts can be heard on many recordings of many different artists. He possesses a mellow, laidback personality, and his drumming is anything but. Jeff "Tain" Watts plays all styles of jazz equally well.

Jeff "Tain" Watts is much in demand. His versatility and his uncanny sense of time enable him to fit in with and direct musicians of diverse styles. During an eighteen-month period beginning in September, 1996, Watts played in the San Francisco Bay Area six times with four different groups. He played twice the Michael Brecker Quartet, which included Joey Calderazzo on piano and James Genus on bass. Watts also played twice with Branford Marsalis, once as part of a trio with Reginald Veal on bass in December, 1996, and sixteen months later with Marsalis's quartet, which consisted of Marsalis, Watts, Kenny Kirkland on piano, and Eric Revis on bass. In September, 1997, Watts was the drummer on a quartet date led by Kenny Garrett on alto sax, with Kenny Kirkland on piano and Nat Reeves on bass.

This photograph was from a date with Charnett Moffett's trio at Yoshi's in September, 1996, on which Kei Akagi on piano also played. I chose this photograph because the group was what used to be referred to as the rhythm section, and Watts's playing was decidedly different here. I've noticed that when a drummer isn't accompanying or driving a horn player, his body and face appear to be much less tense.

WATTS

INTERVIEW, OCTOBER 29, 1997

How did you get into jazz music?

Part of it was from high school. Jazz education was at a different state than it is now, at least in my school. [In high school] we played some stock arrangements that kind of had the feeling of jazz, but the passion of it didn't really come across to me at that time. I started playing classical music, and then I played a lot of R & B. What really brought me to jazz was just wanting to be a more well-rounded player.

How would you describe your breaks into the jazz-music business?

Part of it was going to Berklee. [When I was there], it was a particularly good time at the school. And meeting Branford [Marsalis], that pretty much started my career. He's pretty much responsible for 60 to 70 percent of my career.

Is that right?

Yes, because that's when I moved to New York. I left school to play in Wynton's [Marsalis] first band, and that pretty much started [my career].

Other than Branford and Wynton Marsalis, who are some of the musicians who have most influenced you?

The musicians in Wynton's first band, Kenny Kirkland, Branford Marsalis, Wynton had influence on me as peers, studying this music. But then as far as my personal growth musically, other than them, I would have to say Elvin Jones and Ed Blackwell and Art Blakey; those are some of the first people who interested me as far as jazz music.

A certain amount of my approach has come from listening to all kinds of music and just trying to reinterpret the jazz idiom, you know, swinging. . . .

JEFF "TAIN"
WATTS

A lot of people say that in the last ten to fifteen years there has been a strong resurgence in the popularity of jazz. Do you think that's true?

I guess they've gotten back around to marketing it to a certain degree. I guess it's more popular than it was in the late '70s to early '80s, but the music had changed, and the fusion thing was going on. And I'm not anti-fusion because that helped me get into jazz music— that helped me get into the lineage of the music.

And Wynton Marsalis had a lot to do with it. The way I feel about art is that you have the choice to participate in it or not. It's like a force in the universe. And it's going to continue whether you decide to put in the work and participate in it or not. So you have a choice of participating in this great music or just allowing it to pass by, but it's going to go on anyway.

But I'll give Wynton credit for being very, very responsible. When he emerged, it was the nexus of a whole lot of things. He was pretty much in the right place at the right time, but also his preparation was equal to the opportunity that was presented to him. A lot of it is timing. It's kind of like Michael Jordan. It was a good time, and they were able to find an angle on him , but also he was very responsible to the music and doesn't just settle for being a reluctant figure here.

Tell me some of the most memorable gigs that come to mind for you.

Just the many, many nights with Wynton's band or with Branford's band because at the time we started playing together, we were all pretty much growing at the same time, and different people had different areas of strengths and weaknesses, and a lot of what we played from a vocabulary standpoint wasn't like textbook jazz, but through force of will, it was something that was viable from the start. We didn't have

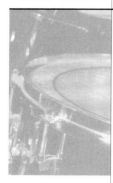

to be ashamed as far as our convictions were sincere in playing the music. But other than that, I've done some work with McCoy Tyner, and every measure of that was rewarding and educational to me, an inspiration.

With respect to the drummers out there of your generation, do you have a chance to interact with each other?

Everybody has a chance to check each other out. Everybody does. I don't know how it is on other instruments, but people who play other instruments have told me that there tends to be more of a kinship amongst drummers just because of the nature of the instrument—and we all have sympathy for each other for having to carry all that stuff around.

Yes. Leon Parker told me one reason he became somewhat of a minimalist is because he got tired of carrying around that drum set.

Yes, that's right. So you kind of have sympathy for each other. You kind of know what each other is going through. It's kind of like when it snows really bad outside, and people are looking at each other, even in New York, just having some empathy.

What is the drummer's role on the bandstand?

In [jazz] music, the primary role is to really dress up the music and to make it feel good and not leave any doubt. If anyone has any doubt about how the music should feel from a dancing standpoint, just to try to reinforce that. But then beyond that, you're trying to enhance things, to know when to support and when to instigate and when to color.

What's your favorite part about your job: the composing, recording, or performing?

I don't know. It all goes together. It's all one thing after a while for me. It's all good—just those opportunities you mentioned. Sometimes I sit back and reflect and say this is my workplace. It's really bizarre.

In general, I just allow the drums to take me on a trip. The drums take me to a studio to make a recording that people will hear thirty years from now. The drums take me around the world. The drums allow me to meet musicians.

Tell me about your goals.

I just want to really take some time to refine my craft and study some composition and some philosophy. I'm going to be composing a record early next year, so I'm going to be focusing on that.

I've done just about everything you can do in jazz except lead a group, so I want to do that. I want to focus on that and contribute some music and help some other musicians develop, to do a certain amount of teaching, and just have fun.

JEFF "TAIN" WATTS
SELECT DISCOGRAPHY

As a Leader

- *Simply Music*—with Joey Calderazzo and Sylvain Gagnon— Lost Chart Records

Collaborations With Other Artists

- *Underground*—with Courtney Pine—Antilles
- *The Dark Keys*—with Branford Marsalis— Columbia
- *Bloomington*—with Branford Marsalis— Columbia
- *The Beautiful Ones Are Not Yet Born*—with Branford Marsalis— Columbia
- *Crazy People Music*— with Branford Marsalis— Columbia
- *Trio Jeepy*—with Branford Marsalis— Columbia
- *Live at Blues Alley*—with Wynton Marsalis— Columbia
- *J Mood*—with Wynton Marsalis—Columbia
- *Black Codes (From the Underground)*—with Wynton Marsalis— Columbia
- *Hot House Flowers*—with Wynton Marsalis— Columbia
- *Whistle Stop*—with Ellis Marsalis—Columbia
- *Ellis Marsalis Trio*—with Ellis Marsalis—Columbia

CHAPTER 8

JAZZ PROFILES

Dee Dee Bridgewater

Kurt Elling

Kevin Mahogany

THE VOCALISTS

Biography

DEE DEE

B orn and raised in Flint, Michigan, Dee Dee Bridgewater (DOB 5/27/50) has lived in France since 1986. From a music loving family, she grew up listening to, and influenced by, the vocalists her parents played around the house. Bridgewater moved to New York in 1970 and soon became the lead vocalist for the Thad Jones/Mel Lewis Orchestra. She also collaborated with legends Sonny Rollins, Dizzy Gillespie, Dexter Gordon, Max Roach, and Rahsaan Roland Kirk.

The night in December, 1997, that Dee Dee Bridgewater came to Kuumbwa to sing was a very bad one for me. I was just recently out of the hospital and recovering from major surgery. I wasn't going to miss her for anything, however. After listening to her for more than ten years, I had my first opportunity to see and hear her live.

Earlier that day she'd given a workshop at Cal State Monterey Bay University, and she appeared to be super-tired when she came on stage. In addition the weather was damp and drizzly. She announced that she'd partially lost her voice and would be singing only in the lower registers. I couldn't tell because she put on a magnificent performance. Her stage manner overwhelmed the audience. She had us where she wanted us.

Bridgewater really connected with a few young and teenage girls in the audience. She spied one eight- or nine-year-old with a pillow. She asked to borrow it because she didn't feel well. The photograph you see here shows her clutching the pillow and really belting out a song. Even though I have more glamorous shots of her, I chose this one because I think it tells you a lot more about Dee Dee Bridgewater.

BRIDGEWATER

The mid-1970s brought an exciting opportunity—Broadway. She won a Tony award for her role in *The Wiz*, and she portrayed Billie Holiday in *Lady Day* (garnering a Lawrence Olivier nomination for Best Actress/Musical in London). She also performed in *Sophisticated Ladies*, *Cosmopolitan Greetings*, *Black Ballad*, *Carmen*, and *Cabaret*.

Bridgewater has returned to the jazz scene and, a phenomenal vocalist, was awarded a Grammy in 1998 for her latest release, *Dear Ella* (Verve), a tribute to legendary vocalist Ella Fitzgerald. With her varied talents, Bridgewater will most likely spend time acting again, but for the time being, the jazz community is indeed blessed to have Dee Dee Bridgewater back.

DEE DEE BRIDGEWATER

INTERVIEW, FEBRUARY 8, 1998

Who were some of your earliest musical influences?

I just always listened to whatever music my parents had in the house. So I remember when I was really young being impressed by people like Harry Belafonte, and Johnny Mathis, and Lena Horne, and Diahann Carroll, and then I discovered Nina Simone, and Nancy Wilson was my first big idol.

I remember being kind of infatuated with Dionne Warwick and all those albums she did with Burt Bacharach. James Brown—I used to sneak out of the house to go hear James Brown. The whole Motown scene was a big thing for me being from Flint, Michigan, and Motown being in Detroit. So any time Motown would have artists in concert in Flint or outside of Flint, I would sneak and go see them.

***Your scatting is wonderful. Did you develop it,
or is it something that just comes natural to you?***

I've tried to develop it through the years in a certain way, but it's something that just kind of came naturally to me, and now in retrospect I really am beginning to believe that it was because my mother listened to a lot of Ella Fitzgerald when I was in her tummy and also as a young baby. And I think that that had an effect on me. I really do because I don't remember consciously ever listening to Ella [Fitzgerald] or Sarah [Vaughn]. . . . So I just have to believe that this came through osmosis because [scatting] was always something I thought you were supposed to do.

Living in France you certainly have been exposed to a lot of the European jazz audiences. A lot of people say that the Europeans and Asians have much more appreciation for jazz music than Americans do. Do you agree?

Yes, I agree that there's a deeper respect for the music. And the fact that [jazz] is a music that has its origins with black Americans and comes from the United States, I know that Europeans really want to hear the music coming from the hands or the mouths of the players of the music who are of African-American descent. [The Europeans] feel that we are the original players and, therefore, we are the ones who play this music the best.

[In Europe] there's a big debate on whether or not European musicians can play as well as American musicians based on the heritage factor and the environmental factor, and I know that that is definitely a truism. And there is even a kind of reverse racism that goes on in Europe because of the fact that European [jazz] festivals will not hire Europeans to headline their festivals. They will put them in a festival, but [the European musicians] are not the headliners. The Americans are the headliners.

Who are some of the vocalists you listen to today?

Ella [Fitzgerald]. I mean I really don't listen to anyone, but when I was selecting material for the tour in October of 1996 with Jacky Terrasson in the States, I had to listen to a lot of Ella. I went back and listened to a lot of her early, early works,

which is where I ended up taking most of the songs I put on my *Dear Ella* album. I had to listen to her a lot, and I hadn't done that ever. So that's the first time I really started to listen to her. And then I was asked by Verve to select songs of Sarah Vaughn for a compilation album that they were doing on Sarah. And that was the first time I really sat down and listened to Sarah.

So otherwise I don't really listen. I think I should, but I have a really flexible ear, and I notice that if I listen to any singer for any length of time, then I'll start—bits and pieces of that singer will start filtering its way into my singing—so I don't like to do that. So I don't like to listen [to singers]. I don't really listen to music. I'm on the road all the time, so when I come home, I like silence.

What are some of your goals?

To produce other artists. Since I've done my last three albums for Verve Records, I really am growing to like producing and putting creative elements together. And the *Dear Ella* project, that was a huge endeavor for me. Before I had never done orchestra producing or big-band producing. To hire the contractors, to hire the musicians, and to give my ideas for arrangements, and to have those ideas come to fruition, and all of that planning I had to do. I loved it. It gave me a real charge. And now I would like to produce other artists. And I'm working on some film projects that I would like to eventually produce that I would star in.

And aside from that, I would like to do original material now. I'm very interested in writing lyrics. It's not so much that I'm tired of standards, but I know that I'm going to be married to standards because of the *Dear Ella* album. And there are so many people who are asking me to do concerts, tribute concerts to her. So I know I'm going to be kind of married to her.

I'm enjoying working with Ray Brown's trio. I work a lot with Ray Brown in Europe, and hopefully eventually we're going to start doing work in the States. And that's usually around Ella also.

I want to do Latin music where I would incorporate Cuban, Puerto Rican, and Brazilian composers. And a big dream of mine is to do something that's really artistic where I don't have to bear in mind sales.

Do the record companies inhibit musicians artistically?

Well, for me it's not a problem because I'm completely free to do whatever I want to do. Basically all I have to do is tell the record company, okay, guys, I'm going to go into the studio at such and such a time period. I intend to record my next album, and it's going to be this music, and they have no say. . . . I'm totally free because I have a producer's contract, not an artist's contract. . . .

Isn't your situation atypical?

It's totally atypical, totally atypical. I think most artists eventually find some kind of hindrance by being signed directly to a label because in the end the label can have a say about what the artist records and can make decisions about who they record with.

If one of your children or a youngster were to come to you for advice about being a jazz musician, what would you say?

My second daughter is a singer, and she signed with Virgin here in France, and she's doing kind of eclectic music, but it certainly is jazz-tinged. And her way of singing certainly is jazzy, and she does an occasional concert or club date where she sings jazz. And I've just told her to follow her heart and really be true to what she wants to do. . . .

Most people that we call singers today are not singers. And even musicians today cannot stand up to the mettle of your basic, well-trained, young jazz musician who can play everything. I think that young kids today are not getting a real idea of what real music is and what real musicians and real singers are because most of these kids can't sing. They're fabrication. They go in the studio, if it's not right, if a note isn't right, they just push a lever, push a dial, and drown out the note. And it's not until you hear them in live performance that you go, oh, my God, they can't sing. The groups can't harmonize. Most of the stuff today is about marketing.

DEE DEE BRIDGEWATER
SELECT DISCOGRAPHY

As a Leader
- *Dear Ella*—Verve
- *Prelude to a Kiss: The Duke Ellington Album*—Featuring Dee Dee Bridgewater with The Hollywood Bowl Orchestra/John Mauceri—Philips
- *Love and Peace: A Tribute to Horace Silver*—Verve
- *Keeping Tradition*—Verve
- *In Montreux*—Verve
- *Live in Paris*—Impulse!

Biography

KURT

A native of Chicago, Kurt Elling (DOB 11/02/67) continues to live there. The son of a music minister, he began in music playing the violin and French horn and discovered jazz while attending Gustavus Adolphus College in St. Peter, Minnesota. Elling entered graduate school at the University of Chicago's Divinity School. Taken with jazz by this time, however, he began gigging regularly at the Green Mill, a local jazz club. Feeling jazz vocals as a calling, he left his graduate studies just short of graduation in January, 1992.

In the last few years, Elling has taken jazz singing to a different level. Not content with simply scatting, he has developed a style he calls "ranting," which is singing improvised lyrics—a true innovation. His self confidence enables him to reach for such daring artistry.

ELLING

INTERVIEW, NOVEMBER 6, 1997

Please describe for me the earliest musical experiences you can remember.

The earliest musical experiences that I can remember are those of the Lutheran Church. My father is a church musician, and he's the choir director, and so I'm sure the first thing that I ever heard was Bach at a pipe organ.

Your singing style is certainly different from any style I've ever heard, and I think it's probably different in a lot of respects from that of anyone else out there today or from the past. How did your style come about?

It's never been that I've said I want to be radically different from everybody else. That isn't really the goal. The goal with me has just been—I mean, you construct or create in reaction to everything that you've seen in your life.

And when I would go out to jam sessions or when I would go to hear local jazz singers and even some of the ones who were on the national scene when I was coming up, I would want to be knocked out, and I wasn't getting knocked out. And they were doing things that I already knew from Ella Fitzgerald records, and I already knew from such-and-such records. And they were just copying this lyric, or using that arrangement, or just not really saying very much. And that kind of pissed me off because the people whose music I had fallen in love with were all people who were really exciting and swung really hard. . . .

I have a very strong sense of what I hear based on what I've been taught by tradition based on the people whose work I respect and whose opinions I respect. And Betty Carter is

KURT ELLING

one, and Mark Murphy is another, and Jon Hendricks, and Tony Bennett, and Frank Sinatra. But each one of those people—those are four or five radically different singers. They each have their own thing. It's because they're such strong artists that they couldn't help themselves. They had to be that which they are.

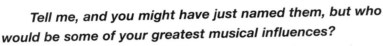

Tell me, and you might have just named them, but who would be some of your greatest musical influences?

Those four or five. And it's my life. It's listening to those recordings. It's all the years of watching my dad conduct different high-school choirs and knock people out. The showmanship and the planning that goes into a concert where people are so happy to be there. I learned a lot of stuff from my dad about how to run a show. And the spirit that that can take on, the spirit of nobility and the spirit of real connection with people.

I've learned a lot from watching old movies of Frank [Sinatra] doing his thing, just swinging really hard. And Tony Bennett, too. I remember when I was like in sixth grade or something, we had our TV, and it was Tony Bennett in a white dinner jacket with the Woody Herman Band. And the band was swinging really hard, but then Tony came out and just hurt everybody—and he just took it to the next place.

I've learned a lot from the cats who are on the scene here in Chicago, who have been open and helped me out and have said, hey, have you tried this side? or wow, that thing you do, that sounds really good.

Let me ask you about something you describe as "ranting," which is where you're basically improvising lyrics. Do you do that every live set, and how do you do it? I mean, it's one thing to improvise musical notes, but quite another to improvise lyrics.

Well, it's a little bit of everything. I certainly rant at least once a night. There are a couple of tunes in the show where it regularly happens.

And yes, it is difficult to come up with new information every night, but the process of doing it has more to do with trying to be open to that experience of what I have in my head. It isn't that you step up, and now you start. It's that you're acquainted with your interior life. It's that you understand what you really feel today and what you really are worried about, or who you love and what that feels like. If you're not able to articulate it, you don't feel it. If you can't articulate it, it doesn't exist. So my opinion is if I can be in contact with my feelings about my experiences going through a given day, and that's the difficult work of the artist on a spiritual level.

Does your typical audience know who you are and know what to expect from you?

No.

No?

Not once I leave Chicago.

Do you think they know that when you're ranting you're improvising?

Not all the time. But how can I say? It's not for me to prescribe the depth of their experience or the nature of their experience. And ultimately it's not important to me that they

know, oh, now he's doing this, now he's doing that. It's really a lot more important for me that they just go and flow with us because the experience people have, it's about them. It's about how open they are and how intent they are on listening and how much they're willing to feel what we're trying to communicate with them.

Do you have specific plans in mind that you can share with me?

I have a number of ideas that are slowly taking form, but I don't have a master plan of what's going to happen four records from now. . . . I'm really just taking everything one situation at a time and trying to make records based on the material that I feel is, first of all, most coherent for the situation I'm in, given the kind of material that I've been writing and that I'm acquainted with. And really telling stories that I feel strongly about when it's time to make that record and have that coherent experience for people.

What advice would you have for someone who might want to make a career in jazz music?

Work hard. Know that it will take ten times more work than you think for it to be worth something.

KURT
ELLING
SELECT DISCOGRAPHY

As a Leader
- *This Time It's Love*—
  Blue Note
- *The Messenger*—
  Blue Note
- *Close Your Eyes*—
  Blue Note

Biography

KEVIN

F rom Kansas City, Kevin Mahogany (DOB 7/30/58) is one of the premier jazz vocalists of his generation. Growing up, he was influenced by the music of his church. Starting out on piano and later moving to saxophone, Mahogany didn't concentrate solely on vocals until his college years at Baker University in Baldwin City, Kansas.

Mahogany has released six recordings as a leader, and each has been critically acclaimed. He also has started *The Jazz Singer*, a jazz magazine devoted to the jazz vocalist. With a style that evokes memories of legendary jazz vocalists, Kevin Mahogany is a truly entertaining artist.

MAHOGANY

INTERVIEW, JANUARY 26, 1998

When did you make the switch from playing saxophone to focusing on vocals?

Part of it was in college because I had to choose which degree program I wanted to be in. I didn't really have to, meaning it wasn't necessary for the curriculum, [but] I had an instructor who wanted me to choose. So when I was in college was when I first started focusing more on vocals than instrumental.

What led you to make the decision, to make the switch?

I just felt like I had reached a plateau instrumentally. And I wasn't interested in a solo-type career on saxophone or clarinet or any other instrument. I enjoyed the values of vocals more in that respect.

Can you point to anything in particular that led you to choose jazz music over any other type?

It was just a conscious decision on my part to come back to a style of music that I had been playing for a long time.

Over the last ten to fifteen years, I believe there has been a resurgence in the popularity of traditional jazz music. Do you agree with this, and, if you do, have you thought about why that might be?

Resurgence, okay. I get into semantics sometimes here, but if there is a resurgence, I don't know why. In some ways, I think a lot of it is just a matter of exposure to it. I think [jazz] has always been good music. That was never the problem.

Early on jazz was the "pop" music of its time. Now it's not in that type of position anymore. But resurgence in the sense of Carnegie Hall Jazz Band, these larger groups and venues that have been establishing grants and funding and knowledgeable people speaking of this topic, I think we've formed a curiosity again about the music that has carried over.

KEVIN MAHOGANY

I think a lot of it is people, as they get older, their tastes change, and jazz is one of those things they tend to gravitate toward a little later in life. And then you also have to give credit to a lot of these younger artists who are playing a music that was born before even some of the older cats were and doing it well. And when people see their peers showing an interest in this type of music, then they tend to take a little more interest themselves, as opposed to, you know, when you used to say, oh, this is old-people's music. You weren't interested in what the old people were listening to, but definitely interested in what your peers are listening to.

Who are some of the younger artists you enjoy listening to?

I would say Nicholas Payton is one of those guys. I think he's an incredible musician. Javon Jackson, Russell Malone, who plays with Diana Krall. Of course, I enjoy listening to Joshua Redman, Mark Whitfield.

I really enjoy listening to the instrumentalists. There aren't as many younger vocalists because to really reach that level of competency, it takes experience which comes with age.

The lifestyle of a jazz musician must be difficult in terms of the amount of time you are on the road, living out of a suitcase a lot of the time. What kind of toll does that take on you?

It's a physical toll. It wears you down physically as well as mentally. It's not easy at all. It can be pretty tiresome. But at the same time, you have to realize that if this is the life you choose, then you have to be prepared to accept those consequences, and that's just part of the consequences, of course, being on the road and traveling.

What advice would you have for someone who is thinking about becoming a professional musician?

I pass on information when we do jazz clinics and while I'm out on the road. For the most part, if it's something you

really want, then I would tell you that you have to persevere. There are going to be good and bad times, more bad than good before any of it works out.

And you have to be prepared for it mentally. But if this is really something you want to do, and if you feel like you just won't be able to live your life without doing this—there has to be that much desire within you, you know, this has to be next to breathing for you—then regardless of whatever happens, then you have to stick with it and stay with it until you make a decision that it is over. You don't let someone else make your life decisions for you.

What are some of your goals?

Just continued growth. I look at my music as a career, not just as a job. And in a career, there's growth. And that's obviously what I want to do.

I've started a magazine for jazz vocalists that I hope will be successful also. It's called *The Jazz Singer*, and that's one of the projects I'm working on. And I'm hoping to eventually develop some other artists or work with some other artists under my own type of production-company type of deal, and just continue spreading the word about vocal jazz and helping some other artists who aren't quite as lucky as I am.

Let's talk about the new jazz museum in Kansas City. Is it getting a lot of traffic, and do you think it is helping to educate the public about jazz?

Yes, on both questions. It is getting a lot of traffic through there, and it's helping to educate the public. They do a lot of clinics and seminars with professional musicians, so in that sense, it helps because those are artists you would not usually have access to. And for a lot of kids, you get to see them free of charge. That's one of the things I think we all had when we were younger—meaning musicians my age—had some clinic or something we went to and got to hear those you usually

wouldn't have access to. I remember a clinic I got to go to and hear Cannonball Adderly, and that, of course, was the only time I got to hear Cannonball Adderly.

So those are the kinds of benefits that the museum is bringing to the inner-city youth and anyone who comes down and partakes. In that sense, [the museum] is very successful, and I think it can continue that way as long as we have people out there who want to learn.

Did you enjoy taking part in Robert Altman's film Kansas City?

Oh, yes. I enjoyed my part in the movie, and I would love to do more if the opportunity came. I don't really consider myself an actor, but I would sure have fun trying. . . .

[Taking part in the movie] was probably better than most of our regular performances because of the caliber of all the musicians all the way around. I'm not saying the bands we play with are bad, but this was a veritable "Who's Who" of musicians. And, of course, you play up to the level of the other artists. And when you've got arguably the world's best musicians on stage, it's going to make you sound probably better than you are.

KEVIN MAHOGANY
SELECT DISCOGRAPHY

Solo Albums
- *My Romance—Warner Bros. Records*
- *Another Time, Another Place—Warner Bros. Records*
- *Kevin Mahogany—Warner Bros. Records*
- *You Got What It Takes—Enja*
- *Songs and Moments—Enja*
- *Double Rainbow—Enja*

Collaborations With Other Artists
- *Kansas City—Original Motion Picture Soundtrack—Verve*

Index

TEMPTED ALL NIGHT

This Large Print Book carries the
Seal of Approval of N.A.V.H.

TEMPTED ALL NIGHT

LIZ CARLYLE

THORNDIKE PRESS
A part of Gale, Cengage Learning

GALE
CENGAGE Learning

Detroit • New York • San Francisco • New Haven, Conn • Waterville, Maine • London

Copyright © 2009 by Susan Woodhouse.
Thorndike Press, a part of Gale, Cengage Learning.

ALL RIGHTS RESERVED
This book is a work of fiction. Names, characters, places, and incidents either are products of the author's imagination or are used fictitiously. Any resemblance to actual events or locales or persons, living or dead, is entirely coincidental.
Thorndike Press® Large Print Core.
The text of this Large Print edition is unabridged.
Other aspects of the book may vary from the original edition.
Set in 16 pt. Plantin.
Printed on permanent paper.

LIBRARY OF CONGRESS CATALOGING-IN-PUBLICATION DATA

Carlyle, Liz.
    Tempted all night / by Liz Carlyle.
      p. cm.
    ISBN-13: 978-1-4104-1485-4 (hardcover : alk. paper)
    ISBN-10: 1-4104-1485-X (hardcover : alk. paper)
    1. Large type books. I. Title.
PS3553.A739T46 2009
813'.54—dc22   2009004816

Published in 2009 by arrangement with Pocket Books, a division of Simon & Schuster, Inc.

Printed in the United States of America
1 2 3 4 5 6 7 13 12 11 10 09

TEMPTED ALL NIGHT

PROLOGUE

Fortune, good night;
smile once more, turn thy wheel.

London, February 1830

It's generally said that a man can be known by the company he keeps, and Tristan Talbot was likely the only fellow in London who went dicing with his manservant. That his servant disdained the Three Shovels as beneath his dignity served only to further illuminate the level to which Tristan sometimes sank. And illumination was direly needed at the Shovels, for the place was dark as a den of thieves.

Actually, it was a den of thieves. And rogues and sharps and bawds — even the occasional gentleman out for a low-class lark. From somewhere deep inside the low-ceilinged alehouse, raucous laughter rang out — one of the sharps, Tristan noticed, who was rapidly plucking his evening's pigeon with a slick hand and a pack of marked cards.

Distracted, Tristan shoved his tankard away, and passed the dice to the chap who sat opposite. Across the room, the door burst open. Through the miasma of smoke and gloom, he looked at the woman who darted in, slamming the door behind her. She was little more than a shadow on the threshold, lingering in a puddle of feeble, bilious lamplight, and looking faintly unsteady on her feet — not that he was any arbiter of sobriety, mind.

He tried to listen to the ribald joke someone farther down the table was telling. But the girl — something in her posture — nagged at him, drunk and detached though he was. Then he realized. It was *fear.* The constant glancing over her shoulder. The gray cloak pulled tight about her, as if she might shrink from view. Lord knew he'd seen it all often enough on the battlefield. Could he have but seen her face, he knew it would have been stark. Pale.

But what business was it of his? Most of the females who chanced to come in here were just birds of the game, looking for a warm hearth and a dram of gin. On the other hand, she wasn't flashing her wares, he thought, flicking her another glance.

Instead, her gaze searched the dingy room as if it were the bowels of perdition.

The Bowels of Perdition.

Now that, Tristan decided, was the perfect name for a public house. Especially in this part of town.

He had a sudden notion to buy one, just for the pleasure of naming it. But like most anything remotely approaching ambition, it would not likely see the morning still in Tristan's head.

He drained what was left of his porter, and watched the girl approach the tapster. She set her hands on the edge of the bar and leaned tentatively across, pleading in a voice so quiet the tapster had to bend over it to hear. He shook his head, and turned away.

Tristan forced his attention back to the game. Foresby had pushed the dice away, his face red with drink and dissatisfaction. The smithy from Clerkenwell — Tristan was too sotted to recall his name — sent them rumbling down the rough wooden trestle table with an artful flick of his wrist. The crowd roared, Foresby dropped his head into his hands, and the smithy swept up a pile of coins, his mouth curling into a stump-toothed grin.

The play went on and Tristan wagered

again, but he couldn't keep his eyes on the table — an invitation to be rooked, and he knew it. By God, the chit was quarreling with the tapster now. Beneath his coat, Tristan's skin prickled.

Foresby cursed, and shoved away from the table. "Damn my luck," he said, jerking to his feet.

Tristan looked down at the two single dots. Foresby was plagued by the twins tonight, that was bloody certain.

"Sorry, old boy," he managed, thumping Foresby's back as he went. "You — Clerkenwell — cast 'em down."

The smithy snatched up the dice again. The play went on as the argument at the bar escalated. The tapster walked away, the set of his shoulders rigid. Somehow, Foresby had joined in. Tristan looked up to see him catch the girl by the upper arm. She flinched and jerked back, but Foresby followed her, pressing her up against the bar.

Tristan had shoved back his chair before he knew what he was about. "I'm out," he snapped. "Play on."

In six strides, he was there. Foresby had his face in the wench's, leering.

"Take your hands off me." Her voice quaked. "This instant, or I shall —"

"Or you shall what?" Foresby whispered.

10

Tristan shoved himself between them. "You're casting next, Foresby," he said amiably. "Quit your wenching, and get back to business."

Foresby smiled over Tristan's shoulder. "Oh, I think I've found something to occupy me right behind you," he said. "That saucy piece has quite a mouth."

Though he couldn't quite see the girl, Tristan could feel her fear rising. "Just let go of her arm," he suggested. "The lads are waiting."

"Mind your own business," said Foresby. "I'm pockets to let, and in the mood for some cheap amusement."

Uglow, Tristan's man, had risen from his chair and moved to the door, his massive form blocking it, his arms implacably crossed. Tristan shoved his leg harder and dropped his voice to a whisper. "I asked you to leave the wench alone," he said quietly. "Now, do you really want to take me on? In this shite hole?"

"You're drunk, Tris," he growled. "Go back to your dice."

"Aye, drunk as a lord," Tristan agreed, setting a heavy hand on Foresby's shoulder. "But sotted and staggering, Foresby, I'm still twice the man you are. Now, shall we

11

step outside? Or will you let the wench pass?"

Foresby let the girl go long enough to shove Tristan. "Bugger off, Sir Galahad."

"Tut, tut," said Tristan. "The unanticipated hazards of an Eton education —" Here, he paused to strike Foresby an upper cut that snapped his head so far back he fell, cracking it against the bar. "— can make a chap too brash with his tongue."

Foresby shoved himself up on one unsteady arm, and touched his bleeding mouth with the back of his hand. "By God, name your second, sir. I demand satisfaction."

Tristan grinned, and waved him up. "Come get it now, old boy," he suggested. "Duels at dawn come too bloody early for me."

After a moment's consideration, Foresby came off the floor and launched himself, fists and elbows flying. It was a short-lived fight. Though neither of them was sober, Foresby was mismatched in height, reach, and suicidal inclinations. He managed, however, to land a blow that swelled one eye and sent blood spurting from Tristan's nose. But when it was over seconds later, Foresby was on the floor holding what looked to be a broken jaw and cursing Tristan to the devil. The girl had vanished.

12

Tristan dragged a sleeve across his nose and looked round to see her cowering deep in the shadows, her face half turned to the wall. The tapster went back to his tankards. Uglow abandoned his guard post. And everyone else went back to their dice and their drink and their cards, shrugging.

Foresby got up and cast the girl a vengeful look. "Slut," he said.

In the gloom, the girl startled like a rabbit. Realizing Uglow no longer blocked the door, she turned to run, but Tristan caught her by the arm and hauled her hard against his side.

"You're going with me," he said, giving her no choice.

He dragged her back through the faint yellow light and into the damp of the unlit alley beyond. Near the door, a barefoot boy sat cross-legged in the thick brume. Tristan dug deep into his pocket, then tossed down a coin. "That you, Lem? Fetch my horse round — and be quick about it."

"Straightaway, gov." The boy leapt up, and vanished into the fog.

Unsteadily, Tristan leaned back against the building and studied her — not that he could really see much. He still gripped her hand, and could feel her quaking with terror. "Haven't been about much in this part of town, have you, love?"

She shook her head. "I — I need ter go," she said, her voice oddly gruff.

He let his gaze drift over her. Something . . . something just didn't fit. But damned if he was sober enough to know what. "Stay put," he said quietly. "I'm taking you home."

"No!" She jerked, and darted away.

He dashed over the cobbles after her and drew her back, surprisingly steady on his feet as the fog swirled around them. "Whoa," he murmured. "To *your* home, love. Foresby's actually one of the nicer chaps you'll meet in this part of town, if you take my meaning."

He felt the fight go out of her then. "Oh. Th-thank you."

Though he couldn't really see her, he cast an appraising glance in the direction of her face. "Now what was it, I wonder, that sent you bolting into the Shovels? The devil at your heels?"

He heard her swallow hard. "It felt like it," she confessed. "Someone . . . followed me here. I could hear their footsteps in the fog and —" She stiffened again with alarm.

Callidora. The great black beast materialized from the fog, her footfalls muffled and disembodied, Lem's head barely reaching her breastplate.

Tristan let the girl go long enough to fling himself up into the saddle, then leaned over and offered down his hand. She looked at it, then flicked a hesitant glance up at him. "Oh, I'd suggest to you take it," he said softly. "I'm drunk, aye, but I'm at least half a gentleman — and that's the best offer you'll get round here."

With a quick nod, the girl dropped her gaze and let him haul her up.

"So you had business in the Shovels?" he asked, lightly tapping Callidora's flanks.

"Just looking for someone."

"Aye, well, you found someone," he remarked. "Got a name, love?"

"No."

"Odd, neither do I," he said lightly. "So, where shall I set you down?"

For an instant, she hesitated. "In the Haymarket, if you please," she finally said, ". . . if that's not too far?"

"Precisely where I was headed," he lied.

The girl said not a word but sat sideways before him, her spine stiff as a duchess. Unable to resist, Tristan leaned forward and drew in her scent. She smelled rather like a duchess, too — and he'd smelled one or two rather intimately. Not even the faintest hint of sweat or must clung to her skin, and her hair held the distinct fragrance of lavender.

She must have sensed his nearness, and glanced back, eyes widening disapprovingly. It was a good thing, he decided, that the gloom obscured his face for he likely looked a horror. He drew back, and spent the remainder of the journey blotting the blood away.

It was rather a miserable ride, too, with her amply rounded arse pressed altogether too near. Despite his inebriated state, Tristan felt Old Reliable starting to rouse, and visions of how he might otherwise have spent an evening with the chit began to dance in his head. Not that he wasn't enamored of Callidora, for he was. But there was much to be said for a good feather tick and a round-arsed wench beneath you.

In the Haymarket, she stopped him near an especially dark corner. He dismounted before her, then lowered her to the pavement with his hands set firmly at her waist. He misjudged the distance, perhaps, lowering her a little closer than was strictly necessary, and a pair of exceptionally well-endowed breasts brushed lightly down his coat front.

Oh, Lord. Old Reliable indeed.

"Thank you," she said in her odd, rough voice.

"It was my pleasure." *Or could be,* twitched his cock. "Look, I don't suppose —"

In the gloom, she lifted her gaze to him. "Yes?"

"I don't suppose your gratitude would extend to warming a chap's bed tonight?"

The girl drew back. "Certainly not."

"Ah, a pity." He flung himself back into the saddle. "I'm a handsome devil, you know, in the daylight — when my nose isn't swollen."

"I'm sorry you're bloodied," she said hesitantly. "I do fear you'll be in pain when you sober up."

Was that a hint of sympathy in her tone? On those rare occasions when his charm failed, he could sometimes persuade a woman to capitulate out of pity. "Listen, are you quite, *quite* sure?" he asked, glancing back down. "I was awfully damn brave back there."

"I said *no,*" she replied more firmly.

He set his head to one side, and looked down at her a little wistfully. "Aye, well. It was worth a shot."

"I daresay." She darted into the fog, then looked back at him. "But . . . But I thank you, sir. For your kindness."

Somehow, he managed to grin and tip his hat with a grand, sweeping flourish — while *not* tumbling back off his horse. At that, she turned round and walked back again. "Tell me, do you just *do* that?" she asked, her voice quizzical. "Just . . . drunkenly proposition every female you meet? And do they actually say *yes?*"

Atop the horse, he nodded, the reins draped lightly through one hand. "A great many, aye — and often when I'm sober."

Clearly this escaped her. "Old? Young? Ugly? What are your criteria for these propositions?"

The fact that the word *criteria* didn't precisely belong in a servant's vocabulary sailed right over his leaden head. "I ask the ones I like," he said after considering it. And after all, he consoled himself, there were plenty of other women who would say *yes* if she did not. The girl, too, seemed to know this. She nodded pensively, then set off up the Haymarket again.

Yes, *plenty of others.*

But she was a lush little morsel, he thought, glumly watching her walk away. There was something about her that was significant in a way he couldn't quite put his finger on. And the hell of it was — for all that she had an exquisite backside and a

18

fine pair of charms — he was probably too drunk to remember her.

Suddenly an odd frisson ran down his spine — an old instinct he'd thought long dead. He sensed a foreboding stillness in the air. Disembodied footsteps in the fog behind him. He looked about. But there was nothing. Nothing but a soldier's intuition . . .

"Miss?" he called after her into the heavy brume.

He sensed rather than saw her turn. She did not speak.

"Be careful," he said. "Won't you?"

There was no answer save the rapid click of her heels vanishing into the fog.

CHAPTER 1

'Tis a vile thing to die, my gracious lord,
When men are unprepar'd and look not
for it.

London, April 1830

Lady Phaedra Northampton made her way
down to Charing Cross, her strides long and
purposeful — mannish, her mother would
have chided — as she weaved her way
through the afternoon jumble of bureaucrats
and shopkeepers. All of them had seemingly
set off in search of luncheon at once,
crisscrossing her path in a sharp-elbowed
frenzy as if conspiring to impede her march
across Westminster. But sharp elbows were
the least of her concerns.

Desperation — and a rash, reckless idea
— had driven her from the house, and
despite the chill, Phaedra had left Mayfair
without a hat. How foolish. And how unlike
her. Now she pushed back the high collar of

21

her heavy gray cloak, cutting a glance over her shoulder. Just behind Phaedra, her maid scurried along, a hand clasped to the top of her bonnet against the wintry gust. Other than that, there was nothing. Why, then, did the hair on the back of her neck keep prickling so? Phaedra tucked her portfolio closer, and picked up her step.

"Ooh, miss, do slow down!" Agnes complained. "I want to find Millie as bad as you, but I'm taking a stitch."

Phaedra glanced back, realizing in some shame that her maid had been practically trotting since they'd left Brook Street. Checking her pace, she noticed a familiar black and yellow barouche pulled to the pavement ahead. *Drat.*

Agnes, too, saw it. "That'll be Lady Blaine, miss," she said warningly.

Lady Blaine, indeed! To Phaedra, she was still Eliza, a little slip of a girl from their home village. Unfortunately, there was no avoiding her.

"Do you think she knows the truth about Priss, ma'am?" Agnes's voice trembled. "Or that Millie's gone missing?"

"She could not possibly," said Phaedra with more confidence than she felt.

"Phae! Oh, Phae!" The wheedling cry rang from the door of a milliner's shop. Eliza came with unfashionable haste toward them, her husband staggering in her wake with a stack of bandboxes which nearly reached his nose. The girl wore a dress of yellow trimmed in deep green, and a green cloak which was a bit insufficient for the weather. The cloak's collar was turned up at a jaunty angle, and embroidered with a chain of white and yellow daises which, Phae inwardly considered, looked hideous, and a little silly.

"Phae, what luck!" said Eliza. "When did you arrive in London? Why did you not tell me?"

"Good afternoon, Eliza." Phaedra spoke cordially if a little hurriedly. "We came up some weeks past."

"Oh, how *exciting* for you!" Eliza had drawn up in front of them, eyes wide. "How very weary you must have been of being stuck in Hampshire the whole winter."

"Actually, I prefer Hamp—"

"But *London,* Phae!" Eliza interjected. "And the *season!* I have scarcely left Town, you know, since my marriage last autumn." She shot a doting glance back at Blaine, a minor baronet so young his forehead was still pimpled. Phae almost suggested he lift the bandboxes higher.

But Eliza was quivering with excitement.

"Listen, Phae! I have quite the greatest news ever. Guess! Guess!"

"Why, I could not possibly," said Phaedra.

"Oh, just try!" Eliza was almost hopping up and down with excitement.

This was the point at which, of course, Eliza would announce that she was *enceinte.* Phaedra had been through this little post-season ritual many times. "Just tell me, Lizzie." She forced a smile. "I know I will be very happy for yo—"

"We're to give a ball!" Eliza interjected, giving Phaedra a swift, explosive hug. "The last Thursday in April!" She set Phaedra a little away. "Now you all must come, Phae! Do say that you will?"

"You know I do not go out much, Lizzie," she said quietly. "I thank you for asking. Mamma and Phoebe will be thrilled to come, I am quite sure."

Eliza's lower lip came out. "Phae, you really are not so firmly on the shelf as all that!" she said. "Indeed, I am quite persuaded that *this* shall be your year."

"I do not need a year." Phaedra smiled. "Besides, Eliza, this is to be Phoebe's year."

"I cannot think, then, why you bother to come each season if you think Town pursuits so very silly."

"And let Mamma come alone?" The words

24

slipped out before Phaedra could bite them back.

"But she would not be alone." Eliza blinked innocently. "There's Phoebe. They would be together."

Yes, thought Phaedra grimly, *and together they would find twice as much trouble.*

But she was being churlish. She gave Eliza another hug. "Do get in your carriage now," she said, urging the girl toward it. "That cloak is not warm enough to stand here gabbing. Come round for tea next week. Phee will wish you to see all her new finery."

Eliza's eyes lit up. "Why, I should be pleased to offer my sense of Town style," she said, stroking her gloved fingertips over her daisies. "How excited the dear child must be. Why, I remember my first season as if it were yesterday."

"That's because it *was* yesterday," Agnes muttered behind her.

In short order, Lord Blaine had tucked his bride back into their carriage, and secured a rug across her knees. "She's still just a flighty little chit in an ugly cloak," Agnes complained as the carriage drew away. "But she's right about one thing."

"I can't think what," said Phaedra, resuming her march toward the Strand.

"This *could* be your year."

Phaedra cut a stern glance over her shoulder. "Don't be ridiculous, Agnes," she said. "Every year is my year."

She was distracted suddenly by a figure in a dark topcoat and an odd, fur-trimmed hat. He pushed away from the shelter of a doorway far to her right, then his head turned toward Agnes and he stiffened. At that instant a black and red mail coach came clattering up from Charing Cross, fresh horses prancing wildly, passengers clinging to the roof, the box, and all but bursting out the doors. When the dust and clatter were gone, the doorway — a tobacconist's — was perfectly empty. She had not even seen his face. "Did you notice that man?" she asked Agnes.

"What man, miss?"

"I thought —" Phaedra shook off the ill feeling. "No, it was no one, I daresay."

Good heavens, she was becoming as fanciful as Phoebe and Mamma. Phaedra forced herself to stroll down to the Strand. She passed her favorite bookseller's — a tatty little shop that sold musty volumes of history and geography. Beyond that was a brass shop where one could buy candlesticks, pokers, and firedogs. A stationer's. A coffin maker and, next door — incongruously — a pie seller, his window trays rapidly emptying. Phaedra turned right into the doorway of a bay-windowed shop, pausing just long enough to read the shop's only marking, a discreet brass plaque:

MR. GEORGE JACOB KEMBLE
PURVEYOR OF ELEGANT ODDITIES
AND FINE FOLDEROL

Agnes, too, hesitated. "He might be dining at such an hour, mightn't he?"

"Then we shall simply wait." Phaedra grasped the cold brass handle and pushed in the door. "Have faith, Agnes. It is possible Mr. Kemble can help us find your sister."

Overhead, a discreet little bell jangled as Phaedra's feet sank into an impossibly thick Turkish carpet. Inside, the shop smelled faintly of camphor, polish, and of the vinegar which was doubtless used to shine the glistening acres of glass cases. Phaedra's gaze swept over a row of Imari vases, a collection of Meissen figurines, and an entire shelf of bejeweled perfume flacons. Oriental carpets hung from the walls, chandeliers dotted the ceiling, and suits of armor were tucked into the corners.

"Mercy," said Agnes. "Looks as if half o' Blenheim Palace got shoved in here."

27

Just then Phaedra's quarry appeared from the rear of the shop, throwing open a pair of heavy velvet panels with more drama than was strictly necessary, and setting the brass curtain rings to jangling. Mr. Kemble was a lithe, elegant man of indeterminate years with quick, dark eyes which always set Phaedra's nerves a little on edge. "Good afternoon, Kemble."

A strange expression passed over his face. "Lady Phaedra Northampton!" he said. "And in my humble shop, no less."

"I wish a moment with you privately, Kemble," she said, laying her portfolio atop one of the glass cases. "A pressing personal matter which —"

The door jangled again. All eyes turned to the slight, dark young woman who entered, her jet eyebrows snapped together. She wore a gown of striped yellow muslin under a sweeping green cloak. Her maid had been left standing just outside the door.

"Hullo, George," she said, nodding at Phaedra as she passed.

"Miss Armstrong," said Kemble smoothly, coming at once from behind the counter. "To what do I owe the pleasure?"

"George, I want another of those heads," she said bluntly.

Kemble folded his hands neatly together

28

and smiled. "My dear Miss Armstrong, you already have a head," he answered. "God only knows the trouble you'd get into if you had a second."

"Lud, not that sort of head," she said, passing easily over the insult. "The white china sort, like the one Papa pitched through the window last year. It was one of the Georges, but I can't think which."

"Ah, the Chaffer bust of George II," said Kemble knowingly. "My dear child, I do not uncrate those by the box load, you know. The Chaffer was rare. And since the marquess saw fit to destroy it in his little temper tantrum, I fear you must all bear its absence stoically."

"What, you can't just get us another?" The girl's black brows snapped back together. "Good Lord, George. It's his *birthday.*"

A sort of verbal fencing match ensued, the girl insisting rather tongue-in-cheek that perhaps Mr. Kemble could conveniently *steal* her a head if he hadn't one in stock, and Mr. Kemble parrying just as tartly that he might as easily steal the Marquess of Rannoch a modicum of self-control, and they'd all be the better for it.

Bemused, Phaedra watched, making several observations at once. Firstly, that the girl had a temper — probably got honestly

29

from her father if he'd thrown such a masterpiece as a Chaffer porcelain through a window. Secondly, that the girl was called "Miss" but her father was a marquess, which meant she was either adopted or illegitimate. And lastly, that the girl was dressed to the nines in Parisian fashions which had cost someone a bloody fortune — but unfortunately, she had topped the gorgeous ensemble with a cloak embroidered in daisies just like Eliza's. It seems so oddly incongruous on such a dark, elegant creature, and with her nerves already on edge, Phaedra let out a little burst of laughter. Swiftly, she slapped her hand over her mouth.

Too late. The argument sputtered away, the girl and Mr. Kemble turning to look at her.

But Phaedra was saved by the ring of another bell, this time not the door, but a loud *clang-clang-clang* that seemed to come from above. A hand bell, Phaedra thought.

"George — ?" boomed a disembodied voice from somewhere above them. "George? What's Jane done with my book now?" There was a muffled series of bumps, then the sound of glass shattering.

"Oh, Lord!" Kemble cast an exasperated gaze upward. "The Sevres teacup."

"It's Maurice again," said Miss Armstrong irritably. "I swear, George, I have never seen a man savor a broken ankle so."

As Phaedra wondered who Maurice might be, Mr. Kemble gave a tight smile, and turned to bow toward Phaedra. "Ladies, I do beg your pardon. It is the housekeeper's half-day and Jean-Claude is at the post office. I shall be but a moment."

He returned through the green curtains, this time leaving them open to reveal a staircase to the right. Through the curtains Phaedra could see a rear entrance flanked with windows, and several worktables set about a cavernous back room. They watched as Mr. Kemble's elegant trouser hems disappeared up the steps.

Miss Armstrong turned to Phaedra and smiled warmly. Phaedra returned the greeting, but hers was a perfunctory smile. She knew Miss Armstrong's type. Pretty and vivacious. Fashionable and flirtatious. The *ton* was littered with their beauty, and with the almost-beauties like Eliza, none of them with two thoughts in their heads worth speaking aloud. Amidst her contemplation, however, Phaedra realized Miss Armstrong was . . . well, *quivering.*

"You were laughing at me!" she declared.

Heat washed over Phaedra's face. "I beg

31

your pardon?"

"You were *laughing*," Miss Armstrong repeated. "At my cloak, I daresay."

"Why, I — I was not," Phaedra fibbed, face flaming.

"Liar," the girl answered on a strange gurgle.

"No, please, I —" Phaedra realized the girl was choking back laughter.

Miss Armstrong burst into giggles. "I daresay I cannot blame you; it's perfectly hideous." Her eyes danced with merriment. "But my aunt Winnie chose it, and I haven't worn it once, and now she's taken notice. So I said to myself, well, it's only George, and after all, *he* must have something to poke fun at, mustn't he?"

"Oh," said Phaedra vaguely. "Yes, I daresay."

But Miss Armstrong was surveying her more closely now. "I'm sorry," she managed. "Have we met?"

"I think not." But politely, Phaedra extended her hand. "Lady Phaedra Northampton. How do you do?"

To her shock, Miss Armstrong squeezed her hand almost affectionately. "So pleased to meet you," she said. "I'm Zoë. Zoë Armstrong — and I *do* know you, come to think on it. Your mother lives opposite Aunt

Winnie in Brook Street. I often stay with her during the season."

"Yes, we reside there when we are in Town," Phaedra replied. "Along with my brother, Anthony Hayden-Worth."

"Oh, yes!" said Zoë brightly. "Mrs. Hayden-Worth left him and went back to America, did she not? A pity, that. One hates to see such a *desperately* good-looking man going to waste."

Phaedra blinked at the girl uncertainly. She was frightfully plain-spoken, but what she said was perfectly true — except that Tony wasn't exactly going to waste. It might be better for all of them if he were. Then Phaedra and Agnes would not be here, dealing with the aftermath, and searching for a needle in a haystack. "Actually, Tony has gone to America, too," said Phaedra abruptly. "I believe his wife wishes a divorce."

"Indeed?" Zoë did not look shocked. "Such things are easier done there, I daresay."

Suddenly Phaedra's thoughts were distracted by something — a shadow, she thought, hovering at one of Mr. Kemble's rear windows. She glanced toward it, and just as quickly, it was gone. Perhaps there had been nothing at all.

But Miss Armstrong was still speaking. "In any case, I used to see you coming home from your morning walk," she continued. "How refreshed and brisk you always looked. At that hour, I am still languishing in my night-clothes, of course, and drinking my chocolate. But I do so admire your zeal."

Phaedra was still trying to figure out Zoë Armstrong when a faint noise sounded at the back door — a sort of whimper and scrape, like a dog wanting to be let in. A vagrant in the alleyway, perhaps. She turned back to Miss Armstrong. It was very odd. Dashing girls like her rarely gave Phaedra's sort a second glance, writing them off as bluestockings, wallflowers, or just hopelessly unfashionable.

Phaedra was all of those things, she supposed. Indeed, she had embraced them.

But Miss Armstrong seemed to find her interesting, and was rattling off an almost apologetic story about how her father had come to break the Chaffer bust in a fit of temper over her cousin Frederica's having fallen for a terrible rake. But Frederica and the rake had married and, it seemed, were living happily ever after. Phaedra had missed most of the details in between.

"And now that my stepmother is with child again," Miss Armstrong finished brightly, "I'm to stay with Aunt Winnie for the season. Papa is hoping quite desperately that this year I will *take* — but this is my second season — well, my third, almost. And I've been in Town most of my life. I really do think it is quite hopeless."

This last was said with a beaming smile which suggested Miss Armstrong was in no way cast down by her lack of marital prospects. The girl went up another notch in Phaedra's eyes. As to Zoë's eyes, they were not just animated, but sparkled with a keen intelligence with which Phaedra would not first have credited her.

"I daresay I could go in the afternoons," Phaedra blurted out.

Miss Armstrong lifted her eyebrows. "Could you? Where?"

"For my walk, I mean," she answered, feeling a little silly. "If you wish to take some exercise, I could go in the afternoon. I . . . I no longer walk in the mornings anyway." That was not wholly true, but Phaedra did not elaborate.

Miss Armstrong's face lit with pleasure. "Why, how very kind you are."

"And I wasn't laughing at your cloak," Phaedra hastily added. "It's just that, well, a friend of my sister's — a rather silly friend, actually — was wearing one just like it not ten minutes past."

"No — !" said Miss Armstrong hotly. "You can't mean it."

"I fear so," said Phaedra, edging ever so slightly into the girlish spirit. "And the two of you are as different as chalk from cheese."

Miss Armstrong's face had darkened. "Devil take Madame Germaine!" she swore. "I knew that old hag had shifty eyes. An original design, indeed! She knows very well I shan't wear so much as a garter if someone else has one like it."

"I'm very sorry," said Phaedra contritely.

"Well, don't be," said Miss Armstrong. "Now I have a reason never to wear the silly thing again. Daisies, indeed!"

Just then, the bump at the door came again — several bumps, in fact, like a slow dirge.

"Oh, bother," said Zoë, walking through the green curtains to call up the stairs. "George — ? *George!* I think you've got a delivery at the rear."

Phaedra followed her into the back, looking curiously over the workroom as Agnes tentatively trailed behind.

Zoë had a hand on her hip, glowering up the stairs. "Oh, bother," she repeated as the thump came again. "Let's just open it."

But as Zoë stepped toward it, the door

suddenly gave, the hasp flying back with a *crack!* A hunched form in a dark coat came staggering in. A gray muffler slithered to his feet, stained blood-red. Eyes wide and glassy, the man collapsed, his knees buckling. He toppled onto the floor along with his fur hat, something tumbling from his out-stretched hand as he fell.

Behind them Agnes stifled a scream.

A thick wooden knife handle protruded from between his shoulder blades.

"Good God!" said Miss Armstrong, drawing back. Then, less steadily, "George!" she cried. "Oh, George! You'd best get down here *now!*"

Her hand over her mouth, Phaedra sank down beside the bleeding man. *The man near the tobacconist.* The hat . . . and his face. Oh, dear Lord. Fighting down a surge of panic, Phaedra stripped off her glove and set her fingers beneath his ear.

"Oh, lawks a'mighty!" whispered Agnes. " 'E looks like 'e's . . . oh, gawd!"

"Hush, Agnes," Phaedra ordered.

"But, oh, miss!" Agnes wrung her hands. "Is 'e dead?"

Phaedra could see an ominous pool of blood oozing from beneath the man's shoulder.

Zoë Armstrong knelt beside her. "Good

God," she said again. "Poor devil."

"Yes, he's quite dead, I fear," Phaedra answered, withdrawing her hand.

"Who do you think he is?" Zoë whispered, turning the man's head with one finger to better show his face.

Phaedra swallowed hard. "I . . . I'm not sure."

"Should we roll him over?" asked Zoë. "Go through his pockets? That's what they do in novels, you know."

"What on earth is going on?" Phaedra whispered, almost to herself. On impulse, she reached for Zoë's hand. "Miss Armstrong, I think we should call Mr. Kemble again. We shall need a doctor — or a constable, perhaps."

But Mr. Kemble was already clattering back down the stairs. "Good heavens, Miss Armstrong, what have you done n—" Then, upon seeing the prostrate body, he said, "My God! What's happened?"

"George, he just staggered in!" Miss Armstrong rose. "I had nothing to do with it, I swear."

"I cannot feel a heartbeat." Phaedra's voice was surprisingly calm given the terror rising in her throat. "Have you a doctor close at hand, Mr. Kemble?"

"Yes, yes, just round the corner." Kemble

was peering down at the body.

"Who is it, George?" asked Miss Armstrong stridently.

Slowly, Kemble shook his head as he studied the man's profile, stark white against the dark, polished floorboards. "No one I know," he said almost disbelievingly, "— and I know *everyone*."

"Everyone who's apt to turn up murdered, you mean," Miss Armstrong added.

Kemble seemed not to have heard her. "My dear ladies, I do beg your pardon," he said. "You must go upstairs at once." Then, springing into motion, he snatched a Holland cloth off a tarnished suit of armor and tossed it neatly over the dead man.

The next half hour passed in something of a daze. Miss Armstrong's maid, who looked to be made of stern stuff, was sent at a run to the Bow Street police station. Despite their protestations, Mr. Kemble whisked Phaedra and Miss Armstrong to his flat upstairs where he seated them in an elegantly furnished parlor, and busied Agnes with the making of tea.

Miss Armstrong glumly watched him go. "This is nonsense," she said, tossing her green cloak disdainfully over a leather armchair. "Tea, indeed! As if we were swooning, faint-hearted females."

"It is rather silly," Phaedra replied, chewing at her thumbnail, her mind racing.

"Now we're missing all the excitement." Miss Armstrong flung herself into a chair and crossed her arms over her chest. "I mean, I'm terribly sorry the poor man is dead, to be sure. But there will be constables now, perhaps even a magistrate. Perhaps we shall have to go and give a statement? He was a gentleman, don't you think, Lady Phaedra? Or something very near it?"

"No, not precisely a gentleman." Phaedra's voice trembled a little. "An upper servant, I daresay."

"Or — or a bank clerk!" said Miss Armstrong. "Or perhaps just one of George's disreputable friends. Perhaps he lied to us."

Phaedra lifted her gaze to meet Miss Armstrong's. "Does Mr. Kemble know a great many such people, Miss Armstrong?"

"You must call me Zoë," she said swiftly. "Especially after *this*. Oh, yes, lots of George's friends are rotters."

Phaedra managed a shy smile. "Have you known him long?"

"Oh, all my life!" she said, waving her hand airily. "When I was little, George was Papa's valet."

"Was he?" said Phaedra, surprised.

"Well, it was mostly an act of mercy on

40

George's part," said Zoë. "To be frank, Lady Phaedra, Papa hadn't any taste."

"Please call me Phaedra," she suggested. "Or just Phae, if you prefer."

Zoë's eyes brightened. "Do you think, Phae, that there shall be something in the *Times* tomorrow about this?" she asked, clutching her chair arms. "Won't that be exciting?"

"I fear your family will not find it so," Phaedra warned. "My mother shall be mortified. Certainly she will not wish me to speak with a policeman. She would think it much too far beneath us."

A grin tugged at Zoë's mouth. "Yes, just think of the scandal!"

Just then, a commotion rose up from below. Zoë leapt up, and strode from the parlor in a swish of muslin. Curious, Phaedra followed.

A man stood at the foot of the stairs — a short, red-faced man wearing a bright green waistcoat fit so snugly across his ample belly it looked as if the buttons might explode. He was trying to push his way past Kemble, who was blocking the steps as they snarled at each other.

The red-faced man pounded a beefy fist on the balustrade. "Aye, an' I 'ave a right ter speak wiv any witness ter a murder," he

41

was shouting. "Stand aside now, Kem, and let me do me job!"

"They did not witness a murder, you dolt." Kemble stuck out a well-shod foot, nearly tripping the man. "The knife was already in his back."

"Even worse!" roared the man, his color deepening. "Now I don't give a cock's tail feather wot manner o' fine ladies these are, I'm ter speak wiv 'em, and speak wiv 'em now!"

"Not in my shop, Sisk," Mr. Kemble retorted. "I shall give you their names as the law requires. Then you may call upon their families and ask permission."

"Aye, and that'll be the end of it," the police sergeant growled. "I'll be sent round back an' left ter cool me 'eels till kingdom come."

"So you would have me permit what their families will not?" Kemble demanded. "You'll rot in hell first, *Sergeant* Sisk."

Her mouth set in a peevish line, Zoë Armstrong started down the steps. "George, don't be ridiculous. We are perfectly happy to —"

"*You,* Miss Armstrong, will not put one more foot down those stairs," Kemble interjected. He half turned on the staircase, his face suddenly unrecognizable in its wrath. "Get back in that drawing room, miss, or by God I shall come up there and put you in it — and your father will thank me for it, too."

Something in Mr. Kemble's expression must have persuaded her. For the first time, the wind went out of Zoë's sails. She turned meekly, and darted back down the corridor, Phaedra on her heels.

CHAPTER 2

A woman is a dish for the gods,
if the devil dress her not.

Despite being on the far side of forty, and possessing a vast quantity of unruly red curls, Lady Swanstead was generally considered a fetching creature. She looked especially fetching, thought Tristan Talbot, with a grape stuck in her navel. A succulent, swollen, sleek-skinned grape just on the verge of being past its prime — and all the sweeter for it. Much like the lady herself.

Just then Lady Swanstead shuddered with pleasure, dislodging Tristan's fine metaphor. The little green orb rolled down her belly, caught the crease of her thigh, wobbled south, then vanished into the soft nest of red between her legs and left her giggling.

"My God, madam!" said Tristan, lifting his head from the breast he'd been nuzzling. "You do know how to challenge a man's

44

viticultural expertise."

"Viti— *What?*" The lady's words ended on something of a shriek, for Tristan was already retrieving his grape. Without the use of his hands.

For Tristan, it was an easy task — and one which took a while. With the morning sun warming his lover's tender skin, and the softness of her expensive bed beneath him, he saw no need to hurry. His fingers, languid upon her thighs, were dark as sin against her pale, pink flesh. She watched him, mesmerized with pleasure, as she had done almost the whole of the night.

Lady Swanstead had begun to cry out most charmingly when the tentative knock came upon her bedchamber door. Fleetingly, Tristan hesitated, lifting his head to look up at her. Her eyes rolling heavenward, Lady Swanstead moaned, and pushed his head back down. Tristan cheerfully obliged her. He was in the business, really, of cheerfully obliging women. It was very nearly the only skill he honed nowadays.

The desperate whisper, however, was harder to ignore.

"My lady!" said a soft, female voice through the door. "My lady, a message."

"Oh, bother!" said Lady Swanstead, rolling up onto her elbows. "Did I not say, Jane, that I wasn't to be disturbed tonight?"

There was an embarrassed pause. "But it's morning, ma'am," came the whisper. "And Lord Hauxton's come — his footmen, I mean — and he's sent his carriage."

"Blast!" Tristan swore, letting his head roll back onto Lady Swanstead's thigh. "How the devil did he run me down?"

But Lady Swanstead was grappling with the message's implications. "Dear heaven, *Hauxton?*" Unceremoniously, she shoved Tristan off, pushed away the fruit platter, and sat abruptly up in bed. "He knows you're *here?* With *me* — ?"

Tristan cast a bereft glance at the fruit, especially that rare, hothouse banana. Yes, he'd had some particularly wicked thoughts of . . .

But his lover was scrabbling about for her dressing gown, which had vanished in the tangle of bedcovers.

"Come, love, don't fret," he cooed. "Perhaps my father has discovered I'm here, but that does not mean he knows *why.*"

Lady Swanstead cut him an exasperated glance. "Oh, for pity's sake, Tristan, don't be a fool." She had risen, and was winding her pink satin bedsheet about her creamy breasts. "When you call upon a lady of the *ton,* everyone knows *why.*"

Tristan let his hand fall. "So it's not my erudite conversation, then?" he said a little flatly. "Well. I am crushed to hear it."

She was gracious enough to blush. With a yawn, Tristan stretched, and rolled onto his belly, sprawling languidly across the lady's bed.

"My lady . . ." came the whisper again. "What must I tell his lordship's men?"

Lady Swanstead gave up all pretense of propriety. "Oh, very well, Jane!" she said tartly. But her eyes, Tristan noticed, had strayed back to his bare buttocks as he plucked another grape from the platter and languidly chewed it. "Lord Hauxton's beloved son will be down in a trice," she finally said. "Tell them they must simply wait."

Drawing her favorite woolen blanket tighter around her knees, Phaedra sat by the hearth in her bedchamber and let her head fall back against her chair. Good God, she was so cold this morning. Utterly bloodless, despite the roaring fire she had ordered built up at dawn.

The stirring of a new day ordinarily heartened her — the hum and clatter of a house coming smoothly to life beneath the touch of a well-trained staff. Phaedra busied herself by overseeing the running of her family's households, and ordinarily took great satisfaction in its success, for in life, she philosophized, one must find satisfaction in what one had, not what one dreamed of.

Behind her, servants were pouring brass cans of steaming hot water into the old slipper tub. Below, in the street, she could hear the wooden rumble of the costermonger's cart drawing up to the kitchen stairwell to unload the day's vegetables. Everything was normal — and yet, nothing felt right. Her trip to Mr. Kemble's had served only to make matters worse.

"Phaedra, darling!" Her mother, the Dowager Lady Nash, popped her head into the room, and made a *titch-titching* sound. "Oh, dear. You've dark circles again. It's that murder business, I do not doubt."

"No, Mamma, I was up reading." Phaedra sat up a little straighter. "Was there something you needed?"

A frown creased Lady Nash's high, beautiful brow. "Yes, I wish to know if we're still short a footman." Her voice was edged with petulance. "Phoebe and I are to go shopping with Aunt Henslow this afternoon. We shall need help carrying our packages."

"We cannot justify four footmen, Mamma,

with Tony away." Phaedra dragged a hand through the heavy, brown-gold hair that still hung loose to her waist. "You must make do with one today. I'll find a new groom in the summer, and move Litten to the household staff. I promise."

But Phaedra's mother believed that a lady's station in life was measured by the number of footmen trailing her through the Burlington Arcade. "By autumn we'll be back at Brierwood. What good will he do us then? Heavens, Phae. We are not precisely *poor*."

"No, we are quite rich." Phaedra forced a smile. "And with just a nip here and a tuck there, we shall stay that way. You must think, Mamma, of your grandchildren, not about impressing your elder sister."

Her mother's lips twitched with irritation. "Oh, very well!" she finally said. "Pinch your brother's pennies to your heart's content, then."

"Thank you, Mamma."

Lady Nash paused to shake a finger at her daughter. "And you, miss, need to keep better hours," she chided. "Reading all hours of the night until you look haggard as an old crone! We might hire three or four footmen, I vow, on what you spend for candles and oil."

When the door thumped shut, Phaedra let her head fall back again. Though she was not quite two-and-twenty, she felt suddenly very old. Yesterday she had watched a man die. Worse, there was a little part of her which could not escape the fear that perhaps, to some small degree, he had died at her hands.

Oh, surely, surely not? Phaedra had wanted only to right a sin; a sin of the flesh and of human weakness. Not her own, no; that one was long beyond her. But God knew the world was rife with others — and this one had fallen to her. Yet thus far, she had failed.

"Miss, are these yours?" Her brow furrowed, a housemaid approached, a folded pile of clothing in her hands. "Shall I put them away?"

Phaedra glanced down at the brown twill gown and rough cloak, and realized her error. "No, Helen," she calmly lied. "Agnes and I were mending yesterday. Leave them for her."

The housemaid bobbed. "Your bath water's ready, miss, whenever you like."

"Thank you, Helen. I'll be but a moment."

Phaedra opened the folio which lay across her lap, noticing as she did so that her hand shook. The eyes of a dead man looked up at her, narrow and faintly exotic in appearance. Mr. Gorsky, perhaps, had possessed a hint of Mongol blood.

Alas, no more.

Phaedra pulled the charcoal sketch from the portfolio. She dared not show it to anyone now. After a quick glance over her shoulder, she tossed it, unseen, onto the fire. The red and gold flames licked up the corners first, curling them into spirals of black ash. Then the center burst into color, exploded, and was gone. Gorsky was beyond helping Priss — or anyone — now.

Twenty minutes after leaving Lady Swanstead — having persuaded her into bed for one last effort at sealing his reputation — Tristan was seated inside the shadowy depths of his father's coach, retying his cravat as they rumbled from the white-walled elegance of Belgravia toward the staid streets of Marylebone.

Despite his having taken his pleasure long and hard with Lady Swanstead, Tristan's mood was a black one. He did not like this business of being run to ground like common prey. But by virtue of his lofty position within the Government — not to mention his nearly incalculable wealth — the Earl of

Hauxton's resources were many, and his will nearly inflexible.

In the past, however, that iron will had done him little good where Tristan was concerned. But things changed, Tristan ruefully acknowledged. Boys grew into men, green recruits into hardened soldiers. And old men died. Thus, as it had ever been said, to everything there was a season — even, perhaps, Tristan's obedience to his father.

Tristan stared through the window at the muted morning sunlight and considered it. Yes, now he was at Hauxton's service, though in the past he had been quick to refuse his father anything — sometimes even the smallest of things, and often out of petty spite, too.

Tristan was not proud of it. He was not by his nature a mean-spirited man. Quite the opposite, in fact. His father himself had often suggested Tristan's greatest fault was his breezy nature — his mother's shocking *joie de vivre,* his father often called it — which was a rather poor choice of words when his mother had been not French, but a hodge-podge of itinerant Mediterranean peasantry. Sadly, her *joie de vivre* had not long survived her marriage, and the only shock — so far as Tristan could see — was that his haughty father had ever deigned to marry her to begin with.

In Cavendish Square, Lord Hauxton's massive mansion sat glowing white in the sun, as solid and impervious an edifice as the man himself had once seemed. The portland stone of its façade reflected not just light, but warmth as well, Tristan noticed as he climbed down from his father's carriage. At the wide, pedimented door, Tristan forced aside his old frustrations and went up the steps. Pemberton, his father's butler, awaited him in the hushed entrance hall.

"My lord." The servant bowed and hastened toward him, his expression relieved. "You have come."

"Afternoon, Pemberton," said Tristan, sliding out of his greatcoat. "How does he go on today?"

In one smooth motion, the butler caught the coat and thrust it at a waiting footman. "Little changed, sir," he answered, waving Tristan toward the grand staircase.

Pemberton's shoes clicked neatly on the polished marble floor alongside the swift, heavy ring of Tristan's boot heels. "The doctor bled him again this morning," he continued, "and left a tincture of laudanum to be taken every hour."

Tristan cut a knowing glance at the servant. "Aye, but he's refused it."

Pemberton's smile was wan. "His lordship says it is merely his body which is failing him," he dryly remarked, "and that he refuses to hasten his mind along with it."

A prudent choice, Tristan considered as he mounted the sweeping staircase. God knew his father's brain was well worth saving. Brilliant and cunning. Incisive. Calm. Utterly Machiavellian. Which made Lord Hauxton one of England's most valued statesmen.

Inside the earl's stately bedchamber his personal secretary and three of his aides were hovering near the bed. Ink pots, papers, and files were everywhere. At the sound of Tristan's heavy tread, the earl lifted his gaze to the door, his expression instantly sharpening. But his face was the color of death, his eyes drawn. And when their gazes caught, Tristan felt a sudden and unexpected rush of some nameless emotion — grief, perhaps, muted and distant though it was.

Hauxton broke the contact and turned to the others. "Leave us," he commanded, lifting a regal hand from the counterpane.

His black-coated staff leapt to attention, fluttering out like a flock of crows flushed off a fencerow, taking their papers and files away with them. One of them paused before Tristan on his way out. "My lord," he said, bowing stiffly at the neck. "You are well, I trust?"

"Well enough, Nebbett," said Tristan. "And you?"

"Quite, thank you," he answered, tucking a leather folio under his arm. His eyes, Tristan noted, were less than warm.

With a lazy smile, Tristan watched him go. "Oh, and give my warmest regards to your wife, Nebbett," he added when the man reached the door. "I have not seen her in an age."

Nebbett looked at him, his mouth tightening. "You are too kind, my lord."

When they were gone, Pemberton closed the door with a quiet *click,* leaving Tristan alone with his father.

"Nebbett doesn't like you," remarked his father dryly. "I wonder why."

Tristan smiled. "I can't imagine."

Hauxton cut him a chiding glance. "Kindly do not antagonize my staff, Tristan," he said. "Nebbett may be a pompous prig with an indiscreet wife, but he is like my right hand — and I can ill spare it just now."

Tristan refused to be baited. He strolled toward the massive half tester bed which was hung with heavy crewelwork curtains. "I collect, sir, that Whitehall cannot function in your absence," he said lightly.

"It seems not." His father's eyes swept up Tristan's length.

"So they must send half your staff up here to bedevil you whilst you're bedridden?" Tristan pressed. "What you need, sir, is to rest and to recover."

"Balderdash!" said the old man, twisting restlessly. "You sound like Pemberton. I am not going to recover, Tristan. We both of us know that. Indeed, I cannot hope to hide it much longer."

Tristan's father had never been one to mince words. Nor was Tristan. "Perhaps not, sir," he acknowledged. "Well. You have my undivided attention now. How do things go on at the Foreign Office?"

"Poorly, sir, very poorly." His father's shoulders seemed to roll forward from the stack of pillows, and even his nightcap seemed to sag. "The Belgians grow unhappier by the day, and now there is trouble brewing in Poland — talk of revolution. Mere murmurings so far, but disconcerting nonetheless."

"Revolution?" Tristan echoed. "Good God, another? Is no one on the Continent happy with their political lot in life?"

"The Poles find the Russian yoke a heavy one, I fear," said his father.

"Have they any chance?"

"None," said his father a little bitterly. "The Russians will mow them down like winter wheat."

Fleetingly, Tristan considered the implication of his father's words. More war, and all the inhumanity it brought with it. Oh, *revolution* was a lofty-sounding word — sometimes even a noble concept — but it was war just the same. The blood of the innocent was just as red. The end result was always the same.

But it was no business of his. Not any longer. Roughly, Tristan cleared his throat. "I am sorry for your troubles, sir," he said. "Nonetheless, I fail to see what could be so urgent as to call me —"

"— from Lady Swanstead's bed?" his father interjected. "A matter which is a vast deal more important than a woman's pleasure, Tristan — something which you might, by the way, consider leaving to *Lord* Swanstead? Pray sit down."

Tristan folded himself rather awkwardly into the small chair by the bed.

His father's gaze turned inward for a moment, as if he saw not the vast, luxuriously appointed bedchamber, but another time and place. "The Home Office is looking into a stabbing which occurred yesterday afternoon in the Strand," he finally said, his voice edged with fatigue. "It is a death which greatly concerns me."

"My sympathies, sir."

"Not that sort of concern," his father snapped. Then, as if remembering to whom he spoke, Hauxton gentled his tone. "It is a matter of some political importance — possibly."

It was on the tip of Tristan's tongue to tell his father he didn't give a damn about politics — *anyone's* politics. He had learned at an early age the treachery of men and their governments. But today his father's color was ashen, his hands tremulous, though he tried to conceal it.

"Of whom are we speaking?" Tristan asked quietly.

"A man called Gorsky," said his father. "A Russian. But his name is being kept quiet for now."

"He was attached to the Russian embassy?" Tristan suggested.

"God, I hope not." Hauxton scrubbed a hand down his long, thin face. "Ostensibly, he was a . . . a sort of business agent."

"Indeed?" Tristan tried to look as if he cared. "For whom?"

"For a rather infamous brothel in Soho, as it happens."

A sour smile curved Tristan's mouth. "Is that why you called me here?" he asked. "My expertise in brothels? I assure you, Father, I need rarely resort to whorehouses. The Lady Swansteads of this world are all too willing to oblige me."

The earl's tremulous hands fisted angrily. "Good God, Tristan, I do not need your frivolity just now."

Tristan paused. "No, you never have, have you?" he murmured, fighting down the urge to walk out. There had been enough of that already, he supposed. "Well, go on. Your dead Russian brothel chap — your concern with him is . . . what, pray?"

His father seemed to shift uncomfortably. "Nothing, perhaps — or perhaps a vast deal," he finally said, his voice still strident. "Damn it all, I hate being confined to this blasted bed!"

Against his better judgment, Tristan took one of his father's cold, thin hands into his own. For a moment, he stared at the contrast, his dark olive skin against his father's pale, bloodless fingers. They could not have been more different — and in more ways than coloring. And yet now, as the end of his father's life neared, Tristan was beginning to feel the faintest stirring of kinship. Not belonging, no — that he would never feel — but it was instead the sense that a part of him was leaving this cold, mortal coil, and the understanding that his life would be forever altered by it. How strange it felt after all these years of believing it did not matter.

"I'm sorry you are ill, sir," he finally said, then tactfully changed the subject. "What does the Foreign Office care about this dead man?"

To Tristan's surprise, Hauxton did not remove his hand from Tristan's grasp. "Do you know the Russian statesman, Czartoryski?"

"The Polish prince?" Tristan acknowledged. "I know of his work at the Congress of Vienna, of course. You are acquainted with him, are you not?"

"I once was," he answered, "when he resided in London as a young man. At that time, there was amongst his entourage a young courtesan named Vostrikova. Some said she was a spy planted by the Russian empress to ensure the prince's loyalty."

"She did not trust Czartoryski?"

His father's smile was dry. "The Russians trust no one," he said. "A wagonload of tinkers could scarce leave Mother Russia's domain without a spy planted in their midst."

"And all this has something to do with the death of this Gorsky fellow?"

Hauxton looked pained. "I am not sure," he confessed. "When the prince last left London, this courtesan remained behind. That was years ago, of course. Over time, she inveigled her way into a great many Government beds, and when her looks began to fail, she opened the brothel in Soho."

"Indeed." Tristan lifted one eyebrow. "How the mighty have fallen."

His father managed a sarcastic smile. "Oh, Vostrikova's is no ordinary brothel," he answered. "It is a very private affair, offering things . . . well, things money can rarely buy. And catering only to those men amongst the highest echelons of power and privilege."

"Ah," said Tristan softly. "Which further explains my knowing nothing of it, then."

Hauxton's smile faded. "No, men of your sort are not invited there."

Men without influence or power — that's what his father meant. Tristan took no offense. He was what he had chosen to be, whether his father liked it or not.

He released his father's grip, and relaxed

in his chair. "I do not see how I may be of help to you, sir," he said, casually opening his hands. "You obviously suspect this Gorsky fellow of some sort of duplicity, but as I said, I do not know him."

His father stared into the shadowy depths of the room. "Gorsky was assassinated in broad daylight," he finally said. "And there were witnesses. Two young ladies of good family."

"Most unfortunate," Tristan murmured. "Did they see the killer's face?"

"I am not perfectly sure what they saw," his father acknowledged. "That is what I wish you to discover."

Suddenly, Tristan understood why he had been summoned. "No," he said firmly. "No, I am sorry, sir. That is what all these new police constables and magistrates are for, I believe."

"Bah!" said the earl. "Utter fools, the lot of 'em."

"You've often said the same of me, sir."

At that, the earl began suddenly to fidget with the gold brocade coverlet, picking almost nervously at a loose thread. "I have never believed you a fool, Tristan. You have a great mind if you would but use it. And your exploits in Greece have proven your instinct for . . . well, let us call it *reconnaissance*."

Tristan jerked from his chair. "Greece proved nothing but my naïveté, sir," he countered. "And persuaded me to mind my own damned business. What do you want of me?"

"Only that which I have wanted these last three years, Tristan," said his father. "I want you to accept a position at the Foreign Office. I want your help."

His father wished him to become one of the black-coated, file-toting crows. It was not the first time his father had pressed him; indeed, it had become a point of contention between them.

"One might better make a silk purse out of a sow's ear," Tristan muttered. "It is out of the question, sir. I've no stomach for politics. You will not persuade me."

"I long ago gave up in trying to persuade you to do anything."

Hauxton watched in silence as Tristan began to roam the room, going from window to window, and then to the small bookshelf by his father's writing desk, lined with volumes of history and politics. As always, he felt trapped in this house. Caged, like a beast, by bars made, not of metal, but of his own childhood longings. His father's unmet expectations. His mother's grief. Oh, he could leave, of course. Nothing held him here — nothing but a sense of duty, a new and somewhat unwelcome sentiment.

He looked down and realized he had wandered to his father's burnished mahogany dressing table; the same dressing table which had doubtless served two or three generations of Talbots before him. His father's pocket watch, seal, and cravat-pin were laid out as if they had just been taken off to await the morrow, when the earl would put them back on again, and return to his office in Whitehall, or to the king's side, or to some foreign nation caught in the throes of a political upheaval which wanted sorting out.

But Lord Hauxton would not be returning to Whitehall. And when next he wore his cravat-pin, it would likely be the undertaker's doing, not his valet's. The knowledge saddened Tristan far more than he might have expected.

It was his father's voice which pierced the silence. "Then at the very least," he said, his voice weary, "will you speak with the families of these girls, get permission to interview them, and see what you can learn? You are charming and handsome — someone whom they won't find threatening. I need to know what they heard. What they saw. Or even sensed."

"Murder is the concern of the Home Office," said Tristan, still looking at the dressing table.

"Indeed, and they have assigned someone," said the earl. "One of Peel's henchmen — a quite competent fellow by the name of de Vendenheim. But the Home Office wishes only to know *who* so that they might provide the killer with a speedy trial and a swift execution."

"And your objectives are different?"

"Quite," said the earl. "I wish to know *why*. And at whose behest."

"And if it was a random killing?" Tristan suggested. "A raving lunatic? Some common cutpurse turned violent?"

The earl fell back into the plump softness of his pillows. "Then I would be deeply relieved," he confessed. "But it is not. I sense it with every fiber of my being."

Tristan picked up the cravat-pin and rolled it pensively between his fingers. "Your political instincts, sir, are unfailing," he said. "But your choice of emissary is not. I fear I cannot oblige you."

The earl swore softly beneath his breath. "God's truth, Tristan, have you no sense of duty?"

The question stung, especially when it had been duty which had driven him here. "Why the hell should I?" he snapped, turning from the dressing table.

His father seemed almost to shrivel before his very eyes. He clutched his hands, an almost childlike gesture, and Tristan felt something rend inside his heart. "Perhaps because I am your father, and I am begging you?" said the earl quietly. "There. I have said it, Tristan. I am begging. Does it please you?"

Strangely it did not. And it struck him that this was perhaps the first time in his life that his father had asked — rather than ordered — him to do anything. Tristan looked again at the withered and ashen man who had thinned to a mere caricature of himself these past few months, and felt the one thing he had never wished to feel for him. Pity.

Or perhaps his father was merely playing clever politics again. A direct order Tristan could flout. But a request from his aged and dying father? No, that he could not.

"Very well," he said at last. "Tell me everything you already know."

The Marquess of Nash was not a happy man. His hands clasped tightly behind his ramrod-straight spine, he was standing before the massive desk in his wood-paneled library, and trying not to curse aloud in front of the ladies, which this afternoon included his flighty stepmother, Edwina, the dowager marchioness, and his two younger half sisters.

"A most unfortunate business," he said, watching his stepmother pour tea. The news of yesterday's unpleasantness in the Strand had fallen upon the marquess's ears early this morning, and he had summoned Edwina and his sisters to his house in Park Lane at once so that he might get to the bottom of it.

His stepmother set down the silver teapot. "Well, I think it perfectly sordid, people getting themselves stabbed in public," she twittered. "I vow, I very nearly fainted when I heard."

Phaedra's cup chattered as she picked it up. "Mamma, pray do not start again," she murmured. "I scarcely think the gentleman meant to flout etiquette by falling dead of a stab wound."

The dowager turned on the narrow settee. "Well, at the very least, Phaedra, they should keep such vile business to the East End where one expects it," she declared. "Phoebe had to fetch my hartshorn —

didn't you, my love?"

"Just so, Mamma." Phoebe's eyes were lowered — spuriously, the marquess was sure.

"— and to think that there was Phaedra!" his stepmother went on. "Caught in the middle of it! And poor Phoebe getting ready to debut."

"I daresay no one will come to my ball now," Phoebe complained, poking out her lower lip. "Phae has ruined everything for me."

"What nonsense, Phee!" Phaedra groaned.

Nash wanted to groan, too. The sad truth was, Phoebe and Edwina hadn't an ounce of common sense between them, and Nash knew it. For years he had depended — perhaps unfairly — upon Phaedra's looking after them. And before that, Edwina's sister, Lady Henslow. Otherwise, God only knew what would have become of the pair. They would have fallen down a well, starved to death, or mortgaged the family estate to buy new hair ribbons. And Tony — for all his political savvy — wasn't much better. Phae was the steady one, and the fact that it had been she in the wrong place at the wrong time was just damned bad luck. He hoped.

"Pray do not be so dramatic, Phoebe," said the marquess. "People love nothing so well as a scandalous story. Now we may oblige them."

"Still, the situation *is* awkward, Nash." His stepmother relished drama. "I daresay Phaedra shall have her name in the newspapers."

"No one in this family," said the marquess tightly, "shall have their name in the papers. I have already spoken to Lord de Vendenheim at the Home Office."

Phaedra hung her head. "Thank you, Stefan."

Lord Nash felt something inside him soften. "You are welcome, Phae." He smiled across his teacup. "No harm has been done, has it? Well, save for that poor devil with the knife in his back. He was Russian, by the way. You doubtless had not heard."

Something strange sketched across Phaedra's face, and was just as quickly concealed.

They passed the remainder of the hour talking about Phoebe's come-out ball, his stepmother darting from topic to topic — food, wine, hemlines, gossip — like the rattle she was. But it was an almost comfortingly familiar sort of blither to which he'd grown accustomed — perhaps even fond of.

"Well!" said Lady Nash, rising once the tea was cleared. "Phoebe has a fitting for her ball gown shortly, and Aunt Henslow will be waiting."

Nash turned his gaze on Phaedra, and steepled his fingers pensively. "What of you, my dear?" he asked quietly. "Are you to have something new to wear to Phoebe's come-out?"

His sister shook her head. "I had not thought to go to any balls this season."

"It would be my greatest pleasure, Phae, to purchase a lavish new wardrobe for the both of you," her brother pressed. "Do please consider it. We shall call it a gift from a doting brother."

"Thank you." Phaedra looked away. "I have considered it already."

Lady Nash pursed her lips and shot her elder daughter a dark, cutting look, but said no more.

Nash forced a smile. "Then if you've no fitting today, my dear, perhaps you can be persuaded to remain behind?" he lightly suggested, motioning toward the nearby chessboard. "I haven't had a worthy partner in an age."

"Oh, Nash!" His stepmother patted his hand affectionately. "With a child in the house and another on the way? You cannot possibly have any time for chess!"

"Very little, 'tis true." Nash rose, his smile

still muted. "Will you stay, Phaedra?"

"Yes, of course," Phaedra was wise enough to recognize an order from the head of the family, however politely it might have been issued.

Soon, in a bustle of reticules, hats, and shawls, with cheeks kissed all around, Lady Nash and her youngest daughter took their leave. Her spirits low, Phaedra followed her eldest brother to the back of the library, to the elegant marquetry table beneath the windows at which they had so often played. Phaedra scarcely spared it a thought, for her mind was elsewhere, numbed by worry, and by a measure of grief for the dead man. Whatever else he might have been, he was a human being — something others seemed all too willing to forget.

"Is there anything else, Phaedra, which I should know about what happened in the Strand?" asked Stefan quietly. "Something, perhaps, you did not wish to say in front of Edwina and Phoebe?"

Fleetingly, she hesitated. It would have been such a relief to unburden herself to her elder brother. But she dared not. "No. There is nothing else."

"Good." Nash smiled wolfishly.

Oh, she was in trouble. She knew it.

His hands were clasped rigidly behind his

back again as he strolled along a wall of paintings. Phaedra knew it had always fallen to him to be the disciplinarian. The one who fixed their scrapes and covered over their scandals. He also put roofs over their heads and paid their allowances, and the fact that Stefan was eldest had little to do with his position of leadership. He was by his nature a strong man, a man one did not willingly anger. And to almost everyone — even to her mother, Tony, and Phoebe — he was *Nash* — more title, it often seemed, than mortal man.

Was she in trouble? Was Stefan to scold her for what had happened at Mr. Kemble's?

No, she thought not. Her brother was a fair man. And he, above all of them, understood her, though he was many years her senior. Even her mother had often remarked that of the four of them — Stefan, Tony, she, and Phoebe — only Phaedra and Stefan were remotely alike. Phaedra often knew what Stefan was thinking — sometimes before he did. Moreover, he confided in her. *Trusted* her to help him guard the family. And until now, they'd had no secrets from one another.

"This isn't about yesterday, is it?" she said, clasping her hands in her lap.

He stopped pacing. "No, it is about the gown, actually."

"The gown?" Her brow furrowed.

"The gown you are *not* being fitted for this afternoon," he clarified.

At that, Phaedra leapt up. "Oh, please, Stefan, not you, too."

He closed the distance between them swiftly, and caught her shoulders in his hands. "Phae, why not? I . . . I could work something out. Lady Henslow, perhaps, could help us?"

"No." Her voice was bitter. "Aunt Henslow has helped quite enough already, don't you think?"

His lips thinned, and still holding her shoulders, he shook his head. "God's truth, I blame myself for all this," he said. "Phae, my dear, you are not yet two-and-twenty. Your whole life — a normal life — could be before you. Marriage. A family, perhaps."

She jerked from his grasp, and went at once to the window which looked out over Park Lane. "Yes, now that you have Xanthia, your notions about wedlock have rather altered, haven't they?" Her voice was laced with bitterness she could not hide. "You have become conventional."

"You say that as if it is a dread disease."

She shook her head. A deep, boundless

sorrow seemed to swamp her, dragging her heart into the pit of her stomach and leaving her awash in grief and shame. Instinctively, as it so often did, her hand went to her belly, resting over that dark void inside her womb. Yes, it was easier to pretend. To pretend that it did not matter. To cloak herself in her wit and her intellect, and tell herself that she felt whole and happy as she was. That a part of her was not missing. Her face must have crumpled a little.

"May I no longer count on you, Stefan?" she whispered. "Will you gainsay me now — after all these years of standing by me?"

His expression suddenly altered, his brown eyes going soft. He drew her into his arms, and she went willingly. "Never, *zaichick*," he murmured against the top of her head. "But just know that — if you wish, and only if you wish — I will arrange things for you."

Phaedra was glad Stefan could not see the tears which had sprung to her eyes. "Arrange what?" she snuffled, clinging to him as she had not done since she was fifteen.

"A husband, Phae," he murmured, tightening his embrace. "Someone good and kind."

Phaedra laughed through her tears. "You mean some desperate old widower with eight children."

"No, I mean someone who might give you children of your own."

She shook her head, her hair scrubbing his chin. "It won't work, Stefan."

"A marriage can be arranged, my dear, at the very least."

"Stefan, you *promised*," she whispered.

"And I shall keep that promise," he said quietly. "Do you wish me never to speak of this again?"

"That is precisely what I wish."

She felt his arms begin to slide away. "Very well." His voice was sad. Resigned.

"I know you mean well," said Phaedra, dashing away her tears with the back of her hand. By God, she would not be a weak and sniveling thing — not even in the face of Stefan's sympathy.

Her brother tipped up her chin. "But do buy some new gowns, Phae," he said firmly. "A whole wardrobe, actually — one with a little color this time — or at the very least, a gown for Phoebe's come-out, and another for Xanthia's gala in June. Please do not disappoint me in this."

"And that is an order?"

He ran the pad of his thumb beneath one teary eye, taking care not to smudge her spectacles. "For your sake," he repeated. "Your not being seen about town with your sister might well cause more speculation than the alternative."

"If you insist, then."

"I do," he said. "Now, chess?"

Phaedra shook her head. "You are very kind," she said. "But I have much at home to do."

"Ah, linen to sort or a housekeeper to chide, I do not doubt." Her brother smiled warmly, and much of the tension seemed to vanish from the room. "Or a book, perhaps. Busy Phaedra, always obsessed with your duties and your dusty tomes."

"Today it is a book." Phaedra brightened her expression. "I am rereading the Langhornes' translation of *Plutarch's Lives.* I feel a little guilty, for it is much faster-going than the original Greek."

But it did sound desperately dull, she inwardly admitted, when said aloud. And later, looking back on it, Phaedra realized that her entire life had become dull — that she had made so, for there was a sort of comfort in predictability. What she did not know, however — and what was to prove utterly *un*predictable — was how swiftly and how thoroughly that quiet life was about to end.

CHAPTER 3

Mark how his virtue, like a hidden sun,
Breaks through his baser garments.

In Long Acre that afternoon, Tristan dressed with a good deal more care than usual, biting back impatience as he did so. The day was to take him to staid Mayfair instead of boat racing upriver on the Thames with some raucous, rough-elbowed companions as he'd planned. There, they would have tossed out blankets in a sunny, sheltered spot along the riverbank, and spent the afternoon skulling against one another, and wagering as to which of them would have the day's strongest back.

There would have been tankards of cool ale from the nearby public house, and undoubtedly one or two of the tavern wenches would have come out to cheer them on. But today, instead of old breeches and a nice, baggy shirt worn soft with age, he was to rig himself out as a gentleman. There would be no buxom wench with her round, squirming rump planted squarely in his lap and her arms twined round his neck.

Instead, he was to call upon the elder of the two ladies who had had the grave misfortune to witness the murder in the Strand — a bluestocking of uncertain age. Tristan sighed, and reached out his hand for a fresh neckcloth. He hoped he did not end the day strangled with it. Lady Phaedra Northampton, he was forewarned, was the younger sister of the Marquess of Nash, a hard-eyed, unrepentant turfite whom Tristan knew from racing circles. And Lord Nash, though reportedly mellowed by his marriage, was not a man whom one lightly angered.

Perhaps Tristan was destined to become the diplomat his father had long dreamed of. He finished off the knot, and let his hands fall.

"Crumpler-peg, m'lord?"

Tristan looked around to see his man, Uglow, thrusting something out between his sausage-like fingertips. "Thank you."

The cravat-pin stabbed securely into place, Tristan peered at himself in the old, mottled mirror which hung haphazardly above his washstand. He had never bothered to purchase a proper cheval glass or any other decent sort of mirror in which one might examine oneself. Other than to pay his tailor's bills in a relatively timely fashion, and to forswear the wearing of any shade of pink, Tristan had never given much thought to his wardrobe. Suddenly, it occurred to him that relying solely upon Uglow's somewhat dubious opinion today might be a mistake.

"How do I look?" he nonetheless asked, giving his cuffs a neatening tug.

The crease in Uglow's slab of a brow deepened. "Togged out ter the nines, sir," he finally decided. "A right proper gent."

Tristan laughed. "First time the phrase has been applied to me, I daresay," he remarked. "Now check the boots. Like mirrors, are they? Today, old boy, they'd better be."

"Aye, but not like *your* mirror," said Uglow with umbrage. "I thinks I knows, sir, 'ow to give a boot a proper lick by now."

"Sorry, Uglow," he said. "Guess I'm out of sorts."

Uglow grunted, and handed Tristan his coat. He slid it on; then, at the last possible minute, Tristan returned to his makeshift dressing table, and pawed through the top drawer until he found his small leather jewelry case. The trefoiled and befeathered crest of the oh-so-noble Talbot family winked up at him in solid gold. Tristan slid his signet ring on a finger of his right hand, marveling as he did so that he could not even remember the last time he'd worn it.

Ten minutes later, Tristan was thundering down the narrow flight of stairs which led from his maisonette to the street. At the livery stable near Covent Garden market, Callidora was saddled and waiting. It was but a short walk to the home of Anthony Hayden-Worth, Lord Nash's stepbrother, with whom Tristan's quarry made her home in London. But Callidora made a striking first impression with her black satin coat, flashing hooves, and wide, snorting nostrils. She was big, too, for a mare so elegantly boned; sixteen hands of broad-chested, long-legged, sidestepping witchery.

A former cavalry horse, Callidora had come home with him from Greece, in part because Tristan could not bear to leave her behind. She was half Arab, the black part — and half Andravida, the big, broad part. And as with Tristan himself, perhaps, her looks were deceiving. Despite all the flash and show, Callidora was no longer young. She was also tame as an overfed housecat, and totally subservient to his commands.

Usually. Which just proved a man could never entirely trust a female.

In Brook Street, he had almost reached Grosvenor Square when Callidora went prancing sideways, eyes inexplicably shying at two newsboys on the corner. Suddenly, a cry rang out. Newsprint and fists exploded. One chap shoved the other up against a costermonger's cart, flailing unmercifully. Wind sent a sheet of newspaper flapping low across the street. Still dancing, Callidora tossed her head and skittered across the road into the path of a coal wagon turning the downhill corner from Duke Street.

"Whoa!" cried the driver, drawing up hard. A scuttle's worth of coal went cascading over one side.

Across the square, a tall, elegant lady in a gray dress froze in midstep, then drew back onto the pavement, her eyes rolling.

As Tristan tried to settle his dancing mount, the costermonger leapt down. He tried to part the two chaps — the larger of which was rather a brute. But the costermonger was old and bent. The big fellow swung at him. The costermonger jerked, hitching up against his barrow, dislodging a peck basket laden with parsnips. A cabbage tumbled down with it. Coal, cabbage, parsnips; all of it rolled beneath Callidora's feet as the men fought on. The horse reared high, coming down mere inches from the cart just as blood exploded over the old man's coat.

In a trice, Tristan was out of the saddle, stripping off his gloves as he went. "Keep her head," he ordered, pressing the reins into the old man's hands.

Wading into the fray, Tristan yanked the larger fellow off the small chap effortlessly. The brute whirled and gave him a fist in his face for his trouble. "Bugger off!"

Head snapping and blood stirring, Tristan threw back a good left. He caught the chap square in the right jaw. "By God, I'll teach you to pick on someone smaller," he said, grinning.

The thug grinned back, and came at him.

The coalman jumped down, shaking his fist. As Tristan and the brute circled about, throwing punches, the coalman began to shout that someone needed to pick up his lost wares. Callidora was still wheeling her hindquarters, her eyes wild, her velvety black nostrils big as the parsnips she trod upon.

Just then, the big chap lunged. A tactical mistake. Tristan was slender, but he was tall and strong — and a much better wrestler than boxer. After a few flips and flops, and a great deal of grunting, he had the bully down if not out.

"Ho, there!" a deep voice boomed behind Tristan. "What's all this?"

Tristan was astride the chap, trying to wrestle him into submission, but the smaller fellow had plucked up, and began kicking his assailant repeatedly in the ribs.

"Ow, ow!" The bully tried to roll Tristan off. "Le' me at the li'l shite!"

The small chap kicked him again.

"Stop, damn you!" Tristan ordered, cutting a glance up at the lad. "Stop kicking hi—"

It was his last clear, conscious thought. Tristan collapsed, rolling to one side. A great, roaring blackness rushed in.

When he awoke — mere moments or perhaps even days later — it was to find the rooflines of Brook Street wheeling above him like a giant jigsaw puzzle, interspersed with shafts of twinkling sunlight, and an oddly split vision of the lady in gray. She looked down at him indignantly, lips wordlessly moving, blue eyes swimming behind a pair of stern gold spectacles. Tristan decided to blink until the vision went away. Christ, his head hurt.

"Oi, Mr. Pimkins!" said a cockney voice through the haze. "Wot a constable you are!

Yer clouted a proper gentry-cove."

The swish of skirts rattled near Tristan's ear. "Stand back, you fools," said a sharp, female voice. "Stand back, I say. Mr. Coalman, get this gentleman up, if you please."

Someone — perhaps a pair of someones — hefted Tristan up beneath his arms and hauled him to his feet. The lady in gray appeared to be gone, and so was his hat. Light, cool fingertips were riffling through the hair on the back of his head.

"Well, this is rather a mess." Ah, the tart-tongued female was behind him now. "And it's going to need a stitch."

Tristan moaned, and tried to sit down, but he was hitched back up again.

"Oh, Mother Mary and Jesus!" A man in a blue police uniform swam before Tristan, all bulbous nose and fretful eyes. He still clutched the tool of Tristan's undoing — a heavy tipstaff, its royal coat of arms glittering in the sun. "Gawd, they'll 'ave me job for this!"

"Stop whimpering, Pimkins," said the female, stepping round. Her voice was husky; a seductive bedroom sort of voice.

Tristan shook his head, and the newsboys came fully into focus. So did the female. Yes, it was the lady in gray who'd been rolling her eyes on the corner. Her throaty voice

84

aside, Tristan did not like disapproving females; he much preferred the cheerful, willing sort. He leaned back against the costermonger's cart and tried to blink her away again.

But the lady in gray was in command now. "Clear these lads off Brook Street, Pimkins," she ordered, stabbing her finger at the pair. "Brawling in the street, indeed! If I ever see either again —"

"Oi, it's my corner!" the larger lad interjected.

"Is not!" cried the second.

And if I ever, the woman ground out, "see either of you this side of Grosvenor Square again, my brother shall have the both of you before the magistrate. Do I make myself plain?"

The smaller of the two hung his head.

"Well, go on!" The police constable pointed up Duke Street. "You 'eard the lady. Off with you."

With one last resentful, sidelong glance, the hulking bully slunk away, seizing up his bundle of newspapers by its twine cording as he went.

"But it's *my* corner, m'lady," cried the smaller chap, shuffling one foot. He was a slight lad of perhaps seventeen in a shabby brown coat, a head shorter than the lady in gray, with the heels of his boots worn down to nearly nothing. "You know it's my corner, for you see me out 'ere every day."

Tristan had given up trying to blink the woman away and was watching her now, mildly fascinated. Her heavy chestnut-gold hair was twisted up in a simple arrangement, but despite her dull gray gown, she could never have been mistaken for a servant. No, she was every inch a wellborn lady — a lady who was still tapping one toe. The angry glint in her eye, however, was relenting.

"You shouldn't have been kicking a man when he was down," she finally said to the newsboy. "That's hardly cricket, is it? If you'd fetched Pimkins to begin with, we would not have this — this *addled gentleman* to deal with."

"Aye, m'lady," said the fellow glumly.

"I'm not addled." Tristan tried to prove it by shaking himself off and standing up straight.

The woman cut him a disdainful glance. "You may go up to Oxford Street for the rest of the month," she said, still addressing the newsboy. "Hawk your papers there."

"Aye, m'lady, but there's a score o' blokes hawking Oxford Street," he said. "This is my corner. An' I got a sick mother and three starving sisters ter feed as is."

The lady glowered. "Have you indeed?" she said. "And do not lie to me, for I shall discover the truth."

"Aye, she will, too," Tristan muttered grimly. "They always do."

The lady shot a disdainful glance at him, lifting one brow. "What do you know of horses?" she asked, returning her gaze to the lad.

Again, the shuffling feet. "A bit, m'lady."

Aye, the arse from the ears, perhaps, thought Tristan.

The lady sighed. "Well, you can shovel manure as well as anyone, I daresay," she muttered. "Go round to the mews and ask for Feathers, the coachman. We've need of a groom."

"Yes, m'lady." The fellow's eyes widened, and he tugged on his forelock. "Th—Thank you. And God bless you." Then he darted away as if he feared she might change her mind.

Tristan dragged both hands through his hair. The throb in his temples was fading, only to be replaced by a deep, settling ache at the base of his skull. Oddly, a pair of footmen had come down from a nearby house. One had gathered up the coal and the vegetables, and the other had taken charge of Tristan's mount.

Suddenly, the lady's gaze turned to Callidora, narrow and oddly assessing. "Go back to your watchbox, Pimkins," she said absently. "I shall see to this gentleman's head."

"Aye, my lady."

At last, she looked back at Tristan. Whatever it was about the horse which had distracted her was apparently forgotten. "Can you walk, sir?" she asked, her voice perhaps a little gentler. "Or may one of the footmen help you?"

"I'm fine, ma'am," he muttered. "Thank you."

"You are not fine." She set one small fist on her hipbone. "You are bleeding. And likely concussed — if you actually have a brain in that pretty head of yours." This last was added under her breath.

"I heard that," said Tristan, rubbing one temple with his fingertips.

She narrowed her eyes. "Come with me, sir," she said more authoritatively. "That wound must be seen to."

Tristan was looking about, trying to get his bearings. "Thanks, but I've a call to pay hereabouts."

"Very well, suit yourself," she said, lifting both hands. "You are obviously hardheaded. But I do hope, sir, that you are aware you look a fright. Your hands and knees are filthy, and blood has soaked the back of your collar."

Tristan had not been aware. He looked down to see that Uglow's fine boot polishing had been all for naught, too. *Damnation.* He considered walking to his father's. No, better to take his chances with the lady in gray. His father might become apoplectic, and in his weakened condition . . .

"If I might just wash up a bit, ma'am?" Tristan suggested, returning his gaze to her sharp blue eyes. "I daresay I should forgo my call for today."

Her mouth twitched almost charmingly. "I would recommend it, yes." She lifted her hand and one of the footmen came running.

"Yes, Lady Phaedra?"

"Be so good as to help this gentleman into the house, Stabler," she said. "Then fetch a basin of hot water and some towels. The back parlor, I think, will do nicely."

But Tristan barely heard the last.

Lady Phaedra.

Wasn't that the name? Or was he indeed addled?

He cocked his head a little to one side. "You are —" he began uncertainly.

She looked at him, and arched one delicate dark eyebrow. "I am what?"

"You were in the Strand yesterday," he said more certainly. "When — yes, when that foreign chap got himself stabbed."

She lost a little of her color then, and visibly stiffened. "Indeed," she murmured in her low, throaty voice. "One begins to wonder if one has become a magnet for violent lunatics."

With that, she whirled about, the hems of her gown furling out to reveal a pair of slender, well-turned ankles, and just a hint of a lace-trimmed underskirt. Intrigued, Tristan followed her across the street to the town house from which the footmen had come. Her spine remained stiff as a poker.

Lady Phaedra went up the steps before him, and to his pleasant surprise, her gray skirts slithered nicely over a lush, round arse which seemed somehow out of character, given her dowdy gown and disapproving expression. And something about her . . . yes, there was something vaguely familiar.

She turned to thank the footman, who now held the door, and Tristan realized in some shock that she really was quite remarkably pretty, with legs that must have gone on forever. As if it were second nature — and it was — Tristan's mind began to consider his options. Or perhaps it was not his mind, but another part of his anatomy altogether. But to Tristan's way of thinking, all women had potential. This one, perhaps, a great deal of it.

Yes, divested of that drab dress, with her thick, chestnut-gold hair down around her waist . . .

Oh, good Lord! His head still hurt like the devil. He still had the burden of his father's mission hanging over him. And Lady Phaedra Northampton was still Lord Nash's younger sister — younger *unwed* sister, he added. Indeed, the girl could not have been five-and-twenty, despite what he suspected were her efforts to appear otherwise.

She escorted him into a small parlor. "The light will be better in here," she explained.

Though the front rooms of the house, Tristan had noticed, were grand indeed with French furnishings and a generous amount of marble and gilding, this room was furnished with soft, well-worn chairs, an ancient game table, a great many books and magazines, along with a rug in shades of deep red and gold which was comfortably worn.

Once inside, she wisely left the door open, and went at once to draw the brocade draperies wide to the sun. Her motions were quick and neat, he noticed. Efficient. But not unpleasant. The actions of a woman with much to do — and a vast deal of experience doing it, he thought. A serious-minded woman. Oh, far too serious. Tristan considered *that* a challenge.

"Kindly remove your coat, sir," she said, going to an old walnut cupboard and throwing open the doors. Tristan did so, watching her assessingly. She seemed awfully comfortable ordering a chap to take his clothes off. And not the least afraid of him. Perhaps there was hope . . .

No. There was no hope. None. *Stop!*

But the devil in Tristan goaded him. "Lady Phaedra, this is frightfully risqué."

She turned about, skirts whirling again. "I beg your pardon?" she said stiffly.

"A gentleman never undresses in front of a lady to whom he's not been properly introduced." Tristan flashed his best shameless grin — the one which never failed to charm.

It worked. A faint glow flushed up her cheeks. "You already know my name, I collect," she said coolly. "What is yours?"

Tristan swept off an imaginary hat, and made her a presentable leg. "Tristan," he said. "Tristan Talbot, ma'am, at your service."

For an instant, she froze. "Tristan?" Lady

Phaedra murmured. Then, lifting one shoulder almost imperceptibly, she retrieved a basket of mending from the cupboard and swept across the room toward him. "Pray be seated. I wish to look at your head."

She tilted her head toward a low-backed chair which was turned opposite the bay window, but he was fleetingly distracted. A little yellow garter trimmed with white lace lay atop the neatly folded mending, the little silk rose in its center hanging by a loose thread. He flicked a quick glance up at her, saw her rush of color deepen, and looked back again. *Hers.* Yes, as incongruous as it seemed, the delightful confection was hers. Now that was interesting.

"Just some warm water, ma'am, and a little privacy in which to tidy myself will do," he said more seriously.

"Nonsense," she answered. "You are going to need someone to gently cut your hair and bathe away the blood. And then, I think, a surgeon will be in order. You are going to need a stitch or two to pull the wound together."

"Thank you, but I haven't time," said Tristan. "Besides, I'm sure I've suffered worse."

"You've taken multiple blows to the head, then?" she remarked. "Why am I not surprised?"

"Aye, a great, thick-headed skull like mine is occasionally good for something," he answered, a wry smile tugging at one corner of his mouth.

"Nonetheless, you must be stitched."

"I wouldn't bother," he said. "After all, as you point out, there's probably not much of a brain in there. And all that brawn's likely padding it."

She tilted her head, and eyed him like an irritated governess. "Come now, Mr. Talbot," she said. "One mustn't be a coward."

Tristan laughed. "I'm no coward," he said. "I'm in a hurry."

The lady pursed her lips. "Very well," she said. "Then I shall do it."

That gave him pause. Then, "Fine," he said. "Have at it."

At that, Lady Phaedra faltered a little, and set the basket down.

He'd called her bluff, he realized. "Have you ever stitched anyone up?" he asked more gently.

"No," she admitted.

Tristan shrugged. "I have," he said. "It's no great thing. Have you any brandy?"

Her countenance brightened. "Yes, that might dull the pain, mightn't it?"

"Actually, I meant for you." He looked at

94

her and grinned.

She pursed her lips again, but humor glinted in those keen blue eyes. "Sit," she said as if he were a disobedient mongrel.

Well, what harm was there, really, in playing along? After all, he *had* come to talk to her. And she was dashed pretty in a classic, somewhat rigid way. The door was open, and servants were passing back and forth. Perhaps because of her age — or her demeanor — no one seemed alarmed at his presence in her company.

She was tapping one toe, her gaze pensive. "I'm curious, Mr. Talbot," she said. "Have we met before?"

"I can't think where," he said honestly. He would have remembered those gorgeous eyes. That bedroom voice.

Just then, the footman returned with a basin, a brass water can, and some small white towels draped across his arm. A second servant followed with Tristan's lost hat, now freshly brushed, and placed it top down upon a small table behind the door. The gloves Tristan had so impulsively stripped off lay neatly draped over the rim. When the water and towels were set down, Tristan's coat was wordlessly whisked away — to be shaken and brushed, too, no doubt.

Someone had trained the staff very well indeed.

"Mr. Talbot?" his hostess pressed.

"Oh, why not?" he said when the servants vanished. "A chap ought to play his weakened condition for all it's worth, I daresay. After all, a pretty girl's ministrations could hardly go amiss."

At that, her face warmed fiercely. She stabbed a finger at the chair. "Sit, please, with your back to the light."

This time Tristan did as he was told, though he was loath to give up his vantage point. Lady Phaedra Northampton had a beautiful blush — the innocent sort of pinkish rush which started along her cheekbones, then deepened. The sort of blush which the ladies of his acquaintance were scarce capable of, unless it came out of a paint pot.

That thought brought home to him again his hostess's marital status. "Is your mother at home, Lady Phaedra?" he gently probed. "Perhaps you ought to fetch her."

She stood behind him now, pouring the water into the basin. "Untie your cravat, please," she said. "Then bend your head forward, but gently."

He did so, their hands brushing as she reached around him to unfurl the cravat

96

from about his neck. Her touch was cool as she unwrapped it, her warmth hovering just behind his back. She stepped to his side, neatly folding the linen strip, the center of which was indeed badly bloodstained, and laid it gently across a chair. Her fingers, he noted, were long and thin, her nails cut short.

"Your mother, Lady Phaedra?" he repeated.

She returned to tuck one of the towels round his neck. "My mother is out, Mr. Talbot," she said, stabbing the cloth round the inside of his collar. "And the door is open, with servants going to and fro. So if the two of us remain here together — even given your shocking state of dishabille — I think I can safely assure you that no announcement of our betrothal will be forthcoming."

"And you don't even sound disappointed about it," Tristan teased as he listened to her wringing out the towel. "Are you this unaffected by all the gentlemen who come calling on you, Lady Phaedra?"

For an instant, she hesitated. "Do you mean to mock me, Mr. Talbot?" she finally said, sounding a little breathless. "You are hardly a gentleman who's calling — well, not in the way you suggest. Indeed, nothing could be more ludicrous."

"Ludicrous?" he countered, not even sure why he goaded her. "How you do wound me, Lady Phae— *Ouch!*"

She had touched him lightly with the moistened towel. "You have wounded yourself, Mr. Talbot," she returned. "You were wrestling in the street like some common thug. Some would say you got what you deserved."

"Well, perhaps I am a common thug," he suggested lightly. "But I wasn't about to let that big chap beat the smaller one senseless."

Lady Phaedra kept bathing his wound. Could he but see her, Tristan was sure her lips would have been pursed again. "Now why do I suspect," she finally said, "that you are the sort of fellow who rather enjoys a good round of fisticuffs?"

"And why do *I* suspect," he returned, "that you are a good deal more tenderhearted than you let on? After all, this common thug sits comfortably — *ouch!* — ensconced in your parlor, and you do not know me from Adam, do you?"

Again, she hesitated. "No, but I know a solid gold signet ring when I see one." He could feel little bits of his hair being snipped away at the nape of his neck, but her touch was gentler now. "And, to be perfectly honest, I recognized the Talbot crest whilst you were out senseless."

"Did you, by Jove?" Perhaps that explained why she'd let him in the house. The Talbots — save one — were notoriously high in the instep.

She set her capable, long-fingered hands to either side of his head, the tips of her fingers touching his cheeks. Something soothing and cool seemed to emanate from her touch. He closed his eyes and gave himself over to it, the throb in the back of his head instantly easing.

"Tilt your head a little lower, please," she said, gently urging his chin down. "Now which of the Talbots are you, pray?"

She released her embrace, and Tristan reluctantly opened his eyes. "Ah, now *that* is a part of my reason for being here."

"I can't think what you mean." He heard her dunk one corner of the towel into the warm water again and steeled himself. "Your reason for being *here?*"

"Just so," he said. "My call, you see . . . well, I was coming to call upon you."

He heard her hand stop. "Upon me?" Her voice was no longer soothing, but sharp. "But I do not know you, Mr. Talbot."

"On behalf of my father," he belatedly added. "I know it's irregular, but I thought your mother would be in. My father, the Earl of Hauxton, sent me."

"I . . . I know who Hauxton is." She sounded breathless again, and he wished to the devil he could see her face. "But he does not know me, I do assure you. Moreover, he has but one son."

"Aye," said Tristan a little sadly. "And that would be me."

She came round to stand in front of him, one hand on her hip. She looked a little peevish. "So you . . . *you* are the Viscount Avoncliffe?" she said. "Why did you not simply say so?"

Avoncliffe, indeed! What a wretched title. It sounded like something out of one of those overwrought novels he saw the ladies whispering over. It sounded silly. Romantic. Besides, he wasn't really the viscount *anything.*

"My reputation precedes me, does it?" he said, vaguely annoyed. But why? He'd earned his black name honestly. "Avoncliffe is just a courtesy title, as I'm sure you are aware. To the people who know me, I am just . . . Tristan."

"How perfectly absurd." But she dropped her fist, and circled behind him again. "In any case, returning to your earlier statement

— what could Lord Hauxton possibly want of me?"

Tristan cleared his throat, then winced against the pain. She was blotting the blood from his hair again. "Well, it's like this," he began. "My father is in the Foreign Office, and —"

"Your father *is* the Foreign Office," she corrected. "And the king's Privy Council. And half a dozen other things. Everyone knows that."

"Yes, well, one does not like to presume," said Tristan wryly. "In any case, he's got a bee in his bonnet over that chap who got killed yesterday — I can't explain it, something to do with his being Polish."

"Polish?" she said sharply. "I thought Gorsky was Russian."

"Aye, Russian," said Tristan smoothly. "Whatever the difference is."

"There is a vast deal of difference," said Lady Phaedra irritably. "Especially if one is Russian or Polish. Now do be still, Mr. Talbot. I have reconsidered my fainthearted-ness, and decided to stitch you up after all."

"Have you?"

"Yes, I begin to think I should enjoy inflicting a little pain upon you."

Behind him, he heard her rummaging through the wicker basket. "I am sorry," he said, genuinely contrite. "It must have been perfectly dreadful for you. I never thought — and your family — of course they will not wish you to have to think about what you saw."

But in truth, she did not seem like the weak, weeping sort. He looked around, and saw that she was threading a needle with some sort of heavy black thread, but her hand was shaking ever so slightly.

On impulse, Tristan turned in the chair, and set one hand over hers. "I am sorry," he said again. "My father . . . I wish he did not find this necessary. But he does, and he's ill and cannot come himself. I make a poor emissary in his stead, I do assure you."

Lady Phaedra exhaled a little tremulously, and let both hands fall. Tristan did not release his grasp. "It's all right," she said a little wearily. "Now, I am going to take three stitches in this cut, because I know that if I don't do it, you shan't get it attended to at all."

She was right about that, but he did not admit it.

"And when I am done," she continued, "I shall answer all your questions, Mr. Talbot, then send you on your merry way — provided you promise never to trouble me with this business again."

Suddenly, it didn't seem such a bad bargain. A little discomfort for a few more moments in her company. Besides, pain did not much bother Tristan. He had learned to endure it.

"All right," he said quietly. "If you think stitches necessary."

"I do." She lifted her gaze to his eyes, her expression a little sad. "I'm afraid Mr. Pimkins's blow has cut quite deep. If you are sure you won't see a proper surgeon . . . ?"

Tristan smiled, and turned back around. "I trust you, Lady Phaedra," he said. "I don't think it will be too bad a job. I'm pretty stoic about such things."

True to his word, Tristan sat perfectly still whilst her work was done, hissing through his teeth a time or two, and wincing at every stick. Funny how a chap could get himself bayoneted in the heat of battle and scarce notice the pain, then whimper like an abandoned pup over a darning needle. But the work was soon done, and the scissors and needle restored to their basket. Tristan's freshly brushed coat was returned and draped carefully over the chair from which it had been taken. Then Lady Phaedra asked the footman to fetch tea to, as she put it, "buck him up a bit."

What Tristan really wanted was the brandy, but he didn't say so, and when the tea came, he drank it as if it were the elixir of life, just to please her. She was not smiling back at him yet, but some of the disapproval had lifted from her eyes.

"Now," she said when the saucers were set down again. "I should like to ask you just one thing, Mr. Talbot — is that *really* what you prefer to be called?"

Tristan dropped his voice. "I think I should permit you to call me anything you pleased, Lady Phaedra," he teased.

The irritated governess look was back. "Very well," she said tartly. "What does Lord Hauxton care about the death of a man he cannot possibly know?"

"Very little, most likely." Tristan waved his hand vaguely. "It is just that there is some diplomatic issue with the Russians — something almost certainly unrelated to this dead man — but my father just wishes to be sure. The Russians might come round asking questions. One of their citizens turning up dead and all that."

Lady Phaedra seemed to accept his answer. "Yes, I see," she murmured, smoothing her hands down the front of her skirts. "What did he wish you to ask me?"

"My father should like to know just what

you saw," he said. "Describe it exactly —
particularly what the man said and all that."

"Why, he said nothing," she answered.
"Indeed, I think he was all but dead when
he fell through the door." She proceeded to
describe the scene in what sounded like
exacting detail.

"Yes, yes, I see," said Tristan when she
was done. "And Miss Armstrong, was she
there the entire time?"

"Indeed, but she can tell you no more
than I," said Lady Phaedra. "Then Mr.
Kemble covered the body, and sent us
upstairs to his parlor. A policeman came —
a sergeant, I believe — but Mr. Kemble
wouldn't let him speak to us. I thought the
sergeant might come by here later, but as
yet he has not."

"No, I believe this matter has been sent
down to Whitehall," said Tristan, scrubbing
his chin. "Might I ask what took you to the
Strand at that time of day?"

"Oh, just shopping," she said swiftly. "Isn't
that every lady's favorite pastime? Mr.
Kemble owns a sort of curiosity shop — a
very elegant sort of place, I might add."

"I see." Tristan would not have taken Lady
Phaedra for a lady who shopped for sport.
But most of the upper-crust females whose
beds he warmed did so. Why should she be

any different? "This Mr. Kemble — he is an agreeable sort of man?"

"Well, I don't know quite how to answer that," said Lady Phaedra. "He is a man of strong opinion, certainly. And he has quite good connections, I know, in the Home Office. I believe his friend there, Lord de Vendenheim, has been put in charge of the matter."

Tristan was silent for a moment. He wondered if Lady Phaedra was somehow protecting this Kemble chap — a man who, his father had already informed him, had connections in a great many places, most of them far less savory than the Home Office. After all, it was his back door through which the dead man had come crashing, and in Tristan's experience, there was no such thing as coincidence. No, Gorsky had been looking for someone.

His father would likely send Tristan next to see de Vendenheim — either that, or summon the poor devil up to his sickbed for interrogation. Then again, Robert Peel mightn't wish Hauxton to run roughshod over one of his own. It would not be the first time the Foreign Office and the Home Office had bumped heads.

But none of this was Tristan's problem. Finding no further excuse to linger, he set his hands on his thighs. "Well," he said, rising. "I thank you, Lady Phaedra, for your candor. I hope that your family will not object to our having spoken."

Phaedra rose as he did. "I am of an age, Mr. Talbot, when I am afforded more than a little latitude in what I do and whom I see," she said quietly.

He pulled a chagrinned expression. "Nary a breath of scandal, then?" he said. "You are quite certain no one is going to demand I make an honest woman of you?"

Now why the devil had he said that? The notion was ludicrous, and Lady Phaedra did not look pleased. "Mr. Talbot, pray do not poke fun at me," she said. "I wish to ask you something quite serious."

Tristan sobered his expression. "Yes, of course."

She opened her mouth, then closed it again. For the first time, she looked a little uncertain of herself — and quite breathlessly beautiful. "I wish to know what you mean to do about Mr. Pimkins," she finally said, her hands fiddling nervously with bit of trim on her cuff.

"Mr. Pimkins?" Tristan watched her long, elegant fingers, wishing, oddly, that she still touched him. "Why? What the devil does he want?"

Her lips thinned. "Do you mean to make a complaint?" she clarified. "He was quite careless, it is true — he wasn't aiming at *you* — but he really is not a bad sort."

"Oh, that!" Tristan jerked his gaze from her hands and laughed. "No, no, once one leaps into a mill like that, one must simply take one's licks. I'll heal up quickly enough."

He heard her exhale slowly. "Thank you," she said quietly. "Mr. Pimkins thanks you. He . . . he has a wife and a large family."

Despite her tart tongue, she really had been concerned for the poor devil, he realized. And he supposed, given who his father was, he likely could have had Pimkins's head on a platter. But Tristan had never invoked his father's name for a damned thing, and certainly didn't want to do so now.

Some of her worries eased, Phaedra sent for her guest's horse to be brought round, then watched as Talbot wound his ruined cravat back around his neck, and shrugged into his coat. She felt a little drained. Shaken, perhaps. But what, really, had he learned from her? Oh, he was a handsome, charming devil — and he knew it, too — but from what little she'd heard, the Earl of Avoncliffe was not known for his intelligence. He was a pretty face, and no more.

His father must have been desperate to send him.

His attire restored to relative order, Talbot followed her to the threshold. Phaedra stepped slightly behind the door to pick up his hat from the table where Stabler had left it. But when she turned back, she realized he had pushed the door half shut and followed her. In the small, confining space, he stood so near she could smell a hint of soap and something like bergamot swirling in his enticing male heat. Her heartbeat ratcheted up. Awkwardly, she handed him the hat.

"I fear you are going to have a bit of a bald spot near your nape, Mr. Talbot," she managed. "I — I had to cut some of your hair off."

I had to cut some of your hair off? As if he would not have noticed her snipping at it! Suddenly, Phaedra of the sharp tongue and even sharper vocabulary felt on the verge of stuttering. Tristan Talbot was watching her with a strange new glint in his eye.

"Well, then," he finally said, "there is but one more thing I should like to do."

"Yes?" The word came out breathlessly. "What?"

He held the hat behind his back now. "I should like to thank you properly," he said. "Or perhaps I should say *im*properly?" And with that, he leaned in to her and set his mouth to hers.

It was a sweet, ethereal thing, hardly a kiss at all. His lips, smooth and pillow-soft, settled gently over her own. His eyelashes lowered in a sweep of soft black fringe.

The room stilled, and for an instant, there was just the two of them on earth. Phaedra stood stock-still, something bottoming out in her stomach, then bursting into a faint warm heat as his mouth lingered, almost molding over hers. That a man so uncivilized could be so tender — oh, the sweetness of it sent her reeling.

Then just as suddenly, it was over. He drew back, the ever-present grin upon his face, the mischievous twinkle back in his eyes. Save for his lips, Talbot had not even touched her. Nonetheless, Phaedra stood there like the veriest idiot, swaying ever so slightly on her feet.

"There," he said quietly. "Let that be a lesson to you."

She felt her face color. "A . . . lesson?"

The man had the audacity to wink at her. "It's never safe for a pretty girl to be alone with an arrant scoundrel," he said. "Even a slow-witted one such as I. But I thank you, Lady Phaedra, for your kindness — and for that most memorable kiss. I think it will warm my heart for a day or two, at least."

Then he stepped from behind the door, and started down the hall. Jerking herself into motion, she darted after him. His hat tucked neatly under his arm, Talbot was pulling his gloves on as he went striding through her house, acting very much as if he owned it.

He was right, she told herself, watching him. He was nothing more than a charming rapscallion with a handsome face. There was no need to sway on one's feet. It was hardly enough of a kiss to warrant a good slapping. Besides, she had invited it. Something about her — something wrong, and all too apparent — had assured him he could get away with it. Still, she was angry.

She stepped before him, yanked open the door, and shot him one last chiding look. "I would box your ears, sir, if I thought it would do a bloody bit of good," she said, her voice low and tremulous. "Now good day to you, Mr. Talbot."

To her consternation, Talbot threw back his head and laughed. "Lady Phaedra!" he said. "What shocking language!" Then he dashed down the stairs whistling, his long, limber legs so steady one would never have guessed he'd taken a stupefying blow to the head.

But then, as if to torment her, he hesitated on the last step. With his gloved hand still resting along the wrought-iron railing, Tristan Talbot turned back, some dark, inscrutable emotion sketching across his face. "Just one last question, Lady Phaedra, if I might?"

"Have I any choice?"

His eyes snapped to hers, suddenly black and utterly penetrating. "The dead man," he said quietly. "You called him Gorsky."

The mood had shifted ominously. Phaedra felt her heart still. "Did I?" she answered too sharply. "But is that not his name?"

"So it is." There was nothing of the laughing rogue in him now, just a grim, almost lethal seriousness. "But who told you?"

She hesitated a heartbeat too long. "I . . . why, my brother, I believe," she lied.

His black gaze cut through her, keen and quick as a carving knife. "Are you quite sure of that, my lady?"

"I . . . yes, quite."

He held her eyes ruthlessly, and she dared not look away. "I see," he finally said, his voice dangerously soft. "Good day to you, then, Lady Phaedra. I thank you for your time."

He turned, and Phaedra felt her knees sag. She had the sudden sense of having badly misjudged something. Of having seen, perhaps, only what he wished her to see — an unsettling thought indeed. Just then, something to the left caught her eye, and she noticed the slight, dark figure standing on the pavement below. "Miss Armstrong!" she said in some surprise.

"Hullo, Phae." Zoë looked up at Mr. Talbot almost coquettishly. "And Avoncliffe!" she murmured. "Bleeding again, I see. But still alive."

The man doffed his hat. "Much to the disappointment of my enemies," he said, bowing. "Miss Armstrong, you are looking well."

"I ought to," said Zoë dryly. "I haven't anything else to do, have I? So, are you and Phae friends?"

Talbot turned back to Phaedra and winked. "I am not perfectly sure," he said, his mood light again. "Phae? *Are* we friends?"

Phaedra ignored him. "Mr. Talbot called to ask some questions on behalf of his father," she said, coming partway down the steps. "About what happened yesterday."

"Did you indeed?" said Zoë cryptically. "How interesting."

"Yes, but we're finished — for now." Talbot took his horse's reins from the approaching footman. "What are you about, Miss Armstrong? Some sort of mischief?"

"No, I've come to ask Phae to a card party," she said. "My cousins and I are having a few friends over Thursday evening. Nothing too exciting."

"Nonetheless, with you at the helm, it will be the social event of the season," Talbot teased.

Zoë's gaze shifted to Phaedra appraisingly, then back to Talbot. "Are you still living in that bolt-hole over in Long Acre, Avoncliffe?" Her voice was laden with boredom. "I shall ask Aunt Winnie to send you a card, though the wagers will run a bit dull for your taste."

"You are all generosity, Miss Armstrong," he said, laughing. "Yes, I am still living in my humble abode. Now, lovely ladies, much as it goes against my grain, I fear that I must leave you."

"Oh, what nonsense." Zoë went up the steps past him. "From what I hear, Talbot, you have a whole gaggle of lovelies awaiting your attentions."

His grin deepened, and then Talbot made another sweeping bow to Zoë. "Miss Armstrong, might I call upon you — and your aunt, of course — tomorrow?" he asked more seriously. "Would one o'clock be too early?"

Now at Phaedra's side, Zoë pressed the back of her hand to her forehead. "Lud, the scandalous Lord Avoncliffe calling upon me!" she declared. "Aunt Winnie is like to faint." She dropped the hand and the sarcasm. "Yes, come round if you must — but make it two. I shall try to be up."

"Two it shall be, then."

In the street, Talbot's mount was already beginning to wheel her hindquarters impatiently, her velvety black nostrils wide and puffing. It was awfully big and awfully black, Phaedra noticed, not for the first time. But then, there must be a hundred such horses in London, mustn't there? It had been so dark that long ago night, and she so frightened. She had not worn her spectacles, and he — well, he had been utterly foxed. But she had heard a name. Not Talbot, though. And not Avoncliffe. She wracked her brain, but nothing came.

And it scarcely mattered. The horse wheeled to the right, and Talbot went with her, swinging himself up into the saddle effortlessly. He lifted his hat one last time, and in a bolting clatter of hooves, he was gone.

CHAPTER 4

I will upon all hazards well believe
Thou art my friend that know'st my tongue
so well.

"Oh, my!" said Zoë, following Phaedra back
to the parlor. "Lord Avoncliffe! Delicious to
look at, is he not?'

"Is he?" said Phaedra vaguely. "I did not
notice."

"What a liar you are, Phae!" Zoë slid out
of her cloak without invitation. "I say, I hope
you don't mind my sneaking over to see
you," she continued. "It's dull as ditch-
water across the way, and I wondered how
you were after yesterday."

"Oh, no, I'm very glad to see you," said
Phaedra honestly. On impulse, she gave Zoë
a swift hug. "My mother and sister are out,
though."

"Excellent," said Zoë, her eyes glittering.
"Then we can talk — about Avoncliffe, I

mean. He's far more exciting than any old murder."

"Is he?" Phaedra smiled, smoothing her skirts as she offered a seat. "But you seemed perfectly bored to see him."

Zoë flopped across the settee. "Well, I have a reputation to maintain," she said, draping one hand limply off the back. "The dead-bored debutante, perishing of ennui. And after three seasons, it's pretty near the truth." Suddenly she sat up straight again. "By the way, why was his cravat all bloody?"

Phaedra explained, keeping her voice as nonchalant as possible.

"Oh, Lud, that sounds like Avoncliffe!" Zoë rolled her big brown eyes. "He has frightfully rough edges — something ladies of the *ton* seem simply mad for."

"He did seem more brawn than brain," Phaedra answered. "How well do you know him?"

Zoë had begun to play with one end of her cashmere shawl. "Oh, well enough to know he's a scoundrel," she said. "I met him, I daresay, through my cousins. They run with a raffish sort of crowd. Which is not to say Avoncliffe is never seen in good company — he is occasionally, but just long enough to get what he wants."

"A womanizer, of course." Phaedra had

begun to chew pensively at her thumbnail. She really did wish the man had not kept calling her *pretty* in that deep, rumbling voice of his.

"A womanizer, and perfectly brazen about it." Then Zoë hesitated as if a thought had just popped into her head. "I do hope, Phae, you did not see him alone?"

Phaedra jerked her thumbnail away. "He was bleeding," she protested. "I had the door open the whole time."

"Oh." Zoë pondered it. "Well, I hope he minded his manners. He's a very bad man, that one, but Aunt Winnie says he's a frightfully good kisser."

Phaedra lifted both brows. "And she would know?"

Zoë cut her a sly glance. "You'd have to ask Aunt Winnie," she said. "She might well. I do know there was a frightful row over him at a masque in Belgravia last season. Lady Holding and Mrs. Butler nearly scratched each other's eyes out in the ladies' retiring room. Avoncliffe is hotly in demand, if you know what I mean."

Good Lord. Phaedra felt suddenly out of place again, as if Zoë knew the secrets to the universe, and she was still hopelessly naïve. Zoë cut a glance at the door, then turned round again. "They say he's part Gi-

118

tano — a sort of Gypsy — and part Sicilian," she continued in a conspiratorial whisper. "And Aunt Winnie says his mother was a flamenco dancer. Do you know what that is?"

Phaedra felt her eyes widen. "*Lord Hauxton* married a flamenco dancer? So Talbot's what? Spanish *and* Sicilian?"

"And God only knows what else." Zoë lifted a shoulder lightly. "Of course one does wonder if it's true," she admitted. "But I don't care. My mother was a dancer, too — and a bit of a mongrel. Whatever he is, I think I should rather like him to kiss *me*. All that black hair and warm skin — he looks so deliciously wicked."

Once again Phaedra felt her face flood with heat.

Zoë was looking at her strangely. "What?" she said innocently. Then she hesitated again, eyes widening. "Oh, no!" she breathed. "Phae, he *didn't* — ?"

Phaedra's blush deepened. "Oh, my word!" said Zoë, sliding forward on the settee. "*Did* he kiss you? Why, the gall of that man! You are not the sort of girl a man like that kisses."

For an instant, Phaedra turned her face away, shame washing over her. *Zoë couldn't see it.* The ugly truth was, she was exactly that sort. She was wrong, somehow — dark inside — and some men sensed it. Some could see what she tried so hard to hide. The raging emotion that threatened to consume her. But Tristan Talbot — he seemed different, somehow. His kiss, at least, had not been lascivious, precisely. More . . . *playful.* "No, we are different, Zoë, you and I," she whispered.

But Zoë had cut her gaze away, her chin dropping. "Yes, you are the kind of girl a man marries," she said, her voice uncharacteristically quiet. "I am the kind they try to kiss in a dark corner."

"Oh," said Phaedra softly. Zoë, it seemed, was the naïve one here.

Zoë shrugged away the moment. "So, if I am to be kissed, Avoncliffe looks like a good bet." She looked up again and smiled. "But there! You kissed him first, Phae. Just do be careful, please? I think he really is a decent sort, but he can be perfectly dangerous."

"It wasn't really even a kiss, Zoë," Phaedra confessed. "It was a just *peck.* The merest little thing. Besides, I really mustn't see him again."

Zoë laughed. "Oh, I think I see intrigue in your eyes!" she said. "Have you any experience with men?" When Phaedra did not answer, and merely stared down at her

120

clasped hands, Zoë leapt from her chair. "Come on, let's go for a walk in Hyde Park. I want to show you something."

Phaedra suddenly welcomed the offer. Perhaps fresh air would rid her head of Tristan Talbot's intriguing scent. She sent a servant scurrying off for her cloak and bonnet, and in short order, she and Zoë were going back down the front steps, Agnes trailing dutifully behind.

While they walked, Zoë talked of her many seasons in Town, and of her father's increasing frustration that she was not wed. At the end of it, she sighed. "What of you, Phae?" she asked. "Does your family not press you?"

Phaedra shook her head. "They do not," she said quietly. Then, after a time, she continued. "Zoë, have you ever been in love?"

Zoë hesitated. "I thought I was," she finally said. "But he became haughty and high-handed and, like a bad case of the 'flu, I got over it. What of you, Phae?"

"I was in love once," Phaedra confessed. "Desperately. Foolishly. But I was young and it . . . it did not end well."

Sympathy sketched across Zoë's face. "Oh, Phae, I am so sorry," she said, catching Phaedra's hand and squeezing it hard.

"What happened?"

Phaedra could not bear to tell the whole of it. "He died," she said simply.

"Oh." Zoë's voice was quiet. "Oh, my poor dear. Do you miss him still?"

Somehow, Phaedra lifted her face to the sun. "No," she answered, drawing in the warmth. "No, but I cannot yet bear to speak of it. Not . . . all of it. Forgive me?"

"What is there to forgive between friends?" Zoë flashed a weak smile, and hooked her arm through Phaedra's. "Even new ones such as us?"

"Thank you, Zoë."

They walked on in silence, arm in arm now. The warmth of the day was just beginning to wane, and the scent of spring was in the air. Along the street, an open carriage sped past, a barouche filled with elegant ladies and gentlemen. The horses' hooves clopped briskly as they flew, requiring one of the ladies to seize hold of her very fetching pink straw bonnet. They were dressed for spring, Phaedra realized, glancing down at her drab skirts. The season was truly upon them, and for the first time, Phaedra wondered if she had made the right choices with her life. People like Zoë Armstrong and Tristan Talbot seemed so full of life, and happy with what they were. So certain of their own emotions. Why wasn't it thus for her?

They reached the park, and Zoë followed the edge of the Serpentine Pond, idly chattering. At Hyde Park Bridge, however, all pretense of seriousness vanished. Zoë plunged into the shrubbery, her eyes alight, dragging Phaedra by the arm. "Come, let's hide in here."

Phaedra cast Agnes a staying glance, and followed. Zoë was up to some sort of wickedness. Deep within the shadows sat a bench. Zoë drew Phaedra down beside her, extracted a cheroot case from her skirts, and thumbed open the lid. "Look what I have!"

"Zoë!" Phaedra sniffed it as Zoë drew it beneath her nose. "Do *ladies* smoke those?"

"Why shouldn't we?" Zoë stuck it in her mouth and struck a vesta on the bench.

"My word! Where did you get it?"

"From my cousin," she said round the cheroot. "Lord Robert Rowland."

Phaedra knew she should have been scandalized, but the emotion seemed beyond her. In the last two days, she'd seen a man murdered, kissed a handsome scoundrel, and befriended a little gamine as wild as Phaedra was proper. Now she found herself merely wondering what a cheroot tasted like. "Lud, Zoë, but you are a corrupting influence," she muttered.

"I am, aren't I?" Puffing on the cheroot until her eyes watered, Zoë settled back onto the bench with a little cough. "Now," she said. "I simply *must* hear all about Avoncliffe's kiss. Precisely how did he go about it? And did he steal it? Surely he must have done?"

"He stole it." Phaedra felt suddenly lighthearted, rather like a schoolgirl. "I was handing him his hat. I didn't know what to do."

"Not to worry!" Zoë waved her cheroot airily. "I shall advise you."

"You are very kind, I'm sure," said Phaedra, "but as I said, I don't mean to see him again."

"But he might turn up at my card party," Zoë complained. "Then where would you be? No, you'd best let me help you. Next time it mightn't be just a peck. You'll want to be prepared."

"Well, I certainly shan't kiss him again, Zoë."

Zoë tossed her a disparaging glance, and passed Phaedra the cheroot. "Have you any notion, Phae, how the ladies of the *ton* vie for his attentions?" she whispered. "Believe me, there's scarcely a female in London who wouldn't like have Tristan Talbot's tongue in —" Here, she had the good grace to stop and blush. "Oh, I do apologize. I have been eavesdropping on Aunt Winnie too often."

"Yes, and you just said he shouldn't have kissed me at all," Phaedra reminded her, still pinching the smoking cheroot.

"Try it," Zoë encouraged, "but don't inhale!"

Phaedra took a tentative puff, then blew out the bitter smoke on a cough. The truth was, she was embarrassed by her response to Talbot's kiss. She understood, logically, that women threw themselves at men like him. And she understood too well that men — most men — would take what they could, and never feel a modicum of guilt. Perhaps she was no better. The rush of emotions Tristan Talbot had reawakened in her today were about as welcome as a case of smallpox — and about as useful. She passed the cheroot back to Zoë, and looked away.

"You will come to my card party, will you not?" Zoë pressed. "Oh, do say you will."

Abruptly, Phaedra turned to face her. "There is something you should understand about me," she said quietly. "I — I am not like you, Zoë. I am not much accustomed to society."

Zoë looked at her in some surprise, then blew out a plume of curling white smoke.

"Phae, you are hardly young," she said. "No, don't scowl at me — you are just a little older than me, I know — but what I'm saying is, surely you must have been to balls and dinner parties?"

Phaedra shrugged. "A bit, yes, but I never really . . . came out," she admitted. "I mean, there was no ball. No sparkling white dress. I just . . . it just wasn't what I wanted. I do go about in society sometimes. To musicales and literary readings, mostly."

"Literary readings?' Zoë drew back, aghast. "You poor, poor girl."

"It's what I want," she said again. "I like to read. I enjoy music."

"You poor, poor girl," Zoë repeated. "You have a vast deal of catching up to do. You are missing the exciting bits."

"What, the pretty, dimwitted scoundrels like Talbot? Or whatever his name is?"

"With a face like that," said Zoë, flicking the ash off her cheroot, "who cares if he's possessed of a brilliant mind? But listen to me, my dear. That one is a little dangerous. Do not mistake good humor for stupidity. Now, about the season —"

"It scarcely matters, for I do not care for the whirl of society," Phae interjected, kicking a small stone near her toe. "I do not go to balls and parties. I am not interested in marriage."

Zoë looked at her incredulously. "Lud, who mentioned marriage?"

"Is that not what the season is for?"

"Not to me!" Zoë laughed. "I've done everything I can think of to avoid marriage. Just ask Papa. No, going about in society is to meet people, you gudgeon."

"To . . . meet people?"

"Yes, and to laugh and be gay," Zoë added. "And to torment the men just a little, perhaps?" Here, Zoë paused to bat her long black lashes. "I mean to enjoy life, my dear. I suggest you do the same. One can always say *no* to a marriage proposal. I've done it half a dozen times."

"Oh."

Phaedra sat in silence for a time as Zoë took one last puff, then knocked the ash from her cheroot and restored it to her case. "Phaedra, listen to me," said Zoë, fleetingly solemn. "You mustn't let an old tragedy blight the present. Get out in the world. Have some fun."

Phaedra considered it. Socializing just for the pleasure of it? Flirting with men to torment them? *That* sounded dangerous. Fleetingly, she wished to return home; to retreat into the safety of her parlor and her books. She desperately feared another kiss from

Tristan Talbot. She did not like the sensations his mouth sent shivering through her body. That awful swell of something churning and thwarted inside her. It brought back the shame, and reminded her yet again that she was not all that a lady should be.

Suddenly, Zoë leaned nearer. "Honestly, Phae, you could just *slay* men with those brilliant blue eyes of yours," she said, her voice low. "Just think of it — you could break a heart or two just for sport."

"Zoë, I . . . I cannot."

"Pish!" said Zoë. "They deserve it — most men, anyway. The nice ones, well, just avoid them. That way, no one gets hurt."

But people *did* get hurt. Hurt in ways no one could foresee, or ever repair. Phaedra knew that firsthand. Nonetheless, she contemplated Zoë's words as they strolled back through Mayfair. The truth was, despite her fears and failures — or perhaps because of them — there was a part of her that had begun to long for a little excitement. Just now, however, she had more pressing concerns. But perhaps . . . perhaps she should accede to Stefan's wishes. Perhaps she should buy those new gowns after all. She was no longer sure. She did not trust herself enough to choose — not even such a small, foolish thing as a new dress.

Half an hour later, Phaedra said good-bye to her new friend, leaving her at her front door across the street. Zoë waved good-bye, her smile sunny as ever.

Inside, Stabler took Phaedra's cloak and hat, and informed her that her mother and sister had retired to rest before dressing for dinner. The evidence of their afternoon's activity still sat by the front stairs — a tower of bandboxes and what looked like four bolts of fabric carefully wrapped in brown paper.

"She wished me to remind you they are to dine with Lady Henslow and her daughter," Stabler explained. "Your mother begs you will reconsider joining them."

"Thank you, but I cannot," said Phaedra hastily. "I mean — I have some reading to do. Urgent reading. Indeed, I do not wish to be further disturbed this evening."

"Of course, miss." The footman gave a slight bow. "I shall inform her ladyship."

"Thank you, Stabler." Phaedra felt suddenly swamped with fatigue. "I shall be in the parlor."

Phaedra returned to stand behind the chair in which Talbot had sat, its back still turned to the bay window. Was it her imagination, or did his warm, clean scent still linger there?

Agnes followed her to the doorway, then hesitated. For the first time, Phaedra noticed her unease. She turned to fully look at her. "What is it, Agnes?"

The maid's hands were clasped rigidly before her. "I did not get a chance to tell you, miss," she said quietly. "I had a letter in the afternoon post."

Phaedra's hand clenched the back of the chair. "From your great-aunt?"

"Just so, miss. I'm sorry. There was no news at all of Millie."

"Nothing?" But Phaedra saw the answering sadness in Agnes's eyes.

The maid shook her head, and let her chin fall. "No, miss," she answered. "Nary a word."

"What of Priscilla?" she asked hollowly.

"Aunt Kessie says Priss is a handful." Agnes's eyes had brightened. "But she cut another tooth. And she does not ask for her mother quite so often now."

"Oh, Agnes," said Phaedra sorrowfully. "I'm not at all sure that is a good thing. And your aunt is too old for this."

Phaedra left the window and sank into one of the worn brown armchairs. Her walk with Zoë Armstrong had been a pleasant diversion. But here, alone in the parlor, real life had already begun to intrude, and the full weight of their trouble was sinking back in upon her. In her mind's eye, she could still see little Priscilla, her plump hands fisted, her blue eyes pooling with tears. It wrenched at her heart to think of a child — any child — motherless. Priss was too young to understand why or where her mother had gone. Phaedra didn't understand it, either. It was the ultimate mistake — the ultimate sin — to abandon one's child. It was, perhaps, unforgivable.

"Are you going up to Soho tonight, miss?" Agnes's words cut into her consciousness.

Phaedra looked away, blinking back the hot press of tears. "Yes, though I don't know what good it will do," she answered. "I shall go as soon as it gets dark. If anyone should knock on my door —"

"Yes, miss," Agnes interrupted. "I'll make a lump with the pillows, and tell them you've a headache."

Phaedra bit her lip nervously. Yes, Agnes knew exactly what to do, she reassured herself. They had been at this for weeks now. So long, in fact, that she really was feeling quite desperate.

Phaedra clenched her hands so tightly her short nails dug into her palms. Damn it, it was just like Tony to be away from home at such a time. As usual, he had created a crisis, and left someone else to deal with it. Usually the job of salvaging Tony and his political career from impending ruination fell to Stefan. But Phaedra did not dare dump this tragedy in Stefan's lap. The last contretemps he had extricated Tony from had nearly ruined the both of them — and at a time when Stefan had at last met the woman of his dreams. Now he had a child to love and another on the way. He was finally happy.

No, there was no possible way she could allow this to fall on Stefan's ears. Besides, he might well throttle Tony this time. Slowly she rose from the chair. "I am going upstairs to try and get some sleep," she said to Agnes. "Wake me when it is dark, will you? And bring me your cloak and another dress — your dark blue, I think, fits me best."

Still wringing her hands, Agnes bobbed. "I will, miss," she said quietly. "And thank you."

The woman at the desk slammed another drawer, this time so hard a figurine fell from the adjacent shelf, shattering. The door sprang open at once, and the pale, broad-shouldered man who entered bowed, then stared down at the shards of fine Bohemian porcelain.

"Madame, what has happened?"

Her hand shaking with rage, Madame Vostrikova yanked open the topmost drawer and stabbed a finger at it. "The sphere, Lavrin." She spoke in staccato Russian. "What has become of the sphere? Tell me, for God's sake, that you have it."

His eyes widening, the man hastened behind the broad mahogany desk, and began to rip open the drawers for himself.

"You waste your time, Lavrin," she said, staring down at the back of his head. "And what is worse, you waste mine."

Lavrin opened the bottom drawer and stood, horrified. "It is gone!"

"My God, yes, it is gone!" Madame rolled her eyes. "This is Gorsky's work — that faithless bastard!"

"But Madame —" Lavrin folded his hands and stepped back, just out of her striking distance. "Madame, his rooms were searched."

She turned on him, quivering with rage. "Then search them again!" she said hoarsely, stabbing a finger at the ceiling. "Rip up the floorboards if you must."

Lavrin winced. "Madame, it will not be found there, I tell you," he insisted. "Perhaps he . . . he took it elsewhere?"

"Don't be a fool, Lavrin," she retorted.

"He didn't know anyone. And after the boy was sent north, Gorsky was always followed and he spoke to no one."

"Perhaps, Madame, he took it with him that morning?"

"It would have been found." She shook her head, her ice-blond hair catching the sunlight. "When they searched him, it would have been found. It would have been brought to me."

Lavrin puffed out his cheeks. *"Da,"* he said hesitantly, "if there was time."

She whirled on him, incredulous. "*If* there was time?" she said. "Do you mean to suggest, Lavrin, that I hired an assassin who did not take time to search the body for incrimination?"

Lavrin lifted both hands, palms up. "I do not know it for certain, Madame," he said. "But yes, it is possible."

Madame thrust a bejeweled finger in his face. "Then you will find him," she said to him. "You will find him, Lavrin, and you will ask him. And if this bumbling fool has allowed my sphere to be lost — *then you will kill him.*"

"Yes, Madame," he whispered.

She rammed the bottom shut with her shoe, causing Lavrin to jump. "And what of those girls?" she snapped. "Have we their

134

names yet? Something? Anything?"

Lavrin drew back another inch. "Our source at Bow Street says they saw nothing," he said soothingly. "Even the papers contained no mention."

"So they are from influential families," said Madame pensively. "Their names have been hushed up."

"Or they saw nothing," Lavrin said again.

At that Madame sneered and slammed the top draw shut with a resounding crack. "My dear Lavrin," she answered sourly. "After a dozen years in this business, can you still be so very naïve?"

That night, a light fog rolled in off the Thames, settling over London like a gossamer shawl — albeit a shawl which stank of low tide and was tinged with coal smoke. Phaedra drew her chair as near to the window of her rented room in Soho as she dared, and peered through the fly-specked glass at the town house across the street.

All the windows were lit, some more brightly than others, as they had been every night she'd sat in this squalid little chamber. And yet she saw nothing. Save for the occasional messenger or servant, no one came. No one went. Indeed, she sourly considered, for such an infamous whorehouse, business seemed remarkably slow. Frustrated, Phaedra drew a handkerchief from her pocket, and scrubbed at the dirty glass as if the effort might reveal something of the house's secrets. A sudden knock at the door jolted her upright.

"Yes?" She was annoyed to hear her voice waver.

"Thompson?" The rough female voice was not especially warm. " 'Tis Tuesday, dearie."

Phaedra rose from her rickety wooden chair. "Aye?"

"If yer means to stay on, there's the rent to be paid," the voice reminded her.

Phaedra snatched the worn leather purse Agnes had lent her, and threw open the door. Mrs. Wooten, the lodging house owner, squinted at her through the gloom, a stub of a tallow candle held high. "One shilling three pence," she said, extending a knobby hand. "If yer stayin'?"

"Aye, another week, mum, if you please," said Phaedra, trying to sound like Agnes as she pressed the coins into Mrs. Wooten's palm.

The old woman fingered them for a moment, then, apparently satisfied, dropped them into her pocket. "That'll do nicely, dearie," she said, glancing up. "Yer found work, I hope?"

Phaedra set the purse away. "Aye, in a millinery," she lied. "In Piccadilly. The pay isn't much — but I can afford to stay on here."

"Odd hours for a milliner, in'it?" Mrs. Wooten remarked.

But the old woman looked disinterested, and Phaedra did not explain. Mrs. Wooten had made it plain when the impoverished widow Mrs. Thompson had let the room weeks ago that she wanted only the rent — paid in full, once a week — and cared little enough where the money had come from.

"Mrs. Wooten," said Phaedra as the woman turned to go, "I was just wondering . . ."

"Wot?" Despite the gloom, suspicion glinted in her eye.

Phaedra motioned toward the window. "That fine, big house across the way," she remarked. "Who lives there?"

"Now why would yer be arskin'?"

Phaedra shrugged. "The windows are all lit up late into the night," she answered. "Yet no one comes or goes. So I just wondered at it."

"Curiosity kilt the cat, din'it?" said the old woman sagely. "I'd stop wondering, if I were you. The doings wot goes on there is none o' my business, and none o' yours, if

137

you're sharp."

"I see." Phaedra stepped back from the door. "Well, thank you, Mrs. Wooten. And good night to you."

Unexpectedly, the old woman's face softened. "If yer makin' a living on your back, lovie, it's naught ter me," she said quietly. "But yer don't wants ter do it there, awright? Keep ter the streets. 'Tis a good deal safer."

"Oh." Phaedra pressed her hand to her chest. "Thank you, Mrs. Wooten. I did not realize."

The woman's expression further relented. "Don't know much about the place, meself," she admitted. "But I knows a lot o' fine carriages come and go — through the back lane, dearie. Not the front. And a lot of pretty girls gets dragged out o' that house and put in them carriages — and some of 'em don't want ter go and don't never come back. So keep ter the streets, awright?"

The back lane. The carriages went through the back. What an idiot she had been!

Phaedra tried to look contrite. "Thank you, Mrs. Wooten, for warning me."

She shut the door, and turned to survey the narrow, tawdry room. She had wasted precious time confined in this dark garret, a chamber so low and so small it would not have held her mother's wardrobe. She returned to the window and craned her head as far to the left as she dared. Even without her spectacles, she could make out the street corner, and the shadow, perhaps, of the back lane beyond.

On impulse, she snatched Agnes's cloak, put out the lamp, and went out and down the steps. Shivering against the damp, she crossed the street, darting around a hackney cab and into the narrower side street almost opposite her window. For a time, the cobbles shone in the faint gaslight. Soon, however, soaring walls loomed up on her left and right, oppressively close, shutting out the air and what little light there had been. It was this — the sense of being entombed by brick and mortar — she most hated about London.

Phaedra turned left into the darkness, moving gingerly along the back lane. She discerned the rear of Mr. Gorsky's brothel by drawing her hand along the garden wall, counting off the gates as she went. Through the faint light which spilled from the windows, she could see the yard behind was long and narrow, without garden embellishments of any sort. The gate stood open and Phaedra could smell the privy just inside it.

Just then, the back door swung wide. A stout woman wearing a white smock came out of the house swinging an old-fashioned lantern in one hand, and a bucket in the other. She trudged down the path, hung the lamp on a peg, and stepped up into the privy to empty her bucket. Phaedra crept round the gatepost, keeping just to the shadow's edge.

"I beg your pardon," she said as the woman came out.

The servant whirled about, eyes wide. The privy door slammed behind her.

"I beg your pardon," Phaedra repeated. "I . . . I was looking for work. As a servant, I mean. In the house."

The woman just shook her head.

"Might there be a place vacant?" Phaedra pressed. "Or someone I might speak with?"

The woman's hand went fleetingly to the collar of her dress. Then she snatched her lamp from the peg, and darted back up the path again, leaving the bucket behind.

Phaedra's shoulders sagged as the door thumped shut and darkness fell over the garden. The woman was even less helpful than Gorsky had been. Indeed, she had been perfectly terrified to speak. Perhaps Gorsky should have been so terrified . . .

Phaedra shuddered. She was increasingly certain the dead Russian had been watching her, perhaps looking for an opportunity to speak with her alone. But why? The day she had so boldly — and foolishly — dropped the knocker at his brothel's front door, the man had denied any knowledge of a flame-haired Hampshire servant girl who might be working within the house. Indeed, it was as if Millie had come to London, entered the house, then vanished from the face of the earth.

Perhaps she had.

No, thought Phaedra, jerking herself up short. She would not give up. Millie might be a naïve country girl, but she had grit. She was a survivor. Phaedra had to get inside that house somehow. It was the only possible way to find her. But perhaps, as Mrs. Wooten had warned, Millie had been one of the unfortunates who had gone out the back way, and not come back in again.

At that dreadful thought, Phaedra shuddered again, and backed slowly into the alley. A hard, unyielding presence caught her up short. Her scream was muffled by a hand slapped firmly over her mouth. A strong arm lashed round her waist, dragging her into the pitch black of the opposite wall. Her voice muffled, Phaedra flailed desperately.

"Shush, don't scream," rumbled a warm, husky voice. "I mean you no harm."

Phaedra fought like a wildcat then, throwing back an elbow while doing her best to stomp upon his toes. The man chuckled deeply in her ear and swung her around, forcing her chest against the brick. "Hold still, for God's sake." The rumbling voice was gentle and — had she not been too panicked to realize it — oddly familiar. "Just listen."

"No! Let me go!" Phaedra shouted, but the words were muffled against his hand.

With a grunt, the fiend shoved a long, hard-muscled leg between hers, pinning her. Phaedra's palms were flat against the damp brick. She could feel the broad wall of his chest against her back, and the cuff of his boot scrubbing her inner thigh. The heat of his body pressed against her, searing her length. Angrily, she thrashed again, then somehow got her mouth open and bit down hard. Leather gloves saved him from the worst of it, and he did nothing but chuckle again.

"Why, you little vixen!"

"Fiend!" she cried into the leather. "Help! Help!"

"Stop shouting and I'll remove my hand," he offered. "Just tell me what you know about that house. That's all I want. Just information. I heard you speaking with that servant."

His mouth was warm against her ear, stirring the loose strands of hair at her temple. The scent of hot, aggravated male surrounded her; a hint of bergamot and male perspiration. A familiar, enticing scent.

Oh, Lord. Surely not? Against her better judgment, Phaedra stopped struggling. His weight sagged against her as the tension left his body. "Very good," he said quietly, "I shall remove my hand. Be so good as to tell me what you know about that house."

"N-n-noffink," Phaedra croaked, trying to mimic a Cockney accent. "Just arskin' for a bit o' scullery work, I was."

"Scullery work, eh?" Phaedra realized in some embarrassment that his other hand all but grasped her left breast. "Now why do I not quite believe that?"

"Believe wot yer please."

His mouth was still at her ear, his nose almost buried in her hair, and Phaedra's fear was melting into something more treacherous. He drew a deep breath. "By God, you don't smell like any scullery maid I ever met."

"Filled your 'ands wiv a few, 'ave you, gov?"

Throwing back his head, her assailant

laughed richly. And that was it. Phaedra was certain.

Please, please, please, she silently prayed. *Don't let him guess.* "Let go!" she protested, wiggling more desperately. "Let go! I tol' you wot I knows."

"Let go?" he murmured. "That's a hard task, love, with a handful of ripe breast and that plump little arse of yours wiggling against my nether regions."

Phaedra went instantly rigid.

His lips skated down the turn of her neck. Phaedra shivered. "Are you sure, my dear?" he murmured. "There's something about you I can't quite —"

"Let me go!" she interjected. *"Now."*

"Ah, well," he murmured, his grip relaxing. "The lady demurs. Another time, perhaps?"

She shifted to slip away, but made the mistake of casting a wary glance at him, as if she might see through the pitch black night. He must have felt her turn and laughed again, catching her mouth with his. It began teasingly, almost innocently. But in an instant, it shifted, his lips moving hungrily over hers, his hand coming up to fully grasp her breast.

Almost against her will, Phaedra opened beneath him, eliciting a deep groan from him as he thrust inside. This was no stolen peck behind the parlor door. Their tongues tangled and stroked, causing a heat to well up from Phaedra's belly, all the way to her throat. His palm rolled over her breast, cradling it as his erection began to swell in earnest against her backside. He made a soft sound of pleasure in the back of his throat, then fleetingly lifted his mouth as if to speak.

Phaedra seized her chance. She jerked from his grasp and bolted — not from him, but from herself — running down the alley and into the side street as fast as her legs could go. And all while she knew that he was allowing her to escape. Oh, yes. With those long, hard-muscled legs of his, had Tristan Talbot wished to catch a woman, she would never have stood a chance.

CHAPTER 5

Speak, cousin; or, if you cannot,
stop his mouth with a kiss,
and let not him speak neither.

"Eliza says that to catch a proper husband, one must master watercolors." Snaring her lower lip between her pearl-white teeth, Lady Phoebe Northampton leaned forward to dab at her canvas horizon with her brush. "There!" she said, leaning back again. "The perfect fluffy cloud, is it not, Miss Armstrong?"

"The whole thing is perfect," said Zoë appreciatively. "With that kind of talent, you shall doubtless land yourself a duke before the season is out, Lady Phoebe."

Phoebe laughed, her cheeks blushing prettily. She had always been able to blush on cue, her sister noted — unlike Phaedra, who seemed to blush over the most seemingly insignificant things, and at the worst possible moments.

They sat in the back garden of Tony's house, the late afternoon having turned shockingly warm and sunny. Zoë Armstrong had provided a bright spot in Phaedra's day by dropping by again unexpectedly — this time to hand deliver the invitation to her card party, and to make the acquaintance of Phaedra's mother and sister.

Now, a full hour after her arrival, the Dowager Lady Nash was still looking at the card. "Well, I cannot think what's best, Miss Armstrong," she chirped. "Phoebe and I are engaged to dine with friends. To permit Phaedra to come alone as you suggest . . . oh, I just do not think . . ."

Zoë Armstrong slid forward on her garden chair and looked at Lady Nash plaintively. "But it is quite informal, ma'am," she wheedled. "Just a silly group of young people to play a few hands of cards. And we are just across the street. Wait — I have an idea."

"What?" asked Phaedra suspiciously.

She, too, was torn. Such frivolous entertainments were not for her. But there was something in Zoë Armstrong's attitude — her rather refreshing view of life — which struck Phaedra as liberating. Infectious. Something that made Phaedra wonder if

147

perhaps she had made a mistake in letting life overlook her. Perhaps marriage and a so-called normal existence were not life's only options. Oh, she had long told herself that. But Zoë Armstrong seemed to live her conviction — and to get away with it.

She returned her attention to Zoë, whose bright smile still shone upon her mother. "The three of you must come to call beforehand, Lady Nash," she suggested. "We shall have a cup of tea. Afterward, Aunt Winnie will keep a watchful eye on Lady Phaedra. She is the most frightful dragon, I do assure you. Nothing untoward will escape her notice." Then, with mischief in her eye, Zoë turned to Phaedra and winked.

Phoebe laid down her brush with a clatter. "Oh, let her go, Mamma," she said, turning from her easel. "Phae needs to get out of the house before she turns into a piece of furniture — a footstool, most likely."

Suddenly, Phaedra jerked to her feet. She was rather alarmed to find herself almost excited by the prospect of Zoë's card party, an excitement which had more to do with Zoë's guest list than was strictly wise. Fleetingly, she closed her eyes, still able to feel the strength of Talbot's long, lean body pressed to hers. The searing heat of his hand on her breast. Dear God. She must be quite mad.

"I do not know, Zoë," she murmured, her hand settling lightly over her abdomen. "I . . . I haven't anything to wear."

"Wear my new pink silk," Phoebe suggested, snapping shut her paint box. "It's too long for me anyway, and too low, Mamma says." This last was added with a disparaging glance at Lady Nash.

"You are a debutante, Phoebe," her mother protested. "And the neckline is far too daring. I can't think where my mind was to have let you order it."

Phoebe shrugged and stood. "Then Phae might as well have it," she said equivocally. "I've a dozen more anyway. Come upstairs with us, Miss Armstrong. You must see if it will do."

"No," said Phaedra two minutes later in Phoebe's bedchamber. "No, this isn't right for me. I prefer gray. Or brown."

"Oh, I *love* it." Zoë whispered the words almost reverently.

Of course Zoë loved it. Her wardrobe was dashing. *Zoë* was dashing. Phaedra was not. And yet, when she looked down at the shimmering pink silk draped across her arm, Phaedra longed for a bit of adventure. The pale fabric looked almost opalescent against her ivory skin, and the high waist was encircled by a wide satin ribbon in a daring shade of green.

"You must have it," her sister declared. "You can wear the pink sapphire necklace Nash gave you for your twenty-first. It is to die for, Phae, and you've never even had it out of the box."

"No," she repeated, letting it slide onto the bed in a crush of fabric. "I . . . I cannot. My figure — it is too ample. This is too revealing."

"Nonsense!" declared Zoë, snatching it up again. "Phae, it is perfect! You will be quite the most striking lady present."

Phaedra looked at her in confusion. "Why are you doing this, Zoë?" she asked quietly.

Still clutching the gown, Zoë folded her arms across her chest, and let her gaze trail down Phaedra's white chemise. "Because I have decided, Phae, that you are to be my project this season," she said musingly. "You are going to save me from expiring of my terminal ennui."

"Ah, is that it?" said Phaedra dryly.

"No, not all of it," Zoë admitted. Then she hesitated. "Phae, are your breasts bound under that shift?"

Phaedra colored furiously. "They just need smoothing out, that's all."

Phoebe giggled. "She thinks they are too large, but they're the same as mine."

Zoë shook her head and made a *tsk* sound. "What nonsense," she said. "Unwrap that frightful rag at once. Now, listen. I have a tidbit of fascinating news to share."

"Indeed?" Phaedra eyed her suspiciously. "Of what sort?"

"The *very* fascinating sort." Zoë fanned her face with her empty hand as if overheated. "The wicked Lord Avoncliffe sent his acceptance this morning. It seems *something* about my silly little party has intrigued him. Now will you please try on the dress? And the necklace. What about those spectacles? Must you absolutely wear them?"

"Only for reading, but she won't admit it," said Phoebe, leaping from the window seat from which she'd been observing. "Now who is Lord Avoncliffe, Phae? How did you meet him?"

"He is no one," said Phaedra. "And yes, I need my spectacles."

"Oh, he's someone," Phoebe sang, "and I'm going to tell Mamma."

Zoë looked down her nose. "Really, Lady Phoebe," she murmured, her tone as haughty as a duchess. "I should have thought you more grown up than that. After all, what is a season in Town without its little

151

intrigues?"

Phoebe hesitated. "Oh, well . . . yes, I daresay." She flashed Zoë a conciliatory smile. "And Phae only wears the glasses to make herself appear smarter than the rest of us."

Phaedra surveyed them both with steady eyes. "That is not hard to do when you both are so very silly," she said. "And there is no intrigue. Lord Avoncliffe is a handsome gentleman who thinks far too well of himself. Moreover, I can't think why it matters what I wear."

"Because we all wish to see something besides gray with that marvelous hair of yours," Zoë urged.

It was on the tip of Phaedra's tongue to refuse her, and to do so with the tart-tongued gracelessness she generally reserved for people who meddled in her business — in other words, Mamma and Phoebe. But she said nothing. It had been a long time since Phaedra had had a friend near her own age — one who could match her in wit and intellect — so she was loath to disappoint Zoë.

Moreover, there was a second, more troublesome reason for her hesitation. Phaedra turned her face to the shaft of afternoon sun which spilt through the window and looked at the garden beyond. The feel of Tristan Talbot's full, soft lips upon hers was not yet a distant memory. And last night — the taut, barely-leashed strength in him. His spicy-clean scent teasing at her nostrils and the warmth of his mouth near her ear. Phaedra closed her eyes as the dreamy, seductive listlessness began to melt through her again.

Oh, foolish, foolish girl! Had she not learnt her lesson long ago?

Apparently not.

Apparently, she had not changed at all. Her passions, it seemed — those foolish fantasies and that dark, unseemly hunger — still lurked just below the detached demeanor she had so carefully crafted these last few years. Phaedra's will was little more than a façade, and one which was destined to crack, it would now appear, at the merest blow. A kiss. A tiny, teasing kiss from a scoundrel who would likely never wish to kiss her again. And yet this knowledge — this shameful certainty — could not stop her from yearning to be an utter fool.

"Phae, please," Zoë gently pressed. "Take Phoebe's dress. We are friends now, are we not?"

Phaedra turned back, draped the dress carefully across her arm, then lifted her gaze to Zoë and Phoebe. "Thank you both, then," she said quietly. "I shall take it."

For the third time in as many days, Tristan Talbot found himself rigging out as a proper gentleman, then digging through his old jewelry case. Uglow watched wordlessly as Tristan again slid the heavy signet ring onto his finger, then helped him into his coat.

Tristan looked down as his hand slid from the sleeve. The chunk of gold seemed to weigh down his hand much as he was weighed down by duty, and by the hope that this time, in some small way, he would not fail his father.

As much as he hated to admit it, there was a part of him that felt challenged for the first time in a long while. There was the vaguest sense of purpose stirring inside the void which constituted his conscience, rather like an acorn rolling about in an empty ale keg. And yet there it was, clattering round and round, the sound not entirely unwelcome.

"Shall I 'ave the gig brought round, sir?" Uglow's deep voice sounded as if it had risen from a tomb — a tomb in Whitechapel, of course.

"Just my stick, old boy," said Tristan, giving his cuffs one last tug. "I think I shall walk."

Perhaps, he considered as he set off, the spring air would clear his head. His morning had been spent with his father again, and with chasing ghosts, or so it felt.

In the past several days, he had had meetings with both the young ladies who'd witnessed the murder — the former of which had been almost disconcertingly memorable, if not useful. For her part, Zoë Armstrong had wanted only to tease, and to talk of Lady Phaedra, a topic Tristan would as soon have avoided.

Following that, he'd interviewed three separate members of the Metropolitan Police. His nights had been spent lurking about Madame Vostrikova's and discovering all he could about her notorious establishment. All of it had been to no avail, unless one counted the sweetly chaste kiss he'd stolen from Lady Phaedra behind her parlor door. He still had a dead Russian on his hands, and no one knew anything. No one had seen or heard anything. Even worse, perhaps, no one cared.

No one save his father. And his reasons were not precisely altruistic.

Perhaps Lord de Vendenheim, Peel's man in the Home Office, cared? Tristan was about to find out.

The walk to the Travellers' Club was less

than a mile beneath high, blue skies. Gossamer clouds scuttled across Westminster, whilst beneath the sun's glory, everyday London went about its business. Tristan set a steady pace along the choked streets, his rarely used walking stick in hand.

The Travellers' Club was not a stodgy sort of establishment in the style of Brooks's or White's Club. It was a place for adventurers and men who had seen a little of the world. A great many foreigners belonged, thus the club boasted one of the best libraries in London, along with newspapers in half a dozen languages. The food was decent, the coffee notoriously strong, and the billiards tables level. Cards, of course, were played all night. It was perhaps the one small slice of London society in which Tristan did not feel out of place, and though he rarely visited, they never failed to remember him.

In Pall Mall, he entered the cool, shadowy depths of the club's entrance hall and handed the stick over to the elderly porter who greeted him.

"My lord." The servant bowed.

"How do you do, Fleming?" Tristan passed him his hat. "I'm looking for a chap named de Vendenheim. Can't say as I know him."

Fleming motioned toward the morning

156

room. "The vicomte is alone at a table by the windows, my lord," he said. "A very tall, very dark man. You cannot miss him."

Tristan thanked him and went in. Fleming was right. De Vendenheim was a man one noticed. He was taller, even, than Tristan himself, and almost as dark. Observing Tristan's approach, he snapped shut his newspaper and came at once to his feet, unfolding himself with an elegant grace.

He was not, however, an especially elegant man upon closer inspection. His clothing, Tristan noted with approval, was of good quality but hardly fashionable. His long, olive face had a cast as foreign as Tristan's, with hard cheekbones accented by a pair of dark, hooded eyes which looked deeply cynical. The newspaper, too, was foreign. Italian, Tristan thought, glancing at it.

He extended his hand. "Good afternoon, de Vendenheim," he said. "Thank you for coming."

"Had I any choice, given who your father is?" The words were not accusatory, merely blunt.

Tristan's smile was muted. "No more choice than I, I daresay, when he bade me look into this wretched business," he answered, sweeping his hand toward a table.

"Shall we sit, sir? Perhaps have some coffee?"

De Vendenheim's eyes were grim. "At least it's strong here."

Tristan sent one of the servants off to fetch a pot, then sat, stretching out his booted legs. "Owing to my father's health," he began, "I had little choice but to accept his request to help him in this matter. I should like you to understand that. Though what, precisely, I'm to do thus far escapes me."

De Vendenheim was studying his face. "I'm given to understand you worked reconnaissance for a time in Greece," he remarked. "I daresay Hauxton thinks you have something to offer."

Tristan laughed, but it was cold and flat. "I was a mercenary," he corrected. "I made war for sport — or helped to make it — because I was young and idealistic, and it seemed like an exciting life."

Something bleak and knowing passed over de Vendenheim's visage. "Ah, I see," he finally said. "And did you find it so?"

Tristan looked away. "For a time, I suppose," he said. "War always sounds exhilarating to those who have not seen it firsthand. It always sounds . . . so bloody noble."

"And instead it is merely bloody." De Vendenheim's mouth twisted. "In that, sir, we do agree. I have most assuredly seen it firsthand, and do not care to do so again."

Tristan surveyed his tight countenance. "Napoleon," he guessed. "You are from the Continent, I collect."

"Alsace, amongst other places," he said, sorrow softening his hard black eyes. "But there is little left of the Alsace that I remember."

The moment was weighted by a shared understanding, and with a poignancy Tristan had not felt in a long time. Sharply, he cleared his throat. "Look here, de Vendenheim, I don't mean to cause any trouble for you fellows at the Home Office. I think I can manage my father. But part of the problem is that he's sick — or more honestly, he's dying. And for a man with his sense of duty, the powerlessness which the end brings is almost more than he can bear."

"I'm sorry. I did not know." De Vendenheim seemed to relax, his shoulders rolling almost imperceptibly forward. "Well, go on. What did you wish to ask?"

Tristan relaxed into his chair as the servant returned with a silver tray. "I've already spoken to the Metropolitan Police and the two young ladies who witnessed the death," he said, observing as the servant tipped the pot and lifted it high, filling the cups expertly. "If you'll just tell me what you've learnt of this dead chap, I'll be on my way."

De Vendenheim took his cup, then mechanically repeated much of what Tristan already knew. Gorsky was a Russian who had been in England for many years. He lived in a flat in the rear of one of Vostrikova's houses, had no family, and was widely believed a homosexual which, given his profession, made a perverse sort of sense.

"Yes, I've managed to learn a bit about Mr. Gorsky's brothel myself," said Tristan. "I gather the sort of clientele they attract prefer not to be seen entering the front door."

A ghost of a smile touched his lips. "They are also not the sort of clients who will welcome your father's interference," he said. "The house caters to the kind of perversions most men would rather keep secret."

"Like what?" asked Tristan flatly.

De Vendenheim turned his hand palm up, a gesture of resignation. "Flagellation," he admitted. "Sodomy. Bondage of all types. Young girls — and more recently, boys, too. Unimaginable cruelty, in some cases."

Tristan knew all this, of course, but he'd wished to have de Vendenheim confirm it. Nonetheless, hearing it recited aloud made him wince.

De Vendenheim shrugged. "It is not for me to judge the depravity of other men's sexual appetites," he said, "so long as no one unwilling is involved. But the madam who owns the brothel is said to be able to procure anything on a whim — anything needed to tempt the jaded palates of her wealthy customers. And that has the stench of *un*willingness about it."

Tristan sipped at his coffee. "I saw two fine unmarked carriages pull through the back lane whilst I watched the place last night," said he pensively.

"While you *watched?*" Anger sketched across his face. "I hope to God you weren't seen."

Tristan lifted a steady gaze. "My dear fellow," he said quietly, "there's not a chance in hell."

De Vendenheim looked at him for a moment, then nodded tightly as if acknowledging his opponent's skill. "I trust you were not, then."

"The carriages stopped but an instant," said Tristan, resuming his tale. "Both times, women were bundled out the back door and into the carriages. One of them appeared hunched forward beneath her cloak, and there was something . . . something in her posture." He set the coffee down again and looked at de Vendenheim very directly. "I wondered, frankly, if she were bound."

De Vendenheim's jaw hardened. "I do not doubt it," he gritted. "I fear a dead man in the Strand will be the least of this foul business before all's said and done."

"What do you know of the proprietress?"

De Vendenheim appeared to sneer. "Her name is Vostrikova," he said quietly. "Lilya Vostrikova. I've tried like the devil to find her, but they claim she's away at her country house in Bordeaux."

Tristan returned his gaze to de Vendenheim. "My father tells me Madame Vostrikova was once thought to be a spy," he said, "and that she came to London with Czartoryski, the Russian statesman."

"Yes, but he's a Pole," said de Vendenheim meaningfully. "And just now, trouble is brewing in Poland and Russia is not happy. Czartoryski is stuck in the middle of it."

Tristan had eyed an unusual knot in the woodwork of the tabletop, and was absently circling it with his fingertip. "Trouble is always brewing in Europe," he said noncommittally. "Which reminds me — do you not find it interesting that this dead man somehow found his way to one of the very few people in London who has a connection to

Russia?"

De Vendenheim lifted his angular black brows. "Kemble, do you mean?" he murmured. "Certainly he has business associates there, and knows a little of the language. But what does that suggest?"

Tristan's finger stopped in midmotion. "Actually, I meant Lady Phaedra Northampton."

"Lady *Phaedra?*"

"Indeed." Tristan watched him steadily. "Do you know her?"

"I do," he said stiffly. "The lady is a paragon of virtue."

"But her half brother, Lord Nash, is Russian, is he not?"

"I . . . why, yes," de Vendenheim admitted. "In part."

Tristan could sense the man's hesitance. "Wasn't Nash mixed up in that French scandal over gun running to the Greek revolutionaries a year or two back?" he pressed. "I daresay *that* got Russia's attention."

A deathly silence fell across the table. The man's face had gone black as murder. "I should like to know, Lord Avoncliffe, just who you have been speaking with," said de Vendenheim icily. "This is not a topic to be bandied about in club rooms."

163

"Oh, I am not *bandying* it," said Tristan, his voice equally cold. "I am stating it as a fact. I know he was in Paris. I know he spent weeks meeting with the French authorities. And I know, Lord de Vendenheim, that a great deal of Greek money changed hands in that misbegotten deal."

"And *I* wish to know who told you all this so that I can relieve him of his employment." De Vendenheim looked as if he were about to pound his fist upon the table. "This is a serious business, you fool."

Tristan leaned very slowly into him. "I fear you forget yourself, my lord." His voice was lethally soft. "And you forget that I have contacts — close contacts — all over the Hellenic Peninsula. Indeed, I have watched their sons and their brothers die in the mud and the blood of Greece. I do not need some insignificant English bureaucrat whispering drawing room tittle-tattle in my ear."

De Vendenheim drew back, his gaze lowering. "Your pardon," he said stiffly. "Again, I forget your past."

Tristan inclined his head. De Vendenheim realized he had misjudged his adversary. People often did that, he had noticed. It was his appearance, perhaps — he had been cursed with boyish good looks. Or perhaps it was his mongrel lineage, or his less-than-serious attitude about life.

Whatever the cause, Tristan was often thought something less than brilliant, and indeed, he was often perfectly stupid, but not in the way people generally believed. *Esse quam videri.* That was his motto.

"Are you going to answer my question, de Vendenheim?" he asked calmly.

"As you wish." The man glowered across the table. "Lord Nash is part Russian, but he has no contact with the government and scarcely any family. A couple of elderly cousins, both of whom have one foot in the grave. You may trust we looked into it. Yes, he did go to Paris, but as . . . as a sort of an emissary of the Government. If you do not believe me, you may ask Mr. Peel. Or your father, perhaps."

He was lying. Tristan realized it at once. And yet not wholly lying, either. Tristan watched him warily for a moment, judging his next move. "Very well," he finally said. "You believe the two young ladies were just innocent bystanders?"

"I do."

"And your associate, Mr. Kemble?" asked Tristan. "He was innocent, too?"

De Vendenheim gave a bark of laughter. "God, no," he said. "Kemble wasn't even born innocent. But in this matter . . . yes, I

165

believe him above suspicion."

Tristan smiled, and pushed away his coffee cup. He wasn't sure he believed it. "Well, it would seem Mr. Gorsky had the remarkable misfortune to be simply in the wrong alley, leaning on the wrong door, at the wrong time," he said, rising. "Rather a bad streak, if you ask me. But you, however, are in luck."

De Vendenheim sounded unimpressed. "How is that, sir?"

Tristan extracted his pocket watch. "I am about to be late to a card game," he said, looking at it. "A very important card game."

He looked up to see that de Vendenheim had pinned him with a hooded *why-am-I-not-surprised* stare.

Tristan tucked his watch away, bade his companion good evening, and headed toward the door, whistling. Behind him, de Vendenheim snapped his newspaper. "By the way, Talbot," he said, just as Tristan's foot touched the threshold. "We pulled a dead man out of the river last night."

Tristan turned. "Is that something new?"

De Vendenheim shrugged. "This one was," he answered. "The River Police found a note in his pocket written in Russian — and a very nasty slash across his throat."

■ ■ ■ ■

Aunt Winnie, the Dowager Lady Nash soon learned, was Mrs. Weyden, a rather merry widow who was not, as it happened, anyone's aunt, but rather an old family friend of Lord and Lady Rannoch. The marquess was a hard-edged, rather unsociable Scot with more money than Croesus and enough temper to match. Lady Rannoch had given him two children with a third on the way, and had brought two young siblings and an orphaned cousin into the marriage.

In addition, Mrs. Weyden had two sons whom Zoë Armstrong also accounted as relations. And somewhere in the picture, Zoë had explained, was an elderly uncle, Sir Hugh, upon whom she doted. Zoë had grown up with a large, rather raucous family, something Phaedra rather envied.

Lady Nash, of course, had begun to dither over the entire business by early evening. "Dear, dear!" she clucked as they started down the steps. "Mrs. Weyden is said to be a little *outré,* Phaedra. And Miss Armstrong — well, there is the unfortunate mystery of her parentage. Indeed, this mightn't be quite the thing."

"It is too late, Mamma," Phoebe warned,

lifting her hems and stepping onto the pavement. "Besides, Miss Armstrong's father *is* a marquess. And if Lord Rannoch trusts Mrs. Weyden to chaperone his daughter, she must be quite nice."

"It is too late," Phaedra agreed, almost wishing it were not. "Besides, the whole affair will be a dead bore, I am sure."

This was madness, she thought as Lady Nash dropped the knocker. Not the fact that she was attending a simple card party. Phaedra was not a complete recluse. No, the madness was this dangerous, wholly irrational sense of euphoria. An almost girlish giddiness which seemed to lift her from her slippers. Moreover, an evening spent in frivolity was an evening *not* spent looking for Millie. Phaedra had not fully considered that before accepting Zoë's invitation.

Mr. Talbot likely would not turn up, but if he did, perhaps she might learn something from him pertaining to Gorsky? And that might help find Millie. The thought consoled her, but only slightly.

They were politely received into a small but fashionable parlor by Mrs. Weyden. The room was decorated in shades of deep red and yellow, not in the French fashion, but in a darker, heavier style which Phaedra thought might be Dutch. A bombé commode chest with an ornately carved cornice and ball feet dominated one wall, while bowls of flowers seemed to be everywhere. It was a room which was at once foreign and pleasantly inviting.

Zoë made a pretty curtsy to Lady Nash, and thanked her again for allowing Phaedra to keep her company for the evening. Tonight Zoë wore shimmering gold, a confection of lace and ruching which was cut square across the neckline, with full sleeves to the elbow. She looked especially small and dark — like a porcelain doll — and utterly charming.

After exchanging half an hour of pleasantries, Lady Nash and Phoebe floated out the door, and as so often was the case, Phaedra was forgotten. Phaedra did not mind. Being forgotten about, she had learned, allowed one a measure of freedom. Sometimes a dangerous measure.

Zoë drew Phaedra into the withdrawing room where the card tables had been set up. Servants were already scurrying in and out with trays of crystal and platters of refreshments, and one of the housemaids was mixing lemon juice into a massive silver punch bowl. She was eyeing the arrangement almost gleefully. "I have a notion, Phae," she whispered. "If the cards are too dull, we shall roll back the rugs and waltz! You do dance, do you not?"

Phaedra smiled lamely. "A little, but very ill," she said. "Country dances, mostly."

"Oh, a country dance won't do." Zoë was drifting about the room, nibbling at the various refreshments. "Avoncliffe will wish you to waltz with him — especially in that dress."

"Zoë, pray do not be silly." Phaedra shifted uncomfortably.

Zoë spun around, a sliver of cucumber pinched delicately between her fingers. "Oh, he will," she said confidently. "Besides, I think the waltz should be the only dance allowed. Avoncliffe is famous for it, by the way. Yes, he will certainly ask you. Indeed, I believe he might be bewitched by you, Phae."

Phaedra rolled her eyes. "Oh, he's nothing but a handsome fribble, Zoë," she chided. "You cannot believe him serious."

"Oh, I don't know." Zoë closed the distance between them. "When he came to call on me yesterday, he asked a score of questions about you."

"About *me* — ?"

A mischievous smile curled Zoë's mouth. "Of course I dared not mention any of it in front of your mother and your sister."

"What sort of questions?"

Zoë cast her eyes upward as if pondering it. "Let's see, he asked how long I'd known you," she answered. "How did the two of us come to be shopping together. That sort of thing. Oh — and Lord Nash. He seemed most interested in the fact that Nash was your half-brother."

Phaedra hesitated. "What can my brother have to do with anything?"

"I couldn't say." Zoë shrugged. "By the way, is it true Lord Nash is Russian? I did not know."

Phaedra instantly stiffened. "Stefan's mother was related to the Russian royal family on one side," she acknowledged. "But her father was Montenegrin. Stefan was born there. It is his home — after England, of course."

"Oh, then that's not quite the same thing, is it?" Zoë snapped off one end of the cucumber between her flawless white teeth.

But Phaedra's mind was working furiously. What bearing could Stefan's background possibly have on the Foreign Office's investigation? Surely Talbot did not think Stefan was involved? Good Lord. Nothing could be further from the truth. Horror flooded through Phaedra — horror that swiftly turned to irritation. By God, she would not have Talbot dragging this mess to Stefan's doorstep. That was precisely what she had striven to avoid. What she *had* to avoid.

A quarter hour later, the drawing room was swimming with guests, most of whom were soon drinking champagne, and all of whom seemed to know one another well. It was a shockingly boisterous crowd, and certainly not drawn from the highest echelons of the *ton*.

Phaedra wanted, inexplicably, to see Tristan Talbot again. Perhaps if she did, she could convince herself that she had been right about him all along; that he was just a handsome ne'er-do-well of no special significance. And that the kisses they had shared had meant nothing. Still, there was a raw, unrestrained sensuality in him that called to the deepest, most hidden places in her soul, to those feelings she wasn't sure she wished ever to feel again.

Mrs. Weyden had returned to stand by the door and greet everyone — not with a smile or a curtsy, but by kissing both their cheeks in a most familiar way. Zoë lifted one shoulder. "She lived a long while in Flanders," she whispered by way of explanation. "I think they must kiss like the French there."

To her acute discomfort, Phaedra sensed it the moment Tristan Talbot entered the room. It was not a sort of raised-hackles awareness — though perhaps it should have been — but more of a shimmering, disconcerting warmth. She was standing by the piano with a glass of lemonade, chatting with one of Mrs. Weyden's sons, when a faint stillness settled over the room, as if all eyes had turned toward the door.

Phaedra, too, turned. The awareness sharpened, piercing and acute. Their gazes met, and Talbot's hand — engaged in passing his elegant, gold-knobbed stick to the footman — froze. A look passed between them; something swift. Heated. A bolt of raw desire shot through Phaedra, utterly unexpected.

And then the moment passed. He cut his glittering gaze away. The murmur of the crowd resumed, if indeed it had ever paused. By the fireplace, someone laughed. Crystal tinkled on a tray. Talbot bowed elegantly over Mrs. Weyden's hand, then lifted it to his lips, making her titter almost nervously.

Phaedra felt instantly shaken. *Heated, indeed!*

Dear God, what a goose she was. Had she no moral compass at all? To feel such lust for a man one hardly knew and didn't especially like. Her mother was doubtless right. Lust was a wayward, shameful emotion, something true ladies did not feel. Brothels like Mr. Gorsky's existed for a reason. Gentlemen, Lady Nash had once said, might need to taste a little sin from time to time, but they did not wish to come home and converse with it over the dinner table. No man would ever wish to wed a woman who could scarce control her own passions.

But despite all this well-remembered advice, Phaedra could not suppress a surreptitious glance in Talbot's direction. He was striding across the room on his long, muscular legs to greet Zoë. Indeed, he had scarcely seen Phaedra at all.

Somehow, she turned back to Augustus Weyden and brightened her smile. "You were telling me, Mr. Weyden, of your life in Ghent," she said. "How often are you there?"

"Half the year, thereabouts," he answered, setting a light hand under her elbow. "It is something of a Mecca for painters, and we are a family of artists, you know." He paused to gesture across the room with his wineglass. "Come, Lady Phaedra, I see my brother has just arrived."

Phaedra passed the next hour going mechanically through the motions of making idle conversation, offering her hand to those gentlemen whom she did not know, and curtsying when appropriate. Her manners, she knew, were flawless. Lady Nash's flightiness notwithstanding, she understood what society demanded of a marquess's daughter, and had ruthlessly instilled it in both of hers. But all the while, she watched Talbot.

The man drew people like bees to a field of clover, she noted peevishly. The older women, a trio of Mrs. Weyden's friends, hovered about him for a time, flirting and fanning a little too furiously. When he gave them no encouragement beyond his beaming, sideways grin, they drifted away one by one, their void filled by a knot of fashionable young men. They surrounded Talbot like a litter of fawning puppies, almost tumbling over one another in their efforts to angle for his attention.

Mr. Popularity, she thought a little sourly. Yet another thing she and Talbot would never have in common.

A raconteur of noted skill, apparently, Talbot was soon holding up both hands, palms out, and laughing until he at last gave in to their pleadings for some sort of story. The small crowd was soon near stitches as the tale — something to do with runaway horses, a pack of foxhounds, and a half-naked magistrate — built to its crescendo. From time to time, his booming, good-natured laughter would ring out, and Phaedra would be unable to stop herself from turning to look once again.

It should be against the law, really, for a man to be so unnaturally handsome.

But was there any harm in looking? All the other females in the room were; the young ones surreptitiously, the older ladies almost avariciously. Talbot's skin was like warm honey, his hair a dark mass of unruly waves which would have looked unfashionable and far too long on any other man.

Above his sinfully full lips, his cheeks were smooth and lean, giving over to high, perfect cheekbones, putting Phaedra in mind of some sleek, sensuous Sicilian prince — not that she'd ever seen such a creature. His jaw was a hard angle, and a pair of thick, inky eyebrows rose to an arch near their ends, almost as an afterthought.

Only his nose saved him from perfection. Hawkish and arrogant, it was Lord Hauxton's, beyond question. Had anyone questioned Talbot's paternity, that nose could have hammered a nail in the coffin of doubt. Somehow, Phaedra managed to turn away and distract herself by chatting with another of Zoë's friends, a Miss Miranda Reesdale, a rather plump, pretty lady who seemed amiable enough. Nonetheless, she was almost relieved when Zoë called for the card playing to commence.

Suddenly, Phaedra felt a warm, heavy hand settle lightly at the small of her back.

"Is it too much to hope, Phae, that we might pair off?" someone murmured in her ear.

Phaedra turned to look over her shoulder. "I beg your pardon?" she managed, forcing herself to ignore the surge of heat against her spine.

Tristan Talbot grinned down at her, sending more warmth instantly to her cheeks — and to some other places as well. "The two of us," he said again. "Might we partner?"

But she was looking at him in stupefaction, somehow distracted by his thick, black eyelashes, which were impossibly long, and by his mouth as it moved to form the words. *A harlot's mouth,* she thought. Full, beautifully sculpted lips that settled over you like butterfly wings. And oh, how she wanted it.

But he had a lean, hard warrior's body to go with that lush mouth, she reminded herself, and the insidious ability to seem far more benign than he was. She must be careful. She must not gaze too long upon that mouth, and let her mind wander. And yet, that plump, sensuous swell in the middle of his bottom lip was so —

"Lady Phaedra?" he repeated. "Have you a partner for whist?"

The card game. "I . . . no, th-thank you," she stuttered. "I am engaged to play with Mr. Upjohn."

Talbot's hand did not move, but instead made a warm — and entirely inappropriate — little circle at the small of her back. "Lucky devil," he remarked, his gaze drifting over her face. "Ah, well. Another time, perhaps?"

Another time, perhaps. The same words he'd spoken just two nights past, his body pressed to hers in the alleyway. The words he probably spoke to every winsome woman who turned him down. If any of them did.

Suddenly, a flash of certainty struck. Yes. That long-ago night in the tavern . . . She was quite certain now, though it had been dark, and he had been battered and bloodied. Drunk, too — and yet oddly chivalrous. Was she forever destined to keep bumping into the infernal man in dark, dangerous places — and, in truth, be thoroughly charmed by him? Still, she could ill afford to turn to mush now. "Pray take your flirtations elsewhere, Mr. Talbot," she said coolly.

178

"You have no rapt audience here."

The irrepressible smile deepened. "Ah, perhaps not," he acknowledged. "But even a big dumb ox likes a challenge now and again."

"Kindly take your hand from my spine before someone notices." Her voice was quiet and a little unsteady. "Really, Mr. Talbot. Or Lord Avoncliffe. Or whoever you are. I am not a challenge to you. I am not . . . anything to you."

"You are a most remarkably beautiful woman to me," he countered. "That pink gown, by the way, is simply stunning, and the greenish ribbon is a dashing touch."

"Thank you," she said stiffly.

"But I think I like you best in gray, and with your spectacles sliding down your nose." He leaned into her, and dropped his voice. "You look so very stern and disapproving. Like a repressed governess looking for a wayward pupil to punish."

Phaedra's eyes widened. "I beg your pardon?"

"I could volunteer," he murmured, his grin widening — if such a thing were possible.

Her eyebrows snapped together. "Volunteer for what?"

He gave a speciously innocent shrug. "I

cannot say," he admitted. "It is very hard for a wayward pupil to choose his own punishment. There are so many to consider."

"I could slap your face," she suggested tartly.

"That wasn't the part I had in mind," he answered.

"Nonetheless, it strikes me as ideal," she answered. "Really, Mr. Talbot. I am a lady. I am not supposed to have an earthly clue what you are talking about. Kindly allow me to at least feign innocence, and go ply your naughty wares with one of those ladies who looks eager to buy them."

He lifted his perfect, angular eyebrows. "I can be cheaply had," he offered, eyes sparkling. Then he sighed. "You are perfectly right, I know. I should pretend. But you are no green miss, Phae — I don't know how I know that, but I do — and you're no fool, either."

No green miss.

He could not know the blow he had struck her, however true his words might have been. Talbot saw. They all saw — once they got close enough. It was why he had dared to kiss her to begin with.

Good God. Her imagination was running wild. Phaedra drew in a steadying breath.

"You presume to know me very well, sir, upon one short meeting."

"Ah, but it was one short, *memorable* meeting," he countered. "In fact, not one instant of it has escaped me. Tell me, Lady Phaedra, why do you not have a husband at your age? — not that I'm offering, mind — it would never do. Still, a man does wonder."

Phaedra set her head to one side and studied him for a moment. "Does it never occur to anyone of your sex, I wonder, that perhaps there are women who simply do not wish the annoyance of a husband?"

His eyes widened in surprise, then just as quickly fell again. "Explanation accepted," he said swiftly. "Which rather clears the decks for me, since I find you so charming to flirt with."

Phaedra let her gaze fall to the floor. "Flirting can be a dangerous business, Mr. Talbot," she said. "Not for you, perhaps. But for me. Now kindly excuse me."

And on that, she walked away, abandoning him to the now-empty corner. Her hands, however, were shaking. That cursed, inevitable question. Even from the likes of Talbot, whose morals certainly left no room to suspect hers. And flirting? Good heavens, she did not flirt.

The other guests were now milling around

the card tables as Zoë organized who was to sit where. Phaedra and Mr. Upjohn were seated with Miss Reesdale, who, Phaedra learned, was betrothed to Mr. Upjohn's elder brother, who was not present tonight. She was partnered instead by another of Zoë's distant relations, Lord Robert Rowland, a young man known vaguely to Phaedra as something of a scoundrel — and the source of Zoë's illicit cheroots.

Like Tristan Talbot, Lord Robert was too handsome for his own good. He flirted outrageously with both she and Miss Reesdale, and kept leaning just a little too near them, his voice a little too solicitous. Phaedra found herself able to ignore him. *He was just a handsome man.* A boy, really. He would not weaken her will or her knees or any other part of her body simply by sharing a card table with her, and engaging in a little harmless flirtation. He was not Tristan Talbot, who — Phaedra was beginning to suspect — ran deep and still and dark beneath his patina of aimless charm. Perhaps that was why Talbot drew her. *Tempted* her. It was an unsettling thought indeed.

The four of them played whist, but in a rather desultory fashion, and for stakes which were, of course, almost laughably low to the gentlemen. It hardly mattered. Miss

Reesdale wished to gossip, and to talk about her wedding, a topic which the gentlemen warmed to with surprising grace.

Phaedra tried not to envy Miss Reesdale her excitement. A wedding, after all, was thought to be the high point of a woman's life. Well, second only, perhaps, to the birth of her children — and Miss Reesdale's marriage would doubtless be blessed with children. She would grow old with a husband whom she likely would respect, possibly even adore. She would have her own home, and be permitted a measure of freedom which society allowed only to married women.

But there were other things in life, Phaedra consoled herself. And for the most part, she already had a household to run. Tony's wife was in exile. At Stefan's seat in Hampshire, his wife Xanthia was present but perhaps two or three months a year, and was happy to leave the running of things to others. Phaedra lived a life of luxury under her elder brother's gentle protection. Her close and loving family involved her — so much as she would allow — in everything they did. Few spinsters had it so well. And yet it was not enough.

Whose fault, however, was that? This loneliness — this awful aching emptiness she sometimes felt — would never be filled. Never be quieted.

Her surging guilt was interrupted by the heat of someone's gaze. She turned only slightly, and gave a careful, sidelong glance. From across the room, Tristan Talbot was watching her, his eyes flashing with dark fire, and he assuredly was not grinning. Indeed, he looked nothing like himself.

"Lady Phaedra?" A cool hand touched her wrist.

She turned back to see Miss Reesdale blinking at her.

"Yes, I beg your pardon," said Phaedra a little breathlessly.

"Currants or plums?" she asked, her eyes wide. "For the bride cake?"

Phaedra managed a smile. "Oh, plums," she said with certainty. "I attended eight weddings last year, and everyone had currants."

"Did they indeed?" Miss Reesdale's fine eyebrows drew together. "Well, one wouldn't wish to be ordinary."

"For my part, Miss Reesdale, I *adore* plums," said Lord Robert, covering her hand with his as his gaze swept down her purple gown. "The plumper and the sweeter the better."

"Robin," said Upjohn warningly, "don't

make me call you out." He grinned good-naturedly, tossed down a ten of clubs, and shoved the hand to his left. "If you keep flirting with my sister-to-be, I shall feel duty bound to kill you."

"What?" demanded Lord Robert. "What did I say?"

"Oh, don't come the innocent with me," said Upjohn. "Even Avoncliffe over there has been eyeing you disapprovingly — and he is the master of scoundrels."

Miss Reesdale was giggling now, and blushing prettily. Phaedra turned to Lord Robert and smiled dryly. "It would appear, Lord Robert, that your reputation precedes you," she said. "Miss Reesdale, I believe the trick was yours?"

"Oh," said Miss Reesdale vaguely. "Oh, dear. I have forgotten — what is trumps?"

"Hearts, my dear," said Lord Robert, winking at her. "How could it be otherwise with two such beauties at the table?"

Finally Miss Reesdale tossed down a card.

"Your cousin is a lovely girl," Phaedra remarked to Lord Robert as the play went round again. "It has been my great pleasure to make her acquaintance."

"Who?" Lord Robert looked up from his hand. "Oh, Powder Keg! Yes, she's cracking good fun."

Phaedra's brow furrowed. "Powder Keg?"

Mr. Upjohn leaned nearer. "Robin's brother nicknamed Miss Armstrong that when she was twelve," he said conspiratorially, "and it stuck."

"Aye, and the truest things are said in jest," declared Lord Robert, laying down a trump and sweeping up the hand. "Zoë's positively explosive."

"Speaking of that —" Mr. Upjohn paused to rummage through his coat pocket. "Who d'you like for the pigeon this season, Robin? I've got ten guineas on Sir Edgar Haverfield."

"Sir Edgar?" Lord Robert blew out his cheeks and pondered it. "No, he can't be such a fool as all that. Not two years running."

Upjohn lifted one shoulder and extracted a small leather folio from his coat. "I'm writing it in the book," he declared. "Wager against me at your peril."

"I beg your pardon," twittered Miss Reesdale. "What are you gentlemen wagering *on?*"

"Hearts." Lord Robert declared, tossing down the king of spades.

"But that's a spade," Miss Reesdale protested.

"Heart*break,*" Lord Robert clarified.

"Specifically, whose heart Zoë will shatter this season."

"It's become an annual ritual," Upjohn chimed in. "When all was said and done, I pocketed forty pounds on Sir Edgar last year."

To her shock, Phaedra found herself laughing with the three of them, then she considered the plight of the ill-fated Sir Edgar. "Lord Robert," she said, lightly touching his coat sleeve, "really, I think we ought not encourage this."

But when she looked up again, Tristan Talbot was still watching her, his visage dark as a thundercloud. His roguish smile had vanished. Phaedra drew her hand away, and dropped her gaze to her cards.

From across the room, Tristan observed the card games unfolding in Mrs. Weyden's drawing room. In the end, her guests had tallied up to an odd number, so Tristan had politely — and happily — bowed himself out of the game. He had not come, after all, to play cards.

Indeed, he wasn't perfectly sure why he had come. Pondering it made him twist a little uncomfortably in his chair. Mrs. Weyden leaned across the tea table solicitously. "More claret, Avoncliffe?" she asked, holding out the decanter.

Tristan nodded, though he'd been drinking it steadily this last hour or better. "Thank you," he said. "You keep a fine cellar, Mrs. Weyden."

He watched halfheartedly as she poured, the ruby red liquid swirling thickly into the bowl of his glass. They lingered by the fire now; he, his hostess, and one of her admirers, Sir Bertram Peck, a jovial chap whom Tristan knew from the racing circuit. Taking his glass, Tristan rose to stretch his legs, pacing nearer to the fire which danced in the grate. He felt restless, impatient for something he could not quite put his finger on. It was a novel frustration for him. Indeed, since leaving the battlefields of Greece, Tristan could count on one hand the times he'd felt such chafing dissatisfaction.

Sir Bertram had one hand draped across the settee on which he reclined, his glass lifted in the other as he regaled their hostess. "Yes, last year's Derby left me plump in the pocket, I don't mind saying," he was bragging. "So this year I did it, Winnie. I bought that colt I'd been looking at, the one I mentioned last week?"

"Yes, yes, Hot Pursuit!" Mrs. Weyden

looked rapt. "One could never forget that name."

Sir Bertram slapped his thigh. "A good one, ain't it?" he agreed. "Anyway, he's three now, so I'll have him at the Guineas next month. You should come up with us to Newmarket, old thing — you, too, Avoncliffe."

Tristan, however, was again observing the card players over the rim of his wineglass — four of them in particular — and was compelled to stir himself to attention. "I thank you, Sir Bertram," he said, propping one foot on the brass fender. "But just now my father's health precludes it."

"Quite so, quite so!" said Sir Bertram with gruff sympathy. "Completely understand, old chap. Next year, perhaps?"

Tristan smiled and gave a little bow. "Nothing would give me more pleasure, sir."

But that was a lie, he realized, returning his gaze to the cards. Pulling the pins from Lady Phaedra Northampton's hair, he was increasingly certain, would be vastly more pleasurable than any horse race he'd ever seen — and he'd had some bloody good fun on the circuit in his day.

In his day? Tristan shuddered. God, those sounded like his father's words. Like a man who was cresting the hill of middle age and getting ready to peer down that slippery slope into the fog of the other side. Perhaps it was the fact that he'd recently turned thirty. Or perhaps his father's impending death was troubling him a great deal more than he comprehended.

Was that why he couldn't get his mind off Lady Phaedra? If he was going to look about for a serious flirtation, why not that saucy minx, Zoë Armstrong? She was rich and beautiful, and though some might sneer at her bloodlines, he certainly did not. But he wasn't looking — had never looked — and never really intended to. But there was something . . . something in the turn of Phaedra's face. The sweet, soft line of her cheek. Something deeply feminine which made his heart bottom out. Desire shot to his loins, hot and sweet. Tristan jerked to a halt and drew a deep breath.

Steady on, old boy, he told himself.

But Lady Phaedra had turned her face just so that afternoon in her parlor when she'd dashed behind the door to fetch his hat. His reaction then, whilst cloaked in frivolity, had been irrepressible — and a little dangerous. He had no wish to end up wed to Lady Phaedra Northampton.

But he certainly would like to bed her. All that tightly bound emotion and tightly bound hair were just waiting, he was sure, for some man to set them loose. And that dusky voice. Those *breasts*. Good Lord. Enough to fill a man's hands and then some. How on earth had he missed those the first time round? Perhaps because he'd been distracted by her wide, intelligent eyes. That was surely a first.

Oh, he wasn't serious. He kept to the riper fruit on the low hanging branches, and God knew it was falling in his lap. Ladies who would swiftly invite him to their beds — if not, perhaps, their drawing rooms. Still, he found himself thinking of the Northampton chit at least a dozen times a day. And strangely, every element of his investigation of this murder in the Strand seemed to lead back to her in some small, subtle way. Was he just going a little mad? Or was something deep inside his mind trying to tell him something?

Perhaps he was becoming mildly obsessed by her. Certainly he was obsessed by this wild-goose chase his father had set him off on. He wondered if his father had known that this would happen. Hauxton was a cagey devil, one who understood the darker side of man better than most. He sensed what drove people. What frightened people. It was a part of what made him such a grand and imperious statesman.

Just then Zoë Armstrong approached, bearing down upon her aunt. "Aunt Winnie, we've grown tired of cards," she said in a wheedling voice. "May we not dance? Mrs. Hankle has volunteered to play the pianoforte."

There was no question, of course, of denying Zoë. Across the room, the gentlemen were already drawing back the chairs, and Lady Phaedra was helping Upjohn throw open the four French windows which gave onto the terrace. Indeed, she was looking into the darkened gardens beyond it almost longingly. Inwardly, Tristan grinned. Perhaps opportunity beckoned. And he'd never been a man to pass *that* up.

CHAPTER 6

Dance on the sands, and yet no footing
  seen:
Love is a spirit all compact of fire.

With its crackling fire and tasteful brocade furnishings, Madame Vostrikova's parlor was an oasis of elegance in a sea of sin. Reaching across the narrow table, Lavrin moved his pawn forward two spaces and set it down with a quiet *click*.

"The man they call de Vendenheim is asking questions again, Madame," he murmured, straightening up. "It seems Mr. Peel is taking an interest in our little contretemps."

In the shimmering lamplight, Madame Vostrikova sipped pensively at her wine. "You are wise to warn me, Lavrin," she murmured. "The Home Office, of course, oversees the actions of the police. We will watch carefully, and hope it is no more than that."

"And if it is?"

She surveyed him across the table, her eyes hooded in the lamplight. "Then you will persuade them to lose interest," she said coolly. "Do you comprehend me?"

"*Da,* Madame." Lavrin watched her long, thin hand hover over the board. It little mattered, he knew, which piece she chose. He would fight the good fight, but in the end, he would lose — deliberately, if need be. He was not such a fool as Gorsky had been to tempt Madame's viciousness. Certainly he would not lose his wits — or his life — over a pretty piece of flesh, be it male or female.

Madame slid her bishop diagonally left, capturing the space. "You are quiet, Lavrin," she murmured. "You disagree with my strategy?"

Lavrin lifted one shoulder. "De Vendenheim knows the owner of the shop where Gorsky was found," he answered. "Coincidence, I hope. I theorize that Gorsky knew he was being followed and slipped into the alley to hide. Still, you are wise to be cautious."

Madame Vostrikova considered it. "Gorsky spoke to no one before he died, and he carried nothing on his person," she said. "Your assassin confirmed this, did he not?"

Yes, with a knife to his throat, thought Lavrin. But why risk Madame's wrath? "He was quite sure of it," he answered.

"Still, it bears watching." Her dark gaze flashed. "It is your move, Lavrin, is it not?"

Lavrin chose his next piece — and his next words — with care. "De Vendenheim was seen at the Travellers' Club this afternoon taking coffee with Hauxton's heir," he murmured, flicking a quick glance up at her. "Of course, they are both members, so it likely means nothing, but I mention it, in case —"

"In case I was thinking of having *your* throat slit?" A smile twitched at Madame's mouth. "On that point, my dear Lavrin, I think we needn't worry. Lord Hauxton's son is too busy with the organ between his legs to have much use for the one behind his eyes, *da?*"

Lavrin smiled faintly. "You have Hauxton's assistant now in your pocket?"

"Soon, Lavrin, soon." Madame's gaze darkened. "Nebbett is bringing us some fascinating letters. And in return, I shall give him the young girl whom you found in Calais."

"The girl who was chosen for Lord Cotting?"

"Cotting caught sight of the other redhead," said Madame, lifting one shoulder. "The tavern maid. Besides, the French girl is a beauty — not worth wasting on Cotting, for he knows nothing useful after all. He is — what is the term? — a bag of wind?"

Lavrin chuckled. "A disappointment, yes," he admitted. "But the French girl, she's a fighter."

Madame laughed. "Oh, my friend, have you so little faith in me?" she said. "I had her gagged, then ordered Hettie to rip out her nest with a hot sugar wax. The little bitch is smooth as an egg now, and looks no more than twelve. Can you imagine what a fiend like Nebbett will do for a taste of that?"

Lavrin jumped his knight over a pawn and took the space. "I hope, Lilya, that she does not prove more trouble than she is worth."

"If I get what I want from Nebbett, the inconvenience will little matter." Her eyes were drifting over the board, keen as a hawk's. "A pity Hauxton himself did not possess such tastes. What a juicy little plum he would have made for my pudding."

"There is always the son," Lavrin suggested. "He is, I believe, what the English call a wastrel."

"And therefore utterly useless," said Vostrikova. "Unless he means to step into his father's shoes?"

"There have been rumblings of envy at the Foreign Office," Lavrin answered, moving carelessly. "There are rumors Hauxton wishes him to join the Foreign Office in some secret capacity."

"Indeed?" Madame's mouth curled into a sinister smile as she lifted her next piece. "Then perhaps, Lavrin, I shall wish to reconsider my strategy? That one, most assuredly, can be led around by his cock."

Then Vostrikova set her queen back down. And in that instant, Lavrin realized that — as so often happened when one dealt with the devil — his end was to come swiftly.

"Ah, Lavrin, my friend," she said quietly. "I believe that I have you in check again."

Phaedra set her palms flat against the sturdy wooden column which supported Mrs. Weyden's pergola, then let her spine settle back against it. Forcing her shoulders to relax, Phaedra drew in the scent of spring — blossoming trees and freshly turned earth — while she watched the garden shadows dance to the sway of the lanterns behind her.

Mrs. Weyden's drawing room had grown unbearably hot, and despite the chill of the evening, Phaedra had seized the first moment to escape the stifling air — and the awkward expectations. She was in no mood for the lively exertions of a country dance, and the waltz . . . well, she simply did not dance the waltz, though that was precisely what Zoë had ordered the pianist to strike up.

This one was a light, lovely piece. Schubert, she thought. Fleetingly, Phaedra closed her eyes and allowed herself the pleasure of mentally swaying to the soft, tinkling notes which drifted through the drawing room doors.

"I must confess," said the quiet voice through the gloom, "that I did not much care for the way Lord Robert Rowland kept ogling your bodice tonight."

Eyes flying open, Phaedra gasped.

Tristan Talbot surveyed her from the opposite column, his arms thrown casually over one another, his long legs crossed at the ankles, the picture of perfect masculine repose. How long he had been relaxing there — still as death itself, apparently — was anyone's guess.

"Really, Mr. Talbot." Phaedra's whisper was sharp. "Must you lurk about like that, frightening people?"

"I beg your pardon," he murmured, coming away from the column to pace toward her. "I did not mean to startle you."

"Don't be ridiculous," she returned. "You meant precisely that. Otherwise you would have made your presence known when I came out here five minutes ago."

"I beg your pardon," he said again, his voice a soothing rumble. "But I was not here five minutes ago."

"What nonsense," she said tartly. "You could not possibly have walked past me."

"Could I not?" he murmured. "Perhaps, then, it was magic?"

But distressed by his earlier comment — and her reaction to it — Phaedra had grown wary. "Indeed, I think I should go inside."

"Wait." He caught her gently, his broad, long-fingered hand surprisingly warm upon her arm. "I am sorry, Phae. Have I really upset you?"

He had, but she was not about to tell him so. The problem was not with him, but with her — with her deep, perplexing attraction to him. She was beginning to wish to see beyond the lighthearted façade to those still and dark waters she sometimes glimpsed within. But what if she were just being foolish again? What if the façade was all there

199

was? She had been mistaken before — and let her heart make irreparable misjudgments.

Inside the drawing room behind her, the music fell away. The dancers parted amidst light applause and laughter. "I merely wish to be alone," she finally said, turning to go.

"Not if you go in there, you don't," he said, drawing her incrementally nearer. "It's turned into rather a madhouse."

Phaedra glanced over her shoulder to see that indeed, the crowd appeared to have swollen, and that couples were now crowding the floor as they attempted to square up for a quadrille. She returned her gaze to Talbot and saw nothing but kindness in his face. But handsome men, she knew, were not to be trusted. She shook him off, and stepped back. "Very well," she retorted. "Let us remain, sir. There was something I wished to say to you."

Talbot stood very near her now, his eyes assessing as they drifted over her face, and then perhaps lower. "My, my," he said dryly. "We really aren't flirting anymore, are we?"

"No, we are not." Phaedra tilted her head, attempting to catch his gaze. "Up, up, if you please, Mr. Talbot! Kindly look at me, not my bosom. You and Lord Robert are scoundrels cut from the same cloth, I fear."

His head did jerk up then, his eyes wide with shock. But the lazy grin soon slid back into place. "I can scarce deny the truth," he agreed. "I take exception to him, I suppose, because I've a pretty fair notion what the cad is thinking — and after all, Phae, I did see you first."

The words were seductive. Possessive. They flowed over her, warm as molten honey. "You have no claim to me, sir," she managed. "Nor am I fool enough to believe you wish one. Now, let us concern ourselves with the trouble at hand. I demand to know why you have been asking questions about my elder brother."

With a nonchalance she sensed was feigned, Talbot scrubbed the toe of his evening slipper across a mossy vein in the flagstone. "Oh, just curious, I daresay," he answered. "The coincidence, you see, struck me."

"What coincidence?" she demanded.

Talbot rocked back onto his heels, his gaze focused somewhere in the depths of the garden. "Well, this dead chap — Gorsky — he was Russian, you know."

Something cold washed through Phaedra's veins. "So you have said."

"Actually, my dear, *you* said it." Talbot's gaze snapped to hers, dark and penetrating, with a speed which left her breathless. "And your brother — he is part Russian, is he not?"

"A quarter, perhaps," Phaedra retorted. "But he knows nothing of Russia — hasn't been there for twenty years or more. Nash is decent man, Talbot. A good brother, and a good patriot. *You leave him out of your tawdry pokings-about.* Do you hear me?"

Talbot was watching her assessingly, like a lion in the sun wondering if he should bestir himself to take down his prey. She had said too much, she realized. And too angrily. Suddenly, he shifted his shoulders as if restless, and crossed his arms over his broad chest. "Do you know, Phae," he said quietly, "I rather admire you — and envy your brother. No one in my family ever looked out for me. The whole lot of 'em likely couldn't stir up a teaspoon of indignation on my behalf."

She opened her mouth to rail at him, then abruptly shut it when his words sunk in. There was a look deep in Talbot's eyes that was suddenly all too solemn. All too tender. Was that what his life was like? No familial devotion? No one to count on? That, she could not imagine. She was reminded of her wish to see beyond his beautiful façade — but every glimpse seemed to shake her.

Good heavens, she thought, glancing away. She really did not need this just now. Not desire and compassion and — yes, a bit of admiration for the man. "Just leave Nash alone, Talbot." Her voice had softened. "He does not deserve the trouble you would cause. Please believe he had nothing to do with this mess."

"You seem awfully certain of that," he murmured. "And perhaps that's one of the reasons, Phae, I keep getting the oddest notion there's something you aren't telling me."

"I don't have to listen to this," she returned, her voice low and tremulous. "And I certainly don't have to tell you anything."

She spun about to go, but again, Talbot caught her arm. This time his grip was unrelenting as he jerked her to him. His eyes bore down on her, narrow and dark. "Can you not accept, Phaedra, that *I* am not your enemy?" his voice suddenly edged with emotion. "That I wish only to help you? To protect you from whatever it is that you fear?"

"To *protect* me?" Her eyes searched his face, wondering if he spoke the truth. "Is that what you are trying to do?"

He had the good grace to drop his gaze. "I begin to fear so."

For an instant they stood there, toe-to-toe, his fingers digging into her arm, their breath coming harder than was wise. Suddenly, something like surrender — but not surrender at all — softened his visage, and Talbot cursed softly. Then his lips came down upon hers.

It was a kiss almost artless in its simplicity, his lips opening hungrily over hers. Phaedra wanted, suddenly, to believe him. To lean on him, and be enveloped in his arms and in his strength. Something like a groan escaped her lips. Against her will, her palms skated up the front of his coat, then her fingers curled into the soft black wool of his lapels. In an instant, Talbot had one hand at the back of her head, and an arm banded about her waist. He drew her to him in a crush of pink silk, then, somehow, Phaedra's spine was against the pergola column again. His mouth was insistent, driving her head back. Relentless.

His lips molded over hers again and again, seductive and irresistible. And when his tongue teased lightly across her lips, Phaedra melted against him, a liquescent cascade of womanhood pooling at Talbot's feet. She opened without the merest hint of protest, inviting his tongue to slide silkily along hers, then responding in kind. The house, the music, the twenty-odd people just beyond the terrace; all of it spun away. For long, mindless moments, they deepened the contact, his fingers plunging into her hair as his tongue plundered her mouth, claiming her as his.

His leg was between hers now, his groin throbbing urgently against her thigh. Dimly, Phaedra recognized the hard bulge for what it was — for what it meant — and yet she urged herself against it. The kiss was endless. Drugging. Phaedra swam in sensation and yearning, aching desire. A dream — a fevered, sleep-tossed fantasy of Talbot naked in her bed — came to her, vivid as the morning's sun. And then somehow, his lips were torn from hers, and Phaedra was left swaying in his embrace, blinking her eyes as if dazed. Talbot cursed again, and drew away.

"Good God," he uttered. "I must be mad." The words were spoken beneath his breath, with a vehemence she would never have expected. She looked up at him, muted and a little disoriented.

Then the glower relented. "My dear, you are on the verge of ruination here," he murmured, letting his hand drop. "And I am on the verge of losing my notoriously unreliable self-control. Where is that sharp tongue of yours, Lady Phaedra, when I really deserve it?"

The sounds of the night returned to her, and the tinkle of Mrs. Weyden's pianoforte again wafted from the drawing room. The *chink* of crystal, and the trill of distant laughter. All of it brought her back to what she'd just done. "I do beg your pardon," she whispered, taking a step back. "You must think that I am . . ."

He gave a rueful smile. "What I think, my dear, is that it is I who should beg pardon," he answered. "And the only thing I am imagining is how beautiful you would be with your clothes off and that glorious chestnut hair down about your waist — a fantasy neither of us can afford just now."

Phaedra's blush deepened.

Suddenly, he grabbed her hand, and pulled her toward a towering tree in the center of the garden. In the full glow of one of the lanterns, a pair of swings hung from a tree. Talbot urged her to sit down, then took the opposite swing, setting some distance between them.

"Well, that was not easy to do." His eyes flicked over her as if checking for damage. "But at least we are in view of the French windows now. No harm, I pray, was done."

But great harm had been done, Phaedra

acknowledged. Tristan Talbot had kissed her again, lessening her precious control, and inside she still trembled. He had awakened the thing within her — that tempestuous creature she did not know and could scarce restrain. And with him it was worse — far worse — than ever. Phaedra looked away, and blinked her eyes rapidly.

When she turned around, he was looking at her quite intently. "Now," he said softly, "our little indiscretion aside, Phae, don't you think you'd best confide in me?"

For an instant, Phaedra thought he was asking for a different sort of confession altogether. "Confide in you?"

Though he looked incongruous in the swing, Talbot had begun to move with that languid, catlike grace which laced his every motion. "About Gorsky," he clarified, pushing absently back and forth with one heel. "You need to tell me everything you know, Phae. It might be important to the government, but more troubling to me is that *you* could be in danger."

Phaedra felt her resolve weakening. "I don't know anything about Mr. Gorsky." She forced out the words. "The man fell dead at my feet whilst I was minding my own business."

"Liar," said Talbot. His voice was soft but certain.

"How dare you!" Phaedra moved as if to leap from the swing, but he stopped her.

"Phae, you knew his name," said Tristan, his voice gently accusing. "You *knew* his name."

Suddenly, she understood. "I — I explained that," she protested. "My brother mentioned it."

Tristan shook his head. "No, love, he didn't," he answered. "Lord Nash couldn't have known it. Not unless he was somehow involved. I checked with my father. Gorsky's name had been provided to no one outside the Foreign Office."

Phaedra closed her eyes, and let the horror wash over her. She was caught out in a lie of her own doing. Caught out with no way to explain it — and no way to keep Stefan out of it — unless she dared tell Talbot the truth. The notion should have been absurd. And yet she found herself considering it.

Suddenly, a group of young people burst onto the terrace. Phaedra realized the music had stopped abruptly. "No more quadrilles!" commanded Zoë, in the lead. "Another waltz, if you please, Mrs. Hankle, and we shall dance it here, beneath the stars with room to spare."

At that, Zoë lifted her arms heavenward, and went spinning across the terrace. Lord Robert Rowland seized her hand, and spun her back again, yanking her unceremoniously into his arms. Zoë fell backward in the crook of his elbow, Lord Robert lowering her almost to the floor. Everyone laughed, and the music began. The couples spilled across the terrace and onto the grass.

Talbot twisted his swing around, and made a gallant gesture of extending his hand. "My lady, might I have the pleasure?"

Phaedra shook her head. "Thank you, no."

Talbot unfolded himself from the swing and stood towering over her. He offered both his hands. "Come, Phae," he ordered. "We'll raise fewer eyebrows if we blend into the crowd."

Still, she hesitated.

"You do not waltz?" he gently prodded.

Lamely, she lifted one shoulder. "Not in a very long while," she confessed. "And never in public."

"In the schoolroom, then?"

"Yes. Something like that."

His smile returned, fainter and less flirtatious now, deepening the ever-present dimple to the right side of his mouth. "Then there is no time like the present, my dear," he said, the words rumbling softly in his chest. "Come, put yourself in the hands of a master."

And so she did. Because it seemed easier to dance than to answer his questions. Because she had not waltzed in an age, and she yearned to feel the music moving through her. And because his body looked warm and solid, his arms open and inviting. Knowing all this, and fearing it, too, Phaedra set her hand to his broad shoulder, and allowed him to draw her close. Too close.

With a smile, he took her hand in his, and swept her under the pergola. But instead of daintily clasping it as was traditionally done, he entwined his fingers through hers, palm to palm, as if to hold her captive. Effortlessly, Talbot twirled her away from the pergola and toward the other dancers. His hand was heavy at her waist, but his steps were light and sure. His familiar heat and scent surrounded her like a comforting, sensual embrace.

He brushed his lips over the shell of her ear. "You are perfect, Phae," he whispered against her ear. "Weightless. Lovely. Someone should waltz you round the drawing room every day of your life."

"How silly you are, Mr. Talbot," she managed.

The sounds of the music rose and fell, their bodies moving as one to the rhythm. Though she was tall, against him she felt perfectly matched. He led her expertly. Fluidly. And when Talbot spun her into an especially sweeping turn, something inside Phaedra seemed to lift, and become buoyant just beneath her heart. It felt like . . . joy, which was odd when, mere moments earlier, she had felt an instant of terror.

But there was no terror in Talbot's arms. And no lack of strength or skill. His lithe body was like quicksilver flowing over the smoothest of glass. They wove unerringly through and around the other dancers now, flashes of light and color spinning round Phaedra in an effortless whirl. Awed, she lowered her gaze to the simple diamond pin in the folds of his cravat, marveling at his command of his body — and of hers. She felt buoyant, as if she might trip over her own two feet, and something in Talbot's elegant step would have carried her gracefully forward.

His lips brushed her ear again. "However much we may quarrel, Phae," Talbot whispered, "our bodies seem to know one another perfectly — and perhaps *that* is what we should most worry about?"

She should have laughed. Or rebuked him.

But it was a giddy, oddly magical moment. Even the moon had come out, peeping over the rooftops of Mayfair. Everyone twirling about them was smiling and gay. And no one else, Phaedra noticed, was cutting much of a dash. Instead they were laughing and moving in a most relaxed and companionable way. Most were also watching Talbot; some in admiration, others with envy. A few, however, were otherwise occupied. Lord Robert Rowland had twirled Zoë beneath the shadowy, vine-laden pergola, and looked very much as if he meant to steal a kiss.

Talbot, too, noticed it. He tipped back his head and laughed, the corners of his eyes crinkling most attractively. They stood so near, she could feel the laughter rumble deep in his chest. "Rowland never gives up, does he?" he murmured against her ear. "Before the night's out, that impudent pup will have kissed every female here — save one, I hope."

Phaedra opened her mouth to speak, but at that instant, Talbot looked down at her, and something in their gazes caught. That stab of desire sliced through her again, sudden and piercing. She could not catch her breath. His eyes held hers, deep, unknowable pools which commanded her and left her trembling. As he spun her around, it was as if her feet left the grass, borne upward by some magnetic force which drew her to him. There was nothing of the light-hearted rogue in him now, just the searing warmth of his body pressed improperly near, and the sense that he held her in some sort of thrall.

Phaedra wanted to demand what sensual spell he had cast, but words would not come. There was only the heavy heat of his grip on her waist. The glittering emotion in his eyes, which in this moment verged on ruthlessness. And suddenly, something more consuming. The slow burn of longing, more fierce than anything she'd ever felt. The rush of need for something desirable yet dangerous.

The weakening of her resolve frightened her, and left her angry with herself — and unfairly, with him. Somehow, she forced her face into a dispassionate mask. "You are quite the dancer, Mr. Talbot," she managed. "Zoë said you were famous for your skill in the ballroom."

Talbot's gaze darkened. "Yes, a gift from my mother, I daresay," he murmured, drawing her fully against him. "But I have other skills, my dear, which are equally honed — and for which I am equally renowned."

"Why, Mr. Talbot, I do believe you are

bragging again," she murmured, drawing a little away from him. "But you needn't. Your reputation precedes you."

"My reputation for what?" A smile quirked his mouth. "Hedonism?"

She managed to hold his gaze. "Yes, actually."

The strange look in his eyes intensified. "You kiss like a hedonist," he murmured, drawing her into the next turn. "And what is the harm in it?" he continued when she stiffened in his arms. "Passion, Phae, can be a beautiful thing. I enjoy women. They enjoy me. I am not breaking hearts for sport, or corrupting innocence."

Phaedra felt suddenly unsteady on her feet. "Blithe words, sir," she answered. "Nonetheless, there is a darkness in you — a hint of bitterness which I am not sure you mean others to see. So, not a total hedonist, I think?"

His mouth twisted, and his eyes flashed. "You have a vivid imagination, my lady," he answered. "Let us not become too serious in our flirtations, *hmm?*"

"I do not flirt," she said.

"And I do not bare my soul," he returned. "It would be a dashed dull business anyway."

She felt a flash of irritation, but at that

moment, something brushed her arm. Talbot spun her smoothly to a halt. Mrs. Weyden stood at the edge of the terrace, a hint of chagrin in her eyes.

"I do beg your pardon, Lady Phaedra," she said beneath the music. "But your mother and sister have come."

Phaedra dropped her arms and stepped back. Talbot did likewise, but his hands slid away with a reluctance she did not think was feigned.

Beyond Mrs. Weyden's shoulder, Phaedra could see her mother and Phoebe inside the drawing room, clutching their reticules and looking at them quite pointedly, burning curiosity writ plain across their faces.

"Oh, Lord," Phaedra muttered.

"Phae." Talbot seized her arm. "Introduce me." His voice was low and surprisingly rough.

Phaedra stepped away. "I . . . I cannot."

Some nameless emotion flared in his gaze. "Cannot or will not?" he asked, ignoring Mrs. Weyden's presence. "Which is it, Phaedra?"

"Not now," she hissed.

"Or *not ever?*" he suggested, his dark eyes taking on a vaguely bitter cast. "Fine. But this is not over, Phae."

With one last wary glance, Mrs. Weyden

drew away, and hastened toward the drawing room.

Phaedra felt a rush of panic. "There is no *this*, Talbot," she whispered. "Are you quite mad?"

His lips thinned. "By God, you just kissed me as if there was a *this*."

She forgot that the other dancers were still whirling about them. That her mother and sister still watched, eyes agog.

"Let us not become too serious in our flirtations, my lord," she retorted. "Must you force me to admit I am not immune to your charms? Fine, you have done so. But women like me don't mean anything to you. Pray do not pretend they do. We have nothing further to discuss."

He still held her arm. "There is still the matter of a dead man in the Strand," he gritted, that cold, penetrating look back in his eyes. "Do not even think of toying with me, my lady. Or you will rue the day."

Phaedra's eyes widened. She could hear her own heartbeat pounding in her ears now. "I . . . I cannot believe you serious."

"Believe it," he snapped, releasing her. "Send word of a time and place to meet me — or *I will come to you*. In Brook Street, no less. In front of your fine family."

This time it was she who grabbed his arm.

"Wait just one moment, sir," she hissed, anger surging. "Do not dare put words into my mouth. I have already invited you into my home, and gladly. But neither I nor my brother nor anyone in my *fine family* knows anything of this business in the Strand."

"Madam, you are a liar," he said, his voice cold and quiet. "*You* are involved. And for your own safety, you had best tell me why."

She pursed her lips for a moment, then spun on her heel and walked away.

"Phae." Behind her, his voice had softened only a little. "I *will* find out."

Phaedra drew in her breath roughly. But when she glanced over her shoulder, Tristan Talbot was striding toward the shadows of the pergola.

Lady Nash hastened to meet her at the French doors. "Who was that?" she demanded, her voice sharp. "Who were you quarreling with?"

Phaedra looked round again. Talbot had melted into the gloom. It was as if he'd never been there at all. "No one," she said quietly, turning back around. "He is no one. Come, Mamma. I think it's time we went home."

CHAPTER 7

Things without all remedy
Should be without regard; what's done is
done.

The mansion in Cavendish Square lay in shadows, the streetlamp near it having gone out again, as it had long been wont to do. Tristan went up the polished white steps, and let himself in with the key he had never returned — and, to his father's credit, had never been asked to return.

That thought only served to increase his restlessness; that chafing dissatisfaction which had followed him from Mrs. Weyden's and into the night. He rolled his shoulders beneath the wool of his coat, then pushed the door open on silent hinges.

Inside the grand vaulted entrance hall, all was silent. Sconces flickered along the walls, casting faint shadows up the massive marble staircase. As with his visit to Mrs. Weyden's,

Tristan wasn't sure why he was here. Nonetheless, he stripped off his gloves, set down his hat, then went upstairs, helping himself to a candlestick as he went.

He found Pemberton propped in a chair by his father's bed, his hands folded over his belly, his chin sunk deep in the folds of his cravat. Tristan touched the butler lightly on his hand, and when he roused, set a finger to his lips.

Pemberton's eyes blinked against the candlelight, his expression one of unconcealed surprise. "Lord Avoncliffe," he murmured, rising awkwardly. "Good evening, sir."

"Go to bed, Pem," Tristan whispered, inclining his head toward the door. "I shall sit with him the night."

Pemberton blinked again. "My lord, are you sure?"

"Quite," said Tristan. "Go. Get some rest."

"We are taking shifts," said the butler. "One of the footmen will relieve you at three."

Tristan shook his head. "He needn't bother, thank you." He already knew he would not sleep this night. He was feeling guilty for the cold words he'd spoken to Lady Phaedra, but lust and frustration were fraying at his temper. Infernal woman.

Pemberton bowed, and went to the sideboard. Tristan sank into the still warm chair, and looked at his father's frail form barely distinguishable beneath the bedcovers. The butler returned with a galleried silver tray set with a flagon of port and a decanter of cognac. One of Lord Hauxton's Venetian crystal glasses sat alongside them. He placed the tray on Hauxton's bed table, bowed again, and left the room as quietly as Tristan had entered.

Tristan took up the decanter, and poured a dram of the heavy amber liquid into the glass. It was going to be a bloody long night, he thought, tossing off the brandy in one swallow.

What in God's name had he been thinking this evening? To have flirted with Lady Phaedra Northampton as if she were some practiced courtesan? And flirtation hadn't been the half of it. He had actually felt a stab of jealousy tonight. It was unheard of. When it came to women, he was a man who cut his losses so fast the strings were still flapping in the breeze as he walked away. And then on the heels of jealousy, the anger. The utter certainty that Phaedra was a liar. *Good God.* It made him remember why he no longer did this for a living.

Tristan blocked that thought from his

mind, and savored the burn of alcohol as it trailed down his throat. His eyes went again to the man in the bed. Hauxton's nightshirt was fastened neatly at the throat, his nightcap securely in place. His thin, long-fingered hands lay upon the coverlet in smooth, perfect symmetry. Even in repose — even as he waited for death — Hauxton was the perfect English gentleman.

Tristan set down the glass, and laid his own hand alongside his father's, almost laughing aloud when he realized how nearly identical they were. Not just the thinness, or the length, but the short nails, a little flatter than most, with faint vertical ridges. The broad palms, and the thumbs which turned at the very same angle. But where his father's hands had been pale even at his most vigorous, Tristan's were brown as a sepoy's.

Tristan's eyes trailed back up to his father's sandy hair, now swept with white, and then to the nose. Ah, the famous Talbot nose, sharp and arrogant. Like the fingers, it attested to their kinship more plainly than any birth record could have done. As a child, he had not failed to notice how his father's relations remarked upon the nose and sighed with relief as age brought it burgeoning forth in all its Talbot glory. Even then, he had known that the sighs meant something — something which left him acutely uncomfortable and a little angry. Now he understood what he had been too naïve to grasp at the age of twelve. They had not believed him Hauxton's child.

They had certainly not wished his misbegotten blood to mingle with their bluer, more perfect hue, but they had feared even more a total imposter in their midst. How in God's name had his mother survived the suspicion? That cold, quiet condescension which, even now, could cut him to the quick?

In truth, he supposed, she had not. She had left England when he was but a child, and died within the year. Tristan could still remember the shouted quarrels and the slamming doors. The deep, wracking sobs, and his mother sitting by his bed, her face bloodless, her eyes limpid with grief, a handkerchief clutched in one tremulous hand as she stroked him with the other.

He could still hear his father's parting words, too, shouted over the dinner table that night, loud enough to carry up the stairs. "Go, then, damn you!" Hauxton had cried. "You faithless bitch! But for this marriage, I would have been Prime Minister by now — and *you,* Carlotta — by God, *you were not worth it!"*

This last had been followed by the shattering of crystal. His mother's doing, no doubt. The only display of emotion Hauxton ever allowed himself was the rarely raised voice. And at dawn, the carriages had come. Tristan could still see the trunks being carried down by the footmen in solemn procession, their white gloves and white wigs stark against the dark leather and wood as they bore them on their shoulders. He did not know who he had been angrier with, his father for letting her go, or his mother for leaving. But there had been no question of Tristan's going with her. The heir to an earldom could not be raised abroad. Certainly he could not be raised by a horde of near-landless mongrels — at least that's how it would have appeared to the English aristocracy.

Just then he was recalled to the present by his father, who stirred restlessly on the bed. His eyes fluttered opened, and he stared at Tristan, blindly at first, and then with a lucidity which was surprising.

"Tristan," he muttered, lifting his head. "You have come home."

It was not home, but Tristan had not the heart to correct him.

"Indeed, sir," he answered, laying his hand

over his father's fingers, which had begun to pick almost nervously at the coverlet. "Now go back to sleep. You'll need your strength on the morrow. After all, someone must run the country."

His father's faint smile held an unmistakable irony. "I fear I must soon give my little portion of it over into someone else's hands," he answered. "You . . . you had something to tell me? Something about the Russian, perhaps?"

Tristan patted his hand. "No, sir," he answered. "I have learnt little, and it will wait."

With that, his father nodded, his nightcap scrubbing the linen pillowslip, then drifted off again, leaving Tristan alone with his thoughts. He poured another tumbler of the cognac, halfway to the brim this time, then fell back into the deep armchair, cradling the glass against his waistcoat.

He had made a fool of himself with Lady Phaedra tonight — and even worse, he had made her angry. Oh, the business about Gorsky and her brother, that he did not regret. There was something strange going on, and his twitching cock aside, he would get to the bottom of it. But kissing her again — and kissing her as one might a light-skirt, not a virginal young lady — deeply. Posses-

sively. It was madness. Which only emphasized the paradox.

He did not kiss virginal young ladies.

Like most men of his ilk, he avoided them
like the plague. Even had his intentions
been honorable — which they weren't —
Tristan had no interest in tutoring an
untried female in the ways of passion. Which
emphasized the second paradox. Lady
Phaedra did not kiss like an untried female.
She had not panicked. Had not backhanded
him as he deserved. Indeed, the woman had
gone toe-to-toe with him and scarcely
blushed when it was done. Only later had
she become outraged. Only when he had
pressed her for an introduction to her family.

She had refused. And he — perhaps
unfairly — had leapt to an ill conclusion.
He had let his temper snap. It had been a
long time since a beautiful woman had
shaken him so thoroughly. Made him behave
so stupidly. Really, what had he been thinking from the neck up? Had he thought to
court her? The lady said she did not want a
husband — and by God, he believed her. It
was not just a frivolous protestation to whet
the challenge in a man.

But she was not immune to his touch.
Indeed, Tristan had felt a passion in her

which even still left him reeling. Repressed sensuality simmered just beneath the surface of her every move. Her every glance. Could no one else see it? He hoped not. Prayed not.

In a day or two, he would approach her again. There was nothing else for it. But this time, he must persuade the truth from her with logic. He thought that tonight, perhaps, he very nearly had. In the garden earlier, he had seen something — something like resignation and perhaps even relief in her eyes. The wish to unburden her soul. It was a look he well knew from his time in Greece, and took no joy in. Then Miss Armstrong had burst onto the scene, and the moment had been lost.

Tristan sipped pensively at the brandy, then set it down again. He had lost the taste for it. Instead, the taste of Lady Phaedra was still on his lips, and the warmth of her hand yet lingered in his. If he closed his eyes, he could still feel the strains of the music, and her body swaying as one with his.

God's truth, but this was very odd.

Perhaps he needed that brandy after all. He picked it up, and slowly sipped it down.

In his sleep, his father's breath hitched a little alarmingly. Tristan looked at him, and again felt that strange, utterly submerging wave of grief wash over him. In a few weeks — days, perhaps — the great Lord Hauxton would be dead. And whatever chasm lay between them would never be breached. All the unspoken words, all those small, seething resentments. Tristan's deeply entrenched sense of having failed at the one thing he had been born to do. Yes, all of it would still remain. There was no grave deep enough to bury all of that.

Was that why he had come here tonight? To mourn what could have been? Should have been? To wallow in his anger and mull over the missed opportunities — opportunities, perhaps, to put things right? Or had it even been within his power to do so? He could not change who he was, or the color of his skin. He could not alter his father's choice to make an improvident marriage, then resent himself for his own weakness in having done so.

And why tonight, of all nights, had he come here? What was it about Lady Phaedra Northampton that had the power to drive him to the one place no one would have expected? *Home.* Or what there was of it. His elbow propped on the chair arm, Tristan bent his head and pinched hard at the bridge of his nose. The swell of grief rose up, and he found himself clenching his jaw against the pain. He wanted to laugh bitterly at himself and at his own folly. But was it tonight's folly? Or the folly of the last twenty years?

Somewhere in the depths of the house, a clock struck two. As he had learned to do in the army, he forced his mind to empty and his body to relax. Slowly, the stillness of the great house settled over Tristan, but little peace came with it. It was going to be a long night. Just he and his dying father — and the lingering warmth of Lady Phaedra's lush body pressed to his.

Phaedra arrived home, still trembling inside with emotion, to find Agnes waiting in her bedchamber, a basket of crewelwork on her lap. She set it aside, and came at once toward the door.

"Good evening, miss."

"Good evening, Agnes," said Phaedra, setting aside her reticule. "You needn't have waited up."

"What, and leave you to take that great pile of hair down by yourself?" Agnes chided. "You aren't accustomed to anything so fancy. Do sit down, miss, and let me brush it out."

"Thank you, Agnes." Phaedra tossed aside

her shawl and sank down onto the stool at the small, giltwood dressing table. She watched in silence as Agnes pulled the pins from her hair, her mind running back over the events of the evening, particularly the end of the evening.

She was very angry at Tristan Talbot, and more than a little unsure how to manage him. And Phaedra was — as her brothers so often remarked — a managing sort of female. Talbot, however, was not amenable to management. What was worse, all his flirting, dancing, kissing, and jumping to conclusions had left her head in a whirl. One instant he was naught but a handsome rogue, and the next . . . dear Lord. His eyes had the look burning coals. Piercing. Accusing. Tempting. Damn him.

She must have cursed aloud.

"Did you see him, then, miss?" Another pin rang out as Agnes tossed it into the crystal dish on the dressing table. "Did you winkle anything out of him?"

No, thought Phaedra dryly. *I thought it made more sense to let him kiss me silly.*

But what she said was, "I'm sorry, Agnes. I did see him, but I did not much advance our cause. Never fear, however. I mean to see him again tomorrow — if, that is, you can help me?"

Agnes looked up and caught her gaze in the mirror, the brush stilling. "Anything, miss. You have only to ask it."

Phaedra thought through her hastily made plan one last time. It would do, she thought. Talbot might be a little dangerous, but there was honor in him, she believed. Pray God she was not wrong. Her track record on that score was dismal, it was true, but she must learn to trust herself again. She hoped Talbot would not let her down.

"I must get a note to Mr. Talbot in the morning," she said when Agnes put the brush down. She rose and went to her writing desk by the windows. Sitting, she extracted a sheet of foolscap from the drawer, and lifted the lid from her inkpot.

Agnes had followed her. "And you wish me to take it to him?" she suggested.

"Yes, and tell no one," said Phaedra. "Should my mother discover —"

Agnes laid a hand on her shoulder. "She won't, miss," said the maid softly. "I'd die first."

Phaedra nodded, and bent her head to the task. "Mr. Talbot lives in Long Acre," she explained, scratching out the note. "I don't know where, precisely. You'll have to ask about. Can you do that?"

Agnes swiftly nodded. "For little Priss, my

lady? Aye, I'd run down the devil himself."

"That's about what it amounts to," said Phaedra, fanning the ink. "So start with the vintners. Then go on to the tobacconists, the chop houses, and — oh, yes — the gunsmiths. I won't ask you to enter the brothels or the gaming hells until all hope is lost."

"Aye, a man of large appetites, is he?" said Agnes, grinning. " 'Tis to be expected, I daresay, from a fellow such as that one."

"My thoughts exactly," said Phaedra dryly, folding the sheet of foolscap.

Agnes lifted one shoulder, and snatched up the note. "Aye, well, from the little glimpse I caught of 'im, a girl could do worse."

Phaedra was silent for a moment. "We must hope, then, Agnes, that Talbot is as much a man as you think him," she finally said. "I believe I am going to have to bring him into our confidence. I am going to have to tell him about Millie — and about Tony, too, I fear."

At that, Agnes paled. "Oh, lawks, miss," she said. "Mr. Hayden-Worth will be frightfully angry."

Phaedra's lips thinned to a tight line. "Well, perhaps Mr. Hayden-Worth should have thought of that before leaving others to tidy up his messes," she replied. "Or before he set about easing his frustrations with a poor tavern girl he'd no business bedding, come to that."

Agnes hung her head. "Oh, you don't know Millie, miss," she answered. "Ever so determined, she was, to have him. And so sure of herself, too. It's why she run off to London, you know. She said if Mr. Hayden-Worth didn't want to keep 'er up, some other fine gentleman would."

"Yes, because Tony put grand ideas in her head," Phaedra gritted. "And now it is Priscilla who must pay the price. Her mother has vanished, and her father is an ocean away — not that he would be of any help, mind. So that beautiful child — *our niece* — is left all but an orphan."

Agnes wrung her hands. "Perhaps —" she awkwardly began, "— oh, perhaps we ought to tell his lordship of all this, miss?"

Phaedra's head jerked up. "Stefan?" she said sharply. "No, Agnes. No, that really would not be wise. You must trust me on this."

Phaedra was not about to tell Agnes the truth. That Stefan would likely throttle Tony. That not long past, Stefan had been required to pay off Tony's blackmailers for an entirely different sort of sexual indiscretion, then bribe the French *commissaire de police* to free Tony's wife from smuggling charges. Those escapades had cost Stefan a bloody fortune, and all of it had been hushed up by the Government at great political cost.

Tony's meteoric career in the Commons had been saved yet again. But Stefan was now at the end of his tether when it came to Tony and his bollixed-up relationships. And Phaedra — well, like everyone, she still loved Tony. One could not help it. For all his indiscreet behavior, he was a good man. And a brilliant politician who, despite his own confused proclivities, had England's best interests at heart.

Once he obtained a divorce from Jenny — once Tony could settle down in some sort of permanent, loving relationship — Phaedra prayed he would be able to lead a happy, relatively normal life. She just had to keep Stefan from killing him first. A sharp *pop* of cinders in the hearth bestirred her to the present, and to Agnes's fretful gaze. "No," she said again, her voice quiet in the gloom. "No, Agnes. There can be no question of Lord Nash's knowing. We are stuck, I fear, with Mr. Talbot."

Agnes looked unconvinced. "But what can he do, miss, that we can't?"

Phaedra lifted her gaze to the maid's. "He can get me into that house, Agnes," she said softly. "And once I am inside, I *will* find Millie."

"Oh, miss," said Agnes. "That sounds frightfully dangerous."

"And another thing, Agnes." Phaedra's voice was pensive. "I wish you to bring down one of Tony's best evening suits. You must pin it up on me, then take it to a tailor — not his usual fellow, mind. I shall want a hat and gloves, too. Oh — and that wig Jenny used to have. The one she wore as Puck to the Midsummer Ball? Can you find it?"

"Oh, I don't like the sound of this." Agnes wrung her hands again. "But yes, miss. I'll do my best."

But Phaedra was trying not to think of the danger. And she was trying not to think of the small shiver of excitement which ran down her back when she considered the prospect of being alone — completely and utterly alone — with Tristan Talbot.

"Will there be anything else, miss?" Agnes asked.

Phaedra looked at her blankly for an instant. "Oh, yes," she answered. "One of my yellow garters has gone missing. Have you seen it, by chance?"

"I put one in the mending last week," she said. "One of the little roses had torn away."

"Yes, I recall." Phaedra furrowed her brow. "Oh, well. It will turn up, I daresay." A mislaid garter was the least of her worries. Abruptly, she excused Agnes for the night, left the desk, and crossed the room to her bed. When the door clicked shut, Phaedra knelt to say her evening prayers. But her usual prayer of thanks did not come. Instead, she simply set her forehead against the turned-down sheets, and prayed for strength.

God forbid anyone should know the dreams that tormented her each night, she thought, climbing wearily into the bed. And God curse the day Talbot had walked into her life with his long legs and seductive smile to awaken all her feverish fantasies — then magnify them tenfold.

At precisely seven sharp, Lord Hauxton's valet came in to strop the earl's razor. On his heels came a housemaid to draw the drapes and sweep the grate. A footman followed as if precisely timed, bearing a breakfast tray containing exactly what it had contained for the last forty years: one soft boiled egg, tea, a rasher of bacon, and two slices of toast.

Roused by all the precision marching, Tristan rose and shook off the remnants of sleep, a little disconcerted to realize he had actually drifted off.

Soon Hauxton was hoisted up in the bed, shaved, dressed in a fresh nightshirt, and given a fork which he then used to push his food impotently about the plate. Tristan paced back and forth by the windows, explaining what little he had managed to discover.

"And you are quite sure, Tristan, that de Vendenheim was lying to you?" his father asked when Tristan had finished his tale. "About Lord Nash's involvement in those arms shipments?"

Tristan turned to face his father. "He was not completely honest. That is the best I can say of him."

Hauxton surveyed him, one eye narrowed. "Quite so," he murmured. "God knows you have your faults, Tristan. But you have a solid grasp of human nature." It was as close to a compliment as his father ever came.

"What was he lying about?" Tristan demanded.

"Nash was involved in the scandal, but the guilt lay with his stepbrother's wife," said his father. "Peel helped Nash cover it up to spare the family. His stepbrother, you know, is quite an up-and-comer in the Commons."

"Yes, Anthony Hayden-Worth," said Tristan, pacing toward the bed. "He was ahead of me at Eton. What happened to the wife?"

Again, Hauxton smiled, this time a little sourly. "Nash exiled her to America," he said, pushing his breakfast tray away. "Her father owns Carlow Arms Manufacturing in Connecticut."

"Carlow?" He gave a low whistle.

"Yes, the temptation of easy money, I collect, was too great for Mrs. Hayden-Worth and her father," said Hauxton. "They got in bed with some duplicitous French diplomats running guns to the Greeks."

Tristan gave a low whistle. "So that's who it was!"

"But Nash was innocent, and his brother was . . . well, merely foolish for having let his wife run wild. It cost Nash a small fortune in bribes to extricate her."

Tristan caught his thumbs in the waist of his trousers and stared pensively at the frail form in the bed. "And you are sure?" he asked. "Nash is clean in this Gorsky business?"

Hauxton nodded. "Quite sure."

And there went his theory regarding Lady

Phaedra. The thought should have made him happy. And it did. But underneath it all was the realization that he'd called her a liar to her face. That she had been telling him the truth about her brother. None of them were involved. And he had no further excuse to see her again.

But that was probably a good thing. Sharply, he cleared his throat. "I have been thinking, sir," he said. "I have a plan."

Hauxton paused in the middle of sipping at his tea. "Go on."

Tristan studied the swirling pattern of his father's Oriental carpet. "I wish you to tell a lie," he finally said. "A very public lie. I wish you to put it about that I am to help manage your tasks in the Foreign Office until you are well again."

"I think, Tristan, that you would be perfectly capable of doing that someday, would you but set your mind to it," he answered. "I do not think, however, I will be getting well again."

"I know we both fear that, sir," Tristan answered. "As to the work, you know my feelings in that regard. But what I wish you to say is that I am your go-between until you can return to the office. I wish people to believe that I have access to all of your files and all of your staff. That I am — and have been for some time — wholly in your confidence."

Hauxton was looking at him quizzically. "Yes, I see," he murmured. "And this will achieve . . . what?"

"I have been compiling a list, sir," said Tristan. "A list of all the known clients of Madame Vostrikova. I've had but limited success."

"As I said, it is a business which is conducted with the utmost discretion," said Hauxton. "I wonder you've managed to find anyone at all."

"I have been watching the house at all hours," Tristan admitted. "And asking around. Calling in a few favors and notes-of-hand. Oh, and I bribed a scullery maid. I've come up with about a dozen names."

His father looked impressed. "Yes, and all very affluent, I do not doubt," he said. "That sort of vice comes dear."

"Oddly enough, not everyone on the list is wealthy," he answered, beginning to pace back and forth across the carpet. "What they are is *powerful* — in one way or another. High-ranking military officers. Active members of Parliament. Government bureaucrats — all gentlemen, of course, but some of rather modest means."

Hauxton was leaning attentively forward.

239

"Yes? Go on."

Tristan turned to face his father. "Did you know Madame Vostrikova requires a . . . a sort of business contract with her clients?"

Slowly, Hauxton shook his head.

"She requires them to state what services they are seeking, and set forth an agreed upon price," said Tristan. "Sometimes this contract stipulates a particular person whose services are being engaged, a time frame, and if the time frame is lengthy, it might provide for an annuity for the woman —"

"— or man?" his father interjected.

Tristan shrugged.

"It's possible."

His father looked perplexed. "Men have been known to draw up contracts and annuities for their mistresses," he muttered. "But the other — surely no one would be so imprudent?"

"When it comes to sexual appetites, there is nothing so imprudent as a man with a stiff cock," Tristan remarked. "They will do incredibly foolish, remarkably shortsighted things to get a particular itch scratched, and worry about the cost to them afterward."

Hauxton lost what little color remained. His face went suddenly stark, and the trembling in his hands visibly worsened.

Tristan lifted his gaze to the earl's, and understanding struck like a blow. His father, he realized, was thinking of his own marriage. Of his desperation to have that delicate, desirable thing which society and its strictures had placed just beyond his reach.

Well, he had taken it anyway. And they had all paid a price.

Sharply, Tristan cleared his throat. "Some sexual perversions can be almost addictive," he continued. "I've heard that Madame will allow you to sample the wares perhaps once, just enough to give you a taste of whatever depravity you desire. And then — if you let her — she will enslave you to it."

"In writing?"

Tristan shook his head. "That is the rumor," he answered. "Though it is hard for me to credit it."

"Dear God." Hauxton's hands drew into knobby fists. "Have you the list?"

Tristan extracted a scrap of paper from his coat pocket and passed it to his father.

His faded eyes ran down the names. "Dear God," he said again. "Are you sure?"

"Not remotely," said Tristan, going to the lamp by his father's bed. He took the note, lifted the glass, then touched it to the flame. He dropped it, smoldering, onto this father's breakfast tray.

Hauxton watched it burn. "Yes," he said when the paper had turned into a curl of black ash. "Yes, I daresay that was for the best."

A moment later, the door again opened. The black crows began flocking in, bringing with them their file boxes and their campaign desks, and alighting about the room in preparation for the day's activities. Tristan took the opportunity to make his bow to his father and flee, thanking God that he was not one of them.

He walked the mile back to Long Acre at a brisk clip, hoping to clear his head. For once, he had done what his father asked, and remarkably, Hauxton had seemed pleased with what he had thus far accomplished. In the past, Tristan had never given a damn whether his father was pleased or not. But today . . . yes, today he had almost begun to care. Then his father had shattered whatever nascent sense of camaraderie that had existed between them.

Nonetheless, Tristan had done his duty, and would continue to do so. Now if he could just expunge that vision of his father's face from his memory. That pale, stark look of recognition, and of regret. For if a man regretted his marriage, well, did he not also regret his children?

Hauxton did. On occasion, he'd even said so. When Tristan had pushed him beyond the range of bearing with his pranks and poor marks. His running away to become a mercenary. And later, with the choices he had made in leading his life. Many a truth was said in jest, or so the old saying went. Tristan had always believed the same could be said of rage.

"A woman came round looking for you, sir," said Uglow when he arrived home.

"A woman, eh?" he said as Uglow lifted the coat from his shoulders and set it aside for brushing. "Buxom and pretty, I hope?"

"Aye, a proper looker," Uglow agreed. "But all business, if yer knows wot I mean."

Something in Tristan's chest leapt. "Was she indeed?" he said, unbuttoning his waistcoat. "With chestnut hair, by any chance? And spectacles?"

Uglow looked at him oddly, the deep furrow returning to his brow. "Reddish-yellow hair," he said. "Left yer a letter."

Tristan's heart settled back into place and his brain kicked in. Lady Phaedra would never be so scandalous as to call upon a gentleman in his bachelor quarters. And he had no business hoping she had done so.

"On yer desk," Uglow grunted, pointing.

Tristan followed Uglow's finger, then

243

hastened across the room, his waistcoat flapping open. The note was sealed in red wax, but the impression was perfectly ordinary. Roughly, he slit it open.

You wished me to name a time and place:
Tomorrow night. Half past nine.
The house opposite Gorsky's.
Ask for Mrs. Thompson.

Mrs. Thompson? Who the hell was Mrs. Thompson?

Then his parting words last night came back to him. Tristan whistled softly through his teeth. The note was written in a fine, tight copperplate with a sharp nib and nary a drip in sight. The foolscap was the heavy, ivory sort. The expensive sort. He knew who the note was from as surely as if he'd watched her write it out.

The house opposite Gorsky's. She meant across from Vostrikova's brothel, of course. A sudden chill settled over him, and with it came a strange frisson of excitement.

Good Lord. His gut had not been wrong after all.

Which only begged one question. What on earth was Phaedra Northampton up to?

CHAPTER 8

Stars, hide your fires,
Let not light see my black and deep desires.

The following afternoon a heavy dampness swept up from the Channel, creeping across Surrey and Sussex to swathe London in a murky brume. Tristan pulled on his oldest boots and the worn leather overcoat which had served him well during his years on the Continent, then set out on foot just as dusk approached. He had long ago learned the power of reconnaissance, and the importance of never walking into a situation one did not control.

Soho, being filled with dens of iniquity of one ilk or another, was well known to Tristan. He pulled down his hat brim, turned up his collar, and strolled past Madame Vostrikova's as dark settled in. The damp clung to his skin like a cool, wet froth, settling over his face and seemingly into his lungs. At the top of the street, a crested coach turned from the alley and went spinning through a puddle, throwing up filth which spattered across his boots.

Tristan looked down and cursed. On days like this, he almost — almost — missed Greece. But the spray of water, he reminded himself, was better than the spray of blood. Particularly one's own. Or that of an innocent, and God knew there were always plenty of innocents.

The house he watched stood three floors high, plus cellar and garret, and was tucked between a rather disreputable-looking coffeehouse and a shuttered linen draper's. At half past seven, someone lit a lamp on the first floor, but no one came or went through the front. Tristan crossed the street and ducked into the coffeehouse just as the drizzle turned to a dull roar that bounced off the pavement and rattled the downspouts.

"I'm looking for lodging," he said over the din, addressing the boy who'd brought his coffee. "What do you know of the house next door?"

The lad eyed him up and down. "I knows it ain't for the likes of you."

Apparently his old coat was not quite battered enough. "A bit dodgy, eh?" Tristan smiled. "Not a nunnery, is it?"

The boy shrugged and took the coin Tristan offered. "No, but not quite a doss house, neither," he said. "There's a girl or two works out o' there, though. Ask at the public house on Greek Street."

"The Pillars of Hercules?" Tristan knew it well.

"Aye, tell 'em you want ter see Cross-eyed Polly," the lad suggested. "She'll know 'oo's workin' tonight."

Tristan knew Polly, too. He rather liked her eyes. But he did not require a tankard of ale or anything Polly's friends might be selling. Tristan finished his coffee, then went around to the alleyway. The rain was coming down hard now. Grateful for his hat and coat, he made his way to the rear of the house, finding it as unremarkable as the front, save for the piles of old barrels and trash which had accumulated between the house and the privy.

A ditch ran along the garden wall, fetid and murky in the feeble light. Tristan stepped gingerly over it, almost tripped over a hissing cat, then picked his way through the rubbish to the kitchen windows. Through the rain that dribbled off his hat, he could see a girl sitting at a roughhewn table, peeling potatoes. Otherwise nothing stirred.

It was a deceptive sort of calm. He was being drawn into something he could not control. His father had cast a lure; a lure he had known Tristan would be unable to resist. And now a piece of the puzzle lay inside that house — something tangled up in his own obsession over Phaedra Northampton — but in what shape or form, he did not know. He was inexplicably afraid for her.

Tristan rose from the window, took the knife from the cuff of his boot, and slipped it into the depths of his coat pocket. Then he went back to the front and dropped the knocker. A pockmarked crone in a faded smock answered the door, and a frightful smell — something like unwashed bodies simmering in stewed cabbage — assailed his nostrils.

"Good evening," he said, raising his voice over the rain. "I'm looking for Mrs. Thompson."

The woman eyed him up and down a little nastily. "Aye, no doubt," she muttered. "A milliner's assistant, indeed!"

Tristan looked down his impressive Talbot nose, mimicking his father's most imperious glare. "Mrs. Thompson," he said again.

"If you please."

"Mind yer boots, then," she grumbled, gesturing toward a frayed rug. "Follow me — and be quiet about your business, sir. I run a respectable lodging 'ouse."

Deeply curious now, he shook the worst of rain from his coat and followed the woman up the twisting staircase until they could go no farther. A narrow door sat at the top of the steps. She rapped on it with the back of her gnarled hand. "Thompson!" she wheezed. "Yer got a caller."

The door creaked slowly open to reveal a nearly dark room. A woman in a white cap stood just inside, her form draped in shadow. "Aye?"

Tristan strained to see through the gloom, but the woman moved and sounded nothing like Phaedra. A frisson of apprehension ran down his spine. Who else, he wondered, might lurk there in the dark? His hand went to the knife, taking a firm grip on the hilt.

The crone leaned across the threshold. "If yer meanin' to entertain gents up here, Thompson, I'm to get 'alf," she said, her voice like gravel. "I said as much when yer took the room."

"Very well," said the woman in the shadows. "I shall settle with you later."

"Aye, that you will," said the crone. Shooting Tristan one last glower, she descended the steps.

Tristan did not wait, but pushed his way inside and shoved the door shut. One hand still on the knife, he yanked the woman to him and spun her about, his arm hooked over her throat. Her worn white cap slid to the floor.

The woman gasped in outrage, but the scent of Phaedra's fragrance and clean hair was unmistakable. A rush of relief flooded him. He released her throat and grabbed her arm.

"What the devil do you think you're doing?" he demanded, hauling her toward the lamp's meager light. "Have you any notion the danger you might be in?"

Remarkably unshaken, Phaedra regarded him disdainfully, one hand at her throat. "Danger?" Her usual cultured voice had returned. "From what? Ruffians like you?"

He looked down into her flashing blue eyes, and he felt the unwanted stir of raw, almost angry lust. "Yes, by God, perhaps." Then, before he realized what he meant to do, he yanked her to him and kissed her hard, with his lips and with his tongue, far more roughly than he should have done. But instead of slapping him senseless, Phaedra turned her face into his, opening her mouth. Water trickled from his hair onto her face, but she rose to him, and gave back as good as she got.

It did not last. Somehow, she pushed away from him, but she was shaken. Hell, *he* was shaken. "That coat smells like a wet dog, Talbot," she managed, her voice unsteady. "And you are dripping on my floor."

"Aye?" He yanked off his sodden hat, angry with himself for wanting her. "It's raining torrents, in case you hadn't noticed."

"Fine, give it to me." She made an impatient motion with her hand. "You may as well stay."

"Oh, I'm staying." He slipped the knife back into the depths of his pocket and slid out of the coat. "Now," he said darkly, "explain to me what you're doing in this place."

Phaedra hung the sodden garment on a peg, then yanked a chair from an old deal table which was wedged into the corner. "You asked to meet me, you will recall," she said. "I do not need your permission to be here."

"No, you need the palm of your brother's hand on your backside for pulling this dangerous ruse," he returned.

She planted one hand on the table and leaned into him. "It sounds as if you're in a mood to do the job for him, Talbot," she whispered. "And here I'd thought you were all blithe charm and aimless flirtation."

"Aye, well, the truth will out, won't it?" He spoke with cold certainty. "You are playing a treacherous game, here, Phae."

She tossed him a speaking glance, drew out the adjacent chair, and sat. Reluctantly, he followed suit, his gaze drifting about the room. His eyes having adjusted to the light, Tristan could see that the garret was small and narrow, the rain loud on the roof which lay just inches above their heads. The chamber held a hearth with a hob, an old oak cupboard, and — to his acute discomfort — an old barley-twist bed tucked under the rafters in the rear. Save for the rickety table and chairs they sat in, the low room was devoid of any decoration.

He returned his gaze to Phaedra. Her lips were faintly swollen from the roughness of his kiss. Frustrated, he tossed his hat onto the table, and plowed a hand through his damp hair. Good God, he did not need this; did not want the hot rush of desire which seemed to strike him every time he saw the girl. "All right," he said quietly. "Let's talk."

Phaedra reached for the lamp which sat on the table and turned up the wick. The flame cast dancing shadows across the planes of her face as she leaned over it, magnifying the length of her thick, feathery lashes and heightening her extraordinary cheekbones.

Tonight she had again eschewed her spectacles and twisted her hair into a tight, plain knot. She wore drab, loose clothing that clearly was not her own. With that habit of keeping her face turned slightly away from one's gaze, as if she wished to melt into her surroundings, she could have been a servant or even a shopgirl. She looked . . . anonymous. And he sensed she'd had years of practice at being anonymous, in one form or another.

"I let this garret a few weeks ago," she said. "Shortly after we came up from Hampshire."

His eyes never left her face. "Why?"

Phaedra drew back an inch. "I do not care for your tone, Talbot," she retorted. "Indeed, I liked you better as a frivolous scoundrel. I begin to wonder why I should I talk to you at all."

Because if she didn't, he was going to kidnap her this instant, and give her over into Nash's keeping — or, if he gave into his baser nature, something worse. Either way, she'd be safe — from everything save him. Somehow, Tristan held his tongue.

He turned one hand over, opening it. As if it had been planned, the hammer of the rain on the roof just above them relented to a dull rattle, and a calm settled over the room. "Phae, you should talk to me because I am on your side," he answered, forcing his tone to soften with the rain. "Because I care for you and your safety. This is a questionable neighborhood, and this place —" Here, he paused to cast his gaze about the tawdry garret. "God's truth, Phae, you don't belong in a place like this."

He watched in the flickering lamplight as something in her eyes softened. "It is perfectly wretched, isn't it?" she murmured. "And yet better than what a great many in London enjoy. But I chose it because it has the perfect vantage point. It overlooks Mr. Gorsky's front door."

Tristan's jaw hardened. "You have been watching him."

"Yes." She cut an assessing glance at him. "Or watching the house, I should say."

His hands fisting, Tristan closed his eyes and swallowed hard. "Good God," he whispered hollowly. "It was *you*. In the alleyway that night. When I . . . when I tried to —"

"— to tempt me into your bed?" she dryly suggested. "Or would there even have been a bed involved in the bargain? Alas, I was

254

compelled to decline the honor. I'm sure, though, that you would have been all that legend suggests."

"Phaedra," he managed. "For God's sake. This is not funny. What if I had —"

"You wouldn't," she swiftly interjected. "Whatever else you may be, you are too much a gentleman for that."

"You don't know that," he warned her.

"Oh, but I do." She gave a swift, oddly muted smile. She was keeping, he sensed, some sort of secret from him. "Trust me, Talbot. I know the difference between a man who understands *no* and a man who presses his advantage unfairly."

He looked at her for a long moment, wondering what she meant as he studied the angles of her face in the lamplight. The high forehead and slightly sharp nose. The wide, intelligent eyes and the mouth which, strictly speaking, was too wide, and yet looked perfect on her face.

Yes, she had always been vaguely familiar to him. But why? Even that night in the alley, it had been as if he'd known her on some visceral level he could not quite explain. If he closed his eyes, only for an instant, he could still feel her round, perfect backside pressed against his swollen . . . ah, but as she said, what was there now to talk about? "I think," he said darkly, "that you'd best tell me what you know of Gorsky."

"Almost nothing," she swore, setting one hand flat upon the table as if it were the Bible. "You must believe me."

"Go on."

"I met him quite by accident," she continued. "I called there once, you see. At the house across the way. And . . . well, when I refused to leave — rather loudly, I might add — the girl who'd answered the door sent for him."

Somehow, Tristan hid his terror. He reached across the table and covered her hand with his. "Why would you go to such a place, Phae?" he asked. "Surely you comprehend the risk to your reputation?"

"I was looking for someone," she began. "And for a reason more important to me than my reputation."

"Who?"

She stared into the gloomy depths of the room. "A girl from our village in Hampshire," she whispered. "My maid Agnes's younger sister. Her name is Millie, and she worked in the village tavern. She's barely nineteen, you see, and she ran away to London just before Christmastime. To seek her fortune."

"Yes?" asked Tristan skeptically. "And how

did she mean to do it?"

Phaedra dropped her gaze. "On her back, of course," she admitted. "Millie has this cloud of brilliant red hair — just a lovely, almost ethereal creature. And I think she imagined that —"

"That a rich man might be persuaded to keep her?" he interjected.

Phaedra nodded. "Yes, poor girl," she murmured. "She told her aunt that she was tired of being poor, and that she meant to make a fortune to support Priss, her daughter. But Millie is too young and to naïve to understand what she is giving up. *Her child,* Talbot. And if I could find her — oh, surely I could convince her what an unforgivable mistake that would be?"

"I don't know," he said honestly.

Phaedra hung her head. "I am sure, too, that Millie never considered when Priss was older, she would realize that . . . well, that her mother was a fallen woman."

Tristan was willing to bet she'd thought of it, and didn't give a bloody damn. He leaned back in his chair and tossed one booted ankle across his knee. "And this child," he prodded. "Has she a father?"

Phaedra stared into the lamplight for a long moment. "Must I say?" she asked.

"Will you refuse to help me if I do not tell you?"

He was beginning to have a deep, uneasy suspicion as to why she'd summoned him here. "Phaedra, I can't help you even if you do," he answered. "You are in danger. One man is already dead. That house — those people over there — they are treacherous."

At that, Phaedra reached out, and set both her hands on his forearm. "Talbot, listen to me." Her words were low and hoarse. "You don't understand. *They have Millie.*"

"They have her?" His eyes searched her face. "Phae, how do you know?"

Phaedra released his arm and let her shoulders sag. Her every gesture spoke of a bone-deep weariness. It made Tristan wonder how long she'd been at this — worrying herself sick and skulking around all night, he did not doubt. He wished he could have saved her from it.

"Millie's letters home all came from this house," Phaedra whispered. "She had taken a room here from Mrs. Wooten. In one of her letters she told Agnes that she had found a place with a woman who lived across the street. This woman . . . she had promised to help Millie. And to — I don't know — to facilitate her entrée into whatever world one would call it."

"The demimonde," said Tristan. "At least that's what your Millie likely hoped. But what those people over there do, Phae — it is nothing like the simple arrangements gentlemen make with their high flyers. What they do — what they sell — are sexual perversions of the worst sort."

Phaedra let her head fall back against the upper slat of the rickety chair. "Oh, Lord," she breathed. "I just knew it was something dreadful. Millie's last letter came near Candlemas. And after that . . . nothing."

Tristan leaned into her. "Phaedra, you cannot be sure," he pressed. "If she went there, she may be gone already. She may have been given over to a man for his use, and taken away. That often happens in that house. Or, sadly, she may have come to a bad end."

He regretted his hard words the moment he saw her gaze soften. "Oh, Talbot," she whispered. "Oh, please do not say that. I could not bear to think of Priss motherless."

"Tristan," he said quietly. "Phae, I think at this point you should call me Tristan."

She laughed, but there was a faintly hysterical edge to it. "I should be calling you Avoncliffe," she said. "*That* is your name."

He took her hand in his, and this time he

did not release it. "I would like you to call me Tristan, Phae, when we're alone — which, of course, we never should be. I shouldn't have come here, and now that I see you are alone, I ought to leave. If I were any sort of a gentleman, I would."

"You are concerned for me?" The edge was still in her voice. "Good God, with everything else we have to worry about. Please. Tristan. Just . . . stay. Help me think what to do."

He tightened his grip on her hand. "Phae, I'm staying, but I'm certainly not the sort of man your family would wish you to keep company with," he said. "I think we both know that's why you did not want me to meet your mother."

Her smile was wry in the lamplight. "Do have a care, sir, when you leap to your conclusions," she warned. "My mother long ago lost whatever discernment she possessed in regard to finding me a husband. You will do quite nicely, I can assure you."

His mouth curled into a smile. "Have you been so very difficult?" he murmured. "One can scarce imagine it."

"I know my own mind," she said.

"And you are not looking for a husband." He squeezed her hand once more, then let it go. "That is a shame. But God knows I am not looking for a wife. Look, Phae, let me see you safely home to Brook Street. I'm afraid I must insist."

"No," she said firmly. "Not until I've found Millie."

"We must accept that she may have vanished into the netherworld of London. Phae, it happens."

"No," Phaedra retorted, fisting both hands. "No, I cannot accept that. I won't. Priss is not even two years old, Tristan. She *needs* a mother."

The tone of her voice was determined. Almost ruthless. Tristan knew, then, what he was up against. A little roughly, he shoved back his chair and jerked to his feet to walk away. It was either that, or drag Phaedra over his knee for a spanking. Or into his lap for something worse. He began to pace the narrow chamber, dipping his head unthinkingly to avoid the low ceilings.

"You are dragging your hand through your hair again," she said from her chair. "What does that mean?"

That he was losing his mind. That he was questioning everything he'd ever wanted.

As to going home, Phaedra would not be persuaded. He already knew it. She wanted him to help her. And if he did not . . . well, God only knew what she might do. Bumble along on her own, no doubt, and get herself killed as Gorsky had done. The frightening thing was, in some ways, helping her did not seem so illogical. They both wanted the same thing. They wanted to know just what was going on inside that house.

"Tell me about Gorsky," he finally said, knowing he would regret it. "Tell me every word that passed between you."

And so she did. In the end she had, it seemed, made rather a scene at Vostrikova's, demanding her Millie be brought down and refusing to leave without her. But Gorsky had denied any knowledge of the girl, turning aside even Phaedra's most emotional pleas. Then Phaedra had resorted to threats — and made the mistake, perhaps, of invoking her elder brother's name.

"Of course I would never have gone to Stefan," she explained. "I daresay Gorsky knew it, too. He was enough of a predator to sense my desperation. There was a look, Tristan . . . this sort of dead yet watchful look in his eyes."

Tristan knew, strangely, just what she meant. He had seen such men on the battlefield; weary and without sentiment, from the years of enduring man's inhumanity to man. "He has seen so much degradation," Tristan murmured, "he likely did not care."

At that, Phaedra lifted a delicately arched eyebrow. "So I thought, at first," she said. "But at the end, there was perhaps a hint of . . . well, of *empathy* in his eyes. I had the oddest feeling he was considering helping me. Nonetheless, he did not relent."

Suddenly Tristan stopped pacing. She had just made a very good point. "Your threat, Phae, about Nash," he said a little sharply. "Why didn't you simply go to him to begin with? Why try to handle this tawdry business on your own?"

At that, Phaedra hesitated. "I . . . I cannot involve Stefan in this."

Tristan swiftly ran through the logic. "The child is his?" he asked. "The child is his, and he does not know? Or he doesn't wish his wife to know?"

"Oh, no!" said Phaedra sharply. "You must not think such a thing."

"Then the child is Mr. Hayden-Worth's," said Tristan more certainly. "And you didn't wish Lord Nash to know that his brother had seduced a young village girl."

Phaedra said nothing, but the blush of truth was upon her face. The notion made a certain amount of sense, too. Nash had already dealt with the expensive scandal

Hayden-Worth's wife had caused the Government. Perhaps he was at the end of his tether when it came to his stepbrother?

On the other hand, Tristan had always heard that Hayden-Worth's sexual preferences ran in an altogether different direction. But then, he *had* taken a wife. Which might or might not mean a damned thing.

Phaedra was looking downcast. "If you could but see her, you would understand," she said, her voice laced with pain. "She is such a rosy-cheeked, pretty little thing — Priss, I mean. But she cried for a whole day and a whole night after Millie left. It . . . It breaks my heart. I would take her, Tristan, if I could. I would take her and raise her as my own — but I cannot."

Tristan sat back down again, and drew his chair closer. "I confess, Phae, I don't care who your brother's been bedding," he said. "But this child —"

"She's my *niece*," Phaedra interjected. "She's my *blood*, Tristan. I have a duty to her, don't I? Even if her paternity is a secret?"

Little in a country village was secret. But he would permit Phaedra this one small fantasy. "And you are to be commended for wishing to do your duty," he said quietly, his mind still turning matters over. "Tell me, Phae, did you ever speak to Madame Vostrikova? Could she identify you?"

He prayed to God the answer was *no*.

Apparently, it was. Phaedra was looking at him blankly. "Who is Madame Vostrikova?"

Tristan hesitated. "The brothel's . . . er, owner, if you will," he said. "You did not know?"

Phaedra shook her head. "I didn't even know Gorsky till I rang the bell," she repeated. "But the day he died . . ." Her expression went suddenly stark.

Tristan leaned forward and took both her hands. "Yes?"

Phaedra sighed. "Tristan, I think Gorsky had been following me," she answered. "That day, I saw him hiding in the shadows on my way to Mr. Kemble's shop. But when he saw Agnes, he . . . well, he seemed simply to vanish."

"Indeed," Tristan murmured. "And then you went on to Mr. Kemble's?"

Phaedra nodded. "I had sketched Gorsky, you see. From memory. I'm not a bad hand with pencils, so I drew a passable likeness, and was taking my folio down to Mr. Kemble's to see if perhaps Gorsky was anyone he recognized. I thought . . . oh, I don't know. I thought Kemble might be able to help me somehow. He . . . knows people who know things, if you know what I mean."

Tristan did know, but another alarm bell was clanging in his head. "Phae," he said urgently, "this sketch. Did anyone else see it?"

"No." She shook her head. "No, not even Mr. Kemble. Zoë came in, you see, and we got distracted. Later, after Gorsky was stabbed, I took it home and I burnt it. It just seemed . . . safest. I knew he had died for a reason. I just sensed it."

"Good girl," said Tristan.

She lifted her gaze to his, her eyes wide and grieving. "Tristan, what in God's name is happening?" she asked. "Did I . . . did *I* cause that man to be killed?"

"You did not," said Tristan firmly. "His choice of a dangerous career working for an evil woman is what killed him. But what I should like to know is who did it."

She cut a swift, assessing glance at him. "I think you already have a theory."

He hesitated, uncertain how much to tell her. "It is said that he and Madame Vostrikova had a terrible row over something," Tristan said reluctantly. "Specifically . . . well, a young man."

"A young man?"

"Vostrikova had engaged a young lad to work for her," he answered. "A very pretty young man. God only knows how she got him. Kidnapped him or drugged him or just enslaved him with money or perhaps with something worse."

"Oh," said Phaedra softly. She had begun to toy with a button on the front of her smock. "Yes. I . . . I think perhaps I comprehend."

Tristan almost hoped she did not, but he plunged ahead. "Gorsky, it is said, developed an attachment to the lad," he continued. "I really should rather not explain it further, Phae, if you do not mind. Suffice it to say Gorsky began to take objection to Vostrikova's use of the boy, and —"

"Boy?" Phaedra's head jerked up. "I thought you said he was a young man?"

The lad had been fourteen, or so Tristan had been told, and Vostrikova had leased him out to a peer with a penchant for pretty boys and a seat in faraway Lancashire. It had taken twenty pounds and a passage to Jamaica to get the scullery maid to tell him that much, and she hadn't known the man's name.

But Tristan wasn't sure how to explain such vile things to Phaedra. Still, if the man was a government nabob — and Vostrikova ensnared no other kind — then he would be found sooner rather than later. Lancashire just wasn't that large a place.

"He was a young man," said Tristan quietly. "And Vostrikova sent him away. That's all I can say. But it was the root, I begin to think, of a falling-out between Vostrikova and her henchman."

"What happened to the boy?" She had defaulted, Tristan noticed, to the more diminutive term. Yet again he realized Phaedra was not naïve. She understood the world could be a wicked place.

"I saw de Vendenheim this morning in Whitehall," said Tristan. "I gave him what information I had. They are looking for the lad. He will find him."

"So he will." Phaedra relaxed into her chair. "He's perfectly ruthless when right is on his side — and sometimes even when it isn't. No one keeps secrets from de Vendenheim."

Her remark brought home to him yet again the importance of getting Phaedra out of this mess. He simply prayed she was still beyond Vostrikova's notice, and that Gorsky's murder while following her was just a crime of opportunity. Everything he had learned thus far suggested as much. But Gorsky, he suspected, had been looking for a private moment in which to approach Phaedra.

Perhaps he had wished to unburden himself. Or, more likely, he'd wished to see Vostrikova punished for sending the object of his affection away. And Phaedra had the right connections for that: two prominent brothers, one rich and powerful, the other politically influential — and both of them untainted, so far as Tristan could discover, by any association with Vostrikova.

One word to them of the blackmail, treason, and outright enslavement which went on under her roof, and the infamous madam might never have seen the outside of a prison cell again. Yes, Gorsky, he suspected, had been looking to strike a bargain with Phaedra.

"You have been very brave, Phae, in trying to find your Millie," he said quietly. "And it was very clever of you, taking this room."

"Little good it's done," she answered. "As we now know, most everyone comes and goes through the rear."

"Yes, well, they have the sort of clients with much to hide," said Tristan. "As you have probably guessed, Madame Vostrikova is running a very particular sort of brothel."

In the candlelight, a lovely shade of pink graced her cheeks. "Indeed, I collect the place is thought quite dangerous," she answered. "People will tell Mrs. Thompson things they won't so willingly share with Lady Phaedra."

"There are some wicked goings-on in that house, it's true," he acknowledged.

Her gaze drifted up him, and to his shock, there was a heated flicker of sensual assessment in her eyes. "Anything you haven't done?"

"Oh, a thing or two, I daresay," he answered, wishing to the devil his cock didn't rouse every time she came within three feet of him. "My appetites, Phae, are pretty conventional by comparison to that crowd."

"What do you think of them?" she asked quietly. "These men, I mean, who wish to engage in such things? Are they . . . evil? Or merely depraved?"

Tristan shrugged. "So long as those men aren't hurting anyone — well, anyone who doesn't wish to be hurt — then it's no one's business, I daresay. But Vostrikova doesn't stop at that."

She looked away, color flaming up her cheeks. "What about women, Tristan?" she whispered. "Are there women who enjoy wickedness? And if they do, aren't they just like those men? If they . . . if they just can't stop thinking about it, are they — I don't know — wrong, somehow? Do they tempt men to be bad?"

"Some, perhaps," he agreed, not entirely certain what she was asking. "Yes, there are women who are sirens of a sort, I suppose."

Her eyes flashed with an emotion he'd never seen before. "I'm tired of being ignorant," she rasped. "I don't know what's happened to Millie. And I don't understand anything. Everyone walks dainty circles around me, and I'm sick to death of it."

He lifted her hand from his arm, but did not release it. "My dear, we're treading dangerous ground," he replied. "Come, let me take you home."

"Please don't think me ungrateful," she retorted, turning a little away from him. "But I mean to play this role until I know what's happened to Millie. And in some ways, Tristan, being Mrs. Thompson has its advantages."

"What do you mean?"

She lifted one shoulder. "This place might be a hovel, but I may do as I please here," she answered. "People believe me an impoverished, lower-class widow, not some virginal, pampered princess who might faint if she learnt anything of the real world — the world beyond Temple Bar and Covent Garden. The world of Mr. Gorsky and those poor women who must work there. There is beauty, Tristan, in truth, even when it is an ugly truth."

He thought he understood, strangely, what she meant. A woman like Phaedra — especially when unwed — lived in a gilded cage. A beautiful existence, but a cage nonetheless.

She rose, and he followed suit. Her chin was up, her shoulders straight but delicate, and the sudden, fierce longing to protect her surged inside him again. But it wasn't what she wanted, he knew. Moreover, the notion doubtless would pass, as did most of his more honorable impulses. God knew he was no guardian angel. Nonetheless, he lifted his hand, and set the back of his fingers to her cheek. It was warm and soft, like the rest of her body, he did not doubt. "Let me, Phae," he ordered. "Let me deal with this Millie business for you."

Her eyes flashed. "No, I mean to see this through," she said. "I won't be mollycoddled, Tristan. Not by any man."

"By God, Phae, I am not *any man*," he said darkly, gripping her upper arm. "I weigh thirteen stone and stand better than six feet. I have a knife in my pocket and a pistol in my boot, both of which I am extraordinarily skilled in using. I've been shot, stabbed, and beaten half to death so often it doesn't much bother me. Furthermore, I have the full faith and authorization of the Crown behind me. But aye, I'm a just man."

"Well, when you put it that way, you sound such a tempting package." She cut a curious glance at him. "We will work together, Tristan. It mayn't be what you want, but that is my offer."

He jerked her closer, his frustration deepening. "You aren't in a position to offer me anything, my dear," he gritted. "Certainly not what I *want*."

She looked at him boldly then, her body mere inches from his. "What *do* you want, then, Tristan?" she murmured, her voice low and throaty. "Just say it. I am, after all, Mrs. Thompson tonight."

"What the devil does that mean?"

She lowered her lashes seductively. "I am . . . anonymous," she answered. "I am, one might argue, that same woman you met in the alleyway. The one you invited to your bed."

"I'll show you want I want, then." The words came out low and rough. He kissed her again, this time more sensuously. Phaedra made a soft sound in the back of her throat, then reached up to curl one hand behind his head, to avoid the wound she had so carefully stitched. Slowly, he thrust inside her mouth, tasting her deeply and languidly, half waiting for her to shove him away. The intimacy of the kiss — what he suggested — was unmistakable.

But she did not push him away. Instead she slid her tongue sinuously along his, making him shudder with barely tethered restraint. Eventually, her mouth slid from his, skimming lightly along his jaw. "Another time, perhaps," she whispered, her lips moving up to brush his ear. "Those were your words to me in the alley that night. Did you mean it? I've seen how they all look at you, fanning and whispering."

"Careful what you wish for, love," he rasped.

"It's wrong, I know." She sounded breathless. A little frightened of herself. "My mother says . . ."

He ran this thumb across her cheek. "What?"

Phaedra's eyes closed, her lashes like dark lace across her skin, and something inside him tore. "Mamma says a real lady shouldn't feel lust," she whispered. "But you know things, don't you? About pleasing women, I mean?"

He made a sound of disbelief. "If real ladies do not feel lust, Phae, why are they forever handing me their cards?" His opposite hand came up to cradle her face, and he was shocked to see it tremble. "Your mother is wrong, Phae. Passion is beautiful. Normal. *Necessary.*"

"I am tempted, Tristan," she murmured, the second hand joining the first, flat against his chest as she leaned into him. "Can you live up to your lofty reputation?"

He didn't like her choice of words, but he'd earned his notoriety, he supposed. And now he was treading in dark water, for there was something about her that called to what was left of the gentleman in him, and made him think of foolish, fanciful things. Alone, in this cocoon of quiet intimacy, with the seductive rumble of the rain just inches above their heads, and that old spindle bed tempting him, Phaedra was beginning to make a frightening amount of sense.

Desire had been simmering in his loins since the moment he'd entered this room, growling and snarling at the chit. His mask was down — that jovial, devil-may-care façade he reserved for the rest of the world — with her, it no longer worked. And he wasn't sure he wished it to.

Phaedra turned her face into the curve of his hand. "Tristan," she whispered against it, her tongue lightly brushing his palm.

"Can you make me stop . . . aching?"

So be it.

Tristan let his fingers slide into the fine, soft hair at Phaedra's temples, and felt his breath shudder from his lungs. "A month, then," he whispered. "Give me one month, Phae, to deal with Vostrikova. And I promise you, I will discover what happened to Millie. Will you do that? Will you trust me?"

She licked her lips, and cut her eyes away. "Yes," she said softly. "I . . . I shall try."

Still cradling her face in his hands, he bent his head and took her mouth roughly. If his kiss beneath the pergola had been too bold, this one was an outright pillage. He drove her head back, surging inside with long, deep strokes which left no doubt of his body's intention. To take. To thrust. To taste until he was sated.

Perhaps he hoped, somewhere deep in his mind, that she would turn tail and bolt down the stairs. If so, he was to be disappointed. Phaedra's mouth molded hungrily to his, her body rising until her breasts were flat against his chest. It was as if she melted into him, her hands sliding around his waist, then up, to the heavy muscles of his upper back.

Her every motion was seduction itself, but without guile, without the calculation he'd come to expect of his lovers. She did not mean to tempt him. She simply did, answering his lust with her own. Later he realized he should have questioned her grasp of what was about to happen, but in those first heated moments it was beyond him.

She said no more, but instead slid her hands beneath his coat, pushing it off his shoulders. Tristan let it go. Her fingers tugged at the hem of his shirt, drawing it from his trousers, and he gave one last thought to ordering her to stop. It didn't last. She set her palms to the bare skin of his ribs and he shivered, then drew her back into his arms for another kiss.

Only a cad would do this to an innocent, he told himself. But Phaedra kept touching him — touching him in a way that was not at all innocent — and driving him past the point of control. He was not perfectly sure who undressed who. He remembered only her hands on his bare flesh, and her breasts rising and falling beneath the thin lawn of her shift. And his fingers fulfilling his fantasy — pulling the pins from her hair as he watched it spill down in heavy, chestnut waves. Stripped to the waist, he pulled her to the bed and drew her between his legs. "I shouldn't," he murmured, his mouth going to her collarbone.

He kissed her there longingly as she stood before him, then untied her shift and pushed the fabric off one shoulder. To his surprise, her breasts were bound with a strip of cotton wrapped twice around. He tugged it loose and they sprang free like large, ripe fruit, their tips already taut and erect, begging for his mouth. His lips captured one through the fabric, and she cried out, her hands spearing into his hair as she stilled his head.

"Tristan," she murmured.

Lazily, he circled her nipple with his tongue, his hand going to the other breast, weighing it, then lightly thumbing the nipple until she arched into his palm with another thready cry of pleasure.

His head swam with the scent of her hair. He fisted his hand in her hem and dragged it almost savagely to her waist. His cock was shoving at the fabric of his trousers now. He untied her drawers and felt the soft linen breeze down her legs. Tristan forced himself to resist the urge to free his straining weight; to pull her into his lap and thrust up and inside her on one triumphant stroke. It would not do; not for a woman of no experience.

Instead he found the swell of her firm buttock and filled his hand, squeezing it. Good

God, he wanted to take her like this, he realized. On her belly. On her knees. On top of him. Any way he could have her. But not yet. Not yet.

When she moaned against his mouth, he stood and lifted her greedily to him. In response, she pulled her lips from his, her eyes glassy, her breath rough. Without speaking, Phaedra set her hands to work at the buttons of his trousers, almost tearing them free in her awkward eagerness.

He was a man who ordinarily took his time with such things, but he shucked his trousers and boots in a fevered rush. Dimly he realized they were approaching a point of no return. Phaedra did not mean to stop him. He knew that this was inevitable. Knew he was going to lie her down on that shabby little bed, thrust himself deep inside her, and make her his forever. The realization frightened him. Awed him. And did not slow him down one whit.

When he turned to face her, his erection heavy and jutting through his drawers, Phaedra's eyes widened. But undeterred, she came into his arms, setting her warm palms against his chest, this time stroking her fingers down the hair which dusted his chest and ran down his belly. "I want you," she murmured, as if convincing herself. "I want this, Tristan."

When she touched him lower with her light, clever fingers, he gasped. "Minx," he said again. "You're going to have me. Get on the bed."

With one last glance at his jutting manhood, Phaedra did as he asked, settling onto it almost girlishly, one leg tucked beneath her. Dimly he recalled that, no matter how passionate she might be, she was untutored. He followed her to the bed, his drawers hanging low on his hips, dipping his head beneath the low, peaked rafters. He bent over her to kiss her again, hotly and open-mouthed, twining his tongue sinuously in a seductive dance of need.

When they came apart gasping, he slowly drew the shift over her head. Phaedra lifted her arms and bent her head slightly as the fabric slid away, a vision of beautiful, feminine surrender. Only then, when the linen had drifted to the floor and Phaedra sat naked before him did he fully comprehend the beauty of her body.

His eyes swept over her as his mouth went dry. Phaedra was made for sin, with wide hips, lush, slightly pendulous breasts, and legs almost as long as his own. Legs which went on forever — until they didn't. And there lay her glory, a nest of dark gold curls which invited a man's tongue — and some of his other appendages — to linger. "Phae, you are made for this," he whispered. "Those gray gowns — yes, I can see why you had to wear them."

She lifted her gaze to him and said nothing, but merely raised her arms as if to draw him to her. Tristan did not need another invitation. Pure longing and a raw, pulsing need hammered in his head and throbbed in his rod with every beat of his heart.

He set one knee to the bed and crawled over her, pushing her onto the mattress as he went. When her head lay back against the bolster, her brown-gold hair fanned out like a pheasant's wings, he kissed her again, his arms braced over her head. Beneath him she squirmed, then her body arched to his like a magnet drawn to north, brushing her curls against this heated cock. With one hand, he pushed her down again. "You wanted me to live up to my reputation," he whispered, his tongue stroking along the shell of her ear. "Lie back, sweet, and let me make you grateful."

"Yes . . . all right."

Without explanation, he slid down the bed and pushed her thighs wide. He shifted his weight between her legs, ignoring the insistent throb between his own. Phaedra sucked in her breath when he set his lips to her belly, and shivered when he thrust his tongue into her navel, languidly circling.

She gasped again when he spread her flesh wide with his fingers. He set his mouth where his fingers had been, and she shuddered beneath him. Lightly, teasingly, he stroked his tongue through her open flesh, and Phaedra whimpered softly, then cried out his name.

"Shush, shush," he whispered. "Hold tight."

Her nails dug into the tattered coverlet, her hips arching. Then Tristan plunged his tongue deep into the silken folds of her womanhood, lightly licking at the silken pearl of her arousal. Phaedra's trembling deepened, and one hand lashed out to grasp his shoulder.

Softly, he laughed. "Relax, my sweet," he murmured. "Relax and let it take you."

"I — I thought you would come inside me," she whispered uncertainly. "I think . . . that this could be more dangerous."

"Oh?" he murmured, just before stroking her again. "In what way?"

He flicked a quick glance up to see that her head had rolled back against the bolster. "Addictive," she whispered into the low rafters, quivering again. "Utterly . . . enslaving. Oh, God. I fear I will dream of this."

"Oh, that is the very idea, love," he said. "I would gladly have you as my slave and bend you to my will."

And bend her over the bed. And over his knee. And perhaps, he considered, *given that fine, plump arse of hers, over the kitchen table.* One look at her lush, ripe body and a man's mind began to run hot and mad.

Ah, but his turn was next, he consoled himself. Tristan dipped his head and lapped at her with light, teasing strokes until she shook and the bed began to shake with her. Phaedra's fingers went to the head of the bed, seizing at the spindles of the old oak headboard and entwining her hands through them as if she might cut off her own blood. As if she feared being cast out to sea on the waves of her own passion.

"Hold me," she whispered, wrenching at the spindles. "I can't — *oh.* Hold me."

Tristan watched her writhe, awestruck as her hunger deepened, almost exploding himself. Passion possessed her — left her gasping — and yet Phaedra could not reach it. On impulse, he spread his upper arms across her legs and held her immobile, fully exposed to his mouth. It seemed to be just what she wanted. It drove her near the edge.

She cried out softly at first, and then her

panting rose to a breathy, urgent rhythm as he suckled her little nub. Then her head went back one last time on a silent, open cry. She shuddered, and shuddered again, and then was spent.

When Phaedra again lay limply, her hands above her head relaxing and her fingers slowly curling into her palms, Tristan crawled back up the bed, biting back his own burning need. Steeling himself for what was to come. *He could still stop,* he dimly reminded himself.

A better man than himself would have. But Phaedra lay beneath him, her heavy breasts still tipped with tautly budded nipples, her eyes somnolent with pleasure, her legs open to take him, and Tristan knew he hadn't the strength. He had committed himself to the inevitable. To her. He knelt over her, and drew his hand up through the warm folds of her flesh, then probed deeper with his fingers. One finger and then a second slipped inside as Phaedra watched him. She was ready and slick with her own need, her womanly passage open for their joining. Their union as man and woman. Lover and beloved.

There was no point in postponing the inevitable, for like any sort of pain, keen and quick was best. Tristan took himself in hand and probed gently. As if she were made for him, he slipped easily inside. Phaedra moaned, but not in pain, her eyelashes dropping shut. Tristan, too, closed his eyes, drew back, and thrust deep.

And there was . . . nothing. Nothing but warm, feminine flesh enfolding him. Welcoming him. Drawing him deep as if drawing him home. Tentatively, he rocked himself back and forth inside her.

Well. This he had not expected.

Phaedra touched him lightly, a little uncertainly, her hands settling over his shoulders. He opened his eyes and smiled down at her. He began to move back and forth, and it was like turning up the wick on a lamp. Heat and flame sprung at once to her eyes. "Yes," she said, holding his gaze. "Ohh! Tristan. Like that."

There was no hesitation, and no pain. Just a clear blue sea of pleasure ahead of him, stretching to infinity. Tristan set a rhythm of deep, perfect thrusts, sliding their bodies together even as he reined back his own eagerness. He knew without asking that Phaedra would reach the stars with him. Already her need was growing. She drew her knees up, and moved restlessly beneath him as their bodies slickened and slid and moved as one, making the old bed creak.

"Yes," she said again, closing her eyes and licking her lips. "Oh, God."

It had been a long time since Tristan had seen a woman lose herself so deeply and so quickly. Phaedra's need was a palpable thing, and it served only to ratchet his own desire to a feverish pitch. And yet it challenged him. Drove him. On impulse, he picked up her knee and hitched it over his shoulder, deepening his thrust.

Phaedra opened her eyes, and looked at him hungrily then lifted her other leg and followed suit. "Oh, yes," she murmured, hooking it over his shoulder. "Like that, Tris. *Ohh — !*"

He dragged her fully against him, both hands grasping the slender turn of her waist, driving himself home again and again as he ruthlessly stilled her to his thrusts. Phaedra took him deep, her face a mask of welling passion.

For long moments he loved her, until the rain had stopped and the streets beyond the little garret grew still. Until he was panting, perspiration trickling down his throat, dripping onto her pale, perfect breasts. Again and again he thrust, rocking into her, driving them into an upward, feverish spiral. The ropes of the old bed were groaning in protest even as Phaedra's sobbing height-ened. She was on the edge, and he was about to explode. And still there was no end.

Good God, he thought. *She was going to kill him.* She was supposed to be an untutored virgin, and he the indefatigable Lothario. *And she was going to kill him.*

Phaedra had both wrists twisted almost painfully through the wooden spindles of the bed now as she writhed and sobbed beneath him, seeking her release. And suddenly, it dawned on him that what she craved — whether she understood it or not — was to be controlled. To be restrained in some way. Her own passion was almost beyond her. The raw eroticism of the notion shocked him.

Her knees tightened over his shoulders, dragging her feminine heat to his groin, increasing the friction of their bodies, and still she could not find her edge. Abruptly, he stopped, and bent over her to kiss her, fumbling at the edge of the bed.

Her eyes flew open and she looked at him beseechingly, her gaze moving over his face. "Tristan?" she whispered uncertainly.

"Give me your hand." The words came out thick and husky.

Obediently she disentangled it from the spindles. Already her thumb had turned faintly blue. He encircled her wrist with his cravat, once, and then again for good measure, lashing it tight. He held it up for her to see.

"Is this what you need, Phae?" he rasped.

She opened her mouth soundlessly. "I don't know what I need," she whimpered. "I just want and want — and for what, I don't know." She turned her face away and closed her eyes.

"Give me the other hand," he said more gently.

Willingly, she did so. He bound both wrists together, tightly but not so tight as to lessen the blood flow, then shoved them high above her head. Deftly, he lashed both hands to the spindles until he was sure she could not escape.

"Pull hard against it," he ordered.

She did so, her eyes widening, her throat working up and down. It was understood. She was his to command now.

"Does it hurt?" he asked.

She shook her head, her thick hair scrubbing the bolster. "Not . . . not in a bad way."

He set his hands to either side of her face and kissed her deeply with his lips and with his tongue — and perhaps even with a little bit of his heart. "There," he said when he was done. "You're bound to me, love."

She looked at him unblinkingly, her eyes

still soft with need. "Yes," she whispered eagerly. "Yes, Tristan."

He gave the knots a hard yank. "See, Phae?" he whispered. "You can't get free. No matter how hard you fight it, you can't get free of me. Now let yourself go, love. Come to me."

She nodded, and swallowed again. Still hard enough to hammer nails, Tristan thrust inside her, tentatively at first. Phaedra closed her eyes, drew down on the knot, and gave a hum of pleasure. He picked up the rhythm, driving inside her, thrusting over and over, gliding against Phaedra's sweet, perfect center.

Her warm, sleek skin tightened and pulled around his cock, milking the pleasure from his flesh. And when he thought he would surely, surely go mad from the pain and the pleasure, Phaedra began to writhe and to sob in earnest. She rose high against him again and again, tears streaming from the corners of her eyes.

The secret to Phaedra was simple. She needed someone — or something — to control her. *It was,* he *thought, the damnedest thing he'd ever seen.* And probably the most erotic.

"Tristan, Tristan, yes," she chanted. "Oh, yes. Oh."

He strained and strained for that last sweet stroke, and when they came together, it was in a blinding, white-hot fury that seized his every muscle and every nerve, shattering him into a thousand shards of light, each of them a piece of her. Each of them a piece of his heart.

When he returned to the mortal world, he was bent over her, his hands planted to either side of her shoulders, and drenched in sweat. Phaedra's hands were still bound tight to the bed, her knees still hooked over his shoulders. He bowed his head and let their foreheads touch.

It had been life altering. And there was nothing more to be said.

Gently, he lifted her leg and shifted to her side, then unfastened the knot which bound her. Phaedra did not open her eyes until he was done. Then she watched as the cravat slithered off the bed, and licked her love-swollen lips uncertainly. "You can say it now," she whispered. "The earth won't split and swallow us whole."

Tristan drew one finger down her cheek and smiled into her eyes. "Say what, Phae? That you are beautiful and passionate?"

She swallowed hard and held his gaze, and even then, he could sense what it cost her. "No. That I wasn't a virgin."

"Were you not?" he murmured, plucking a thick curl of her hair and twining it round his finger. "Can't say as I ever had a virgin myself. But then, it really isn't any of my business, is it?"

She shifted her gaze away, and looked at her wrists, which still bore the faint lines of his cravat. "You must think me disgraceful," she murmured. "That I am . . . terribly wrong, somehow. The way I'm made, I mean. And your cravat — I never dreamt such a thing . . ."

"But you liked it, aye?" He trailed a fingertip down her breastbone, and dropped his voice to a more serious tone. "Phae, love, there's nothing wrong with you. It's just bed play. Many people find that erotic."

"Do they?" She cast him a dubious glance. "I wish I understood. My body is so . . . hungry. And my mind is so . . . not my own. Not . . . when I'm like that."

He reclined on one elbow and looked down at her. "You have no idea, do you?" he murmured. "Such passion is a gift, Phae. You would be a treasure to any man whose bed you graced."

Gently, she chaffed her wrist. "You do not find me . . . strange?"

"I don't find you anything but charming," he murmured, rolling forward just far enough to kiss her nose. "Well, and bull-headed, of course. You just haven't learned to leash your own desire. To trust yourself. You are so passionate, Phae, but so caught up in thinking it's wrong — when it isn't. It's beautiful. Natural. And all that confusion . . . it just overwhelms you. Give yourself time, love. Give yourself time to learn to govern your own body."

Her soft gaze searched his face. "And what if . . . what if I cannot?"

He winked at her. "Then I daresay I shall just have to keep doing it for you," he said, laughing. "Oh, what a bloody shame that would be!"

She fell silent for a time as if pondering it. Tristan rolled to one side, then flopped flat on his back to let the cool of the room settle over him. Beside him, Phaedra shifted onto her left side, a few inches away. When the silence began to feel heavy and a little expectant, he rolled back again. "Phae." He dipped his head and kissed the turn of her neck as he held her. "Do you want to talk? About . . . anything else?"

She shook her head. "No," she murmured. "Let's not spoil it."

Once again it came home to him how very different she was from any other woman he had known. He opened his mouth to press the issue, then closed it again. Instead, he shut his eyes and drew in the scent of warm, spent woman, and felt that unfamiliar instinct — that surging wish to protect her — tug at him again. He had done it. He had committed . . . to *something,* surely?

Steady on, old boy, said the devilish imp on his shoulder. *And keep your mouth shut. You don't owe her a bloody thing.*

It was true, perhaps, Tristan realized. The heat of lust had given way to the languor of enervation, and his cooler, more rational mind was beginning to function again. Phaedra had not been a virgin. He had not — well, taken anything from her save his own pleasure. He had not irreparably damaged her in any way.

No, someone else had done that. And he wanted — suddenly and fiercely — to kill them. But *why?* Why wasn't he thanking his lucky stars? He had leapt into this mess believing himself some sort of martyr, ready to do the right thing — and that fact by itself was damning. But now to learn his martyrdom was not needed . . .

He should have been relieved. And he was, he supposed. Yet beneath it lay an odd sort of anger. Not with Phaedra, no. He was not yet so sunk in self-absorption as to believe he could hold her to a higher standard than himself. So she wasn't a virgin. There had been someone — perhaps more than one someone — before him. And there he was, back to those paradoxes again. For never had he met a woman more innocent, more artless, and more wholly unaware of her own charms than this one. Certainly he'd never met one so deeply, innately passionate. None of it — nothing about this whole blasted night — made sense to him.

But there was no resolving the matter just now. There was still the shadow of Gorsky's death lingering over them, and the business of the house across the street. He still needed to somehow convince her to leave matters to him. Oh, she'd promised him a month, but she'd lied through her teeth, perhaps unconsciously, but a lie all the same. Just now, however, he hadn't the energy for that sort of fight. So he kissed the round of her shoulder, and drifted off with Phaedra in his arms.

CHAPTER 9

Jesters do oft prove prophets.

That night, Phaedra dreamed of Priss, and of Hampshire in the spring. They lay on blankets in Brierwood's bottom, just a slow, lazy walk from the village. Even in sleep, Phaedra could hear the rhythmic *swoosh-swoosh-swoosh* of the mill in the distance, and feel the faint rumble of the millstones deep in the alluvial earth.

Priss sat on her round bottom, her fat baby legs crooked out beneath her, a white-brimmed bonnet shading her cheeks from the sun as she played with a fistful of daisies.

"No, Priss, like this." Agnes sat up on the blanket to show her how to make a small bouquet. "Not squishing from your fingers all higgledy-piggledy. Then we tie it up with ribbon."

Her blue eyes wide beneath the white bonnet, Priss stuck out her bow lip, and watched intently as Agnes looped the ribbon around.

Priss gurgled with laughter and flailed one hand. "Like *dis*," she said, rolling over to half crawl onto Phaedra. She laid her fist on Phaedra's chest and opened it, depositing her flowers in a tangle of green and gold. "For you," she said proudly. "Dis for you, Phae."

Phaedra looked up into the child's round face and felt a flood of maternal affection, and a deep, lingering sadness she could not explain. "Thank you, Priss," she said. "It is the most beautiful bouquet I ever received."

But Priss faded away and for a fleeting instant, became another, more distant memory. It was all mixed up together. In her head and in her heart. And when she blinked her eyes, Phaedra was looking not at the child that haunted her, but at Tristan Talbot.

He was waiting. Waiting for her to explain. She opened her mouth, but no sound came out.

"Phae?" he said quietly.

"I tried," she finally whispered. "Oh, Tristan, I tried."

Tristan set his hand to her feverish cheek. "To do what, Phae?"

Phaedra swallowed uncertainly. "I . . . I don't know," she murmured. "I wanted to save her."

"The child?" His touch was tender. "You were saying something about a child."

"Was I?" she rasped, awake now. "I — I don't want to think about that now."

The rain had cleared to an ethereally brilliant night, the full moon centered in the narrow attic window. Tristan loomed beside her in the darkness, propped on one elbow, steadily watching her with eyes which once were dancing, but tonight were remarkably solemn.

"Make me," she whispered. "Make me not think about it." And when she lifted her arms to him, he turned her onto her back and mounted her, entering on one swift thrust.

In the silence of the room he rode her, capturing her wrists in his strong, long-fingered hands and forcing them high above her head. Pinning her to the bed. Impaling her. Driving her again to that exquisite, perfect height. Sweat slicked his body, the sinewy tendons of his arms and the layered muscles of his chest glowing in the lamp-light. She came not in a whirling firestorm, but in a quiet, shuddering release. This time, however, Tristan jerked himself from her body, spilling his seed onto her stomach as he cried out on a silent shout, his head going back, the tendons of his neck straining.

Then Tristan fell against her, and again Phaedra drowsed, not entirely certain if any of it had been real, or just another of her feverish dreams. She wasn't sure how long she slept entwined in Tristan's arms, but when next she began to rouse, it was in a cold sweat, with a vision of Gorsky's disembodied face swimming in the gloom before her.

Not Gorsky's cold visage as he had turned her away at the door in Soho, nor Gorsky's bent head as he lurked in the shadows of the tobacconist's. No, it was Gorsky's mask of death. The glassy, wide-eyed stare of a man who had seen his end coming; seen, perhaps, the very face of his killer. He had fallen face-first in a heap at Phaedra's feet, one hand outstretched as if pleading . . .

As if pleading.

Through the fog of sleep, Phaedra tried to recall. Yes, his hand had been outstretched . . .

She must have cried out in the darkness.

"Phae?" Tristan's voice cut through the haze. "Phae, what is it?"

Phaedra opened her eyes and looked at Tristan. Was she sleeping? Or awake? The rain had picked up again, thundering on the roof above the bed. She was awake. "His hand," she murmured. "Gorsky's hand. He . . . he was reaching out to me. He was clutching something."

"Clutching something?" Tristan muttered, dragging a shock of wavy black hair off his forehead.

Phaedra set a hand to her heart, and jerked upright. "There was something in his hand," she said

"Phae, what are you talking about?"

"Something tumbled from his hand — and it sounded . . . I don't know. Wooden, almost? And it rolled. Yes, it rolled across the floor."

"Wooden?" he asked. "Are we talking about Gorsky?"

"My God." Phaedra's hand lashed out, catching his wrist. "What time is it?"

Tristan glanced at the window. Even through the rain, he sensed the full moon was fading. "Late, blast it," he said. "Dawn can't be more than an hour away."

Phaedra leapt from the bed, and snatched something from the floor. "My God," she said again, dragging her shift over her head. "We must hurry."

Propped on one elbow, he reached out for her hand. "Wait, Phae." And then he asked the one question — that simple but telling question — the one he'd never asked of any woman. "When will I see you again?"

Caught in midmotion of snatching her stocking from the floor, Phaedra went perfectly still. For a long moment, she said nothing, as if she did not trust herself to speak. "At nine o'clock," she finally said. "That's when Kemble opens. Number Eight, in the Strand."

He sat up, snared her wrist, and pulled her between his bare legs. "The Strand?" he said, setting his hands on her slender waist. "What about . . . well, what about *us,* Phae?"

"Us?" she echoed hollowly.

Tristan, of course, wished to snatch back the phrase as soon as it left his mouth. If he'd had a ha'penny for every time a woman had said that to him . . . ah, well. The shoe was on the other foot — at least this morning — and to his surprise, it pinched a little.

Phaedra's eyes softened, and an emotion which might have been regret sketched over her face. "Tristan, there is no us," she said in her quiet, husky voice.

There is no us. Well. No expectations here, then. And he couldn't afford to bed her again anyway. Women like Phaedra you married — or you left them alone. Which meant another clean getaway for the infamous Tristan Talbot. He forced himself to smile up at her.

"As you wish, love," he said, releasing her hand. "Nine o'clock it is."

"Un balai! Un balai!" Mr. Kemble was on his knees in his workroom floor, his snug, elegant arse stuck high in the air as he peered beneath a row of cabinets. "Jean-Claude! *Dépêche-toi!"*

Tristan watched as Kemble's lean, dark-haired assistant leapt from the floor and went rushing toward a closet tucked beneath the stairs. He returned with a broom, and knelt to tentatively offer it.

"Merci," grunted Mr. Kemble, snatching it.

Kemble, of course, had been surprised to see Phaedra and her maid awaiting him when he came down to unlock the shop at nine. He had been even more surprised to see Tristan, and had surveyed him up and down with open suspicion.

The vague awkwardness between Tristan and Phaedra had likely been palpable to those around them. Tristan had felt it the moment he joined her on the pavement outside Kemble's door. Her unwillingness to quite hold his gaze. The stiff formality in her language which could not be wholly explained by the very public place in which they stood. Regret and uncertainty seemed to linger in the air between them.

Or perhaps it was only Tristan who felt that press of unspoken questions. That diffident uncertainty of an awkward morning after. They were lovers who did not yet fully know one another — and likely never would. The thought left Tristan strangely melancholy.

But Phaedra's focus now was on finding the object she was so certain Gorsky had dropped. She was watching Kemble ply his broom, her expression chagrinned. "I can't think why I didn't remember this sooner," she said for the tenth time. "But there was just so much blood . . ."

"You were in shock, as any rational person would have been," said Tristan, observing as Kemble eased the broom beneath the last piece, a massive chinoiserie armoire, and drew it gingerly across its width.

Kemble flicked an irritated glance up at Tristan. "Anything?"

Tristan glanced down at the side legs of the armoire. "Dust balls," he said.

Kemble hissed through his teeth. "Try to make yourself useful," he snapped. "Look behind the blasted thing. Perhaps I pushed it through."

Tristan strode round the wardrobe and leaned as far back as he could. "Well, it's dark behind there —"

"No, seriously?" Kemble acerbically interjected.

"— but I think I see something far to the right."

Phaedra, too, had knelt on the floor now, and was trying to look under it. "Perhaps it's stuck?" she said unhelpfully. "Perhaps if we moved it?"

"What, and get a hernia?" said Kemble, horrified. "One's trousers would never fit smoothly again."

Tristan stood to the left of the offending furniture. With a grunt, he braced his hands at both the front and the back, gave it a good shove, then lifted and pivoted it forward on its right rear leg with a horrendous scraping sound. A dusty, cavernous space opened up behind it.

Kemble's broom clattered to the floor. "Good God," he said, scrambling to his feet. "All that brawn is good for something after all."

Jean-Claude, Tristan noticed, was eyeing him with a newfound appreciation.

At least someone was. Phaedra was too busy attempting to squeeze behind the armoire. "I am the smallest," she said, her voice muffled behind the wood. "So if I can just wedge in here —"

"Shall I simply heft it up again?" asked Tristan dryly. "After all, I live to serve you, my lady."

The barb sailed over her head. "Oh, look!" she said brightly. "Here it is!"

She backed out of the space, a cobweb caught in her hair, and held out her hand. A wooden sphere slightly smaller than a cricket ball rested on her palm. Tristan and Kemble stepped nearer, studying it.

"I haven't a clue what that might be," Kemble admitted.

Tristan was somewhat surprised to hear it, given the contents of Kemble's shop. Every oddity in the world seemed to rest upon his shelves or hang upon his walls. But the ball was indeed a curiosity. It was made of a golden, lacquered wood and cut with little squares rather like a spherical chessboard. Each of the squares was inlaid with a tiny letter in a darker wood.

"It looks Cyrillic," said Phaedra.

"Yes, Russian, I believe," Kemble said, poking at the ball.

He was likely right, Tristan realized. Each square contained a letter of a Cyrillic-style alphabet.

Kemble took the ball, and turned it over and over. "I can read a little Russian," he said. "But this doesn't actually *say* anything so far as I can see."

Tristan held out his hand. "May I?"

"By all means." Kemble dropped the ball into his palm.

Experimentally, Tristan pressed with his pinkie finger on one of the squares. The wood gave with a little *snick,* and the wooden bar slid through to protrude on the other side.

"Interesting," said Kemble. "Press another."

He did so, but the ball seemed locked. Tristan returned the original letter to its place by pressing on the opposite end of the bar. The letter clicked back into place, and the ball was smooth again. He pushed another, and again, the bar slid through.

"It is a puzzle ball," said Mr. Kemble thoughtfully. "I've seen such things from Eastern Europe, but never in this shape. And certainly never this complicated."

"I think you're right," said Tristan pensively. "I saw a similar device once on a dead Turk — a spy, actually. But square in shape, and far more rudimentary."

"What does it do?" asked Phaedra.

Tristan shook his head. "I think, if one presses the right letters in the right series, the thing will open to reveal a secret," he said. "A gem or a *billet-doux.* Something like that."

"What series of letters?" asked Kemble sharply.

"That can be decided, I daresay, only when the ball is open," said Tristan. "Or perhaps by the woodcarver who made it."

"So we cannot open it?" Phaedra sounded crushed.

Kemble lifted his gaze to Tristan's. "I think we ought not try," he said quietly. "We'd be better served by taking this straight to de Vendenheim. The boys in the Home Office can have a look."

"Quite right," said Tristan, turning the thing over in his hand. "And the sooner the better. Shall I do the honors?"

Kemble tossed a well-manicured hand. "Oh, God, yes," he said. "I avoid Whitehall at all cost."

Phaedra's shoulders fell. As he tucked the ball into his coat pocket, Tristan regarded her quietly. He did not like the look of dejection in her eyes. He knew what she was thinking. Gently, he set his hand on her arm, and drew her a little away. Mr. Kemble and his clerk returned to one of their worktables, and discreetly occupied themselves by poking about in a pile of old silver.

Tristan caught her keen blue gaze with his

own. "Phae, remember that month we discussed?" A look of guilt sketched across her face. "You cannot go with me, my dear," he continued. "It was brilliant of you to remember this. But you cannot go. Your brother will hear of it."

Fleetingly, she hesitated. "And you promise to let me know what you discover?"

Tristan watched her warily. "Is that an invitation to call upon you?"

Phaedra snared her lip between her teeth. "I suppose it is," she finally answered. "In fact, my Mamma and sister and I would be pleased, Mr. Talbot, if you could take tea with us this afternoon."

"Thank you," said Tristan solemnly. "I shall try to be there."

In the Strand, traffic was picking up with carriages rattling up and down the street, and pedestrians pushing past him on the pavement. Tristan retrieved Callidora from the lad he'd paid to hold her. After running a judicious eye over the horse, Tristan fed her a lump of sugar from his pocket, then threw himself into the saddle and reined her round for the journey deeper into Westminster.

In the end, however, Tristan's journey was of little use. He arrived in Whitehall at half past ten, only to be told that his quarry was out, and that he should come back that afternoon. Frustrated, tired, and with his emotions oddly raw, Tristan turned round and went up to Cavendish Square to check on Hauxton whilst he cooled his heels. It was quite possibly the stupidest thing he could have done.

Pemberton let him in with the news that his father was perhaps a little stronger, and had taken a bit of his breakfast. Tristan went upstairs to find that the black crows had flapped off in search of tea, leaving a measure of quiet, if not the peace that went along with it.

On being presented with the puzzle ball, and the story behind it, his father offered his usual stiff compliments on Tristan's good work, turning the ball over and over in his hands. "And who did you say found this?" he asked after a time.

Tristan cleared his throat a little sharply. "Lady Phaedra Northampton."

"Yes, the one who witnessed the murder," said his father, laying the wooden ball aside. "What manner of female is she, this Lady Phaedra?"

"Why, she is a woman of great intelligence and refinement," said Tristan stiffly.

"But a girl of some years?" said his father. "Not, I collect, a chit from the schoolroom?"

"No, sir," Tristan agreed. "She is, I should guess, not above four-and-twenty."

"Is she a beauty?" asked his father.

Tristan started at the question. "I believe she is generally thought quite plain," he answered, "but only to those who have not looked closely."

His father lifted his graying eyebrows. "Yes, I see," he murmured. "And you have been paying her a marked amount of attention, I believe? I trust you will recall, Tristan, that she is an innocent, unwed girl of impeccable breeding, and not your usual fare. Indeed, I hope you are not engaging in a flirtation merely in order to further this investigation."

The accusation stung. "What, you want your murder solved *and* tied up with a pretty pink ribbon?" he asked a little snidely. "Since when do you give a damn, sir, if I flirt with a woman?"

Hauxton removed the silver spectacles from his nose, and sighed. "I had harbored some faint hope, I suppose, that it was more than just a flirtation," he said wearily. "But indeed, your life is none of my business, Tristan. You have made that abundantly clear these many years."

Tristan jerked from his chair, and strode to the windows which looked out over the square. *My father is ill,* he reminded himself. But Hauxton's barbed questions stung more than they should have, and his ugly assumptions hurt far more than usual. The fact that his warning was not wholly uncalled for only made matters worse. Phaedra was not the sort of woman a decent man dallied with, but that was precisely what he was doing, wasn't it?

"I am scarcely good enough, sir, for my own family," he finally said, his voice less steady than he would have wished. "I can assure you I'll never be good enough for the Northamptons."

A heavy silence settled over the room, broken only by the rhythmic *clop-clop-clop* of a lone rider in the square below, and by his father's labored breathing. And Tristan waited, counting off the strikes of the horse's shoes. Waited for the apology that never came. Waited for his father tell him to go to hell and get out for good. Waited for *anything* save this bloody damned impasse which seemed to loom eternally between them.

Of course, when his father finally spoke, it was the latter. "The circumstances of your birth were regrettable, Tristan," he acknowledged, "and I know the Talbot line has not always been as welcoming to you as they might have been. I am sorry for it."

Tristan whirled on him, incredulous. "Not as *welcoming?*" he echoed. "My own grandmother could scarce bear to look upon me. To this day, your cousins barely acknowledge my existence, whilst your brother sat 'til his dying day perched like a vulture over the doorstep, hoping to God I'd perish at the hand of a murderous Turk or some irate, unhinged cuckold."

"Yes," said his father dryly, "and you tried your best to oblige him."

Tristan shook his head. "And you call the circumstances of my birth regrettable," he continued. "My mother, sir, was not *regrettable*. Not to me."

Hauxton folded his hands one across the other atop his bedsheet. "You are my son, Tristan," he said quietly. "And I have tried to make the best of that. I wish only that you had done the same."

You are my son. He always spoke the words as if they were a curse to be borne.

Tristan left the windows and snatched up the wooden puzzle. "I should leave you now, sir," he said tightly. "You need your rest."

Hauxton took up his spectacles again. "By the way, Tristan, I have done as you asked," he calmly replied. "You are now, ostensibly, assistant to the Under-Secretary of State for

Foreign Affairs with a staff and full access to the very highest state secrets. It's been put about that you've been serving unofficially here since my illness."

"Yes, the word's out already," said Tristan mordantly. "I just came up from Whitehall where I had to poke people's eyeballs back into their heads right and left."

The sarcasm escaped Hauxton. "What, then, is your next step?"

"To get inside that house," said Tristan. "I am acquainted with a few of her patrons. Amongst them, I've subtly suggested I might possess, shall we say, certain unnatural itches that might require scratching."

"And what will this accomplish?" asked his father. "You may but pique Vostrikova's curiosity and get your throat slit."

Tristan shrugged. "Either that, or I'll get bound, gagged, and caned by a pair of buxom blondes in black corsets."

Hauxton's lip curled with distaste. "Your comments strike me as deliberately obscene."

"What strikes me, sir," Tristan retorted, "is that doing your dirty work is rather like making haggis. You might take a bite when it's finished, but by God, you don't want to know how the job got done."

"Tristan, you don't —"

"No, *you* don't understand," Tristan interjected. "You have sent me on a vile errand, sir. To do it I must consort with people whom even I consider offensive — and that's saying something. And I'll quite likely be required to engage in behaviors that are dangerous and disgusting. But you want to know what Vostrikova is up to, and there is only one way to find out. To get invited inside."

Hauxton waved his hand weakly. "Fine, just brief de Vendenheim," he managed. "Then just . . . finish the job, Tristan."

His hand already on the door, Tristan hesitated. Yes, by God, he meant to finish it, for he had the bit between his teeth now. Just as his father, devil take him, had known he would. Besides, he had to unleash his roiling, thwarted emotions on someone. It might as well be Madame Vostrikova. "I have given you my word, sir," he answered with a tight nod. "And I shall keep it. Good day to you."

He went back down the elegant spiral staircase, cursing himself and cursing his father. He wondered how the devil Hauxton had got wind of his flirtation with Lady Phaedra so quickly.

There was only one way, of course. Hauxton had set spies on his spy. Cursing one last time beneath his breath, Tristan restored the wooden ball to his pocket, and let the front door slam behind him.

Phaedra arrived home at midmorning, enervated yet on edge, only to find Zoë Armstrong on the doorstep, her hand poised to drop the knocker. Her maid stood dutifully on the middle step, something frothy draped across her arm. On seeing Phaedra's approach, she lightly touched her mistress's elbow.

"Phae!" Zoë turned round, and came back down the steps. "What luck!"

"Hello, Zoë." Phaedra tried to brighten her smile. "You're up early."

Zoë pulled a long face. "Papa insisted on having breakfast with me," she said on a sigh. "It was time to have The Talk."

Phae opened the door and they went in together. "What sort of talk?" she asked, handing their cloaks to Stabler.

Zoë took the dress from her maid's arm, and looked around conspiratorially. "Let's go up to your room," she said. "I wish you to see my new ball gown — and I want to hear all about Avoncliffe."

After inviting Zoë's maid to go belowstairs for a cup of tea, Phaedra went up the steps,

314

Zoë chatting amiably behind her. "Now The Talk, you must understand, is an annual ritual," she said. "We have it just before every season commences, with Papa looking all solemn and proper — as if *he* wasn't once the worst rakehell in Christendom — and telling me how I must mend my ways."

Phaedra closed her door and motioned Zoë to a chair by the windows. She was glad, she decided, for the distraction. Zoë's effervescence was the perfect antidote for her blue mood, and it would keep her from dwelling on the night of passion she'd just spent in Tristan Talbot's arms — those long, strong, beautifully sculpted arms which she'd been trying desperately not to think about since bounding out of bed this morning.

Indeed, it had taken all her strength not to beg Tristan to linger into the wee hours of dawn and make love to her yet again. She had wanted, shockingly, to forget about Millie and Gorsky and duty and obligation — and to think only of herself and this beautiful man who, at least last night, had seemingly understood her better than she understood herself. Only when Phaedra had grasped the turn her mind was taking this morning did the alarm bells go off in her head and send her all but bolting from the room.

She forced her attention to her guest. "So the talk is about . . . what, exactly?"

Zoë had flung the gown onto Phaedra's bed, and flopped into the chair with a huff. "Oh, the talk is all about decorum and discretion and delicacy," she answered with an airy gesture of her fingers. "It is about the importance of my behaving myself, making a good impression, and finding myself a suitable husband."

"Then I begin to see why it is necessary to repeat this talk." Phaedra managed to grin at her. "You are failing on two of those counts rather miserably, my dear."

Zoë rolled her eyes. "And you are supposed to be my friend," she said. "Hurry, Phae, and look at my dress. Then let's go out to gossip and shop."

"Shopping again?" asked Phaedra.

"Phoebe said you might choose patterns and fabrics for new gowns this morning," Zoë explained. "And I mean to go along, else you'll have that frightful rag wrapped round your dumplings again, and your bodices yanked up to here." Zoë chopped a hand dramatically across her throat.

"I beg your pardon?" Phaedra picked up the dress and cut a curious, sidelong glance at her. "My *dumplings?* Remind me again, Zoë, why we struck up this strange friendship."

Zoë grinned. "It is because I am the anti-Phaedra," she said. "You are drawn to me because I am exactly what you try not to be."

"Indeed?" Phaedra fluffed out the hem of Zoë's dress, amazed at the layers of ruffles. "So I am the opposite of you?"

Zoë laughed. "Yes, we are extremes, both of us," she said. "And deep in our hearts, perhaps, we hope we will rub off on one another. Deep in our hearts, perhaps, I should like to be a bit good like you, and you should like to be a bit bad like me."

But Zoë had no idea how bad Phaedra longed to be. There was a sensual, twisting hunger inside Phaedra that frightened her, a thing she could never wish on her younger friend. She thought of Tristan's neckcloth bound about her wrists and shivered.

"Zoë, you are perfectly silly," she said. Then swiftly, she changed the subject. "This gown is utterly gorgeous, by the way. Try it on."

Zoë leapt at once to her feet, and Phaedra began to undo her buttons. It really was an odd sort of friendship, she mused, but in some inexplicable way, Phaedra longed for

Zoë's company. Zoë was refreshing — and a little dangerous. And like Phaedra, she did not suffer fools. Though Zoë might pretend otherwise, she was smart as a whip.

They had been meeting at least once a day for tea, or to shop and gossip, and in the process, Zoë had made Phaedra feel almost girlish again. Between Phoebe and Zoë, she had somehow been persuaded to take up Stefan's offer of an opulent new wardrobe. And Phaedra was beginning to look forward to it. Indeed, with Zoë, Phaedra felt more herself — the self, perhaps, that she could have been had her life turned out a little differently.

At last the new gown was pulled over Zoë's sleek, dark hair, spilling to the floor in a cascade of ruby-colored silk. "Breathtaking," said Phaedra, doing up the back. "What is it for?"

"Lady Kirton's charity ball," said Zoë on an unladylike yawn. "It's the big season opener this year. Have you a card for it?"

"I daresay," she answered. "Mamma usually goes."

"Then my nefarious plan proceeds apace," said Zoë, turning round. "This year *you* shall go, too."

"Oh, I think not." Phaedra busied herself neatening the ruffles of Zoë's new gown.

"Lord Robert and Mr. Upjohn will be there," Zoë wheedled in her singsong voice. "Perhaps even Avoncliffe will turn up. Which reminds me, Phae — where the devil were you last night?"

Phaedra's hand stilled, and she looked up again. "I beg your pardon?"

Zoë tucked her head and grinned. "Last night," she said. "I came round about one and threw rocks at your window."

"Zoë!" Phaedra rose from the floor. "Why?"

Zoë lifted one narrow shoulder. "Well, I went to the musicale at Mrs. Hendrick's and it was just frightful," she complained. "So Aunt Winnie claimed a headache and we left. But I got home and I was bored and I knew, of course, that you'd be up reading, so when the rain let up, I slipped out with a fresh cheroot and came to get you."

"Zoë!" With a muted smile, Phaedra turned her and began to unfasten the buttons. "You will make me scandalous before the season's out."

Zoë's grin deepened. "What's scandalous, if you ask me, is that you weren't home," she answered, winking over her shoulder. "Especially when I know for a fact your mamma and your sister were at Mrs. Hendrick's."

Phae said nothing.

"So — ?" asked Zoë.

"So what?" Phaedra looked down at her work.

"*Who* were you with?" Zoë was still trying to catch Phaedra's eyes.

"How do you know I was with anyone?" she finally answered.

"If you'd been home, Phae, you'd have already complained that you didn't hear any rocks," said Zoë, wiggling the red dress down her hips. "But you *haven't* said that."

"I didn't hear any rocks."

"Too late!" Zoë's grin deepened. "Besides, I cracked a pane of glass, I think. It made a frightful noise — and no one could have slept through that."

Phaedra felt her face flame. "Shush, Zoë," she begged. "I *cannot* be caught."

"As wicked as that, was it?" Zoë feigned a look of contrition, and tossed the dress aside. "You'd better tell me, Phae. If anyone thought they saw you — well, I can at least be your alibi."

"Oh, thank you, Zoë!" Phae collapsed onto the bed beside the heap of red silk. She really wished she could talk to someone, but not even to Zoë could she tell the whole truth.

"I went for a walk," she finally said.

"To . . . To meet Mr. Talbot — Avoncliffe — if you must know."

"Oh, Lud!" Zoë slapped her hands to her cheeks. "I knew it. I just *knew* it. He's smitten, Phae. Everyone noticed how he singled you out the other night. But, oh, Phae, have a care with that one!"

"It isn't what you think," Phaedra lied. "I just needed his help with something."

"Yes, a lot of women do, I've heard." Zoë giggled. "And he's known to be quite obliging."

"Zoë!" Phaedra's shoulders fell. "Really!"

"Yes, *really!*" Zoë's tone was low and vaguely appreciative. "I begin to wonder, Phae, if you are the anti-Zoë after all. Did he kiss you again?"

Phaedra's blush deepened, and she turned to the window. Perhaps she shouldn't have told Zoë of that first kiss. But she had — in one of those whispered, girlish confessionals which Phaedra had always thought herself above — because, for the first time in her life, she *really* needed a friend.

"He *did* kiss you," said Zoë, following her across the room. "But was it a kiss, Phae. Or was it a *kiss?*"

Phaedra lifted her gaze to the glass, and looked at Zoë's watery reflection. "It was a *kiss,*" she whispered. "Oh, Zoë. It was . . .

very much a kiss."

"Oh, Lord." Zoë's eyes were like saucers. "Avoncliffe is either the greatest cad that ever breathed — or for once, he's deadly serious. Either, I daresay, is possible."

"What on earth do you mean?"

Zoë shrugged. "Well, I've never thought Avoncliffe a bad sort," she mused. "He's . . . well, he's not a *rake,* if you know what I mean. He's a scoundrel. And there's a difference."

Phaedra closed her eyes, willing the vision Zoë's words conjured to go away. A rake, a scoundrel — what was the difference to her if she fell for him?

"But he's a good sort of scoundrel, I collect." Zoë was clearly pondering aloud. "I've never heard of him trifling with virgins. Have you quite a large dowry, Phae?"

"Yes, as it happens," said Phaedra. "Not that I mean to use it."

Zoë ignored her. "No, that's not it," she mused, shaking her head. "Avoncliffe needn't marry you for your money."

"*Marry* me?" Phaedra turned from the window.

Zoë looked at her as if she were a silly child. "Phae, if you keep sneaking out to kiss Avoncliffe, eventually, you *will* get caught," she warned. "Even I know that.

And then Lord Nash will demand he do the right thing. And Avoncliffe might just do it, especially if it spares you a scandal."

Phaedra leaned back against the window frame and crossed her arms over her chest. "Even if you're right about him, Zoë, *I* won't do it," she said, regarding her friend solemnly. "You forget that."

"Oh, you'll marry him," said Zoë knowingly. "Depend upon it. For they will assail you with all sorts of talk about family honor and scandal and how you will ruin Phoebe's marriage prospects, and blah, blah, blah, and you will surrender, Phae. You will cave in like a house of cards."

"But you don't cave in."

"That's because I'm selfish," said Zoë, sitting back down on the bed. "You aren't like that, Phae. You'll do it."

Phaedra stood silent for a moment, half afraid that Zoë was right.

Zoë tilted her head to one side. "Surely, Phae, you've not fallen in love?"

Phaedra just clasped her hands. "Oh, Zoë, surely I have not? This is just . . . infatuation. Isn't it?"

Zoë shrugged, and brightened her smile. "Well, it mightn't be so bad," she said cheerfully. "As a husband, Avoncliffe's hand wouldn't be a heavy one, and at least you'd have him in your bed. A definite advantage, that. Besides, he needs an heir. He'll have to marry eventually."

That brought Phaedra's foolish fantasies up short. "I think *you* should have to get married," she said mordantly. "I think you should marry Lord Robert Rowland, instead of just sneaking off into the dark with him."

"Marry Robin?" Zoë laughed uproariously. "Now *that* will never happen. Besides, the woman who takes him on will have naught but hell to pay. Surely, Phae, even I do not deserve *that?"*

But Phaedra couldn't hold her gaze. Zoë's words were a stark reminder of the risks she was running, and of the fact that she was scarcely a suitable bride for anyone. As the firstborn son of an earl, Tristan would inherit uncountable wealth, and with it the hopes and dreams and weighty expectations of three hundred years of history. And he would be required to bear a son in turn. He would be required to take a wife who was fertile. Fondness or affection or even love would likely not enter into it.

No, even if a man were willing to take a tarnished bride, he could never take a woman who might never give him children. Life simply did not work that way.

"I'm sorry, Zoë. I oughtn't tease you

about Lord Robert." Phaedra had gone to her desk, and absently picked up her letter-knife. "And I'm afraid I cannot go shopping today. I must stay in."

"Oh, I don't care a fig about teasing," she answered. "But why can we not go order your new gowns?"

Phaedra turned from the desk with a twisted smile. "We're stripping the rugs and draperies upstairs for spring cleaning," she said quietly. "And then — well, Mr. Talbot is coming to tea with Mamma and me, if you must know."

Zoë's eyes widened as her grin returned. "Oh, Lud! Sounds like a case of honorable intentions to me. Truly, Phae! After last night, why — what if he *offers* for you?"

Phaedra tried to shake her head. But the hot press of tears had risen behind her eyes, and she felt suddenly as if a welled-up dam were about to burst. Her lips trembled, and she felt her face begin to crumple.

Zoë sprang off the bed at once, her eyes going soft. "Oh, Phae!" she said, circling an arm around her shoulders. "My dear, what is wrong? What did he do? That cad! I shall kill him with my bare hands!"

Phaedra bit her lip, and shook her head. "It's not Tristan. Not . . . like that, I mean."

Zoë drew her back to the bed, and urged

her to sit. "Then what, Phae?" she whispered. "Did something happen last night?"

"No," Phaedra whispered. "Not last night."

"Oh, my poor Phae!" Zoë extracted a lace handkerchief and began to blot Phaedra's cheeks. "Oh, please, my dear, do not cry. Whatever is wrong, why, we shall fix it."

To see Zoë suddenly so solemn and so affected was the last straw. And as Phaedra's tears spilt out, the words went with them. "Oh, Zoë, you are a dear, but no one can fix this! And it happened a long time ago. I had an illness, you see, and afterward, the doctors told me . . . they told me I was likely barren. That I likely couldn't have children. Now do you understand?"

"Oh, Phaedra! Truly?" Sorrow welled in Zoë's eyes.

Phaedra let her head fall against Zoë's shoulder. "I don't think about it often," she whispered, blinking hard. "I *don't.* Really. But then I met *him.* And I don't want to marry him, Zoë. Truly, I don't. And he doesn't want me. But it's just that . . . it's just that . . ."

"It's just that if you *did* want him," Zoë whispered, drawing a warm, heavy hand down Phaedra's hair, "you wouldn't have him, would you? You would do the honorable thing."

"I would do *nothing,*" Phaedra said, snuffling against Zoë's shoulder. "That's what I always do. I keep to myself, Zoë. Because it is too hard to explain something so personal, then watch disappointment dawn in a man's eyes. To see the pity there, and then watch him draw away. I could not bear it."

"No, nor could I." Zoë said nothing further for a long moment. Instead, she simply stroked Phaedra's hair. "I am so sorry, Phae," she finally murmured. "So very sorry. Someday, perhaps, you will find a man to whom such things won't matter? But regardless, you may always depend, of course, upon my confidence — and my friendship."

"Thank you, Zoë."

And there was really nothing more to be said. They sat there together on the bed, clutching one another in a tight embrace, until the slanting sun left the window to rise high above the roofs of Mayfair. Then Phaedra kissed her new friend's cheek, and walked her to the door, all the while thinking of the afternoon that was to come, of the tea which she had to get through, and of the heart she must somehow preserve, whole and intact.

■ ■ ■ ■

When Tristan returned to Whitehall that afternoon, he was escorted up by a harried, black-coated civil servant who looked very much like one of Hauxton's crows, to find Lord de Vendenheim in a small office at the top of the stairs. To his shock, a great black dog the size of small pony lay flopped out before the desk, his massive jowls drooling faintly on the carpet. Upon seeing Tristan, the hellhound licked his chops, then — apparently judging him too sinewy for a decent meal — drifted off to sleep again.

"Good Lord," Tristan muttered, stepping lightly past him.

It took less than ten minutes to brief de Vendenheim on the progress of his investigation. Then Tristan extracted Phaedra's prize. Unfortunately, de Vendenheim knew less about the sphere than either Tristan or Kemble. The vicomte stood by the window which overlooked the river and street below, turning the ball over in his fingers. "And it fell from Gorsky's hand, you say?"

"Yes, Lady Phaedra saw it," Tristan answered. "She recalled it suddenly late last night."

De Vendenheim's head jerked up, his eyes

sharp. "Late last night?"

Tristan hesitated. "Or so she said."

De Vendenheim returned his focus to the wooden sphere. "We have experts, of course, in the Cyrillic languages," he said musingly. "But I don't know how long it will take to find one."

"Blast," Tristan muttered. "Time is of the essence."

"And you think I don't know that?" de Vendenheim snapped. "But what I don't know is whether or not this blasted chunk of wood says anything. Perhaps the letters are random? Or perhaps it's Cicero's lost *Consolatio?* How the hell would I know?"

Tristan ignored his outburst. The vicomte's frustration was understandable. "All we really need just now," he mused, "is someone who reads Russian fluently."

De Vendenheim lifted his gaze to Tristan's, and his eyes lit with understanding. "Exactly!" he said. He retrieved his coat from behind the door. "Lucifer!" he said to the dog. *"Vieni qui!"*

"Where do we go?" asked Tristan.

The vicomte was already throwing on a sweeping black cloak. "To Mayfair," he said, shoving the ball into his coat pocket. "To one of the few Englishmen who can read Russian like his mother tongue — and perhaps the only one whom I trust."

Understanding washed over Tristan like a cold bucket of water. But there was nothing for it now. De Vendenheim was half out the door, the massive dog on his heels. Tristan hastened after them. He had wondered, vaguely, what Phaedra's powerful elder brother was like. Apparently, he was going to find out.

"By the way, I hear you've gone to work in the Foreign Office." De Vendenheim flicked him an appraising glance as they went down the steps. "Is it true?"

"Utter balderdash," said Tristan quietly. "Still, it may bring me to Vostrikova's notice."

De Vendenheim glanced at him again. "Then be careful, Talbot."

Lord and Lady Nash lived in a town house so vast it seemed at first impression to span half of Park Lane. *"Sta' fermo!"* said the vicomte, looking down at the dog. The great beast flopped down upon the top step, settling his head onto his paws with a sigh that shuddered his jowls.

Tristan and de Vendenheim were whisked into an elegant chamber overlooking Hyde Park which the footman called "the gold parlor," but which would have constituted two withdrawing rooms in most London homes. The room positively dripped with gilt, and its walls were hung with champagne-colored silk; a chamber which spoke of elegance and of calm. Yet they had scarcely been seated when a clamor arose in the hall beyond the parlor's gilt doors. The happy shrieks of a child, a barking dog, and above it, a woman's voice cautioning quiet. Eventually, the racket settled down, and the woman's voice could be heard in the parlor.

"Is he indeed?" she said, her heels clicking across the marble.

A lovely, dark-haired lady appeared at the door, a child propped on her hip, and a small, barking spaniel at her heels, nominally leashed by a red ribbon. It was Lady Nash, Tristan decided, judging by her attire. A footman brought up the rear, one suspicious eye upon the dog, a creature so small he would scarce have made a snack for the beast out front.

"Max!" The lady hastened in, somehow managing to embrace de Vendenheim despite her encumbrances. The vicomte, Tristan judged, was a good deal closer to Lord and Lady Nash than he had disclosed.

De Vendenheim presented Tristan as Mr. Talbot, and some inscrutable emotion flared in the lady's eyes. "But you are also Lord Avoncliffe, are you not?" said the marchioness, her keen gaze sweeping over him. "At long last, I have the pleasure."

"I'm generally known as Talbot," said Tristan, wondering at her words. Still, he made her his most elegant bow — and his best bows were very elegant indeed. Unfortunately, the tiny spaniel — a feathery black-and-white concoction — chose that moment to launch himself at Tristan, somehow ending in his arms, his tongue making quick work of Tristan's face.

More gleeful shrieking ensued as Lady Nash attempted to claw the dog away. De Vendenheim bent to catch the dog's ribbon, which Lady Nash dropped. Somehow, amidst a vast deal of apologizing and brushing at Tristan's coat, she managed to pass the squealing child to de Vendenheim, capture the dog, and thrust him at the footman.

"This is Chin-Chin," she said, roughly tousling the dog's ears. "He is my brother's dog, a wicked creature whom my son begs to have visit. I should have let Lucifer eat him."

His nose aloft, the unfortunate Vernon toted the barking creature away. The child followed them with his bereft gaze, then stuck a consoling thumb into his mouth.

"Do sit, gentlemen, please." The lady took

the child from the vicomte, and relaxed onto a brocade divan.

"Young Luke is growing apace," remarked de Vendenheim as she bounced the babe on her knee. "You have been out enjoying the weather today, I collect?"

Lady Nash laughed. "No, indeed, we've just come from Wapping." She turned to Tristan and smiled. "My family has some shipping interests, Mr. Talbot. Luke has his own nursery above our counting house, and a lovely nurse looks after him whilst I work."

Whilst she worked? How very odd. And if he did not miss his guess, the nursery was about to become a little more crowded. Lady Nash looked like a pale, vibrant madonna, with lively eyes and luxurious dark hair. Precisely the sort of woman he would ordinarily have made note of, just in case disillusionment should strike her marriage, or a case of ennui should overcome her better judgment.

Today, however, he watched her clinically, wondering at the sort of man her husband was. Wondering if she was a good sister to Phaedra, and what manner of family they constituted. A close-knit one, perhaps. The lady still dandled the child on her knee, and there was neither a nurse nor a governess in sight.

"Well, I shall leave you," she finally said after they had passed a few moments in pleasant conversation. "Nash should be down shortly. Mr. Talbot, it was a pleasure. I'm frightfully sorry about Chin-Chin."

Tristan came swiftly to his feet as she rose. "The pleasure was mine, my lady," he said. "I rather like dogs."

"Well, not at the expense of a good coat, perhaps." She smiled musingly, shot him one last lingering look, then hitched the child onto her hip and left.

From his chair, Tristan could see the sweeping staircase, and the tall, dark man who was swiftly descending it. He met Lady Nash at the foot, embraced her openly, then kissed the boy on the cheek.

Lord Nash, most assuredly. The gentleman came into the room, his presence instantly commanding. He stood perhaps an inch taller than Tristan, and just a little less lean. His dark eyes swept over the room, and Tristan had the oddest impression he took in everything at once.

The man shook de Vendenheim's hand, and turned his piercing gaze on Tristan. His clothing was stark, dark, and extremely expensive. His eyes were set at a slightly exotic angle, his hair swept off a high, aristocratic forehead in a style which, like

Tristan's, was too long and too dark to be strictly fashionable.

"Talbot." Lord Nash bowed stiffly at the neck. "Pleased to meet you at last."

There it was again, thought Tristan. That faintly expectant remark which suggested . . . *something.* Tristan's hackles went up like a wolf scenting an enemy, and he felt his posture stiffen. But Nash turned his attention to the vicomte at once, and listened attentively to his story about the wooden sphere. Tristan, it seemed, was forgotten.

"Why have I heard nothing from Phaedra of this sphere business?" he demanded when de Vendenheim was done.

"I believe she recalled it just last night," said the vicomte.

"Last night?" His head swiveled like a hawk's, his gaze again nailing Tristan. "Is that correct, Talbot?"

Good God. He lifted his hands. "That's what she said, sir."

"She summoned you to meet her at Kemble's?"

Ah, thought Tristan, there was the slippery slope Lord Nash was inviting him to slide down. "Someone sent word round, I collect," he said breezily. "I was abed myself."

Nash held his gaze for a long moment,

then looked down to study the sphere, turning it lightly in his hand. "These are nothing but letters arranged more or less in alphabetical order," he said after a time. "There is no secret message here."

"Have you seen such things before?" asked the vicomte.

Nash shook his head. "This inlay, however, is some of the finest I've seen," he said pensively. "It might be Hungarian, or even Italian."

"Or Polish?" Tristan suggested.

Nash looked at him strangely. "Possibly."

De Vendenheim made a tight, frustrated fist. "I wish to the devil we knew how to open it."

"I don't think opening it is the issue," said Tristan.

The two men looked at him blankly. Tristan shrugged. "There's more than one way to skin a cat," he suggested. "You gentlemen must merely decide whether you wish to have the sphere, or whether you wish to have what is inside."

De Vendenheim and Nash exchanged glances. "By God, I want what's inside," said the vicomte. "I don't give a twopenny damn for the beauty of the thing."

Tristan took the sphere from Nash, slid one of the wooden bars all the way through, strode to a spot beyond the opulent Oriental carpet, and set it on the marble floor. He flicked a quick glance at the two men. "You are quite sure?"

De Vendenheim looked at him dubiously. "Quite certain," he answered. "But short of a hacksaw —"

His words were cut off by the splintering of wood.

Tristan set his boot heel back down, and stood looking over what was left of the sphere. "Simple physics," he said.

"Look." De Vendenheim went down on one knee by the shards of wood. "A scrap of paper." Carefully, he pulled apart the mangled bars of wood and plucked the tiny fold of foolscap from it.

Nash still sat in his chair, his fingers thoughtfully steepled as the vicomte unfolded the scrap. "May I translate for you, old fellow?" he said when de Vendenheim did not speak.

"No," said the vicomte hollowly. "No, that won't be necessary."

Tristan was watching the vicomte. "You look a tad pale, de Vendenheim," he said. "Might I have a look?"

The vicomte cast him a dark glance, then with obvious reluctance, passed the paper over. It was nothing but a list of names. The first was unknown to Tristan, but the next were vaguely familiar. *The black crows.* Three of them, anyway. He glanced at de Vendenheim. "You recognize these men?"

The vicomte hesitated. "All work within the Government, yes. This ball was how the Russians let her know whom they wished her to turn."

"Or Vostrikova's way of telling *them* whom she had already turned." Tristan extended the paper to Lord Nash, who held up both hands, palms out.

"I am well out of this, gentlemen," he said quietly. "I do not work for His Majesty in any capacity save for my service in the Lords."

"As you wish," said de Vendenheim, taking the paper.

Nash stood and rang for a servant. "Vernon," he said when the footman appeared, "kindly sweep up that mess, and wrap the pieces for Lord de Vendenheim."

De Vendenheim tucked the paper away. "Well, I must be off. Be so good as to have that broken wood sent down to my office, won't you, Nash?"

"Certainly, old chap," he said, his voice oddly quiet. Nash turned his glittering gaze upon Tristan. "Talbot, if you would be so kind as to stay? I should like a word."

De Vendenheim cast him an almost sympathetic look, and hastened from the room. Nash's suppressed emotion was now all but palpable. It was wrath, Tristan thought. The knowledge, strangely, did not frighten him. He had taken on bigger fellows than Nash and come out on top. If Nash wished to throw down a gauntlet, Tristan would simply have to pick it up.

He sat, and lifted one eyebrow inquiringly.

Lord Nash regarded the man who sat opposite him with a measure of icy disdain. Talbot was a handsome devil, he'd give him that. Personable and more clever, too, than he'd been given to understand. But there were many handsome, clever, personable men in the world, and bloody few of them — to borrow de Vendenheim's apt phrase — worth a twopenny damn. It remained to be seen, so far as Nash was concerned, to which side of the bar Talbot fell.

"You are aware, Talbot, that Lady Phaedra Northampton is my sister?" he said quietly. "That I am, in fact, her guardian?"

"I am aware, yes," he answered.

"Then kindly explain to me, sir, whose idea it was for you to meet surreptitiously with her? It was inappropriate, and you know it."

Despite his olive skin, Talbot seemed to

lose a little of his color. "Surreptitious, sir?" he repeated. "I wasn't aware you'd learnt of it."

"No," said Nash dryly. "I daresay you were not. But servants talk, Talbot. And in this case, I also pay their salaries. A fact you would be prudent to remember."

"You are speaking of Brook Street, then?" Talbot's shoulders appeared to sag with relief. "I meant Lady Phaedra no harm, I assure you."

Nash jerked to his feet. "Yes, Brook Street," he said, pacing across the room. "What else would I mean?"

Talbot smiled faintly. "I wasn't certain," he answered, standing at once with Nash. "I also had the pleasure of seeing your sister at a card party."

"Indeed," said Nash. "A party at which you were seen whispering in her ear, and waltzing with her — and far too closely — or so the Dowager Lady Nash has informed me."

Talbot's gaze swept almost disdainfully down him. "Lady Phaedra is not permitted to waltz, sir?" he asked brusquely. "What a pity. She dances beautifully — when she can be persuaded. And I think, sir, if you'll forgive my saying so, that she has spent entirely too much time *not* dancing."

Lord Nash regarded his quarry for a long, silent moment. "Have you any notion, Talbot, how long it had been since my sister put on a beautiful gown and spent an evening in frivolous pursuits?"

"Too long, I'd say," Talbot snapped.

"Precisely," said Lord Nash. "And now that she has done so, it leads me to wonder why."

"I have no idea, sir."

Nash felt the muscle in his jaw twitch. "No, I thought perhaps you did not." He carefully considered his next words. "You are known to me, Talbot, only by your reputation — and of late, there has been nothing in it to recommend you."

"How kind of you to concern yourself," he said coolly.

The marquess ignored the sarcasm. "But," he continued, "I am aware, too, of your past exploits on the battlefield. Whatever you lack in brains, you apparently make up for in ballocks. That, at least, says something about you."

"Could you kindly come to your point, sir?" Talbot's voice was cold. "We have a murderer on the loose, you'll recall. And witless, well-hung ox that I am, I still harbor some faint hope of helping catch the bastard."

Talbot had a point. Moreover, it had been but a year or two since Nash had had this same discussion with his wife's brother — but then it had been he on the receiving end of the interrogation, and not without reason. He sensed, however, that Talbot, for all his blithe manner, was not a man to be pushed. There was a dark shimmer of dangerous waters beneath all that nonchalance, and though Talbot had spent the last several years as a skirt-chasing wastrel, his near-suicidal exploits in the revolution were the stuff of legend, as was his sudden departure from Greece after the bloody Siege of Tripolitsa — an atrocity in which the Greeks had massacred every Jew and Turk within the city walls, slowly torturing even the women and children.

Talbot, apparently, was amongst the many who had quickly turned their backs on the once-romanticized Greek cause — and Nash thought more of him for having done so. And he had to admit that, from the carefully veiled look he thought he'd glimpsed in Talbot's eyes, combined with Edwina's twittering, he had begun to think it possible that there might be *something* between this man and Phaedra. And despite his grave misgivings, he found himself loath to crush it out.

He was spared these few moments to temper his words since Vernon had returned with the broom and a small box. *Ashes to ashes, and dust to dust,* thought Nash as the footman swept. Nothing — not even solid wood or stone-cold hearts — lasted forever.

He turned his attention back to Talbot as soon as Vernon left the room. "Our discussion is finished, sir," he said quietly. "Go and find de Vendenheim, then catch your killer. Just don't —" His voice caught embarrassingly, and Nash was compelled to look away.

"Just don't what?" asked Talbot softly.

Nash swallowed hard, cleared his throat, and returned his gaze to his unexpected guest. "For God's sake, do not hurt my sister, Talbot," he answered. "She has been hurt so very much already. If you wish only to trifle with a pretty female, I beg you, go and find another. Phaedra does not deserve it."

Talbot regarded him steadily. "I think, sir, that your sister is a very strong woman," he finally said. "Stronger, I believe, than you give her credit."

But Nash just shook his head. "Now that, Talbot, simply proves how little you know her," he said. "Behind her carefully crafted façade is in truth a woman as fragile as spun glass."

Talbot was looking into the depths of the room as if mulling over Nash's words. "I must confess, Nash, that I do not see her that way."

"Few people do," said Nash. "And that is why, sir, I will be very, very slow to give her over into another man's hands. Do you understand me?"

Talbot looked deeply perplexed, and deeply unhappy. He lowered his eyes, and gave a faint bow of his head. "I believe, my lord, that we have reached an understanding."

"I hope, for your sake, sir, that we have," said Nash stiffly. "For if my sister should ever be hurt at your hand, you will not live to tell the tale."

Talbot looked unafraid. "I shan't do anything to hurt Phaedra, sir." His voice was strong and confident. "In that regard, your threat is unnecessary." And with that, Talbot bowed again, and quit the room, his gait long and utterly relaxed.

Her arms crossed beneath her face, the girl lay naked, prostrate upon the narrow cot, a shaft of afternoon sunlight cutting across the welts which striped her buttocks. The old woman who leaned over her made a *tut-tutting* sound, and dabbed again at the worst of the lashes, a swollen ridge of flesh already purpling beneath the skin.

At the sting of the cloth, the girl started, hissing through her teeth.

"Lie still, Flora, or she'll be in 'ere," the old woman whispered. "On yer like a hawk, that one, and a'pecking at yer eyes."

"It in't my fault!" the girl cried into her arms. "A right bastard, 'e is — and stark starin' mad, Hettie. I . . . I couldn't bear it."

Too late, the door burst open. A tall, lean form towered on the threshold, her ice-blond hair contrasting sharply with the black bombazine of her gown. The girl sobbed, and turned her face to the wall.

"What's happened here?" Madame Vostrikova stabbed her finger at the girl, her ruby ring catching the shaft of sunlight, sending shards of blood-red fire through the room. "Why is Flora not upstairs earning her keep?"

The old woman set down her basin and cloth, hesitating.

"By God, I asked a question." Madame swished into the narrow room, her hand raised to strike.

The old woman flinched. "Lord Horrowood sent 'er back down, ma'am. Flora took ill on 'im.'"

"Took *ill?*" Madame's voice was shrill. "If that little bitch has disgraced me, she had best pray it's fatal."

"She fainted, that's all," said the old woman. "Horrowood was taking 'is pleasure, and, 'e got too rough, Madame. Plain as that. These wounds are like ter turn putrid. She'll not sit for a week and then some."

Madame strolled slowly to the table, then, with a swift snatch of her hand, seized the girl up by her mass of rich, red-gold curls. The girl's eyes shied round like a frightened colt as Madame bent over her.

"Now you listen, you little cunt, and you listen well," she whispered. "I need Lord Horrowood, and you are getting paid to deliver him, do you hear me?"

"In't like I din't try, mum," said the girl on a gasping shudder. "I did try, I swear ter Gawd. But the whip — 'e wanted the big one, mum — and I . . . I couldn't take it."

"Why you craven little guttersnipe." Madame shoved her face-first into the table. "I dragged you out of Whitechapel, dressed you, fed you, and put a roof over your head — and this is the thanks I get?"

"I'm sorry," cried the girl, her voice muffled by the cot. "I'll go. Just . . . let me go back, awright? I'd rather be a threepenny uprighter back in Brick Lane."

Madame laughed richly. "Oh, that's as much a fantasy as Horrowood's," she answered. "Now get up, get dressed, and get back to work or the lashes he striped across your bottom will pale in comparison to the next you'll wear — for they'll be laid at *my* hands."

"Ye—" The girl's voice hitched on a sob. "Yes, Madame."

The melancholy *tick-tock, tick-tock* of the longcase clock accentuated the stillness of the Dowager Lady Nash's drawing room, and cast a sense of impending doom across an otherwise tranquil scene. To quell her impatience, Phaedra sat up perfectly straight in her chair and began to rearrange the pleats of her skirt.

"Just think of it!" The dowager twitched a little nervously at the lace of her fichu. "A gentleman paying a call upon Phaedra!"

Phoebe leaned forward and plucked another lemon biscuit from the tray which had been brought in early at her wheedling. "Well, I don't know if one can call Avoncliffe a gentleman," she said, studying it. "But he's certainly handsome enough."

Phaedra snatched the tidbit from her

347

sister's hand. "Must you eat all the best biscuits, Phee, before he even gets here?" she complained. "And Lord Avoncliffe is every inch a gentleman. His appearance, however, is of no consequence to me."

Phoebe eyed her warily. "Well, it certainly would be to me."

"He is unaccountably *dark*," said the dowager a little uneasily, "and I hear he keeps very low company. And Mrs. Hendrick claims that Lady Hauxton was part Gypsy. But still . . ."

But still, Phaedra mentally filled in the blanks, *his father is rich, and my daughter is desperate.*

She did not say the words aloud. Instead, she smiled dotingly. "His breeding is exceptional, Mamma, but it needn't concern you," she answered. "He is merely grateful for my help to his father and wishes to call and thank me. I am sure the thought of courting never crossed his mind."

Lady Nash looked unconvinced. "I thought you said you meant to invite him to walk in the garden?"

Phaedra hesitated. She did indeed need a moment alone with Tristan in order to discover what he'd learned from de Vendenheim, and to reassure him that last night had not meant . . . well, anything either of them needed to worry about.

From the very first she had assumed that last night was something of an anomaly, a thing of beauty to be seized fleetingly, like a firefly, and then released into the night. Tristan, however, had surprised her. His parting words had suggested that perhaps he wished to see her again. Indeed, he had acted a little wounded, but perhaps that had been nothing but his male pride stinging a little at her hesitance. Doubtless he was accustomed to females flinging themselves at his feet.

But what either of them wanted or expected scarcely mattered now. Zoë's wild ramblings had brought home to Phaedra the very real risk of continuing to see him again alone.

For Priss's sake — and for Millie's — Phaedra would insist he keep her apprised of his success in investigating Gorsky's death. They had made a bargain. For one month, she would stay out of his way — God knew she'd accomplished nothing on her own — but she must insist that Tristan call upon her from time to time. And if her mother and Phoebe wished to read something more into it, it was a price she would have to pay. To ensure Priss's happiness, it would be worth enduring Phoebe's teasing and her mother's expectations.

Tick-tock, tick-tock.

The clock, Phaedra decided, was getting louder.

"I vow, Mamma, how much longer must we wait?" Phoebe's sharp voice cut into the silence. "Can we not at least have the teapot brought in?"

Lady Nash flicked a glance at the clock. "Oh, not yet, my sweet, for —"

Her words were cut off by the butler's entry. He came forward bearing a silver salver, a calling card placed squarely in the center of it. It was the third which had arrived this afternoon, but to her disconcertion, Phaedra's heart leapt with hope again.

The butler bowed to the dowager. "The Duchess of Reyferry, madam," he intoned, "accompanied by her niece, Lady Anne Jenkins-Smythe."

Phoebe's eyes widened. "Oh, Lud! And I wore my second-best muslin!"

Lady Nash's hand quivered over the card, then abruptly she snatched it back. "No, Winston," she said hastily. "We are not in."

"*Not in* to the Duchess of Reyferry?" Phoebe seized her mother's chair arm. "Mamma, are you quite mad?"

Lady Nash pursed her lips and shook her head. "I'm sorry, Phoebe," she said. "As I said, I wish us to give Lord Avoncliffe our full attention."

"But I long for a card to her ball!" Phoebe's lip came out. "Really, Mamma, the others were nobodies, but you must see *her.* This is my big chance."

Lady Nash leaned forward, and tucked a wayward curl behind Phoebe's ear. "We must think of Phaedra, my pet," she said consolingly. "She hasn't the opportunities you have."

Winston bowed again, and left.

Phoebe fell back into her chair.

Tick-tock, tick-tock.

The clock struck the hour — an unfashionably late hour for callers. Phoebe scowled across the tea table, then leaned forward to snatch the lemon biscuit again.

"He isn't coming, I tell you," she said, looking venomously at her sister. Then she bit into the morsel with her sharp, white teeth.

The clock went on in the cavernous silence.

And she was right. No one came.

Tristan lingered in Grosvenor Square, one elbow propped on the iron railing as Callidora knabbled and tugged at what little grass her velvety lips could reach through the bars. The afternoon was all but gone, he thought, his gaze focused down Brook Street.

He was cold, he realized, letting his boot slip from the fence's stone footings. His fingers which clutched Callidora's reins were growing stiff from immobility. Or perhaps from being clenched in wracking uncertainty.

Good God. He was not a man who suffered uncertainty. There was nothing to mourn, or to rail against, for Nash had taken nothing from him that had ever been his to claim. So why, then, did he still stand here, gazing like a mooncalf at her front door and wondering about what could have been? What was this dark, welling emptiness? He felt, strangely, as he had felt watching his mother's trunks go down the steps.

Had Phaedra waited for him, he wondered? Had she even noticed he had not come?

He had watched through the early afternoon as society's *crème de la crème* paid their incongruously named morning calls. Three fine carriages had drawn up at the Northamptons' door, their well-dressed occupants descending and going up the steps only to be turned away and sent back down again.

Tristan snorted and drew a hand down Callidora's sleek, black neck. If the occupants of those crested carriages were being turned away, he had even less hope, perhaps, than he had realized. But hope — or the lack of it — had little to do with why he still stood in the middle of Mayfair with the wind whipping through his hair and Callidora wanting her dinner. He was accustomed to being less than welcome. No, he lingered here, his hands going numb and his heart heavy, because he knew, deep down, that Nash was right. And his father was right. Even if they would throw open that door to him, he had no business pursuing Phaedra.

Oh, he didn't fear Nash. He feared hurting a girl who didn't deserve it. Even if his heart were pure, his life was unsettled. His mission quite possibly dangerous. Did he really want to involve her in this mess? Did he really want *her?* He was beginning to fear he did. Still, some would say he was a rogue and a rotter to his very core, and incapable of being what Phaedra deserved or needed.

And it might not matter. Phaedra had made it plain: she did not wish to be bound by marriage. Initially, he'd thought that suited him. But now he was wondering *why* she resisted, and the fact that he was so curious was a dangerous sign.

A woman as fragile as spun glass.

Nash was right on that point, too, Tristan thought, watching as a tow-haired housemaid came out to sweep the Northamptons' doorstep. Tristan, however, hadn't recognized that frailty for what it was until someone thrust it in his face. Perhaps, as Phaedra had once accused, his gaze had not traveled much beyond her breasts.

That was a shame. Especially when there was no denying the fact that an unmistakable melancholy lingered in her eyes if one but looked for it. No woman made the cold, hard choices Phaedra had made — not without a damned good reason. She had been terribly hurt, her brother said. And it took no great leap of logic to figure out what had happened. Someone had promised her undying love, gained her family's trust, then taken what he wanted from her and left, possibly breaking her heart in the process.

Tristan wondered if the bastard was still alive to tell the tale. Not likely, he judged, based on what he'd seen of the Marquess of Nash. That was as well, he supposed. Tristan would have been tempted to do the job himself. Not out of possessiveness, or even misplaced male pride — no, he had no right to those things. He would have done it because of what it stripped from her. Opportunity. Love. Hope — hope for something a little better than a clandestine tumble with London's most arrant womanizer.

But so far as fleeting physical affection went, Tristan might be the best she could do now, and the realization scarcely warmed the cockles of his heart. In fact, for the first time in his life, he was almost ashamed of what he had let himself become. A lady's last resort. A whore, even.

He watched emotionlessly as a lamp flared to life behind a second floor window. A bedchamber, most likely. Perhaps even Phaedra's. Fleetingly he closed his eyes and watched her undress again. In his mind, he could see her peeling away the muslin gown she doubtless wore, and then the shift which lay beneath it. Unwinding that coil of magnificent chestnut hair which hung nearly to her waist. Lord, if ever a woman had been made for a man's embrace — for a man's worship — it was she.

Just then, the clock at St. George's struck the hour, the sound low and mournful beneath leaden skies. Tristan pulled out his pocket watch and cursed. He was late for a meeting at a coffeehouse in St. James, where he was pursuing a friendship with an old school chum — and a client of Vostrikova's. Tonight they would laugh, and talk of women, then go on to dine, or perhaps visit a gaming hell or two. And with a little luck, the conversation might turn to the topic of where a man might go to slake his less salubrious desires.

On impulse, he extracted the band of ruched lace and yellow silk from his coat, and looked at it, so innocent and dainty in the broad palm of his hand. The little rose still dangled by its loose thread, tenacious as his foolish infatuation. He'd stolen it the day she stitched up his head, and he still wasn't sure why. On impulse, he looped it over one of the iron fence posts as if to leave it. Then abruptly, he changed his mind and shoved it back into the depths of his pocket.

With a soft *whuff* of her velvety nostrils, Callidora cropped one last mouthful of spring grass, then cut a baleful glance up at him. Tristan drew her head up, and slicked his hand down her neck one more time. "Come on, old girl," he said, shoving his boot into his stirrup. "There's nothing more for us here."

CHAPTER 10

> O but they say the tongues of dying men
> Enforce attention like deep harmony.

Phaedra endured the next weeks with a measure of stoicism, biting back her impatience and hurt. When tempestuous, wicked dreams woke her in the dead of night, she got up and sluiced her face in cold water, then forced herself to read a chapter of *Pilgrim's Progress*. She tried not to think of Tristan Talbot, and of the tea that never was.

Her mother, however, glossed it over for days after, patting Phaedra on the arm as if she were a child again, and declaring that Phaedra could do far better anyway. It was a cold comfort.

On the morning of Lady Kirton's charity ball, two weeks after that fateful night in Tristan's arms, she awoke bent double with cramping pain. By the feeble light of dawn, she climbed down from the bed with a heavy heart, and went to the washstand only to have her secret fears confirmed. The blood between her legs lay bright red upon the facecloth, damning evidence of the void within. Phaedra fell to her knees, sudden sobs wracking her body.

It made no sense. Oh, she *knew* it made no sense! She should have been thanking God above for her good fortune at having been saved, this once, from her own stupidity. Her wicked, wayward passions. Except that it wasn't good fortune at all. It was a tragedy all over again — a smaller tragedy, yes — but it was heartbreak all the same.

Somehow Phaedra dragged herself up, and through the tears, made a fold of white linen, then crawled back into bed to bury her face in the pillow. Awash in misery and self-pity, for once she let herself give in to it. She cried as she had not cried since girlhood.

She had wanted Tristan's child.

She had wanted it for days, deep in her heart, even though she'd known it was all but impossible. Indeed, she had barely dared hope — not in her conscious mind. Not until she'd seen the blood. What, precisely, she would have done about a child so far as Tristan was concerned she hardly knew. And it scarcely mattered. She could have raised a child alone. She was *sure* of it now. And the scandal — her mother's wailing, Stefan's disappointment, even Phoebe's blighted chances — none of it would have mattered to Phaedra could she but have the opportunity to hold her own child in her arms.

Oh, it was wrong, and it was selfish, and she would not have given a damn. She was sick of being Phaedra the Good. Phaedra the Dutiful. But she was not to have that chance. Indeed, she was scarcely able to have her cry and sleep long enough for the blotches to leave her face before Phoebe came twirling into the bedroom, bursting with conversation about the gown she was to wear to Lady Kirton's, and the flowers and fawning she expected to receive the following day.

"Gentlemen would send you flowers, too, Phaedra," her mother twittered over breakfast, "would you but apply yourself."

But there was little need for Phaedra to apply herself to anything, Phoebe declared, when Zoë Armstrong was doing everything for her.

There was some truth to Phoebe's barb. During those early weeks, Zoë took her vow to make Phaedra her season's project quite seriously. Dresses and fripperies arrived almost daily, both frothy and flounced, in shades from shimmering sky blue to deepest emerald, and invitations which in the past would have been summarily rejected were accepted at Zoë's cajoling — and sometimes her berating.

So as the season opened in earnest, Phaedra went out. The eyeglasses did not. She danced a little, flirted not at all, and as the days passed, watched a bit of the worry fall from her brother's face even as she looked in vain for Tristan around every corner. Under Zoë's tutelage — heavy handed though it was — Phaedra learned to bare her ample décolletage if not proudly, then at least without embarrassment, and to flutter her fan a bit. And she realized, too, that she need no longer fear being seduced by every handsome man who cut an assessing glance her way.

Oh, her old defenses were still firmly in place, though their shape and substance had altered. Gone was her armor of gray wool and linen binding. And in their place was the dawning knowledge that her voluptuousness was not a sin, and that the passion she'd once feared ungovernable now craved but one outlet — not that it brought her much comfort to know she was half in love with a scoundrel. A scoundrel who did not keep his appointments and likely wasn't going to keep his promises, either.

And through all of this, Phaedra tried to consider the possibility that Millie simply might not be coming back. That Priss might have to grow up with neither mother nor father, and that Phaedra must somehow make it right from a distance. Rationally, she understood that she was fighting not Priscilla's fight, but another fight lost long ago. In her heart, however, she believed none of this.

But she did believe, strange as it seemed, in Tristan. She had promised him a month, and she trusted that he was keeping his bargain. He might not be communicating with her as he'd promised, and had doubtless grown tired of flirting with her, but he was a good deal more apt to find Millie than she. But when two weeks turned to three, and she had heard not a word from the man, even this slender reed of hope began to slip her grasp and Phaedra grew exasperated.

It was the day of Lord and Lady Blaine's long-promised ball when Zoë next accompanied Phaedra to Bond Street. Phoebe was laid low by a case of the sniffles — or a case of having danced until three in the morning, depending upon how one looked at it — and Phaedra was called upon to go down for the final fitting of her sister's gown.

"Oh, do remember, Phae, to slouch, or the hem won't be quite right!" Phoebe pleaded, waving a handkerchief from her bed. "That cat Eliza will tell everyone at Brierwood if I go dressed like a rustic."

"And buy yourself a little something, my dear — a new hat, perhaps?" her mother called out from her chair by the bed. "Miss Armstrong, do help her pick something out. Your taste is always *comme il faut.*"

"Oh, and my yellow slippers!" cried Phoebe. "For Aunt Henslow's garden party on Saturday. Pick them up, Phae, won't you?"

"Very well," said Phaedra. She dragged Zoë toward the door to make her escape before the shopping list lengthened.

"I wish you were coming to the Blaines' ball tonight," she said to Zoë as they strolled along Brook Street, their maids following dutifully behind.

"I do, too," said Zoë morosely. "But I have to be here." She gestured toward an elegant double-fronted town house which Phaedra had often passed.

Phaedra turned to study it. "Isn't that the Countess of Kildermore's house? Lord

Robert's mother?"

"No, it belongs to her eldest son, the Marquess of Mercer now," she said darkly. "I go there with Papa every year. To a birthday party for the countess."

"What, you do not wish to go?" Phaedra crooked her head to look at Zoë.

"I don't know what I want." Zoë was uncharacteristically quiet. "At least, Phae, you know that much. In a perfect world, you'd want Avoncliffe — not that he deserves you, mind, given this disappearing act of his."

Phaedra cut a sharp, sidelong glance at her. They had had this argument a dozen times already, and Phaedra had grown tired of pretending Zoë was wrong. "I miss him," she quietly admitted. "I miss his wicked grin and that warm, dark skin. Those little crinkles at the corners of his eyes. Oh, he's a shameless cad, I know. But I miss him so much. Zoë, am I an utter gudgeon?"

"Yes," said Zoë glumly. "And I think, perhaps, that I am, too."

In Bond Street, however, Zoë shook off her doldrums by impelling Phaedra to buy a new straw bonnet with a wide blue ribbon which, Zoë swore, perfectly matched her eyes. Then they picked up the shoes and visited the modiste, who made the final tucks in Phoebe's gown and promised to deliver it later that afternoon.

"Now, let's go have an ice," Zoë said as they stepped out of the shop.

"One of these days, Zoë, you are going to turn into an ice," Phaedra warned. "*And* get fat."

But Zoë did not snap back with her usual biting retort. Phaedra glanced over to see that her friend's gaze had darkened warily. "Well, well," she murmured aside. "I see Avoncliffe is back to his old tricks."

With a sinking sensation, Phaedra looked farther down the pavement to see Tristan coming up the street, his head thrown back in laughter, his beautiful eyes twinkling. In the crook of one elbow he carried two bandboxes, and on his arm was a beautiful, dark-haired woman of perhaps something less than forty, her ardent gaze fixed firmly on his face.

"The devil," Zoë muttered. Then she lifted her hand, and waved merrily. "Avoncliffe! Oh, Avoncliffe! How do you do?"

Phaedra realized it the instant he spotted them. His gait hitched, and she could almost feel his hesitance. But left with no alternative, Tristan drew up beside them on the pavement. The light, however, faded at once from his eyes, and his companion's mouth turned into a faint pout.

"Good morning, Miss Armstrong," he said, bowing. "Lady Phaedra. How do you do?"

"Quite well," said Phaedra, surprised at the jealousy which stirred in her breast.

"Do you ladies know my friend, Mrs. Nebbett?" he asked.

"Oh, you know us silly debutantes, Avoncliffe," said Zoë lightly. "We scarcely know anyone over thirty. Ma'am, how do you do?"

Mrs. Nebbett's eyes flared at the subtle dig. Swiftly, Tristan made the introductions. Zoë and Phaedra curtsied, as did Mrs. Nebbett, but her smile was stiff and perfunctory. Clearly, she had better things to do, thought Phaedra maliciously.

"Mrs. Nebbett's husband works for my father," Tristan remarked conversationally.

"Indeed?" said Zoë. "I collect Mr. Nebbett is not a fan of shopping?"

"Mr. Nebbett's hours have become intolerable of late," the lady returned. "Today I needed help with my packages, and Avoncliffe kindly offered his arm."

"Ah, well, sometimes one's work must suffer in a good cause," said Tristan cheerfully. "And a beautiful lady is always a good cause — at least that's always been my philosophy."

Zoë was eying him up and down. "Yes, I hear you've become gainfully employed yourself, Avoncliffe," she remarked. "Civilization as we know it has just altered, has it not?"

Still clinging to his arm, Mrs. Nebbett looked vaguely affronted. "Indeed, Lord Avoncliffe is now an assistant to the Under-Secretary of State for Foreign Affairs." She cut a doting glance up at him, setting her dark ringlets to bouncing. "It is a *very* important post — dealing with the highest state secrets."

Zoë widened her eyes. "And here I was imagining him shoveling out grates and sharpening pencils."

Tristan laughed. "Oh, I am just pitching in a bit whilst Father is laid low," he remarked, tucking his companion's hand more snuggly over his arm. "And what better way to help than to squire Mrs. Nebbett up and down Bond Street?"

"Yes, after all, every man has his field of expertise," said Zoë a little snidely.

Just then, a bewigged servant approached, attired in a red coat and gray velvet knee breeches — a livery Phaedra did not recognize. He bowed to Tristan, and glanced round at the ladies apologetically. "My lord, forgive me," he said. "Pemberton asked me to tell you that you are needed in Cavendish Square most urgently. A matter of state business, he told me to say."

"Well, duty calls!" said Zoë brightly. Then she waved a cheery good-bye, and seized Phaedra by the arm. "Have a lovely day, both of you — and, oh, Mrs. Nebbett! Watson's is having a sale on their jacquard silks just two doors down. You really mustn't miss it."

"Jacquard silks?"

"Yes, they cast the light upward so beautifully." Zoë's eyes widened ingenuously. "My aunt declares they can take five years off one's complexion."

For an instant, Mrs. Nebbett could only stare after them, her mouth hanging slightly open.

"Zoë, that was rude," hissed Phaedra as they walked away.

Zoë's gaze narrowed. "Well, don't you just want to scratch her eyes out?"

When Phaedra said nothing, Zoë yanked her arm, turning her around to face her. "Well, don't you, Phae?" she demanded. "Come, admit it. You'd like to smack that simpering smile off her face — or at least I hope you would."

"Zoë!"

"No, listen to me," said Zoë hotly. "I know

you're in love with him, Phae — and it was his doing, not yours. After all, he has kissed you. *More than once.* And you are not the kind of girl a man so lightly kisses. Even if you're barren as the bloody desert, you deserve something a little better than a sudden disappearance, and that cat in your face."

But Phaedra was, apparently, exactly that sort of girl. Tristan had clearly forgotten her, and he had been none too pleased to see her again, either. That much had been painfully apparent.

"She used to be his paramour, by the way," Zoë added spitefully. "When he first came back from the war, she sunk her claws in and made a frightful fool of herself. He cannot possibly want her again."

"Zoë," she said wearily, "what is your point?"

"My point is, if you want him, Phae, go after him."

"What? Now?"

"No, not *now*," said Zoë impatiently. "You must think of another way — but punish him first, Phae. Make him suffer. Break his heart. A man will never respect a woman who cannot bring him to heel."

"I don't know how," she confessed.

Zoë caught her by her shoulder. "Tease

him," she whispered against Phaedra's ear. "You are the cat, *ma chère*. He is the mouse. You must bring him to *your* claws."

Tease him? Phaedra scarcely knew how to begin.

Zoë's ice forgotten, they walked back to Brook Street in silence, Phaedra pondering what Zoë had said. It was true. *She was in love with Tristan.* There was no halfway to it. And it had not taken Zoë's outburst to make her realize it, either. No, the mere vision of that woman's hand on Tristan's arm had brought it home to her more acutely than anything else could have done, for she had felt not just jealousy, but a hot, righteous anger, and on its heels, that deep and lingering sadness again.

But a woman could not hold a man to an unspoken promise, or to a fantasy. Still, Tristan Talbot had spoken one promise aloud to her. He had sworn to search for Millie, and made a vow to keep her apprised of his progress. And to that promise, at the very least, she could hold him accountable.

It took Tristan all of ten minutes to send Mrs. Nebbett back to Whitehall in the company of his father's footman, and make his way up to Cavendish Square. He had not needed the footman to tell him what the matter was. And in that moment, he hadn't given a damn about Mrs. Nebbett or what information he might pry out of her. He cared only about seeing his father.

He burst into the shadowy great hall to find Mrs. Wight, the housekeeper, quietly sobbing at Pemberton's side. The butler himself looked pale and rather shaken.

"You've come, sir," he said, stepping forward. "Thank God. I sent for you at once, but it took Simpkin a while."

Tristan's jaw was set grimly. "How bad, Pem?"

"Quite, sir." Pemberton started toward the stairs. "His lordship has been asking for you all morning," he continued as they hastened up. "Well, until perhaps an hour ago. Dr. Glockner is with him now. I think, though, that it won't be long."

Tristan felt hollow. Cold and still inside. "But he rallied yesterday, Pemberton," he muttered. "What the devil happened?"

"Dr. Glockner says that is often the way with the mortally ill," said Pemberton. "They have one last good day, and then . . ." He lifted a hand impotently.

Tristan nodded, and pushed open the door to his father's bedchamber — the same heavy oak door he'd been going in and out of, sometimes twice a day, for almost a month now. Indeed, throughout the whole of his life, Tristan couldn't remember ever having spent so much time in his father's company. There had always been his father's duty to the Crown. Always — *always* — that had come first.

And the fact was, it had been nothing but the same duty which had caused Hauxton to call his son to his bedside these last weeks, Tristan realized, looking down at his father's ashen, emotionless face. And nothing but duty which had prompted him to answer. They needn't delude themselves. He did not regret, this once, doing his father's bidding. Indeed, the challenge of it had awakened something long dormant — a grim sort of determination — inside him. But the sad truth of it did not escape him.

He leaned over the bed, and picked up his father's hand, which was already cold and limp to the touch. He flicked a quick glance at the physician, who had respectfully backed away.

"No." The doctor formed the word softly, and shook his head. "But it won't be long . . . my lord."

Tristan ignored the belated honor. He pulled his usual chair to the edge of the bed and sat, feeling — perhaps for the first time in his life — old and worn. Seeing Phae again had damn near broken his heart, and driven home to him an unfathomable truth. Was he now to have a second loss to be endured on its heels?

As if it had been agreed upon, Pemberton drew the physician from the room and quietly closed the door.

The physician, he realized, was right. Already Tristan could hear the faintest hint of what he knew would become a death rattle in the back of Hauxton's throat. God knew it was a sound a man never forgot. After the fall of Tripolitsa, soldiers' bodies had lain so thick upon the ground, one could scarce enter the city walls without trodding upon the dead and dying. The sounds of death drawing nigh had rasped from the mounds of bodies, a ghastly testament to the barbarity of their end. And then the worst — the systematic slaughter of the women and children — had begun.

The truth was, wars were made by men like Hauxton. And yet Tristan was grateful his father was to have the comfort of dying in his own bed, never knowing what war truly was. He looked down to see that every emotion had fallen from Hauxton's face, and that his pallid skin now lay smooth, unfurrowed by worry. But it was, apparently, something of an illusion.

Tristan laid his hand over his father's, clasping it between his own. "I am here, sir," he said quietly. "If you need me, I am here."

To his surprise, his father's eyes flickered open, but his gaze was unfocused. Unseeing. "Tristan."

Gently, Tristan squeezed his hand. "Are you in pain, sir?" he asked. "Do you need your laudanum?"

"No." Hauxton's mouth tried to turn up in a sneer. "Just tell . . ." he finally managed. "What . . . news?"

Work. Always, it was work. But what else was there to speak of? It was the only thing he and Hauxton shared. The only thing they had discussed since his father's lecture about Phaedra — a lifetime ago, it seemed. And so Tristan began this bedside chat as he had every conversation he and Hauxton had shared these last many weeks.

"I dined with James Ridler again last night as planned, sir," he reported. "I now have an open invitation to visit Vostrikova's brothel and — as Ridler put it — sample the wares. As soon as you're feeling more the thing, I'll —"

"*No*. Mustn't . . . wait." The words were a thready rasp with a hitching breath between. "What . . . else?"

Tristan was reluctant to continue. "I spent much of the morning with Mrs. Nebbett as we'd planned," he finally said. "It seems her husband's finances took an upward turn last month — a card game at White's, or so he told her. And I confirmed that Nebbett has indeed been bringing home diplomatic correspondence. No doubt he is sharing it with Vostrikova."

"Corres . . ." Hauxton managed. His eyes fell half closed. "Wha . . . sort?"

"Really, sir. This *must* wait." Damn it, was even his father's dying breath to be devoted to England?

"What . . . *sort?*" Hauxton rasped, his voice barely audible.

Tristan closed his eyes, and swallowed hard. "Letters from Whitehall to our man in Warsaw, from what I found hidden in his desk," he answered. "The Russians are trying to ascertain if England will hold firm to their side should war break out."

"Damned . . . conniving . . . bastard." A shudder ran through his feeble body. "*Trusted* . . . Nebbett."

And suddenly Tristan realized why his father had involved him. Hauxton had suspected, with his unfailing political instinct, that traitors lurked within his midst. So he had called Tristan — the one person he knew who was well outside his circle. It was a cold comfort now, as he watched his father lay dying, to know he was little more than the instrument of the man's revenge. That he was a mercenary still; a mercenary bought not with money, but by the immutable need for his father's approval.

Hauxton tried to speak, but the words just gurgled in the back of his throat.

"*Stop,* sir." Tristan squeezed his father's hand more firmly. "This is not necessary. You need to rest."

Hauxton drew a deep, rattling breath. "You . . . stop it," he whispered, squeezing Tristan's hand. *"Promise . . . stop her. All of them."*

"Yes, sir." Tristan hung his head. "I will do my best, sir."

And with that, his father's hand relaxed and went limp within Tristan's grasp.

The rattle in his throat deepened. Hauxton's eyes were still half open. His legs as leaden as his heart, Tristan went to the door and allowed Pemberton and the physician to return. There was a flurry of activity as the doctor threw open his satchel and extracted his stethoscope, whilst Pemberton unfastened Hauxton's nightshirt.

Glockner set the wooden tube to Hauxton's chest and listened. "It is very faint," he reported. "He shan't last the night. I'm sorry, my lord."

So Tristan sat back down in the chair, joining in the long, dark vigil. Sometime around midnight, the rattle became a quiet gurgle. Then Hauxton's breathing began to hitch in long, expectant pauses. At three in the morning, he drew what would be his last. Tristan got up and waited, leaning over the bed in prayer, willing his father to live.

Breathe again, he begged. *Just one more time.*

Just one more chance. Yes, that, really, was what he begged for. Even after all these years, he wanted one more chance with his father — to do what, he did not know. But Hauxton did not breathe again.

"I am sorry." The doctor laid a heavy hand on Tristan's shoulder. Pemberton withdrew a handkerchief, and softly blew his nose.

Tristan reached across the bed, drew down his father's eyelids, then fastened the throat of his nightshirt. He gave his father, insofar as it was possible, a small measure of dignity in death.

He turned to the butler. "I must go now," he said quietly. "But you must do one more thing for him, Pemberton."

"Yes, my lord. You have only to ask."

Tristan looked back and forth between the

two men. "Allow no one into the house," he said. "Say nothing of his death yet, particularly to anyone at the Foreign Office. Just tell them he is too ill, and they cannot come in on my orders. Trust me, this is what he would have wanted."

"Very well," said the butler uncertainly.

Tristan laid a hand on the butler's sleeve. "There was one last task my father bade me finish, Pemberton," he said quietly. "But I need time. And it will go far easier if no one knows he is dead."

"Yes, my lord." Pemberton's voice was more certain this time. "I shall arrange for the undertaker to come here, and have your father laid out in the state drawing room."

"Thank you, Pemberton," he said, noticing that the butler was looking at him with extreme deference.

Suddenly Tristan realized why. This — the servants, the house, the duty, all the burdens his father had borne — they were now his to bear. It was nothing he'd ever wished for. But whatever the cost, he would at least see this miserable business finished first. He would let his father rest in peace, his will carried out.

In the end, perhaps, that was all that mattered. In the end, he supposed, that's what families were for.

■ ■ ■ ■

Phaedra rose early the following morning and girded her loins for the trouble she knew was to come. Saturday was the day of Lord and Lady Henslow's annual picnic at their Thames-side estate in Richmond, and to call it a gala affair was a true injustice. This being Phoebe's come-out season, she and Lady Nash were to travel down early to prepare for the festivities. Phaedra, however, was not.

"I can't think *why* you must be so stubborn, Phaedra," her mother complained over breakfast. "Most young ladies would kill for an invitation. My elder sister will think you no longer hold her in any affection whatsoever."

Phaedra looked down at her plate a little guiltily. She did love Aunt Henslow — and dearly. But her aunt understood Phaedra's reluctance to move about in society. And sometimes, if Phaedra were honest, it was just a little hard to bear her aunt's company. "I have never gone to Aunt Henslow's picnic, Mamma," she said quietly. "And I don't mean to start. Besides, I think we might turn out all the second floor bedchambers for cleaning whilst you're away.

Pray do not quarrel with me."

Her mother, of course, did quarrel. She railed, complained, and finally, wheedled, until at last there was a series of loud bumps in the corridor beyond, and two footmen came past the door bearing a huge traveling trunk high on their shoulders. Her mother sprang up to implore them not to drop it, lest the locks spring and all her finery tumble down the front steps into Brook Street.

Phaedra took the opportunity to get up and poke about on the sideboard, though she ate little. In truth, she had no appetite, and had scarcely slept. A tangle of dreams had tormented her night; sweet dreams of Priss in her arms, and dreams of Tristan all caught up with them, in ways which made no sense at all. Twice she'd awoken in a tangle of sheets, feverish and yearning, the feel of his hands warming her body, the scent of him teasing at her nostrils.

How could one both welcome and dread seeing him again? Was this really about Priss now? Or was she, as she had said to Zoë, an utter gudgeon, chasing after a rogue she'd foolishly fallen for? Her mind in a whirl, Phaedra was barely able to wait until the trunk had been loaded into the family's traveling coach, and her mother and sister handed up inside.

"Do try, my dear, to keep your nails clean and the smut stains from your face," said Lady Nash, leaning down to have her cheek kissed. "We will have Lady Huston's soiree to attend on Tuesday."

As soon as the carriage had vanished, Phaedra went belowstairs and shocked the staff by giving most of them two days off, then hastened up to her bedchamber and rang for Agnes. "They are gone," she said when Agnes came in. "Now pin up my hair — as tight as is humanly possible."

"Oh, miss," said Agnes quietly. "Oh, I *do* hope you know what you're doing."

Phaedra hoped so, too.

According to Agnes, Tristan Talbot lived in a first-floor maisonette, its entrance wedged between a secondhand bookseller and a shop stuffed full of dusty, dubious-looking crockery. Ordinarily a bookshop would have caught Phaedra's notice, but she hastened to the next door with scarcely a passing glance, and dropped the knocker hard.

"In for a penny, in for a pound," she reminded herself. But her shield of righteous indignation had begun to tarnish during her march across Covent Garden, and she was beginning to fear this intrusion was just a

little less about helping Priss than was wise.

Too late. Phaedra could hear heavy footfalls coming down the stairs. A great beast of a creature opened the door, his slablike forehead deeply creased as if he could not quite make out the slight young gentleman standing upon his master's doorstep.

Phaedra, however, knew him at once. Still, the reminder hit her a little sideways, and left her knees shaking more than they already were. Though the taproom at the Three Shovels had been desperately dark that long-ago night, the man's width, breadth, and utterly bald pate gave him away. Somehow, Phaedra found the presence of mind to hand him a card.

"Mr. Hayden-Worth to see Avoncliffe," she said, dropping her voice an octave. Surely the man would not know Tony was three inches taller and a good deal older?

As she stripped off her gloves, the brute scowled down at the card which his massive thumb almost obscured. "The master's still abed," he said flatly.

Phaedra pushed past him and into the tiny entranceway. "Yes, afternoon comes frightfully early, doesn't it?" she said dryly, handing him her hat and her walking stick. "Kindly get him up. My business is urgent."

The scowl deepened, if such a thing were

possible. Phaedra got the impression they didn't get a great many callers, for though the foyer held a decent mahogany table with a well-scrubbed lamp and a fine Chinese bowl, there was no salver for receiving cards. Tony's card still pinched between his massive fingers, the servant led her up the stairs into a long, narrow sitting room hung with hand-colored prints — mostly hunting scenes — then vanished through an interior door between two overstuffed bookcases which stretched to the ceiling.

Phaedra gazed about the room, drawing in the scent of musty books and some exotic blend of tobacco, the smell sweet and oddly seductive. An old leather sofa stretched across most of the back wall, the table before it worn with the evidence of boot heels flung thoughtlessly upon it. A faded Turkish carpet covered the floor, and a stout Jacobean desk, cluttered and black with age, sat between the windows which overlooked Long Acre.

Here and there Phaedra noted various *bibelots:* an ornate Persian platter of etched silver, a wicked-looking scimitar glittering upon the wall, an ancient telescope, the wood worn smooth, the brass warm with age — all of it from Tristan's travels, no doubt. It was every inch a man's room, she thought, looking about it with mild approval.

Though Phaedra could still hear the rumble of an occasional carriage in the street below, the house lay silent, and she began to wonder if Tristan had simply gone out the back to avoid her. It little mattered; she'd run him to ground eventually. Impatient, she crossed the room to the bookcases, and let her eyes run over the shelves. It was a remarkably eclectic assortment of history, philosophy, old racing sheets, their corners dog-eared, and even the occasional novel. To calm her nerves, Phaedra reached for one.

"I don't know who you hope to fool in that rig," rasped someone behind her.

Phaedra dropped the book, and spun round. "*Must* you keep doing that?"

In the narrow room, he seemed suddenly larger — and angrier — than she remembered. With his dark shadow of beard and flashing black eyes, Tristan looked like the devil himself. He stood in his shirtsleeves and stocking feet, his cuffs rolled up to reveal a pair of dark, well-muscled forearms dusted with dark hair, and his tousled hair made it plain he'd just risen from his bed.

He regarded her through slitted eyes. "What's this about, Phae?"

"You are late, Talbot," she said, keeping her voice low.

"Late?" He had begun to jerk down his cuffs. "For what?"

"For tea," she snapped, pushing past him toward the narrow sofa. "By about three weeks."

Tristan's manservant returned, a garment of flowing red silk draped over his arm, and looking as if he didn't quite know what to make of her. At least someone was fooled.

"Uglow, a word?" Tristan took the garment — a dressing gown — and spoke quietly as he drew it on over his open shirt. The servant nodded and vanished. An instant later, a door slammed in the rear and heavy steps went trundling down a flight of stairs.

Tristan turned his glower back to her. "Your pardon, Phaedra," he said, his voice laced with barely suppressed rage. "But I am not accustomed to receiving ladies in my shirtsleeves."

Phaedra let her gaze run down the red silk. "Oh, I've seen you in somewhat less formal attire, Talbot," she said. "Or had you forgotten?"

"I've forgotten nothing," he snapped. "And you'd best have a very good reason for turning up here like this."

His words stung, and she realized in some humiliation she'd hoped for a different sort of welcome. But she turned to hold his gaze directly. "Oh," she said quietly, "I have a very good reason."

Some nameless emotion sketched across his face then. Joy? Terror? In two strides, he had crossed the room to seize her by the upper arms. "Phae, *good God* — ?"

The fervency of his words shocked her, and she staggered back a step. It was just a fleeting, subtle glance, his eyes falling to her belly so quickly most women would not have noticed. But Phaedra did. And suddenly, she knew.

"Oh," she whispered, her brow knotting. "Tristan, no. Not that." He held her gaze bleakly for a long moment, and there was a silent pleading in his eyes. For what, she did not know. "No," she said again. "Really, you cannot possibly have feared —"

"Three weeks, you said." He was still holding her gaze, watchful and intense. Suddenly, his ruthless grip relaxed. "No," he whispered, putting her away in a swirl of red silk. "No, you wouldn't know, would you?"

She followed him across the room. "Listen to me," she said. "I *do* know. You needn't worry."

"How can I not?" He turned again, his eyes bleak, his emotions clearly frayed — all most uncharacteristic. "I worry for you — that you might have been seen coming here. And worried about that, yes." Again, he flicked a quick glance down. "I am not a total cad, Phae."

"And I'm concerned with the child who *is*, not the child who will never be." She set a hand on his arm, the shimmering red silk soft against her fingers. "Tristan, I . . . I cannot have children. I am barren, or likely so. Please put it from your mind."

He looked at her again with that deep, penetrating gaze of his. "Barren?" he echoed. "How can you know?"

Phaedra cut her eyes away, toward the door through which the servant had vanished. "It is a long story," she answered. "I had a fever once, and some . . . complications. That's all. It happens, you know."

"No, it doesn't." His voice was firm. "Not like that. And it doesn't explain —"

"Why I've dressed up in my brother's clothes and come to call?" Her mouth twitched. "Is it really that obvious?"

He hesitated. "Well, you're good with voices, and the walk's about right," he grimly admitted. "All in all, a damned good ruse, but if you're not carrying my child, you'd better have a damned good reason to go with it."

"Why, I never ceased to be amazed how quickly an indolent scoundrel can turn into a judgmental tyrant," said Phaedra, releasing his arm. "What is *your* reason for *your* behavior, Tristan? I have heard nothing from you in all these weeks. We had an arrangement, sir. You promised to keep me informed."

He paced across the room. "Oh, no," he said warningly. "You'll not turn this around on me, my girl."

"So you make a habit of that, do you?" she snapped. "Kissing a woman senseless, then bending her to your will so that *you* get the bargain you want?"

He spun around, the red silk whipping round his ankles again. "We had no bargain," he gritted, stabbing a finger in her direction. "I promised you nothing. And trust me, Phae, if you were bent to my will, you'd be bent over that sofa right about now."

"Oh, now *there's* a fantasy," she retorted. "You said we would work together to find Millie."

"No, my dear, *you* said that." He had returned to stand before her, tall and whipcord lean, his lips drawn thin with implacability. "Think back carefully, Phae. I may be a scoundrel, but I don't make women promises I cannot keep."

She started to turn away. "Tristan, you swore —"

"No, I said I'd find out what happened to her," he interjected, grabbing Phaedra hard by the shoulders. "And I asked you to stay out of harm's way. Is that really so difficult? Do you really trust me so little?"

"*La*, sir, I don't know," she said speciously, laying a finger to her cheek. "Let's see, you spent yesterday — and likely last night — tending to your Mrs. Nebbett. One can only infer what you spent the other twenty days doing."

"No, I spent *yesterday* wheedling information out of Mrs. Nebbett," he said, his voice rising to a near shout. "And I spent last night praying by my father's deathbed. And I do not need you, Phae, to come here now to tell me how to do my job —"

"Tristan, I —"

"And I don't need *you*," he shouted over her, "scaring the bloody hell out of me because I have to worry what dangerous ruse you'll pull next. Whether yours will be the next dead body they pull out of the river with a slit throat. Do you understand me, Phae?" He jerked her hard for emphasis, but Phaedra was still stuck on the word *deathbed.*

She raised an unsteady hand to her forehead, only to feel the stiff, foreign curls of Jenny's wig brush her hand. It all seemed so ludicrous now; so suddenly unimportant. "I beg your pardon," she managed to whisper. "Your father . . . he . . . he is gone?"

"He is gone." The words were flat. Almost emotionless.

She looked up to see Tristan's eyes swimming with unshed tears. The full import of it struck her. "Oh, my God." She set her palms to the lapels of his dressing gown. "Oh, Tristan, I am so sorry. I did not know."

The room went perfectly still for a long, awful moment. "No one knows," he finally rasped.

"No one?"

"The doctor. The household." He released his grip on her shoulders, and shrugged. "It must be kept quiet for a time."

She drew back, meaning to ask him why. But the raw pain in his eyes stripped away every question. Every shred of anger. "I am so sorry," she said again. "You must have loved him very much. And he you."

He shook his head once, but it was a slight, uncertain movement. "I thought I loved him not at all," he managed. "And that he loved me no better."

"Oh, Tristan, that cannot be true." Firmly, she set her hands to his lean, unshaven cheeks. "There is too much grief in your eyes for that. And your father, perhaps he was not a demonstrative man — so many of his ilk are not. But how could anyone, once they truly knew you, not love you?"

"Phae." He dragged a hand through his thick hair. "Phae. You are a fool for coming here."

"No," she said with quiet confidence. "I am not that. Not any longer."

And suddenly, it seemed the most natural thing on earth to kiss him — no, it seemed *necessary.* As necessary — and as inexplicable — as her need to come here today. Phaedra rose onto her tiptoes, and set her lips lightly to his, and it was as if time spun away. As if she stood again in the parlor in Brook Street, tucked behind the door with Tristan's mouth upon hers in a sweet, gentle kiss.

But this was a kiss of pure seduction. His tousled black waves fell forward as that beautiful harlot's mouth softened over hers. Molding to her lips in pliant, coaxing strokes. Sending that sweet, hot ribbon of need twisting through her. Drawing her fully into him.

Then just as abruptly, he lifted his mouth and left her staggering. "Go now," he said thickly. "I'll deal with your Millie, and send word, I swear. Go home, Phae."

Impulsively, she brushed the corner of his mouth with her lips. "Is that really what you wish?" she asked, her eyes dropping shut. "I think not."

"Go home, love," he rasped. "I'm so bloody tired and ill-tempered. I'm not myself, Phae."

She opened her eyes, and searched his face. His expression was stark, his eyes soft with grief. "I think that perhaps you are more real than I have ever seen you," she whispered. "At least you are angry. Sorrowful. Worried. At least you *care*."

His mouth lifted at one corner, a dry, humorless smile. "Aye, as I said — not myself."

She shook her head. "That man who laughs all the time and cares for naught," she said. "That charming knave on Mrs. Nebbett's arm. Tristan, tell me, is that really you? I . . . I need to know."

He closed his eyes wearily, as if he feared what message she might read there.

Acting on instinct, Phaedra slid her palms up the red silk of his gown, then kissed him again, twining her hands behind his neck. It was to have been a kiss of compassion, and of reassurance. But there was a hard edge to him today, something brittle and desperate. And when he drew his tongue hungrily across the seam of her lips, she opened. Something inside him snapped — like a burning lamp sent crashing to the floor in a cascade of flame as he thrust inside. Heat washed through Phaedra, welled up and surged through her every vein. She could feel it in him, too; that same helplessness as his mouth moved over hers. The sense of inevitability, and of rightness.

His lashes still wet with tears, his face twisted with grief, Tristan held her to him. She responded, opening fully, giving willingly whatever he needed to take. He slanted his mouth over hers, the sensuous swell of that bottom lip dragging faintly over her own, his unshaven cheeks raking her. His arms came fully around her, powerful and warm as he lifted her to him. With each breath, she drew him deeper inside herself, luxuriating in the clean scent of plain soap and warm male skin. Phaedra felt herself relaxing into the supple strength of his body, as if the lee of his broad chest might shelter her.

"Phaedra," he whispered.

She felt weak, without will or good sense,

unable to pull her mouth from the soft temptation of his lips. Her heart cried out for him; it was no longer just her body. She kissed him again, more boldly, and let her hands slide beneath the red silk. Her palms stroked down the hard slabs of muscle at his back to the curve of his spine, and lower still, pulling him into her. Offering what comfort she could.

He accepted, thrusting deep, his tongue parrying with hers, his hands roaming over her, heavy and seductive. She could hear her own heartbeat now. She knew what was going to happen, and welcomed it. Whatever he needed — whatever they were together — it was right in this moment.

Somewhere by the sofa, he shoved the coat from her shoulders, still kissing her desperately. Her neckcloth followed, a trail of white across the opulence of the Oriental carpet. In the swirling heat and madness, Phaedra hitched up against something, and a pile of magazines cascaded to the floor. *The bookcase.*

Unthinkingly, her hands went to the close of his trousers, slipping loose the buttons. A snatch of some long-ago eulogy sketched through her mind. *Even in death there is life.*

These past weeks, *she* had felt alive. Alive for the first time in more years than she could bear to count. Back from the dead of a shuttered and hopeless life. She wanted to drink it in — the pleasure and even the pain — all of life's richness she had so long denied herself.

Her waistcoat slid away, allowing her shirt to fall open down her throat. Tony's trousers slithered to her hips. Somehow, she stepped out of one leg, and hitched the knee about Tristan's waist. He tore his mouth from hers, then on a soft curse, turned her, and swept his arm across the desk. The Persian platter went clanging to the floor in a cascade of quills, paper, and ink pots.

Roughly, he lifted her, perching her on the edge of the desk heedless of the windows to either side. The wood was cool against the flushed heat of her bottom. Tristan fumbled at the fall of his trousers, pushing down the snarl of linen drawers. His manhood sprang free, swollen and jutting, far more intimidating in the light of day. Uncertainly, Phaedra slid one hand down the hot, silken length of it, causing him to moan. Emboldened, she drew him near. Tristan entered roughly, on one hard stroke, burying himself deep and letting his head fall back.

"I'm sorry, Phae," he choked. "Oh, God."

"Don't be sorry." Her lips brushed down

his cheek.

He thrust, and thrust again, each stroke deep and shuddering, lifting her off the wood, the desk and even the prints hanging above it shaking at the impact. Phaedra clung to him as if clinging to sanity, taking his kisses deep and returning them in full measure.

"I'm sorry, I'm sorry," he said thickly.

Then Tristan thrust one last time, coming inside her on a low, inhuman groan. The rush of his seed surged into her in a hot, satisfying flood. And in a minute — three, perhaps — the storm was over. She fell against him in a tangle of limbs and linen shirts, their breath coming in deep, heaving gasps.

"Phae," he rasped. "Oh, God. Tell me you wanted that."

"I wanted that," she whispered, her nose buried against his damp neck.

His arms wrapped around her, Tristan responded by pulling her off the desk.

Phaedra wound both legs round his waist as he carried her through the door into the depths of the house. Halfway down the darkened passageway, her second shoe fell off, and she lost the last leg of her trousers. Tristan turned into a shadowy room — his bedchamber, she realized, for the cool, still air was redolent with his scent. They collapsed onto the bed, their bodies still joined, the roping beneath creaking in protest.

Hesitantly, he lifted his hand and tucked a bit of her hair beneath the cap of Jenny's old wig. "Well, that was utterly humiliating," he murmured, his eyes roaming over her face. "A world record, I daresay, of the worst sort."

She kissed him again, settling her mouth softly to his cheek. "Sometimes it's best to just take what one needs at the moment," she whispered. "Sometimes, Tristan, that's what lovers are for."

"And what about you?" he asked. "Do your needs count for nothing?"

She smiled, a muted Madonna-like smile. "You needn't play Lothario for me," she murmured. "I did not give myself to you so that I might get something in return."

"Did you not?" he asked lightly, one hand cupping her face. "Why, then?"

She glanced away, hesitating. "Because I care for you far more than I might wish, I daresay," she finally answered. "If the guilt is more than you can live with, make it up to me."

"Phae." The word was soft; almost as soft as the kiss which followed. "I oughtn't be —"

She laid a finger to his lips. Her anger — and his — had burnt down to ash. "Do not speak to me, Tristan, of *ought*," she said quietly. "I know what I want. Who I am. I have been changed by this. By you. Oh, my dear, I'm not naïve. I know exactly what we are doing. And exactly how far it should go."

"How far?" he rasped.

She looked away.

"Phae." His voice sounded pleading. "What do you want of me?"

"Just . . . this," she replied. "Must we speak of it now, and ruin it? Your father is dead, Tristan. Mourn him however you must — or simply celebrate being alive. Nothing else matters just now."

It wasn't quite the answer Tristan had hoped for, strangely. His heart still thudding, he let his eyes roam over Phaedra. He was glad — selfishly, disconcertingly glad — she had come. And God knew he hadn't honor enough to send her away again.

Lingeringly, he let himself savor her every aspect, taking in her strangely seductive contrasts. The cropped brown hair which only accentuated the feminine turn of her neck. Her fine-boned wrists encircled by deep, white cuffs. The starched, masculine shirt, and beneath it, the tantalizing swell of womanly breasts that rose with her roughened breath, threatening to burst from her linen binding.

In the dreams which had begun to torment him nightly, Phaedra wore only the most feminine of fabrics; layers of lace and virginal white silk. Frothy, ephemeral garments which slithered inch by inch down her body as he painstakingly unfastened each button. Row upon row of tight, tiny, impossible buttons, as if Morpheus meant merely to tempt him. To deny him what he burned for. Night after night, she came to his bed, her smile knowing, her eyes unreadable. And never were the buttons fully undone. He would awake shaking, in a sweat; purity and salvation always just beyond his reach.

Perhaps it was what he deserved. But Phaedra was here, in his bed now, and his desire for her was but barely slaked. With a hand which trembled, Tristan folded back the opening of her shirt, exposing the creamy swells of her cleavage to his gaze, mesmerized by the contrast of his dark fingers against her pale skin.

The vision was not enough. He lifted her gently, drew the shirt from her body, then closed his eyes and bent over her, setting his cheek to hers.

"I need you to say it, Tristan," she whispered, her breath stirring against his ear.

"Say what, love?"

"Tell me you are glad that I am here."

He gave a dark, sensual laugh. "You shouldn't be here at all."

"I think we are well past *shouldn't* by now."

He closed his eyes, and inhaled deeply of her scent. Of lavender and warm, sensuous woman. She was right. Things between them had changed inexorably, shifted and altered into something more undeniable, for good or for ill. Keeping his distance from her would not change that now. It probably wouldn't even keep her from getting hurt. "I thank God you are here, Phae," he finally admitted.

She sighed beneath him and began to twist free of the linen binding. Tristan rolled onto one elbow and stripped off what remained of his clothing. When he looked down at her again, he could see some nameless emotion flickering in her eyes. Desire, yes, and something more. A hint of uncertainty, perhaps?

He wanted to laugh bitterly. Any woman who considered throwing her lot in with his ought well to feel a healthy dose of doubt. And suddenly, he wanted to strip that doubt away. For once in his life, he wanted to be worthy of something better and greater than himself. And when Phaedra parted her lips, and looked at him, he kissed her gently, cupping her face with one hand as his tongue lightly explored her mouth.

She tasted sultry and a little tart, like wild strawberries warmed by the sun. Her heavy breasts lay fully exposed now, a shaft of midday light cutting through the sheer draperies to cast her in a faint, warm glow. Cupping one breast in his hand, Tristan bent his head and touched his tongue lightly to her nipple, making her shudder beside him. "They are too large," she whispered self-consciously.

He laughed deep in his throat and lifted his head to look at her. "You have the silliest, most endearing notions," he said, smiling down at her.

She cut an uncertain glance away. "I always wished for a pair of pert little teacup breasts," she said. "Not something . . . not something that made me look as if I were made for sin — a body made merely to tempt men to wickedness."

He flicked an appreciative glance over them. "You are made for adoration, Phae," he corrected. "A lush beauty in the full flower of womanhood. What could be more pure and perfect than that?"

She shot him a chiding glance. "You are only saying that to get what you want."

At that, he threw back his head and laughed. "I already got what I wanted," he corrected. "Now I am merely lingering, worshipful."

Her hand slid down to grasp the hardening rod of his erection. "What a frightful liar you are," she whispered, her soft blue gaze catching his.

He closed his eyes again, the breath shuddering from his body on a low, hungry growl. "I am a liar," he admitted. "I want to make love to you, Phae — and your perfect breasts. Slowly. Exquisitely."

And in that moment, it mattered not at all that, despite her fears, he might leave her with child, or that her brother might kill him for it. It mattered only that he knew what brought her satisfaction. That he knew the sounds of her need, and the scent of her body. He knew how she liked to be taken — with control and yes, a little domination. And he knew the unalloyed pleasure of spending himself inside her.

Slowly, he touched her, circling one taut nipple with the tip of his finger until she sighed with pleasure. But his hands still trembled imperceptibly with each stroke, and with the knowledge that he had been given — at least for today — a precious gift.

Phaedra's hands came up to cradle his face, drawing his mouth to her breast as her bare foot slid up the length of his leg. Deftly, she curled her limb around his, like a cat seeking the pleasure of a stroke. Somewhere amidst the pleasured sighs, Tristan pushed the mop of curls away and unwound her real hair, the glorious golden brown coils spilling down her shoulders and over her breasts. The tangle of clothing was kicked off the bed and the covers shoved fully down. The expanse of white sheeting was his canvas, and she was to be his masterwork.

Tristan let his hands and his mouth roam over her until her soft gasps of pleasure filled the cool stillness of the room. Her breasts, her belly, her long, beautifully sculpted thighs. He let his hand run up the length of her leg from ankle to the crease of her joining. He let his tongue toy with the sweet, hard nub between her legs, but only enough to make her arch with pleasure.

"Tristan," she rasped when he licked his way up, and plunged his tongue into her navel. "Tristan, *wait.*"

There was an urgency in her voice which made him lift his head.

Her long, brown lashes fluttered almost

shut, and the tip of her tongue came out to toy with one corner of her mouth.

He drew himself up and lay down alongside her. "What is it, love?" he murmured, nuzzling her left breast. "Shall I stop? Go faster?"

She shook her head.

He drew a finger down the smooth white length of her breastbone. "Come, Phae," he whispered against her throat. "We are lovers now. Tell me. Let me please you."

She turned her head away, her throat working up and down. "I want what you did in the garret," she whispered. "I want . . . I don't know how to explain it."

He shifted the weight of his body atop her, bracketed her face in both hands, and kissed her long and deep. "You wish to be fully beneath me?" he said when she was breathless. "You wish . . . something more?"

Her eyes still closed, she nodded. "Sometimes it feels . . . like too much," she said. "Too *good*. As if I cannot trust myself to . . . to . . . I do not know. I . . . I don't understand myself."

Something dark and knowing surged inside him. "You want me to possess you," he murmured huskily. "To control you."

"Yes." The word was a hungry whisper. "I wish you to —"

"I think I know what you wish," he whispered.

A sigh of relief escaped her. "I am . . . wrong, somehow," she whispered. "But this — this will be our secret, Tristan. Yes?"

"You are not *wrong*," he said. "You are a deeply sensual woman, Phae, but for some reason, you don't trust yourself. So, for now, you want a strong lover who dominates. And there is no shame in that, so long as it is done gently and with . . . with deep affection."

She looked at him in confusion.

"Phae, in time you can learn to master your own desires," he said. "Or do you wish me to master you? I will, love — gently — but only if that's what you want."

When she did not answer, he rose from the bed and went to the lowboy by the windows. When he returned, he laid a coil of soft rope across her belly, then stretched himself back out along her length. What is that?" she asked without looking at it.

"A *kinbaku* rope from the Far East." He picked up one frayed end and teased lightly at her nipple. "This one is made of silk, and very soft. It is used to heighten sensual pleasure, if a person is so inclined."

Her face flushed with pink. "I cannot believe you own such a thing," she sputtered. "You are more wicked, I daresay, than even Zoë knows."

Tristan laughed, and did not tell her the truth — that the silk rope was a recent acquisition, bought in the East End in a moment of reckless melancholy. He had not thought ever to use it, and wasn't perfectly sure he should do so now.

But Phaedra had twisted the other end of the white rope about her wrist and was looking at it, transfixed. "How do you use it?"

"Oh, I think you have some idea, my sweet," he murmured. "I can simply tie your hands to the bed, and mount you."

"Oh, my," she said huskily.

"Or I can tie your legs open."

"Oh," she breathed.

"Or I can bind this round your breasts and then to your wrists," he suggested. "That, I daresay, might keep my naughty girl in her place?"

"Yes." Her eyes flew open, her gaze clear and hungry. *"That."*

Dear God. Tristan swallowed hard. But he had bought the rope, and offered it to her. "Sit up," he said, his voice roughening.

He wrapped the rope twice beneath her breasts, knotted it to one side of her spine, then twice above her breasts until the rope pressed down tight upon her pale mounds. Carefully, he worked the rope through her cleavage. Good God, it was a beautiful, highly erotic sight.

"Lie down," he rasped.

A smile flirted at the corner of her mouth. "My, you are getting tyrannical already," she murmured.

"I must admit, my dear," he said darkly, "that the notion of finally having you obey me is rather intoxicating." He drew the silk up her throat, and stretched her arms high, binding them together in gentle coils from her lower wrist to above her thumbs. He knotted the rope to the bed and sat back on his haunches surveying his handiwork.

Not a bad job for an amateur, he thought.

Phaedra's eyes widened as she tested the knot. *"Oh,"* she said softly as her breasts lifted against the strain.

Tristan let his gaze drift over the ropes which pressed into the plump mounds and felt raw lust surge. God, he was very much afraid a man could get used to this. The eroticism of having Phaedra — bossy, meddlesome female that she was — fully bound and immobile beneath him was dizzying. But as he bent over her and kissed her deeply, he realized that the real eroticism came not from the control, but from the trust — the trust which Phaedra so willingly offered him. It grieved him to wonder how long she'd felt such shame, unable to unburden herself to a lover who would not judge. How lonely her life must have been. Perhaps he understood more than she might guess.

And in that moment of stark, clean realization, as their mouths sought solace in one another, it was as if something inside him broke under the pressure of craving her. Dear God, he was in too deep to ever get out of this, and suddenly weary of his life spent pleasuring other women. Tired of rising from their beds so cheerfully apathetic, often unable to recall their names or even why he had wanted them in the first place.

Whatever she needed, Tristan burned to drive Phaedra mad with pleasure. To enslave her with it, and bind her to him forever. He nudged her legs wide with his knee and braced himself over her on one arm. He took her mouth again, more roughly, and drew his fingertips through the damp, feminine heat between her thighs. The dew slicked his fingers, and sent desire shafting through him, red-hot and searing. His cock throbbed insistently. To tamp down his impatience, he shifted his weight lower, and settled one arm across her thigh.

Slowly he slipped two fingers inside her as she watched beneath heavy eyes. Phaedra's passage tightened, pulling him into her; drawing him deeper into the sensual haze. He wanted to lose himself. To thrust his flesh into hers and claim her once again. Instead, he kissed her there, then held her gaze as his tongue teased deeper.

She gasped, the ropes drawing taut, then relaxing again. Something passed between them; a look of acceptance and surrender. "I have you under my control, Phae," he whispered. "There is no escape unless you beg for it."

No escape unless you beg.

Phaedra heard the words and shivered. The ropes which bound her pressed into her flesh, tight but not painful, yet confining all the same. Binding her to his touch. Laying her out like a feast for his eyes and for his body. She felt the weight of Tristan's erection throb against the tender skin of her inner leg, and gave herself up to the torment.

Using his thumb, he opened her more fully, and set the other hand on her inner thigh, gently urging her wider. His tongue stroked into her warmth, sin and sensation washing over her. It was decadence unimaginable. When she struggled, and tried to shift away, he laughed and nipped gently at the tender flesh of her belly. "Mind what you do," he growled. "You are under my control, remember?"

Oh, she remembered. And it frightened her a little.

His tongue stroked deeper, the stubble of his beard rough against her skin. Beneath the pressure of the rope, Phaedra's nipples had hardened to pebbles. He was drowning her in desire and that swirling hot madness. He stroked again, this time sliding one finger inside her, and Phaedra's hips bucked off the mattress.

In response, he licked lightly at the very center of her madness. Enslaving her with his mouth and his hands and his rope, until at last the rush of sensation swamped her. She cried out, pleading, and then was lost in him. The waves crashed in, dragged her down into a world of drugging, lethargic pleasure.

When she resurfaced in the present, limp and trembling, Tristan was braced over her, the tan, sculpted muscles of his arms taut, his eyes dark with desire. She licked her lips uncertainly. "Untie me?"

Slowly, he shook his head. "I don't think so, love." The words rasped from his throat. "Not unless you beg me."

With a tentative smile, Phaedra let her eyes rake down Tristan. His was a warrior's body; lean and hard, with scars across his arm and his hip — God's perfection marred by man's inhumanity. And he was all the more beautiful for it. She let her eyes feast on fine shoulders as wide as her thighs, and the sleek turn of his waist. Between the two points there lay nothing but honey-colored muscle layered over strong ribs and dusted with a hint of dark, curling hair which winnowed away to nothing at his navel. And below that, *oh* . . .

Phaedra was shocked to feel the return of desire. She lifted her hips in invitation. "I'm not begging," she whispered. "Not for that, at any rate."

With his knee, he nudged her leg wider, then he set his hand to her mound. "Have you any idea, Phae, how beautiful you are?" His black Gypsy eyes enthralled her, shook her just a little. "Have you any notion how desperately I want you?"

She managed a feeble grin. "You probably say that to all the girls you tie up," she whispered.

He looked at her blankly, his eyes still dark with need. "I have no idea," he muttered. "Right now I can't even remember ever making love to anyone else."

With that, he drew one hand down his cock and closed his eyes, as if savoring the moment. Then he settled himself over her and thrust, his head going back as he buried himself inside her again.

He thrust inside her rhythmically, his arms rigid with muscle, his belly drawn taut. She could understand why women might fight over this. Tristan made love like he danced, with a raw, physical grace. Living life to the fullest, seeking pleasure only in the present. There was glorious, wild beauty in it — and a life lesson, too, she feared.

She let her head fall back into the softness of the bed, and rose to him, taking his strokes with equal abandon. His scent — bergamot and soap and his own sensual warmth — teased her nostrils. She wanted desperately to please him, as he had pleased her. The afternoon light was strengthening now as the sun shifted over the roofs of Covent Garden. It shone over him, bathing his honeyed skin in a golden glow. With his dancer's grace, he deepened his rhythm, moving inside her with sweet, perfectly timed strokes.

She felt her hunger spiral higher, and gave herself up to him. Their skin was damp now, their bodies sliding wetly against one another. "Phae," he cried, his hair falling forward to shadow one eye.

Boldly, she rose to him, watching him in the fading light. That masculine beauty, the utter magnificence of his body, was her undoing. She cried out and felt the stars fall. Felt herself tumbling headlong into the unknown, Tristan's arms tight and strong about her.

Long moments later, she stirred to feel the weight of Tristan's leg thrown over hers. He lay facedown beside her, his lips pressed to the turn of her neck, one arm banded about her waist in a sweet, possessive gesture. She was his. Whether he knew it or not — whether it ever came to anything more than this — she was his. She was, headlong and hopelessly, in love.

His body spent and still shuddering within, Tristan sensed Phaedra stirring. Somehow, he found the strength to kiss her lightly below her ear. *"Ummm."*

"Oh, my." Beneath him, Phaedra exhaled on a shudder. "Tristan. That was . . ."

"Ummm," he moaned again. "Perfect."

"Yes, *perfect*," she sighed. "Let's do it again."

He lifted his head and looked at her through a shock of inky, disordered hair. "You cannot be serious."

Phaedra's face colored furiously.

She *was* serious. Well, he had never been one to resist a challenge. He laughed, and rolled onto his elbow. "Greedy puss!" he muttered. "You are insatiable."

She looked away. "Sometimes I'm afraid I might be," she said softly. "But you make this seem so beautiful. So . . . *normal.* Can you? Do it again?"

He reached over the edge of the bed and felt for the knife he always left inside his boot. Then he lifted the rope which stretched down her cleavage, unsheathed the blade with his teeth, and slipped the knife between her breasts. He jerked up, slicing the ropes cleanly.

In a moment, Phaedra had shaken her hands free of the remaining coils. He tossed the knife onto his bedside table with a clatter, and seized her wrists, turning them this way and that in a shaft of afternoon light. He looked down to see the embarrassment had faded from her cheeks. He bent to kiss her, gently and lingeringly.

"Now," he said when he had thoroughly ravished her mouth, "to answer your question — *yes.* I can do it again." Already he felt the faint stirring of lust. "But this time, Phae, we do it without the rope."

"Without the rope?"

"And with you on top."

Her eyes widened. "But I . . . I don't know
—"

He cut her off by setting his hands to her
waist. "Oh, I'll show you," he promised, rolling onto his back and taking her with him.
"This time, Phae, you are in control — and
for as long as it takes, love."

It took a while. She was sweetly slow and
uncertain. Inexperienced as she was, Phaedra would take time to become comfortable
in her own skin, he knew. And admittedly,
he was not at his best. Perhaps his age was
finally telling. Or perhaps it was the fact
that he was spent — not just physically, but
emotionally, by an exhausting mélange of
grief and lust, and by the disconcerting
realization of just how deep he was where
Phaedra was concerned. But in that moment — in that perfect time and place — it
scarcely mattered. His body was soon joined
again to hers, and fleetingly, the world was
his.

Chapter 11

O, how this spring of love resembleth
The uncertain glory of an April day!

Long moments later, Tristan lay sated beside Phaedra, twining a lock of her chestnut hair round and round his finger, and pondering what he ought to do about his rapidly deepening feelings for the girl. Nothing yet, he thought, regrettably. There was too much hanging over them. His father's death, and this business with Vostrikova to finish. Her family's disapproval. Her obsession with this motherless child and missing tavern maid. And above all, the danger.

But when his gaze drifted over her face, sweetly softened in sleep, he felt his heart lurch.

Suddenly, the *thump* of the front door roused him. Tristan glanced at the clock. *Half past three.* Bloody hell. It was Uglow returning, most likely. He could hear heavy feet trundling around in the sitting room. A few moments later, the floor in the passageway creaked ominously.

Phaedra's eyes fluttered wide. Tristan set a swift finger to her lips, and drew the bedcovers up. The footsteps continued, slow and heavy, stopping just outside the door. Instinctively, Tristan rolled to one side and snatched up his knife.

A slow, heavy knock sounded, a dirge upon the wood. "My lord?" Uglow's voice sounded strained. Unnatural.

Tristan dropped the knife. "Aye, what?" he said impatiently.

There was a long, pregnant pause, then the door opened just a crack to reveal the servant's broad back. "My lord," said Uglow solemnly. "I'm afraid I've got ter give me notice."

"What, this minute?" Tristan sat up in bed, and pinned the door with his dark gaze. "Are you mad?"

"I've been through it wiv you, sir, the thick and the thin," he said grimly. "Put up wiv yer wicked women and vile habits. Them murderous Turks trying ter slice me throat wiv their nasty, crooked knives. But even a chap like me draws the line at *this*."

Tony's trousers sailed through the air, landing on the bed with a *whuff.*

A horrible realization dawned.

"Uglow!" Tristan snatched up his silk robe from the floor. "Wait. No. It's not what you think."

Uglow hesitated, then slammed the door shut. "It's an unnatural act, sir, wot yer about wiv that lad," he said through the wood. "And I'll 'ave no part in it."

Beside him, Phaedra spurted with laughter, then clamped a hand over her mouth. Tristan shot her a dark look. "Wait, Uglow." He rolled out of bed, shoving his arms into the red silk robe. "And you — be quiet," he said, whirling around to Phaedra. "Not a peep till I return, do you hear me?"

She grinned, and drew the covers to her nose. "Oh, yes, my lord and master!" she said in her gentleman's voice, a little too loudly. "Please, oh, please don't tie me up and have your wicked way with me again!"

"Awright. That's it!" Uglow's heavy tread carried away from the door.

Tristan stabbed a finger in Phaedra's direction. "You. Will. Be. *Quiet.*"

Then he slammed the door behind him.

A quarter-hour later, with Uglow somewhat mollified, Tristan returned, the robe wrapped tight about his waist, to find fresh water in the basin, and a damp towel tossed over the wash stand. Phaedra was sitting up, her hair tidied, and wearing her brother's shirt.

"I am very angry with you," he said, slamming the door. "Your reputation could be in tatters right now."

She looked at him and grinned. "Nonsense," she said, "and you know it. By now you will have persuaded him that I am some insatiable, faithless wife out on a lark behind her husband's back."

Tristan felt his face heat. That was, in fact, precisely what he'd told Uglow. Not that Uglow quite believed it, for the old boy had a nose for trouble. But he did believe, at least, that Tristan was bedding a female, which was a damned good thing considering Uglow's prudish notions. Over the years, Tristan had come to depend upon the chap pretty thoroughly.

He shucked the robe, sluiced cold water down his face with both hands, then hastily bathed. The intimacy of it — Phaedra in his bed, him striding about stark naked, and the two of them sniping at one another just a little — all of it felt perfectly natural. Comfortable. Seductively so.

She felt it, too, he sensed. Bedcovers pulled up to her chin, Phaedra watched him towel off his chest and groin with a warm, appreciative gaze, but with a casualness which suggested they did this every day of the week. Despite his frustration, it was an oddly comforting notion.

He tossed down the towel and returned to bed.

"Well, we are even, Tristan," she said, falling back into a pile of pillows. "I came here angry with you."

"Aye, you were." Tristan crawled between the sheets, weary. "I'm sorry for it, but I daresay it won't be the last time."

At that, she looked at him strangely. He lay back down, but she did not. Instead, she sat up, folding and refolding the hem of the coverlet, her brow in a faint knot.

Now, ordinarily, this was the point at which Tristan would deliberately drowse off to sleep, and hope his lover's gratitude would outweigh whatever she was about to scold him for. If that didn't work, he usually rolled out of bed and pled a forgotten engagement. But he was beginning to fear his running days might be coming to a precipitous end. Ah, well. There was nothing else for it. He rolled back to face her, and took her hand.

"What is it, Phae?" he murmured, planting a kiss atop her fingers.

She trembled on the verge of some uncertainty. Then finally, she spoke, blurting out the words. "Why did you not come to tea, Tristan?" she demanded, her low, warm voice uncharacteristically unsteady. "Was the prospect so very dreadful?"

For a moment, he weighed what to tell her. But they were beyond prevarication, he supposed. "I spent much of that afternoon with your brother," he admitted.

"Regarding the puzzle ball." Her voice was impatient. "Yes, I heard."

"And afterward, we . . . well, we spoke of you. He explained some things to me."

"What are you saying?" Phaedra looked at him, incredulous. "That Stefan warned you away from me?"

Tristan averted his eyes. "He warned me not to hurt you," he whispered. "And given who I am, it was not an unreasonable request."

Her lips had gone white with anger. "Oh, it wasn't a request, it was a *threat,*" she said, her hands fisting in the coverlet she'd so neatly folded. "I know Stefan. I shall throttle him. I swear it."

"Phae, love, he was right." Gently, Tristan caught one hand, and smoothed out her fingers with this own. "I might hurt you. God knows I'd never wish to. But my life has hardly been one of sober rectitude. My reputation, as your brother so tactfully put, has little to recommend it. And now this business I must settle for my father — it might not end well."

Some of the anger went out of her then. "What do you mean to do?" she asked. "Tristan, what is going on? Your father is dead. And whatever you are about, it is far more than a murder investigation. Even *I* have figured out that much."

He kissed the back of her hand again, and drew her back against him, cupping his body about hers. "I promised my father to see this through," he said, brushing his lips down her neck. "And I mean to do it. But you, Phae — much as it pains me, I think you should go home now. Before you're missed."

She cut a sidelong glance at him, as if measuring his reaction. "Oh, we still have some things to talk about, Tristan," she said. "Besides, Mamma and Phee have gone to Richmond, and I gave half the servants two days off — not that they'd dare question me. Agnes will make my excuses if trouble turns up."

He exhaled slowly, and considered it. He had little doubt she'd covered her tracks pretty thoroughly. "You must be mad, Phae," he said, brushing his lips over her cheek. "And I am weak. Too weak to do what's right, and send you packing."

She turned, and wiggled her rear against his groin, tucking herself spoonlike against him. "Please, let us just have this, Tristan," she whispered. "For a few more minutes, may we not just pretend?"

But pretend what? Inexplicably, he burned to know what was in her mind. How odd when, mere moments ago, he'd wished to avoid it.

But Phaedra did not say, and he had not the heart to ask. Instead, he circled one arm about her, and set the palm of his hand on the slight swell of her belly. It reminded him yet again of his reaction this afternoon upon seeing her. Of the foolish assumption he'd leapt to — and it had been, disconcertingly, a little more than an assumption. God help him, for one fleeting instant, he had felt *hope.*

He let his eyes roll heavenward at the thought. He had always been inordinately careful in that regard. And yet he had not been careful with her. Five times he'd made love to her, and only once had he taken even the slightest of precautions. If he wanted to bring down Lord Nash's wrath, and ruin Phaedra's life, he could scarce have chosen a better method.

Except that Phaedra believed herself barren. She had come to him an innocent, but not a virgin, so he had known there was a tragedy in it somewhere. But perhaps the tragedy was worse than he'd first imagined. He rolled up onto his elbow a little, and kissed the turn of her shoulder, his hand still stroking, wondering at what her life had been like, and feeling something pluck painfully at his heart.

Phaedra felt Tristan's hand circling her belly, and with it, the pendulous weight of unspoken words. She cut an uncertain glance up at him. "What is it?"

She was soon to wish she had not asked. He held her gaze watchfully for a long moment. "Phae, who was he?" he finally whispered. "Can you tell me?"

She knew, of course, what he asked. But just for an instant, she closed her eyes and let herself pretend she did not. But before she could speak, he did. "No." His voice was sharp. He fell back onto the mattress, striping away his warmth and comfort. "Christ, I'm sorry. Forget that. I have no right — and, today, of all days . . . I'm sorry, Phae."

She rolled over to look at him, her gaze drifting over his haunting brown eyes and that full, sensuous mouth. "I understand," she murmured. "You are curious about my first lover." But even as she spoke it, she hated the word. Even now it chilled her.

Tristan set the back of his hand to her cheek. "None of this matters to me, Phae," he said quietly. "I don't need to hear it."

She shot him a chiding glance. "Two lies, Tristan, one on the heels of the other," she murmured. "I know what you said earlier — in the sitting room — what you accused me of. But I trust you. I do. I might be a fool again . . . but I do not think so."

"What do you mean?"

But Phaedra had made up her mind. If Tristan wished to ruin her, he already possessed enough ammunition. "His name was Edward," she began, lying down on her shoulder to face him. "And I shan't tell you his last name, for it ceased to matter long ago."

He threaded a hand gently through the hair at her temple.

She plunged on. "I'm telling you not because you asked," she said, setting a finger to his lips. "But because I wish to. You said, Tristan, that I did not trust myself. Sexually, I mean. And I think that might be true."

"All right. Go on." He squeezed her hand.

Phaedra nodded, closed her eyes, and let herself remember. That year was fixed in her mind, as deep and as permanent as the etchings on a gravestone. "Edward came down to Brierwood for the summer," she began, as if she'd rehearsed it a thousand times. "He was an acquaintance of Tony's from Oxford. It was the year my father died."

"So you knew him?"

"No, but I found him fascinating," she admitted. "Of course, I was, by all accounts, a strange girl. Bored, and too bookish, I daresay, for my own good. Edward and Tony talked so passionately of the things that interested me — of history and philosophy, and of politics — not fashion or furbelows like Mamma and Phee."

He smiled gently. "And so you fell in love?"

Had she? Phaedra was no longer sure. "I was infatuated with him, in the way foolish girls often are with beautiful blond men," she said. "I had read too much poetry, I daresay. And he . . . he flattered me with his attentions. Mamma and Tony thought it charming."

"Your mother hoped, perhaps, for a match between you?"

Again, she could not hold his gaze. "Mamma imagined he thought of me as a younger sister," she murmured. "Her attention was absorbed by Phoebe. Phoebe would not apply herself to her studies, and the governess despaired of her."

"And so you were the good girl?" said Tristan quietly. "The one who could be counted upon to do the right thing?"

"Yes."

"And then he broke off the courtship?" said Tristan, as if trying to make it easier for her. "I am so sorry, Phae. He was a fool, though it is a story old as time itself, I suppose."

"No, he did not break it, precisely." She closed her eyes. "Tony went back to London to stand for Commons, so Edward left. And I was too stupid to know what had happened. That I had conceived a child."

His hand reached out to touch her face uncertainly. "Phae, Tony was two years ahead of me at school." She could hear realization dawning in his voice. "And he was standing for Commons? How . . . how old are you?"

She knew where this was going. Subtraction was no great task. "I shall be two-and-twenty next month," she answered.

A dark emotion sketched across his face. "Phae," he whispered. "Phae, how old were you then?"

She turned her head and gazed at the dressing table which sat by the window.

"Fifteen," she whispered. "I had just turned fifteen."

Tristan sat up and turned toward her. "And he was a grown man," he said, brushing his knuckles down her cheek. "Oh, my poor girl."

A sour smile curved her mouth. "Edward was not a man," she said. "He was a reptile in a well-cut suit. But I was too sheltered to know it. I was so naïve, Tristan, I did not even grasp *what I had done* with him. What I had *given up.*"

"Phae." He smoothed both hands down her face, a cool, gentle caress, and she began to tremble. "Phae, love, did he force you?"

"No." She shook her head. "*I let him.* Because I loved him so much — or believed I did. Papa was gone, Stefan lived in London, and I . . . I just liked that someone paid attention to me."

"Christ," Tristan whispered.

But Phae pushed on. "That summer we read together in the gardens, and Mamma let him teach me to waltz, and I believed — oh, Tristan, I believed myself in heaven. He would even play battledore with me. Can you imagine? He . . . he began to kiss me when no one was looking. Then one night, he slipped into my room. He said that if I loved him, I must prove it. So I let him do what he wanted. More than once. And . . . I wanted it, too. Even then, I think I wanted it — or I wanted *him,* at least. That is not force, is it?"

"No," he gritted. "That is a lamb being left unprotected from a rapacious wolf. How old was that bastard?"

"Twenty-three," she confessed.

She could see the horror of it sickened him. He dragged a hand through his hair. "Your mother must have been heartsick."

Phaedra's hand lashed out, seizing his arm. "Mamma does not know," she whispered. "And no one, Tristan, must ever tell her. *Not ever.*"

Tristan looked at her incredulously. "What do you mean, *she does not know?*"

Phaedra searched for the right words to explain the emotional tangle that was her mother. "Mamma is a good person," she began. "But she is little more than a child herself, Tristan. She is just not terribly bright. I don't mean that to sound unkind, but her priorities are — well, though Stefan loves her, he calls her a pretty featherbrain."

"I am sorry," said Tristan stiffly. "But still, Phae, how could she *not* know?"

"Because I did not tell her," said Phaedra insistently. "I didn't even know the words to use. I was that ignorant, Tristan. Finally, my governess noticed my figure rounding."

Tristan was still reeling with the ugliness of it. "Phae, I am so sorry." He had hoped, he supposed, the tale would take a less tragic turn, but he had known in his heart it would not. "What did she do?"

"Stefan was my guardian, and her employer," said Phaedra quietly. "She was terrified, of course. But she wrote to him with her fears. And Stefan knew there was no point in telling Mamma. She would have shattered quite utterly."

"You were but an innocent," Tristan whispered again, his gaze turned inward. "Far too young to be wed."

She flashed a withering smile. "By then I was five months gone," she said. "Those hideous empire waists . . . And there was no question of marriage. Edward had made off with a coal heiress from Northumberland — a girl richer, even, than I. Mamma read it to us from the *Times* over breakfast one morning, not knowing . . ."

The pain was still stark in her eyes. And given Lord Nash's reputation, Tristan could easily guess what happened next. "Did Nash kill him?"

Phaedra wrapped her arms around her chest. "Not quite," she whispered. "I begged him not to — not for Stefan's sake, but for

Edward's. Because I still thought I loved him. Pathetic, isn't it?"

"Oh, Phae." Tristan lifted a hand and tucked a tendril of hair behind her ear. "My poor girl."

Phaedra managed a faint smile. "Stefan came straight down to Brierwood first, of course," she went on. "And announced I was to go abroad with my Aunt Henslow. She has always been more a mother to Mamma than a sister. So Aunt Henslow took me to France — a little holiday, Stefan told Mamma."

"What did they tell you?"

"That Aunt Henslow would . . . take care of things," she said. "Stefan left it to her — he was quite beyond himself with grief and rage, and wanted only to get his hands round Edward's throat. He said later — and I believe him — that he did not quite grasp what Aunt Henslow meant to do."

"What . . . did she do?"

Phaedra shrugged. "I thought, foolishly, that I would have the child," she said, "and that it would be . . . I don't know . . . taken somewhere safe? But when the doctor came to our flat in Paris, he said I was not quite six months along . . . and then he did something to me."

"Christ Jesus," he said again.

"And it did not go well." This time, her voice cracked pathetically, and her face with it. "I had a little girl, Tristan," she said through welling tears. "The loveliest, most beautiful little girl. They thought, you know, I was too addled to comprehend, that I would not remember seeing her."

"Phae, shush, shush," he cooed, dragging her into his arms.

"But I did see her, Tristan," she cried against his chest. "She was scarcely a babe at all, and she did not breathe, and so they took her away, and I do not know what became of her. *I do not know what became of her,* do you understand? She had fingers and ink-black hair, but she did not make a sound, and I kept thinking — *cry, cry, and they will have to give you to me!* But she just lay there in the doctor's hand, still as death. And then they just took her away."

"Oh, Phae." He rocked her, his lips pressed to her hair, and tried not to cry with her. "Oh, my poor, poor girl."

"They still won't tell me where she is." Her voice was barely audible through the sobs now. "I know, of course, that she is dead. They caused her to come too soon. I know that now. But I didn't understand it then. I thought that every child should have its mother, or at least know that it was loved and wanted. I had believed someday we would be together. Instead, I fear, they buried her in some pauper's grave."

If that, thought Tristan grimly. Likely the child had been thrown out with the evening's rubbish. "I am sure, Phae, that they gave her a lovely service," he lied. "I am sure she is very much at peace."

"Do you think so?" But there was no hope in her voice. "I don't remember very much after that. I became deathly ill, and Aunt Henslow was terrified. When the fever finally broke, the doctor told us I was . . . damaged somehow. Scars, he said, from the infection. Aunt Henslow cried, and asked if I could still have children, and he said it was highly unlikely. That I should go home, and make a quiet life for myself. And so that's what I did. Until Millie ran away, and left Priss behind."

Tristan drew a hand down her hair, his chest tight with grief. This was what Nash had referred to; the thing which had left the anguish — and perhaps even that hint of rage — in his eyes. *Fragile as spun glass,* he had said. Dear God. Tristan was beginning to grasp the horrifying depth of this obsession Phae had with Priss, and with finding the child's missing mother.

"Phae, I hope we find Millie," he said

softly. "But reuniting one mother and child . . . well, it won't reunite *you* with your daughter. I'm sorry. Tell me you understand that."

"I understand," she said, her voice rising. "I am not such a fool, Tristan, as all that. I understand my own motivations. My own *heart.*"

"Why then?" he pleaded.

"Because Priss is my flesh and blood." Phaedra's voice was tremulous with emotion. "And because Millie does not understand the terrible price she will pay for what she has done. *I do.* She is too naïve, Tristan, to know how this will haunt her. She needs to be there for her child. To keep Priss safe. *She has that choice,* Tristan. The choice which was taken from me."

But she might not have a choice in this, either, Tristan considered. Millie quite likely knew exactly what she had done, and probably didn't care. On the other hand, there was a chance — a slight chance — that the girl was the naïve village innocent Phaedra so clearly believed her. In which case . . . dear God.

"What happened, Phae, to the man who abused you?" he asked. "What did Nash do?"

She flicked an uncertain glance up at him.

"Thrashed him half to death with a horse-whip," she said. "But I'm not supposed to know."

"A horsewhipping was but half what he deserved," Tristan gritted.

Phaedra snuffled, and dashed her wrist across her eyes. "And then Stefan went down to Oxford, and thrashed Tony," she added. "He said Tony had brought a vile scourge into his home, and that Tony was as responsible as Edward for what happened to me."

"Well," said Tristan slowly, "I don't see a flaw in that logic."

But her eyes held a quiet grief now, the tears and the anger gone. "For better than a year, Tony kept his distance," she whispered. "Mamma knew, of course, that they had quarreled over something. She began to cry over it, heartsick, and finally Stefan relented. Not too long after that, Tony married Jenny. But that didn't work out so well, either."

Tristan was beginning to wonder if Tony hadn't got what he'd deserved. He remembered Mrs. Hayden-Worth vaguely, for she'd run with a fast, dangerous crowd. "So Edward lives in Northumberland with his rich bride and nothing worse than a few scars on his arse, savoring his wife's money," he said grimly. "God's truth, there is no justice in this world."

"A little, actually," she said. "When I was eighteen, Edward got caught in the schoolroom with his wife's niece. That rich father-in-law of his shot him through the heart — but it was hushed up."

Tristan felt his fists relax. "So how do you know?"

"Stefan told me." She gave a withering smile. "He thought it might make me feel better, I daresay. I don't know how he learnt of it, nor do I wish to." .

Tristan rolled toward her and tucked one arm under his head, uncertain what next to say. His first instinct — to promise he'd kill the bastard who'd done this to her — was futile now. His second — to hold her in his arms and pledge her a lifetime of security and happiness — was just about as irrational.

He settled for simply holding her, tucking her spine to his chest, and wrapping his body protectively about hers. Quietly, he kissed her, just below the ear on that soft, perfect pulse-point that so often caught his gaze. "What will you do, love, when all this is over?" he asked, half afraid of her answer. "When your Millie is restored to you, and you can give up your Mrs. Thompson and your trousers and all your reluctant forays into society?"

Phaedra turned her head, and cast her gaze up to the ceiling. "Go home, I hope," she said. "Back to Brierwood."

He gazed at her pensively for a time, then lifted his hand and stroked a finger over her face, memorizing the lines of it. "Lady Phaedra Northampton," he murmured, drawing his finger down to the tip of her nose. "I'm going to miss you when you're gone."

She laughed, a forced, light sound. "Oh, not for long, I daresay."

He picked up one of her long, chestnut curls and wrapped it round his index finger again. "What is it, Phae, that you miss so much? Why couldn't you linger in Town awhile? I should love nothing better, I think, than to go to one of those elegant society balls and waltz you round beneath your brother's nose."

She wriggled partway onto her side and looked at him. "I miss Priscilla," she said in a voice of quiet confession. "Oh, Tristan, she is the sweetest child ever. Fat, still, like a little cherub, you know? With pink apple cheeks and a little bow mouth and a laugh — sometimes an ear-splitting shriek, actually — that just warms your heart. Every day, Agnes and I walk to the village to play with her."

"I suppose I can understand that." His smile softened, and he drew her onto his shoulder. "Well, just rest in my arms for a little while, Phae, and dream of Priss. You will be back in Hampshire soon enough."

"Just for a little while?" she echoed, a hint of petulance in her tone.

He laughed. "A very little while," he corrected. "For I've got a hard night ahead. And you need to go home soon. Please."

Of course she ignored him, twisting around in his arms like a restless child. "Why, I have no plans for the evening," she murmured, her eyes searching his face. "What are yours?"

Tristan was instantly wary. "I'm going to Vostrikova's," he admitted. "I've managed to get myself invited to have a look round the place."

"No!" She sat halfway up in bed. "You've gained entry to that house?"

"And I haven't forgotten Millie," he hastily added. "I swear it."

But Phaedra's brow had knotted. "Tristan, what is going on? And don't take me for a fool. Stefan would tell me little about the puzzle ball. But I know this is no longer about a dead Russian in an alleyway — and I suspect it never was."

He toyed with the fraying hem of the coverlet, wondering how much to tell her. He wanted suddenly to unburden himself to her as she had done to him. To offer her at least a little trust, and, if he were honest, to deepen the circle of intimacy which surrounded them.

"No, it never was," he admitted. "Vostrikova is a Russian spy. Has been for years, we think."

Phaedra's eyes widened. "So that's why your father was involved," she whispered. "My word. A spy running a brothel catering to the Government's most powerful — that opens up a whole cesspit of intrigue, doesn't it?"

Tristan smiled at the analogy. "Vostrikova is an expert at exploiting men's weaknesses," he answered. "So I have acquired a few to tempt her."

"What is your plan, precisely?"

"To get in and get out quickly," he admitted. "Or as quickly as I can. Vostrikova has a suite of rooms in an adjoining house. That's where business gets done. The whole place is a rabbit warren, by the way. Not one house, but three, connected up and down, attics to cellars."

"So your aim is to get into her private office," said Phaedra musingly.

"Eventually, yes," he said. "Tonight, I hope."

"To search for what?"

"Correspondence," he said. "Encryption codes. A list of those men whose loyalty to the Crown has been compromised. And I mightn't have time to be subtle. As soon as I'm out, she'll probably know she's been had."

"You'll doubtless need to pick a lock or two," she murmured. "Can you?"

Inwardly, he sighed. Phaedra was quick — too quick for his comfort. "Your Mr. Kemble taught me," he answered. "A clever chap, that one."

Phaedra did not seem surprised by this revelation. Still, something was weighing on her. "Tristan, you do not owe me an answer to this," she finally began. "But I should just like to know . . ."

He cocked his head and studied her. "Yes?"

Her lashes swept down, a tentative, shy gesture. "What if you have to . . . to *do* something whilst you're there?"

He knew at once what she meant. And Phaedra was blushing three shades of pink. This, he had not wished to consider. Oh, when he'd begun this task, he'd assumed that participating in Vostrikova's debauchery would be unavoidable. But that was a sacrifice — a strange choice of words, admittedly — he was no longer willing to make.

"No," he said finally. "I've never availed myself of prostitutes, Phae, and I don't mean to start now."

Her shoulders relaxed, and she looked away. "In any case, you cannot do this alone," she said quietly. "It will be dangerous."

"I won't be alone," he said hastily. "De Vendenheim will have men stationed round back."

She nodded, remarkably cool and composed. "All right," she finally said. "So, who killed Gorsky? And why?"

He cast her an appraising glance. "Vostrikova had him killed," he admitted. "Then she had her assassin garroted. But de Vendenheim and I picked up the second killer three days ago, boarding a ship to Estonia, and he'll talk soon enough. No one else knows save Peel and . . . well, my father did."

"I'm impressed," she murmured. "But that does not explain *why* she did it."

"There is no honor among thieves, Phae," said Tristan, measuring his words. "Gorsky was her henchman, but when they fell out over the boy she'd sent away . . ."

"Revenge is always dangerous." She made a little shooing motion with her fingers. "And — ?"

He lifted one shoulder. "Not long before their quarrel, you had dropped by, bandying about your brother's name, and threatening to bring the full force of the British government down on Gorsky's head, so perhaps he got creative," Tristan admitted. "After their quarrel, he likely saw a way to exact vengeance. Perhaps he'd been following you, wondering if it was safe to approach you."

"He wanted to speak to me," she whispered. "But he hadn't terribly good English."

"And that might be a part of it," Tristan admitted. "The man had no friends, for Vostrikova kept him on a short leash. Perhaps he meant to turn on her, and knew your brother spoke Russian? Or perhaps he merely wished to sell you information? We shall never know. He died before he could speak to you — and we hope Vostrikova knows none of this. Indeed, it is doubtful she does."

Phaedra had gone bloodless. "We?" She pressed a hand to her heart. "Tristan . . . who is *we?*"

This, too, he had hoped to avoid. "De Vendenheim," he confessed. "And me."

"You told him?" Her clutched fist went to her heart. "You told him I'd gone to that house?"

"Phae, what choice did I have?" He opened his hand, palm up. "The more we learned, the more likely it looked. At some point, I had to err on the side of your safely. I told him that you'd been there."

Her gaze was distant, her voice a whisper. "And he has not told my brother." Her knuckles were white now. "Not *yet.*"

"No, and he won't." Tristan caught her hand. "He swore to me, Phae. But I could not leave you exposed. And I could not watch over you myself." *Not all the time,* he silently added.

But he had been watching her, far more often than he wished to admit. And if he had to observe her dash down her front steps in another seductive, low-cut ball gown with Zoë Armstrong laughing on her arm, he was beginning to think he might to have to cut off his own cock, or suffer the inconvenience of a perpetual third leg. The thought of her dancing in another's arms, perhaps meeting someone she might fall in love with . . . he had felt like the greenest lad, but he had burned nonetheless with jealousy.

But Phaedra was still pondering his words. "Exposed?" she asked. "What do you mean, *exposed?*"

"De Vendenheim set someone to keep an eye on you whilst we investigated," he admitted.

"*Spies* — ? Surely you jest?"

"No, *guards.*" Tristan looked at her chidingly. "Your Mr. Kemble, mostly, or one of his henchmen. Uglow once, though he's a hard one to hide. One of them is likely hanging about in Long Acre this minute, if they realized who you were when you left Mayfair."

"In Tony's kit?" She laughed. "Impossible."

Having seen her in disguise, Tristan agreed, but kept silent. There was no point in encouraging bad behavior. Still, she did look awfully fine in trousers . . .

"Besides, I went out through the garden," Phaedra continued, dragging the hair back off her face. "And I've never seen anyone observing me."

"Then they are doing their jobs," said Tristan firmly.

Her worried gaze searched his face. She grasped the seriousness of it, at least. "And you? What have you been doing?"

"I've spent the last weeks cultivating

certain — shall we call them friendships?" he answered. "I have been drinking a little too much, and bragging a bit too loudly about my new Government post and my father's connections. And I have quietly compiled a list of Vostrikova's customers."

Phaedra's eyes widened. "To get you inside."

"That's the plan," he said grimly. "But it's been a near run thing. One does not precisely invite oneself; that would look too suspicious. Now, my dear, I've told you all I'm at liberty to say, and a good deal more. Dress, and I shall ring for Uglow to follow you home."

But Phaedra's brow was still furrowed, and her mind, he could see, was far away. "This is all very interesting," she murmured. "But how does any of it help us find Millie?"

Tristan looked down at her, his arms crossed over his chest. "*Us,* is it now?"

The afternoon sun swirled through the room in a kaleidoscope of fractured light, burnishing her hair and shooting it with gold. Fleetingly, he considered kissing her again to dissuade her from whatever she was about to say. It was useless, of course. She lifted her intelligent gaze to his. "If you found Millie, you could help her escape," she said, her voice perfectly calm. "But you do not know what she looks like."

"Describe her." He forced a tight smile. "Don't leave out a single detail."

She scowled. "I suppose she looks like half the prostitutes in London," she answered. "Young, pretty, and nubile — except that she has red hair. But even that won't narrow it down much."

Phaedra obviously hadn't met many of London's fair nightingales, not to mention the uprighters working the East End. "How tall is she?" Tristan persisted. "What color are her eyes?"

Phaedra looked at him askance. "They're prostitutes, Tristan," she said. "They won't be taking tea in the drawing room, and you can scarcely take time to go knocking on doors. You already said you may have to get in and get out quickly."

Tristan didn't deny it. And it wasn't that he didn't wish to help Phaedra, he did. He'd simply never believed Millie much of a victim. She hadn't been snatched from her own village, as so many of the younger girls were. Millie had gone looking for trouble. On the other hand, Vostrikova had been known to hold women captive, and even to sell them into what amounted to sexual slavery. The knowledge troubled him.

Phaedra leaned across the bed. "Tristan,

this may end up like a kettle with its lid blown off," she said. "If this goes badly — if Vostrikova knows she's been compromised — we shan't get another chance. She'll be on the next boat bound for the Continent, and those girls will be scattered to the four winds or worse. And I will *never* forgive myself."

But *I will never forgive you* was what she meant. And she had a point. Tristan scrubbed a hand across the stubble of his beard and considered it. Good God, one prostitute in a house with perhaps two dozen, and a suite of rooms which would need a thorough pilfering . . .

Phaedra sensed his vacillation. "Please, Tristan." Her voice was low and tremulous now. "Perhaps Millie seems like a small concern to the Government, but to me *she is everything.* Priss needs a mother. Now, are you going to help me? Or must I go back to doing it on my own?"

He answered with icy certainty. "Out of the question."

"Tristan." She eyed him very deliberately. "Do not patronize me. You are not my master."

"There's always the silk rope." He eyed her grimly. "That seems to tame you down just a tad."

"You sliced it to bits with your knife," she retorted, setting her head at a stubborn angle. "More fool you. Now, about Millie?"

Slowly, he exhaled. "All right," he finally said. "I will find out what's happened to her. I swear it, Phae — and I don't promise what I cannot deliver."

"You need to *find* her," she gently pressed. "Or find out where she was taken. And to do it, you're going to need someone to go in with you. Someone who can poke about and ask questions whilst you slip downstairs."

He had known, of course, it would come to this. "I was invited alone," he said. "I'm not sure Vostrikova will welcome anyone else."

"Oh, I think she might." Phaedra was clearly thinking out loud now. "By now she will have heard your father is terribly ill."

"Aye, the doctor ordered his staff out on Wednesday," said Tristan grimly. "And today the house is shut up. Tomorrow we'll have to announce it."

"But there's been a Lord Hauxton somewhere in the Foreign Office for the last century," Phaedra reminded him with a smile. "And then there is your infallible charm. That package will prove irresistible to Madame Vostrikova. She is a woman who lays long-term plans, I'll wager."

Tristan, of course, already knew all this. He was surprised, however, at how quickly Phaedra grasped it. "Very well, I shall take someone," he finally agreed. "One of de Vendenheim's chaps will have to do."

Phaedra smiled dotingly. "Thank you, Tristan," she said. "But none of them knows what Millie looks like. And I rather doubt, frankly, that they can pass for the sort of gentlemen Vostrikova entertains."

This time Tristan dragged both hands through his hair. He already knew where this was going. Fleetingly, he considered locking her in the house, and setting Uglow to watch her. But that made him little better, perhaps, than Vostrikova. And Phaedra was not a fool.

"Draw a sketch," he said hastily. "I'll fetch you paper and pencil now."

"I think that's risky." Gently, she took his hand in hers, lifted it to her lips, then, with a neat little jerk, snatched the gold signet ring from his pinkie finger.

"Phae — !"

With a sweet smile, she slid it onto the third finger of her right hand, then held it up in the shaft of afternoon light. "I always wanted to be a Talbot," she declared. "I think I shall be Harold, your first cousin."

He lifted both brows and shot her a dark look. "I quite loathe my family," he said. "And they loathe me."

"But you are about to inherit, my lord." She turned the ring this way and that, admiring the way it caught the sun. "All is generally forgiven in such cases."

He sighed. "Do I even have a cousin Harold?"

She tossed him a disdainful glance. "You dare to doubt Lady Phaedra's exhaustive knowledge of Debrett's?" she asked haughtily. "Harold is Uncle Tobias's eldest."

"Aye?" His glower deepened. "Go on."

"They live in Wiltshire, near your seat, and not far from Hampshire." She lowered the ring and smiled. "Unfortunately, they don't come up to Town very often. Still, young Harold is of an age where a lad might like to taste a little of the city's sin. And a doting elder cousin might oblige him."

His mouth twisted sourly. "No doubt."

"And if you should ever perish, God forbid, of one of those dread diseases the girls at Vostrikova's pass round," she said brightly, "young Harold — most conveniently — will become heir apparent. So I am sure Vostrikova would love to make his acquaintance, too."

Tristan sighed. The frightening thing was,

Phaedra was quite probably capable of pulling it off. And he would much rather go in with her than without her. She was perfectly capable of thinking on her feet, and might well prove an asset. But if something went wrong, he'd kill himself. Assuming Phaedra's brother didn't get to him first.

"Phae, love, it's just not safe. And — God's truth, the debauchery — no lady should be subjected to such filth."

She lifted one shoulder in a casual, effortless motion. "Better I should go with you than on my own, as I did last time," she answered. "Besides, as you have already observed, I am hardly a demure innocent. I rather doubt that place will shock me."

"Love, this will go far beyond any bed games you and I might play," he cautioned. "But more importantly, what if I cannot protect you?"

"Tristan, you *can*," she pressed. "But you shan't need to. You'll be downstairs doing the dangerous work, and providing a distraction. I'll slip out the back to Kemble's men. Now, just listen. I have a plan, and it's a good one."

"I was afraid of that," he answered. "Does it include our hiring the services of a redhead for the night?"

Phaedra's eyes widened. "Oh, at the very

least," she answered innocently. "Frankly, I'd suggest we hire two or three. This is a big night for Cousin Harold. I'm not sure he'll wish to share."

CHAPTER 12

I will wear my heart upon my sleeve
For daws to peck at.

Owing to the cloudless day and a stiff breeze, the stars made a rare appearance that evening, coming out to wink over London like a spattering of tiny jewels. But it took Phaedra another several hours of threats and outright begging to bend Tristan to her will, and another thirty minutes for her to twist her hair up snugly enough to permit the wig to be pulled back on.

When that was done to his satisfaction, Tristan made her practice her walk, her voice, her hand gestures, then he sat her back down and begged her again to give it all up.

But the truth was, she looked like a young English blueblood just down from Cambridge, all coltish legs and sullen disdain, projecting that quintessential air of aristocratic entitlement — a parody, perhaps, of her youngest brother at that age. And after all, it was his suit.

When she refused to capitulate to Tristan's final entreaties, as he'd known from the first she would, he sighed and rolled out the rough floor plan of Vostrikova's houses, sketched from what little information he'd managed to elicit from tradesmen and patrons. And through it all, he wished Millie the tavern maid to the devil.

This undertaking was not safe; he knew that. But he knew, too, the awful pain in her eyes, and the desperate need to make things right when something in your life had gone horribly wrong. That burning wish to expiate one's sins, real or imagined. It was a part of what had driven him from Greece as a young man. The carnage and the hopelessness, and the knowledge that he had not the power to repair it — nor even hinder it — no matter what he did. So Tristan had drowned his guilt in apathy. Numbed himself with licentious living. Phaedra, however, had chosen a different path.

Yes, in her heart, Phaedra believed that helping this child *would* change things; would somehow bring her life aright again. And if she felt, in even the smallest of ways, that this might atone in her heart for the child they had taken from her, who was he to say it would not? Yes, it was irrational. But the heart, he was beginning to understand, so often was.

Out of an abundance of caution, Tristan sent Phaedra out the front with instructions to go round the block and into the alley which skirted the rear of his house. They would make their way to Vostrikova's on foot, through the back lanes.

After counting off three minutes, impatient and on edge, he went down the back stairs and out into what passed for a garden. He saw her there, a lean, willowy form waiting by the gatepost, the feeble lamplight of the stable opposite casting a faint glow about her feet.

He picked his way through the dark, past the dustbins and outbuildings, silent and unseen. For a moment, he watched her, the passions and whispered secrets of the afternoon they had passed in each other's arms still sweet and heavy in his heart. And it occurred to him that this might be their last moment alone; if by some miracle Phaedra found her tavern maid tonight, she might hasten back to Hampshire.

He wanted, suddenly and desperately, to kiss her one last time. But when he reached out through the gloom to touch her, everything altered in an instant. Something lashed about his throat. A cord. *A garrote.* A vise-like arm whipped out of the dark. On a strangled cry, Tristan found himself hauled hard against something immobile, spun about, then hurled face-first into the weeds, a knee rammed hard against his spine.

"Tristan!" Phaedra's voice was harsh. "Stop! Unhand him!" He heard the sound of her kicking someone as he clawed at the choking garrote.

"Ouch! What?" His assailant's voice rasped in the gloom. "It's *Avoncliffe?*"

"Yes! Let him up!" Phaedra demanded.

"What the devil?" His assailant's knee relented and the garrote relaxed. Blood surging, Tristan forced his attacker off, rolled, and came up swinging. His fist whistled through the air, just an inch from Kemble's nose.

Phaedra thrust out a hand. "Wait! Stop!"

Tristan glared into the gloom, and spat out a curse. "Good God, man! Are you trying to kill me?"

Kemble bent, and in one smooth motion, picked up Tristan's walking stick, tossing it to him. "If I were trying to kill you, my lord," he said quietly, "you would be dead now."

Tristan snatched the stick from midair,

something in the man's voice sending a shiver down his spine. The mincing dandy was gone, and in his place was someone altogether more threatening. But Tristan was not easily intimidated. "Then what the hell *are* you doing?"

"Keeping her safe, you idiot." Kemble's gaze swept Phaedra as if she were a piece of his fine porcelain.

"Not from *me,* for God's sake!" Tristan bent down and snatched up his hat.

Kemble smiled and brushed a bit of grass from his sleeve. "Now, I wonder, Avoncliffe — would her brother share that view?" he mused. "Tell me, what have you naughty boys been up to all day?"

Heat flooded Tristan's face. He stabbed a finger toward Long Acre. "Have you been out there all afternoon?"

"*And* all night," said Kemble, tossing them a knowing glance. "Until about three minutes ago."

"You followed me." Phaedra sounded breathless.

"I did." Kemble was shooting his cuffs back into place. "And if Avoncliffe here had been the rear-attacking, stick-wielding assailant he looked to be, both of you would be kissing my boots for it right about now."

Tristan felt the fight go out of him then.

"You are right, of course. I am sure my approach in the dark looked like something altogether different than it was."

"It looked rather as if you were about to press your attentions on an innocent, unmarried, gently-bred young lady," said Kemble. "Perhaps even lure her into your home — or your *bed* — for some sort of nefarious high jinks. Thank God I was *entirely* mistaken."

Tristan did not miss the acidity in his tone.

"Mr. Kemble, really!" Phaedra drew herself up very straight.

"I, however," Kemble continued, undeterred, "am willing to listen with an open mind." Here, he flashed a lupine smile at Phaedra. "My lady?"

"With all respect, Kemble," she said quietly, "it really isn't any of your business."

Tristan hitched Phaedra to his side. "You may congratulate me, Kemble," he said tightly. "This afternoon, Lady Phaedra made me the happiest man on earth —"

"Yes, that's what I was afraid of."

"— and generously consented to be my wife."

Lady Phaedra drew away in horror. "Good God. *Tristan.*"

Kemble sighed deeply. "Oh, spare me the theatrics, Avoncliffe." He extracted a silver snuff box, smooth as a cat in the dark, and languidly deposited a dainty pinch on the back of his hand. "I would not wish a wedding to you on my worst enemy. Just tell me what's going on here."

Phaedra sagged with relief, and something sharp pierced Tristan's heart. "I'm on my way to Vostrikova's as we'd planned," he snapped.

Kemble took his snuff, then looked up. *"And — ?"* he said leadingly.

"And I'm going, too," said Phaedra, her chin rising.

Kemble flicked a dark glance at her. "I trust, my dear, that you know what you are about?" he murmured. "It is a vile, dangerous place. You're quick-witted enough, God knows. Still, your reasoning today, on any number of issues, quite escapes me."

Swiftly, Phaedra drew Kemble deeper into the shadows, and explained.

"Ah," said Kemble when she was done. "And who is the father of this child, I wonder."

"Not," said Phaedra darkly, *"Stefan.* And that is all I shall tell you, Kem."

Kemble was silent for a moment. "Well, well," he said quietly. "Mr. Hayden-Worth's tastes are more varied than I'd have guessed."

Phaedra actually cursed beneath her breath. "I *never* said the babe was his."

In the gloom, Kemble tossed his hand, once again the consummate dandy. "My dear girl, I am the soul of discretion," he answered. "Far be it for me to question what a man does after dark — or who he does it with. Now, how did you plan this joint assault on Vostrikova's bastion of perfidy?"

"Much as you and I discussed with de Vendenheim," said Tristan. Swiftly he explained what Phaedra would do. When he was done, he hesitated. "Do you think, Kemble, that she will be safe?"

Again, Kemble's quick glance flicked over her. "So long as she doesn't mind Vostrikova's muck on her shoes, yes," he answered, bending over to tug something from his boot. "Lady Phaedra is no one's fool."

Tristan exhaled with relief.

Until Kemble pressed the pistol into her hand.

In Soho, they were admitted through the rear, then escorted to the front of the house where Madame Vostrikova kept her private rooms. They were shown upstairs to a sitting room to find their hostess awaiting them on the landing. After a perfunctory introduction, her dark eyes looked Phaedra over, only the slightest flicker betraying her annoyance.

"Welcome," she said, "to my humble establishment." Then Madame Vostrikova linked her arm with Tristan's and strolled with them up the remaining stairs, fluttering her lashes like a thin, aging coquette.

The woman, Phaedra thought, was perfectly chilling. Ice-blond hair contrasted dramatically with the shimmering black silk of her gown, and she put one in mind of a straight razor, glistening with danger, ready to lay open one's throat at the slightest provocation.

She was, however, a flawless hostess with manners that would have done a countess proud. "Let me offer you a glass of my very best wine," she said, going at once to the sideboard. "It comes from my private vineyard in Bordeaux, and is reserved for only my most special guests."

"What an intriguing establishment you have created here, Madame." Phaedra watched as Tristan held his wineglass aloft with a studied languor, the pink liquid swirling above his long, thin fingers. As he had done since their arrival, he surveyed their hostess like a tomcat eyeing a bowl of cream, and wondering whether to trouble himself to lick it up.

Madame Vostrikova set down her crystal decanter, and turned from the sideboard. "I am delighted, my lord, at your interest."

"Interest is, perhaps, too mild a word," said Tristan. "Cousin Harold and I could not be better pleased. This wine, by the way, is excellent."

"*Spasiba,* my lord." Madame had settled into a chair opposite, studying them both from beneath hooded eyes. "You will find I offer my patrons only the very best of pleasures — both sensual and otherwise."

"They do say you are a woman of extraordinary discernment, Madame." Tristan's square, flawless teeth were white against his skin as he smiled over his glass. "What, precisely, do you call this?"

Madame Vostrikova preened just a trifle. "It is a claret, my lord," she answered. "But of a traditional sort — thus its pale color — scented with anise and cardamom. A far cry from that bland rubbish the French try to sell us nowadays."

Phaedra took another sip, her eyes running over the dark, elegant sitting room. The walls were hung with a deep blue silk, the furniture faintly Asiatic in style, and on the whole, it looked to have cost a small fortune. So far, nothing about Vostrikova's establishment resembled anything remotely like a brothel, or what Phaedra had imagined a brothel might look like.

"What do you think of my special claret, Mr. Talbot?" Madame Vostrikova asked.

Phaedra feigned a look of aristocratic boredom. "I like it well enough, thank you," she said, dropping her voice an octave, "but I should prefer something darker and more full-bodied — a redhead with large breasts, perhaps? That is, after all, what we came for."

Suddenly, Vostrikova's eyes sparkled with malice. "Indeed?"

Tristan severed the mood with a hearty laugh. "Ah, the impatience of youth, Madame," he said with a dismissive wave of his glass. "I fear Harold has not yet learnt to temper his appetites."

"Has he not?" said Vostrikova, eyeing Phaedra watchfully. "A wiser man might know how to savor that which is offered him."

"Precisely so." Tristan grinned. "Perhaps you have a young mistress who specializes in such disciplines? Someone who might teach the poor lad . . . well, shall we call it *patience?*"

The madam returned her languid gaze to Tristan's. "*Da,* my lord," the woman purred. "Anticipation is half the pleasure. But frankly, I did not expect Mr. Talbot. His visit is . . . most extraordinary."

"Ah, I understand completely, Madame!" Tristan set his wineglass on the elegant marquetry table by his chair, his every move speaking of blithe indolence. "Perhaps we should take up no more of your time."

For the first time, Madame's expression faltered a trifle. "Already, you must go?"

Tristan opened one hand. "It might be best," he said smoothly. "I have promised Harold here a night of debauchery, and I should hate him to be disappointed. After all, I have my reputation as the family sybarite to maintain."

Madame Vostrikova rose gracefully with Tristan. "You will come again, I hope, my lord?" The word *alone* remained unspoken.

Phaedra shot Tristan a scornful glance. "Devil take you, Cuz," she uttered, jerking to her feet. "I thought you said this was a prime place for a bit of sport!"

Tristan ignored her, smiling seductively at their hostess. "I should like to call again, of course, Madame," he said, leaning very near. "Regrettably, my new duties in the Foreign Office grow more pressing by the day."

Her sharp, angular brows flew aloft. "How sorry I am to hear it."

Tristan threw back his head and laughed. "As am I, Madame," he said. "I begin to quite long for my old life as an utter wastrel. Instead, at my father's insistence, I shall be going abroad for a few weeks."

"But this is dreadful news!"

Tristan shrugged. "Alas, I must go," he complained. "Otherwise, Hauxton has threatened to cut off my allowance. I fear my father finds me a bit too indolent and self-absorbed for his taste."

"Ah, well," said Madame. "You will travel to someplace exciting, I hope?"

Tristan hesitated. "To Warsaw," he finally answered. "There is unrest in Poland, and my father wishes me to go there in his stead, and press Great Britain's interests with their government. Indeed, he has written down every word I am to say — as if I haven't a thought in my own head."

"Has he?" said Madame, her eyes gleaming. "Then I hope they are very clever words?"

Again Tristan laughed. "Madame, you are too kind," he said. "I would not dare bore so great a courtesan as yourself with my father's dull state secrets. Come, Harold, fetch your stick and your hat. We have taken up quite enough of Madame's time."

Madame Vostrikova paused, frowning, her

hand on the door. Tristan, Phaedra realized, had played her like a professional sharper, whilst looking like the witless, pretty face Phaedra had once believed him.

Phaedra struck a petulant pose by the door, throwing her arms across her chest. "I thought you were to show me a bit of fun, Cuz," she said to Tristan.

"I'll take you to Mother Lucy's, perhaps," said Tristan in a tone of mild exasperation. "Kindly do not make a scene, my boy." He turned and set his hand on the doorknob.

"Wait," said Madame Vostrikova.

Tristan dropped his hand and looked at her.

"It is a little irregular, my lord," she said with a quiet smile. "But after all, Mr. Talbot is your cousin and heir. And he is so young. One hates to disappoint the very young."

Tristan laughed jovially. "One hates to disappoint the old and jaded, too, Madame, I hope?" He smiled hugely. "Have you relented after all? Will you take us on tonight? I would account it a very great favor."

"And we want redheads," said Phaedra in a low, dark voice. "That's what Tris promised me, and by God, that's what I want. A pair of them — three, perhaps, if my cousin is feeling energetic."

Tristan widened his eyes. "Ah, the gauntlet has been thrown down!" he said. He turned back to Vostrikova. "Madame, I suppose blood will tell. Can you accommodate our whims?"

Madame looked faintly pleased. "Just redheads, my lord?" she murmured. "Can I not offer you something . . . more exotic?"

Yes, thought Phaedra, *something more worthy of blackmail, perhaps?*

Tristan tilted his head toward Phaedra. "Soon, Madame," he said quietly. "For tonight — for the lad — just the women, I think?"

Vostrikova smiled. "I comprehend," she said. "My assistant Mademoiselle LaFoy will show you upstairs. I shall go and procure a pair of girls — *da,* Mr. Talbot, red-haired, if I can."

At the last instant, however, Tristan caught her wrist. "Your pardon, Madame," he said quietly, "but my cousin has a bit of a vicious streak in him. And I — well, I have some tastes I should as soon keep private. Your girls are . . . prepared for such things?"

Madame Vostrikova's mouth curled into something which might have been a smile, or might have been pure bloodlust. "Trust me, my lord," she said quietly. "You will not be disappointed."

"Well, *Harold,*" said Tristan when the door was shut, "you very nearly managed to get us thrown out on our collective arses before we'd even had a good toss."

"Bugger off, Tris," said Phaedra. They had agreed to stay in character in case Vostrikova kept an ear to the door. Phaedra threw herself into one of the chairs, mimicking Tony in one of his snits. "I've escaped Papa and his prudish notions for one night at least, and I mean to make the most of it."

"Do you indeed?" murmured Tristan. "Uncle Tobias must be so proud."

"Yes, and pour us some of that brandy, won't you?" said Phaedra. "I should like something harder than that pink rot."

Tristan eyed her a little nastily, but he poured a dram and brought it to her. "You'll mind your manners, my boy," he said, pressing the glass into her hand. "Madame Vostrikova has invited us here for a free taste. The next time you'll pay — and dearly — for your buxom redhead."

Phaedra snorted, and sipped at the brandy. "Vostrikova still has a fine pair of dumplings herself," she remarked. "Old enough to be our mother, but still . . ."

Tristan almost spat out a mouthful of wine. "Dumplings?" he uttered after swallowing. "God's truth, Harold! The words a lad learns at Cambridge nowadays."

Phaedra shrugged. After one last glower in her direction, Tristan began to pace, his pretense of indolence fading. Now that she knew him, Phaedra could sense the tightly-coiled energy in his step, the restlessness which he barely suppressed.

They fell into silence for a time, Tristan's footfalls heavy and rhythmic on Vostrikova's Oriental carpet. To dispel her own anxiety, Phaedra picked up one of the black books which lay upon a side table. The volume was bound in opulent, ornately tooled leather, with nothing but roman numerals embossed in gilt on the spine. Curious, Phaedra opened it, almost choking when she did so.

Tristan came at once to her side. "Oh, for pity's sake," he hissed. "Give me that!"

Eyes wide, Phaedra clutched it. "No, I think not," she murmured, her voice a little unsteady. She flipped through a few of the pages, which were little more than lavish, hand-colored prints, exquisitely detailed, and set with French captions, each drawing more vulgar than the last.

"Good Lord," Tristan said as the next page fell.

"Indeed," she murmured. "Look, Tris. Isn't this one intriguing?"

Tristan's hands were clutched tightly behind his back now. "Yes," he said tightly. "I daresay."

"What do you think she's doing on her knees like that?" Phaedra asked.

"I couldn't say," he gritted.

Phaedra looked up and grinned shamelessly. "Hazard a guess."

He bent lower. "Put the book away," he said quietly.

"Well, I think she's got his — er, his *cock* — in her mouth." Phaedra managed to maintain her gentleman's voice — and vocabulary. "I must remember that technique. I daresay it might prove useful someday."

"I daresay it might, *Harold*." Tristan's fingers, she noticed, were digging into the arm of her chair now.

"Ever tried it?" she asked lightly. "Perhaps you ought to have a go at it sometime."

"Good Lord," he choked, jerking upright.

Phaedra turned another page to find a similar drawing. This time the kneeling lady was servicing her lover orally as he reclined on a pile of pillows, whilst a second gentleman knelt behind her.

"My word!" This time, Phaedra's voice slipped a trifle. "That is . . . that is most remarkable."

Tristan was pinching the bridge of his nose now, as if the pain might distract him. "I believe," he said tightly, "that this is Madame's private pornography collection, Harold."

"And obviously meant to be shared," said Phaedra calmly. "That's why it is here, laid out upon the table, wouldn't you say? Now this second chap — the one on his knees behind her — where do you think his cock is?"

"Harold — !"

Phaedra pointed to the lady's ample buttocks which were tilted high in the air. "I ask, you see, because it appears to me to be stuck in her —"

Tristan seized the book from her lap at the very instant the door swung open. Phaedra jerked to her feet, and let the book go.

"*Bonsoir,* gentlemen." Another woman in black swept into the room, this one much younger. "I am Mademoiselle LaFoy."

"Bonsoir, mademoiselle." Tristan bowed, and laid the book aside.

Phaedra tried not to gape, and sketched an awkward bow.

The woman wore a garment that was part evening gown and part corset. The corset half, however, did not quite cover her nipples, but instead thrust them up in a way which looked mortifyingly painful. Her inky hair was swept high and tight, her lips stained bloodred, and long drops of what looked like onyx swung from her ears. Her gaze fixed upon Phaedra, the woman did not walk so much as slither, drawing the length of a slender black riding crop through the opposite hand as she came.

"*Alors,* Madame tells me we have an insolent young man with us this evening," she said, her voice deep and throaty as she drew up in front of them. "Tell me, my lord, does your cousin need to be taught a lesson?"

Tristan's eyes glinted with humor. "Indeed, I'd rather enjoy a thorough caning of his buttocks right about now, how —"

"Tristan!" Phaedra almost squeaked out the word.

"— *However,*" Tristan continued, "another day, perhaps? I have promised the lad his first orgy — well, just a little family affair, really."

At that, Phaedra elbowed him sharply.

"Ah — with redheads, of course," Tristan belatedly added.

Disappointment sketched across her face. "*Très bien,* my lord." Mademoiselle LaFoy inclined her head, and drew the crop through her hand one last time. "A pity.

Now if you will follow me, gentlemen, I will take you upstairs."

They followed the young woman back into the corridor through which they had passed earlier, but this time turning up a flight of stairs and progressing deeper into the house. Every few yards they passed through a series of doors which existed, she explained, to afford maximum privacy to Madame's clients.

With a sinking sense of disappointment, Phaedra realized just how difficult her task was to be. All the individual chambers along the way appeared to be locked. She saw no salons, and no public rooms of any sort, just wide, elegant corridors decorated with small bookcases containing more black leather books, and consoles topped with vulgar *objets d'art.* Fine paintings lined the walls depicting all manner of unnatural sex acts between puckish sprites, goat-footed satyrs, and even marauding Romans. Phaedra goggled at each as they passed, often to find herself hitched up by the arm, and dragged onward by Tristan.

"You cater to a variety of tastes, do you not, *mademoiselle?*" asked Tristan lightly as they started up a second flight of stairs. "You supply both males and females?"

"*Oui,* my lord," said Mademoiselle LaFoy.

"And of any age you wish. Shall I bring you a young —"

"No, no." Tristan waved his hand in obviation. "*Merci, mademoiselle.* Given my new career, you must understand, I can ill afford any rumors."

The woman drew herself up as if insulted. "My lord, I remind you we specialize in discretion," she answered. "You may contract with Madame for any sort of services you wish with complete anonymity."

Tristan hesitated as if torn. The woman tossed a nasty glance at Phaedra. Clearly they thought Cousin Harold a hindrance to what might otherwise have been an evening of true vice.

"Not tonight, I think," he finally answered. "But I am intrigued, most certainly."

At the end of the passageway, the woman stopped, tucked the crop beneath her arm, and unlocked a door, a slab of solid oak some three inches thick. She pushed it open to reveal a sitting room furnished in the same dark elegance as the rest of the house. To the right through double doors was the largest bed Phaedra had ever seen, and to the left a smaller, darker room.

Mademoiselle LaFoy went to an armoire by the windows and opened it to reveal a set of deep drawers. Implements of black leather and burnished metal hung from hooks inside the doors. Though Phaedra recognized almost nothing, the effect was chilling. The woman turned to face them, her breasts jutting almost into Phaedra's face. "My lord, we supply a variety of implements to heighten the pleasure of your visit," she explained. "Our girls — and our boys — are well trained to tolerate them."

"Excellent," said Tristan. "And the door, I see, is quite thick. The walls, too, look double-plastered. I expect the sound does not carry?"

She smiled faintly. "It does not," she answered, waving a hand down the length of the armoire. "May I show you anything in particular? Or supply you with something more . . . exotic?"

Tristan made a pretense of opening the drawers. "No, I think this will do nicely," he answered. "What is in there?" He jerked his head toward the dark room.

Mademoiselle smiled faintly. "I shall leave you to discover that for yourself," she said. "Now, may I fetch you a late supper? Some refreshments, perhaps?"

"A bottle of brandy," said Tristan, "and some champagne."

The woman nodded, and withdrew, closing the door behind her.

Swiftly, Tristan began to move through the room, running his hands and his eyes over the walls, lifting the draperies, and even peering behind the artwork.

"What are you looking for?" asked Phaedra, following him.

"Peepholes," he answered. "Cubbyholes. Anything of that nature."

Phaedra moved to the opposite wall and began to search. "Do they use such things?"

"Most brothels do," he said, lifting a portrait of a lady pleasuring herself with some sort of implement. "But here, I think not." He let the painting drop. "I gather Madame focuses on the art of blackmail."

Phaedra finished her wall and moved toward the dark room.

"Don't!" Tristan cautioned.

But it was too late.

He caught her there, just inside the doorway, her eyes running over the walls. "My God," she whispered.

He jerked her arm roughly. "Come on, Phae," he said, forgetting their ruse. "You do not need to see this."

But as with so many of life's horrors, the room transfixed one's gaze, making it impossible to turn away. The only light came from a narrow, grated window near the ceiling, well beyond any human's reach. Chains and racks hung from bare walls like medieval torture devices. A narrow metal cot was bolted to one wall, and beneath the window sat a sort of padded wooden horse such as one might store a saddle upon, with iron manacles affixed to the wall above. The rest of it, she could not bear to contemplate.

At the sight of Phaedra's pallor, disgust dashed over Tristan like a bucket of ice water, cold and sickening. He drew her forcibly from the room, and pulled her into his arms. She dived into the embrace, and buried her head against his neck.

"Phae, I'm sorry," he murmured, setting a hand to the back of her head. "That room contains pure filth. Vostrikova specializes in it. She *addicts* men to it. Do you see now why I did not wish to bring you here?"

She lifted her head from his shoulder and stared into the depths of the narrow room, her eyes bleak. "Tristan, I know I like . . . the things you do to me. But that room — it just seems *vile.*"

He forced her face back to his, and kissed her lightly on the nose. "Phae, what you enjoy is sex play," he explained. "You like a dominant partner, yes. But that room is for men — perhaps even a few women — who enjoy inflicting pain. Who are excited by the sexual humiliation of others. It is a far, far cry from the things we have done in bed together."

"I know." He felt her relax as she tilted her head toward the armoire. "What of the other things? Are they so wicked?"

He laughed. "Oh, a little, perhaps," he admitted. "There are some small but relatively harmless whips, and some manacles, but made of velvet, not metal. Some sex toys from France and the Orient. No one is apt to get hurt using any of those things."

Her eyes widened with curiosity. *"Velvet manacles?"* she whispered.

Tristan flashed a wicked grin. "I'll get you a pair," he answered. "But only if you promise to take turns."

"Take turns?"

"Well, it seems only fair," he answered, smiling down at her. "I think I should rather like to be chained to the bed and ridden to exhaustion."

She licked her lips uncertainly. "Have you . . . have you ever done that before?"

"I cannot recall," he lied, his eyes twinkling. "I don't remember anyone before you, Phae."

And that, he thought regretfully, *was another lie he'd told all too often.*

But this time, it was perilously near the truth. In fact, Tristan did not wish to contemplate just how far he had fallen. Particularly not here in this hellish, disgusting place. He did not want Phaedra surrounded by this filth. He did not want her to question, even for an instant, her own desires.

Struck with an urge to protect her, and to shut out his fears, too, Tristan drew her fully against him. Perhaps Phaedra was a little different, he thought, tucking her head beneath his chin. But there was nothing *wrong* with her, save that she was ashamed of her own passionate nature. She had been introduced to sexual desire in the worst possible way, by a wolf who'd preyed upon her youth. A bastard who'd seduced her when she was physically ready, but emotionally naïve. And that left a deep and ugly wound; one which could be healed but slowly, with trust and with patience — and with love.

He looked down to see Phaedra watching him, the deep blue of her eyes softer now.

"Phae, my dear," he said quietly, "when we leave this place — when all of this is over — forget this. And forgive me for ever letting you come here."

There is nothing to forgive," she answered. "You've done what I asked. And this place would be no less evil had I remained ignorant of it."

"Phae." He set his lips softly to hers in a kiss of reassurance. Her long lashes lowered in a sweep of velvet, and in his arms she trembled, not with passion or fear, but with something he could not quite name. Perhaps she, too, sensed the deepening significance of what lay between them.

Suddenly, the door flew open. Tristan broke the embrace, and looked round to see Mademoiselle LaFoy on the threshold, her eyes dancing with amusement.

"Oh, pray do not let me stop you!" The woman's lips twisted into a smile as she entered. "*Alors,* I have brought for you Sally and Flora —" Here, she paused to lift her hand toward the girls who followed her, "— but perhaps you no longer require their services?"

Without missing a beat, Phaedra resumed her surly pose. "We wanted girls with red hair," she protested, pointing at the smaller of the two girls. "Hers is blond."

Mademoiselle LaFoy's eyes glittered maliciously. "Flora has reddish-gold hair, Mr. Talbot," she said tightly. "And I can assure you, she will give total satisfaction."

"But her hair," said Phaedra slowly, "*is not red.* Take her away and bring us another."

Tristan held out a staying hand. "Harold,

dear boy, she is a fetching chit," he said. "But have you anyone with darker hair, *mademoiselle?* We will, of course, keep Flora, too."

"We have no one else of that coloring," said Mademoiselle LaFoy tightly. "I can bring you a brunette, if you wish."

Tristan drew the girl called Flora to his side. The girl was terrified, her eyes shying wildly. "Thank you, *mademoiselle,*" he murmured. "Flora will do nicely."

"*Merci,* my lord." Mademoiselle LaFoy bowed ever so faintly. "Ah, and here are your refreshments."

A maid set down a tray laden with bottles and glasses, bobbed a swift curtsy, and vanished.

"We shan't wish to be disturbed before daylight," Tristan ordered, already stripping off his coat. "See to it, *mademoiselle.*"

"*Oui, bien sûr,*" she said, inclining her head. "Good evening, gentlemen." Then Mademoiselle LaFoy withdrew, closing the slablike door with an awful *thud.*

The girl called Flora let out a little whimper. Her heart sinking, Phaedra let her gaze run over them, taking in their tawdry, low-cut gowns and painted faces. Until this moment, she simply had not accepted that Millie might not come. Certainly she had not expected these poor, thin, worn-down creatures, both of whom drew her sympathy. Neither remotely resembled Priss's mother. The smaller, Flora, was frozen in fear, like a spring rabbit caught in the garden, a pitchfork bearing down upon it.

Tristan poured two glasses of champagne and pressed them into the girls' hands.

Flora looked down at it, unblinking, as if she'd never seen such a thing.

"Wot would yer 'ave, sir?" asked the girl called Sally. "We can undress, the two of us, and lie wiv the both of yer together, if yer likes it that way?"

"Oh, let's not rush into anything, my dears." Tristan was pouring himself a brandy. "Sit down. Let us get to know you a little."

The girls exchanged uneasy glances, but they sat, clutching their glasses awkwardly. Tristan paced along the floor in front of them. "Tell me, girls, do you like your positions here?"

Sally hesitated. "Just come on two days past." She lifted a bony shoulder. "But it's a roof o'er me head, in't? And summink ter eat every day?"

The girl sat defiantly before them in her cheap, brightly-hued gown, her bosom exposed and her fingers bitten to the quick, and Phaedra wanted suddenly to cry. *Something to eat every day?* For that she had been compelled to sell her body into slavery? Oh, Phaedra knew, of course, as every upper-class Londoner did, that it happened. But to see it thus . . . dear Lord.

"Flora?" Tristan encouraged.

Flora did not answer, but instead seemed to curl inward on herself like a morning glory at day's end. The girl could not have been above sixteen years old. "I likes it fine, sir," she finally whispered, refusing to look at him.

Tristan knelt, and lifted her chin with one finger. "How long have you worked here, may I ask?"

But of course he could ask, thought Phaedra. He could do anything he damned well pleased. These poor girls were paid to indulge his every whim — and likely beaten if they did not.

Flora's wild eyes trembled. "A year September, my lord," she whispered.

"I see." Tristan stood, and tossed off what was left of his brandy, then turned to look at Sally. "My dear, can you make your way back to your quarters without being seen or scolded?"

Sally looked at him oddly. "We 'ave ter do

it, 'ere, my lord," she said. "Vostrikova's rules."

"No, I mean you are dismissed," he replied. "My friend and I will amuse ourselves with only Flora tonight."

Flora gave a little cry, then slapped a tremulous hand over her mouth.

Sally looked as if she couldn't decide whether to be affronted or afraid, but she set aside her glass and flounced across the floor toward Tristan. She lifted one hand and stroked it slowly down his face. "Oh, but yer such a fine, big buck of a man, milord," she murmured. "Why would I wants ter leave?"

Tristan smiled faintly, lifted her hand away, and lightly kissed the back of it, as if she were a highborn lady. "Thank you for that heartfelt compliment, my dear," he said quietly. "But we have changed our mind."

The siren's façade fell away, and something like panic sketched over Sally's face. "No," she said abruptly. "I — I can't go. Madame will flay my backside for a week. I can give satisfaction, milord. I promise."

Tristan smiled and pressed some coins into her hand. "Look, you're a smart girl, Sally," he answered. "Find a quiet corner and put your feet up. I'm afraid I must insist."

Sally edged toward the door. "And you'll not tell old LaFoy?"

"She'll never know," Tristan assured her.

"Suit yerself, then." The girl cast them one last look as she went.

Flora, however, looked on the brink of tears. Tristan drew Phaedra aside, and tilted his head toward the girl. "Do you think she knows anything?"

Phaedra shrugged. "Perhaps, but you don't have time for this. Go. Leave me to question the girl. If she's been here a year, surely she must know what happened to Millie."

"My logic exactly." Tristan tossed Flora another glance. "But I don't like the look of her. She is not well. Whatever you learn, Phae, we are going to have to get her out of here."

Phaedra agreed. "Leave that to me," she answered. "You have until the clock at St. Anne's strikes midnight. One way or another, we'll be in the old scullery as planned. Now *go.*"

His eyes filled with worry, Tristan lingered only long enough to interrogate Flora about the locations of closets, pantries, and servants' stairs throughout the house — things he'd been unable to ascertain from Vostrikova's customers. The girl answered him in a flat, monosyllabic voice, and if she cared why Tristan asked, one couldn't discern it. Phaedra got the impression that it had been a long time since Flora had cared about anything. Tristan was right. The girl had to be snatched from Vostrikova's clutches. Phaedra's only worry was for how many more there might be just like her.

At the door, Tristan tipped up her chin and kissed her hard. "Be careful, Phae, for God's sake."

Phaedra nodded, fighting down the fear that welled up in her chest, then pushed him out the door. She returned to the girl's chair. "Are you all right, my dear?"

The girl squeezed her eyes shut as if she expected to be hit. "Y-yes."

"Flora, we mean you no harm," she said, no longer bothering with her deep voice. "Listen, I haven't time to explain all this. Do you wish to leave here? To go home?"

Her face crumpling, she nodded. She was quite remarkably beautiful, despite her tears and her terror.

Phaedra took her hand, and gave it a squeeze. "Then we will take you away tonight," she said. "Vostrikova will not use you again, I swear it."

The girl was watching Phaedra oddly, as if wondering what to make of her. Phaedra rose and withdrew to the window. To her shock, the rain had returned, a downpour which slicked the cobbles with a yellowish sheen beneath the lamplight. The street looked gray and forbidding.

"Flora, I need information," she gently pressed. "We are looking for someone. I am sure she is here against her will. Her name is Millie Dales, and she is tall with red hair. Is she here?"

Mutely, Flora shook her head.

They were too late, thought Phaedra sickly. The events of the evening weighed down on her, and tears sprang to her own eyes. What a naïve fool she was! Tristan had been right.

"Not tonight," the girl whispered.

"What?" Phaedra's head whipped round. "What are you saying? That she *was* here?"

The girl snuffled wetly. "Bin gone a week, I reckon?" she answered. "Comes and goes, Millie does. Madame puts 'er out on loan."

Hope leapt in Phaedra's heart. "So she's coming back?"

The girl snuffled again and nodded. "Tomorrow, per'aps? I think that's right."

Phaedra crossed the room and grabbed both her hands. "Flora, listen to me," she begged. "We are going to get you out of here — and Millie, too. But first you must tell me *everything.*"

■ ■ ■ ■

It took Tristan better than a quarter hour to work his way back through the rabbit warren of corridors and stairs, sliding in and out of closets and pantries when he heard footsteps or voices. Some of the doors were locked, but devices Kemble had lent him — four long, slender bits of metal, worked infallibly — if a little more slowly than one might have wished.

It was Madame Vostrikova's habit, Tristan had learned, to play chess in the evenings with one of her bully boys. Her offices were on the ground floor of the last house, whilst her private rooms were two floors above it. To enter, he crossed over by way of the attic, through a sort of lumber room crammed full of old furniture, with plenty of places to hide.

Apparently he was not the only one who thought so. Near the exit, he stepped round a dark corner, almost stumbling into an old divan. A footman and one of the girls were putting it to good use, caught in the throws of passion. Impatient, Tristan slid behind a wardrobe and waited for the sighs to die down. He was not ordinarily the voyeuristic type.

When the girl had drawn her skirts back down, and both had slipped away, Tristan crept through, and let himself out onto a flight of narrow, dusty stairs. Sliding through the shadows, one ear constantly cocked, he made his way down the next three, far grander, flights which opened dramatically to the front hall below. On the last landing, he caught the sound of a sharp, feminine voice. The sitting room door above him opened, light spilling down the steps. Tristan sucked in his breath and pressed himself behind a potted palm.

"*Da,* my wool shawl, Lavrin," Vostrikova commanded. "And you, girl! Put more coal on the fire."

The door closed. A man moved past, going down the stairs. The same squat, thuggish chap who'd let them in, too well dressed to be a servant. In the gloom, he did not notice Tristan. He descended swiftly and crossed the hall, his heels ringing out on the marble floor below, then fading. In the distance, the clock at St. Anne's struck eleven, the sounds reverberating off the front of the town house.

Tristan exhaled, then eased down to the ground floor. Vostrikova's private offices were just along the entrance hall, the first rooms a visitor might see upon arriving.

Working by feel alone, he snicked the first lock and let himself into a large, square antechamber. Gaslight fell through the window, casting a ghostly sheen over the chairs and settees which lined two walls. The room held a desk and a set of glass bookcases to the rear. Tristan made a mental note to riffle them if time permitted.

The next door took a little longer, but not much. This room was smaller, but richly appointed in shades of red and gold, with costly mahogany furnishings. The well-polished desk stretched to infinity. It held nothing but a lamp and an ornately carved rosewood box. Gently, Tristan lifted the lid. Cheroots — fine, sweet Cavendish, too, he thought, drawing one beneath his nose.

Behind the desk was a chest, four drawers deep, stretching from window to window. It took but a moment to spring the lock, then Tristan lit the lamp and set to work. The drawers held ledgers, receipts, and correspondence, almost all of it in English. After half an hour of meticulous searching, his suspicions were confirmed. Nothing of value there. He turned to the desk. Again, nothing save the usual clutter. Wax. Ink. Letter paper. A tidy pile of tradesmen's receipts.

Sighing, he made quick work of the rest of the room, lifting his lamp high to peer behind pictures and furniture, taking a calculated risk that no one observed from the street. Judging by the volume of rain which rattled through the downspouts, he thought it unlikely. He tried not to think of Phaedra, and of where she might be at this moment. He knew too well that losing one's concentration was the most fatal of errors.

Frustratingly, his search yielded nothing, so Tristan returned to the chest. On impulse, he extracted one of the bottom drawers and studied the cabinet's interior. He rapped on the bottom with the back of his hand. Yes, too high, and too hollow. He wedged his fingers between the frame and the wood skirting. *Ah.* The skirting was actually hinged; dropping down to reveal two, more shallow drawers — little more than trays.

Carefully, he drew them out, marveling at the tidy stacks of letters and ledgers. This, without question, was what he wanted. Tristan flipped through the correspondence. Most was in Russian, but what he could read was damning. Names, dates, all manner of schemes laid bare — years' worth. And far too much to be shoved beneath one's coat, unfortunately.

He looked about the room and saw the long fold of black wool tossed casually over the desk chair. *Madame's lost shawl.* The irony of it pleased him.

Hastily, Tristan spread it on the floor and piled his loot atop it. He rolled it into a tight bundle and tied it up with a long length of packing cord he'd seen in the desk. De Vendenheim's men were supposed to be watching the house. Tristan hoped to heaven they were awake.

He carried the bundle and lamp to a front window, threw up the sash, then thrust the lamp out into the rain, waving it back and forth three times. Hastily, he ran the cording out the window, lowering his bundle down the side of the house, the wool of Madame's shawl scrubbing along the brickwork.

At the ground floor balconet, he hesitated. He might manage to swing the bundle beyond it and onto the pavement, but a passerby might find it first. And then there was the rain. Best to go on as he'd begun. His cord, of course, was several feet to short. At the end of it, he cast up a prayer and let go. The bundle landed on the flagstone below the basement stairs with a *whump!*

He hung out the window another moment, wondering if anyone below had heard it. This section of the cellars was supposed to be used for coal, wine, and the like, with little traffic. And indeed, no one came out below to see what the matter was. Tristan withdrew, and shut the window.

At that very moment, however, a carriage came clattering down the street. A sleek black gig, moving fast. It drew up before the window. Swiftly, Tristan fell to a crouch. The driver leapt down, whipping his reins round a lamppost. In the pool of weak gaslight, there was no mistaking the man's face. George Nebbett bounded up the stairs — the *front* stairs — looking as if the hounds of hell were on his heels. Softly, Tristan cursed beneath his breath.

This could not be good.

In an instant, Nebbett was pounding on the door like a madman. Tristan turned down the wick and considered his options. There were voices in the hall now; Nebbett's, followed by a servant's voice, stiff but politely solicitous. Tristan glanced about the room. If anyone came in, he had no way out, save for the windows, both of which overlooked the stairwell — easily survivable as falls went — but escape meant abandoning Phaedra inside the house. He would have to find another way.

He hadn't long to consider it. Footsteps were coming down the passageway; one set heavy, the other light and quick. Angry words were exchanged. The lock rattled in the antechamber door. *One more to go.* Tristan knew with a spy's instinct he was about to be caught out.

There was nothing to do save brazen it through. He turned the lamp back up, lit himself a cheroot, and threw his boot heels up onto Vostrikova's fine mahogany desk.

At the pounding which reverberated through the corridors, Phaedra froze on the back stairs, thrusting Flora behind her. If Tristan's intelligence had been correct, this part of the house should have been quiet now. It wasn't. In an instant, servants' voices rang out. Fast, light footsteps echoed beyond the door, heightening the urgency in the air. Phaedra hesitated, listening.

"I do not like my evenings interrupted, Mr. Nebbett." It was Vostrikova's voice carrying sharply down the corridor. "Surely this is tomorrow's business?"

Phaedra leaned out. At the opposite end of the passageway, she could see Vostrikova descending the front stairs, her face tight with anger, a ring of keys clutched in her hand.

"Madame, it cannot wait." Phaedra could make out the profile of the thin gentleman who lingered in the hall, a sodden hat clutched in his hands. "I've just this instant received alarming news."

Vostrikova dismissed the servant, then motioned the man to follow her. "Come in," she said, rattling her keys. "But be quick." Her black silk skirts swished around the corner.

The man vanished after her. The sound of Vostrikova's key in the lock was unmistakable.

Good God, where was Tristan? From the diagram Tristan had shown her, Phaedra knew those were Vostrikova's private offices. Her heart was pounding in her ears now. Fleetingly, she closed her eyes. Surely, surely he had had time to get out?

But it was not likely. She knew it. Biting her lip, Phaedra reached into her coat pocket and extracted the little pistol Mr. Kemble had given her. Her pulse ratcheted up another notch. "Go on down without me, Flora," she whispered over her shoulder. "Hide in the old scullery until one of us comes."

The girl eyed the pistol and scurried away. Phaedra hastened across the open corridor and slid into the shadows, her back set to the wall. She eased toward the front of the house until the voices came clear. The weight of the gun was cold in her hand, like a dead, unnatural thing. She gripped it harder, remembering Kemble's instructions.

"I tell you that bastard's been at my papers!" The man's voice rang out, strained. "Twice he tricked my wife into leaving him alone in my library. She admitted it tonight, the cuckolding bitch."

"Was anything disturbed?" Madame demanded. "Out of place?"

"Well, no. N-nothing I could see." The man was blustering now. "But there's trouble afoot, I tell you. We are caught out."

Vostrikova's sharp laughter rang out. "You are such a coward, Nebbett," she answered. "Everyone knows Avoncliffe is nothing but a pretty fribble." But there was an uneasy edge to her voice.

Phaedra was near the foot of the stairs now. She flicked a quick glance up, the turns of the stairs fading into the gloom as they rose.

"You may think him a fribble, Madame," said the man. "But he was once sly enough to bed my wife under my very nose — and did it again yesterday, for all I know."

Hastily, Phaedra crossed the foot of the steps, and set her back alongside the open door.

"Half the *ton* has bedded your wife, Nebbett." Madame's voice rose. "My God, man! Does this domestic drama really warrant disturbing my chess game?"

Phaedra peeked round the corner into a sort of antechamber. "You've not heard the worst." The man called Nebbett had his hands clasped prayerfully before him. "Lord Hauxton refuses to see me now. The staff has been ordered not to let me in."

"He's ill," snapped Madame. "He'll be dead any day, you fool."

"You don't know Hauxton!" Nebbett cried. "He'll work until they pry the pen from his cold, rigored fingers and drive the nails into his coffin. No, Madame, I tell you — *I am found out!* Please, please, you must help me."

"Help you?" Vostrikova sounded incredulous.

"Madame," he said, clutching at her sleeve, "do you know what they do to traitors in this country?"

Vostrikova laughed richly. "I know what they do to traitors in *my* country, Nebbett," she answered. "In England, your death will be a luxury — swift and painless."

"At least give me back the letters," Nebbett begged. "You've had time to read them by now. They cannot mean anything to you."

Vostrikova shook him off, then relented.

"Oh, very well, if it will rid me of you." She turned to unlock the door behind her.

"I need them all," Nebbett stressed. "I must replace them tonight."

"Be quiet, you fool," Vostrikova hissed. Phaedra watched a little sickly as the door swung wide. "Your letters are safe in my office."

"Not anymore, they aren't." Phaedra heard Tristan's voice ring out cheerfully in the gloom.

"My God!" Nebbett cried, plunging into the room, Vostrikova stalking after him.

Phaedra strained round the door, but could see only Tristan's boot heels — *propped upon the desk!* The audacity of the man! Emboldened, she crept in after them, terrified but determined, positioning herself to the left of the last door. Their attention was wholly focused on Tristan.

Vostrikova had paced to the edge of the desk. "My Lord Avoncliffe." Her voice was oddly calm. "You surprise me — and I do not like surprises."

"Neither does His Majesty's Government," said Tristan, puffing smoke from one side of his mouth. "By the way, Madame, these are damn fine cheroots. You must give me the name of your tobacconist."

Nebbett seized the madam's arm. "Kill

him!" he hissed. "Call your bully boys! He has the letters!"

Phaedra watched as a grin curved Tristan's mouth. "Not anymore, I don't," he said. "Hell, I'm so witless I couldn't even read 'em — so I've sent them off to the powers that be."

"You lie!" hissed Vostrikova. She made the curious gesture of folding one hand over the other. "No one has come or gone from this house. The letters are still here, and *I will find them,* my lord."

"Have a look round, then." His grin deepening, Tristan uncurled himself from his seat and stood, planting one tall boot boldly in the middle of the chair, as if he owned the place. "Pull open your secret drawers if you wish. But you will find them empty."

Suddenly, Vostrikova leaned forward, whipping something long and glittering from her sleeve. "By God, I will not let you ruin this!" she cried brandishing the knife. "Nebbett! Seize him!"

"*Seize* him?" Nebbett cringed.

"Do it!" Vostrikova snarled. "Or I swear to God, I'll slit your throat next."

"No one," said Phaedra in her own voice, "is slitting anyone's throat." She stepped into the fray, the pistol held straight out in both hands, elbows locked, just as Kemble had shown her.

At last, Tristan's grin faded. His color went with it. Vostrikova turned, her eyes glittered wickedly. "Well, if it isn't *Mr.* Talbot," she whispered, the knife trembling. "You little bitch. I should have seen through you at once."

"Phae." Tristan was half turned from the door, one hand out. "Phae, I have it under control."

"But she has a knife," Phaedra whispered. "And I just —"

Everything happened in a flash then. Vostrikova glanced past Phaedra for an instant. Phaedra sensed rather than saw something lunge to her left. She was jerked back, a thick arm whipping round her throat. The cold kiss of steel brushed her windpipe below. "Drop the gun," a deep, foreign voice rasped in Phaedra's ear. "I assure you, my blade is far faster."

Nebbett fell back, his face ashen. "Lavrin! Thank God!"

"Just do as he says, Phae." Tristan's voice was utterly calm. "Everything's fine."

Across the desk, she watched him. Almost imperceptibly, he nodded, then winked with one eye. He had a plan. Phaedra flung the gun away. It skittered across the carpet and vanished under a low, heavy chest.

"Kill her, Lavrin!" Vostrikova's voice and her blade trembling with rage. "Kill her now!"

The man hitched his arm tighter, crushing Phaedra's windpipe. It was as if time leapt forward then. In one seamless motion, Tristan struck his hand across Vostrikova's wrist, his opposite hand going to his boot. "Phae, *drop!*"

Phaedra went limp, taking her attacker with her. A blade of light came hurtling across the desk. The blade caught him — she knew not where — and he cried out. He fell over her like a dead weight. Nebbett shrieked and bolted from the room, slamming the door, snapping the lock behind.

Phaedra shifted, and a dark, thickset man rolled to the floor behind her, writhing in agony, the knife buried deep in his right shoulder. It had all happened in an instant. *It was over.*

"Tristan," she uttered. She sagged with relief, too witless to look for her gun. Suddenly, the wounded man — Lavrin — staggered to his feet, dazed with pain. Vostrikova seized the only weapon to hand — the lamp which burnt on her desk — and circled toward Phaedra.

"My papers, Avoncliffe!" she demanded,

holding the lamp high, the glass chimney chattering. "Show them now! Or I swear I'll send her to a fiery death!"

Phaedra pressed herself back against the wall. Vostrikova was in front of the door now. If she sent the lamp crashing to the carpet, the whole room would soon be ablaze, trapping them. The madam's grip was unsteady, her eyes wide with rage.

Tristan held up both hands. "You win, Madame," he said, easing from behind the desk. "Just put the lamp —"

"Get back!" she cried. The flame flickered eerily up the walls, casting dancing, lethal shadows.

"Lilya, no!" Lavrin struggled to hold up one hand. He lurched toward her, the knife still sticking from his shoulder.

Later, Phaedra could not have said whether he fainted, or merely lost his balance. But he tumbled into Vostrikova, striking her in the ribs. She lost her grip on the lamp. It crashed to the floor. Oil splashed, flames rolled across the carpet and onto her skirt. Vostrikova fell back against the door, screaming and beating at them with her hands.

Somehow, Phaedra found the presence of mind to grab Lavrin by the ankle. Then Tristan was beside her, pulling the other.

They dragged him off the carpet, the knife jiggling in his shoulder. Vostrikova was screaming, flailing at the flames, making them worse.

"Roll!" Tristan shouted at her. "Roll on the floor!"

"No!" she shrieked, backing against the door. "No, noo!" Heat and light filled the room.

"Phae! With me!" Tristan dragged her to the window, and threw up the sash. "Crawl out," he ordered.

Phaedra did not hesitate, but sat on the sill and swung both legs through.

"Good God!" she cried, looking down.

Swiftly he kissed her. "It's not far, love. I swear."

But she did not have time to consider it. Tristan shoved her hard. Phaedra slid down the side of the house, brick scraping at her back. She landed at the foot of the stairs, collapsing onto something hard and fat, striking her head on the bottom step. Oblivion washed in around her, black and engulfing, then Phaedra knew no more.

CHAPTER 13

'Tis not the many oaths that make the
   truth,
But the plain single vow that is vow'd true.

Shivering and disoriented, Phaedra woke to a shaft of pale morning light cutting across her bed. Lifting her head from the pillow, she looked about the room, something nebulous and fearsome just beyond her grasp.

But there was nothing. Only Agnes, going about her usual morning tasks. Drawing her draperies. Pulling out her old slipper tub. In the street below her windows, the daily clatter of carriages and carts had started up, and the cooing of pigeons carried in from the sills.

Phaedra fell back into the pillow. *She was in her room. Her own bed.* And yet the darkness nagged at her. Her legs felt leaden beneath the bedcovers, her hands bloodless.

Tristan.

She rose up little, holding a hand to block the light. "Agnes — ?"

Her maid tossed down the brush she was cleaning, and swooped down upon the bed, her brow fretful. "Awake, are you, miss?" she said, peering into Phaedra's eyes. "Oh, what a fright you gave me!"

Phaedra's brain felt swathed in cotton wool. "What happened?" she asked, rising onto her elbows. "I . . . I can't think."

Agnes settled herself on the edge of the bed. "You fell, miss. Do you not remember?" She stroked the hair back from Phaedra's forehead. "Ooh, what a nasty lump you have!"

Phaedra's hand fluttered to her temple. "A lump?" Yes, snatches were returning now. "Tristan?" she uttered, catching Agnes's wrist. "He is . . . safe?"

Agnes was smiling at her now. "Oh, aye," she said. "Lost a bit of hair in that fire, but still handsome as they come."

"Thank God," Phaedra whispered.

She knew, of course, that he was safe, though she wasn't sure how. But the vaguest of memories were beginning to stir. Tristan's hand soft against her face. His arms lifting her gently into a carriage. She'd felt his cheek pressed to hers. She had felt . . . tears. *Hers? Or his?* Both, she thought. Dear God. Her fingers fluttered to her lips, pressing hard.

Agnes cleared her throat a little awkwardly. "That Mr. Kemble came round this morning to ask after you, miss," she reported, tidying the bedcovers. "He said Mr. Talbot was quite the hero last night."

"He pushed me out a window," Phaedra said. "I remember that much."

"Trying to save your life," Agnes reminded her.

"Yes." Phaedra's gaze turned inward. "I — I think I hit my head on the steps."

"Aye, they said," Agnes murmured.

Phaedra remembered someone scooping her up, too. A very deep voice near her ear as they ascended from the gloom. The cool rain on her face. She could still feel the burn of smoke in the back of her throat. The cold terror which gripped her — the fear that something dreadful had happened to Tristan.

They had carried her up Vostrikova's front steps. And then she'd seen him, standing in a halo of charred and splintered wood, his face black with soot, an avenging angel battling his way through the gates of hell. Relief surged through her again, more vivid now than it had been last night. *He was alive.*

She was alive. And they were bloody lucky, the both of them.

But the once beautiful Madame Vostrikova was beautiful no more. Phaedra closed her eyes, willing the vision away. The madam had lain upon the carpet Tristan had used to snuff the flames and carry her out; her hair a scorched mass, her face so badly burnt it was unrecognizable, the flowing silk gown cocooning her body in a crumbling, ashen sheath. De Vendenheim had cursed beneath his breath, and hastily turned Phaedra's face away.

That had been her waking dream. The thing she'd wished to escape. She remembered it now, and shuddered. Phaedra forced it away, and looked at Agnes.

"Lord de Vendenheim," she said, her heart sinking. "It was he who carried me up from the stairwell. And by now he will have told Stefan *everything*."

Agnes set a soothing hand over Phaedra's. "I fancy not, miss," she said. "He brought you here in his carriage. He and Mr. Talbot had hard words out in the alley, but I think they reached an understanding."

Phaedra closed her eyes. She could only imagine de Vendenheim's outrage at seeing her in Soho, and of course, he would have blamed Tristan for it. The knowledge sick-

506

ened her. "What of our staff?" she whispered, scarcely caring. "Did anyone see me?"

"Oh, no, miss," Agnes reassured her. "I sent Cook to bed at ten with a strong, hot toddy and a bit of flannel for her throat. I thought she looked a trifle peaked, and I told her so."

Phaedra managed a weak smile. Cook was a notorious hypochondriac, and prone to watching at windows. "Poor woman. By now she must think she's dying."

Agnes shrugged. "Anyways, I was on the lookout, miss, when the carriage came round back," she said. "No one was about. But there was a girl — frightened little thing. Flora, they called her. De Vendenheim was taking her to mission house. Don't you remember coming up the stairs with me?"

"A little, yes." She felt gingerly at the knot on her head.

"By the way, I told Cook you tripped over the carpet last night," Agnes went on, pointing at the edge of Phaedra's dressing table. "That marble edge is frightfully hard. Anyways, I put you straight to bed. And here you've been from that moment 'til this — and I dare anyone to say different."

Phaedra dragged both hands through her

hair. It felt filthy and matted. "Vostrikova —
?"

Agnes's face softened. "That Kemble fellow said she was alive, but just. Very polite, he was. He said to tell you the other chap — the chap with the knife in 'im — was taken up by the magistrates." She gave a little shiver as she rose from the bed. "Ooh, miss, it chills me to think what went on last night."

"Yes, well, you're not the only one," said Phaedra dryly. "I made a fool of myself — and I almost got Mr. Talbot killed."

"Oh, miss, I'm sure you did not!" Agnes shot her a reproachful glance, then went to the bell pull. "Now you must put it all out of your mind. What you need is a good, strong cup of tea."

A few minutes later, the tea was poured and a parade of footmen carried in water for Phaedra's bath. When they were gone, she threw back the covers and rose, the teacup rattling in her hand. She had to see Tristan. Had to assure herself . . . of something.

But what? He was well enough; she knew that much. And what more was there between them now? He had done as she had asked. He had helped her find —

"Millie!" Phaedra set her cup down on

her dressing table. "Oh, Agnes! I forgot to tell him about Millie!"

"Millie?" On her knees, Agnes turned from the tub, eyes wide. "Did you find her, miss?"

"Millie is supposed to come back today!" Phaedra threw off her wrapper. "Hurry, Agnes, lay out my blue walking dress. We must be there when she arrives."

Agnes looked doubtful. "I'm not to let you stir until Mr. Talbot comes, miss," she answered. "He said so last night. Said he'd come round this morning to check on you."

Phaedra drew her nightgown off. "Did he?" she answered. "Then I must hurry. Here, help me wash my hair."

An hour later, Phaedra was in the family parlor, alternately pacing the floor and staring out the windows across the garden. She remembered it now — coming up that path on Tristan's strong, solid arm, the scent of scorched wool sharp in her nostrils. The horrors of the night washed over her; the ugliness of all she had seen, and the sadness which came with the certain knowledge of how less fortunate women lived.

She thought again of Flora, and of Sally, so hardened, and so accepting of her fate. Of that dark, narrow, horrid room. But she thought most of all of Tristan; of how very

509

much she owed him. Of how desperately she ached to touch him with her own hands and reassure herself that all was well. He had said he would call this morning — and he would. Above all else, he was a man of his word. And then she would ask him for one last thing — one last favor, though God knew she had no right to do so.

Moments later, she heard the knocker drop at the front door and knew with a woman's instinct that it would be him. Clutching her hands before her, Phaedra resisted the urge to rush down the passageway and answer it herself. It was time, she supposed, that she began to conduct herself with a little decorum — outwardly, at least.

She had already informed the footmen that she would receive Tristan here, for it seemed somehow fitting. In this soft, comfortable, familiar room, she had first begun to know him. Had first kissed him. And in this room, it was entirely possible she would now bid him good-bye. After all, what more was there to say? What more lay between them? He owed her nothing. Only her need to find Priscilla's mother had drawn them together, and today — one way or another — that ended. Phaedra had resolved it in her heart. If she did not find Millie this afternoon, she would search no more.

There was a noise, the soft sound of shoes on the carpet, and she turned round to see Tristan standing on the threshold. His face was fiercely red up one side, and a little of his hair was scorched away, but that irrepressible humor still lurked in his eyes.

"Mr. Talbot, my lady." The footman bowed, and stepped aside.

He entered the room as he always did; as if he owned it, with an easy, loose-limbed grace. He filled the room with his presence, making her mouth go dry and her heart hammer. For an instant, he stood looking at her, both hands set at his narrow hips, taking her in, something sharp and assessing behind his laughing eyes. He had been worried, she realized.

"Thank you, Stabler," she managed to say. "We require nothing further."

The footman bowed, and withdrew. Phaedra shut the door, and without fully grasping her own intentions, hurled herself at Tristan.

"Phae." His arms came around her, solid and strong. "Always on the edge of propriety."

She made a sound, a sort of choked sob. "Oh, do be quiet!" she said. "I am so tired of being proper. And I am so desperately glad to see you!"

He set her a little away, his gaze solemn and watchful. "It was a hard, strange night, my girl," he said grimly. "And I'm dashed glad to see you up and around."

"Oh, Tristan!" She blinked hard, and gathered herself. "You are burnt!"

"Not enough to ruin my boyish good looks," he said, grinning. Then the expression faded, and he lightly touched the bruise at her temple. "Poor love," he murmured. "Does it hurt?"

"Like the devil," she answered. "And I deserve it. Tristan, I am so sorry for being so rash."

A wicked humor danced in his black Gypsy eyes. "You, Phae? Rash?"

Phaedra sighed. "That pistol!" she said. "Coming into that room. You knew what you were doing — and *I thought I was saving you!*"

At that, he threw back his head and laughed. "Oh, it was going to be a free-for-all no matter what," he said evenly. "Once old Nebbett turned up, my plan was out the window — and you with it, I'm sorry to say."

"Yes, my only regret is that I'll never be able to tell that story at dinner parties," she confessed. "Someday, when the terror has passed, it will likely seem hilarious."

He ran the ball of his thumb over her cheek, then let his arms fall. "Vostrikova died early this morning," he said quietly.

Phaedra was quiet for a moment. "And the house?" she finally asked. "The women and children? They are safe?"

Tristan shrugged. "Little damage was done by the fire," he admitted. "De Vendenheim's men are taking away those who wish to leave. His friend Lady Delacourt runs a mission in the East End."

"And what of you, Tristan?" She set her head to one side. "Was it worth the pain? Did you get what you hoped to find?"

His irrepressible grin appeared, but it was a little sideways. "Oh, my hair looks like a hedgehog cut it, and I blistered up one shoulder a bit," he said. "But yes, we found what we needed, and then some. It's as well Vostrikova died. It saves the Crown a hanging."

"Tristan." Lightly, she took both his hands in hers. "Oh, Tristan. I am so sorry to have dragged you into this."

"You did not drag me," he corrected. "My father did."

She lifted one shoulder lamely. "In part, perhaps," she agreed. "But I still wish to thank you for your help. And tell you that it's over. After today, I'm not going to search for Millie any further."

"After today?" He looked at her in puzzlement.

"Agnes and I are going back this afternoon," she said quietly. "Flora said Millie might return today. Did she tell you?"

He lifted one dark, slashing eyebrow. "No."

Phaedra snagged her lip. "I mean to try one last time to find her," she said after a moment had passed. "If we cannot, we will leave word for her. After that — well, I daresay we must all buck up, and move on. Priss included."

He squeezed her hands, his lips thinning with disapproval. "There's no stopping you from going, is there?"

She shook her head.

For a long moment, he simply held her hands and stared at her. There was an inestimable weariness in his gaze, and for the first time Phaedra noticed the deepening of the lines about his mouth and at his eyes. "Then I shall take you," he finally said. "God knows I oughtn't. But it is better, I daresay, than your going alone."

Phaedra felt the hot press of tears spring to her eyes. "You are too kind," she said, sagging with relief. She had not wished to face that awful place without him. "I thank you."

"Well, don't thank me yet," he warned her. "When we are done, Phae, you will owe *me* something."

"Yes, anything," she said. "You have only to name it."

He gave a bitter bark of laughter. "We are going to have a long talk, my girl," he said grimly. "Just the two of us. And you are going to hear out my every word without so much as a squeak. Are we agreed?"

She dropped her chin, and stared into the snowy folds of his cravat. "Yes, Tristan," she said quietly.

He folded his arms over his broad chest, and regarded her with his dark gaze. "Aye," he said quietly. "We'll see, won't we?"

They arrived in Soho to find Vostrikova's houses swarming with activity. Policemen in their blue, brass-buttoned suits were everywhere, taking statements, carrying out boxes, sending people hither and yon in hackneys, carts, and even on foot. Phaedra ordered Agnes to wait inside the carriage. It was one thing to know, intellectually, what a whore was, but an altogether harder thing to have it thrust in one's face, especially when the whore was your sister. She went up the stairs on Tristan's arm, thankful he'd forced her to wear a veil.

In the entrance hall, a police sergeant stopped him — the same stout, florid man Phaedra had seen in Mr. Kemble's shop so many weeks ago. "My lord, above 'alf this lot already piked orf!" he complained, clearly believing Tristan in charge. "Wot are we ter tell the constables?"

"The truth, Sergeant Sisk," said Tristan. "De Vendenheim says we cannot hold anyone without evidence. Children will be taken in by the parish. As to the others, if they don't wish our help, we must let them go."

"Poor cows," said the man, shaking his head. "The beaks won't like it, neither."

Tristan paused to fish in his waistcoat for a card, then pressed it into Sisk's hand. "If any magistrate should question you, tell them the orders were Lord Hauxton's."

Lord Hauxton. That was Tristan.

Until this moment, the gravity of it had not quite registered with Phaedra. She realized in some shock that Tristan still had his father's funeral to attend to. And then he would have the responsibility of taking on the vast estates, and the many duties required of a peer of the realm. It was a sweeping, life-altering change — one which she knew he did not welcome.

But Phaedra lost that train of thought as soon as she looked up. Her gaze fixed at once upon the staircase, and on the people moving up and down it, and peering over the balustrades as if wondering what was to become of them. Women in all states of dress and dishabille. A pair of young boys — twins, by the look of them — stood barefoot on the upper landing, holding hands as they waited their turn. Three girls who could have scarce been above ten or twelve years were being led down by matronly women in gray serge gowns, bound, Phaedra feared, for the orphanages. And amongst all of them, a few haggard, hard-eyed women who clearly knew what they were about. The professional prostitutes, Phaedra supposed, but her heart ached no less for any of them.

Surveying it, Tristan uttered a soft curse. "I must be mad to have brought you back here."

One of the women pushed past them, carrying a cracked leather portmanteau, her chin high, as if daring anyone to stop her. Phaedra caught the woman's arm, and her eyes flared wide with alarm.

"Wait, miss," said Phaedra gently. "Do you need help? Food or shelter, perhaps?"

The alarm faded to a world-weary gaze. "I wish ter get on wiv me business," she said. "And 'oo are you ter stop me?"

"I don't wish to stop you," she said, as Tristan urged her forward. "I'm just searching for someone — for Millie Dales. Do you know her?"

The woman's gaze darkened, and she jerked her head toward the staircase. "Third floor, through ter the next 'ouse," she said. "The first room yer come to. But that one don't need no help."

They continued up the steps, Phaedra wondering at the woman's words, and at the barely veiled derision in her eyes. Millie's room was easily found. Phaedra peeked around the open door to see that a trunk sat on the floor, all manner of frothy garments hanging out of it.

Millie stood by the window in a pale pink muslin gown with puffed sleeves and a deeply flounced hem, a garment clearly meant for a girl just out of the schoolroom — an odd contrast in the tawdry bedchamber. A portly gentleman was clasping both her hands in his own, and looking almost rapturously down at her.

And thus ended Phaedra's mission of mercy — not with a bang, nor with even a fleeting moment of triumph — but with a whimper, and a sinking sense of the inevitable. "Millie?" she whispered without lifting her veil.

Millie turned slowly around. *"My lady?"* she cried, her eyes widening. "Is that you? Oh, lawks!"

Phaedra rushed to the girl, and seized both her hands. "Oh, Millie," she said. "Come, let me look at you! Oh, thank God. Agnes and I have been so frightfully worried."

But Millie's expression was oddly blank. "Why, I'm perfectly well, miss. Truly. But thank you."

The portly gentleman came away from the window, his brows in a knot. "Kitten?" he said sharply. "What's all this?"

Millie blushed. "My lord, this is a lady from my home village," she said. "She . . . why she is just paying a call on me, as she says, to see that I'm well, what with all the dustup last night. And this other gent —" Running an assessing eye over Tristan's expensive coat and polished boots, she made a swift curtsy. "I am afraid I do not know him."

"Oh, never mind me," said Tristan dryly.

Phaedra caught Millie lightly by the arm and glanced at the trunk, a shiny, leather affair with bright brass trim. It looked sadly out of place given the old portmanteaus and ragged bundles the other women had carried down. "Millie, I don't understand," she whispered. "This house is being shut up."

"Oh, I know that, miss!" she said. "But it's no matter to me now."

"But you won't need those things," said Phaedra, her voice strident. "We've come to take you home."

"Take her home?" said the portly gentleman, his voice sharp. "Whatever for?"

Millie bobbed again. "Oh, thank you, my lady, but with Madame out of the picture, me an' Lord Cotting have come to an understanding," she said. "I'm to go with him."

"To . . . to go with him?" Phaedra echoed. "But you do not have to. Millie, it is over. Madame is dead."

Millie wrinkled her nose. "Aye, so I heard," she answered. "Can't say as I'll miss the old cat."

"We've brought a carriage," Phaedra pressed. "Agnes is waiting outside. We want to take you back to Brierwood."

But Millie was looking at her blankly. "What? And go back to scrubbing the taproom floors?" she asked, drawing back. "Oh, no, miss. Thank you. Indeed, I do thank you. You've always been ever so kind.

But Lord Cotting is letting rooms for me, and I'm to pick out all the furniture."

Phaedra could scarce believe her ears. "But Millie, surely . . . surely you cannot enjoy this life? And what about Priss?"

"Priss?" The gentleman by the window swiveled his head to look at them, one eye narrowed suspiciously. "Kitten, who is Priss?"

Millie cut a low, swift look over her shoulder. "No one, my lord," she said hastily. Then she took Phaedra's arm and dragged her out into the corridor. Tristan followed, looking very much as if he knew where this was going.

Phaedra, however, was confused. She had expected — well, gratitude, she supposed. She had believed by now Millie would have seen the error of her ways. "Millie, I don't understand," she said. "What is going on here?"

"Listen to me, my lady," said Millie under her breath. "His lordship knows nothing of Priss — and you mustn't speak of her again, do you hear? Madame told him . . . well, she told him I was a virgin. And he paid good money to def— to defel—"

"To defile you?" Tristan dryly suggested.

Her eyes widened appreciatively. "Exactly," said Millie, turning to Tristan.

"There's good money to be made in defiling virgins. Indeed, they're ever so popular with gents of a certain age, though I never would have thought it, would you?"

"Certainly I never would have," Tristan put in. "Always found 'em a nuisance, myself."

Millie tossed him an admiring glance. "Exactly," she said again. "But chaps in their dotage are right mad for 'em. And he thinks I am one — or was one, at any rate. And all it took was a bit of chicken blood and vinegar — well, that and a little shrieking and running around the room. 'Til he caught me, tore my clothes off, and tied me up, o'course."

Tristan was looking at Millie knowingly. "Oh, you're good at this, aren't you?" he murmured.

Millie drew herself up proudly. "Madame trained me to put on a proper show," she replied. "I got defiled thirty-two times." Then her face fell. "But only Lord Cotting here took a real shine to me. Still, his wife died last month — can you just imagine my luck? He's a *widower*."

Phaedra's brow was furrowed. "But what about Priss?" she said again.

Millie set a firm hand on Phaedra's arm. "Listen to me," she repeated, leaning near, one eyebrow arched in warning. "Priss will be fine. Aunt Kessie will see her raised up proper, I'm sure."

"Your *great-aunt?*" said Phaedra incredulously. "She's seventy!"

"And I'll send a little money when I can," Millie said hotly. "Really, miss. I'm sorry. But what else am I to do? Go back to Hampshire and wait for Mr. Hayden-Worth? No, thank you. Once the babe come, I thought as how he'd set me up proper, but he didn't — and now Cotting will."

Phaedra set a hand on her arm. "What, exactly, do you want, Millie? I — why, I'll arrange it if I can."

Millie's mouth turned into a pout. "What I *don't* want is to die of boredom in a poky old village," she said. "I'm a good-looking girl, miss, and I ain't about to waste it. You're very kind, I'm sure, but you can't help me."

Suddenly, a shadow fell across the corridor. "Kitten, do look at the time." Cotting had pulled a glittering gold watch from his waistcoat. "My carriage is waiting downstairs. Now put on your new hat, my little pet, and say good-bye."

Phaedra let her hand fall. And that was the end of it. No salvation, and no joy; just a feeling of utter helplessness, like watching someone plummet headfirst off a bridge into the cold and churning waters below, whilst praying fervently they could swim. Millie didn't want Priss, she wanted excitement. And Phaedra wanted to cry.

Tristan caught her elbow, and guided her gently back to the stairs. Together, they went out and back down the steps, his hand warm beneath her arm, Phaedra's stomach in a hard knot as she thought about Priss, and about going home to Brierwood empty-handed.

"Phae, I am so sorry," said Tristan when she was safely ensconced in the carriage again. "Agnes, I'm afraid we do not bring the best of news."

The maid's face went white with anger upon hearing Tristan's carefully-edited version of what had transpired. But Agnes knew, as Phaedra did, the utter impossibility of changing Millie's mind, and that there was always a chance that Millie — selfish and resourceful as she was — might actually land on her feet. Possibly even prosper.

In the end, Agnes accepted Tristan's offer to climb down and say good-bye to her sister. They waited in bitter silence until Millie came down the front steps, her hand on Lord Cotting's arm, a pink lace parasol swinging cheerfully from the crook of her elbow, her head tossed back in gay laughter.

"Always getting above herself, that one," Agnes muttered, climbing down. "And never a thought for the rest of us — especially not for Priss." At the last instant, she turned, looking back at them, her gaze wounded. "I should like to slap her senseless, miss," she said quietly. "But I shan't. I'll let her have the life she wants — much joy may it bring her."

Grief and a deep sense of failure pulled at Phaedra as she watched the maid dash across the lane. "I cannot imagine how Agnes must feel. Indeed, it must be far worse for her than for me."

"I am so sorry, Phae," said Tristan again. "All your effort — your concern for Priscilla . . ."

Phaedra's shoulders fell with fatigue. "There's nothing else for it," she said on a choked sob. "I must give Agnes up. Her aunt will need help raising Priss. I have been selfish."

Tristan scooted across the carriage to sit beside her on the banquette. "No, you have been trying to give Priscilla her mother back," he said, drawing her firmly to his shoulder. "And you feared for Millie as you would fear for any woman out of her depth

with men set on taking advantage of her —
because you know too well what that's like."

"But now I begin to fear who is taking
advantage of whom," said Phaedra. "Am I
really so naïve as all that?"

"Only in the sweetest of ways," he murmured. "But I am afraid, Phaedra, that
Millie is simply not a fit mother for Priscilla. I'm sorry to have to say that."

"No, no, you are right." She tried to blink
back the hot, urgent pressure behind her
eyes. "Priscilla is the dearest, most precious
babe *in all th-the w-world.*" And then, appall-
ingly, she burst into heaving sobs.

The tears seemed to swamp her utterly.
She cried then as she had cried upon realizing she did not carry Tristan's child. She
cried for Priscilla, and for her own foolish
failings. Cried until Tristan's coat was wet
and his handkerchief sodden. And he did
not do her the insult of telling her that all
would be well, or that it did not matter. He
simply held her, his lips pressed to her
fevered brow. He knew, as she knew, that
she cried in part for a child lost long ago.

They sat in silence during the drive back
to Mayfair, Agnes staring out the window,
her hands clasped tightly in her lap. "Thank
you, my lord," she said when Tristan helped
her down at Brook Street. "You are very

kind. Quite as kind as my lady — and that's saying something."

Blushing, Phaedra turned to Tristan. "Will you come in?" she asked. "Perhaps take some sort of refreshment?"

"Most certainly." He fixed her with a grim stare. "You've your end of this devil's bargain to keep now, my girl."

Phaedra remembered then what she had promised, and led the way back to the parlor. He followed her, his boots ringing heavily along the passageway, his height casting a long shadow in the afternoon light. It was odd, she mused, how swiftly a mood could turn. How two people who had just spent hours together — some of them perilously near death — could suddenly feel uneasy with one another.

Inside, the parlor seemed somehow smaller, and Tristan seemed so large. So imposingly *male*. Impulsively, she threw up one of the sashes. Tristan's presence seemed to crowd out all the air. Or perhaps it was the sudden tension in the room. He was going to say something he knew she would not like — she sensed it — though he still radiated utter calm. Absolute control. A pity she did not possess the same.

As if they might shield her emotions from view, Phaedra went to her reading table and put on her eyeglasses which, oddly, she'd scarcely worn of late. Then she rang for coffee. When it came, and there was no further delay to be found, Phaedra closed the door. This time he did not chide her — a bad sign, perhaps.

"You wished to have your say," she said, nervously slopping a little of his coffee onto the saucer as she passed it. "And God knows you've earned the right. All this effort. All this — this *madness* on my part. And now nothing to show for it."

But Tristan did not so much as lift the cup to his lips. Instead, he put it down and strode to the open window, gazing pensively across the gardens just as she had done that morning, one hand set at the back of his neck. A warm breeze blew in, shifting his dark, overlong hair like a curtain of wavy black silk.

She wanted suddenly to go to him. To touch him, and feel those powerful muscles shiver again beneath her touch. To let her hand slide up that broad, strong back, and beg him for . . . something. But what?

Her heart fluttered in her chest. The silence in the room was a heavy, palpable thing. Unable to bear it, she rose and went to him. "Tristan?" she said. But she touched only his arm. "Tristan, what is it?"

He turned and let his hand drop. "It's like this, Phae," he said, his eyes bleak. "I think we should get married."

She drew back an inch, her knees suddenly unsteady. "We . . . we should what?"

"Marry," he said tightly. "Us. I was not jesting when I said it in the alley last night. I have ruined, compromised, and thoroughly dishonored you — and both Kemble and de Vendenheim suspect it."

"No, no, you wait just a moment." But when Phaedra caught him by the shoulder, Tristan hissed through his teeth.

"Ah!" She leapt back, wincing. "Your burn."

He looked at her, chagrin and frustration in his clear, dark gaze. "I sometimes think, Phae, that you are going to be the death of me."

"No. I shan't be." She took a firm step back. "I've caused you enough trouble already. Certainly I'm not going to marry you. And you are *not* the man who ruined me."

At that, something dark and lethal passed over his visage. "No," he said softly. "Not like that, perhaps. But I'm sorry, Phae, that the man who did so is dead. In my quiet moments, I think of little else. I feel cheated of the opportunity to watch that bastard breathe his last."

This time she touched him gently. "Tristan, it's over," she lied. "It's so far in my past, I rarely even think of it. Certainly it has nothing to do with us."

"Damn it, Phaedra, don't you see?" His eyes glittered with frustration. "It has everything to do with us. That man hurt you. And I . . . Phae — I *love* you."

"You love me?"

For once, there was no laughter in his black, flashing eyes. "I wake up knowing it every day, Phaedra," he answered. "Knowing that I have an obligation to protect you — and knowing, already, that I can never make this one thing right, except to simply love you, and give you a good and happy life. Will you let me?"

She opened her mouth to speak, and felt the hot rush of tears against the backs of her eyes. Swiftly, she looked away. She knew pity when she heard it, though she knew, too, that he'd deny it to the last — and might not yet recognize that insidious emotion for what it was. But he would. Someday.

"Tristan," she said quietly, "I decided long ago not to marry. And I have been happy, by and large, with that choice."

"Phae, damn it, did you hear what I just said?"

"Yes, now *you* listen." She felt her impatience spike, and with it the ache in her heart. "You are an earl now — one of the most powerful men in England. You mightn't like it, but you *are* Hauxton. You have duties and obligations you have not had time to consider. You have not even sat down with your solicitors to see how things stand. You have not yet buried your father, nor had time to mourn his passing. How can you possibly know what you want? You don't even know what you have."

He closed the distance between them and set his hands firmly on her shoulders. "Phae, I have never wanted anything in my life," he said. "Nothing I could define. Not until I met you. Until now, my life was simple. My needs were simple. But there is nothing simple about *this*. About *us*."

She searched his face as she searched her mind for the right words — not to tell him how she felt, for that would never do. She searched instead for words of comfort, and of reassurance. For a way of letting him off the hook and sending him on to the rich and happy life fate was offering him, would he but give up this mad notion of saddling himself with a sometimes waspish — and quite probably barren — wife.

But he did not wait for her answer. Instead, he kissed her. Roughly. Possessively. He kissed her in a way he had never kissed any woman before, did she but know it, opening his mouth over hers and taking her without hesitation, possessing her. Claiming her. Tempting her to say *yes* until it seemed his embrace wrung tears from her very heart. She wanted him so desperately.

His hand fisted in her hair and his mouth ravaged hers until her knees shook and her scalp ached and until she wanted to crawl out of her skin and into his, melding with him as one. He slanted his mouth over hers again and again, kissing her without any pretense of grace or tenderness, raking her face with the faint stubble of his beard as he thrust deep and crushed her against him.

She wanted him — wanted him with more than simple lust. He was a part of her, and ever would be. He understood her. She let his tempest draw her in, almost losing herself in the dizzying rush of his rage and need. Her yearning drew her to him, and pooled in her womb with that old familiar ache as he trembled against her.

But her womb was still a cold, black void, and hope was a tenuous thread. All the passion in God's world would not make her whole again, and when the emotional storm raining round them slowed, and Tristan tore his mouth from hers, Phaedra held his dark gaze, shuddering at what she saw in his eyes.

"Now tell me, Phaedra," he gritted, his nostrils flaring, "that I *don't know what I want.*"

She looked away, too unsteady to answer. Too afraid to trust herself.

He gave her a little shake. "Do you think I give a damn about a title, Phaedra? I don't — save for the fact that it makes it a good deal harder for your brother to refuse me."

She shook her head, afraid of how desperately she wished to fling herself at his feet. "This will not do, Tristan," she whispered, tears welling behind her eyes. "It will not."

"Phaedra." He caught her by the chin and forced her face back to his. "Phaedra, do you love me?"

"Oh!" she said softly. "Oh, Tristan. Please do not make me answer that."

"Phae, is this about children?" he whispered. "Because you do not know for sure. You *don't.* Sometimes miracles happen. And it doesn't matter to me, one way or the other."

But it would matter to him in the end, and she knew it. It mattered to all men — especially men of wealth and title. The laws of entail vested everything he had — everything he was or would ever be — on his ability to have a son. She would not take the risk of cheating him of that. Especially when he had scarce had time to grasp what fate and his father's death had thrust upon him.

"You will want children, trust me," she said quietly, steeling herself for her next words. "And if you love me as you say, Tristan, then you will not press me."

"You just don't want me, then?" he rasped, his face a mask of pain. "Is that it? Why, Phae? Is my blood too impure for the mighty Northamptons? No Spaniards, no Sicilians, and for God's sake, no Gitanos allowed climb that lofty family tree? Because if that's it — if it's just lust you feel for me and no more — well, I'm used to that. Just say it, and at least I'll —"

She cut him off, placing her fingers across his lips. "You are good enough," she said, her hand trembling against his mouth. "Good enough for anyone. Please, don't ever say that again. It's ugly and it's *vile*."

"You think I will change my mind." His words were cold.

"I fear it, yes." An almost overwhelming weariness washed over her then, and left her swaying on her feet. "And I will not be the reason you have no children, Tristan. I could not bear it."

He just shook his head. "Phaedra, *please.*"

She wanted him to leave before she did something inestimably stupid. "Go home, Tristan," she said quietly. "To Wiltshire, I mean. Get out of London's filth and go see to your estates and to your earldom, and find yourself some pretty, biddable gentleman's daughter. One who won't drag you through the stews and doss houses of London, and make you wish to rip your hair from its roots."

"Thank you, Phaedra," he said icily, "for that most thorough advice."

She went to the window and stared out into the muted afternoon light, mottled across the garden by the shifting tree limbs and fluttering leaves. "Tristan," she said quietly, "until you are wed, if we are discreet, perhaps we could continue —"

"No," he interjected harshly. "Do not dare to suggest such a vile thing, Phaedra. If you want me, by God, *then you'll marry me.*"

"I cannot think that wise," she whispered. "And once you grasp what your new life will be like, Tristan, you will thank me for this."

"And if I don't?"

She shook her head, opened her mouth, then shut it again. "Well, if you do not," she finally said, "give it a year. And then . . . and then . . . oh, I just don't know!"

"A *year?*" he sneered. Then he rammed a hand into his coat pocket, and closed the distance between them, slapping something down upon the windowsill without breaking his stride. "Your uncertainty is a damned cold comfort, Phae, and I am not a patient man. Now, if you will excuse me, I have a funeral to attend to."

She watched him leave, his gait no longer the lazy pace she'd come to love, but an angry, purposeful stalk. She had hurt him, and more than she'd imagined possible. Suddenly the chill deepened, settling over her and going far deeper than her bones. What if it was not just honor or lust or affection which drove him? What if Tristan meant what he said? What if she could have him, and know he would never, ever regret it? Was it possible? Dear God. What if she had just made the biggest mistake of her life?

But it simply *was not* possible.

Oh, he said he didn't care about children. But he would — and then he would begin to hope; quietly, and with a deepening despair. And she knew too well the awful burden regret could be, a burden which would weigh doubly heavy, she feared, when reflected in the eyes of the person you loved. When you had to watch it fester year after year, until it was nothing but a quiet look of hopelessness. Kingdoms had fallen for less.

Deep in the house, she heard the front door slam. She exhaled on a ragged sigh, and bowed her head. And then she saw it. The thing he'd hurled down so angrily.

She picked it up, the yellow silk shimmering in a shaft of afternoon sun. Her garter — the little white rose still dangling by a thread — a little grubby from a life lived amongst a jumble of pocket change and house keys. She remembered then how long it had been missing — that the day she'd lost it had been the day she'd first kissed him.

First begun to fall in love with him.

And then her tears fell in earnest, the sobs dragged from her chest on a rising swell of grief.

CHAPTER 14

Thy love is better than high birth to me,
Richer than wealth, prouder than garments' cost.

"The potted palm?" Xanthia's voice was querulous as a child's, her mouth fixed in an uncharacteristic scowl. "Or the basket of gladioli?"

"The gladioli," said Phaedra swiftly. She motioned for Stefan's footman to take the palm away. "They are just the right height for a centerpiece."

Xanthia sighed, and fell into a chair, her gaze trailing across her ballroom, which admittedly looked a shambles. "Oh, why, Phae, *why* did I ever begin this?" she asked, plopping a hand high upon her now-rounding belly. "My feet hurt, my temper's short, and everyone knows my giving a gala ball is like a pig trying to waltz."

Phaedra sank down beside her. "You

planned this ball to please Mamma, Zee," she said, gently squeezing her hand. "It was perfectly silly of you, of course. But you are trying to prove to her that you can do it all — raise a family, run a business, *and* be what she wants — Lady Nash, pillar of elegant society."

"*She* is Lady Nash, the pillar. In this family, I'm just the spindly fencepost — and soon everyone will know it."

"Nonsense," said Phaedra. "Now put your feet up on one of those empty chairs whilst I go downstairs and chide Monsieur René about the *mignardises.* Then Gibbons will help us decide where to hang the bunting, all right?"

"Yes, all right." With an exasperated *puff,* Xanthia blew a tendril of hair from her face, then cast her sister-in-law a grateful glance. "Thank you for all this, Phae, and for agreeing to stay," she said quietly. "I know you don't wish to. But Stefan has been so pleased to see you out a bit this season."

"I am happy to be here," said Phaedra.

But that had been a lie, she considered five hours later. Five hours which had been spent in frantic preparation, with vases to be filled, swags to be hung, silver punch bowls to be polished, carried up, and filled. All of her brother's servants — and half of

Phaedra's — had worked tirelessly. And for what?

So that Phaedra's mother could brag to all her friends what a marvelous, talented, socially acceptable daughter-in-law Stefan had married. And so that Phaedra could put on another of her low-cut ball gowns and spend the rest of the night in misery.

Upstairs in one of the guest chambers, Phaedra dressed with the help of Evans, Xanthia's maid, having no maid of her own now. She had sent Agnes back to Brierwood almost six weeks past, and had missed her ever since. They had been grim, lonely weeks with no one save Zoë to talk to — and since Zoë knew nothing of Priss, and certainly nothing of Tristan's marriage proposal, there was limited solace to be sought there.

Zoë knew, though, that Phaedra was desperately, depressingly in love. Phaedra had not even troubled herself to deny it. It would have done no good at all.

"Will you have your dress on now, my lady?" asked Evans, drawing up the muslin sheath which covered it.

"Thank you, yes." Phaedra lifted her arms, sliding into the shimmering, deep green ball gown which had brought her an almost illicit amount of pleasure when Zoë had helped her choose it. She slicked her hands down the front, smoothing away the wrinkles, and wondering why the dress brought her no pleasure now.

Because Tristan was gone.

And because every garment she'd ordered — every scrap of silk or lace she'd worn through those heady first weeks of spring — had been bespoke for just one reason. Because, in her heart, she had hoped to see him wading through some crowded ballroom. Seated at someone's dinner table. Or relaxing at someone's card party, his long legs stretched carelessly out, those black Gypsy eyes dancing with laughter. She had gone out on Zoë's arm, forcing herself to be witty and gay, in the faint hope that he might notice her.

But Tristan had been occupied at the time with other, more important matters. She fully grasped that now. She wished she had grasped it then; wished she'd stayed home alone with her books and mending and her warm fire just as she always had done. For if she had, she would not now need to explain — to Zoë, to Mamma, and even to Stefan — why she no longer wanted to go out at all.

Suddenly her abdomen cramped, hard and fierce, and Phaedra set her hand to her belly. She must have made a little sound, for Evans circled back around from doing up her buttons, her expression one of concern. "My lady?"

Phaedra forced her expression to relax. "My monthly," she said. "It will pass soon enough."

And it would. It always did. This, just as her last, had come like clockwork.

Thank God she had not acceded to Tristan's foolhardy wish to marry, she thought as Evans finished the last button. Otherwise she would have spent every fourth week of her life thus, one hand on her stomach, one hand on her heart, praying to God for something other than the inevitable.

Evans turned her around and smiled. "You look beautiful, my lady," she said. "You'll be quite the prettiest woman there, I am sure. Now sit, and I'll do up your hair — up very high, I think, to show off that long, graceful neck."

"Thank you," said Phaedra, taking the seat before the dressing table.

A short while later, there was a hard knock at the door and Zoë came in, dressed in her favorite purple ball gown. An amethyst pendant the size of a robin's egg hung from her throat, and her black hair was drawn into a knot which was pierced with a long purple plume.

"Phae, hurry!" she scolded. "Aunt Winnie and I were the second carriage to arrive, and now the queue's stretched up to Oxford Street."

Phaedra stood from the dressing table and smoothed her gown once again. "I'm ready," she said, not entirely certain it was true. "How do I look?"

Zoë scowled. "Like a ghost," she said, reaching up to pinch Phaedra's cheeks, her purple plume bobbing with each squeeze. "There. Now you've got a little color."

They went down the stairs together, Zoë chatting gaily. "Robin is coming tonight," she said. "And his arrogant brother, too. They both asked if you would dance with them, so I accepted on your behalf. A quadrille, I think, for Lord Mercer — oh, and a waltz for Robin."

"Zoë, please. Not a waltz."

Zoë tossed her hand. "Oh, it's only Robin," she said. "Besides, you should —"

"Zoë." Phaedra jerked to a halt. "No more *shoulds*. Must we have this discussion again?"

Zoë rolled her eyes. "Lud, Phae, what a stick-in-the-mud you've become," she said as they strolled arm in arm into the ballroom. "But I think you might get rather a shock tonight."

"A shock? Of what sort?"

Zoë snapped out her fan, and plied it coyly. "I have it on good authority that Avoncliffe is back from the country," she said. "Excuse me — *the Earl of Hauxton*. He came up just yesterday — a whole entourage, mind, with two carriages, a baggage cart, and that big, black horse he adores — so I think it's safe to say he did not come alone."

Her knees suddenly unsteady, Phaedra followed Zoë to the punch bowl. "With whom did he come, then?" she asked, unable to stop herself.

Zoë took a cup from a waiting footman and eyed Phaedra across it. "I don't know," she said earnestly. "But I know he got a card for this ball."

Through the swelling throng, Lord Robert edged toward them. "Hullo, Phae," he said, grabbing Zoë's arm.

But Phaedra scarcely saw him. "Zoë, why would he?" she hissed. "Who would have sent it?"

But Zoë just smiled as Robin drew her away. "Now *that*," she said, melting into the crowd, "is a subject best discussed with your brother, I think."

Phaedra did not ask her brother. Indeed, she could not think how. What business was it of hers whom he chose to invite into his home? But why Tristan?

She did not have the entire night, however, to ponder it. She kept Zoë's pledge to Lord Robin, who galloped her around the room in a dance that was more an exuberant jig than a waltz. Lord Mercer, however, surprised her. Though she did not know him well, the young marquess invited her to stroll in the gardens rather than dance, and she accepted gratefully. In sharp contrast to his younger brother, Mercer was a solemn, almost austere gentleman. Quite the tallest man in the room, his dark hair and oddly colored eyes set him apart from the rest of the guests, though he made no effort to draw attention to himself.

Phaedra laid her hand upon his arm, which felt strong and solid beneath his evening coat, and passed a pleasant time conversing about nothing more exciting than the health of the king, which Mercer reported to be in sharp decline. They turned to books, and to their shared interest in the French and German philosophers, both of which Mercer read in their original languages, a fact he let slip casually, and without pretense. After that they talked of breeding bloodstock, a particular hobby of his.

She was almost disappointed when the music ended. But as was proper, Mercer returned her at once to Xanthia and Stefan, exchanged a few polite words, then bowed most formally. Phaedra watched him go with the strange sense that perhaps she had just met a kindred spirit.

Mercer disappeared into the crowd as the orchestra struck up Phaedra's favorite Haydn waltz. Ignoring it, she snapped open her fan to wave it gently over Xanthia, who had finally been persuaded into a chair, and was looking a little limp. "Oh, thank you, Phae." Xanthia cut another grateful glance up at her. "You are too kind."

When she straightened, however, Stefan was speaking to someone in a tone which was warm but a little formal. Perhaps it was her peripheral vision, or perhaps some sort of sixth sense, but she turned slowly, oddly certain of who she would see.

And she was right. Tristan stood before Stefan, more resplendent than ever she'd seen him. He was dressed in formal, flawless black, his linen almost blindingly white, his hair swept back off his face in a mane of ebony waves which did not appear to have been cut during his weeks of absence. With his strong nose and dark skin, his elegant attire could not alter the fact that he still looked barely civilized. Her medieval Sicilian prince, misplaced in time.

"Ah, Hauxton, I think you know my sister?" said Stefan, setting an arm round Phaedra's waist.

"I have had the pleasure." Tristan smiled, but it did not reach his eyes. "My lady, you are looking very well indeed."

"My lord." She made a deep, formal curtsey. "What a shock to see you here."

"And you do not shock easily, do you, Lady Phaedra?" There was a change in him; a wariness she'd not seen before, and it made her heart ache. His smile still guarded, he held out his hand. "I see you are not dancing. Might I have the honor?"

"Thank you, but —"

Phaedra felt a hard jab in the center of her spine. Stefan? Or Xanthia? She tried again, confused. "But you are in mourning," she blurted, then immediately wished she had not.

Beside her, Xanthia hissed.

Phaedra's face colored furiously. "I do beg your pardon. That was impertinent."

Tristan shrugged. "I never did have any sense of propriety."

"Oh, I think society affords a few exceptions, Phae," said her brother solemnly. "Perhaps Lord Hauxton has decided to do his duty by his title and look about for a wife? It is generally thought quite pressing under such dire circumstances."

Phaedra turned round to look at him. "I beg your pardon? Dire circumstances?"

"Yes, I hear his cousin Harold almost came to a bad end recently," said Stefan, his face perfectly straight. "Entangled in that brothel fire over in Soho, someone said. Russian spies caught out. State secrets exposed. It would not do for such a scandalous chap to inherit now, would it?" He lifted his hawkish black brows, and looked pointedly at her.

Dear heaven, thought Phaedra. *Did he know?*

But Tristan ignored the remark, and instead turned back to Phaedra. "Will you dance, my lady?" he said impatiently. "After all, we are *friends,* are we not?"

It seemed the only way to escape Stefan's glare. "Thank you," she said, placing her hand in Tristan's larger, darker one. "I would like that."

Phaedra followed him through the crowd to the edge of the dance floor, then turned to face him, unable to stop herself from drinking him in. When he set his hand at the turn of her back, she laid her palm lightly on his shoulder, and allowed herself to be, well, *poured* onto the dance floor — for Tristan did not simply lead, he melted, taking her with him in an elegant, undulating ribbon of grace.

"I fear he's caught wind of that business in Soho," she whispered when she'd caught her breath and her nerves.

Tristan looked past her and shrugged. "He likely picked up a scrap of gossip somewhere and wished merely to make a point," he answered. "After all, Cousin Harold's exploits are tame in comparison to mine."

She flicked an anxious glance up at him. "Yes, I daresay."

They danced in silence for a long while, Tristan holding her closer than was strictly necessary, his big, warm hand set firmly at the turn of her spine. As always, his body possessed hers. Drew hers. In his arms she felt the stirring of passion remembered; of how it felt to have his long, powerful body stretched naked along hers. Joined with her. She had always believed Tristan danced as he made love — intensely, with perfect rhythm, and with the whole of himself. Tonight was no exception.

But that train of thought would not do. Ruthlessly, she shut it off. "I understand you've been in the country, my lord," she said stiffly. "How did you find it?"

He looked down at her with another faint smile, but for an instant, his dark, glittering gaze was unguarded. "You speak as if we are perfect strangers, Phae," he murmured, his voice husky. "I liked it well enough."

"Did you?" He spun her smoothly into the next turn. "I am glad to hear it."

The smile fell away from his face then. "I am getting on with my new life, Phae," he said quietly. "I am going to do what is expected of me — well, not the Government bit, no. But the estates, the farms, the mines and the quarries — I'm going to do my best to make a success of it."

"And your best will be very good indeed, Tristan." She forced a tremulous smile. "I am quite sure of it."

He whirled her about again, and this time pulled her fully against him, causing glances to cut their way, eyebrows aloft. "Will you be at home tomorrow, Lady Phaedra?" he whispered, his eyes holding hers, his lips pressed scandalously near. "I have someone whom I should like you to meet."

Phaedra did not like the solemnity in his tone. "Someone special, I take it?"

Tristan's cheeks colored faintly, but he did not set her away. "I think she is very special, yes," he answered. "I met her when I was in the country. And I remembered your advice."

"My advice?"

"About finding a pretty gentleman's daughter," he said.

Something inside her froze. "Yes, I see," she managed, trying to keep her step. "And biddable. You did not forget that part, I hope?"

He flashed a chagrinned expression. "Alas, she's not especially biddable," he said. "Still, I think . . . yes, I very much think she is going to be a permanent part of my life, Phae. But I should like your blessing first. Will you meet her?"

Phaedra forced herself to smile. "My brother was not wrong, then?" she said quietly.

Again the faint, tentative smile. "Nash isn't wrong about much, is he?"

Phaedra humiliated herself then by tripping over her own foot. "Bloody hell," she gritted.

Tristan caught her, smoothing over the error so gracefully no one could possibly have seen it. But Phaedra had seen it. And she had had quite enough. If she kept this up — her body pressed too near Tristan's, his rich, familiar scent teasing at her nostrils —

she would most assuredly burst into tears.

Deliberately, she slowed, and Tristan drew her smoothly alongside an arrangement of palms. Then, when no one was looking, he swiftly kissed her cheek. "Your brother is looking daggers at me now," he said. "I had best bid you good night, Phae."

"Yes," she managed. "And thank you. Thank you, Tristan, for trying to help Millie. And thank you for catching me just now."

"With you, my lady," he said, "the pleasure — *always* — is mine."

Then, finally, he flashed a hint of that shameless grin she loved, and bowed with a great flourish, sweeping the floor with an imaginary hat, putting her very much in mind of the night she'd met him, when he'd very nearly toppled from his horse. Someday, perhaps, when the heat between them died down to ash, she would tell him about that. Perhaps they would be able to laugh together as friends.

"Until tomorrow, then?" he asked.

"Tomorrow, yes." Forcing a smile, Phaedra folded her hands together, her nails digging into her own flesh. "Shall we say half past two?"

He looked at her a little oddly. "Very well. Half past two it shall be."

Then he strode through the room, the

552

crowd parting like the sea before him, and vanished from her sight.

The following afternoon, Phaedra was in the library upstairs keeping vigil by the bank of windows when Tristan's carriage came clattering down Brook Street. She had been there since noon, the press of tears hot behind her eyes, her entire body so rigid with the waiting her muscles ached. Again and again she went over the words Tristan had spoken last night, but she could ascribe no other meaning to them save for the worst.

He had met someone. A gentleman's daughter. Someone he wished to make a part of his life.

It seemed too soon, she thought. *She was not ready.* She had thought . . . *what?*

That she would have more time? That Tristan would wait, and press his suit again? Why should he, when she had turned him off so thoroughly? And what had changed? She was no more eligible a bride now than she had been two months ago. And now, her two months of misery were about to grow, she feared, into a lifetime of regret. He had taken her good advice. He was moving on with his life.

Rising onto her toes, Phaedra watched the

carriage draw up, her hands clenched, her nails digging into her palms. She had resolved to wait until the calling cards were brought up, and then to receive them formally, in the withdrawing room. Now her resolve was weakening. She wanted to rush down and get it over with. Or at least receive them in her oasis of safety, the family parlor. But that room held too many memories, both happy and sad, of her time with Tristan.

The carriage was a fine one, an elegant, old-fashioned post chaise made for fast travel and privacy, with the Talbot family crest emblazoned on the side, and bewigged footmen posted to the rear. They wore the same gray and red livery she'd seen that day in Bond Street, their velvet knee breeches fastened with gold buckles. Having leapt down, they were now opening the door and dropping the steps.

And then she saw him. Tristan descended to the pavement wearing his usual tall, shining boots, a coat of midnight blue, his hair covering the collar. He turned, offering up his hand to someone. The lady took it, stepping gingerly down, glancing up at him almost deferentially as she did so, her broad-brimmed bonnet obscuring her face.

She was quite tall and wore a dress striped

in shades of gray. A perfectly ordinary dress. An ordinary woman, too, by the look of her. Would it have been easier to bear, Phaedra wondered, had she been a stunning, round-figured lady dressed in the height of fashion?

Phaedra jerked shut the draperies and turned from the window.

She had thought that she could do this. And she could. *She would.* But it would not be easy with her heart in her throat and regret bitter in her mouth. She paced the floor until Stabler came, his eyes solemn, the silver salver extended, the little patch of ivory taunting her atop it.

"The Earl of Hauxton, my lady."

Just one card. One name. At the time, however, it did not register.

"He asked, of course, for Lady Nash," said Stabler. "But since she is not in . . . ?"

Phaedra felt a moment of guilt for inviting Tristan when she knew her mother would be out, but she could not have borne this with her mother looking on. "Show them into the withdrawing room, please," she managed, taking the card. "And send for tea."

Stabler bowed, and quit the room. Going to one of the pier glasses which divided the windows, Phaedra dabbed at her face with her handkerchief. She did not have Zoë today to pinch some color into her cheeks. Besides, it would not have lasted. With one last steadying breath, she lifted her chin and swept from the room. She was Lady Phaedra Northampton, for pity's sake. She would bloody well act like it.

Her chin was still up, and her color perhaps a little higher when she reached the withdrawing room. The double doors were open to the passageway, and Phaedra swept through, a welcoming smile fixed upon her face. She had no sooner stepped over the threshold, however, when she was taken aback.

The woman in the gray striped dress was Agnes!

Tristan sat nearby, his elbows on his knees, his hands clasped as he leaned forward. On the floor before them a little child toddled, blond ringlets bouncing, her face lifted to Tristan's as if he were the sun, and she the sunflower.

"Dis is Bunnet," said the child, extending him a small stuffed rabbit. "Here. You take 'em."

Tristan smiled back, and suddenly, he looked himself again. "Thank you," he said. "I'll just tuck Bunnet in my coat pocket, shall I?"

"Priss!" Phaedra didn't even realize she'd

cried out before she was on her knees, drawing the child to her breast.

"Oh!" squealed the child. "Phae, you squish me."

"Oh!" Phae set her a little away, and slicked a hand down her shining hair. "Oh, Priss, I did not mean to crush you."

But Priss just smiled, two rows of shiny front teeth beaming up at her. "Phae, me got a top," she said, turning. "I shows you." A basket sat on the Aubusson carpet by Tristan's shiny boot, brimming with toys. Priss toddled to it, and began to rummage.

Still on her knees, Phaedra looked back and forth between Agnes and Tristan, searching their faces for some explanation. "What has happened?" she asked breathlessly, her tangled rush of emotion not yet receding. "Where is your aunt, Agnes? What is going on?"

Agnes would not quite meet her gaze.

"It's complicated," said Tristan. "Just tell me, Phae, that you are glad to see her? To see us?"

"Of course I am glad!" Phaedra cried, her gaze returning to her maid. "Glad to see all of you. How could I not be? Agnes, what is going on here?"

Agnes cut a strange, somewhat dubious, glance at Tristan, and rose. "I'm to let his lordship explain that one, and gladly," she said, bending over to pick up Priscilla. "Little Miss Mischief and I shall just stroll in the gardens, shall we, whilst he does?"

"But . . . I do not understand." Phaedra stood. "Why must you go?"

Agnes, however, just settled Priss on her hip, and tossed Tristan a parting glance. "Good luck to you, my lord," she murmured.

"Agnes, wait!" But Agnes did not wait, and Phaedra's gaze followed them from the room. When they vanished into the depths of the house, she turned to look at Tristan. He stood by the basket of toys, one hand at his slender waist, pushing back the front of his coat. In the other hand he held a sheaf of papers.

Phaedra jerked to her feet. "Tristan," she said sharply, "tell me straight out. What is going on here?"

Wordlessly, he passed her the papers. Eyes wide, she opened them, shuffling from one page to the next. "But this . . . this is Millie's signature," she whispered. "Here. And here. And these seals — all these legal words — what do they mean?"

"They mean that Priscilla is now my ward," he said quietly. "The document was drawn by my solicitor in the City some days ago. And if you agree, Phae, I mean to petition the court to adopt Priss as soon as possible."

Phaedra lifted her gaze to his, mystified. Her relief at seeing Agnes instead of the future Lady Hauxton in her drawing room was giving way to utter confusion. "To . . . to adopt *Priss?*" she managed. "You . . . you cannot do that. *Can* you?"

Tristan lifted one of his dark, slashing eyebrows. "I can if Millie signs away her rights," he answered. "Which, for a price, she did — and pretty cheerfully, I might add."

"You . . . you bought her?"

"That sounds harsh, Phae," he said tightly. "But I am resolved, unless your brother means to step forward and claim his child? I shall do him the courtesy, of course, of waiting until he retur—"

"Oh, Tony will not claim her," Phaedra interjected, handing back the papers. "Tristan, you will not force his hand. Is *that* what you thought?"

Something dark and angry sketched across his face. "Hell and damnation, Phaedra!" he growled, snatching the papers. "Do you think me such a fool as that? I'll give Hayden-Worth the opportunity — to do otherwise would be ungentlemanly — but if he'd meant to do right by that child, he'd have long since done it. Isn't that how all this mess fell to you to begin with?"

Phaedra felt the tears well up again. "But Priss . . . I don't understand."

"The child needs a loving home, my dear," he answered, his tone softening. "With Nash's permission, I've hired Agnes to be her nurse. They are living at my estate in Wiltshire, not so very far from Brier- wood."

Phaedra set one hand to her temple, un- able to fathom it. Good God. What was Ste- fan's part in all this? Did he suspect Tony's guilt? Or *hers?* None of it made sense. "But Tristan, what will you tell people about Priss?"

"That it's none of their damned business," Tristan snapped. "They will assume the worst, of course — people always do. It will be whispered she's my by-blow, and that I adopted her as Lord Rannoch did Zoë."

"Oh," said Phaedra. "Oh, dear."

Tristan shrugged, and tossed the papers onto a side table. "Should it matter to us, Phae?" he asked. "She's a clever, sweet child, and I've never given a damn what people say. As to Priss — well, you tell me — is she better off as Lord Hauxton's pampered bastard? Or as the illegitimate child of a tavern maid? It's not a perfect world. I did the best I could."

Phaedra swallowed hard. "I — I see your point," she whispered. "But I know . . . oh, Tristan. I *know* you are doing this for me."

"Yes," he answered, his voice softening. "I am doing this for you — or I was."

"I don't understand," said Phaedra. "What do you mean?"

He shrugged a little shyly. "A funny thing happened, Phae, these last two weeks," he said. "Life was looking a little empty and a little bleak for me. But she's a taking little thing, Priss."

For the first time, Phaedra smiled. "Yes, she is."

At last he grinned, his square, white teeth contrasting sharply against his honeyed skin. "I've grown dashed fond of the chit," he admitted. "So, yes, I did it for you, and for her, and even for Agnes, perhaps. But I think, Phae, that in the end, it will have been for me."

"Do you?" Her voice was soft. "Oh, Tristan. I am so glad."

His gaze was focused on the door through which they had vanished. "You were right, you know, about my needing a child," he said quietly. "I look at Priss, so smart and so vivacious, and I realize . . . well, that's she's worth a lot of effort. She brightens my life. Gives me a purpose, perhaps, mawkish as that may sound."

Phaedra did not remind him that what he needed was *a blood heir,* and no adopted child, certainly not a female, could ever be that. But the moment was raw, and his eyes were tender. There would be time enough for him to consider that later.

She clasped her hands tightly before her. "I am glad," she said again. "If your heart is set, then Priss is the lucky one."

His gaze fixed on hers, and he shook his head. "No, I think that perhaps I am," he answered. "And ever the gambler, I'm going to try my luck again."

"Yes?" Suddenly, her heart leapt. "In . . . In what way?"

He stepped a little nearer. Until that time, she had not seen the two packages which sat by his chair tied up with red ribbons, one atop the other. He turned and pulled the ribbon free, then with the smaller of the two in hand, he knelt before her.

"Lady Phaedra Northampton," he said quietly, "I did not do this properly the first time, so —"

"Oh, no!" she interjected, her hand out as if to stop him. "Oh, Tristan, please —"

"— so I mean to try again," he pressed

on. "Phae, I love you more than life itself. I should have said so, very clearly, two months ago. Please marry me. Please be the Countess of Hauxton — be Priscilla's mother — and make me the happiest man on earth. Now, love, I am begging you. *Please marry me.*"

Phaedra was shaking so badly, she was compelled to collapse onto the settee behind her. "Oh, Tristan, please get up," she said. "Come sit by me. Let us talk of this rationally."

"No." He leaned into her, his eyes demanding, the box still in hand. "Let us talk of it *irrationally,* Phae. Let us talk of how we feel in one another's arms. Of how we understand one another. Of how we exasperate one another. Why, Phae, would I settle for something less, and live a passionless marriage? Is a child — an heir — worth that?"

"Tristan, you need —"

His lips thinned. "With all respect, Phae, I'm a little tired of your telling me what I need," he said. "I need *you.* And Priss needs *us.* You, me, and yes, probably Agnes, too. And how we'll work all this out, and what we'll say to people, I do not yet know. But I do know that our not marrying because you fear you cannot give me a child is just balderdash, Phae. We will have Priss to love. Let Cousin Harold inherit the rest of it. Whoever the hell he is, he'll no doubt make a fine earl."

Phaedra's hands were shaking now. "I don't . . . oh, Tristan . . . I can't think."

"Don't *think*," he whispered, his gaze level with hers. *"Just say yes."*

She closed her eyes, her hands fisting so that she would not reach out for him.

"Phae, I'll be a good husband, I swear," he said. "I'll never look at another wom—"

"No, you *won't*," she said sharply. "That, I *will not* have."

"Then you'd better say *yes*," he teased, "or you'll have no say at all."

"Tristan," she said, her eyes flying open. "Oh, Tristan. You are a fool."

His eyes were solemn as he shook his head. "No, I've never been a fool, no matter what people thought." Then his expression suddenly darkened to something far more intractable. "Now, I have a ring in this box, my dear. A Talbot family heirloom. Give me your hand, for I am done asking, Phae. You are marrying me. You can say yes. Or I can lay siege to your house for a year or two. Or I can go to Nash, and tell —"

"Tristan," she said warningly.

"Just hold out your hand," he ordered,

"and say *yes.* Please, Phae. Because this is done. And because I love you — and because I think, perhaps, that you love me?"

Slowly, so slowly it quivered, she unclenched her fingers and extended her hand. "All right, then," she whispered. *"Yes."*

He snapped open the box and slid the ring, cool and loose, onto her hand. She drew one last steadying breath, then looked down. A band of diamonds set with three large, perfectly matched emeralds winked up at her. A ring that must have cost a king's ransom two or three centuries past. She embarrassed herself then by bursting into tears.

"Yes," she said again as he kissed away her tears. "Yes, *I love you* — and you know it, too, you wretch! I love you madly, and I have since the first time you kissed me."

"I thought," he said solemnly, "that you might never say so."

She laughed, and said it again for good measure. "Yes, I love you, and you are mad for doing this, but I have not the will to fight it," she answered, snuffling. "Oh, Tristan, I have missed you so! Now, what's in the other box?"

"Greedy puss," he whispered, rising and picking it up. He returned to sit beside her, laying it in her lap. "You may open this one," he said, his voice sultry, yet teasing. "It is for you to wear — or not — as it pleases you."

Her hands still shaking, Phaedra lifted the lid. Inside, on a bed of white satin, lay a set of purple velvet manacles fastened with long gold chains and tiny gold locks, and set at each corner with large teardrop pearls. "Oh, my!" she whispered reverently. She reached out, tentatively, and touched one. The fabric was soft as down.

"Only if you wish," said Tristan softly.

Then he turned on the settee, his hands coming up to bracket her face. He kissed her sweetly, as he had the very first time, but deeply. A kiss rich with the promise of years to come, and of passion unbound and eternal. And when he drew away, his black eyes were dancing again, and his irreverent grin was back in place. "Now, Phae," he said teasingly, *"you* have to give something to *me."*

"Anything." She held his gaze, perfectly serious. "You have only to name it."

"I claim my prize, then," he said. With a sudden twitch of his hand, he jerked her skirts up to her knees, making her shriek.

"Tristan, not here!"

"Yes, Phae. Now." The grin was back, brilliant and wicked. *"I want my yellow garter back."*

Epilogue

Love is a smoke made with the fume of
sighs,
Being purg'd, a fire sparkling in lovers'
eyes.

Wiltshire, January 1833
The Earl of Hauxton was sweating — not
perspiring, not merely damp with exertion
— but sweating great rivulets that ran down
his bare throat to settle in the vee of his collarbone, and from thence trickled into the
light thatch of dark hair that graced his fine,
broad chest.

"Oh! God!" he groaned. "That was —"
"— *exquisite,*" his wife finished.

Atop him, she bent forward and drew her
long, purple feather down his throat, along
his shoulder, and lower still. "*Now do it
again,*" she whispered, gazing down at him.
"Or this time I shall ply my plume without
pity."

His black eyes flashing, her husband bucked his powerful hips, threatening to throw her off. But he wouldn't, and they both knew it. Instead, Phaedra held on with a little shriek.

"Shh," he said gently. "You'll wake the children."

Phaedra lifted one eyebrow. "A good try, my lord," she replied, drawing the feather down his flank until he shivered. "But that pair could sleep through a thunderstorm." The feather came up again, teasing and tormenting. "Do you know, I'm glad we spent Christmas in the country."

He crooked his head to look down his chest at her. "Are you indeed?"

"Yes," she purred, drawing the feather lower. "I find this fresh Wiltshire air quite whets my appetites. Once more — then, I promise, I shall unfasten you."

The earl grunted. "That's what you said an hour ago," he answered. "Where the devil did you get that garish feather, anyway?"

Grinning, Phaedra twirled it. "It's just an old thing of Zoë's," she confessed. "I stole it from her trunk upstairs. She wears it sometimes in her hair."

Her husband grinned. "I think you should wear it in *your* hair," he said, lifting his dark eyebrows suggestively. "Untie me, love, and let's see how it looks, *hmm?*"

"Oh, no, no," said Phaedra. "You are my concubine. And I demand another performance."

The earl looked up at the purple velvet cuffs which bound his wrists to the bed and pulled down as if testing their strength. "Madam, I think you have me," he agreed. "Your tastes, I find, have altered."

She fell against him on a sigh of satisfaction. "Yes, I have mastered my passions," she murmured. "And now I mean to master *yours.*"

"Witch!" he uttered.

She kissed his damp throat, reveling in the heat of his body, and of the scent of strong, lusty male. "Oh, you'll survive," she said, tossing the feather aside. "And I find I rather enjoy being the one in control."

He turned his face into hers. "My love," he said solemnly, "you have always been the one in control."

She peeked at him through a curtain of heavy chestnut hair. "Truly?"

He nodded, his hair scrubbing the pillow. "Aye, since that long-ago day when I kissed you behind the parlor door. Did you ever doubt it?"

She caught her lip between her teeth. "At first," she admitted.

He snorted in disbelief. Exhausted, the encore forgotten, they drifted off thus for a few moments, only to be roused again by a tentative knock at the door.

"My lady?" It was Arnolds, the butler. "My lady, I fear you are needed upstairs."

With a groan, Phaedra rolled herself gingerly away. "What is it, Arnolds?" she asked, scrabbling about for the key to the manacles.

The butler hesitated. "It is Miss Armstrong, my lady," he finally said. "No one is hurt, but I fear Miss Priscilla tied her to a chair in the schoolroom, and set her hair afire with an old tinderbox."

The earl grunted. "Wild Red Indians again," he said. "Didn't you forbid them that game?"

Phaedra sighed deeply. "Thank you, Arnolds," she said, snapping open the first lock. "Yes, I told them, but Zoë's as bad as Priss. I don't feel sorry for her in the least. But still, I daresay we'd best hurry."

The butler's heavy tread fell away, and in a trice they were dressed and rushing upstairs to the schoolroom. They arrived to find Miss White, the governess, already surveying the damage, her hands on her hips. Priss sat — feigning contrition — in one chair, whilst Zoë sat in the other, looking much the same.

As usual, Tristan caved in first. "Oh, come here, Priss," he said, picking up the child, who was pretending to snuffle now. "I expect you've had a scare, *hmm?*"

Phaedra expected otherwise, but she held her tongue. It took but a few moments to elicit the full story, and to hear Zoë's apology for egging the situation on. The damage was to the tendrils at the nape of her neck, and the room still stank of singed hair.

"She's only five, Phae, for pity's sake," said their houseguest under her breath. "I never dreamt she could actually *strike* the bloody thing."

"Yes, well, let that be a lesson to you." Phaedra borrowed Miss White's scissors. "Now look down, Zoë, and I'll snip out these burnt bits."

"I daresay you'll soon grow tired of having me," said Zoë sorrowfully over the *snick! snick! snick!* of the scissors. "I suppose I ought to just pack up my things and go back to Richmond and throw myself on the pyre of Papa's horrid demands."

"Yes, I'll believe that bit of drama when I see it, my dear." The hair cut away, Phaedra put down the scissors and motioned at Priscilla. "What of you, Priss?" she said warningly. "Have you something to say to Miss

Armstrong?"

Priscilla turned her head into her father's shoulder. "I didn't mean it, Papa!" she said, settling her head on his shoulder. "I'm sorry! I didn't mean to do it."

"Oh, I'm fairly sure you did," said Tristan evenly. "Now, how would you like to go into the conservatory, and have breakfast with Papa, *hmm?*"

Phaedra sighed.

"Can the babies come?" Priss cut a doting gaze up at her father.

Tristan cast his wife an enquiring glance and she quickly nodded. After so many years of trying, the twins had been — well, nothing less than a miracle, really, and they rarely left Phaedra's sight. "We shall ring for Nurse to bring them," Tristan agreed. "*If* they are awake."

Half an hour later they were seated *en famille* in the conservatory, with Tristan wiping jam from Priscilla's fingers. Zoë was bouncing Caroline on her knee, whilst Christopher still slept in his basket.

Phaedra sipped her tea, and stared pensively out the windows. The snow was coming down hard now, cold and silent, blanketing the house's vast gardens in a mantle of white. Already Priss was wheedling to be taken out to play — and already Tristan was surrendering.

How much things had changed in just a few short years! After endless months of hoping — though she'd sworn she would not hope at all — Phaedra had conceived. Perhaps the Lord had doubly blessed her for her patience. The twins were beautiful, healthy babes, and some days, Phaedra still wept when she held them.

In Wiltshire, Priss had truly blossomed. She had stopped asking after her mother long before leaving her aunt's cottage, and Phaedra did not know whether that was good or bad. Immaterial, she supposed. Millie still lived under the protection of Lord Cotting, and though they had not married, he was fast growing old, and anything was yet possible. Agnes had shocked them in the spring by stepping out with Mr. Uglow, Tristan's valet. They now lived on the grounds in a cottage where Priss had her own little bed when she visited, and yet a second collection of dolls and toys.

Which left only Zoë to be happily settled — an unlikely hope indeed, for though she claimed to envy Phaedra's happiness, she seemed as disinclined as ever to marry. Instead she lived a peripatetic life, moving from her father's Richmond mansion, her stepmother's family home, her aunt's town house and even spending weeks at a time with Phaedra and Tristan. It was as if she felt she belonged nowhere.

As if he'd read her thoughts, Arnolds came in at that instant, cutting short Phaedra's reverie and bringing fresh coffee with the morning's post. Today there was but one letter. Phaedra picked it up then, her eyebrows rising, pushed it across the table to Zoë.

"For you, Pocahontas."

Zoë passed Caroline to Phaedra and took up the letter, her smile withering. "From Papa," she muttered, slitting the wax with her butter knife. "Oh, Phae, this cannot be good news."

Tristan, who had been engaged in persuading Priss to eat her eggs, turned to face them as Zoë's gaze flicked over the page. "I trust no one is ill?"

"Only me," said Zoë dryly. Then she sighed, and lowered the letter to her lap. "Well, the ax has finally fallen. What day is it, Hauxton?"

"January twentieth," said Tristan. "Why?"

Zoë turned to Phaedra with a sour smile. "Papa says it will soon be time for The Talk," she said. "I'm to have only a little more freedom, Phae — five months and eleven days' worth."

Phaedra's gaze searched her friend's face, which was rapidly losing its color. "And then what, Zoë? You look as if you're headed to Tyburn."

Zoë lifted her chin, her eyes sparkling with anger. "I might as well be. The season is just weeks away, and Papa declares that if I cannot settle on a husband by the end of it, he is going to find one for me. Or I may go home to Scotland. Those are my choices."

Phaedra was taken aback. "Oh, my poor dear," she murmured. "Oh, that really is too cruel. But if you cannot find *anyone,* why, I am sure he will relent . . . won't he?"

"Anyone?" echoed Zoë bitterly.

"No, not *anyone,*" said Tristan helpfully. "Here, let's make a list." When Zoë's eyes shot daggers at him, he clarified. "Of eligible bachelors, I mean. Why, there must be a dozen decent chaps I know who could use a good wife."

"Yes, what about Lord Robert?" Phaedra suggested. "You did once say, Zoë, that if you go round kissing someone long enough, you'll end up married to them. And Robin would do well to settle down, before he kills himself."

Abruptly, Zoë crushed the letter in her hands. "My God, just listen to yourselves!"

"I beg your pardon?" said Tristan.

Zoë fixed him with her darkest glower. "Why, not three years ago, Hauxton, you couldn't spell *matrimony,* let alone fathom it," she exclaimed. "And Phae! You were a confirmed spinster, you will recall. It took me a fortnight just to get you into a proper dress."

Tristan and Phaedra exchanged sheepish glances across the table. "Well," she said quietly, "we were wrong."

"Oh, bother!" said Zoë, shoving back her chair. "I'll find a way out of this, trust me. Papa is in for the shock of his life. Now come on, Priss. Get your boots and mittens. Let's go roll in the snow. I, for one, should like to cool off."

"Snow!" cried Priss, scrambling down from her chair.

Everything followed in a flurry of activity. Miss White swooped in to carry her charge off to be properly dressed for the outdoors, Zoë following. The nurse — a stout, dependable soul — declared it time for the twins' baths, then picked up their baskets by their massive handles and summarily carted them away. Arnolds motioned for the footmen to begin to clear the unused dishes. And in moments, Phaedra and Tristan sat by themselves, eyeing one another across the breakfast table.

"Well, my dear," he said suggestively. "Alone again."

"Yes, my love. What *shall* we do?" A myriad of possibilities passed through Phaedra's mind, then suddenly, she gasped and leapt from her chair.

"What?" Tristan jerked to his feet. "Phae, what's wrong?"

Phaedra felt her face flood with heat. "The velvet shackles," she whispered, grabbing his arm. "Oh, Lud! Please, Tristan, *please* tell me you put them away?"

At that, Tristan threw back his head and laughed. "Oh, Phaedra!" he said as she dragged him toward the stairs. "The servants will have plenty to gossip about now!"